THE KING'S AFRICAN RIFLES

Printed and bound by Antony Rowe Ltd, Eastbourne

THE KING'S AFRICAN RIFLES

*A Study in the Military History of
East and Central Africa, 1890-1945*

BY

LIEUTENANT-COLONEL H. MOYSE-BARTLETT

M.B.E.(Mil.), M.A.(Oxon.), Ph.D.(London)

[Photo: Lt.-Col. G. C. Hill

Sentry of 2/4 K.A.R., photographed in the Field, Portuguese East Africa, 1918

Frontispiece

FOREWORD

By General Sir George Giffard, g.c.b., d.s.o.

I HAD always hoped that the history of the King's African Rifles would be written some day, and on appointment as Colonel Commandant of the Regiment I determined to see what could be done.

The first problem to be solved was financial, for the battalions of the King's African Rifles have no large funds from which to finance the writing of a history. I therefore approached their Excellencies the Governors of Kenya, Uganda and Tanganyika to ask whether their Governments would be prepared to find the money. They most generously agreed to provide the necessary funds.

My second problem was to find an author. In this I was exceedingly fortunate, for Lieutenant-Colonel H. Moyse-Bartlett, who served in the East Africa Command during the late war, volunteered to write the history. This was a most generous offer, as he was Secretary of the School of Oriental and African Studies of London University and a very busy man. The amount of research has been very great, and has entailed the almost complete surrender of his spare time for the past four and a half years. He has written a very interesting and valuable history of the Regiment, and all ranks, past and present, owe him a great debt of gratitude.

It will come, I think, as a surprise to many people to learn for how short a time Great Britain has been concerned in the development and government of East Africa. It all began, as it has so often in our overseas possessions, with individual traders who were eventually absorbed by chartered companies which in turn gave place to governments controlled first by the Foreign Office and subsequently by the Colonial Office. The chartered companies were compelled, in order to maintain order and protect their stations, to raise local forces. As Government took over the administration these forces were transferred and became the regiments of their respective colonies. In 1902 all were combined into the King's African Rifles. It was essentially an active service regiment, and it is most interesting to learn how little time, especially before the 1914-18 war, was spent by officers and men in barracks at headquarters. They lived hard, worked hard, and when necessary fought hard to protect the frontiers of the colonies and to maintain order among a turbulent population. This was splendid training for junior officers and men, and provided the firm foundation for the development of the Regiment, which grew from scantily equipped levies armed with out-of-date rifles discarded by the Army and employed on local expeditions against ill-armed tribes, to a force of all arms equipped with modern weapons and capable of meeting and defeating such a stubborn fighter as the Japanese.

Colonel Moyse-Bartlett has rightly emphasized that the African soldier must have good leaders if he is to give of his best, and the importance for the European leader to learn the language of his men. In the days before the 1914-18 war this was all that was necessary, and officers stayed for long tours of service.

During the 1914-18 war a great expansion of the Regiment took place and hundreds of British officers, warrant officers and non-commissioned officers were drafted into the King's African Rifles. Great difficulties arose owing to the lack of understanding between Europeans and Africans. The same difficulties arose during 1939-45. I have no doubt that, now that African forces are liable for service anywhere, the African soldier should also learn English. It would make for greater efficiency within units and better co-operation when African units are part of mixed formations.

Those who read this book will, I am sure, be greatly impressed not only by the soldierly qualities of courage and cheerful endurance shown by the African soldier, but also by his outstanding loyalty. Those who served with him will read these pages with affection and admiration in their hearts for their African comrades. All of us who served with the King's African Rifles look back on our days with the Regiment as some of the best of our service.

Giffard
General

CONTENTS

PAGE

FOREWORD by General Sir George Giffard, G.C.B., D.S.O. . . v
INTRODUCTION xvii

PART I

THE CAMPAIGNS OF THE EARLY REGIMENTS

CHAP.
1 THE POLITICAL BACKGROUND 3
2 THE CENTRAL AFRICA REGIMENT 12
   (i) The Slavers' War, 1888-96.
   (ii) Minor Tribal Expeditions and the Formation of the Central Africa Rifles, 1896-1900.
   (iii) Foreign Service: Mauritius and Somaliland, 1899-1900.
   (iv) Foreign Service: The Ashanti Campaign, 1900.
   (v) Foreign Service: The Gambia Expedition, 1901.
3 THE UGANDA RIFLES 49
   (i) Lugard and Emin Pasha's Sudanese, 1890-92.
   (ii) The Muslim Rebellion and the Reorganization of the Sudanese, 1893.
   (iii) The Campaigns in Bunyoro, 1893-95.
   (iv) The First and Second Expeditions against the Nandi, 1895-97.
   (v) Mutiny and its Consequences, 1897-1901.
   (vi) The Third Expedition against the Nandi, 1900.
   (vii) The Affair at Ribo Post, 1900-01.
4 THE EAST AFRICA RIFLES 95
   (i) The Armed Forces of the Imperial British East Africa Company, 1888-95.
   (ii) The Organization of the East Africa Rifles, 1895-1901.
   (iii) The Mazrui Rebellion, 1895-96.
   (iv) Punitive Expeditions in Jubaland, 1893-1901.

PART II

THE CONSOLIDATION OF THE REGIMENT, 1901-1914

5 FORMATION AND ORGANIZATION, 1901-02 . . . 123
6 DISPOSITIONS AND ESTABLISHMENTS 132
   (i) Trial and Experience, 1902-04.
   (ii) Reorganization and Definition of Functions, 1904-08.
   (iii) Concentration and Dispersal in British Somaliland, 1909-10.
   (iv) The Second Period of Reorganization, 1910-14.
7 CAMPAIGNS AGAINST THE MAD MULLAH OF SOMALILAND 160
   (i) The First Expedition, 1901.
   (ii) The Second Expedition, 1902.
   (iii) The Third Expedition, 1902-03.
   (iv) The Fourth Expedition, 1903-04.
   (v) The Return of the Mullah and the Formation of the Somaliland Camel Corps, 1905-14.
8 TRIBAL EXPEDITIONS IN EAST AFRICA 195
   (i) Internal Security in the Three Territories.
   (ii) The Defence of the Railway, 1902-06.
   (iii) Punitive Expeditions in the Highlands, 1902-14.
   (iv) The Uganda Border and the Northern Frontier District, 1908-14.
   (v) Jubaland and the Marehan Expedition, 1902-14.

CHAP.		PAGE
9	TRIBAL EXPEDITIONS IN UGANDA	228
	(i) Expeditions in the Central Province, 1902-05.	
	(ii) The Turkana Mission, 1910-11.	
	(iii) Operations of the Northern Patrol, 1911.	
	(iv) The Lango Detachment, 1911-12.	
	(v) Operations of the Northern Garrison, 1912-14.	

PART III

THE EAST AFRICA CAMPAIGN, 1914–1918

10 THE DEFENCE OF THE UGANDA RAILWAY, AUGUST, 1914-FEBRUARY, 1916 259
    (i) The Opposing Forces and the Theatre of War.
    (ii) The Concentration and Deployment of the K.A.R., August, 1914.
    (iii) Initial Operations in the Northern Area, August-October, 1914.
    (iv) The Tanga Expedition and its Consequences, November-December, 1914.
    (v) Operations in the Coastal Area, December, 1914-January, 1915.
    (vi) Defensive and Preparatory Operations in the West and South, 1915.
    (vii) Defence and Preparation for the Offensive in the North, January, 1915-February, 1916.

11 THE INVASION OF GERMAN EAST AFRICA, MARCH-SEPTEMBER, 1916 296
    (i) The Encirclement of Kilimanjaro, March-April.
    (ii) The Advance to the Msiha River, May-June.
    (iii) The Advance to the Central Railway.
    (iv) From the Central Railway to the River Mgeta.
    (v) Invasion from the West: Operations of the Lake Force.
    (vi) Invasion from the South: Brigadier-General Northey's Operations.

12 THE EXPULSION OF THE ENEMY FROM GERMAN TERRITORY, OCTOBER, 1916-NOVEMBER, 1917 332
    (i) The Expansion of the K.A.R.
    (ii) The Advance from Kilwa: Operations around Kibata, October, 1916-January, 1917.
    (iii) The Advance from Kilwa: Operations around Utete, January, 1917.
    (iv) Operations in the South: September, 1916-February, 1917.
    (v) The Pursuit of Wintgens and Naumann, February-September, 1917.
    (vi) Operations of the Kilwa Force, February-August, 1917.
    (vii) The First Operations from Lindi, February-July, 1917.
    (viii) The Operations of the Western Columns, March-November, 1917.
    (ix) The Combined Offensive in the East, September-November, 1917.

13 THE PURSUIT THROUGH PORTUGUESE EAST AFRICA, NOVEMBER, 1917-NOVEMBER, 1918 389
    (i) Preliminary Dispositions.
    (ii) KARTUCOL: The Advance from Port Amelia to Munevalia, April-June, 1918.
    (iii) Operations North of Quelimane, July, 1918.
    (iv) The Break to the North-West, August-September, 1918.
    (v) The Final Phase, October-November, 1918.
    (vi) The K.A.R. in the East Africa Campaign.

PART IV

INTERNAL SECURITY AND REORGANIZATION, 1914–1939

14 THE END OF THE MAD MULLAH 419
    (i) Operations in British Somaliland, 1914-19.
    (ii) The Final Defeat and Expulsion of the Mad Mullah, 1919-20.
    (iii) The Tactics and Strategy of the Campaigns in British Somaliland.

CHAP.		PAGE
15	INTERNAL SECURITY, 1914-30	434
	(i) Jubaland.	
	(ii) Turkana.	
	(iii) The Masai.	
	(iv) The Northern Frontier District.	
	(v) British Somaliland.	
16	DISPOSITIONS AND ESTABLISHMENTS, 1919-39 .	452
	(i) Demobilization and the New Garrisons, 1919-20.	
	(ii) Reorganization and Redistribution, 1921-28.	
	(iii) Reduction and Reorganization, 1929-33.	
	(iv) Reorganization and Rearmament, 1933-39.	

PART V

THE WAR OF 1939–1945

17	THE DEFENCE OF KENYA, 1939-40	475
	(i) Preparation for War, August, 1939-June, 1940.	
	(ii) Frontier Actions, June-December, 1940.	
18	THE DEFENCE OF BRITISH SOMALILAND, JUNE-AUGUST, 1940	494
19	THE ADVANCE TO ADDIS ABABA, JANUARY-APRIL, 1941 .	504
	(i) The Advance to the River Juba.	
	(ii) The Forcing of the Juba and the Occupation of Mogadishu.	
	(iii) The Advance to the River Awash.	
	(iv) The Crossing of the Awash and the Occupation of Addis Ababa.	
20	OPERATIONS IN THE SOUTH AND WEST, JANUARY-JULY, 1941 .	522
	(i) Operations of 21 and 25 (E.A.) Brigades, January-May.	
	(ii) The Battle of the Lakes: Operations of 22 (E.A.) Brigade, April-May.	
	(iii) The Pursuit to the West, June-July.	
21	OPERATIONS IN THE NORTH AND EAST, APRIL, 1941-DECEMBER, 1942	554
	(i) The Situation in the North, April-September.	
	(ii) Ambazzo and Kulkaber, 19th September-21st November.	
	(iii) The Fall of Gondar, 22nd-28th November.	
	(iv) The Blockade of French Somaliland, 1941-42.	
	(v) Commentary on the Abyssinian Campaign.	
22	REORGANIZATION AND DEVELOPMENT WITHIN THE COMMAND, 1942-44	574
23	THE CAMPAIGN IN MADAGASCAR, 1942 .	579
	(i) Diego Suarez and Mayotte.	
	(ii) The Advance on Tananarive: Operations of No. 1 Fighting Group (1/1 K.A.R.).	
	(iii) From Tananarive to Ambalavao: Operations of No. 3 (1/6 K.A.R.) and No. 2 (5 K.A.R.) Fighting Groups.	
	(iv) Commentary on the Madagascar Campaign.	
24	THE CAMPAIGN IN BURMA: OPERATIONS OF 11 (E.A.) DIVISION, AUGUST-DECEMBER, 1944 .	610
	(i) The Turn of the Tide.	
	(ii) The Advance to Sittaung: Operations of 25 (E.A.) Brigade, August-September.	
	(iii) The Advance to Yazagyo: Operations of 26 (E.A.) Brigade, August-September.	
	(iv) The Eastern Flank: Operations of 21 (E.A.) Brigade and 5 K.A.R., September-November.	
	(v) From Yazagyo to Natkyigon, October-November.	
	(vi) The Establishment of the Chindwin Bridgehead, November-December.	

CHAP.		PAGE
25	THE CAMPAIGN IN BURMA: OPERATIONS OF 28 (E.A.) BRIGADE AND 22 (E.A.) BRIGADE, JANUARY-NOVEMBER, 1945	663
	(i) Operations of 28 (E.A.) Brigade, January-April, 1945.	
	(ii) Operations of 22 (E.A.) Brigade, January-November, 1945.	
	(iii) The K.A.R. in Burma.	
26	THE FIRST FIFTY YEARS	683

APPENDICES

A	UNIFORMS	689
B	BANDS	694
C	MEDALS	697
D	INSPECTORS-GENERAL	700
E	STATISTICS OF THE EAST AFRICA CAMPAIGN, 1914-18	701
F	K.A.R. BATTALIONS: WAR OF 1939-45	702
G	SELECT BIBLIOGRAPHY	704

GLOSSARY OF TERMS AND ABBREVIATIONS 715

INDEX 719

ILLUSTRATIONS

Sentry of 2/4 K.A.R., 1918 . . . . *Frontispiece*

	PAGE
Facsimile of Regimental Orders, 1898	81

	FACING PAGE
Advance Guard of 2 C.A.R., Gambia Expedition, 1901	45
Atonga Company, 1 K.A.R., 1902	133
Fort Mlangeni, 1902	133
Fort Mangoche, 1904	137
Yao Sergeant, 1 K.A.R., 1905	137
Askaris, 'F' Company, 3 K.A.R.	224
Breaking up rifles, Marehan Operations, 1912-14	224
1 K.A.R. entering Longido Camp, 1916	296
Landing party, River Rufigi, 5th May, 1916	320
Patrol, 2 K.A.R., Schaedel's Farm, July, 1917	320
Transport, Portuguese East Africa, 1918	391
Column of 2/4 K.A.R. on flooded road, 1918	405

	PAGE
Facsimile of von Lettow's surrender	413

	FACING PAGE
Bomb bursting near Tale Fort, 1920	428
Main gate, Baran Fort, 1920	428
The first car into Moyale, 1928	457
Truck fitted as a troop-carrier, 1938	457
Recruit affixing thumb-print	484
Askaris holding captured Italian flag, 1940	484
5 K.A.R. entering Kismayu, 1941	509
Blown railway bridge, River Awash	520
K.A.R. column nearing Addis Ababa	520
5 K.A.R. crossing River Gidu	542
K.A.R. entering Gondar	542
The landing at Majunga	584
Laying a river crossing near Andriba	584
K.A.R. marching through Tananarive	593
K.A.R. signallers in training	615
East African soldier in Burma	615
Askari in captured Japanese foxhole	615
Corduroy road in the Kabaw Valley	626
K.A.R. sergeant teaching snipers to read a compass . . .	626
K.A.R. in the jungle, Burma	640
East African troops marching into Kalewa	655
East African troops crossing the Chindwin	657
Mountbatten with the K.A.R.	662
Display by 24 (U) K.A.R.	680
N.C.O., 1904	685
Askari, F.S.M.O., 1939-1945	685

MAPS AND SKETCHES IN TEXT

		PAGE
1.	Nyasaland	13
2.	Operations in Ashanti, 1900-01	35
3.	Operations on the River Gambia, 1901	43
4.	The Witu District	97
5.	British East Africa, Coastal Area	103
6.	British East Africa: Civil and Military Districts, 1897	115
7.	British East Africa: The Central Highlands	205
8.	Military Camps in the Logire Hills, December, 1912	247
9.	The Coastal Frontier Area	271
10.	The Southern Area of Operations	274
11.	Action at Jasin, 18th-19th January, 1915	283
12.	Lake Victoria: Eastern Area	285
13.	The Taveta—Kahe Area	297
14.	Attack on Zuganatto Bridge, 15th June, 1916	307
15.	Outflanking Movement through the Nuguru Mountains	311
16.	Advance round the Uluguru Mountains	313
17.	Attack on Mwanza, 11th-14th July, 1916	323
18.	The Environs of Kibata	337
19.	The Kibata Positions	341
20.	The Environs of Utete	344
21.	Investment of Utete Fort, January, 1917	345
22.	Operations against Lincke	350
23.	Battle of Narungombe, 19th July, 1917	365
24.	Action at Lukuledi Mission, 19th-21st October, 1917	383
25.	Action at Medo, 12th April, 1918	393
26.	Action at Nhamacurra, 1st-3rd July, 1918	401
27.	The Environs of Moyale, 1940	483
28.	Action at the Tug Argan, British Somaliland, 11th-18th August, 1940	499
29.	March of FOWCOL to cut the Gelib—Mogadishu Road, 20th-22nd February, 1941	513
30.	Crossing of the River Awash by 5 K.A.R., 3rd April, 1941	518
31.	Attack on Soroppa by 1/4 K.A.R., 31st March, 1941	525
32.	Area of Operations, 2/6 K.A.R., February-June, 1941	532
33.	Attack on Magado Ridge, 6th-7th May, 1941	535
34.	Attack on Mount Fiké, 1st May, 1941	541
35.	Action at Colito, 19th May, 1941	545
36.	The Gondar—Kulkaber Area	557
37.	Attacks on Kulkaber, 13th and 21st November, 1941	563
38.	The Tadda—Azozo Positions	566
39.	Line of Advance, Madagascar, 1942	581
40.	Advance from Majunga to Marotsipoy, 10th-17th September, 1942	585
41.	Advance from Ankazobe to Tananarive, 19th-23rd September, 1942	589
42.	Action at Mahitsy, 21st-22nd September, 1942	590
43.	Advance from Tananarive to Ambositra, 25th September-16th October, 1942	595
44.	Advance from Ambohimahasoa to Ambalavao, 25th October-6th November, 1942	603
45.	Attack on Jambo Hill by 11 K.A.R., 18th August, 1944	619
46.	Attack on Leik Ridge by 4 K.A.R., 22nd-23rd October, 1944	632
47.	Operations of 22 (E.A.) Brigade on the Tanlwe and Taungup Chaungs, April-May, 1945	675

FOLDING MAPS

	FACING PAGE
I. UGANDA	63

    (a) Map showing the sites of the early forts in Western Uganda, and illustrating the Operations of the Northern Garrison, 1912-14.
    (b) The Central Province.
    (c) Karamoja and Turkana.

II. THE NANDI COUNTRY AND THE GERMAN FRONTIER . . 90
    (a) The Nandi Country; Map to illustrate the Campaigns of 1895-1900.
    (b) The Nandi Country: Defence of the Railway, 1902-06.
    (c) The Southern Frontier of Uganda, 1914.
    (d) The Kilimanjaro Area, 1914.

III. BRITISH SOMALILAND 190
    To illustrate the Campaigns against the Mad Mullah, 1900-20.

IV. JUBALAND AND THE NORTHERN FRONTIER DISTRICT . 227

V. GERMAN EAST AFRICA. Northern Sheet 325
    (a) The Arusha—Dodoma Area.
    (b) The Pare—Usambara Area.
    (c) The Advance of the Lake Force.
    (d) The Area of the Central Railway.
    (e) The Pursuit of Wintgens and Naumann.

VI. GERMAN EAST AFRICA. Southern Sheet 388
    (a) Campaigns of the Kilwa and Lindi Columns, October, 1916-November, 1917.
    (b) Area of Operations, Northey's Force, 1916.
    (c) Movements on Northey's eastern flank, August-September, 1916.
    (d) The Songea Area.
    (e) The Lukuledi Valley.

VII. PORTUGUESE EAST AFRICA 411
    The Pursuit of von Lettow, 1918.

VIII. THE ABYSSINIAN CAMPAIGN, 1941 573
    (a) The Invasion of Italian Somaliland.
    (b) The Advance from Mogadishu to Giggiga.
    (c) The Advance from Giggiga to Addis Ababa.
    (d) Operations in the South and West.
    (e) Northern Abyssinia and French Somaliland.

IX. BURMA 613
    With reference to the Campaigns of the K.A.R., 1944-45.

X. BURMA: THE KABAW VALLEY. Operations of 11 (E.A.) Division, 1944   661
    (a) The Area of Operations.
    (b) The Advance to Sittaung.
    (c) The Advance to Yazagyo.
    (d) The Yazagyo—Kontha Area.
    (e) Operations of 22 K.A.R., 26th-27th October.
    (f) Operations in the Mawku—Mawlaik Area.
    (g) The Advance of 21 (E.A.) Brigade east of the Chindwin.
    (h) Positions south of Yazagyo.
    (i) The Myittha Gorge.
    (j) The Completion of the Chindwin Bridgehead.
    (k) The Indainggale—Indainggyi Area.

XI. BURMA. Operations of 28 (E.A.) Brigade, January-April, 1945 . . 672

ACKNOWLEDGEMENTS

I WISH to record my thanks to General Sir George Giffard for his constant interest and unfailing help at all times during the making of this book; and to Professor C. H. Philips for kindly supervising the first two parts of the work. I am also indebted to Professor Sir Keith Hancock and the authorities of the Historical Section of the War Cabinet for enabling me to see certain unpublished material relating to the campaigns in East Africa during the two world wars; to Lieutenant-General Sir Alexander Cameron, Lieutenant-Colonel C. F. Rouse, and Mr. J. F. Sandon for making available all relative documents at G.H.Q., Field Records, East Africa; to the Chief Archivist, Nyasaland, for a similar facility with regard to the Central African Archives; to the authorities of the Colonial Office for permission to consult their files relating to the K.A.R.; to Dr. R. A. Oliver and Mr. G. W. B. Huntingford for their helpful suggestions and criticisms; to Major-General W. A. Dimoline, Major-General W. H. A. Bishop, and Lieutenant-Colonel M. W. Biggs for commenting on certain events in which they themselves played important parts; to Mr. D. W. King, Deputy Librarian at the War Office Library, for his constant help in elucidating many points of detail; to Dr. G. C. Pether for two medical notes on the Mad Mullah of Somaliland; to Mr. R. J. Hoy, for kindly reading the proofs; to Mrs. A. F. Broomfield, Miss Gillian Glennie and Miss A. M. W. Adams for assistance in preparing the typescript; and finally to all those officers and ex-officers, too numerous to mention by name, who have seen service with the African soldiers whose exploits are described in this book, and have generously allowed me to make use of their correspondence. diaries and photographs.

H. M-B.

INTRODUCTION

MILITARY service and civil administration were synonymous during the early years of British rule in east and central Africa. Civilian commissioners led military expeditions; military officers governed provinces, settled tribal disputes, and constructed roads and public works as part of their normal duties. In British Central Africa the primary problems, the suppression of slave-raiding and the establishment of internal security, involved measures of a police rather than a military character. In Uganda military measures assumed an international significance, bound up with control of the Nile sources and the reconquest of the Sudan. To the regular officer of the 1890's, particularly those who had served with Arabic-speaking troops, Uganda offered a new and valuable field of experience.

By the beginning of the present century, the evolution of civil government in the African territories had brought about, in principle at least, the separation and subordination of the military function. In practice this separation remained for some years incomplete. In Jubaland and along the northern frontiers of British East Africa and Uganda, military measures remained closely knit with civil control, and the dual experience so gained resulted in the recruitment to civil service of many officers whose knowledge of Africa had been gained in a military capacity. This state of affairs lasted until the outbreak of the 1914-18 war. A unity of policy and practice may therefore be traced throughout the period 1890-1914, in which the military officer played a special part in the general extension and development of British rule in the territories of Somaliland, East Africa, Uganda and Nyasaland.

There is also a modern significance in the study of the military history of this part of the African continent. The withdrawal of Britain from the North-West Frontier of India, for so many years the best practical training-ground for her troops, the position in the Sudan and the Near Eastern bases on the Suez Canal, have already placed the territories of eastern Africa in a fresh strategic relationship with the Commonwealth as a whole. This new importance is not merely the result of a geographical accident. In this post-war period, when increased military commitments have had to be met in the tropical dependencies coincidentally with the loss of the Indian Army, the importance to Britain of colonial troops has been greatly enhanced, and the evolution of the African askari, with all his limitations and his special skills, is a subject that well merits the attention of the military historian.

No comprehensive study has previously been made of the military aspects of this branch of African colonial history, and no account has yet been published of the growth and organization of the armed forces concerned, nor, with the exception of an official history of the campaigns in Somaliland between 1901 and 1904, of the local campaigns in which they fought. It has been necessary to approach the subject without the general guidance even of a standard political history of this part of

Africa, and consequently without preconceived ideas of the main trends of policy.

The material I have consulted has fallen into five main categories: published work; parliamentary papers; the relevant correspondence in the Foreign Office and Colonial Office files (now in the custody of the Public Record Office); the archives of the colonial governments, and of the military record office at Nairobi; and various diaries, letters and other papers in private hands. These sources are listed in Appendix G.

Published works consist mainly of the personal narratives of those who took a prominent part in laying the foundations of British rule in east and central Africa: soldiers, administrators, missionaries, travellers and traders. The list shown in the Select Bibliography has been chosen from a wide field. Six military officers wrote accounts of their experiences in Uganda, though one of these books (Ternan's *Some Reminiscences of an Old Bromsgrovian*) was not published until long after the events described. Other books (e.g. McDermott's *British East Africa or IBEA*) were written in justification of recent events, or of personal actions (e.g. Lugard's *Rise of Our East African Empire* and Austin's *With Macdonald in Uganda*). All these works, by virtue of their particular viewpoints, have their value, especially when dealing with such controversial issues as the causes of the Sudanese Mutiny. Private diaries and correspondence have provided first-hand impressions of places, people and actions to supplement other material and my own first-hand experience of the country and of the Regiment.

The parliamentary papers listed in the bibliography cover the complete range published between 1890 and 1920 containing any information of military significance. From this source a great deal of important correspondence is readily obtained, though there were occasions, e.g. in the report of the Jubaland Expedition of 1901, when the full story did not become known until after the publication of the paper. Prior to 1901 most of these papers relate to the stormy course of affairs in Uganda; after that date the more important of them deal with the 'Mad Mullah' operations in Somaliland.

The files of the Foreign Office contain all despatches, drafts, correspondence and minutes relating to the affairs of the African protectorates. During the early 1890's the volume of this material was slight; after 1894 it becomes considerable. Military affairs were not treated separately, but were filed in order of date as a part of the whole. The Colonial Office, on the other hand, opened from the start of its East African administration in 1905 a separate series of files dealing exclusively with the King's African Rifles. It is upon this category of source material that the first two parts of this book have primarily been based, the main outline of the growth of the armed forces reconstructed, and the evolution of colonial military policy traced.

Some useful material from the archives of the governments of Nyasaland, Zanzibar, Kenya and Uganda has been made available to me in England, and I was able to see still more during a recent visit to Kenya and Uganda. Of particular value has been a number of files dealing with tribal expeditions in Uganda around the turn of the century, and the manuscript diary of Captain Claude Sitwell, now in the Secretariat Archives at Entebbe. This diary covers the period May, 1895, to May,

1899, and throws new light on the basic loyalty of the Sudanese troops.

The haphazard treatment of military affairs in the early stages of British administration in tropical Africa and the lack of formal organization before 1895 have made it difficult to discover the details of any settled policy before that date. In particular, the attitude of the Imperial British East Africa Company towards this question remains hazy. It has, however, been possible to show the part played by military officers, to trace the evolution of military policy after 1895, and its integration within the different territories after the reorganization of 1901.

The compilation of accurate maps to illustrate the earlier periods of East African history has presented some difficulty. A group of shallow water-holes, a lonely tree, an outstanding rock, and similar features are sufficient in certain parts of Africa, notably in Somaliland and the N.F.D., to merit place-names in areas otherwise too barren to admit of other means of identification. These names are subject to change in the course of time; villages, first known by the names of chiefs or headmen, have sometimes ceased to be so called after their death; some have disappeared with the exhaustion of the soil, others in the course of tribal migrations. It is hoped, however, that the maps contained in this volume will prove adequate for the understanding of the text.

The first two parts of the book, covering the period 1890-1914, were written as a thesis for the degree of Ph.D. of the University of London.

For the military operations that formed part of the two world wars, the main source material has been the official despatches, unpublished accounts dealing with the various formations concerned, and the war diaries of the K.A.R. battalions taking part. This material has been supplemented by many diaries and other papers in private hands. The campaigns have been recorded from the viewpoint of the K.A.R., but the operations of the Regiment have been set within a general framework descriptive of each campaign as a whole.

Throughout this book officers have been given the military ranks they held at the time, no distinction being made between substantive, brevet, local, temporary or acting ranks. Where possible the regiment to which an officer belonged has been indicated when his name first appears in the text.

When the events described in the earlier chapters took place the 24-hour clock system was not in use; in order to preserve uniformity it has not been introduced at a later stage.

One more point is worthy of mention. It is hoped that this account of the origins, development, and fighting record of a colonial regiment will reveal something of the part played by the African himself in helping to lay and preserve the foundations of British rule in Africa, a factor that has been too little regarded in the past.

H. M-B.

PART I

THE CAMPAIGNS OF THE EARLY REGIMENTS

CHAPTER 1

The Political Background

THE origins of the King's African Rifles lie within the earliest period of British administration in East and Central Africa. Though the Regiment dates officially from 1st January, 1902, when it was formally constituted under its present title, troops had been raised and trained in each territory long before that date. Three regiments were already in existence: the Central Africa Regiment,[1] the Uganda Rifles, and the East Africa Rifles. These, with their Indian Contingents and certain levies in British Somaliland, were reorganized and renamed to form the six original battalions of the K.A.R.

No regiment has ever been more intimately connected with the territories through which it marched and fought, or with the peoples from whom it was recruited. Among the lakes and uplands of Central Africa, the swamps and rivers of Uganda, the mountains and desert of the Abyssinian border, and the waterless bush of Somaliland, the operations of the K.A.R. have played a major part in the development of British Africa. In pioneering days the three regiments were the normal instruments of civilized authority. During the first world war the K.A.R. took part in the conquest of the vast German territory that hitherto had separated its recruiting areas. In the second world war, after safeguarding its own homelands by participating in one of the swiftest fighting advances in military history, the Regiment for the first time saw active service outside the continent.

The establishment of armed forces within the African protectorates was an essential step in the early development of these territories. Before describing the circumstances that led to the formation of the three original regiments, the story of whose organization and campaigns must form the first part of this history, it is necessary to sketch briefly the political and topographical scene in which these events were set.

As early as the eighth century of our era Arab settlements were to be found along the eastern seaboard of Africa. Passing for a time under Portuguese domination, they had become in the early nineteenth century an overseas empire subject to Oman. Slaves and elephants—the black ivory and the white—were the objects of the quest that first took the Arabs to the populous regions around the great African lakes, for in their opinion no other trade was sufficiently lucrative to justify the expense of such arduous journeys. In 1840 Seyyid Said, the ruler of Oman, elected to leave Arabia for the more exotic atmosphere of Zanzibar, and thereafter devoted his energies primarily to developing commerce between

[1] Originally the Central Africa Rifles.

his coastal possessions and the vast and little-known territory that lay behind them. A British Consul was appointed at Zanzibar in 1841.

Before his death in 1856 Said expressed the wish that his dominions should be divided between two of his sons, one taking Oman and the other Zanzibar and the African settlements. The eldest living son, Thuwain, contested this division, claiming Zanzibar (which had passed to his brother Majid) as well as Oman, where in his father's lifetime he had ruled as governor. After an abortive attack on Zanzibar, Thuwain was constrained to submit the matter to the arbitration of the Governor-General of India, who confirmed the division of Said's dominions, mainly because of the evident preference of the people of Zanzibar for the rule of Majid.

In 1870 Majid was succeeded by his brother Barghash, the first ruler of Zanzibar whom it became customary for European nations to address as 'Sultan'. During his reign the influence of Britain, as exemplified in the person of Sir John Kirk, the Consul-General, rapidly became paramount at Zanzibar. This influence could easily have developed into direct political control. In 1877 Barghash offered to Sir William Mackinnon, the Chairman of the British India Steam Navigation Company, who had begun a regular mail service between Aden and Zanzibar, a seventy-year lease of his mainland dominions. Again, in 1881 Barghash offered to the British Government the official guardianship of his heir in terms that would undoubtedly have led to a formal protectorate. But the negotiations with Mackinnon broke down, and Britain refused to undertake the proffered guardianship. Kirk's policy was not to supplant, but to support the Sultan's authority.

There was a disinterested reason for this. Kirk was anxious to secure the Sultan's co-operation in destroying the slave trade, the very foundation on which the prosperity of their dominions was considered by the Arabs to rest. It has been estimated that at the accession of Barghash some 80,000 to 100,000 Africans were killed or captured annually on the continent by Arab slavers and their confederates among the tribal chiefs. The British Navy had long been attempting to crush the slave trade, but the effect of naval patrols in the Indian Ocean was comparatively slight. The trade could never be eliminated at sea so long as it continued to flourish on land.

Throughout the middle years of the century the operations of the Arabs steadily developed, and prosperous communities grew up at well-organized trading centres on the lakes. From Kilwa, Bagamoyo and other ports along the tropical coast their caravans traversed well-beaten tracks to the region around Lake Nyasa; through Tabora to Ujiji and other points around Lake Tanganyika, and thence northward to Lake Victoria and Buganda. At first, their attitude towards the European explorers and missionaries, who were beginning to visit and settle in East and Central Africa, was fairly cordial. This situation was abruptly reversed by the European 'grab for Africa' that followed the action of the German explorer Karl Peters, who in 1884 made a number of treaties with African chiefs and in the following year founded a German East Africa Company that afterwards received a Charter of Protection from the

Kaiser. As similar treaties had been made in the Moshi and Taveta areas by Harry H. Johnston,[1] a young artist, naturalist and explorer who had led a scientific expedition to Mount Kilimanjaro for the British Association, the rivalry thus created put an end to Kirk's policy of preserving the integrity of the Sultan's dominions and brought to the fore the question of his exact status on the African mainland.

The Sultan had planted his flag at various points inland, and now claimed extensive territorial rights. Britain, France and Germany agreed that these should be examined by an international commission. On visiting the coastal ports the members of the commission found garrisons of 'Arab' troops at Dar-es-Salaam, Pangani, Tanga, Vanga, Mombasa, Takaungu and elsewhere. Britain and Germany, the two nations principally concerned, agreed in 1886 to define the Sultan's continental dominions as a strip of coast ten miles deep, stretching from Tunghi Bay to Kipini, and the ports of Kismayu, Brava, Merca, Mogadishu and Warsheikh. The River Umba was to mark the boundary between the British and German 'spheres of influence', the British reaching north to the Tana and the German south to the Rovuma. This arrangement Sultan Barghash had no option but to accept.

Under the presidency of Sir William Mackinnon a British East Africa Association was now formed to take over Johnston's treaty rights. In May, 1887, the Association gained a concession of Barghash's coastal strip north of the Umba, to be administered in his name, and in the same year made a number of treaties with tribes in the interior. In March. 1888, Barghash died and was succeeded by his brother Khalifa, who confirmed the arrangements already nearing completion for a similar concession to the German East Africa Company. On 3rd September, 1888, Mackinnon's Association received a royal charter and became the Imperial British East Africa Company, charged with the administration of a vast but ill-defined territory, to be governed on the lines of a crown colony. It was a heavy responsibility for a small commercial enterprise, and George Mackenzie, the Company's first administrator, who reached Zanzibar in October of that year, was obliged to exercise a liberal measure of tact and discretion. Trouble was forestalled at Mombasa by the presence of two British warships and a body of the Sultan's troops, but Mackenzie made no attempt to hoist the Company's flag, and later on the two flags were always flown side by side within the coastal strip.

Such tact was not shown by the Germans. The Arab *liwalis* on the coast were naturally suspicious of the arrangements that had been made over their heads, and the Germans' open contempt for the Sultan's flag brought immediate conflict with their new dependants. The Director of the Company was fired upon when he tried to land at Pangani; a German warship bombarded Tanga; the coast flamed with resentment and for a time the Germans were forced to withdraw. Britain joined in a naval blockade, intended to prevent the importation of arms. Captain Hermann von Wissman was appointed by the Kaiser as Imperial Commissioner to

---

[1] Later Sir Harry Johnston, Commissioner and Consul-General for British Central Africa, 1891-97.

quell the rising, and ruthlessly fulfilled his charge in 1889 with Sudanese troops and naval forces.

The effect of these events upon Arab policy in the interior was widespread. For the first time the Arabs aimed at establishing their authority over the inland tribes in a conscious effort to forestall or supplant European influence. Relations between Arabs and Europeans, hitherto tolerant and even friendly, became after 1884 violently antagonistic.[1] Most Europeans attributed this to an intensification of the slave trade, but the movement was undoubtedly political, and so comprehensive that there is reason to suppose that it must have been co-ordinated at Zanzibar.[2] At this point it is necessary to examine the nature of the inland territories and the situation that arose there at the time when they were about to pass under British control.

Beyond the seaboard of eastern Africa the coastal plain varies in width from ten to thirty miles, or more in the basins of the great river systems. Inland the country rises to an elevated plateau cut by the eastern and bounded by the western arm of the Great Rift Valley, a vast fissure flanked in the region of Lake Tanganyika by abrupt cliffs, several thousand feet high. Properly speaking the Rift Valley ends here, but the depression continues south-east to embrace Lake Nyasa, the third largest lake in the continent. This broad band of water, deep and navigable though subject to sudden storms of considerable violence, runs for 360 miles from north to south down the wide valley floor, to drain at the southern end through the deeper valley of the Shiré River into the great Zambesi. Beyond the plains bordering the lake, scarped highlands rise to a height sometimes exceeding 7,000 feet. To the south the plateau of the Shiré Highlands is crowned by the steep mountain groups of Mlanje and Zomba. In some respects the country is not unlike Scotland, though the natural scenery varies from the familiar thin acacia groves of the tropical African plains to hardwood and evergreen forests and the pale, delicate green of the bamboo belt in the cooler altitudes. Though not large by African standards, this region of high mountains, deep valleys, woods and rivers forms a distinctive physical unit. Politically, the western plateau and the southern highlands comprise the protectorate now known as Nyasaland.

In 1851 Livingstone first struck the Zambesi in his explorations from the south. Seven years later he led an expedition up the river from the coast, branched northward up the Shiré, and in September, 1859, discovered the lake. Greatly concerned at the extent of the slave trading that harassed and oppressed the tribes north of the Zambesi, his reports met with a sympathetic response in Britain, but a short-lived attempt to found a mission on the Shiré was defeated by sickness and the difficulties of supply. In 1866 Livingstone returned to Central Africa, crossed Lake

---

[1] For a brief but vivid account of the kind of experience that converted the early British pioneers into implacable opponents of the Arab slavers, see A. J. Swann, *Fighting the Slave-Hunters in Central Africa*, pp. 48-50.

[2] R. A. Oliver, 'Some Factors in the British Occupation of East Africa, 1884-1894,' *Uganda Journal*, xv, 1 (March, 1951), 52-55.

Nyasa and continued his explorations among the elevated plateaux to the west, reaching Lakes Mweru and Bangweulu and the southern end of Lake Tanganyika. It was near Lake Bangweulu that he died in 1873. Two years later the Free Church Mission became the pioneer of permanent British settlement in Nyasaland, when the Livingstonia station was first founded at Cape Maclear.

Before long several other missions were also working in the area. After 1878 the missionaries' needs were supplied by a trading concern, the Livingstonia Central Africa Company (generally known as the African Lakes Company and after 1893 as the African Lakes Corporation), which was intended also to foster legitimate trade with the natives. Stations were established on the River Shiré and the western shores of the lake, steamboats appeared on the waterways and a highway was planned, known as the 'Stevenson Road' (after James Stevenson, the Chairman of the Company, who in 1881 offered a substantial sum towards its cost), to connect the north of Lake Nyasa with the southern tip of Lake Tanganyika. This road was built in the first instance as far as the most northerly of the mission stations at Mwiniwanda's, about sixty miles north-west of Lake Nyasa. A few coffee-planters and traders came to settle in the Shiré Highlands, and a British Consul was appointed in 1883. His position was difficult: there was no one to whom he could be properly accredited, and as he had no means of enforcing his authority, he was expected to exercise his functions by persuasion and tact. This official appointment had not long been authorized when the hostility of the Arabs began to develop in earnest.

Though commonly known as 'Arabs' the slavers were usually coastal Swahili with a slight admixture of Arab blood. Their methods were insidious and certain. The slaver would enter his chosen district as a peaceful trader, posing as a friend and using every means to gain the confidence of the local tribes. To all appearance he was himself a chief: liberal and wealthy, surrounded by armed followers (*ruga-ruga*); provider not only of coveted trade goods but also of those instruments of authority and power, firearms and powder. In such circumstances the slaver had no difficulty in securing adherents. The next move was to participate in the perpetual local quarrels. With every advantage on their side, the *ruga-ruga* could not fail to win, and it was natural enough that their master should exact his toll of slaves from the defeated enemy. To conduct tribal raids for the express purpose of securing slaves now followed easily, and so the long caravans to the coast began. Some of the more warlike tribes, notably the Angoni and the Yao, were allied with the Arabs in the conduct of this nefarious traffic, which resulted in a long conflict with British authority known as the Slavers' War.

Nearly a thousand miles north of Nyasaland, the territories that were destined to become the protectorates of East Africa and Uganda offered a very different prospect, both topographically and politically. From the coastal plain the land rises through a waterless upland of desert and sapless bush to the grassy plains surrounding the Athi River. Beyond these plains, still the home of vast herds of game, lies the fertile, wooded country of the Kikuyu, rising to a height of some 7,000 feet near the eastern scarp of the Rift Valley. Beyond the valley floor, the western wall is well defined for many miles on both sides of the Equator by the towering escarpments of the Mau and Elgeyo ranges, that form a densely forested watershed beyond which all streams flow towards the upper basin of the Nile.

The rich abundance of Busoga and Buganda in the warm, luxuriant climate of the lower lands around Lake Victoria is in marked contrast to the eastern side of the watershed. The rain-forests of Mount Elgon and the snow-covered mountain ranges of the far west precipitate the rainfall in a huge catchment area that feeds the branches of the Nile. The navigability of this river system is often checked by rapids and swamps, blocked with sudd, and thick, impenetrable growths of papyrus, reeds and grasses that grow far above the height of a man, so that districts such as Lake Kioga remained for many years largely unexplored. North of Elgon and the Nile bend, the country stretches away to a drier region of plain and mountain, arid and volcanic in the neighbourhood of Lake Rudolf, where thin pasture exists for brief periods after the rains, and only a nomad life can maintain the flocks and herds of the pastoral tribes.

Such was the area of windswept upland, sombre forests and brilliant, tropical sunshine known a hundred years ago as 'darkest Africa' and shown practically blank upon the maps, a standing temptation to all of an adventurous turn of mind.

Rumours of the existence of great lakes and waterways, coupled with the search for the hidden sources of the Nile, drew a number of explorers to this region in the mid-nineteenth century. The presence of hostile tribes in the upper valley of the Nile made progress from the north difficult beyond Gondokoro. Conceiving it easier to approach the great lakes from the east coast, the explorers Burton and Speke reached Lake Tanganyika in 1858, and from there Speke struck north to Lake Victoria. On a subsequent expedition he travelled up the western shores of the lake to Buganda, where instead of a country of scattered tribes and petty chiefs he found an organized Bantu kingdom, flanked by tributary states beyond its borders, with an elaborate system of native law and administration, a fleet of canoes, and a method of levying troops. Speke traced the outlet of the eastern branch of the Nile; Baker, approaching from the north, discovered Lake Albert. The main sources of the White Nile were thus made clear by British explorers.

Egypt was at that time engaged in an expansion of territory that ultimately proved too great for her resources. The Khedive chose Baker to command an expedition into the region south of the Sudan, and afterwards made him Governor of the equatorial province thus acquired, charged with the task of subjugating the country south of Gondokoro and suppressing the slave trade. In 1876 his successor Gordon sent a mission to Mutesa of Buganda, contemplating a possible extension of territory still farther south. The envoy chosen for this delicate task was a German doctor named Eduard Schnitzer, who while serving in Turkish employment had become a Muslim and was now known as Emin Effendi. Two years after his mission Emin was appointed Governor of the equatorial province with the title of Pasha. In 1884, isolated from Egypt by the

Mahdist Rebellion, he was forced to retire south with his troops to Wadelai, and for some time nothing further was heard of him. Eventually the German explorer Junker brought Emin's journals to Europe, where they excited considerable interest and led to a clamour for his relief. This was effected in 1888 by Stanley, who persuaded the somewhat reluctant Emin to accompany him to the coast.

Stanley had first visited Buganda in 1875, and his description of the country and people led to the arrival of an Anglican mission in June, 1877. The first missionaries carried letters from the British Foreign Office that inevitably gave them some official standing in Mutesa's eyes. They were followed nearly two years later by the French Roman Catholic mission of the White Fathers. Though Mutesa was a cruel tyrant he was inclined, if only for political reasons, to favour the Christians rather than the Muslim party, which was already growing in consequence of Arab penetration. In 1884 Mutesa died and was succeeded by his son Mwanga, a profligate youth, who, though his real aim was to stamp out both the recently imported religions, leaned at first towards the Arab party. At their instigation, in October, 1885, he brought about the murder of the Anglican Bishop Hannington, who was at that time approaching the country, and in 1886 there followed a severe persecution of African Christians of both denominations, from which, however, they emerged considerably strengthened. Meanwhile Mwanga was turning away from his Arab advisers and trying to institute a pagan reaction, thus driving the Muslims and the Christians into a temporary alliance. From the first trial of strength in 1888 the monotheistic parties emerged victorious, and Mwanga was compelled to flee for refuge to a Roman Catholic mission station at the south of the lake. In Buganda it was not long before the Muslims and the Christians were at loggerheads, and the former being at first successful, the latter joined forces with the exiled Mwanga and sought to restore him to his throne.

It was at this stage that Mwanga first sought the help of the newly-established Imperial British East Africa Company. Exploratory safaris had been sent inland to make treaties with the chiefs and report on the opportunities for trade, and in the course of this work F. J. Jackson[1] and Ernest Gedge reached Mumia's village in Kavirondo late in 1889. Mwanga heard of their presence and wrote to Jackson appealing for help, but the latter had been instructed not to enter Buganda, as the Company had no wish to become embroiled. Jackson went north to Mount Elgon, seeking for ivory to pay the expenses of the trip, and did not return to Mumia's till March, 1890. By then Mwanga had regained his throne, but a further letter addressed to Jackson had been opened and read by Karl Peters, who had landed on the coast near Witu and travelled inland with the ostensible purpose of 'relieving' Emin, though really to investigate the chances of extending the German sphere in the inland areas. Peters hastened to Mengo, the capital of Buganda, and offered his services to Mwanga in the hope of securing a treaty for Germany. This effort was

---

[1] Later Sir Frederick Jackson, who after many years' service in Africa became Governor and Commander-in-Chief, Uganda, 1911-17.

nullified soon afterwards by the Anglo-German Agreement of 1890, but Peters' action was sufficient to take Jackson to Buganda, where he left Gedge as the Company's representative, with 35 men and all the rifles he could spare. In this way, against its original intentions, the Company first gained a footing in Buganda.

Meanwhile within the coastal strip the Imperial British East Africa Company was called upon to rule a settled Arab community of long standing, where Muslims were already quarrelling with the Christian missions over the question of slavery. Seven years were to pass before the inevitable trial of strength took place, but the Company was faced at once with an unexpected difficulty—the aggressive attitude adopted by the state-supported German Company. Ahmad bin Fumo Luti, a descendant of the old Nabhan Sultans of Patta, had been conquered by Majid in 1860 and had settled in the Witu district, about twenty-five miles inland, north of the River Osi. There he collected about 3,000 malcontents and terrorized the surrounding tribes, who nicknamed him 'Simba'. When the Sultan of Zanzibar sent a punitive expedition to Lamu his action was challenged by the Germans, who considered Simba their protégé and claimed jurisdiction over the coast north of the Tana. On grounds of a vague promise, Germany then claimed the cession of Lamu. Arbitration decided in favour of the British Company, which got the concession instead.

Great hopes were entertained at this period for the future development of the Tana valley. The entrance to the river is blocked by a bar, but access to the sea was gained by a canal linking the Tana with the Osi. On this canal Simba planted an unauthorized customs post which he refused to remove, expecting to receive the support of the Germans. In October, 1888, Germany suddenly declared a protectorate over the coast from Witu to Kismayu. This so disheartened the Directors of the British Company that they called on the Government to declare a protectorate over all their territories. They had already decided to enforce their ultimatum at Witu, and towards the end of December C. H. Craufurd was sent with 150 troops and a maxim gun. The Germans were in no position to back Simba with force, and he retired discomfited while Craufurd occupied the district.

The remaining steps needed to complete the political settlement were soon taken. During 1889 the Sultan of Zanzibar executed an agreement with the Italian Government that resulted in a concession of his ports and their surrounding territories north and east of the River Juba, which thus became the frontier between the British and Italian spheres, with equal rights of navigation reserved to both nations. The vagueness of the inland boundary, however, still offered scope for the German ambition of securing all the great lakes of central Africa. The matter was settled by the Anglo-German Agreement signed on 1st July, 1890. Germany gave up her claim to a protectorate over Witu and the coastline as far as the Juba. The southern boundary of British territory, which ran inland from the Umba to Lake Jipe and skirted Kilimanjaro to include the mountain in the German sphere, was continued westward across Lake Victoria along the line of 1° south latitude, and thence to the boundary of the

Congo Free State. The effect of this Agreement was to include in the British sphere a vast area reaching to the western watershed of the Nile. Britain undertook to facilitate the absolute cession to Germany of the Sultan's mainland possessions then occupied by the German East Africa Company, and Germany agreed to recognize a British protectorate over all the Sultan's remaining dominions.

In March, 1891, the Imperial British East Africa Company assumed responsibility for the administration of Witu. In October the administration of Zanzibar was reorganized under the control of H.M. Agent and Consul-General. These measures were followed by the formal declaration of protectorates over Zanzibar and Witu in November. Thereafter some measure of friendly co-operation between British and Germans in East Africa was secured, though the Company felt that this was often achieved at the expense of its shareholders' interests.

As regards the internal situation created by the attitude of the Arabs, however, matters were to prove very different, for the first British administrations had to be set up in territories infected by their deep and widespread hostility, and well supplied with arms by their trading caravans. It is therefore not surprising that these governments were largely military in outlook during those early years, though their armed forces were left to develop out of makeshift arrangements devised upon the spot, and led by Army officers who were often merely on leave in Africa to satisfy their taste for pioneering and adventure.

Each territory established its own regiment independently. In Nyasaland the assistance of Indian troops was first sought to maintain order in the new protectorate. Around them was grouped a body of native troops that eventually became welded into a single unit known as the Central Africa Rifles. In Uganda certain Sudanese troops, formerly of the Khedive's army, became the nucleus of the Uganda Rifles. In East Africa the Foreign Office, on taking over from the Imperial British East Africa Company, formed out of the Company's miscellaneous forces the East Africa Rifles. The circumstances that led to the formation of these three regiments, with some account of the campaigns fought by each, must be related separately, until the time in 1901 when the growing need for organization on a wider basis brought them together as different battalions within a single regiment.

CHAPTER 2

The Central Africa Regiment

(i) *The Slavers' War, 1888-96.* Map 1.

ON the north-west shores of Lake Nyasa, at the point of departure of the Stevenson Road, the African Lakes Company built in 1884 a trading station at Karonga. It was only a small place; at first merely a store, protected by a low wall open at one side to the lake. But it was a beginning. It represented British influence in the north, along the projected route from the Cape to Cairo; was linked by steamer with the settlements in the Shiré valley, and formed a base from which the Stevenson Road might be completed. Karonga therefore had an importance out of proportion to its size, and when its existence was threatened, the Company felt compelled to react strongly. The result was a conflict with the Arab interest on this part of the lake: the 'North End War'. This led to an extension of hostilities against a number of Yao slave-raiding chiefs south and east of the lake, and the whole series of operations became known as the 'Slavers' War', though the term covered a number of separate expeditions rather than a connected campaign. It was during these operations that the first attempts were made to train the indigenous tribes of Nyasaland as fighting troops.

The threat to British influence first came from a slaver named Mlozi, a 'black', or coastal Arab, and his associates Kopakopa, Msalema, and several others, who built their stockades a few miles from Karonga, overlooking the first section of the Stevenson Road. The original slave routes to the coast had run past the southern end of the lake, from a collecting centre at the village of the chief Mponda, and across the lake from Kotakota's on the western to Makanjira's village on the eastern shore. Now, as part of the Arab movement to secure political control over the inland areas, Mlozi began to develop the more remote northerly route.

Far greater in armed strength than the British and insolent in proportion, the slavers were well able to hold their own in these early encounters. At first Mlozi professed friendship for Monteith Fotheringham, the Company's agent at Karonga, and the Arabs generally traded their ivory at the station. Trouble began in July, 1887, when Mlozi first showed signs of his intention to drive out the inoffensive Ankonde tribesmen and replace them by native allies of his own choosing. Fotheringham, who at that time had only 13 rifles and 34 cartridges for the defence of his post, tried in vain to mediate and prevent the outbreak of a local war. His efforts failed; hundreds of Ankonde were brutally massacred by the Arabs, and in November Fotheringham's half-finished

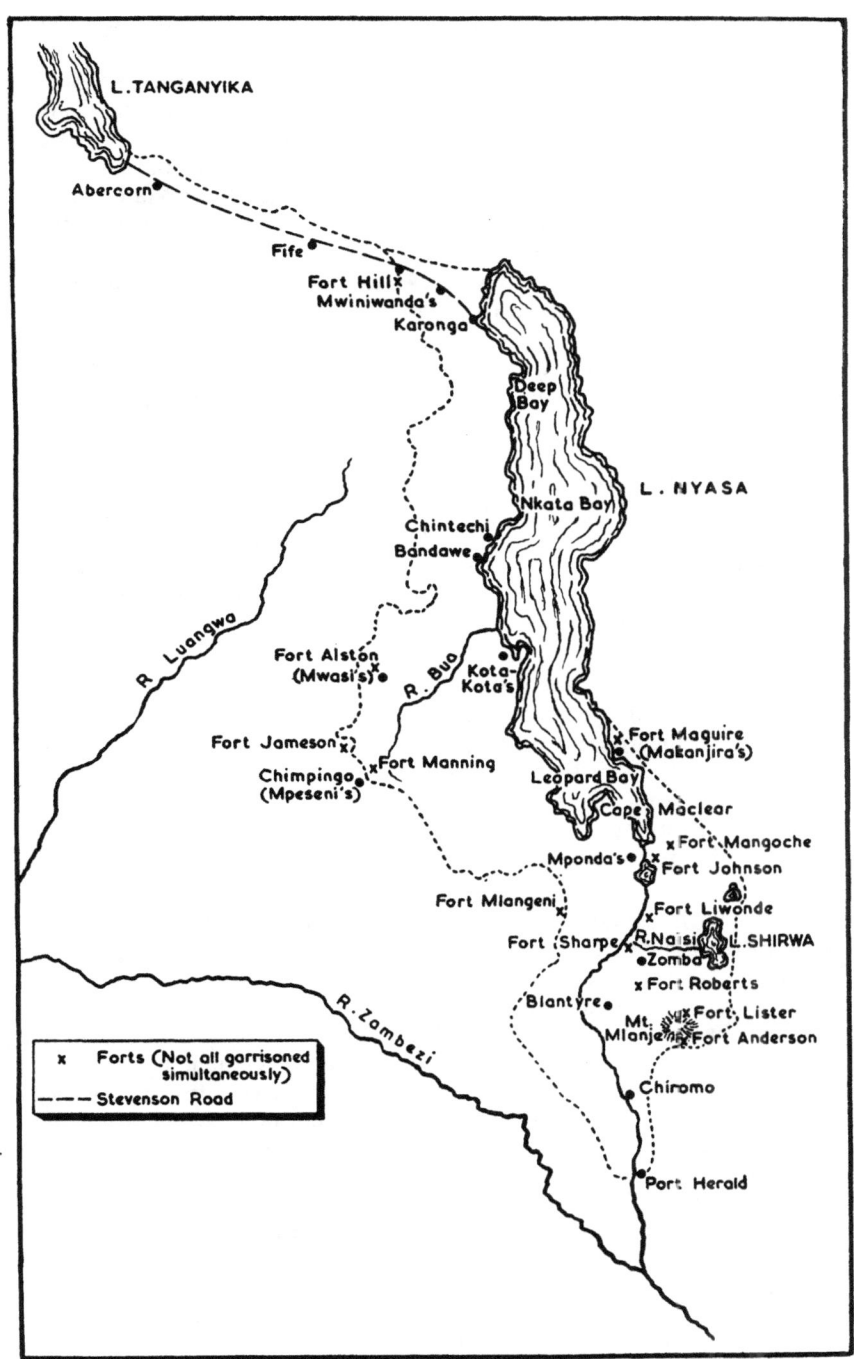

1. Nyasaland

stockade was surrounded. The siege was raised with the help of a large body of Mambwe from the Tanganyika plateau, but these were uncertain allies and for the time being Karonga had to be abandoned.

Although the seriousness of the position was not yet realized at the Company's headquarters at Mandala near Blantyre, the British Consul arrived upon the scene, and while the lake steamer went for reinforcements and supplies, decided with the rest of his European companions to attack the Arabs. This could only be done with the aid of Mambwe and Ankonde allies, and the task of organizing them was deputed to Fotheringham. It was no easy matter. 'I divided them.' he wrote later, 'into what might be termed battalions. . . . Each battalion was commanded by its chief, while the companies or bands—comprising between 200 and 300 men—were led by the head men under the chiefs. The station boys were headed by the whites. All the lines were not of uniform depth, and though our formation might not have pleased an inspecting officer on review day, it must be owned that we looked like our work.'[1] The Arabs were defeated, but so much plunder was captured in the form of ivory, cloth and powder, that the natives were satisfied and refused to continue the campaign. Nothing further could be done until the steamer returned six weeks later, when Karonga was reoccupied and rebuilt. A further attempt at negotiation with the Arabs came to nothing. Mlozi had proclaimed himself 'Sultan of Nkonde' and it was evident that unless the whole of the 'north end' were to fall under Arab control, matters must be fought to a finish.

The North End War was resumed in earnest on 10th April, 1888, when a force of eight Europeans and nearly 500 natives, armed with 270 guns and rifles, left Karonga to attack Msalema's stockade. The village was fired, but a sally from Kopakopa's prevented this advantage from being followed up, and the party withdrew to Karonga. Hostilities then languished, as many of the native allies deserted, disappointed in their hopes of plunder. Nothing decisive was likely to be achieved until the Company produced reinforcements and supplies on an adequate scale.

At this stage Captain F. D. Lugard[2] (Norfolk R.) a soldier too restless in temperament to be satisfied for long with garrison life, appeared in Nyasaland. During the past ten years Lugard had seen active service in Afghanistan, the Sudan and Burma, and now, while on leave from his regiment, had travelled down the east coast of Africa, at first with the idea of joining the Italians in their war against Abyssinia, and then with a half-formed notion of seeking Emin Pasha. Hearing that the African Lakes Company was willing to equip elephant hunters, he decided to make for Blantyre. On his way up the Shiré he heard of the Karonga affair, became convinced that a military expedition was essential to safeguard British interests and decided to offer his services. With the approval of the Acting Consul he agreed to command the relief expedition.

Lugard left Blantyre on 19th May, 1888, with a miscellaneous group

---

[1] L. M. Fotheringham. *Adventures in Nyasaland*, pp. 118-19.
[2] Later first Baron Lugard of Abinger.

of nearly twenty British and South African volunteers. Travelling by steamer, he reached Bandawe on the lake, where he took the advice of Dr. Robert Laws, of the Free Church Mission, regarding the selection of native allies.

At that time the area west of Lake Nyasa was terrorized by the Angoni, the descendants of a Zulu clan that had first crossed the Zambesi in 1835 and travelled north in several migrations, looting, raiding and acquiring cattle and slaves. They were now settled under their chiefs in four main divisions, and the full extent of their authority and power only became known when the members of the Livingstonia Mission visited their country in search of a healthier site than Cape Maclear. The warlike character and military organization of the Angoni made it easy for them to dominate the more peaceful indigenous tribes and assume the status of a ruling caste. Their villages were full of slaves taken in their perpetual raids, particularly against the Atonga, a tribe of fishermen living along the shores of the lake, who had been dispossessed of their inland villages.

Realizing that the Angoni were best avoided, Lugard left one of his company, Alfred Sharpe,[1] to enlist recruits among the Atonga and march them along the coast to Karonga. Sharpe duly arrived with a mixed body of tribesmen, having met and attacked a slaver's caravan on the way. He brought 190 Atonga, who with those already at Karonga raised the number from that tribe to about 220, 50 'Ajawa'[2] and 50 Mambwe. About a third were armed with breech-loaders, and a third with muzzle-loaders. The rest had no firearms at all. Lugard and his Europeans began instruction in musketry, teaching the tribesmen to hold and point their weapons. Exact aiming was beyond them as apparently many were incapable of closing one eye. The Atonga, led by Dzenji, son of the principal chief, were divided into five companies, each under a European. The 'Ajawa' and Mambwe formed a company each, and the miscellaneous elements another. Bullets were cast for the small arms, and hand grenades were made from jam tins rammed with clay and quartz pebbles. Instead of uniforms, each fighting man was given a narrow band of brightly coloured cloth to tie round his head as a distinguishing mark. With these preparations Lugard's 'troops' were ready for war.

Strategically Lugard's operations achieved their object of maintaining a foothold in northern Nyasaland at this critical juncture. Tactically his little army did not meet with much success. The slavers' stockades were twice reconnoitred by night. Under cover of darkness Lugard then assembled his forces and when dawn broke on 16th June led the attack on Kopakopa's. After scrambling across the deep ditches protecting the outside of the stockade, the growing light showed Lugard that what he had taken for a high bank was in reality a substantial mud wall, pierced by loopholes and crowned with a 14-foot stockade. On trying to scale this obstacle in the uncertain hope that the tribesmen would follow, Lugard was shot and paralysed in both arms and the attack had to be broken off.

[1] Later Sir Alfred Sharpe, Commissioner for British Central Africa, 1897, and Governor of Nyasaland, 1907-10.

[2] Yao immigrants.

A grim period followed. For many weeks Lugard sat completely helpless, disheartened by sickness, ill fortune and repeated quarrels among his Europeans. But Karonga was not abandoned. For the time being Fotheringham resumed the command, and a request was sent to Blantyre for a cannon to breach the stockade. Meanwhile Lugard's tribesmen were reorganized in three companies of Atonga, Ankonde and Mambwe respectively, and their regular patrols began to dominate the countryside, attacking the slavers' caravans and practically confining them to their stockades. Lugard grew to have a great regard for his Atonga. Having once gained their respect and convinced them that he was not to be trifled with, he found them ready, cheerful, and willing. They identified themselves with European interests more rapidly and completely than any other tribe, possibly on account of their need for protection both from the Angoni and the Arabs.

At this juncture the Sultan of Zanzibar sent an emissary to assist in arranging terms, but he proved a person of small influence, and after a series of desultory negotiations, finally absconded and threw in his lot with the slavers. In January, 1889, an Armstrong 7-pounder gun reached Karonga. It had been purchased by the Nyasa Anti-Slavery and Defence Committee, which had been established in the United Kingdom by supporters of the Company and the Scottish missions, and passed through the Portuguese customs after special representation from the Foreign Office. Ammunition was scanty, primitive and largely home-made, and the first attack on the stockades was not very successful. The native force kept guard and prevented reinforcements arriving from Mlozi's, while Msalema's and Kopakopa's stockades were bombarded, though without effecting a breach large enough for assault. On the second and third occasions many rounds were fired and most of them found their mark. The worst danger was over; small-pox was raging in the Arab camps, and it was now they who were in a precarious position.

Before the third bombardment, the march of events had taken Lugard elsewhere. Among many Englishmen concerned in the early development of Central Africa, he viewed the situation from the beginning with a soldier's eye, realizing that little progress could be made without a properly armed and disciplined military force. In the light of subsequent events his proposals are interesting. His outlook was strategic and concerned rather with maintaining an open route than with making the country safe for settlement, for he proposed that military headquarters should be established on the Nyasa—Tanganyika plateau, with garrisons at points on both lakes. He suggested that 1,000 troops should at once be raised locally, and placed under Indian officers and N.C.Os.

In October, 1889, H. H. Johnston, who had recently been appointed British Consul at Mozambique, reached Karonga on a mission to the interior. Partly to settle the Arab war and partly to forestall Portuguese interests in Nyasaland, he had travelled inland and negotiated treaties with the powerful half-caste Arab Tawakali Sudi (the 'Jumbe' of Kotakota) and several other chiefs south and west of Lake Nyasa. At Karonga he assured Mlozi that the war would be ruthlessly prosecuted if the terms proposed were not accepted. As these terms, though providing for the peaceful return of the Ankonde and safeguarding the position of the Company, allowed the slavers to retain their stockades, Mlozi and the other Arabs willingly agreed, and the treaty was signed on 22nd October. Johnston then visited Lake Tanganyika, made a treaty with the Mambwe, and on his way back another with the Yao chief Mponda south of Lake Nyasa. It was his suggestion that the territory should be called British Central Africa.[1]

A Protectorate over the whole of Nyasaland was formally proclaimed in May, 1891. Johnston became the first Commissioner, and until 1st July, 1895, was also Administrator of the British South Africa Company for the sphere of influence lying to the west, now known as North-East Rhodesia. Among the members of his staff was Captain C. M. Maguire, of the 2nd Hyderabad Lancers, who was engaged with the consent of the Government of India. Maguire raised 70 volunteers from the Indian Army for service in Central Africa: 40 Mazbi Sikhs of the 23rd and 32nd Pioneers, and 30 Muslim cavalrymen from various units of the Hyderabad Lancers, to form the first armed forces of the new Protectorate.

Johnston set up his headquarters at Zomba. His little army was soon in action, for the Nyasaland region was divided between the slave-trading chiefs, Arab or Swahili in the north and Yao in the south. The Jumbe controlled the west from his headquarters at Kotakota, Makanjira the east of the lake, and Mponda the south. Though a temporary truce had been secured with the Arabs, the conflict had aroused the intense hostility of these Yao chiefs, who belonged to a slave-raiding tribe living along the route to Kilwa and had now spread westward from Portuguese territory, at the expense of the indigenous Nyanja. The Yao were an able people, strong and intelligent, and the suppression of their activities was to involve five years of intermittent war.

Maguire's troops were engaged in four expeditions before the end of 1891. The first took place in July, against a Yao slaver named Chikumbu, who had settled in the mountainous country around Mlanje,. where he dominated the peaceful Nyanja. The occasion of the expedition was an attack on two British coffee-planters. After a few days' hard fighting Maguire put Chikumbu to flight and captured his brother.

A more serious situation arose in September south of Lake Nyasa, where Mponda, who controlled the upper course of the Shiré, was attempting to interfere with the free passage of the river steamers. Johnston and Maguire set out with 68 sepoys and a 7-pounder gun. On reaching the neighbourhood of Mponda's. Maguire thought it advisable to fortify his camp. The work had to be done secretly and at night, as Mponda was highly suspicious. These hastily constructed earthworks revetted with bamboo were called by their constructor 'Fort Johnston', and became the first of a succession of forts established throughout the Protectorate in the next few years.[2] From this camp Maguire moved out to crush chief Makandanji, who had

---
[1] The name was changed to Nyasaland in 1907.
[2] Fort Johnston was later moved down river to a healthier site.

captured some Government messengers. Mponda remained quiet during this action and then cynically captured the refugees. As he refused to give them up his town was bombarded and his warriors driven out. The news of this so disturbed Zarafi, a very powerful Yao chief living twenty miles to the east, that he also subscribed to the peace treaty. Johnston and Maguire then turned their attention to Makanjira, who had been raiding friendly chiefs across the lake. Makanjira's village was bombarded from the steamer *Domira* and afterwards taken and burnt. Ten Zanzibari and ten Makua tribesmen served with the sepoys on this expedition, and Johnston was well pleased with their performance.

The expedition had hardly returned to Zomba when news came of depredations by the Yao chief Kawinga, who lived north-east of the Zomba Range. The main enemy position lay on top of a hill. When Maguire tried to storm it he was wounded in the chest and his attack was repulsed, but Kawinga sued for peace.

Maguire returned to Mponda's to complete the building of Fort Johnston, which was to be permanently garrisoned. Makanjira possessed a fleet of slaving dhows, and information came that two of them were hidden in a small cove. The chance was too good to miss, and Maguire embarked a small force in the *Domira*. On 15th December he landed at the cove with 28 men and was immediately attacked by Makanjira with overwhelming force. Maguire withdrew to the beach, and in trying to get close inshore the steamer went aground. Maguire was shot through the head as he was pulling himself on board, and sank into the water dead. His troops struggled on board with a loss of three killed. Makanjira then enticed the doctor and chief engineer on shore with a promise of surrendering Maguire's body, and treacherously murdered them. Owing to the efforts of the second engineer and the Sikhs, who behaved splendidly throughout, the *Domira* escaped, firing her 7-pounder gun into Makanjira's hordes as she drew away. But the final reckoning with this powerful chief had to be postponed.

Soon afterwards Zarafi attacked Fort Johnston, and the Commissioner hurried north to its relief with a force that included several British volunteers. Mponda remained loyal, and Zarafi's more vulnerable villages on the plain were raided in revenge. For the time being, however, his subjugation could not be attempted, for the morale of the little body of troops was seriously shaken. The Sikhs, who had actually wept over Maguire's death, were by this time reduced to 63 effectives, of whom 10 were suffering from wounds. The cavalrymen were unused to hill fighting and their horses had died from tsetse. Soon afterwards they were sent back to India, and the Viceroy agreed to replace them with Sikhs, on the understanding that the Protectorate would pay wound and family pensions in the event of casualties.

Johnston was careful to explain that these expensive military expeditions were forced upon him by circumstances beyond his control. 'I shall confine my attention mainly to the maintenance of order and security along the great trade routes of Central Africa,' he wrote to the Foreign Office. 'Neither Captain Maguire nor myself have gone out of our way to attack the Slave Trade.' In fact, he had neither the means nor the inclination to prosecute a war for its own sake. The folly of attempting too much with inadequate resources was demonstrated when J. G. King, who had been left in charge of Fort Johnston, was tempted by an offer of help from the Angoni to try conclusions with Zarafi. King's expedition numbered 35 sepoys, about 30 Zanzibaris, 100 Angoni and some porters. At the foot of the slaver's hill-fortress he was wounded and seriously defeated, losing six of his Indian troops killed. Fourteen others were scattered and reached Fort Johnston some days later, and a 7-pounder gun was lost in the bush. The morale of the Yao chiefs, who had grown cautious at the exhibition of British strength, was immediately restored. In reporting this setback Johnston again felt impelled to make his intentions clear. 'I am anxious,' he wrote to the Secretary of State, 'to assure your Lordship that I am not pursuing a bellicose policy in attempting to suppress the Slave Trade along the River Shiré and on the south end of Lake Nyasa. . . . But what I am forced to do is to put down slave-raiding and trading along our narrow and precious line of communications between the Shiré and Tanganyika, because if I allow these nefarious pursuits to continue, I am exposing this line of communication to constant and dangerous interruptions.' For a time, however, Johnston was obliged to remain on the defensive, until the arrival in June, 1892, of Captain C. E. J. Johnson (36th Sikhs) with another 60 Sikhs. These new troops and three gunboats on the lake helped to restore British prestige.

Trouble arose again in February, 1893, with a serious outbreak of slave-raiding on the Upper Shiré. The worst offender was a chief named Liwonde. When one of his caravans made off with some boys from Zomba, Captain Johnson went in pursuit and released them, though their captors escaped. The whole district was in arms, and for a time Johnson was cut off. With the arrival of a contingent of sailors the position was restored ; Liwonde's town was attacked and taken and two more forts were established.

During 1893 the armed forces of the Protectorate were reorganized and strengthened. In that year the time of the first draft of Sikhs expired. Captain Johnson asked that in future only Jat Sikhs should be sent, and it was decided also to increase the number. A draft of 100 arrived under command of Lieutenant C. A. Edwards (35th Sikhs), and a second draft of the same strength under Lieutenant W. H. Manning[1] (1st Sikhs), who was destined to become the first Inspector-General of the K.A.R. Meanwhile the policy of enlisting Africans as regular troops had already begun. Trial was first made with about 50 Zanzibaris and Makua, but the former proved nearly as expensive as Sikhs and were not easy to recruit, owing to regulations at Zanzibar controlling their employment overseas, so they were eventually paid off and replaced by local enlistments. The military force now numbered three British officers, 200 Sikhs, 150 native regulars, and a varying number of irregular levies. Though the Sikhs were still the mainstay of the force, the need to train local troops was at last realized, for the Government of India was growing disturbed at the

---

[1] Afterwards Brigadier-General Sir William Manning, G.C.M.G., K.B.E., C.B., Governor and Commander-in-Chief, Nyasaland, 1910-13.

frequent requests for troops to serve in Africa, fearing that the high rates of pay would interfere with recruiting for the Indian Army.

Two more forts (Fort Lister and Fort Anderson) were built in the Mlanje district. The Nyanja offered no opposition to this, but a Kololo chief named Nyaserera, who had become a leader of the Yao, treacherously attacked and wounded Captain Johnson in his bungalow. Lieutenant Edwards led a punitive expedition and subdued Nyaserera after a brief campaign. Soon afterwards trouble arose with the Mlanje chief Mkanda. By that time the second draft of 100 Sikhs had arrived. An expedition was organized, and after several days' hard fighting among the crags and precipices, Mkanda's strongholds were captured and he fled into exile.

Johnson now felt strong enough to tackle Makanjira in earnest. As a result of this chief's intrigues a rebel named Chiwaura had overthrown the Jumbe of Kotakota, who had been one of the first chiefs to sign a treaty. In November, 1893, Johnson and Edwards marched to the Jumbe's assistance with 113 Sikhs and a few Makua, and attacked Chiwaura's town, a short distance from the lake. The approach lay across an open stretch of marshy ground, and in the hope of saving casualties fire was opened with a 7-pounder gun. This had little effect upon the rebels, and anxious to maintain the prestige of his arms in the eyes of his allies, Johnson ordered the assault. The Sikhs charged gallantly for the eight-foot wall. The first to scale it was shot dead, but his comrades soon reached the top and had the mass of natives below at their mercy. Chiwaura was killed, the town taken, and hundreds of captured slaves released.

Attention was now turned to Makanjira himself. A gunboat chased one of his slaving dhows, manned by 70 fighting men, and forced them ashore, where they were besieged on a hill overlooking Leopard Bay. Leaving his allies to this task, Johnson made an unexpected landing near Makanjira's great township of several thousand huts. While his troops got into position for the attack, the gunboats opened fire. After five hours' fighting Makanjira's warriors gave up, but their chief remained intractable as ever and refused to make terms. His town was accordingly destroyed, and it was decided in view of past experience to leave a large garrison of Sikhs in the district. The fort was named Fort Maguire in honour of the first commander of the Protectorate forces, who had met his death nearby. On 1st January, 1894, Makanjira attacked it, but he was defeated by Captain Edwards, who soon afterwards succeeded Johnson in command.

By this time, though fighting continued along the eastern borders, the interior of the Protectorate was settling down under the protection of some eight or nine forts and a number of smaller military and police posts. Zomba and Blantyre were sufficiently garrisoned by a few police and Sikhs; Forts Anderson and Lister served to keep the chiefs Matapwiri and Kawinga in check; Forts Roberts (a small post on the north-eastern flank of Mount Chiradzulu), Johnston and Maguire were garrisoned by Sikhs; Forts Sharpe and Liwonde guarded the Upper Shiré; and in the north, posts at Deep Bay, Karonga, and in North-East Rhodesia at Fife.

Abercorn, and Rosebery all possessed small garrisons. In addition to the 200 Sikhs, who were serving on a two-year engagement, 40 Zanzibaris had been recruited with the Sultan's permission, 40 Arabs, and 69 Makua from Mozambique, while a varying number of tribesmen—Atonga, Angoni and others—had been raised locally, mainly by the civil authority. The Makua regulars, who had been trained by Johnson, were considered very efficient and received Rs14 a month as privates.

In November, 1894, while on leave in London, Johnston obtained permission to negotiate in India an agreement for two more drafts of Sikhs, to serve in Central Africa for a period of three years. He expressed the highest admiration for the services rendered by the previous drafts, saying that there had not been a single complaint from a native of ill-usage or violence on the part of the Sikhs, which was more than could be said of the Zanzibaris or the Makua. He also requested the services of Edwards and Manning for a further three years, this time on regular secondment instead of leave. In India Johnston found the Commander-in-Chief most helpful, though some of his commanding officers were not anxious to second their men. But the Central Africa Medal had been presented to those troops who had taken part in the previous campaigns, and with this stimulus volunteers were forthcoming in large numbers. Johnston was allowed to select up to twenty from any of the Sikh or Punjabi units: no less than 500 of the 900 men in one regiment alone (45th Sikhs) offered themselves as volunteers, and Johnston considered that he had obtained 'the very cream of the Sikh regiments'.[1] This co-operation was in marked contrast to the attitude adopted subsequently at the India Office, which, owing to representations made in India, became increasingly uneasy at the policy of supplying Indian troops for service in Africa.

Early in 1895 trouble again arose with the Yao chiefs. Kawinga, Zarafi and Matapwiri decided that the time had come to drive the British out of the Shiré Highlands, and Kawinga began operations with a raid near the Scottish Mission. Corporal William Fletcher, R.E., was dispatched there with six Sikhs and a few Atonga. Fortunately he took the precaution of constructing a strong *boma* around his post, for within a few days Kawinga attacked him with 2,000 warriors. Fletcher and his handful of men held on grimly, and when reinforcements of Atonga appeared, sallied out with the last few rounds of ammunition and routed the enemy with a spirited charge.

Meanwhile Captain Manning was marching to Fletcher's aid with fresh troops. Concentrating a force of 55 Sikhs and about 200 Africans, he discovered an unexpected route to Kawinga's stronghold, which he attacked on 17th February and captured after a two-day siege. This put an end to the robberies that were making the roads dangerous for trading caravans. Kawinga escaped, but subsequently became a loyal ally and assisted in the final attack against Zarafi.

Matapwiri was tackled next. In September a mixed force set out from Forts Lister and Anderson, and approaching Matapwiri's village by night, achieved complete surprise and an easy victory. In the following

[1] Johnston to F.O., 12.iv.95. F.O.2, 117.

month, with a punitive force of five officers, 65 Sikhs and about 230 native troops, Edwards took Zarafi's upland villages on the slopes of Mount Mangoche by storm, and the lost 7-pounder was recovered. Zarafi fled to Portuguese territory; Fort Edwards was built and garrisoned until the district was placed in Portuguese territory by the Boundary Commission some five years later. A further expedition against the troublesome Makanjira then practically completed the overthrow of the Yao slaving chiefs.

Success had been quicker than expected, but peace had not yet been secured throughout the whole Protectorate. Mlozi and his confederates, as Lugard had foreseen when he heard the terms of Johnston's treaty, were again threatening Karonga and raiding the countryside for slaves. An attempt at negotiation failed completely, for Mlozi resolutely refused to discuss terms. Six combatant officers (including several volunteers who happened to be in the country on shooting expeditions), 100 Sikhs and 300 native troops were assembled and left Fort Johnston on 24th November, 1895. All available steamers were chartered to convey this force up the lake. On 1st December, in the darkness of a night of pouring rain, Lieutenant H. Coape-Smith (I.S.C.) left Karonga and posted three strong detachments round Mlozi's stockaded town. Early next morning a force of Sikhs and sailors from the gunboats bombarded Msalema's stockade, the nearest to Karonga, and captured it with little difficulty. Kopakopa's turn came next, and then Mlozi's, where the bombardment began soon after 1 p.m. Heavy rain prevented the huts from catching fire, and Mlozi replied with his muzzle-loading cannon and small arms. Early on 3rd December a flag of truce was hoisted, but Mlozi refused terms and the bombardment was resumed. One of the refugees then pointed out his house, and a shell was dropped upon it. Mlozi was wounded, and a rumour spread among his followers that he had been killed. Desperate and angered by this news, the defenders made a furious sortie, which was met by the Sikhs, who fought their way over the walls of the stockade. About 200 of the enemy were killed for a loss of one Sikh and three others killed and six wounded. Sergeant Bandawe of the Atonga, discovering Mlozi's hiding-place in an underground chamber beneath his house, pluckily entered it alone and killed the spearman who was guarding his dazed and wounded chief. Mlozi was tried and hanged on the following day, and the rest of the Arab stockades were then systematically destroyed.

The final defeat of Mlozi may be regarded as the close of the Slavers' War, though some years were still to pass before the slave trade was completely stamped out in Central Africa. Other tribal expeditions were needed, but a marked change took place in the attitude of the Yao chiefs. Johnston reported that a sense of peace and security was settling on the natives, who were leaving the chilly hill-country in favour of the warm plains, with nothing further to dread from foreign slave-raiders and internal disorder. In May, 1896, he handed over to Alfred Sharpe and left for England, where he was created a K.C.B.

Considering the difficulties of the country, the achievements of so small a number of troops were remarkable. But the failure to foresee from the start that so large and troubled an area could not be administered without an adequate armed force unduly prolonged the operations. In Central as in East Africa the optimism of the civil authorities, who assumed too soon that their territories had been pacified and that further punitive expeditions would never be needed, was a constant source of military weakness. One unfortunate result of these years of raiding, bloodshed and lawlessness was that many hitherto peaceful tribes obtained arms and in sheer self-defence became dangerously warlike themselves. For a time, therefore, tribal campaigns continued in Nyasaland, particularly in the area west of the lake, where Fort Hill was constructed some way inland from Karonga, for the protection of the Stevenson Road.

(ii) *Minor Tribal Expeditions and the formation of the Central Africa Rifles, 1896-1900.*

Immediately after Mlozi's defeat, Edwards began to redistribute his forces in a number of stations around the lake and to plan further expeditions against disaffected chiefs, hoping to complete the task of pacification while the effect of his victories lasted. His first move was to send Lieutenant E. Alston (C. Gds.) with 149 Africans and 40 Sikhs to join A. J. Swann, the political officer at Kotakota, in an expedition against the Chewa chief Mwasi, an ally of the Arabs. Mwasi's country lay sixty miles west of Kotakota, and the chief's stronghold was situated on a mountain-side overlooking a plain dotted with villages. Swann had brought 2,400 auxiliaries, who were kept in reserve while Alston attacked with the regular troops. At the sight of Mwasi's warriors brandishing their spears behind the stockades the Makua hung back, so the stronghold was stormed by the Sikhs. Of the nine soldiers killed and five wounded in this action, it is recorded that three were struck by lightning. Mwasi escaped, but an important capture was made in Saidi Mwazungu, the ringleader in the treacherous Makanjira murders of 1891, who now at last paid the penalty. A boma known as Fort Alston was built not far from the site of Mwasi's village, where a small garrison remained for some years to guard the route into North-East Rhodesia.

Johnston had long foreseen that he would be forced some day to try conclusions with the Angoni, whose reputation for ferocity and intractability stood so high that they were now regarded as the most serious native problem.[1] The Angoni did not, of course, offer so difficult a problem as the slavers, who had been protected by strongly-built stockaded villages and were well supplied with firearms. Their arms were those of their Zulu forebears: the heavy stabbing spear, a handful of smaller spears for throwing, some kind of club or axe, and an oval hide shield for protection. Except in the case of certain chiefs, the Angoni villages were not fortified, but they were often built in inaccessible positions that were difficult to take by surprise.

In January, 1896, Edwards sent an expedition against the paramount chief Tambala in Central Angoniland. Tambala's village was perched

[1] *Report by Comr. Johnston of the First Three Years' Administration.* Africa No. 6 (1894) (C. 7504), p. 24, LVII, 711.

on the flat top of a hill with three precipitous sides and a fourth covered with large boulders. Another hill, separated by a deep gorge, stood at a distance of 800 to 1,000 yards, and from this eminence the village could be reached by artillery fire. The operations met only with partial success, for although Tambala's stronghold was captured, the chief escaped and joined the Chewa raider Odete, who lived on Mount Chirenje. To break this alliance Manning left Kotakota on 6th October and five days later was climbing the mountain slopes by a little-used track, with a force of 24 Sikhs and about 80 Africans, half of whom were irregular levies. One by one the raiders' villages were surprised and rushed until finally, against a hail of spears and stones, the main stronghold was stormed on the mountain peak. Odete and other chiefs submitted, and Manning was then free to join Captain Stewart, who was on his way from Zomba to punish the Angoni chief Chikuse for a number of raids south of the lake.

Stewart's column included four military and political officers, 58 Sikhs, 198 African troops and a 7-pounder gun. Marching by way of Liwonde through country thoroughly devastated by raiding, he reached Chikuse's on 21st October. Manning's force arrived next day, and on the 23rd the village was taken. Chikuse and a party of his warriors attempted to break out, but the chief was captured, tried and shot.

The year 1896 saw a complete reorganization of the Protectorate forces. Edwards had always intended to get rid of the expensive Makua and to train Nyasa natives in their place. A few Atonga had been used as irregulars in the operations against Liwonde in 1893. In 1895 more of them had been enlisted experimentally for a year's service, and maintained their good reputation during the expeditions of 1895-96. Fifty Yao and 25 Marimba had been enlisted during the same year, and fought well against Zarafi, Makanjira and the Arabs. Edwards was well pleased with all these local troops, who were good marchers and made keen soldiers, but he considered the Yao the best, on account of their obedience, self-reliance and good marksmanship. Crime was rare and the men were smart.

At the end of the Slavers' War the armed forces of the Protectorate consisted of a commandant, a second-in-command and staff officer, a third officer and quartermaster, six company officers, a sergeant-major of artillery,[1] the Sikh Contingent, and about 300 native troops. These forces were now reorganized and expanded as the Central Africa Rifles (renamed in 1900 the Central Africa Regiment), comprising six companies of 120 rifles each: three of Atonga, two of Yao, and one of Marimba. Enlistment, if for three years, was at the rate of 5/- per month for a private.[2] In view of this increase in local enlistments, when applying for another Sikh Contingent in the following year the Commissioner asked only for 80-100 men, saying that within a few years he hoped to be

[1] The appointment of 'sergeant-major of artillery and transport officer' was abolished in December, 1899, in favour of two extra Indian clerks.

[2] Edwards to Actg. Comr., *Report on B.C.A. Protectorate, 1896-97*. Africa No. 5 (1897) (C. 8438). p. 11. LXII. 15. The establishment was originally eight African companies, but two of these were reorganized as police.

almost entirely independent of Sikhs, provided a few could be secured as drill instructors and N.C.Os. to command small stations.

Edwards did not live to see the outcome of these changes. In May, 1897, he died of blackwater fever, and was succeeded as Commandant by Manning. Following a precedent set in Uganda, Manning's appointment was coupled with that of Deputy Commissioner.

In August, 1897, Manning led an expedition consisting of four officers 51 Sikhs and four companies of Africans to punish the Anguru living in the region south of Lake Chilwa, following a number of highway robberies. Serumba was the chief primarily responsible. Little resistance was met; Serumba was captured, his village burnt, and a fine imposed.

News of much more serious trouble reached Zomba towards the end of the year. In North-East Rhodesia the North Charterland Exploration Company was operating a concession in the Luangwa valley and adjacent territory, with headquarters at Fort Jameson, garrisoned at that time only by some 25 Atonga police. The old Angoni chief Mpeseni had long been suspicious of British influence, and was now unable to control the truculence of his sons and their followers. The situation became so threatening that in December Warringham, the Company's representative, sent an urgent appeal to Kotakota for assistance.

As soon as the news reached Zomba, plans were put in hand for the concentration at Fort Alston of practically the whole of the military forces of the Protectorate. Reports put the Angoni warriors at figures varying from 10,000 to 25,000, and there was evidently no time to be lost. By 2nd January, 1898, Captain H. E. J. Brake, R.A., was ready to leave Zomba with the first detachment of 29 Sikhs and 78 askaris of 'A' Company. The total force, numbering seven officers, 118 Sikhs and all six African companies, with artillery and maxim guns, reached Fort Jameson by forced marches on 18th January. Brake found the flag still flying, and relieved another party, besieged at Luangweni some thirty miles distant, on the following day. His situation, however, was precarious. The rains were at their height; the country was wooded, hilly and almost unknown, even to the Company's officials. In the campaign that followed, the mobility of Brake's troops was greatly impaired by the number of cases of sore feet that had afflicted the askaris after nine days of rapid marching.

Reports came that large numbers of Angoni were massing about three miles from Luangweni. On 20th January Brake was at breakfast when he heard that a concentration of warriors, estimated at 600-700 strong with many more in rear, was assembling near the village, a quarter of a mile east of the fort. With perfect steadiness the Sikhs and askaris deployed before their enemy, who were dancing and waving their spears 300 yards away. 'A' and 'E' Companies fired one volley each; bayonets were fixed, and the line advanced in silence. This was too much for the Angoni, who threw their spears at the troops and then began to give way. Finding themselves outflanked from the direction of the village, the enemy broke into a run. Two rounds from Brake's 7-pounder guns split the retreating mass into groups, who made for the hills, leaving 20 dead behind them.

The troops had hardly returned from the pursuit when they were threatened by another body of Angoni, at least 500 strong, approaching from the west. Four shells, a burst from the maxim, and a charge by 'A' Company that did not get to close quarters dispersed the enemy. From a dying Angoni it was learnt that this party, which was decked out in full war dress, had come direct from Mpeseni's capital Chimpingo to challenge the invaders. These two successful actions convinced Brake that the Angoni could not face his fire, and in spite of their great reputation for bravery were not likely to charge home, however great their weight of numbers. He decided therefore, instead of temporarily evacuating the district as at first intended, to assume the offensive and seek out Chimpingo, the exact location of which was unknown to him. A reconnaissance in extended order discovered the town, but though from a distance the place appeared deserted. Brake felt himself too weak to rush it, as he had with him at the time only about 40 men.

Mpeseni's son Singu, the ringleader of the trouble, was said by a prisoner to have taken refuge in a high range of hills about seven miles south of Luangweni. On 22nd January Brake set out to attack him with Lieutenant J. S. Brogden (R.M.L.I.), Lieutenant A. G. G. Sharp (Leinster R.) and 'D', 'E' and 'F' Companies. The enemy position was located and reconnoitred, but although Brake approached from two directions the Angoni were too wary to be caught. The capture of a small herd of cattle and the destruction of a few villages were all that resulted. On his return to camp Brake found envoys from Mpeseni with a present of cattle. They assured him that the impis had dispersed and that the old king was deserted. Brake realized that Mpeseni was now at his mercy, but decided that it would be folly to leave Luangweni until the power of Singu and Mlonyeni, the two most influential leaders, had been broken.

On 23rd January Brake and Sharp accordingly resumed operations with 'A' and 'E' Companies against Mlonyeni, marching and fighting for fifteen hours and capturing so great a herd of cattle that porters had to be sent out from the camp at dusk to bring it in. The chief's villages were all destroyed, though unripe crops were left standing to prevent famine. With Singu and Mlonyeni both fugitives, Brake considered Luangweni safe from serious attack, and moved on Mpeseni. The old chief had again sued for peace, and asked that the British flag should be hoisted over Chimpingo. On Brake's approach he fled into the bush, and as he refused to return his capital was burnt. Brake followed on 26th January with 'A' Company, caught the retreating Angoni and drove them from village to village until news came that Mpeseni's followers had been reduced to a handful and driven into foodless country.

Singu was surrounded and captured in February by a force under Lieutenant Brogden. He was tried and shot in the presence of the assembled headmen. Mpeseni surrendered, and after a year as a prisoner at Fort Manning, a new fort erected near the Protectorate boundary, was allowed to resume his chieftainship.

It was evident that a proper garrison must be provided for North-East Rhodesia. In return for an annual subsidy of £10,000 paid by the British South Africa Chartered Company, three additional companies of troops ('G' Company, 120 Atonga; 'H' Company, 120 Yao; and 'I' Company,

110 Yao) were raised for this purpose by the C.A.R. Later on other tribes besides Atonga were enlisted in 'G' Company. The original intention was to train all these companies at Fort Manning, but this was modified, 'G' Company being trained at Fort Johnston and 'I' Company at Zomba. The provision of these three extra companies lasted until the reorganization of military forces in 1901.

At the beginning of 1898 the distribution of the C.A.R. was as follows: 'A' Company (Atonga) at Zomba; 'B' Company (Yao) at Zomba; 'C' Company (Yao) at Mlanje; 'D' Company (Atonga) at Mangoche; 'E' Company (Atonga) at Fort Maguire; and 'F' Company (mixed) at Kotakota. A battery of four 7-pounder mountain guns and two 9-pounder field guns, manned by African crews with Sikh instructors, was attached to 'A' Company. One Sikh colour-sergeant served with each infantry company, with three Sikh drill instructors as section commanders, for the authority of the African N.C.O. over his men could not yet be relied upon. The staff of the regiment was drawn from the Indian Contingent, which now numbered 175 Sikhs. Those Sikhs not attached to the battery or the infantry formed a striking-force about 100 strong, stationed at Zomba with porter transport ready to move at short notice. The mobility of this force had been thoroughly tested on the Mpeseni expedition.

Further tribal punitive expeditions were needed during 1898, notably in southern Angoniland during April and May, where a large force of armed Angoni was reported at Dedza. A strong patrol, led by Captain F. B. Pearce (W. York R.) and Lieutenant Brogden, marched through the country and restored order without serious fighting. But the year was chiefly memorable for some far-reaching decisions that brought the C.A.R. into some prominence and ultimately gave the askaris an opportunity to show their merit outside their own country. The rapid expansion of steamship routes during the second half of the nineteenth century led to the establishment of coaling stations in the islands and along the seaboards of the Indian Ocean. The defence of these stations placed an added strain on the resources of the British Army, and towards the end of the century, when the war in South Africa was absorbing all available forces, it was decided to garrison some of them with Africans. In December, 1898, the existing troops of the Central Africa Rifles were designated the 1st Battalion, and authority was issued for a 2nd Battalion, to be enlisted for a term of three years, of which two were to be spent on foreign service. As it was intended for employment outside the Protectorate, the 2nd Battalion was placed under the control of the War Office.

The formation of 2 C.A.R. began at Zomba on 1st January, 1899. The authorized establishment was 19 officers, one warrant officer and 1,084 African ranks, organized in eight companies. The men were recruited among the Yao, Anguru, Atonga and Marimba tribes in the Zomba, Fort Lister, Fort Mlangeni, Kotakota and Chintechi areas. Instructors were drafted from the Indian Contingent, and the men were drilled on evening parades with the rifles of the 1st Battalion. Captain Brake was appointed to command with the rank of temporary major, and was joined by a few more officers in May. In the same month, after a minimum of training, without arms and without proper uniforms, the battalion was ordered to Mauritius on foreign service. Its experiences during the next three years will form the subject of the sections that follow.

Meanwhile in Central Africa the 1st Battalion continued its task of pacification, marching and fighting as required from east to west of the Protectorate and even beyond its borders. On the eastern frontier two Yao chiefs named Nkwamba and Mataka caused trouble on both sides of the border that led to punitive measures by British and Portuguese. Nkwamba had ambushed two European traders and killed a number of their followers. The British punitive force left Zomba under Captain Pearce on 4th August, 1899: nine officers, 119 Sikhs and 269 askaris of 'B', 'C' and 'E' Companies. British and Portuguese expeditions converged on Nkwamba's village in the Namweras hills, which was destroyed on 27th August after slight resistance. Mataka proved more troublesome, and was a nuisance to the Portuguese later, though some confusion was caused by the fact that there were two chiefs of that name, one in Portuguese and one in British territory.

In September an expedition was authorized against the Bemba of the Tanganyika plateau and the chief Kazembe, who lived near Lake Mweru in North-East Rhodesia. Kazembe had previously refused to enter into a treaty with the British, but now sought aid against the last remaining Arab slavers in his district. A force of 12 Sikhs, 60 askaris of 'E' Company and a 7-pounder gun under Lieutenant P. C. R. Barclay (I.S.C.) was sent up to Karonga, where command was assumed by Captain E. C. Margesson (S. Wales Bord.), who came from Fort Manning to meet it. Marching by the Stevenson Road as far as Abercorn, Margesson struck south-west to Kazembe's. The slavers fled into Belgian territory, and an agreement was reached with Kazembe. In the space of some two months the askaris taking part in this expedition marched nearly a thousand miles.

In November, 1900, renewed operations took place in Central Angoniland under Captain L. F. de V. Stokes (R. Lanc. R.), who was in command at Fort Mlangeni. Over 300 villages were punished and about twenty tribesmen killed. In December a mail-carrier from Fort Jameson was murdered. A strong party of troops sent out from Fort Manning discovered that the dead man's rifle and kit were in Tambala's possession, captured and destroyed several stockaded villages, and eventually took Tambala himself as he was escaping through the gorge where his main stronghold stood.

These brief campaigns, coupled with the civilizing influence of the missionaries, which after many years of unrewarded labour was now at last beginning to replace that of the old tribal war leaders, practically completed the pacification of the Central Angoni. The military qualities of the tribe stood the K.A.R. in good stead during later years.

(iii) *Foreign Service : Mauritius and Somaliland, 1899-1900.* Map III.

To describe the foreign service performed by the Central Africa Rifles is to trace mainly the fortunes of the 2nd Battalion, which left Zomba on 23rd May, 1899, on its way to the coast.

The men were allowed to take with them one wife each. On 22nd June the battalion embarked at Chinde in the steamship *Muttra*, with a strength of seven officers, 32 Sikhs, 878 Africans, 220 wives and 77 children—somewhat under strength owing to desertions on the way by those whose hearts failed them at the prospect of crossing the sea.

The *Muttra* reached Mauritius on 29th June. From the start, the new battalion was subjected to a most unfortunate and trying experience, for the news that African troops were coming to garrison the island had provoked an intense resentment that was constantly inflamed by the local press. On 30th June the men landed at Port Louis in the face of a very large crowd of hostile Creoles, kept back by police and a company of the 1st Bengal Infantry. The Bengali band played the battalion to the station, where it entrained at once for its camp inland at Phoenix.

It was the middle of winter. To save expense, all arms, equipment and uniforms were to be forwarded direct to Mauritius, and in the meantime the hastily-raised battalion had only fatigue dress. Rainstorms and cold winds blew daily across the camp, and men, women and children shivered in bell tents while lines were laid out and the building of grass huts began. Pneumonia and bronchitis resulted, and flannel had to be purchased locally to make temporary jackets. Until greatcoats arrived the troops paraded in their blankets, draped around their shoulders with the knot under the left ear. It is related that on one occasion the inspecting officer noticed a suspicious bulge. A prod showed that the cause was something soft, and further investigation revealed a small baby. The mother was sick, and the father was making an honourable effort to combine military duty with domestic responsibility.

Between July and September 11 more officers and a British Sergeant-Major (T. Slattery, Scottish R.) reached the battalion. Strenuous efforts were made to bring the men to a state of reasonable efficiency. On 6th October the British infantry regiment forming part of the garrison (the 2nd Battalion King's Own Yorkshire Light Infantry) left Mauritius for the war in South Africa. In the following month the first annual inspection of 2 C.A.R. was carried out by Major-General J. Talbot Coke, who submitted a satisfactory report to the Adjutant-General of the Forces. Soon afterwards the battalion, together with the 1st Bengal Infantry and the 43rd Company Royal Engineers, was reviewed by the Governor, Sir Charles Bruce, K.C.M.G., and was complimented on its smartness, efficiency and good behaviour.

Notwithstanding these compliments from those in authority, the local press continued to deliver unceasing attacks. When walking out at weekends the men were often attacked by parties of Creoles with sticks, stones and knives. The matter became so serious that early in December orders were issued for troops to leave camp only in parties of ten or more, under the charge of an N.C.O. But by that time the injustice of this unreasoning hostility had had its effect.

On 9th December news suddenly reached the officers' quarters that about 200 troops who had left camp in properly organized parties had assembled near the village of La Caverne and were attacking the Creoles. The moment their officers reached the scene the troops obeyed orders and fell in. No time had been lost, and beyond a few beatings and the scattering of some furniture into the road, little damage was done. The subsequent Court of Inquiry disclosed the prolonged provocation the men had endured, and the instant restoration of discipline by the officers earned the commendation of the War Office.

But it was obvious that the matter would never be forgotten in Mauritius. The press agitation became furious. The Governor agreed to hold a judicial inquiry, and received a deputation of Creoles, who demanded the withdrawal of the regiment and its removal pending embarkation to Flat Island, the quarantine station. Though reconnaissance showed no proper water supply, orders for this were issued on 17th December. While the move was in progress instructions came from England for the battalion to embark and await orders. For the next five weeks the troops were cooped up on board. with 'H' Company and the women and children on the island. while mounting numbers of sick had to be evacuated to the barracks at Fort George.

At last news came that the battalion was destined for Berbera. Early in February, 1900, it embarked in the R.I.M.T. *Clive*, with a strength of 16 officers, one warrant officer, 30 Sikhs and 862 African ranks. Of four men left behind to stand trial for riot at the Assizes, all but one were acquitted.

The decision to send 2 C.A.R. to British Somaliland, the first African battalion to garrison that Protectorate, was the consequence of a disturbing situation that had recently arisen there. The fantastic. violent career of the man who came to be known as the 'Mad Mullah' had begun. For the next twenty years he was destined to defy British authority, and for the whole of that time was never once seen by an Englishman.

Topographically, British Somaliland is well adapted for guerrilla warfare. Most of its tribesmen are inured alike to the pitiless summer heat of the plains and the cold. driving winter mists of the uplands. Behind the coast lies an arid plain that extends in places for a width of fifty miles. Beyond this a broken range of mountains runs roughly parallel to the coast, at an average height of 4.000-5.000 feet. This range continues inland as a high plateau that slopes away to the valley of the Webi Shabelle, or Leopard River. This almost waterless plateau is known as the Haud, and consists of gently rolling plains covered partly with a spare, coarse grass. and partly with thick bush. forest. and barren areas of rock and stony soil. pierced with the stark red pillars of millions of burrowing termites. In the time of the Mullah the inland regions were little known. Apart from the coastal towns of Berbera and Zeila. and the decaying port of Bulhar, there were only three centres of settlement round permanent water inland: at Sheikh. about fifty miles south of Berbera, where the road climbs the escarpment in a tortuous and terrifying course up the long pass and around the final crags and pinnacles to the plateau above; at Burao. forty miles inland from Sheikh; and at Hargeisa. The rest of the country was dotted with nomad encampments. constantly moved by the tribes as they wandered from place to place in the perpetual struggle to pasture their herds of camels, goats and sheep. Britain had administered the country since the withdrawal of the

Egyptians in 1884, first under the Government of India, and after October, 1898, directly under the Foreign Office. The original British garrison was a company of Indian infantry from Aden.

Mohammed bin Abdulla Hassan, the Mad Mullah of Somaliland, became the object of military operations that involved all told troops drawn from six different battalions of the K.A.R. He was born about 1870, near Kirrit in the Dulbahante country. On pilgrimage to Mecca he came under the influence of a reforming Arab teacher named Mohammed Salih. In 1895, supported by the prestige of his pilgrimages, he began to propagate his religious opinions and to advocate a number of puritan reforms among the Somali tribes. These stern doctrines did not prove altogether popular. This apparently convinced the Mullah that a *jehad* was needed against the unbelievers who ruled his country, and drove him in time to a degree of bestial cruelty that converted the interior of Somaliland into a welter of pillage, rape and murder. In his youth the Mullah had had a bone removed from the top of his head, and there is some reason to suppose that the unskilled operation may have caused insanity in later years.[1]

The Mullah's influence over his followers gave him an authority in tribal affairs that from time to time brought him into touch with the British at Berbera. Early in 1899 his messages became very truculent, and report said that he was collecting arms. In August the Mullah established himself at Burao with about 1,500 men, of whom 200 were armed with rifles. Proclaiming himself the Mahdi and denouncing all who neglected to join him, he attacked a rival religious sect at Sheikh. For a time Berbera was thought to be in danger. 'Choose for yourselves,' he wrote to the Consul-General; 'if you want war, we accept it.' The Mullah was accordingly declared a rebel.

At the end of February, 1900, when 2 C.A.R. reached Berbera, the Mullah was endeavouring to raise the tribes in the Ogaden. It was known that arms had been smuggled from Jibouti, and in consequence, though opposition to his cruelties had already arisen among the tribes and the exact number of his followers was uncertain, his power was thought to be increasing. On the arrival of 2 C.A.R. the company of Indian infantry was relieved and returned to Aden. One company of the battalion remained at the coast to garrison Berbera and one company went to Sheikh. The remainder went to Syk, a recently established police post about fifty miles inland covering the Jerato Pass, and then to a better camp site two miles farther south at Adadleh Wells, where stone huts were built within a thorn zariba. In spite of the heat and the barren nature of the country, Somaliland proved a welcome change from

---

[1] Head injuries, treated or not, are often followed by changes of temperament and behaviour, usually for the worse. Whatever the reason for the removal of part of the skull, it is probable that, in unskilled hands, some permanent interference with brain function would remain. Given a fanatical belief, which often incites its followers to war against unbelievers, one may well suppose that a head injury might inflame the mind of the Mullah and cause any sense of justice, humanity and decency to be cast aside to further his own ends, whether due to insane egoism or a burning faith. In a civilized setting injuries of this type may and do lead to personality disorders which bring disaster or notoriety to their victims and to those around them.—G. C. P.

Mauritius. Space was unlimited and there were few local temptations. the unit was free to complete its interrupted musketry training, and active service was in prospect.

Colonel J. Hayes Sadler, the Consul-General, did not consider offensive operations immediately advisable. The occupation of Adadleh and Sheikh was intended to secure the safety of the coast and plans were in hand to garrison Burao. While these were proceeding, news reached Sheikh on 15th June that a party of French adventurers had left Jibouti with arms and ammunition for the Mullah, and was now passing through the Protectorate, ostensibly on a shooting expedition. At that time the Mullah was reported to be contemplating a move on Harrar, so Brake was ordered to Hargeisa with 'A' and 'B' Companies.

At Hargeisa Brake could obtain no news of the Jibouti party. Soon after his arrival he was told to prepare half his battalion for the Ashanti campaign then in progress on the other side of the continent. 'A' Company was accordingly withdrawn from Hargeisa to the coast.

Meanwhile news reached Hargeisa that the French expedition was at Halisa, some seventy miles distant. 'B' Company, 60 rifles strong, surprised and captured the whole party: four Europeans, 30 Sudanese, four Arabs and a few Somali guides, thus scoring the first operational success of the new battalion.

On 20th July, Lieutenant-Colonel Brake embarked in the transport *Dwarka* at Berbera with 'A', 'D', 'E' and 'F' Companies. Major A. W. V. Plunkett (Manchester R.) assumed command of the half-battalion in Somaliland. His headquarters remained at Adadleh, with detachments at Hargeisa, Berbera, Sheikh, and for a short time at Burao. In October great unrest was reported around Hargeisa, where some of the tribes were moving to attack the Mullah's forces at Milmil, near the Abyssinian border. Acting on orders from the Consul-General, Plunkett marched to Hargeisa with reinforcements, and thence towards the frontier. The Mullah was ignorant of his approach, and all his herds and cattle were out grazing, but Sadler had given Plunkett definite instructions not to cross the frontier.[1] Operations were therefore limited to a patrol in force towards Milmil, and an excellent chance of cutting short the Mullah's career was lost.[2]

---

[1] Sadler to Salisbury, 26.x.1900.

[2] Lieutenant-Colonel J. S. Graham, the last surviving officer of 2 C.A.R., has described this incident as follows: 'I well remember our dismay and Plunkett's ire when, the day we were to make our night dash to seize the Mullah, the runner arrived from the Consul-General at Berbera . . . with the order forbidding us on any account to cross the frontier. Our information was that the Mullah had no idea that we had even left Hargeisa. We could see his camp fires and from a spy knew exactly which hut he was in. He was, however, just over the frontier and Plunkett did not dare disobey the order. We were all convinced, and I shall always remain so, that we should have got him with some certainty that night and also have caused very heavy casualties among his followers. As it was we had to make an ignominious retreat to Hargeisa, causing much trouble and expense in the following years.'

The Consul-General made no mention of this in his despatches, but merely wrote of the C.A.R. as 'demonstrating' in the direction of the frontier. The incident is, however, recorded in detail in the regimental records of the Battalion.

On 9th November, after several weeks of very arduous marching, the troops again reached Adadleh. For some time the health of the regiment had suffered severely. Scurvy caused a number of deaths, and the detachment at Berbera had to be withdrawn. At last, after several applications, Sadler agreed to release the half-battalion for West Africa, where it was urgently needed, and 'B', 'C', 'G' and 'H' Companies embarked in the *Dwarka* on 20th December.

Sadler had felt able to spare 2 C.A.R. on account of the progress made in raising a local Somali Levy, and the authority that had recently been issued by the home Government to increase its establishment to 1,500 men. The Emperor Menelik's troops had already been in conflict with the Mullah owing to his depredations in the Ogaden, and the intention was to take combined action in the following year. Command of the Levy was given to Captain E. J. E. Swayne[1] (I.S.C.), with the local rank of lieutenant-colonel. With major operations still proceeding in South and West Africa, and a large-scale expedition being assembled in Jubaland for punitive measures against the Ogaden Somalis, British Somaliland had to be left for the time being to the protection of its own tribesmen.

(iv) *Foreign Service : The Ashanti Campaign, 1900.* Map 2.

The turn of the century was an anxious period for Britain. The strain imposed upon her military resources by the South African War left few troops available for the settlement of tribal unrest elsewhere in Africa. For the first time, therefore, the sole reliance in operations of some magnitude had to be placed upon African soldiers, and companies of both battalions of the Central Africa Regiment were dispatched to the Gold Coast to take part in the second stage of a particularly difficult campaign. The immediate causes of this war arose from the possession of the Golden Stool.

The Ashanti were a powerful and highly organized group of tribes living in the dense, primeval forests north of the Gold Coast Colony. Early in the eighteenth century the chiefs of Kumase had become paramount. The consciousness that the Ashanti were a great people was aroused by their wise man Anokye, who in the midst of a great storm is said to have brought down from the thunderous darkness above a wooden stool decorated with gold, that came to rest on the knees of the chief, Osei Tutu. Anokye affirmed that the spirit and strength of the nation were enshrined in this stool, which thus became a sacred symbol of great spiritual significance. All chiefs were 'enstooled', not crowned, for in Ashanti the Stool was the mark of royal authority, but by the end of the nineteenth century it was not the custom, even for the King of Ashanti, actually to use the Golden Stool as a throne.

This conception of the Stool's mystical function, very imperfectly understood at the time, lay at the root of a rebellion that flared up unexpectedly in April, 1900. Owing to their attacks on the weaker coastal tribes, the Ashanti had frequently been in conflict with British authority

[1] Later Brigadier-General Sir Eric Swayne, K.C.M.G., C.B.E.

on the Gold Coast. Sir Garnet Wolseley had conducted operations against them in 1873-74, and Sir Francis Scott in 1895-96. After the last occasion King Prempeh was deported, and a treaty was drawn up with the remaining chiefs. But the terms of this treaty were never fulfilled. In March, 1900, the Governor visited Kumase and held a meeting of the chiefs. He told them that Prempeh would never return, reproached them for withholding the indemnity imposed by the treaty, reasserted his right to demand labour for public works, and asked why, as representative of the paramount power, the Golden Stool had not been brought from its hiding-place for his use. Owing to the peculiar significance attached to the Stool, this final demand was a serious though unintentional blunder, and precipitated a rebellion among the Kumase, Ofinsu, Ejisu and Adansi sections of the tribe.

On 31st March, guided by a native informer, a party of Hausa troops left for the Bali and Nkwanta districts to search for arms and the supposed hiding-place of the Stool. Needless to say, it was not to be found, and the party had to fight its way back through a succession of ambushes. The Governor telegraphed the Secretary of State, and troops were ordered to the Gold Coast from Nigeria and Sierra Leone. Some of them reached Kumase; the Governor retired to the Fort; the telegraph line was cut, and before long the party was besieged by 40,000 Ashanti warriors, who built strong timber stockades, usually several hundred yards long and four or five feet high, across all roads leading out of the town.

Unfortunately, the relieving troops only reached the Fort after expending most of their provisions and ammunition. The occupants now numbered 29 Europeans and about 750 soldiers and police. Negotiations with the chiefs broke down; sallies against the stockades met with scant success and merely disheartened the garrison. As the stock of provisions grew low and thousands of starving refugees began to cluster around the Fort, it became evident that desperate measures were needed. On 23rd June, leaving three Europeans and 150 men to hold the Fort, the Governor broke out with the remainder, and aided by loyal Ashanti, fought his way across the River Ofin and reached the coast.

By now some 1,400 troops had been ordered to the Gold Coast. Command of this Field Force was given to Colonel J. Willcocks,[1] Commandant of the West Africa Frontier Force, who reached the coast on 26th May. One of his first actions was to appeal for reinforcements. On 19th June four officers, 73 Sikhs and 267 African troops of 1 C.A.R., with a maxim gun detachment, medical officer and hospital staff, left Zomba for Ashanti under the command of Major A. S. Cobbe (32nd Pioneers). In the same month Willcocks accepted also the offer of half 2 C.A.R. from British Somaliland. Meanwhile he marched to Bekwai, where he established his headquarters. On 13th July he set out for Kumase, and in spite of constant attacks on his flanks, bombarded and rushed the stockades on the Peki road and relieved the garrison.

This concluded the first part of the campaign. The second stage, in which the Central Africa Regiment took part, aimed at the defeat and

---

[1] Later General Sir James Willcocks, G.C.B., G.C.M.G., K.C.S.I., D.S.O.

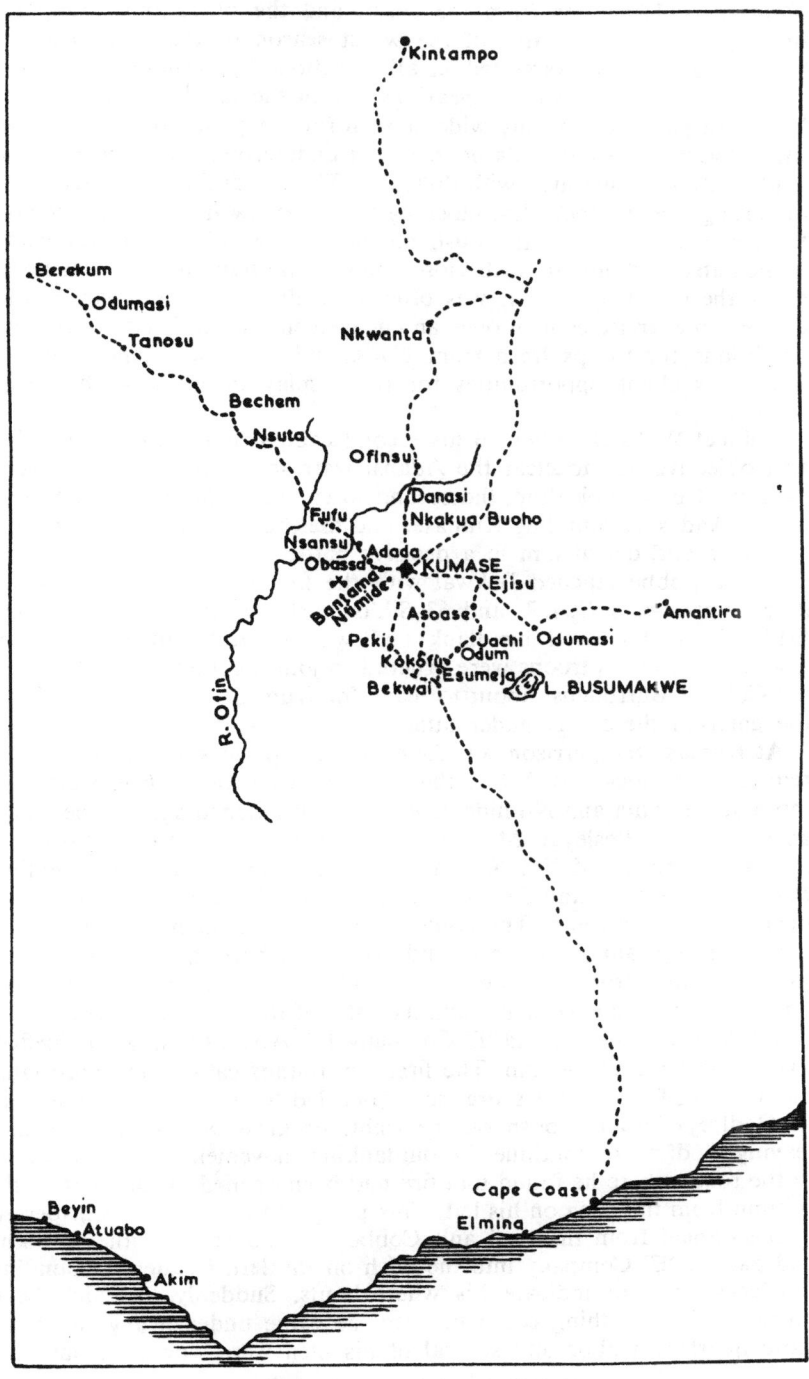

2. Operations in Ashanti, 1900-01

punishment of the Ashanti armies and the pacification of the country. Kumase is 170 miles from the coast, and the operations took place during the torrential rains of the worst season of the year. The vast area of forest was intersected in all directions by swamps and swollen rivers. The villages, built in clearings within the jungle, were connected by native paths, often only wide enough for troops to advance in single file between towering walls of trees and undergrowth so thick that they could only be penetrated with difficulty. The Ashanti pinned their hopes on strong timber stockades, blocking these narrow tracks and extending for some distance into the bush on either side, with their war camps immediately behind. In such close country the fighting unit was necessarily the company, and it was often difficult for the commander of a column to exercise control once an engagement began. These were novel conditions for troops fresh from Nyasaland and Somaliland, but they offered excellent opportunities for the display of initiative by junior officers.

Colonel Willcocks planned his second campaign in three stages. The first objective was to clear the Adansi warriors from the right flank of his line of communication, the second to complete the destruction of all the stockades surrounding Kumase, and the third to drive the enemy to the north and defeat him in a decisive battle.

Major Cobbe reached Bekwai with the first troops of the Regiment (two companies 1 C.A.R. and 63 Sikhs) early in August. By that time Willcocks had cleared his flank and was about to attack the main stockades. Cobbe's troops were ordered to join a column under Lieutenant-Colonel Burroughs, about to leave for Kumase, as reports said that the garrison there was under attack.

At Kumase the garrison was found intact, so work began at once on reducing the stockades. While the West Africa Frontier Force attacked those at Bantama and Ntimide, Cobbe was dispatched against the stockades near the Wesleyan Mission, comparatively close to the Fort. His column consisted of 'B', 'C' and 'E' Companies, 1 C.A.R., totalling 161 African troops and 53 Sikhs, a company of the West Africa Regiment, and a small gun. The column left camp at noon on 6th August. Sniping began almost at once, and 200 yards beyond the Mission, fire from the right front became heavy. Cobbe called in his flankers and opened fire with a maxim gun and the rifles of the two leading companies (West Africa Regiment and 'E' Company 1 C.A.R.). Finding this ineffective he brought up the gun. The first few rounds caused no appreciable diminution of the enemy's fire, so Cobbe led 'C' Company (Lieutenant C. Godfrey) into the bush on the right. Progress was very slow, and leaving Godfrey to continue the outflanking movement, Cobbe returned to the road, where he found that fire had been opened on the rear of the column from the bush on his left. This party of the enemy was dispersed with shrapnel from the gun, and Cobbe then advanced with the Sikhs and part of 'E' Company into the bush on the left, frequently sounding the 'cease fire' to indicate his whereabouts. Suddenly, in thick bush through which nothing could be seen, he came under heavy fire from close quarters. Cobbe and several of his men were wounded, but continued to advance, pouring in volleys meanwhile. Captain Margesson now came up with the rest of 'E' Company. Leaving him to lead the advance on the left, Cobbe returned to the road. Judging that the two flanking parties must now be close to the enemy's position, he ordered a general advance, and almost immediately heard the cheers as his flanking companies charged. The Ashanti fled down the road and into the bush, and their stockade and war camp were captured. The stockade was found to be 300 yards long, five feet thick and four and a half feet high, and so well hidden that Cobbe had bumped into it unexpectedly. The behaviour of all troops in this engagement was excellent, especially that of the advance and rear guards, who were forced to sit on the road for an hour and a half, constantly under fire from an unseen enemy, while the outflanking parties made their slow progress through the bush. 'All ranks, especially those fine soldiers the Sikhs, behaved admirably,' wrote Willcocks in his official despatch, 'and if it were not for this impossible forest we should soon wipe out most of the Ashantis.'

After bringing the garrison of Kumase up to strength, Burroughs' column had been ordered back to Bekwai. Before leaving, he decided to try a night attack with bayonets only, in order to conserve his ammunition. On 7th August a strong stockade was selected and reconnoitred on the Accra road, and after nightfall, marching in single file through the moonlit bush, the column of 500 troops set out, with Burroughs in command. The Central Africa Regiment was represented by 'A' Company (Captain Margesson), whose task was to charge through the stockade in the rear of the leading troops and encircle the left flank of the war camp. A company of the W.A.F.F. was to perform a similar movement on the right.

The alarm was not raised until the leading troops were close to the Ashanti position. In spite of a ragged volley from the defenders, the stockade was carried at the first rush. The West Africans poured through the centre and surrounded the right flank, but the opening was too narrow for Margesson's troops to follow quickly, and many of the enemy escaped. The stockade and several abandoned camps were then set on fire, and the askaris returned to the Fort without having fired a single shot. Next day Burroughs marched back to Bekwai with most of his troops.

Headquarters and four companies 2 C.A.R., numbering six officers, one warrant officer and 483 rank and file, under Lieutenant-Colonel Brake, reached Cape Coast on 13th August and Bekwai a week later. They were sent into action without delay. On 24th August Brake was ordered to Kokofu with 400 men and a 7-pounder gun. There he learnt that the enemy was near Jachi and pushed on in pursuit. On the way 'F' Company, who were acting as advance guard, surprised and rushed the enemy in the village of Odum without loss to themselves. A captured Ashanti said that Jachi was a mile farther on, and that the main body of his comrades was there. Brake sent 'A' Company forward at the double, with 'E' Company in support. As Jachi was approached, the enemy was sighted rushing for the shelter of a large tree that lay across the road. Fire was opened and the Ashanti scattered into the bush. With bayonets fixed, the leading companies then drove the enemy from Jachi, killing 50 or 60 for the loss of one man wounded. Chief Opoku, one of the war captains commanding the Adansi armies, was among the dead. A great deal of gold, silver, and other property was found abandoned on the track and in the villages, and about 140 rifles were captured. Jachi was the first action to be fought by 2 C.A.R., and the result filled the troops with keenness and confidence.

Most of the country south of Kumase had now been cleared of the enemy. A few detachments were left to maintain the peace, the line of communication was reorganized, and headquarters moved from Bekwai to Kumase, preparatory to following the Ashanti armies north and defeating them in the heart of their own country.

While the remainder of the Field Force moved on Kumase, Brake was ordered to march via Jachi and Asoase to Ejisu, twelve miles east of Kumase, where the main Ashanti concentration had been reported. His column numbered nearly 900 men, and included three companies 2 C.A.R. besides West African troops and artillery. The column left Bekwai on 29th August and marched through Jachi and Asoase in pouring rain. Shortly before 10 a.m. on the 31st, when approaching Ejisu with great caution through thick bush, the Ashanti sentries were heard to give the alarm and the scouts ahead were fired on from cover. Enfilading fire poured into the column from a stockade hidden on the bank of a river near the road crossing. Brake brought up the guns, and as they came into action began the familiar outflanking movement, sending his leading companies into the bush on either side of the track, half 'D' Company, 2 C.A.R., following half 'F' Company to the left, and half 'F' Company and two companies of the W.A.F.F. moving to the right. The Ashanti had prolonged their defences with felled trees and rifle pits, and the troops took nearly two hours to outflank them. By that time the guns had breached the stockade, and when word came that the enemy's right flank had been turned, Brake ordered a general assault. The troops went in with the bayonet, and the Ashanti fled to Ofinsu, leaving large numbers of dead, chiefly the result of the artillery bombardment. The Regiment's casualties comprised one officer and one other rank killed, and Lieutenant-Colonel Brake, Sergeant-Major Slattery, and 20 rank and file wounded. Ejisu was burnt and the column reached Kumase on 1st September.

For the next few weeks there was a break in major operations, though several companies of the Regiment were employed with punitive columns destroying stockades and villages around Kumase. The rains poured down, the troops obtained a badly-needed rest, and the opportunity was taken to reorganize administration and supply. A return of the Field Force dated 15th September shows the strength of 1 C.A.R. as five officers, 71 Sikhs, and 263 Africans; and of 2 C.A.R. as eight officers, one B.N.C.O., 10 Sikhs and 487 Africans. The total strength of the Force at that time was 134 officers and 3,234 other ranks. As organization of offensive operations was usually by column, senior officers were often employed independently of their own units.

Major operations were reopened on 21st September, when a column of 950 troops with two guns left Kumase under Lieutenant-Colonel Montanaro to attack the main rebel forces at Ofinsu. On approaching the village of Nkakua Buoho in an area of particularly dense bush, signs of the enemy's presence became apparent and the alarm was raised. Two companies 2 C.A.R. went forward and drove the enemy from a crescent-shaped position concealed in the bush. The village was then occupied and a halt made for the night. Next morning the Ashanti were discovered in force in the bush near Danasi. While the guns went into action a company of the W.A.F.F. began the outflanking movement. As progress through the bush was slow, a company of the C.A.R. followed in support.

Within a short time it became evident that the Ashanti were themselves working through the bush and trying to surround the column. Such initiative was unusual. Cobbe, who had barely recovered from the wound in his thigh, was in command of the main body, consisting of the Sikhs and two companies of the W.A.F.F. Montanaro ordered him up to deal with the threat developing on the left, which he repulsed very effectively with the Sikhs and their maxim gun. Meanwhile the two companies on the right had found an open banana patch, through which they charged with the bayonet. The two wings of the advance then trapped between them the enemy opposing Cobbe, and drove them through Danasi and beyond.

Ofinsu was entered two days later without further opposition. Before returning to Kumase, the surrender of five chiefs was received, and 341 small arms were captured.

On 25th September Brake was invalided home, and command of the half-battalion 2 C.A.R. was assumed by Captain A. F. Gordon (Gordon Highlanders) with the rank of temporary major.

Battle of Obassa, 30th September, 1900.—The pursuit to the north was now pressed in the hope of bringing the campaign to a finish. Danasi was quickly followed by the most important engagement of the campaign, the decisive battle of Obassa. On 28th September reports were received that the Ashanti leader Kofi Kofia, with an army estimated at 5,000 men, mostly drawn from the hitherto unbeaten Achima section, was waiting on the Berekum road. Colonel Willcocks decided to advance against him in person, accompanied by the British Resident and a political officer. His column numbered 1,200 troops with five guns, and included the Sikhs of the Indian Contingent, two companies 1 C.A.R. and three companies 2 C.A.R. It was organized in four sections for the approach march, Cobbe being in command of the main body. The troops floundered cheerfully through the mud in a downpour more intense than any other experienced in the whole campaign. Early on the morning of 30th September, while between the villages of Adada and Obassa, the scouts of the advance guard gained contact with the enemy. Reconnaissance showed that the position extended across the track and overlapped on both flanks. 'E' Company, 2 C.A.R., which was in the lead, was ordered into the bush on the right to probe the enemy's flank. The next troops to arrive, a company of the W.A.F.F., were sent into the bush on the left; and then a company of the West Africa Regiment to the right in support of 'E' Company.

All this time the Ashanti were pouring a heavy volume of fire straight down the track. After twenty minutes the charge was sounded, but as the Ashanti held firm and continued to fire volley after volley at close range, the assault was not pressed. Reinforcements came forward and another company of the C.A.R. was sent into the bush to extend the line still farther to the left. As there was some danger of losing touch, a second charge was delivered on the stockade, which again made little progress.

It was now plain that the undertaking was beyond the capacity of the advance guard and its supporting troops, especially as the guns could not be brought into action. Colonel Willcocks himself came forward. As a former officer of the Indian Army he placed great reliance on the Sikhs, and telling them that he would watch the charge, he ordered them to attack the centre of the stockade in the teeth of the Ashanti fire. As the bugles sounded the Sikhs dashed down the slope with Major Mellis and Captain Godfrey at their head, followed by the rest of the line. This charge decided the issue of 'a somewhat doubtful day'.[1] The Ashanti still fought, but by this time 'E' Company and the West Africans had got through the bush on the right, and charged together across a clearing into the left of the enemy's position. As the Ashanti gave way before the Sikhs they therefore came under a devastating enfilading fire that rapidly spread panic and completed the rout.

Obassa was a hard-fought victory over a most courageous enemy. The Ashanti suffered heavily. They fled to Nsansu, and then, unable to rally, still farther north across the River Ofin. The pursuit was undertaken by Major Cobbe, who set out next day with a column 800 strong, including three companies 2 C.A.R. The Ofin was found to be eighty feet wide and six feet deep, with a strong current, and Cobbe spent five hours bridging it with tree trunks and getting the column across. Beyond the river lay a sticky mass of swamp, and to make matters worse the track was almost destroyed by a violent tornado. It was long after dark before the leading company of the C.A.R. reached Fufu, where the enemy had been reported, only to find the village deserted. Shortly after midnight the tornado blew itself out, but the column had to return next day through rising floods that already covered the improvised bridges.

For a time the heavy rains again put an end to operations. The rest was welcome, but the troops were stricken by small-pox, and 20 men of 'E' Company, 2 C.A.R., died.

The fugitive chiefs had collected in north-west Ashanti, a district hitherto unpatrolled. On 1st November a column under Lieutenant-Colonel Montanaro, that included two companies 1 C.A.R. and two companies 2 C.A.R., left for Berekum, followed by a smaller column of West African troops under Major Browne. The two columns united at Nsuta, and a message was sent demanding the surrender of the rebels, then at Bechem. Kobina Cherri, their chief, sent a prompt refusal, and announced his intention to fight, but when the column reached Bechem no enemy was to be found. The troops then marched through Tanosu

---

[1] Sir J. Willcocks. *From Kabul to Kumasi.* p. 294.

and Odumassi to Berekum, where they were received with great honour by the local chief. Major Browne, who had been left with a garrison at Odumassi, captured Kobina Cherri, and altogether 31 chiefs surrendered as a result of the operations of these two columns.

The organizational capacity and the tactical sense of the Ashanti were on a much higher level than any encountered in the tribal wars of East or Central Africa. But when pitted against Central African troops, armed, trained and commanded by British officers, the Ashanti were worsted in every engagement. Despite the advantages derived from their knowledge of the country, their chiefs could not think strategically or exercise the centralized control necessary to cope with the attacks of several mobile columns, operating simultaneously in different parts of the country. Tactically, however, the Ashanti proved formidable enemies. They were excellent at bush patrolling, ingenious in posting concealed sentries and arranging trip wires, and had a good eye for selecting ground suitable for ambushes. Though well supplied with firearms their marksmanship was generally poor, as they preferred to fire from the hip owing to the large charges of powder. Good use was made of the plentiful timber at hand for building stockades, but the Ashanti had only recently acquired this practice and they never learnt to build defences in echelon to protect their flanks. The morale of the Central African troops was greatly enhanced by their success against such formidable enemies.

On 27th November Willcocks held a farewell parade. When he left for the coast a week later, 2 C.A.R. was called upon to furnish the guard of honour. Willcocks paid high tribute to the battalion in his final despatch, written at Cape Coast on Christmas Day, 1900. 'This was the first occasion in this campaign,' he wrote, referring to Brake's action at Jachi, 'on which this excellent battalion had an opportunity of a fight, and by its discipline and pluck at once established itself as one of the best corps in the Field Force—a reputation it has right well maintained.' Manning also was highly satisfied with the performance of his troops. 'I think we may say without boasting,' he wrote to Sir Clement Hill, the Superintendent of African Protectorates at the Foreign Office, 'that our troops were the best drilled, best disciplined, and best shooting corps employed in the Ashanti expedition. This . . . I put down to the fact that our officers . . . have been trained in the Regular Army and knew their work.'[1]

(v) *Foreign Service: The Gambia Expedition, 1901.* Map 3.

Gambia is the smallest and most northerly of the British West African territories. It is little more than a narrow strip of land bordering the banks of the Lower Gambia, the only river in Africa navigable to seagoing vessels for more than 200 miles. Though partly cultivated, the country consists largely of mangrove swamps lining the numerous creeks

---

[1] Manning to Hill, 31.i.1901. F.O.2, 469, Naso, a native of the West Shire district, wrote some amusing impressions of this campaign which are filed in Central African Archives, K.A.R. 2/1/1-9.

adjoining the river, and of thick bush, bamboo and scrub. The indigenous tribes are the Mandinka, Wolof and Wola.

An agreement with the French, whose territory surrounds the colony, had settled the boundaries in 1889, but this meant little to the native slave-raiding chiefs, who were accustomed to operate indiscriminately on both sides of the frontier, a constant source of unrest throughout the last decade of the nineteenth century. One of these chiefs, Fodi Kabba, had been driven out of the colony in 1892 and had settled at Madina, six miles beyond the southern frontier in French territory, whence he raided impartially in all directions. But it was internal troubles that brought about in 1901 a military expedition that was afterwards prolonged to settle matters with the slavers also.

On 14th June, 1900, two travelling commissioners, Sitweil and Silva, were murdered with their police escort of six constables at the village of Sankandi in the Kiang district, south of the river. The people of the nearby town of Dumbutu were known to be primarily responsible for this treacherous act. Gambia possessed an armed police force of 100 men only, and on account of the Ashanti trouble no troops could be spared from elsewhere to punish the outrage. The result was the growth of a dangerous spirit of disaffection that spread from the south to the northern bank of the river, many chiefs refusing to recognize British authority and informing their people that the country had been handed back to them to administer. In December, 1900, another travelling commissioner, J. H. Ozanne, was forced to escape by night from the large village of Salikeni, owing to the threatening attitude of its people. A military expedition was thereupon authorized, and as the need for further troops in Ashanti was now past, it was decided to employ the four companies of 2 C.A.R. that had just left British Somaliland, and four companies of the 3rd Bn. West India Regiment from Sierra Leone, a total of 802 rank and file. Command of this Field Force was given to Lieutenant-Colonel Brake, who met the half-battalion of his old regiment on arrival at Gibraltar. Three small warships, H.M.S. *Forte, Dwarf* and *Thrush*, were to co-operate and to hold in readiness a naval contingent of 200 men for use if required.

The two essentials for success were secrecy and speed. News of an impending expedition could travel very quickly from village to village by native runners, and the rebel chiefs were well aware that sanctuary lay within reach across the frontier. Dumbutu, the first objective, was only a mile from French territory. The offending village of Sankandi had already been burnt by its inhabitants, who had moved to Nema across the border. Plans were therefore made to synchronize the concentration of troops off Bathurst on 10th January, 1901, and then to move up-river with the least possible delay.

The half-battalion 2 C.A.R. arrived off the mouth of the Gambia River in the transport *Dwarka* on 9th January, to find the other vessels of the expedition assembling. Next morning the flotilla entered the river and anchored off Bathurst, where 'H' Company and the women and children were landed and accommodated in the police barracks. Though H. M. B. Griffith, the Acting Administrator, was very doubtful whether

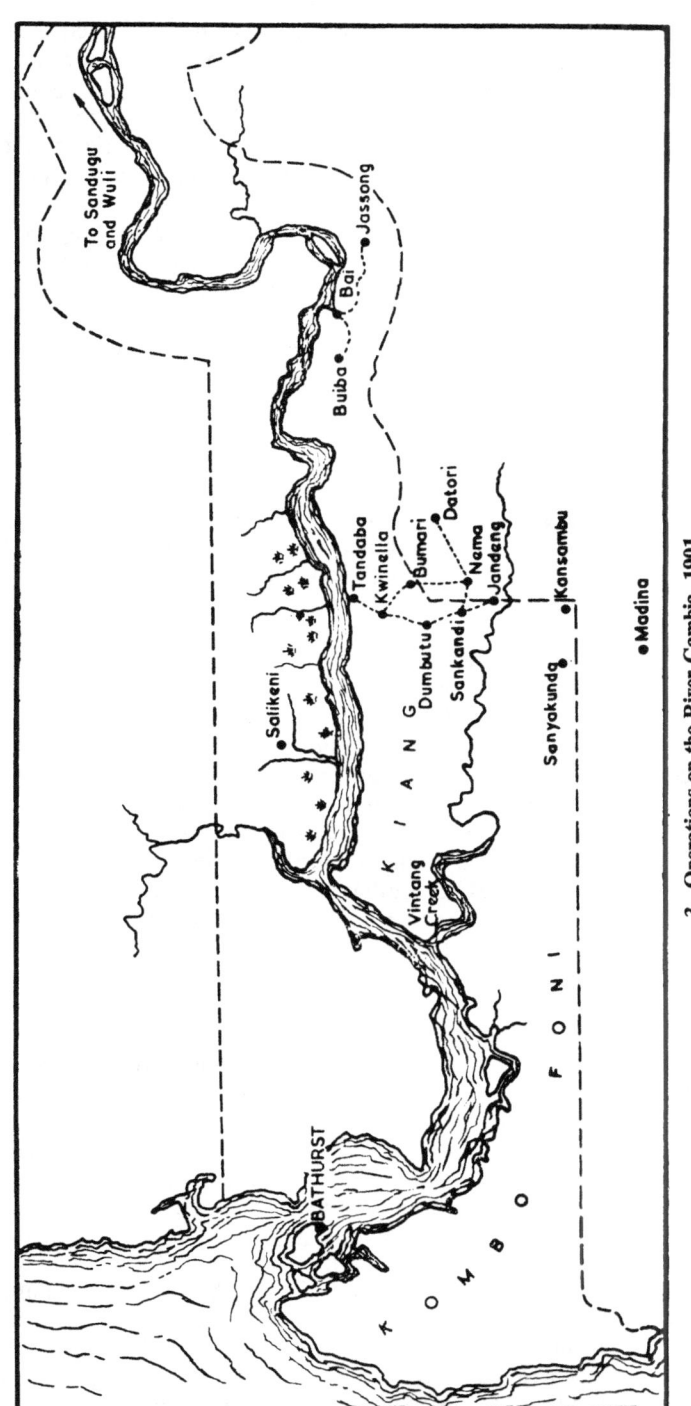

3. Operations on the River Gambia, 1901

a surprise attack was worth attempting, Brake had obtained the sanction of Sir George Denton, the newly-appointed Administrator, to his plan for an immediate advance. The expedition therefore started up-river at 2 p.m. on the same day, timed to arrive off Vintang Creek at dusk to await the rising of the moon. A transport was then sent up the creek with two companies of the West India Regiment, with orders to prevent any natives from crossing to the north bank.

At two o'clock on the morning of 11th January the voyage up-river was resumed by the rest of the Field Force. The objective was Tendaba ('Big Wharf'), sixty-three miles from Bathurst and eight from Dumbutu. It was hoped to land the troops before dawn, and in spite of difficult navigation the ships arrived off Tendaba at 4.30 a.m. Disembarkation began at once, but as there was no pier and shallow water made approach difficult by boat, it was 8.30 a.m. before the landing was completed. Each man carried three days' rations and 100 rounds of ammunition.

Within half an hour the column had left Tendaba. Four miles out it was joined by a screen of 50 native scouts under Lan Sanyeng, the son of a loyal chief who had been killed with Sitwell and Silva. The function of these scouts, who wore bunches of leaves on their heads so that the troops could recognize them, was to capture any natives who might be met on the approach march and so prevent news of the advancing column from reaching the enemy. This they did most effectively, moving in silence through the long grass.

At 11.45 a.m. the scouts reported that Dumbutu was in sight. Going forward to reconnoitre, Brake found that the town consisted of two collections of buildings lying in an open cultivated plain. To the right of the line of march, a patch of scrub and high grass offered good cover, and by moving his troops through this he brought them unobserved to within a quarter of a mile of the town. Brake then ordered Major Plunkett with two companies 2 C.A.R. to outflank the town on the left as rapidly as possible, and take up a position between it and the French frontier. This was done without giving the alarm, and Brake then ordered his troops to advance through the fields.

Part of the town was defended by a stockade, and the position was seen to be crowded with armed men. Surprise was complete, and few escaped before all exits were barred. The natives then raised a white flag, but as the troops advanced a heavy fire was opened from the walls of the compound and the doors of the huts. Fortunately it was very poorly directed and did little damage. Several parties of the enemy tried to break out but were driven back. The headman, Mai Dabu, who had been captured early in the engagement, was sent in under escort to persuade his people to surrender.

On occupying the town it was discovered that more than 60 tribesmen had been killed, including two of the rebel headmen. Three other headmen and over 200 men and women were captured, of whom 35 men were retained later by the Administrator for trial. The Field Force lost one carrier died of wounds, and four askaris (two from each regiment) wounded. Owing to the decision to begin operations at once,

Advance Guard of 2 C.A.R. entering the jungle during the Gambia Expedition of 1901

[*Photo: Lt.-Col. I. S. Graham*

and the excellent dispositions made for the approach march, the affair at Dumbutu proved a most satisfactory start to the campaign, and its effect was salutary. On the following day when two companies marched to Kwinella, a hostile village on the route to Dumbutu, the headman arrested the leading rebels and handed them over without demur. The two companies of the West India Regiment at Vintang Creek likewise met with no resistance, and rejoined the main body on 13th January.

At Salikeni on the north bank of the river 3,000 men were said to be under arms. Hoping again to surprise his enemy, Brake left two companies of the West India Regiment to garrison Dumbutu and guard the depôt and base hospital that had been established at Tendaba, and re-embarked the rest of his force on 16th January. Proceeding downstream, the ships anchored at nightfall off the south bank, some distance from the mouth of the Salikeni Creek. At 4 a.m. the landing party began to embark in boats and lighters. After some delay owing to the *Dwarf* grounding on a sandbank, the ships towed the loaded boats through the heavy current of the main stream to the mouth of the creek, where they were taken over by the steam-cutters.

The landing took place at 8 a.m. Beyond the wharf a raised causeway about five feet wide ran for nearly a mile through the mangrove swamps. The local officials had all agreed that the tribesmen were likely to offer a stubborn resistance, but there was no alternative to advancing along the causeway in single file, hoping that the alarm had not been given. Beyond lay open ground, where the leading companies were able to deploy. Salikeni was situated about two miles from the wharf, at the crest of a gentle slope masked by a patch of rice crops. No natives were seen until this field had been passed. Then the chief, accompanied by a few unarmed followers, approached to announce that no armed resistance was intended. Ozanne, who was present with the column, pointed out the part of the town occupied by the rebels, who were all arrested. A fine was imposed by the Administrator, and about 200 guns were discovered and confiscated. Flying columns similarly disarmed two other towns in the vicinity without opposition.

During the next few weeks columns of troops carried out many hot and toilsome marches through the disaffected areas of the colony. The three companies of 2 C.A.R. were transported to the districts of Sandugu and Wuli, north of the upper reaches of the river, where they visited the villages of two chiefs suspected of disloyalty, and were well received at both. On returning down-river in H.M.S. *Dwarf*, the ship went aground and two days passed before she could be refloated. Two companies of the regiment were then landed at Bai and marched under Major Plunkett to collect the fines imposed by the Administrator on Jassong and Buiba. In February three companies of the West India Regiment marched through Kiang, and three companies of the Central Africa Regiment through Foni and Kombo. This brought the operations as originally planned to an end.

Negotiations had already opened with the French for combined operations against Fodi Kabba, as the presence of so many troops in Gambia offered an excellent opportunity for destroying his power for good. The half-battalion of the Central Africa Regiment was considered sufficient for this purpose, so on 26th February the West India Regiment left Gambia in the *Dwarka* for Sierra Leone, leaving one company behind for garrison duty, pending the formation of a garrison company of the West Africa Frontier Force to be raised locally. On 5th March two French officers reached Bathurst to discuss plans. These were agreed, but several delays occurred, and another fortnight passed before the French were ready to leave their base.

Madina, Fodi Kabba's chief town, was surrounded by mud walls and reported to be full of slaves employed as fighting men. No proper estimate could be obtained of their numbers, or of those at Nema and Datori, two lesser strongholds that were also stockaded. The French expedition numbered 18 officers, 40 Spahis and 400 Tirailleurs, with three 80-mm. guns, and the plan was for their main body to approach Madina from the west while the cavalry worked round to the south. The eastern flank was to be blocked by native levies under Musa Mullah, and the task of the C.A.R. was to line the frontier and prevent escape northward into British territory. The three companies of the regiment were therefore posted at the frontier villages of Kansambu, Sanya Kunda and Jandeng, with strong picquets on all the roads leading from Madina.

At noon on 23rd March the sound of the French guns reached the picquets. The bombardment continued till 3.30 p.m., when the artillery had sufficiently breached the walls and the French infantry stormed the town. Fodi Kabba was killed, together with 150 of his men, for the loss of two French soldiers killed and seven wounded. Some fugitives were captured on the frontier and escorted to the French camp, which was visited by Brake, who was taken into the town to inspect the damage. The French then planned to attack Nema and Dator, while Brake manned the section of the frontier from Dumbutu to Bumari. But the rebel towns had already been deserted, and it only proved necessary to send a flying column to destroy them. This ended the combined operations. The garrison company of the West India Regiment remained in the disaffected area for the time being, and on 30th March the Central Africa Regiment embarked in the *Dwarka* at Tendaba for transport to the Gold Coast.

The secrecy and celerity with which Brake carried out his campaign had pacified the country with a minimum of fighting. Three of the murderers were captured and hanged, and five other ringleaders were deported. The co-operation with the French also served to instil the lesson that the frontier could not be counted upon as a means of escape for criminals. The behaviour of the troops, most of whom were on active service for the first time, proved very good and was marked by constraint towards the persons and property of their defeated enemies. Throughout the operations the heat was intense, and water was often very short.

The Gambia expedition was unique in one respect: it was the only occasion on which naval officers served in command of troops of the regiment on active service. When the C.A.R. arrived in Gambia there was only one officer per company, and for a time Lieutenant-Commander H. F. Shakespear, R.N., of H.M.S. *Dwarf*, Lieutenant-Commander H.

D'Oyly, R.N., of H.M.S. *Thrush*, and Lieutenant Massey Dawson, of H.M.S. *Forte*, helped to fill the breach. Brake paid tribute in his report to their excellent service.

One more task fell to the lot of the battalion before it returned home. A mutiny had broken out in the West Africa Regiment, serving in the Gold Coast, and about 150 men were marching west from Cape Coast to Sierra Leone, plundering freely as they went. The half-battalion left Bathurst in the *Dwarka* on 2nd April, and six days later landed 'B' Company at Cape Coast Castle. The women and children were left at Elmina, and picking up a detachment of 30 men of 'D' Company from Kumase, the expedition then sailed for Akim and Atuabo to join H.M.S. *Forte* in stopping the advance of the mutineers, who were reported to have broken through a detachment of police.

On 9th April, Brake landed three companies at Beyin. Drenched with surf and pouring rain, the troops took up position that night about two miles west of Atuabo. Some marshes a short way inland ran parallel to the sea and formed an effective barrier that would confine the mutineers to the coast road. Trenches were dug across and flanking the road and along the foreshore. The position was well camouflaged with bushes, and a maxim gun was sited to command the approach.

At 8.30 a.m. on 10th April, police scouts reported that the mutineers were in sight. Twenty yards from the position Brake met them and demanded their surrender. The mutineers refused, and drew together, ready for a rush. A second call to surrender was made, again without effect, and the order was given to fire. The mutineers replied, falling back rapidly as they did so, whereupon the troops charged and drove them through Atuabo and into the bush beyond, killing eight and wounding many more. Trapped against the marshes and with all retreat cut off, 128 men were captured by search columns during the next five days. Twelve more were believed to have been killed or committed suicide. The troops re-embarked for Accra on 16th April.

The two battalions of the regiment did not return home together. The Zomba contingent of the 1st Battalion, accompanied by 40 men of the 2nd Battalion, reached Central Africa on 21st January, 1901, under the command of Major Cobbe, having lost two officers wounded and one invalided, and three other ranks killed and 40 wounded. On 3rd June a detachment of 1 C.A.R., consisting of one Sikh (Havildar Jaimal Singh, 14th Sikhs), six sergeants, three corporals, 12 privates and an interpreter, drawn from the Yao and Atonga tribes, embarked for England under the command of Captain C. V. N. Percival (Rifle Brigade). Another detachment of 15 N.C.Os. and men of the 2nd Battalion had left Accra for England on 22nd May, under Captain J. Johnston-Stewart (A. & S.H.). On arrival they were quartered at St. George's Barracks and attached to the 3rd Bn. Coldstream Guards. On 26th June they were inspected in the gardens of Marlborough House by King Edward VII, who presented medals for the recent campaigns in Ashanti and Gambia. The detachment then marched to the War Office for inspection by the Commander-in-Chief, Lord Roberts. During their stay in England the men saw the Royal Tournament, the Military Exhibition at

Earls Court, and a review of the Household troops, but the most lasting impression brought back by either party was a display of Brock's fireworks at the Crystal Palace, and a performing elephant that played a piano at the Alhambra.

The main body of 2 C.A.R. left West Africa in two parties during May and June,[1] and did not reach home until July, when the Atonga were given six months' leave and the Yao four months'. By that time far-reaching decisions on the future of the regiment had already been taken.

---

[1] The B.I. steamer *Dwarka*, which was again used to transport the battalion, came to be known as the Regimental Yacht. A record of her voyages of 1900-01 was later inscribed on the lid of an old ammunition box and mounted at the head of the companion way.

CHAPTER 3

The Uganda Rifles

(i) *Lugard and Emin Pasha's Sudanese, 1890-92.* Map I (a).

TOWARDS the end of 1890 Captain Lugard, who had taken service with the Imperial British East Africa Company, arrived in Buganda. Pressure from the British Government and the general interest aroused in the country by Stanley had obliged the Company to reconsider its cautious attitude, and Lugard came to assure Mwanga of the Company's protection and assistance. By this time Gedge and the handful of men left by Jackson were in a somewhat precarious situation. Mwanga was suspicious, fearing that vengeance might be exacted for Bishop Hannington's murder, but after prolonged negotiations Lugard succeeded in winning his confidence. Mwanga then signed a treaty with the Company, valid for two years, that gave Lugard a recognized status in Buganda. On a small hill named Kampala he pitched his camp.

The country was obviously on the verge of civil war. The Muslim party, with its Arab allies, was preparing a new attack on Buganda from Bunyoro. Moreover, the so-called Christian party had by this time become deeply divided along denominational lines, the Anglican chiefs actively supporting the treaty with the British Company, and the Catholic chiefs remaining suspicious and covertly hostile. Lugard's aim was to compose the differences between the hostile factions and to instruct Mwanga in the art of impartial kingship, but it soon became plain to him that little progress could be made without some independent means of upholding his own authority and maintaining the Company's prestige. He had left Mombasa with 70 Sudanese who had been recruited in Egypt for the Company's service by Captain W. H. Williams, R.A. By the time he reached Buganda he had about 50 Sudanese and Somali 'troops' in whom a semblance of discipline had been inculcated, 270 porters, most of whom were quite useless for fighting, eleven rounds of ammunition per man, and a worn-out maxim gun.[1] In January, 1891,

---

[1] Machine guns were first used by the British Army in the Zulu War of 1879. The Gatling guns then employed, like the *mitrailleuse* on which the French based such mistaken hopes in the war of 1870, were multi-barrelled and thus too heavy and cumbersome for success in a colonial campaign. After many experiments a notable improvement was introduced by Sir Hiram Maxim in 1889, when the recoil caused by the explosion was utilized to load, fire and eject the next shot. The maxim gun was not introduced into the British Army until 1891, and did not become standard until 1894. It is easy to understand, therefore, the importance that was attached to the maxim at this early period and the interest that was aroused by its performance in Uganda. Like other types of machine gun, it was used also in Ashanti, in the Sudan, and on the North-West Frontier of India. The experience so gained proved of great value, but for a long time it was regarded as a weapon suitable only for stopping wild rushes of savages, and a good deal of prejudice subsisted against its use in regular warfare.

Williams joined him with 75 Sudanese, 100 Swahili and another maxim. This reinforcement was timely, and while Lugard devoted his energies to political affairs, Williams took in hand the training of the force on which so much depended. The best of the Swahili porters were formed into a 'Zanzibar Levy', organized in two companies, the Red and the Blue. Membership of this body came to be regarded as an honour, and helped to strengthen the wavering morale of the Swahili. Under Williams' direction discipline improved; drill parades were held daily, and simple military exercises were practised, such as advancing in formation through the long grass and banana shambas without losing touch. Crowds of Baganda collected to watch these exercises.

Another safari reached Buganda from the coast in March, and again the best of the men were taken to strengthen the little military force. The fort, which had been considerably enlarged, now housed seven Europeans and 650 men, of whom 300 had been drilled by Williams. These troops learnt to respond to bugle calls, advance in open order, aim with care, and take cover.

It was not long before they were in action. Kabarega of Bunyoro had joined hands with the Muslim party, and Lugard went west with the Baganda army to meet him. His troops marched in the centre of a vast throng of 25,000 Baganda levies, advancing across country in parallel columns, each with its chief at the head. It was an extraordinary spectacle, often to be repeated in succeeding years, and one that frequently invoked the wonder of officers new to Uganda and unused to the co-operation of such strange allies. Each night while the camp fires lit the surrounding hills, Lugard was pestered by the chiefs for ammunition, for the Baganda army carried some 4,700 firearms. On 7th May, with Lugard's force in the centre of the attack, the Muslims were met and scattered. Lugard wanted to pursue, but his allies refused and the levies broke up.

Sending Williams back to the fort at Kampala, Lugard decided on a course that had long been in his mind. Williams was sure that no more Sudanese could be recruited in Egypt, but Emin Pasha's troops, now under the command of Selim Bey, had the reputation of being the 'best material for soldiery in Africa', and Lugard thought that with their aid the Company might hold both Buganda and Bunyoro. He accordingly marched through Buddu to Ankole, where he made a treaty with the king, Ntale; reached Lake Edward; built a stockade which he called Fort George; marched up the eastern flank of Ruwenzori and built another, Fort Edward; and continued to Lake Albert, where at last he found Selim Bey and his Sudanese at Kavalli's.

Selim was a giant Sudanese of considerable force of character, who had formerly been Governor of Mruli. Emin and Stanley had sent him north to complete the evacuation of Wadelai, but the Commandant there, Fadl el Maula Bey, mutinied and led most of his troops to the hills. Delayed by this, Selim found on his return that Emin and Stanley had already left for the coast. Eventually 800 of Fadl's men rejoined Selim at Kavalli's. Emin had in the meantime returned to the interior in the service of the German Government, and tried to persuade Selim to join him. Selim refused, saying that he was still a loyal officer of the Khedive.

The same objection was now raised in answer to Lugard's proposals. Though Selim was overjoyed to see him, and realized that his men would welcome a return to proper soldiering after their long exile, he insisted that they could not serve under Lugard without the Khedive's consent. Eventually Selim agreed that while awaiting this he would serve in alliance with the British, retaining for the time being the Egyptian flag. A scale of pay was drawn up, ranging from four rupees a month for a private to 420 rupees for Selim. This agreement[1] constitutes the basis of the claim that Emin's Sudanese were the origin of the K.A.R.

The Sudanese presented a motley appearance. Most of the original troops had come from the northern Sudan, and a few were pure Egyptians. Their ranks, thinned by constant campaigning, had been replenished by recruits drawn from many tribes, with the result that most of the original soldiers were now native officers or N.C.Os., largely self-promoted. Some had been at Kavalli's for over two years, and were surrounded by numbers of followers. Lugard held a parade to explain the new agreement, and afterwards the two regiments, all that remained of 3,000 fighting men, marched past, headed by their drums, bugles and tattered flags. About 600 were armed with rifles.

Lugard realized from the first that he ran some risk in enlisting the help of such a body of men. There were insufficient Europeans to exercise control, and without this the Sudanese might become a greater menace than Kabarega to the people of Bunyoro and Toro. Though they had loyally served their Government for several years without pay, the fact that they had perforce grown self-supporting made them eager for followers and slaves. Lugard looked forward to the day when they would become entirely dependent on him for ammunition. Meanwhile he planned to split them into garrisons of manageable proportions in a line of stockaded forts along the southern boundaries of Bunyoro. Before returning to Buganda he built and garrisoned five forts with the whole of the 1st Regiment and part of the 2nd Regiment of Sudanese.[2] Altogether about 8,200 men, women and children were brought away from Kavalli's, including 932 men with arms and 1,153 without. From the 2nd Regiment Lugard selected 89 men under Selim Bey to augment the garrison at Kampala, where the troops were reorganized in three companies: No. 1, Old Sudanese; No. 2, New Sudanese; and No. 3, Zanzibaris.

Lugard reached Kampala again on 31st December, 1891, after an absence of six months. There to his dismay he learnt that the Company, alarmed at the expense of administering Uganda, had decided to withdraw. Funds were, however, subscribed in England and the Company agreed to carry on for one year more.

[1] Dated 13.ix.1891 at Kavalli's. F.O.2, 57.

[2] Lugard's original forts, numbered 1 to 5, were named respectively Forts Wavertree, Lorne, Kivari, Ntara, and Grant. In 1892 Kivari and Ntara were re-sited and named Briggs and de Winton, and Fort Edward was evacuated. Forts Gerry (Portal) and Raymond were built in 1893, and a new Fort Grant in the position shown on the accompanying map. Fort Roddy (originally called Fort Nakabimba) was not built till 1895.

Within a few weeks civil war was again raging in Buganda. Convinced that Mwanga and the Catholic party, acting perhaps under the advice of the French missionaries, were becoming increasingly hostile to the Company, and realizing that his own forces were too small to take independent action, Lugard allowed the incident of a gun stolen by one faction from the other to develop into a *casus belli*, and in the ensuing conflict issued arms to the Protestant forces. The Anglicans, with some support from Lugard's fort at Kampala, were successful in an action fought at Mengo on 24th January, 1892. Mwanga and the French party fled to Buddu. Judging that his restoration was the best means of pacifying the country, Lugard at last persuaded him to return. Signs were not wanting that the Muslims were endeavouring to seduce their co-religionists the Sudanese, and the danger was always present that they might combine with Kabarega to attack Buganda. Lugard therefore sent Selim as an emissary to the Muslim leader Mbogo, who after some hesitation consented to return to Buganda. A division of the country was made between the three parties, six provinces being allotted to the Protestants, three to the Muslims and one, the province of Buddu, to the Catholics. This arrangement soon caused further trouble.[1]

Lugard had fully intended to send Williams and other officers to command the line of forts, but unfortunately was prevented by the pressure of events in Buganda. The Sudanese at Kampala, and some of the garrisons in the forts, behaved excellently, but rumours soon came of oppression and looting elsewhere. There were too many self-promoted officers, and the rapaciousness of their wives and followers became a by-word.

Complaints of Lugard's actions had already been raised in Europe by the missionary societies, and in this critical situation he decided to leave for home. The railway survey under Captain J. R. L. Macdonald[2] had reached Uganda with an escort of Indian troops, and with this party Lugard left for the coast in June, 1892. On the way he noticed an excellent site for a station on a hill near the rocky gorge of the great Eldama Ravine, a deep cleft at the foot of the Mau escarpment, near the forested and well-watered hills of the Kamasya range. Later events proved the military necessity for the post that was established there, but in Lugard's eyes the chief advantage was the suitability of the district for an agricultural settlement. Establishment in colonies appeared the only solution to the future of the Sudanese, for the Khedive disclaimed responsibility for his former soldiers.

With the controversy aroused by Lugard's political methods and motives we are not directly concerned. It is, however, relevant to note that many of the actions for which he was blamed undoubtedly stemmed from the need for reliable military support to back his precarious

---

[1] From the Baganda angle, the events of this period were part of an expansionist movement that had begun long before. 'The establishment of European government marked only the final stage of a political and social revolution, which had started at least eight years before Sir Gerald Portal's arrival, and in which Christianity had played from the first a prominent part.' (R. A. Oliver, *The Missionary Factor in East Africa*, p. 194.)

[2] Later Major-General Sir James Macdonald, K.C.I.E., C.B., LL.D

authority. Local allies were essential, and for this reason Lugard was driven to support the Protestant interest, to the detriment of the impartial rôle he sought to maintain. His introduction of the Sudanese troops created many problems for Uganda in the years to come. They may have been the 'best material for soldiery in Africa', but only if properly disciplined and led. Lugard's line of forts looked formidable on a map, but in practice they were merely a handful of isolated, earth-banked stockades, not even defensible in design, with palisades too high to fire over and without loopholes. As an effective barrier to Kabarega and the gun-running caravans of the Arabs they were of little use except as bases for mobile patrols. But the Sudanese officers had neither the incentive nor the initiative needed, and in fact were soon hard put even to maintain themselves, especially in Forts 3 and 4, which were situated in a foodless area. Political motives caused by the aspirations of other European nations, the importance then attached to the headwaters of the Nile, the desire for economic expansion, the zeal of the missionaries and their supporters at home, were all factors impelling the attempt to do too much with too slender means. There was no time for consolidation. The handful of soldiers and administrators who laid the foundations of the new protectorate in the early 1890's had to rely upon such military resources as lay to hand. The result was an exhausting succession of campaigns, that culminated at last in unexpected disaster.

(ii) *The Muslim Rebellion and the Reorganization of the Sudanese, 1893*. Map I (a).

On his way back to the coast, Macdonald was ordered to return to Uganda. The home government, pressed by France to compensate the Catholic missionaries for their losses in the civil war, realized that the time had come for official action, and decided to send Sir Gerald Portal, the British Agent and Consul-General at Zanzibar, to examine the situation and report on the best means of dealing with the country. In the meantime Macdonald was to conduct a preliminary investigation into the accusations levelled against Lugard.[1]

Portal reached Kampala in March, 1893. While passing through Busoga he found the people suspicious and noticed a number of ruined villages, the result, it was reported, of a visit in the previous year by Captain Williams with some of the Company's troops and a horde of Baganda levies whom it was beyond his power to control. Portal did not therefore begin his task with any liking for military rule, but the discontent of the Muslim party at Lugard's division of provinces soon convinced him that only the presence of the English officers and their Sudanese troops prevented the outbreak of another civil war. Williams had enlisted a second company of Sudanese, thus raising the garrison of Kampala to about 300 men, but soon after Portal's arrival he left for

[1] The Government did not publish Macdonald's report, which was highly critical of Lugard. It will be found, together with the evidence of the witnesses in F.O.2, 60 (7.iv.93).

the coast, taking with him all the enlisted Sudanese but 18 native officers and N.C.Os., who were left in Buganda as drill instructors. Portal was accompanied by several British officers and had brought an escort of 200 Zanzibari soldiers under Captain L. R. Arthur (Rifle Brig.); troops who had been smart enough on garrison duty at home, but who now proved lazy, dirty and utterly untrustworthy. The raising of fresh troops was therefore of immediate importance.

The only solution was to enlist more men from the Sudanese garrisoning the forts. The task of selection was entrusted to Major E. R. Owen (Lan. Fus.) and Captain Raymond Portal (Loyal North Lancs.), who were instructed to enlist up to 450 men. These troops were to be taken temporarily into the British service with effect from 15th April, 1893,[1] at 'very low rates of pay', ranging from four rupees per month for a private to sixty-five for a native officer.[2] In most districts pay had to be issued in the form of cloth, a particularly expensive and uncertain method of remuneration, owing to the wastage by loss, theft, and damage during transport from the coast. In course of time it also proved very unfair, for the price of cloth naturally increased in direct proportion to the distance it had to be carried from the coast, so that the 'rupee stick' kept at every station to measure the appropriate length was shorter for troops stationed in the remoter parts of the Protectorate.

The troops were formed into five companies, each of 125 all ranks. But the status of the unenlisted Sudanese, still in forts flying the Egyptian flag, remained highly anomalous. Owen had been instructed to evacuate Forts 1 and 2, concentrating all Sudanese whom he did not select for Kampala at Forts 3 and 4, where they were nearer to Buganda. Investigation showed that these garrisons had already laid waste a great part of southern Bunyoro, for in the absence of any organized system of supply they could maintain themselves and their followers in no other way. Though realizing that Bunyoro was unlikely to come peacefully under European domination so long as Kabarega was alive, Portal saw nothing to be gained by its forcible subjugation, and therefore came to the decision that the southern forts must be abandoned entirely and their garrisons concentrated in defensive positions on the borders of Buganda.

Selim Bey strongly opposed the policy of weakening the garrisons to provide troops for Buganda. The Muslim party was demanding a revision of the land settlement and the grant of another province, and Selim began openly to support their claims. On being charged with disloyalty he replied with some reason that although as native commandant of the enlisted Sudanese he considered himself strictly under British orders, he was responsible to no one as the acknowledged leader of the thousands of unenlisted men and their followers.

Owen was now placed in command of the forts, but food was so short

---

[1] The earliest enlistments shown in the 'Long Rolls', however, are 1st April, 1893.

[2] Portal's instructions to Owen, 27.iii.93, and the 'Conditions of Enlistment' drawn up by Captain Williams. F.O.2, 60.

that he was unable to concentrate near the Buganda frontier as intended.[1] Kabarega was already attacking the northern forts, and, though repulsed, met with some success in ambushing patrols and foraging parties. In Buganda the issue of civil war once more hung in the balance. In the midst of these troubles, worn out with fever and sorrow at the sudden death of his brother, Sir Gerald Portal left for the coast after only ten weeks in Buganda. Before departing he appointed Macdonald Acting Commissioner and issued precise instructions to guide him in the employment of his troops. They were never to be used for police work, or in small parties unaccompanied by an English officer, but were intended 'primarily for the protection of the persons of the Acting Commissioner and his staff . . . of the property of Her Majesty's Government, and for the repulsion of invasion of Uganda by any foreign enemy'.[2]

Macdonald took a serious view of the Muslim threat. Selim was ordered to Port Alice on the Entebbe peninsula, where Portal had set up his headquarters, to prevent him from intriguing with the Muslim leaders at Mengo. It was planned to raise a reserve force of 250 men from the unenlisted Sudanese, but Selim's attitude prevented recruits from coming forward. By the middle of June Macdonald considered the position critical, for Selim had warned him that he would regard war with the Muslims as a hostile act. Macdonald therefore decided that the time had come for strong action, because if Selim's troops mutinied he had only eight Sudanese from Egypt and 50 Swahilis (about half of whom were incapacitated by jiggers[3]) on whom to rely.

The Sudanese officers were summoned, and Macdonald ordered them to take an oath of allegiance to the Queen. They refused, though still protesting their loyalty. Macdonald then sent for the armed Swahilis stationed at Port Alice. Their arrival raised the number of Swahilis at Kampala to 120. Covered by the rifles of these men and by two maxim guns manned by British officers, the Sudanese company was paraded and disarmed. Without delay Macdonald set out for Port Alice with a force of five Europeans, about forty Swahilis and 2,000 Baganda. Again the Sudanese troops were disarmed without difficulty. Selim Bey was arrested in his quarters, tried for mutinous conduct and treason and sentenced to degradation and deportation. He had for some time been a sick man, and died suddenly of heart disease at Naivasha *en route* to the coast.

Doubt has been expressed whether Selim's conduct merited so harsh a sentence. There is reason to suppose that his message to Macdonald suffered in translation, and his actions never extended to open rebellion.

[1] Disaffection, drought, and the natural fears of Kasagama and the other Toro chiefs at being left unprotected gave Owen an extremely difficult time. From Fort No. 3 he wrote in a letter: 'I have to be a linen draper, a builder, a clerk, a governor, a colonel, and an explorer, all in one, and last, but by no means least trouble, a doctor, without the provision or facilities for any of them.' (M. Bovill and G. R. Askwith, *Roddy Owen: A Memoir*, p. 79.) It was a fair picture of the life led by a military officer in Uganda for the next decade.

[2] Portal to Macdonald, 29.v.93.

[3] In 1893 the jigger, a small insect living in the soil, was a newcomer to Uganda, but Lugard's fort at Kampala was already alive with them.

'There must have been a strong want of tact,' wrote Lugard, 'to convert a loyalty so sincere into hostility, when Selim was even then a dying man.' Portal, who had waited for news on his way to the coast, approved of Macdonald's actions, though he considered his attitude towards the Sudanese unnecessarily alarmist.

The civil war duly broke out, but was of short duration. Deprived of Sudanese help, the Muslims were defeated at Rubaga Hill and driven into their own province. In July the pursuing Baganda army reached Fort de Winton. Owen attempted to arrange terms but without success, and on 18th July the Muslims were caught and defeated in a final battle. It was the last of the politico-religious wars.

In September the delayed reorganization of the Sudanese troops and their followers was carried out. On the 26th Owen reported that the entire garrisons of Forts George, Gerry, Nderi and de Winton, 3,859 persons all told, had been brought into Singo. New forts were under construction there, as it was already clear that there could be no lasting peace until Kabarega had been defeated. Macdonald and Owen selected the sites for Fort Raymond, Fort Grant and Fort Lugard, and throughout September and October the work of building and fortifying continued. The Sudanese garrisons numbered 600 enlisted men, distributed at Kampala (120), Port Alice (200), Fort Raymond (100), Fort Grant (70), Fort Lugard (70), and Fort Lubwa (40), the last named being a new fort in Busoga. A reserve force of 300 men was enrolled among Sudanese living near the forts. So far as internal troubles were concerned, the position in Buganda was now reasonably secure.

Portal's final report examined in detail a number of factors bearing on the situation in Buganda and its dependencies. In his opinion economic considerations argued for withdrawal, but political and strategic factors for remaining. Everything pointed to a coming struggle with the Arabs throughout Central Africa. Even now those on the great lakes and at Tabora were communicating with the Sudan, and to abandon Christian Uganda, which dominated the north and west of Lake Victoria, held access to Lakes Albert and Albert Edward, and controlled the head-waters of the Nile, would seriously imperil the whole position and virtually confine British influence to the coast. The presence of a hostile and jealous neighbour in Bunyoro and of the alien Sudanese and their followers were added difficulties. Portal had a high opinion of the Sudanese as soldiers under discipline, and recorded that their presence had enabled him to remove most of the more expensive but much less efficient Zanzibaris, but he was well aware of the terror the Sudanese had inspired on the western frontiers of Buganda.

Portal thought that the declaration of a protectorate would be the simplest course. He recommended that the Imperial British East Africa Company's jurisdiction should cease, and that a commissioner should be appointed, with 13 English officers and 500 Sudanese troops, over Buganda, Busoga and Kavirondo. After long deliberation, the British Government decided to declare a protectorate only over the area covered by Buganda and its provinces, bounded by Koki, Ankole,

Bunyoro and Busoga, territories in which arrangements were to be limited to agreements with the local chiefs. Such was the intention, but even before the protectorate was declared, a series of campaigns had begun that led inevitably during succeeding years to extensions of the protectorate boundaries.

(iii) *The Campaigns in Bunyoro, 1893-95.* Map I (a).

In November, 1893, Colonel H. Colvile[1] (Gren. Gds.), the new British representative, reached Kampala with two other officers, Captains J. H. S. Gibb (Worcs. R.) and A. B. Thruston (Oxf. Lt. Inf.). From now onward other military officers continued to be seconded for service in Uganda, usually men who had served with the new Egyptian army, partly on account of their ability to speak Arabic, and partly because the future of Uganda was felt to depend on successful resistance to the Mahdi. Colvile found it impossible to work in the vicinity of the Baganda capital, and following Portal's example moved to Port Alice.

A threatening situation was developing in Bunyoro, for Kabarega had taken the evacuation of the southern forts as a sign of weakness. He was rumoured to have an army of 8,000 men equipped with firearms and 20,000 spearmen. Owen reported that an attack was expected on the forts in Singo, and Colvile decided to take the initiative. On his instructions Owen made a night march with 200 men, discovered his enemy awaiting him in a well-concealed position, attacked with small-arms fire for three hours, and eventually drove the Banyoro from the long grass and bush in headlong flight. This action had a salutary effect on Owen's Sudanese and Baganda allies, who had quite expected such a small force to be overwhelmed.

On 1st December news reached Colvile that Kabarega was raiding extensively in Toro and Busoga. Withdrawing 400 men from the garrisons of the forts, he collected a strong force to march into Bunyoro and dictate terms, little realizing the magnitude of the task he was undertaking. On 13th December the expedition left Kampala with seven Europeans. 221 Sudanese, 156 armed and about 200 unarmed porters, a maxim gun, and a steel boat in sections. At Mukwenda's Owen joined the column with another 200 Sudanese from the forts. The force was accompanied by some 15,000 Baganda levies, mostly spearmen.

The crossing of the River Kafu into Bunyoro was made with difficulty through a mass of swamp and slush. Though his army was encamped within sight of the river, Kabarega missed his chance of opposing the passage. Instead he retired to the north, burning his capital behind him. Colvile optimistically followed, hoping either to bring Kabarega to action or drive him from Bunyoro. At Lendui advance patrols discovered a deserted camp, in the form of an elaborate town of grass huts surrounded by a grass zariba. These were the quarters of Kabarega and his court, regularly erected on the march by an army of skilled workers. Beyond Lendui Colvile's advance guard was ambushed at close quarters, but the

---

[1] Later Major-General Sir Henry Colvile, K.C.M.G., C.B.

enemy withdrew after receiving a few volleys. At Kibuguzi the expedition reached the confines of the Budonga forest, where going became difficult through high grass and thorn intersected by ravines choked with dense vegetation. The district was foodless; it was impossible to overtake Kabarega if he refused to fight, and his army and herds were already disappearing into the depths of the forest. Colvile contemplated a march to Mruli, where rumour said that Kabarega had concealed his hoard of ivory on a group of islands in the Nile, but reconnaissance showed that most of the route lay across desert country.

Colvile accordingly recast his plans. He decided to divide Bunyoro with a line of forts, make terms with the chiefs to the south and confine Kabarega to the north. Leaving the Baganda to blockade the forest in the hope that Kabarega would be obliged to eat up all his supplies, Colvile marched west, occupied Kitanwa, and descended the steep escarpment to Kibero on the shores of Lake Albert. The steel boat was assembled and launched. If the new forts were to be properly garrisoned more troops would be needed, and Colvile was anxious to discover if any of Fadl el Maula's Sudanese were still at Wadelai. Owen was sent north to Bugungu, where he had two brushes with Kabarega's foraging parties, but owing to the mass of reeds at the river entrance the boat was unable to ferry his troops across.[1] A second attempt, made solely by water, succeeded in reaching Wadelai, where Owen made arrangements with the local chief to garrison Emin's old fort under the British flag. The 50 natives he enrolled for this purpose received a month's pay in advance, but the experiment was not a success, owing to the bad faith of the chief and the impossibility of proper supervision, and the fort was later abandoned.

Forts were built at Kibero and Kitanwa, garrisoned by 25 and 75 men respectively, and commanded by Sudanese officers. Colvile then selected a site for the headquarters fort on a slight rise 400 yards from the River Hoima, where he left Captain Thruston in command with 200 men. Another fort was built at Baranwa, near the Kafu crossing.

While the construction of these forts was proceeding, Kabarega emerged from the forest. The Baganda took him by surprise, captured 3,000 of his stock and 40 guns, and sent him flying across the Nile to the unexplored region known as Bukedi, 'the land of naked people', accompanied only by a handful of his followers.[2] After this success they were anxious to return home, and as Kabarega was now beyond the Nile, Colvile thought there was nothing to be gained by remaining longer in Bunyoro.

Before long Thruston reported that colonies of natives were settling down peaceably in the shadow of his forts. He had altogether about 600 Sudanese and 60 irregulars to guard the line of communication between

---

[1] '. . . up to our armpits in swamp-water and vegetation, cutting through brambles and trees, legs caught below the water in water plants and covered with animals . . .' (Owen's Diary, 26.i.94.)

[2] In this context the term 'Bukedi' may refer to the district now known as Lango.

Uganda, Lake Albert and the Nile. Fort Hoima was completed as a square stockade with bastions at diagonal corners, capable of being held by a very small garrison when troops were withdrawn for punitive expeditions. Climate and soil allowed the raising of two crops a year, and within twelve months the garrison had 400 acres under cultivation.

Kabarega was now reported at Mruli, and Colvile decided upon another attempt at capture. On 12th April, 1894, Captain Gibb marched north from Buganda with 200 Sudanese and over 5,000 Baganda. Gibb was so crippled with rheumatism that he had to be carried in a hammock. His instructions forbade him to cross the Nile, as Colvile wished to gain the friendship of the Bakedi and so deprive Kabarega of his refuge. On 4th May the column reached the ruins of Emin's old fort at Mruli. A boat was launched on the Nile and some canoes and sheep were captured among the islands, but Kabarega had heard of the expedition long before it arrived and retired across the river with most of his property. Gibb then travelled up the Nile through Busoga, and reached Kampala again on 28th June, quite unfit for further service.

Meanwhile news had reached Thruston that a large body of armed men 'with many flags' had arrived at Muhaji Saghir, west of Lake Albert. On investigation Thruston found them to be some of Fadl el Maula's missing Sudanese, who had left Wadelai to take service with the Belgians. Thruston persuaded their leaders that it was the Khedive's wish that they should join the British, who were now administering Bunyoro. On Colvile's instructions he ferried about 10,000 men, families and followers across the Nile and sent them to Buganda. The march was strenuous and only about 3,000 arrived: a strange collection of Sudanese, Egyptians, Bantus, Abyssinians and even a few pygmies from the Congo forests, armed with ancient breech-loaders and scatter-guns. Colvile selected nearly 400 men for immediate enlistment, bringing his total force to about 1,200 men.

Foraging parties from the forts and the monthly caravans to Bunyoro were frequently attacked. The chief danger to the line of communication was the hill fortress of Musaja Mukuro ('the Giant'), a steep, flat-topped eminence rising abruptly for about 1,000 feet and crowned by a standing camp approachable only by two zig-zag paths. On 20th May Thruston surrounded the hill and, selecting 50 of his best troops, climbed the narrow paths in the face of a hail of rocks and stones. On nearing the top he decided to conserve his ammunition, and having no bayonets drove the enemy out with rifle butts. This was one of the keenest actions ever fought by the Sudanese, and success was largely due to the excellent leadership displayed by the native officers.

Kabarega's escape soon restored his confidence. He returned to northern Bunyoro and sent an army to threaten Hoima. Thruston left the fort to a half-company of Zanzibari and the sick, and marched out with 150 Sudanese and some Baganda to forestall the attack. As usual, the Banyoro were advised in good time of his approach, and Thruston found over 700 riflemen concealed on the side of a ravine. Behind them and on the surrounding heights thousands of spearmen waited to see which way the battle would go.

The Sudanese opened fire and gradually worked their way forward, driving the enemy before them across the stream. But this time the Banyoro showed no sign of conceding a cheap victory. Leaving part of his force to contain the front, Thruston led the remainder over the stream to attack the enemy's flank. A long, stubborn fight ensued in the thick grass and bush before the tribesmen split into groups and scattered. This was the signal for a general flight on the part of the spearmen and onlookers. The engagement was the most important yet fought with the Banyoro, and showed them to be much more formidable adversaries than previously supposed. It cost Thruston 3,000 rounds of precious ammunition, most of which was wasted by firing too high, though over 200 of the enemy were killed.

There could be little hope of lasting peace in Bunyoro while the Arab trade in arms and ammunition continued. Regulations forbidding the importation of arms into Uganda except through a bonded warehouse were not passed until 1896, and at this time such goods were constantly being brought up from the coast through German territory. In July Colvile therefore sent Captain G. G. Cunningham (Derbyshire R.) with 57 Sudanese to establish a post in Ankole. Ntale, the ruler of Ankole, fled at his approach, but a treaty was made with his representative, and after a visit to Fort George, Cunningham returned into Buddu and built a fort at Sango near the mouth of the River Kagera.

Later in the year Kabarega was reported at Machudi, and Thruston was again ordered to attack. He left Hoima on 3rd November with 237 Sudanese on a forced march of seventy-eight miles. This time surprise was achieved, for although Kabarega was warned, he underestimated the Sudanese capacity for marching. Thruston entered the town after dark. When the alarm was raised, pandemonium ensued and a passage had to be forced through crowds of terrified people and animals. Kabarega's lodging was reached just too late: the king had leapt from his bed and fled with a blanket over his shoulders. The royal insignia, a sceptre of brass and iron and a copper spear, were captured, together with a quantity of cloth and ivory and many cattle. As the troops marched back to Hoima, driving the captured stock through a succession of swamps, they were frequently ambushed in the tall elephant grass, which the Banyoro bent over and twisted into barricades covered by fire from unseen marksmen. In one of these ambushes Thruston was slightly wounded in the breast and had a narrow escape from death.

A protectorate was formally declared over Buganda in June, 1894.[1] The news reached Colvile in August, with an expression of the Government's appreciation of the way he had conducted his operations. But a word of warning was sounded. The despatch impressed upon Colvile that campaigns in Bunyoro or anywhere else outside the boundaries laid down for the new Protectorate must be limited to measures 'indispensable to secure the safety and defence of Uganda', and that efforts should be made to secure the friendship of Kabarega and to prevent him from allying himself with the adherents of the Mahdi. This view was reiterated again

---

[1] The Protectorate was not extended to include Bunyoro until June, 1896.

later, when governmental satisfaction at the operations carried out by Thruston and Gibb was coupled with a reminder that such measures could only be countenanced when the 'defence and security of the Protectorate' were at stake.

Hastening to Mengo, Colvile raised the Union Flag with as much military ceremony as could be mustered, while his Sudanese instrumentalists gave their own peculiar rendering of 'God Save the Queen'. At the end of the year, delirious from a sudden attack of fever, Colvile was invalided home. F. J. Jackson succeeded him as Acting Commissioner pending the arrival of the new Commissioner, Ernest Berkeley,[1] who did not leave the coast for Uganda until June, 1895.

Thruston handed over his command in Bunyoro to Captain Cunningham, who brought reinforcements to raise the garrison of Hoima to three companies. By that time four Europeans and some 400 Sudanese were scattered in garrisons at half a dozen points throughout Bunyoro. Unfortunately the sites of some of these posts proved unhealthy, for suitability was largely a matter of trial and error. The Sudanese always suspected witchcraft and seemed unable to understand that men previously strong and well could sicken and die within a few days from natural causes. It was not unusual for native company commanders to arrest a man on the accusation of his fellows and bring him up for trial on a formal charge of witchcraft, a difficulty with which most military officers posted to Uganda in those days had to contend.[2]

The effort to crush Kabarega was continued with still greater intensity in the first half of 1895. Most of the fighting was centred on the Nile, and some of Gordon's old forts were visited for the first time since they were abandoned in 1888. The arduous nature of this campaigning in the unmapped swampy reaches of the Upper Nile can be visualized from the following description, written by Lieutenant S. Vandeleur (Scots Gds.), one of the officers who took part:

'Passing through one of these swamps is a most tiring experience. Now clutching hold of the papyrus at the side, now stepping from one bit of floating vegetation to another, one tries in vain to save oneself from sinking deeper than necessary, until at last a treacherous root gives way, and down one goes into a quagmire of evil-smelling mud and water, only to recommence the whole process again. Except where the papyrus and weeds have been beaten down in forming a passage across them, there is no water to be seen, and from a distance one of these sluggish river swamps appears like a beautiful green lawn of varying shades. This appearance is in reality caused by the great heads of the papyrus with their innumerable little delicate spikes, supported four or five feet above the level of the marsh by the long thin stems growing out of the tangled mass of floating vegetation.'[3]

---

[1] Later Sir Ernest Berkeley, K.C.M.G.

[2] S. Vandeleur, *Campaigning on the Upper Nile and Niger*, p. 48; H. H. Austin, *With Macdonald in Uganda*, p. 259; T. Ternan, *Some Experiences of an Old Bromsgrovian*, pp. 245-47.

[3] Vandeleur, *op. cit.*, p. 20. Vandeleur was killed in the South African War.

Another large caravan of arms and ammunition was on the way to Kabarega, who sent 1,200 men south to meet it. The whole country was full of spies, and the party had no difficulty in evading the column sent out to intercept it. On 25th February two and a half companies from Hoima joined forces at Kunguru with two companies of Sudanese and 2,000 Baganda levies from Kampala for a combined attack on Kabarega's positions across the Nile. When the troops approached the opposite bank they found that the river was 1,100 yards wide, including the thick fringe of papyrus. On 2nd March the crossing was attempted in a fleet of native canoes, covered from the bank by a maxim gun, but so heavy was the fire from Kabarega's riflemen that the operation had to be abandoned. Captains Cunningham and H. G. Dunning (R. Fus.) were both severely wounded, and the latter died on the journey back to Hoima.

This was a serious reverse. It has often been assumed that tribal wars and punitive expeditions in Africa were unequal contests between well-armed, regular troops and ill-organized tribesmen equipped only with primitive weapons. Such was far from the case. Regular troops were so few that they had nearly always to be supplemented by levies from friendly tribes who fought under their own chiefs, and the campaigns often differed but little from the inter-tribal warfare of former times. Moreover, rival forces were by no means always as ill-matched as recent critics have supposed. Many years elapsed before the illicit sale of firearms could be stopped, and the fighting tribes of Africa often showed considerable military skill. Kabarega in particular was an outstanding commander, who, if he had had the good fortune to be approached by Europeans other than through his traditional enemies, the Baganda, might have proved a far more faithful ally than the fickle Mwanga. In point of fact, the realization that these operations in Bunyoro were on a serious scale was already provoking searching questions in the House of Commons.[1]

From April to June another expedition against Kabarega was in the field, for it was considered essential to restore prestige at the earliest opportunity. A new officer, Major Trevor Ternan[2] (Manchester R.), who had served for ten years with the Egyptian Army, where he had commanded the 1st (Sudanese) Battalion, had just reached the Protectorate. He was destined to play a major part in East African history.

After consultation with Jackson and Wilson, Ternan organized a new expedition and on 5th April marched north with about 120 Sudanese, two Hotchkiss guns,[3] and at least 15,000 Baganda. On 20th April he joined forces at Mruli with Cunningham and a column from Hoima. A number of canoes were carried overhead in sections and another fleet

---

[1] *Hansard*, 4th Series, Vol. XXXIII, 1030-31, 13.v.95.

[2] Later Brigadier-General Trevor Ternan, C.B., C.M.G., D.S.O.

[3] The Hotchkiss gun was first registered in 1879 as a 'revolving cannon'. Its large calibre barrels fired explosive shells on the Gatling principle. It was mounted on a small field carriage, and was really too clumsy a weapon for the swamps and narrow bush tracks of Uganda. Considerable difficulty had been experienced in getting these two guns up from the coast.

1. **Uganda**
   (a) Map showing the sites of the early forts in Western Uganda, and illustrating the Operations of the Northern Garrison, 1912-14.
   (N.B. The early forts were established at different dates and were not all in simultaneous occupation)
   (b) The Central Province
   (c) Karamoja and Turkana

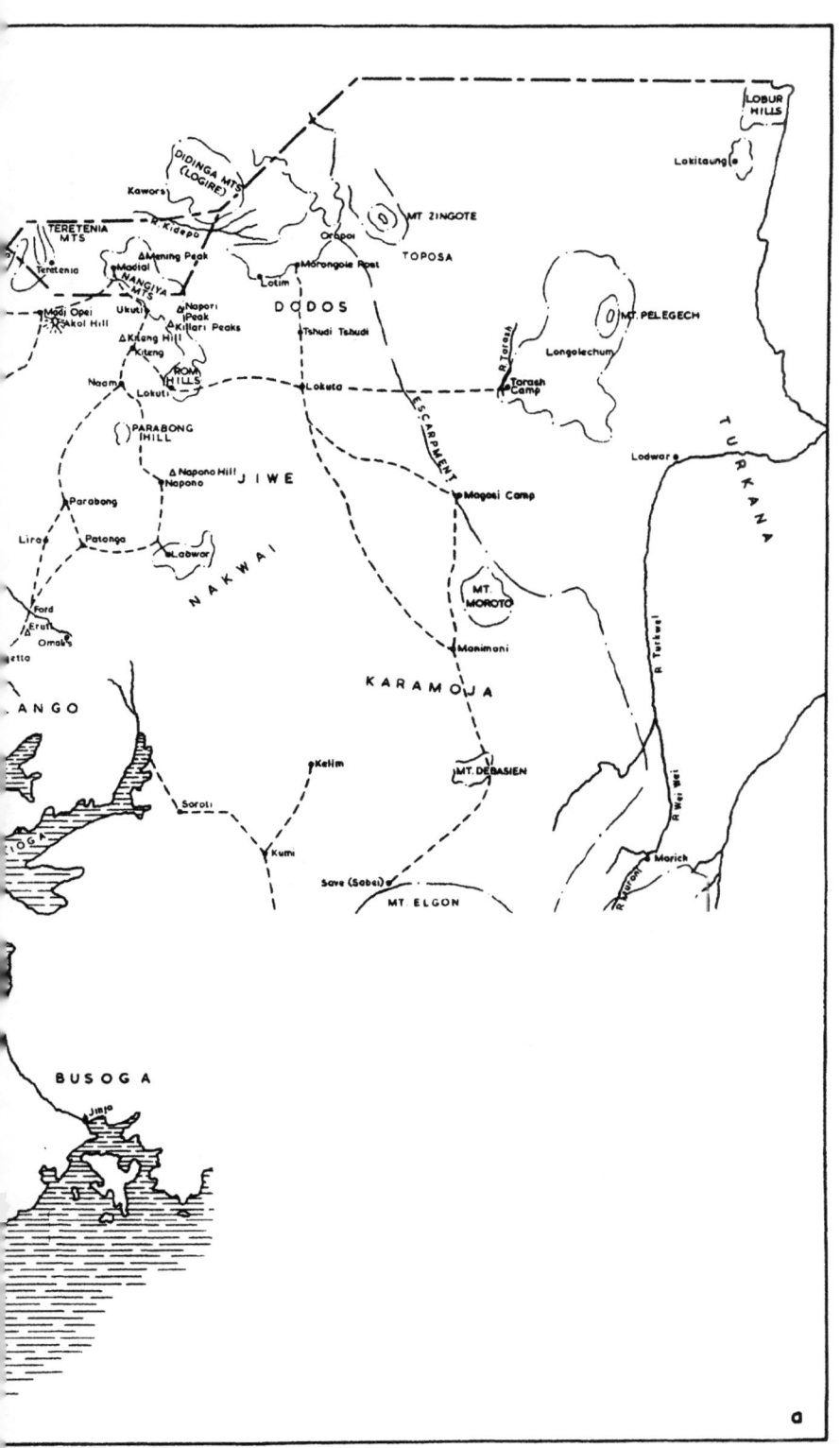

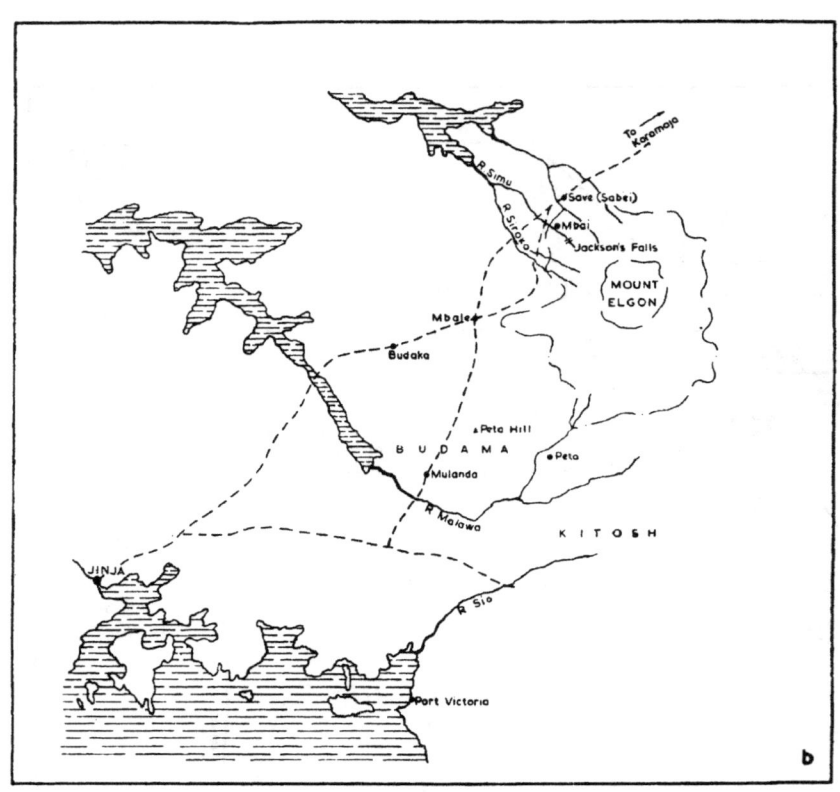
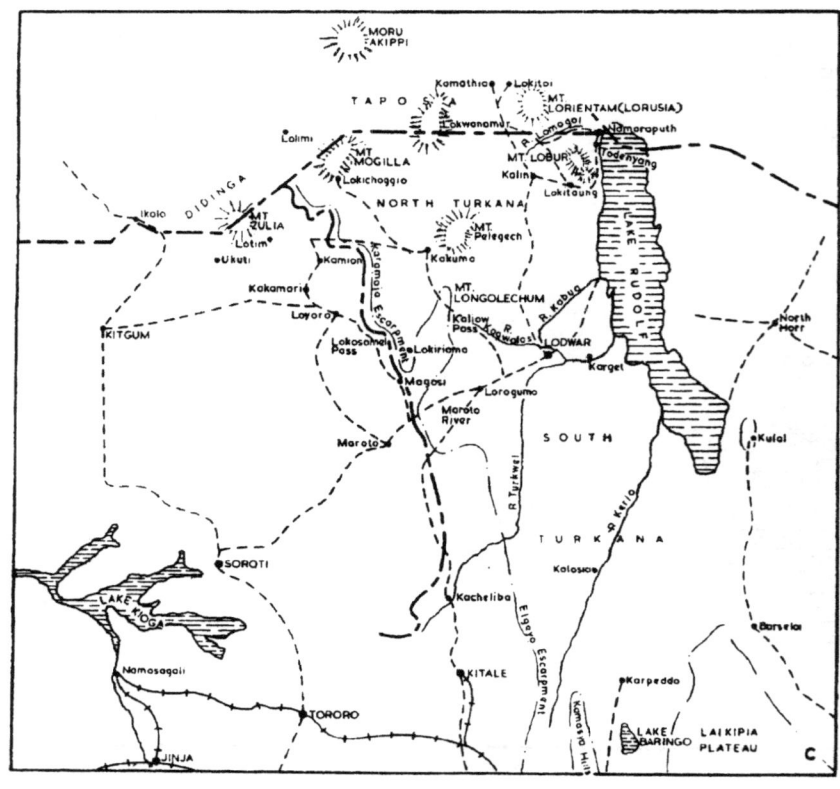

Face page 63

came down the Nile via Lake Kioga. This time the river was crossed under cover of the guns, and Kabarega's position was taken by storm. A column of Sudanese then moved to cut him off from the river while the Baganda took up the pursuit. The Bakedi, who had never forgotten their success in annihilating a Sudanese force from Mruli in 1877, proved very hostile, and though columns followed down both banks of the Nile, once again Kabarega escaped. After following as far as the Murchison Falls and establishing some small posts, the columns returned to Masindi, where a fort was built.

In August Kabarega again attempted to enter Bunyoro. A column of troops from Forts Masindi and Hoima marched to the Murchison Falls, found his settlement and burnt the huts, though again without catching their enemy. Stations were afterwards established at Foweira and near the Falls to extend military control up to the line of the Nile. Masindi became the headquarters in Bunyoro and a new and better route to Kampala was opened up via Mruli and Lake Kioga. These operations, conducted by the largest forces yet employed in Bunyoro, were thought to have convinced the Banyoro that Kabarega's power was broken, and in forwarding Cunningham's report to England Jackson described the results as 'eminently satisfactory'.

In the course of his plans for enlisting more Sudanese, Colvile had raised the question of the status of his troops, suggesting that they should be regarded as part of Her Majesty's regular forces and that commissions should be granted to the native officers. The Foreign Office referred this question to the Colonial Office for advice, asking whether any precedent could be quoted elsewhere in the British dominions. The Colonial Office pointed out that as the status of 'regular forces' was defined by statute, it could not properly be extended to the Sudanese without royal, and perhaps also parliamentary consent, and would in any case involve many difficulties over military estimates, pay and supplies. Governmental policy was to confine the employment of regular forces abroad to the defence of maritime fortresses and coaling stations, leaving the internal defence of colonies and protectorates to locally raised corps controlled by the civil authorities. Troops of this kind were usually called police or constabulary, but it was thought that the War Office would probably raise no objection to some such military designation as Uganda Rifles or Carbineers; nor was there likely to be any technical objection to the grant of commissions to suitable native officers, provided this were done by the highest local civil official. This opinion was submitted to the War Office for comment, where it was confirmed that a variety of reasons made it undesirable for the Sudanese in Uganda to be taken over as regular troops, though there would seem to be little difficulty in their constitution as a Uganda Frontier Force under the administration of the Foreign Office.

This was the origin of the title given to the regiment of 17 companies that was formally constituted on 1st September, 1895, under Major Cunningham's command. The terms of the Uganda Rifles Ordinance that brought the regiment into being provided for a Commandant, chief officers (usually European 'wing commanders'), native officers and under-officers. Privates were to be enlisted for twelve years, but if approved could re-engage for another six, and continue thereafter indefinitely, with the right to claim discharge at three months' notice. This was the first attempt to set the troops of the Protectorate upon a proper footing, but in the troubled period that followed, years filled with constant campaigning and the temporary disintegration of the regiment brought about by the mutiny of 1897, the task of properly arming and equipping the troops proved difficult and slow.

(iv) *The First and Second Expeditions against the Nandi, 1895-97.* Map II (a).

The Nandi are one of a group of people that includes the Kipsikis (Lumbwa), Kamasya, Elgeyo, Marakwet, Endo and other tribes, linked by language and custom, related to the Masai and inhabiting the great tract of country along and beyond the mountainous escarpments west of the Rift Valley. Living in difficult country well suited for defence, the Nandi succeeded in maintaining their independence for many years, first against the Masai, then against the incursions of Arab and Swahili traders (who originated the term 'Nandi', meaning 'cormorants', in view of their fierce, predatory habits), and finally against the first attempts at administration by the British. When the boundaries of the Uganda Protectorate were expanded to include Kavirondo, the Nandi country, and Masailand as far as Lake Naivasha, it became the responsibility of the Uganda Rifles to undertake punitive expeditions into this troublesome area in search of murderers or to exact fines of cattle. Such expeditions were not on the same footing as the campaigns in Bunyoro, but they had their own peculiar difficulties as the Nandi lived in scattered homesteads instead of villages, and had evolved a military system of their own.

The tribe was divided into a number of *pororosiek*, a term that embodied not only a deliberative council concerned with affairs of war, but also the actual fighting unit, composed of young men of the military age-group.[1] Such an organization, which was of course unrealized at the time by the British officers sent to operate in the Nandi country, enabled the tribesmen to plan concerted resistance well suited to the nature of their country, with the result that expeditions against them generally met only with qualified success.

The route from the coast ran close to the borders of Nandi proper. The tribesmen were not slow to take advantage of their opportunity, and during 1895 attacks on caravans became frequent. One example will suffice. A Scots trader named West pitched his camp one evening beside a running stream within the escarpment forest, making no attempt to protect it with a boma, and carelessly stowing all the rifles together inside his own tent. The Nandi crept upon the encampment unseen, murdered West, killed 23 of his porters, and looted the trade goods.[2]

[1] G. W. B. Huntingford, *The Nandi: Tribal Control in a Pastoral Society*, 1953. Chaps. II-IV.
[2] C. W. Hobley, *Kenya from Chartered Company to Crown Colony*, pp. 88-89, says that the murder of West was in revenge for punishment meted out to the Nandi by West's employer Dick, who had accused them of stealing some of his cattle. After this affair the Nandi were 'like an agitated swarm of bees'.

News of this and similar outrages constantly reached Mumia's and the new station at Eldama Ravine, which had been rebuilt on higher ground at the beginning of the year. On 28th August a wounded Swahili reported that the mail party had been attacked, the mail burnt, and the boxes broken. On 7th October another attack on a caravan was reported in which nine men were killed, six wounded and 40 head of cattle stolen. These and similar aggressive acts were the cause of the first military expedition against the Nandi, designed to safeguard the route between Uganda and the coast.

Cunningham had to withdraw troops from Bunyoro to form the expedition, for no garrison had as yet been established in Nandi. On 14th October he left Kampala with a column a thousand strong, including porters and followers. The fighting troops were drawn from Nos. 1, 4, 5 and 9 (Sudanese) Companies, with one maxim gun and a small body of drilled and disciplined Baganda. The column reached Mumia's on 29th October, where further attacks on caravans were reported.

At Mumia's Cunningham was joined by Captain C. H. Sitwell (Manchester R.) who had arrived there in August on his way up from the coast. Sitwell had been ordered to assist C. W. Hobley, the administrative officer, in a punitive expedition in Kitosh and Kabaras, to suppress the perpetual raiding and smuggling of arms stolen from porters. On 15th August Sitwell had stormed a walled village after a desperate struggle in which only the Sudanese among his troops would follow him.[1] After these operations were over he was ordered to await Cunningham's arrival with the Nandi column.

Cunningham now divided his force into two columns, the larger under himself to march due east on Kapiyet, and the smaller of about 100 men under Sitwell to approach from the south. The main column set out through the villages of Kabaras, which the Nandi had recently attacked. Owing to the proximity of such warlike neighbours these villages were surrounded by deep ditches and six-foot mud walls, with narrow entrance causeways, and low doors that could easily be blocked with beams of timber. None of the Kabaras natives would act as guides, and Cunningham had to find his own way into unknown country.

Before long the column came across West's scattered camp, with the skulls of the victims lying near the abandoned table and chair. Some of West's property was recovered from the huts of the first Nandi villages. The column then climbed the escarpment and camped at an altitude of 6,000 feet. Kapiyet was reached on 11th November, but Sitwell's column did not arrive till some days later, having been misled by Masai guides.

Cunningham was prevented by shortage of food from remaining long at Kapiyet. He struck south through Kipsamwite, hoping to discover a shorter route for the Mombasa caravans. While thus engaged his patrols reported that the column was being watched by large concen-

[1] Sitwell had a narrow escape on this occasion, when three natives charged him simultaneously. He shot two, but the spear of the third slid between his left arm and side. Using it as a lever, Sitwell toppled his assailant over and killed him. Shortly afterwards another spear knocked the pipe out of his mouth. (Sitwell's Diary, 15.viii.95.)

trations of Nandi. In the valley of the River Kimondi, Cunningham stood to face a sudden attack, delivered by about 500 tribesmen, who advanced rapidly through the long grass in a formation resembling three sides of a square. It was the first time that the Sudanese had faced the tossing skin headdresses and flashing, long-bladed spears of the Nandi warriors, but they stood firm and their fire checked the attack before it reached close quarters, though the enemy scored a minor success by cutting off and annihilating a party of fourteen men. The Nandi had already captured some rifles from the looted caravans, but fortunately were unable to use them.

After this action Cunningham resumed his march to the south-east. In the early morning darkness of 17th November the Nandi again attacked, creeping up in large numbers towards the boma. The sentries were alert and the men slept with their rifles beside them, so the attack was beaten off, though with all the pandemonium of a 'soldiers' battle'.

At dawn Cunningham struck camp and continued into the Kipture district, crossed the 'Kaimin' (Choimin) River with No. 9 Company skirmishing in advance to drive the Nandi from the ridge flanking the valley, and camped on Taito Hill, overlooking the Lumbwa country and the lake.[1]

With the Nandi still hanging round the flanks, the column next marched into the Sagane valley. Here the tribesmen changed their tactics. As the long line wound down the precipitous mountain paths to the river an avalanche of boulders descended from the cliffs above. Several men were wounded and for a time the porters were thrown into confusion, racing in all directions for shelter. Then the maxim got the range of the line of dusky faces peering over the edge of the cliff and the Nandi suddenly vanished. While the main column camped in the valley, Lieutenant Vandeleur with 50 askaris was sent to reconnoitre a shorter route through the forest to the Eldama Ravine, where he spent one night, drew posho for his men, and returned with a number of cattle, captured on the way back. His visit to the Ravine was timely, as it strengthened the wavering loyalty of the Kamasya, who were supplying the station with food.

Meanwhile Sitwell, finding no trace of Cunningham at Kapiyet, had continued operations on his own account, destroying huts and crops but unable to bring the Nandi to close quarters. On 24th November he was at Kitoto's. Returning to the escarpment, his camp was suddenly attacked at 3 a.m. on the morning of the 29th. Awoken by the noise, Sitwell leapt from his bed to find the Nandi rushing into the camp through a hole in the boma. He shot three with his revolver; the askaris rallied, and after ten minutes' confusion the affair was over. Sitwell returned to his tent, to find it pierced by five bullet holes and four spear holes.

Operations were renewed in December, when a column 400 strong again marched through Kipsamwite and Kipture. Negotiations with the

---

[1] It is possible that the name 'Kaimin' was used both for the Choimin and the Mokong, as the column must have crossed the latter river, and not the swampy Choimin, to reach Taito.

Nandi produced no result, so the escarpment was climbed again and a large herd of cattle was captured in one of the ravines after a running fight. The column then continued across the plateau to Marapa. All this time the Nandi were hovering in the vicinity. On Christmas night a shower of spears came over the boma, and on Boxing Day an attack was made on the column as it passed through a rocky gorge. Mumia's was reached again on the last day of the year. A few weeks later Cunningham and Vandeleur left for the coast on their way to England.

In January, 1896, Jackson arrived at the Ravine to take over the administration of the Eastern Province. The district round Eldama was under development as a supply centre for caravans on the three weeks' journey across the foodless country between Kikuyu and Kavirondo, and many of the Kamasya, who had remained friendly during the Nandi expedition, were beginning to settle round the station. Half No. 6 Company was at Eldama and half at Naivasha, where a station was built soon afterwards. Detachments of N.C.Os. and men from these garrisons were used as escorts along the dangerous section of the road, and as guards for the stores dumped by Captain B. L. Sclater, R.E., who was at work realigning and improving the route.[1] Though a civilian, Jackson was given the title of Chief Officer in the Uganda Rifles, for there were not enough British officers to command every station.

On 10th February the Nandi leaders arrived at Eldama to make peace. The first attempt to administer them now began, with the establishment of a small post at Kipture (Nandi Fort).[2] The tribes did not take kindly to this innovation, and their confidence was difficult to gain. It was not at first realized that the Nandi possessed no tribal chiefs in the commonly accepted sense, but only a religious head, the *Orkoiyot*, who though of great influence possessed no executive function.

Trouble was not long in coming. After a few months of comparative quiet, the leader of a group of southern Kamasya began to stir up trouble, and on Christmas Eve, 1896, raided a village actually in sight of the Ravine station, killing two men, driving off 40 cattle and burning the huts. The road between the Ravine and Kipture again became particularly dangerous, and the station diaries of the period are filled with rumours and accounts of raids.

At the end of 1896 Berkeley was invalided, and Major Ternan became Acting Commissioner as well as Commandant of the Uganda Rifles. After a tour of Buddu in his civil capacity, during which he appears to have heard some rumours of intrigue, despite extravagant outward professions of loyalty from the Catholic chiefs, he turned his attention to the situation reported by Jackson among the Kamasya. Owing to the difficulty of obtaining food, it was impossible at this time to keep a large garrison permanently in the Nandi country, and arrange-

[1] Work on the Mackinnon Road had stopped at Kibwezi. It was now being extended to terminate at the Nzoia River ferry, about three miles from Mumia's.

[2] The Fort enclosed a rectangular area approximately 136 by 76 yards, and was surrounded by a trench 5-10 feet deep. There were entrances to the east, south and west. The remains of the Fort may still be seen about four and a half miles east of Kapsabet.

ments had to be made for withdrawing troops once more from Bunyoro and transporting food from Busoga and Kavirondo. This took some time, and it was 20th May before Ternan reached the Ravine with an expedition drawn from Nos. 1, 2, 4, 7 and 9 Companies, the largest force yet to be sent to the district. By this time the Nandi tribes had earned the respect that was their due as fighting men. Ternan chose the period of full moon to minimize the risk of night attacks, and laid down careful orders for the march. Askaris of the advance and rear guards were forbidden to carry loads. The column marched in fours as far as practicable, with hospital and stretcher parties in the centre and the Swahili porters flanked by files of askaris. Fifty bullocks and ten milch cows were taken as live rations, and this herd followed the column, driven by ten porters and watched by two askaris, a much smaller guard than would have been detailed in later expeditions, considering the strength of the temptation offered to the watching tribesmen. Each night company escorts were detailed for the parties cutting bush for the boma. Immediately inside this barricade came the company lines; then the porters, and in the centre the cattle, food stores, hospital and officers' tents. A gate was left in the boma for each company, guarded by sentries posted outside during daylight and inside at night.

The Field Force marched first to Eldama Ravine, where it split into two columns, one to operate under Ternan against the Kamasya and the other under Grant against the Elgeyo. Each party consisted of five Europeans (all civilian officers except Ternan) and 210 askaris. Mobility was essential, so all surplus stores and cattle were left at the fort, with 25 sick men and a guard of 15 askaris. The regular troops carried 100 rounds of ammunition per man, and as many of the Swahili porters as possible were armed with Remingtons or Sniders and ten rounds each.

Ternan left the Ravine on 22nd May, and for the next fortnight marched through the Kamasya hills and valleys, traversing steep ravines, exploring hidden valleys, searching for scattered huts and granaries in the dense forest and driving off the tribesmen while the Masai herdsmen who accompanied him rounded up the stock. The Field Force orders, which Ternan wrote and published daily for the guidance of his civilian officers, reveal his method of conducting this type of expedition. Captures of stock were recorded in full detail, distinguishing between bulls, bullocks, cows, cows in calf, calves, sheep and goats, each of which had a recognized place in the scale of values when it came to distributing the spoils. Sentries who stole or connived at thefts of livestock were severely punished.[1]

Meanwhile Grant's column was engaged in similar work to the northwest. On 6th June Ternan again reached Eldama. Five days later he left on a night march to surprise a certain village in a long, deep valley on the lower slopes of the escarpment. But though he succeeded in getting his men into position high up on the surrounding hills, the going was so difficult that daylight found them still on the move, and the alarm was at once given from watchers on all sides.

---

[1] The orders also contain more homely details, such as instructions that washing must not be hung out in front of officers' tents.

Both columns now returned to the Ravine, where one officer and eight N.C.Os. and men per company were detailed to reinforce the garrison. Movement on the way back was hampered by heavy rain. A whole company was detailed to escort the cattle and secure the rear, and as most of the askaris were carrying loads the march rate was restricted to two miles per hour to avoid straggling. Anxious not to encounter trouble while thus handicapped, Ternan gave orders that askaris and porters should strike camp as quietly as possible and make no noise on the march.

On 20th June the column passed into friendly country. The proceeds of the expedition totalled 238 cattle and 7,838 sheep and goats. These Ternan distributed in the proportion of two-fifths each to the Government and the Masai and one-fifth to the troops, apportioned according to rank, native officers being the only Africans entitled to a share of the cows and calves. European officers could purchase cattle from the Government share at thirty shillings for a bull and forty-five shillings for a cow, and any soldier could buy a sheep or a goat for two shillings.

The Field Force lost six askaris and porters killed, and five wounded. The troops managed to expend over 6,000 rounds of ammunition in keeping the tribesmen at bay, for their marksmanship was usually poor, and their readiness on the trigger invariably great. Weapons were improving, for Sniders had replaced Remingtons, and now the new Matini-Henrys were arriving. It was not unknown, however, for the troops to remove the backsights as a senseless encumbrance that prevented them from seeing the foresight properly.

While the second Nandi expedition was in progress, despatches from Buganda had convinced Ternan that some kind of political mischief was brewing. Though later news, received after his return to Eldama, was more reassuring, he was anxious in his capacity as Acting Commissioner to get back to Entebbe as soon as possible. The Nandi operations were therefore broken off rather sooner than was desirable, for though some of the tribe had sued for peace, the lesson had not been sufficiently severe to be remembered for long.

(v) *Mutiny and its Consequences, 1897-1901.* Map I (a).

The Nandi expedition of 1897 was barely over when George Wilson, the sub-commissioner at Kampala, uncovered a serious plot. He arrested two Baganda chiefs and charged them with incitement to revolt, but a third, the Mujasi Gabriel, made good his escape. Mwanga, who had recently been fined for smuggling guns, took this action badly, and in July showed his hand by flying secretly to his friends in Buddu and raising the standard of rebellion. Reports came that many people, including a notorious rabble of outlaws known as the Futabangi, were preparing to join him. Prompt action was essential. A force of 70 men with a maxim gun was holding a position near the mouth of the Katonga. To reinforce it Lieutenant C. V. C. Hobart (Gren. Gds.) left Munyonyo, the nearest port to Kampala, by canoe on 13th July with 70 men of No. 2 Company. A mixed force scraped together from three other companies followed by steam launch from Port Victoria. Ternan marched overland with Nos. 1 and 7 Companies, a maxim gun section and about 14,000 Baganda under the Katikiro.

Ternan reached Buganda by forced marches on 16th July. There he instructed his company commanders to leave up to twenty of their most footsore men, for the Sudanese troops were growing intensely weary. The Buddu Field Force now comprised Nos. 1, 2 and 7 Companies and sections of Nos. 3 and 4 Companies. Ternan continued his march through Baja and Masaka. Going was difficult: the column started each morning in the chill before dawn, marching in greatcoats until the first halt and crossing the swamps with ammunition boxes borne clear of the water on the askaris' heads. On entering Buddu the troops were permitted to raid the local crops for food, but were forbidden to burn the huts.

On 20th July Ternan encountered the main rebel force in a strong position on a ridge of hills protected by a swamp. Mwanga's standard was flying on a hill-top known as Kabwoko, and his army was estimated at about 14,000 men. While his Baganda allies concentrated against the rest of the ridge, Ternan decided to attack Kabwoko with the Sudanese. His two maxim guns, each manned by an officer, covered the approach while No. 1 Company deployed to the right and No. 7 Company to the left. A few hundred yards behind, Nos. 2 and 3 Companies advanced in column, followed by the hospital party and No. 4 Company in the rear. The total force numbered 220. The two leading companies moved forward through the bush in single file, firing in volleys at the word of command, with the Baganda levies protecting both flanks. In spite of the thick bush the swamp was crossed and the ridge taken under heavy fire, for the loss of one man killed and 11 wounded. The action lasted for an hour, and Ternan reported that his troops 'behaved exceedingly well'.

After this action Ternan continued his march as far as Simba, where news reached him that Mwanga had fled to German territory and surrendered at Bukoba. Accordingly the march south was halted. On 25th July Ternan received the Queen's message of thanks on the occasion of her Diamond Jubilee and published it to the troops and Baganda chiefs. The askaris with the Field Force were all awarded a special gratuity of one month's pay.

Another encounter with the rebels took place when the Futabangi stronghold was attacked at Marongo on 28th July. Near the entrance to their valley the enemy had prepared an ambush for the little force, but Ternan climbed the forest above the position and turned the tables by attacking from the rear. He recorded the affair in a laconic note scribbled in pencil at the bottom of his daily orders: 'Enemy met with and dispersed this day'. Next day a herd of 700 cattle was captured in the Bwera district. This entailed a strong escort by day and the construction of a cattle boma each night, which slowed the progress of the column. On 31st July congratulatory messages were received from the administration, the missionary societies and the native community at Mengo on the successful action at Kabwoko. So great was the relief at the speed with which Mwanga had been driven out of the country that the fort at Kampala and all the residences were decorated with bunting.

Ternan's prompt action had saved the situation for the time being. He placed Mwanga's infant son, Daudi Chwa,[1] on the throne and arranged for a regency of three chiefs. A flesh wound in the shoulder was troubling him, and as he had been weakened by the cumulative effect of many attacks of fever, he was ordered home on leave by the medical authorities.[2] Jackson took over the duties of Acting Commissioner, and Major Thruston, who after a spell of service outside the Protectorate had returned to his old command in Bunyoro in April, 1897, handed over to Lieutenant W. R. Dugmore (North Staffs R.) and at the end of August left for Entebbe to take command of the Uganda Rifles. He appears to have realized that all was not well with the regiment, but neither he nor Ternan foresaw the seriousness of the trouble ahead.

The forthcoming reoccupation of the Sudan by Britain and Egypt, and the consequent interest aroused in France and Abyssinia regarding the future of the Khedive's former equatorial provinces, convinced the British Government that 'a more accurate knowledge' was needed of the country north of the East Africa and Uganda Protectorates, where the River Juba was believed to rise. An exploring expedition was projected, and Major Macdonald was chosen to command it. Macdonald reached Mombasa in July, 1897, to find that the railway for which he had conducted the preliminary survey several years before now reached nearly seventy miles from the coast. The Government of India had seconded two British officers and 30 men of the 14th and 15th Sikhs as escort for Macdonald's party. Six other officers came direct from England, and Macdonald engaged a caravan of 350 Swahili porters, increased later by another hundred, the biggest caravan ever to go beyond Kikuyu. The expedition was to concentrate at Njemps.

In view of Kabarega's activities on the Upper Nile and the unknown and unsettled state of the country north of the Nile bend, Macdonald's escort was considered insufficient. Before his hasty departure for Buddu, Ternan had received orders to detail three companies of Sudanese to augment it. Pointing out that the pay of the troops at Nandi was six months overdue, he asked Jackson to obtain clothing from Uganda to pay them in full till the end of August. On the completion of the Buddu campaign, Ternan informed Lord Salisbury that there was 'no reason to prevent the troops required for Major Macdonald being forthcoming at Njemps by the date fixed', adding that their replacement by fresh recruits would be difficult owing to the reduced numbers of the Sudanese and their low rate of pay, and that he proposed to raise one or two Swahili companies instead.

The companies selected for Macdonald's escort were Nos. 4, 7 and

[1] On coming of age on 8th August, 1914, four days after the outbreak of war between Britain and Germany, the Kabaka Daudi Chwa was at his own request given an honorary commission in the K.A.R. He was granted the rank of honorary captain on 22nd September, 1917.

[2] Sir Albert Cook, *Uganda Memories*, p. 71, recorded that a medical board found Ternan 'wretchedly ill, and invalided him home as the only way to save his life'.

9, some of the best under Ternan's command. Largely on this account they had been the most frequently employed during the past strenuous years. Discipline, however, had lately become very slack. In No. 4 Company (Mabruk Effendi), Ternan had reduced all the native officers and N.C.Os. by one step, and in No. 9 Company (Bilal Effendi) he had reduced 21 N.C.Os. in rank. The sweeping nature of these punishments was in itself sufficient to cause serious unrest.

But the basic cause of disaffection among the Sudanese was of longer standing. The companies chosen had been campaigning almost continuously for several years in Bunyoro, Nandi and Buddu. Although the pay of a private had recently been increased to seven rupees a month, it was still lower than the average pay of a porter. It was known in Uganda that Sudanese serving in East Africa were receiving fifteen rupees, and those in German territory even more. Rinderpest, shortage of porters and other difficulties interfered with transport, so that the trade goods in which pay was issued were often in short supply. For the same reason the troops' clothing could rarely be maintained at the proper scale. Many of the new officers seconded to the regiment had had no experience of handling native troops, and as most of them remained for one tour only, few made any serious attempt to learn the language. From this the Sudanese inferred a lack of interest in their problems, and when they complained at the prospect of another long and arduous period in the field, which they understood to necessitate a further separation from their wives and families, they felt that the matter was dismissed without proper consideration. They realized also that they were practically the only trained troops in the country, and probably felt that if they took the law into their own hands there was little to fear.

On his way to the coast, Ternan met Macdonald and told him that the companies detailed as escort were on their way back from Buddu to join him. Macdonald therefore decided to alter the rendezvous to Ngare Nyuki, about eight miles from Eldama Ravine.

The three companies, numbering in all 330 men, did not reach Ngare Nyuki together. The first batch of 92 askaris arrived on 17th September, after Jackson had ordered them three times to march from the Ravine. By 20th September all had arrived except 113 men under Bilal Effendi, Jardin Effendi and Suliman Effendi, who were expected shortly. It had been conceded that wives should accompany the expedition and their rations were issued on that day, but Mabruk Effendi, the senior native officer present, asked that the wives should wait and follow with the relief convoy.

The expedition was to march in three columns on Marich. On 21st September the first column, escorted by 69 men of No. 7 Company, set off without trouble under Major H. H. Austin, R.E. Next day the men of No. 4 Company, who formed the escort for the second column, only marched after protest, and most of them deserted that evening. On the 23rd, the day on which the headquarter column should have started, it was discovered that nearly all No. 9 Company had deserted in the night. The remainder of No. 4 Company, which was to have formed the rearguard, then deserted as well, led by Mabruk Effendi. The first column got as far as Njemps, but when runners from Macdonald brought news of what had happened, Austin's men also deserted in the night.

The garrisons at Eldama and Nandi remained loyal, but the men were too few and their attitude too uncertain for them to be used against the mutineers. For several days Jackson tried without success to reason with the men, who had camped near the Ravine,[1] but they broke away and looted the ammunition store. Shortly afterwards they were joined by the men from Njemps, and the whole party then made for Mumia's. After threatening to attack the fort and demanding rations, they eventually withdrew. Meanwhile Macdonald and Jackson, with the European officers, Sikhs and armed porters, were making for Kavirondo by a different route, while warning messages were sent ahead to Kampala.[2]

The mutineers next made for the fort at Lubwa's, which was built on a promontory not far from the outlet of the Nile, hoping to raise the garrison and join forces with the disaffected Muslim element in Buganda. Thruston reached Lubwa's first, and the situation at the fort appeared to be under control when he and his companion Norman Wilson were treacherously seized by Rehan Effendi, the native officer, and made prisoners. Seeing the British flag still flying, Scott, the engineer of the steam launch, put into the fort and was also taken. The mutineers then arrived and were admitted, the whole force numbering about 600 Sudanese and 200 Baganda Muslims. Macdonald followed and occupied a hill dominating the fort with 10 Europeans, 17 Sikhs and 340 half-trained Swahilis.

Before dawn on 19th October about 300 mutineers and 150 Baganda left the fort and approached the hill in fighting formation. Some parleying took place, and then the mutineers, led by Suliman, endeavoured to rush the camp. For five hours the mutineers pressed their attack with well-directed assaults, planned and led by capable native officers. It was greatly to the credit of the Swahilis that, following the example of the Europeans and Sikhs, they stood firm and ultimately, with a well-directed charge, drove the mutineers back to the fort. Macdonald's little force lost 46 men killed and wounded in this action.

The die was cast, and anxious that any waverers should be fully committed, Bilal and Rehan shot Thruston, Wilson and Scott with their own hands and sank their remains in a basket in the lake. After that there could be no further talk of terms.

In England, Ternan found it hard to believe that his Sudanese, who had given him an affectionate leave-taking, could be guilty of serious disaffection. 'Though I subsequently returned to Uganda,' he wrote many years later,[3] 'I was never able to find out the real cause of the mutiny.'

[1] Ravine Station Diary, pp. 23, 27.ix.97.
[2] The stockade that protected Lugard's fort at Kampala had been pulled down and the ditch filled up. The fort was hurriedly rebuilt on a larger scale than before, with strong ramparts of earth surmounted by brickwork and enclosed by a new trench, deeper and wider than the old one.
[3] T. Ternan, *Some Experiences of an Old Bromsgrovian*, p. 320.

Influenced by his opinion, the home authorities were not at first unduly alarmed. Before long, however, further reports from Uganda showed the urgent need for reinforcements. In October the Foreign Office was warned that the local forces were quite unable to cope with the situation, and advised to order to Uganda the 300 Sikhs of the East Africa Indian Contingent, then at Mombasa under Captain W. C. Barratt (1st Sikh Inf.) and Lieutenant T. E. Scott (3rd Sikh Inf.), and to arrange for a battalion from India to replace them. In November the Indian Contingent began moving inland, 150 sepoys under Scott going forward from railhead on the 23rd and another 70 sepoys following soon afterwards. The garrison of East Africa Rifles at Machakos was also relieved and sent to Uganda. Meanwhile the 27th Bombay Infantry had been detailed for service in Africa and left Karachi on 2nd December with 12 officers and 737 troops under the command of Lieutenant-Colonel W. A. Broome. As senior officer it was intended that he should take command of all troops in the Protectorate. Owing to transport difficulties his movement from the coast proved very slow. Though some of his companies went ahead, Broome did not reach Kampala with the headquarters of his regiment until 26th July, 1898, seven months after landing in East Africa.

While Macdonald went to examine the situation at Kampala, the investment of Lubwa's continued. On 24th November Captain E. M. Woodward (Leic. R.) led 12 Sikhs, 190 Swahilis and some loyal Baganda against the outposts of the fort, which he drove in with the object of establishing a closer siege. The heavy losses suffered by the Baganda prevented this, but early in December, after Macdonald's return, a new position was secured. Captain E. G. Harrison (W. Riding R.) had now arrived with 80 men of the East Africa Rifles. On 11th December the mutineers made another sally. The Sikhs and the East Africa Rifles saved the maxim guns when the Swahilis broke and fled. In one of these actions Mabruk Effendi was killed or died of wounds.

Meanwhile at Kampala apprehension had spread lest the troops elsewhere should rise in sympathy. The 300 Sudanese at Kampala were disarmed without much difficulty, but there were nearly 500 in Bunyoro under Lieutenant Dugmore, another 200 in Buddu with Grant and Hobart, and over 100 in Toro under Captain Sitwell.

The alarm occasioned in Uganda, coupled with the recent memory of Selim Bey's alleged conspiracies in the Muslim interest, gave rise to a general distrust of Sudanese troops that has perhaps been too easily accepted as justified. But the immediate grievances that brought matters to a head were confined to the three companies concerned, whose members totalled less than a quarter of the regiment; nor was the movement in any sense a planned conspiracy against British rule. It cannot be doubted that some sympathy with the plight of their former comrades was present among the Sudanese, but the commonly-held view that the loyalty of the regiment as a whole was in question is not borne out by the facts. This can well be illustrated from the diary that Captain Sitwell so diligently maintained throughout his four years' service in Uganda.

The news that Nos. 4, 7 and 9 Companies had mutinied reached Sitwell on 29th October, when he was at Fort Gerry. On the following day he heard of the engagement at Lubwa's and the imprisonment of Thruston, Wilson and Scott. Parading his troops, he read the relative extracts of the letter. His pleasure at their spontaneous reaction is evident from the diary:

'Was interrupted all the time by men saying "That if all the remainder of the regiment mutinied, they would stick to me." Not bad that.'

On 3rd November he recorded:

'Letter from Sudanese officers at Kampala to officers here came in, telling them the news and advising them not to mutiny. Not much need of that.'

Thus forewarned, and with full confidence in the loyalty of his men, Sitwell felt able to take a strong line when the inevitable attempt was made to persuade his native officers to join the rising:

'22 Nov. 1897. Three Waganda came in from Usoga with letters for Bilal Effendi and Saba Effendi, to be forwarded to Masindi, asking them all to join and warn Buddu garrison, all to be of one shaurie. Rehan Effendi brought them all to me and put the Waganda in the chain-gang. Gave them each 50 (lashes) and sent off special mail to Kampala, . . .'

'23 Nov. 1897. Men at work fetching wood for bridge. Tried case of three Waganda, found that they were in the boma at Lubwa's when Thruston and others were murdered. Sentence to be shot. Sentence carried out at 5 p.m. Rehan Effendi commanded the firing party. Mr. Berkeley present.'

All subsequent news of the mutiny recorded in the diary is encouraging: the arrival of Indian troops, casualties among the mutineers, and so on. Early in January Sitwell wrote to Wilson giving his opinion, no doubt forthright, about the 'delay in finishing the show', and when he was ordered to march his men into Masaka to be disarmed, wrote both to Berkeley and Macdonald flatly refusing.[1]

In Buddu, however, the situation was not so stable. After Ternan's departure Grant had again been in action with the rebels, and in December the Mujasi Gabriel made strenuous efforts to persuade the Sudanese garrisons to join him. Macdonald left for Buddu with a force of 200 men, including half Harrison's contingent of the East Africa Rifles. Hearing on the way that Gabriel's men had been dispersed, he was about to return when news came that Mwanga had escaped from German territory and was in Ankole with 1,300-1,400 rifles. Sitwell was ordered to guard the Bwera frontier while Macdonald continued his march, disarmed the Buddu garrisons, and on 15th January defeated Mwanga's army at Kisalira.

This development brought home to the British Government still more effectively the serious state of affairs that had spread throughout the Protectorate. Realizing that after the mutiny the armed forces would

[1] Sitwell's Diary, 21.i.98.

have to be completely reorganized. Ternan submitted his proposals to the Foreign Office without further delay. He suggested that 400 Indian troops should be enlisted as the backbone of the forces, that 700 Sudanese who had not been directly implicated in the mutiny should be retained, and that 700 Swahilis should be recruited. The African troops were to be incorporated in two mixed battalions comprised of six companies, three Sudanese and three Swahili, with an establishment of 13 officers and 702 rank and file per battalion. Asked for an opinion, the War Office agreed in principle with these proposals, though considering them if anything too modest. The Foreign Office therefore lost no time in asking the Viceroy of India whether 400 men, Sikhs or Punjabis preferred, could be recruited for Uganda on the same terms as those supplied for British Central Africa.

The Government of India had become increasingly reluctant to provide troops for service in Africa, especially from the Punjabi regiments, as it was feared that recruitment for the Indian Army might suffer in those provinces nearest to the North-West Frontier. The Viceroy informed the Foreign Office by cable that his Commander-in-Chief could not spare any more Sikhs or Punjabis, and thought it inadvisable to recruit Pathans. The possibility of recruiting Zulus from South Africa was tentatively considered, and a battalion of the Royal Welch Fusiliers, homeward bound from the east, was detained for a time at Aden. But the news of Mwanga's escape was regarded as so alarming that pressure was placed upon the India Office to order the recruitment of a contingent for Uganda without further delay. The 27th Bombay Infantry was accordingly followed to East Africa by a wing of the 4th Bombay Infantry, and in March, 1898, Captain J. T. Evatt (39th Bengal Inf.) was appointed to raise the first Indian Contingent, 400 strong, for service in the Uganda Protectorate.

During Macdonald's absence in Buddu offensive operations at Lubwa's had to be suspended. On the nights of 7th and 8th January, 1898, the mutineers evacuated the fort, using native canoes and the captured steam launch. Woodward was unable to prevent this, as the first troops of the East Africa Indian Contingent did not reach him until several days later. The attitude of the Sudanese in Bunyoro was considered doubtful, and when it was discovered that the mutineers were following the course of the Nile to Mruli, Scott was dispatched there with a column of 100 sepoys and 60 Swahilis to disarm the garrison and if necessary to take over the defence of the other forts as well. Those troops who were likely to prove troublesome at Mruli were sent down to Kampala and disarmed.

Macdonald had meanwhile resumed command. Heartened at his success in Buddu, the Baganda came forward in greater numbers, and with the arrival of the rest of the Indian Contingent from East Africa and the knowledge that other troops were on the way, no time was lost in following the mutineers, who were now entrenched near Lake Kioga. On 18th February they attacked the pursuing column at Kijembo, but were beaten off with loss. On the 24th Captain Harrison with 80 of Barratt's sepoys, 110 men of the E.A.R. and 80 Swahilis attacked the rebel stockade at Kabagambi. In an action lasting two hours the mutineers put up a stubborn fight, but were driven out at last with heavy loss, most of the survivors escaping along the Mruli road. In this action Jardin Effendi was killed.

Harrison followed to Mruli, to find the mutineers on the opposite bank of the Nile. He reinforced the Mruli garrison and then joined Scott at Masindi, where the Sudanese garrison was disarmed. The immediate danger to Bunyoro had been averted, and the defence of the province was in the hands of the sepoys and the E.A.R.

Towards the end of April the pursuit of the mutineers was taken up by Major C. G. Martyr (D.C.L.I.) with a column of 250 troops drawn from the Indian Contingent, the E.A.R. and the armed Swahilis. Crossing the Nile at Mruli, Martyr followed the track of the mutineers for nine miles down-stream, drove them from an entrenched position and destroyed their stockade. At the same time Lieutenant N. Malcolm (A. and S. H.), who commanded the post at Foweira, attacked a body of 50 mutineers, killed about half of them and captured their baggage.

By May, 1898, the situation had eased considerably, though the remnants of the mutineers were still formidable in alliance with Kabarega's Banyoro. Macdonald handed over the conduct of operations to Martyr and prepared to resume his interrupted expedition. The greater part of the 27th Bombay Infantry was then in Uganda, with 150 Sikhs of the Indian Contingent from East Africa and 130 men of the East Africa Rifles. Swahili recruits were being enlisted as rapidly as possible; the first of the new companies was already marching to Uganda, and another 400 men were in training at Ndi.

Throughout June and July operations continued in Bunyoro against those chiefs who supported the rebellion, though Mwanga and Kabarega still eluded capture. In July the mutineers, who had built another stockade near Mruli, showed fresh signs of aggression. To prevent their escape beyond the Nile a force assembled in secret on the farther bank. On 3rd August the advance began in two columns. The first, under Major C. H. U. Price (27th Bom. Inf.), consisted of four officers and 237 men of the 27th Bombay Infantry and one officer and 24 men of the Uganda Rifles. Under cover of darkness Price surprised and overcame an enemy picquet on a hill overlooking the mutineers' fort, then waited for dawn to combine his attack with that of the second column. This was commanded by Major Martyr, and consisted of two officers and 159 men of the Uganda Rifles, one officer and 53 men of the East Africa Rifles, three maxim guns manned by sepoys and a 7-pounder gun. At daylight on 4th August the stockade was bombarded and stormed by the two columns, 40 mutineers being killed and two men of the Uganda Rifles slightly wounded.

This ended the main operations against the mutineers. Macdonald reported that he and Martyr had fought five major and seven minor engagements, and 35 skirmishes. Altogether some 2,000 troops had been employed, and 3,000 Baganda auxiliaries equipped with firearms. Supported by a hastily raised body of several thousand carriers, these troops made many arduous marches throughout an area exceeding 40,000 square miles. Seven Europeans and 280 Indians and Africans were killed, and five Europeans and 555 Indians and Africans were wounded during the mutiny operations.

On 23rd May, 1898, Evatt, now raised to the rank of local lieutenant-colonel, left India with five other officers and 387 men for service in Uganda. His second-in-command was Captain E. J. E. Swayne, known later for his operations against the Mad Mullah of Somaliland, and perhaps the first military officer to make the journey from the coast to Uganda on a bicycle.[1] The Government of India was anxious for the return of the troops loaned specifically for the mutiny operations, and Lieutenant-Colonel Broome was asked to report on the situation. Most of the forts in Bunyoro were then held by detachments of his regiment, but as seven companies of Sudanese had been rearmed, four companies of Swahilis and Somalis were in Uganda and another company was in process of formation, Broome thought that his regiment could safely be withdrawn as soon as Evatt's Indian Contingent arrived.

Meanwhile in the Buddu and Koki provinces the native authorities had shown themselves quite unable to deal with the situation created by Mwanga. Though part of Buddu remained loyal, many of the people were inclined to ingratiate themselves with the rebels, especially along the frontier, where they were actively hostile. In Masaka incendiarism was rife; women were being captured in large numbers and sold in Ankole to traders from German territory, in exchange for arms and ammunition. The chiefs who remained loyal were ignorant, their intelligence arrangements were faulty, and their initiative gone.

Military operations were essential, and Captain M. J. Tighe[2] (1st Baluchi Lt. Inf.) was sent to Masaka in command. Reports from spies showed that 1,000 armed rebels under Gabriel, with about 2,000 spearmen, were in the neighbourhood of Kabula. The speed and secrecy of their raids were remarkable, and their intelligence system so efficient that it was almost impossible to take them by surprise.

Tighe's first object was to restore confidence in the Government among the terrorized and wavering people of Buddu. A mixed force of 122 rifles under Lieutenant Hobart was stationed at Masaka with outposts at Kikoma and Bulusana, to provide a disciplined nucleus for the Baganda levies. A company of Indian troops and more levies were ordered to Buddu. While awaiting their arrival Tighe sent Hobart with a flying column to patrol the frontier, spread the news that military operations were about to start, and establish a network of picquets and patrols.

Gabriel was reported to be planning an evasive withdrawal into Ankole, with the object of enticing the punitive expedition after him and then doubling back to devastate the defenceless Buddu province.

---

[1] Bicycles became a popular form of transport with military officers serving in Africa. Churchill recorded (*My African Journey*, p. 138) that nearly all the K.A.R. officers he met on his tour in 1907 used them.

[2] Later Lieutenant-General Sir Michael Tighe, K.C.B., K.C.M.G., C.I.E., C.B., D.S.O.

The attitude of Kahaya, the young ruler of Ankole, was doubtful, so an ultimatum was dispatched allowing him twenty days to confirm his loyalty, failing which Ankole was to be declared hostile territory.

Late in August the expected reinforcements reached Masaka, and Tighe marched out with two officers, 107 regular troops, 1,200 Baganda armed with guns, and about 2,000 spearmen. Tighe was unused to such allies, and fascinated by the long, parallel files of spearmen marching straight across country on his flanks. Gabriel was reported to be in the hills near Kabula, and by splitting his force into four converging columns Tighe hoped to surround him by night. He soon learnt that rebel-catching in Africa with a force consisting mainly of irregulars was not easy. At dawn on 3rd September, just as the attack was about to start, a number of followers crept up in rear of the main column and by their chattering and calling gave the alarm. The result was that Gabriel and most of his men escaped towards western Ankole.

Selecting a site on a ridge overlooking the rich valleys around Kabula, Tighe built a fort, while Hobart with 57 men of No. 3 Company and several smaller patrols scoured the area seeking news and rescuing captured women and cattle. Excellent work was done by the regular troops on these exhausting expeditions: on one occasion Hobart's men marched fifty-eight miles in two days without water. The Baganda levies often let parties of rebels escape in their anxiety to secure the women and cattle, though repeatedly told that by rounding up the rebels first possession of their booty would inevitably follow. On 13th September the arrival of Lieutenant C. U. Price (130th Baluchis) with an Indian company to garrison the new fort allowed Tighe to join the chase after Gabriel, who was first reported to be at Lusikasi's with 700 men and then mysteriously disappeared.

Kahaya's answer reached Kabula late in September, promising co-operation and hoping that a post would be maintained permanently at Kabula and another in Ankole. Tighe's system of flying columns and patrols had been ranging over a wide area, fighting minor actions and recapturing women and cattle. At last the rebels' main force was discovered near starvation in the Bwera district. Hobart's column covered 130 miles in five days; another attempt was made to surround the rebels, but once again Gabriel and his principal chiefs escaped. At first it was thought that he had crossed the Katonga and was making for Bunyoro, but nothing more was heard of his whereabouts and later reports said that he had been wounded and died unseen in the tall grass.

By October the rebels in the south had been scattered and their leaders were in full flight. A line of outposts was established and the rest of the Field Force returned to Masaka, where Hobart resumed command, with a flying column ready to move at short notice. The expedition had killed 142 rebels, captured 43 and recovered 539 stolen cattle, for the loss of five men killed and 18 wounded.

Meanwhile in the north Martyr was advancing down the Nile, establishing posts at Fajao, Wadelai, Affuddu and Lamogi. The experience so gained proved beyond doubt that easy communication with Khartoum could not be expected by way of the Nile. Major A. H. Coles,[1] who had reached Uganda in July as second-in-command, left Kampala on 24th October with a column nearly 500 strong to continue operations in Bunyoro and the Nile area. Throughout November many small actions were fought around the forests where the rebel leaders concealed their followers and cattle. In December Bilal Effendi was shot by a patrol under Lieutenant C. U. Price. In the same month a rebel chief who surrendered to Hobart reported that Mwanga with 200 rebels and 50 mutineers had crossed the Nile to join forces with the remaining mutineers from Lubwa's. On 9th April, 1899, he and Kabarega were surprised and captured at Kangai by a field force under Evatt that had crossed Lake Kwania by canoe: an unexpected and unspectacular conclusion to two long and troublesome careers.

Colonel Ternan had returned to Uganda and taken over command of troops from Broome late in October, 1898. He now issued special orders for the custody of these important prisoners. An escort of half a company marched them to Kazi, where they embarked by dhow for Port Victoria, *en route* for Kismayu. It was by water that Mwanga had so often made his previous escapes. This time he was thoroughly cowed and left Uganda whining at his fate. Kabarega, on the other hand, remained proud and truculent to the last.[2]

The mutiny in Uganda brought home to the British Government the political and military instability that had always underlain the new Protectorate. Authority had rested upon a loosely organized regiment consisting mainly of Sudanese, and when they failed, the situation was exposed in all its danger. There was neither continuity of command nor of military policy, and the regiment had suffered accordingly. When the crisis arose, no plan existed to meet it and none could be formulated at short notice, either in Uganda or in England. Military experience lay at the War Office; military authority was vested in the Foreign Office; succour was being organized in India. For a time conflicting reports and the shocked incredulity of certain soldiers and administrators who happened to be in London led the Government to view the situation too lightly. Afterwards, when the truth was known, panic measures were advocated, but little could be done beyond hurrying forward reinforcements in the hope that those on the spot would know best how to deal with them when they arrived. In consequence the real crisis in Uganda was met by those loyal troops, Indian and African, who happened to be present in East Africa at the time.

---

[1] Coles had recently retired from the Buffs. Like Ternan, he had at one time commanded the 1st Sudanese Battalion of the Egyptian Army.

[2] The place of exile was later changed to the Seychelles, where Mwanga died. Many years afterwards Kabarega was allowed to return to Uganda. He died of influenza at Jinja in 1923.

It is interesting to speculate on what might have occurred had the British occupied Uganda by way of the Nile instead of from the east coast. It is conceivable that if the first treaty had been signed with Kabarega instead of Mwanga, he might have proved the more dependable ally, and British influence would then have been ranged on the side of the Banyoro against the Baganda. Had this come to pass, subsequent history might have followed a very different course.

Regimental Orders by Lieut-Colonel A. H. Coles, D.S.O.
Commanding Uganda Rifles.
Port Alice 29th Sept 1898.

EXTRACT 26. Nº 108 — PROCLAMATION.
from ORDERS by O.C. Troops U.P.

The following Proclamation has been issued by order of H.M's Commissioner and Consul General for Uganda, to be read three times to all troops in the Uganda Protectorate. "Whereas Bilal Amin Effendi, Rehan Effendi and Gardem "Effendi, formerly Officers in the Uganda Rifles have been "found guilty of Murder and of Armed Mutiny against "the Government of this Protectorate and whereas they are "still at large in Armed Insurrection against His Majesty's "authority — Notice is hereby given that a REWARD "of Rs 2000 (Two Thousand rupees) is offered to any person "who may be able to effect the capture dead or alive of each "or either of the above named men, and bring him or them to "the nearest Government Station, and should such capture "or delivery be effected by soldiers or other persons who join-"ed in the Mutiny, a Free Pardon will be granted to them, "provided that they themselves took no active part in the "murder of the European Officers at LUBWAS in October last year KAMPALA 20-8-98) sg? E.J.L. Berkeley H.M. Comm. & C. General.

Killed and Injured Decr 7

MILITARY 27 ARMS & STORES OF U.P.

The O.C. Troops at each Station is responsible for all Military weapons, ammunition or Military Stores of whatever des--cription, belonging to the Uganda Protectorate, and should render a Monthly Return of their number and condition. At Stations where the O.C. Troops has no suitable Store Building, it is advisable to allow the Arms etc and Stores to remain in the Civil Store, obtaining a receipt for every-thing from the O.C.S + making a periodical inspection of them.

ARRIVALS 28
At Port Alice on 21.9.98 Sergt Bugler Thomson + 38 rank & file
— " —   on 27.9.98 Captain J. Niver
— " —   on 28.9.98 Sergeant Bone
at KAMPALA on 27.9.98 Lieut H.C. Moorhouse + 43 R+file

Facsimile of Regimental Orders by Lieutenant-Colonel A. H. Coles, D.S.O., commanding the Uganda Rifles, dated 29th September, 1898, and containing a Proclamation offering a reward for the capture of the leaders of the Sudanese mutineers

Macdonald was criticized for not taking sterner action in the initial stages of the revolt, and for his alleged tardiness in following the mutineers back to Uganda. On the other hand, he was also accused of provoking the mutiny by his uncompromising strictness in dealing with troops whose language he did not speak.[1] Whichever view may be correct, it is certain that the vigorous action taken by Macdonald at Lubwa's and in Buddu prevented the mutiny from developing into a Muslim rebellion. No over-all plan could possibly have been made for concerted action in Uganda; communications were difficult and for long periods there was in effect no one in supreme command. Isolated officers had to cope unaided with local situations. It was largely owing to their influence that the military revolt was confined to three companies of troops. Thus the crisis had passed before the first reinforcements from India reached Uganda.[2]

The mutiny brought the long years of warfare in Uganda to a head. By flooding the country with troops it settled at last the fate of Mwanga and Kabarega, creating for the first time an atmosphere peaceful enough to make a real settlement possible. In this sense it was a turning-point in the history of the Protectorate. In July, 1899, Sir Harry Johnston was appointed Special Commissioner to report on the country and remodel its system of government.[3] He drew up a new agreement with Buganda, made land settlements, and extended administrative control throughout

---

[1] For example, in the account of the mutiny given in Thruston's *African Incidents*, and in the Parliamentary debates of the time. In the House of Lords, Lord Stanmore spoke at some length on the Government's published reports of affairs in Uganda, and was evidently highly suspicious of the part played by Macdonald, whom he described as 'a leader they [the Sudanese] did not trust.' In his reply the Duke of Devonshire ignored this point. (*Hansard*, 1898, Vol. 54, col. 433 *et seq*.)

Portions of two letters quoted in *The Times* are illuminating. In one (2.ii.98, p. 7) the missionary Pilkington pays glowing tribute to Macdonald's work. In the other (24.iii.98, p. 11) Macdonald shows his coldly autocratic attitude towards the missions when a request is made for release of the missionaries then assisting him.

[2] Macdonald did not abandon his expedition. In July, 1898, when the worst danger was over, he concentrated on Elgon with his Sikhs, 70 Sudanese, and 350 armed Swahilis. He then led a column via Manimani, Bukora and the Rom Hills to the Nangiya and Teretenia ranges, an unexplored region that some fourteen years later became the scene of many frontier expeditions by 4 K.A.R. Near Tarangole (Tirangore) he was joined by some 35 Sudanese ex-askaris, who accompanied him south and in February, 1899, were enlisted in the East Africa Rifles at Machakos. On the way back one of Macdonald's officers, Captain R. T. Fitzpatrick (Leins. R.) was treacherously murdered by tribesmen in the Nakwai Hills while on a foraging expedition.

Meanwhile Major H. H. Austin led a second column through the Suk and Turkana country, following the courses of the Wei-wei and Turkwel rivers to Lake Rudolf. He marched up the western shore of the lake, but found the Turkana unfriendly and experienced great difficulty in obtaining food. On his return he was met just in time by the base party with fresh supplies. These also had not been obtained without considerable trouble, the tribesmen around Mbai having frequently attacked the supply columns from their caves among the crags and precipices. (Vide *Report by Lieutenant-Colonel Macdonald, R.E., on his Expedition from the Uganda Protectorate, 1899*. Africa No. 9 (1899) (C. 9503). LXIII, 567. Also H. H. Austin, *With Macdonald in Uganda*, especially pp. 227-28. and p. 242.)

[3] Full status as a British dependency was granted by the Uganda Order in Council, 15th October, 1902.

Bunyoro, Busoga and Ankole. The Arab-Mahdi danger was over, but the main line of communication, the railway that was now approaching Uganda and the Nile waterway to Gondokoro, had to be secured. Johnston considered that the substitution of a military for a civil administration, caused by the constant wars of the past eight years, had had a bad effect and that the troops had been given too much police work. He therefore created a native constabulary with a nominal establishment of 1,500 men, trained by sergeants of the Metropolitan Police and the regular Army, to free the armed forces of the Protectorate for their proper rôle. By the time Johnston had finished his task there were over 80 civil officials in Uganda, as against 29 serving army officers.

In February, 1899, a Military Ordinance was passed reducing the period of enlistment to four years, with the possibility of re-engagement for a similar term, and allowing for the secondment of British N.C.Os. to appointments as 'instructors' with the Uganda military forces.

In 1900 the Regiment numbered 36 British officers, 21 British sergeants, and 1,952 native officers, N.C.Os. and men, organized in 16 companies each of 122 all ranks, with an Indian Contingent (sometimes known as the 1st Bn. Uganda Rifles) consisting of six British officers, a medical officer, and 402 Indian ranks. Ternan was appointed Deputy Commissioner of the East Africa Protectorate, and Coles was promoted to command the armed forces of Uganda, Lieutenant-Colonel J. T. Evatt of the Indian Contingent acting as Commandant from January to September while he was on leave. Coles returned to Uganda with the local rank of Colonel, but on Johnston's recommendation it was decided not to couple his appointment with that of Deputy Commissioner. With the exception of those who had been through what he termed the 'Indian mill', Johnston thought military administrators too domineering, and 'simply disastrous' when in charge of a large native population. 'The Foreign Office,' he wrote to Lord Cranborne after his return to England, 'has a curious, old-maidish love of the red coat, and delights to lavish her elderly smiles on handsome martinets.'[1]

The maximum pay of the Sudanese troops was raised to 20 rupees a month, but this was later reduced to the Sikh maximum of 18 rupees. Johnston wished to reduce it still further, and gradually to decrease the number of troops as his police force grew, but the optimistic view that he took of a peaceful future in Uganda[2] was not wholly borne out by subsequent events.

It was Ternan who had first suggested the employment of British sergeants as drill instructors and commanders of maxim-gun sections, and a draft of 17 N.C.Os., selected from the Royal Marines and various regiments of the British Army, left England for East Africa in December, 1897. But the main difficulty lay in finding suitable native officers and N.C.Os. Reports submitted by officers serving with the new companies all agreed that the experiment of enlisting Swahilis on regular

[1] Johnston to Cranborne, 6.xi.1901. F.O.2, 464.
[2] Sir Harry Johnston, *The Uganda Protectorate*, Vol. I, Chap. VIII.

engagements was only a qualified success. The men were cheerful, teachable, hardy, and often imbued with greater courage than expected, but they had little sense of responsibility and no ambition. Constant detailed supervision was essential, and Sudanese officers and N.C.Os. had to be drafted to the Swahili companies to provide it.

Unfortunately, the most suitable men were not always chosen. In remote districts such as the Nile Province disciplinary matters were particularly difficult, and a minor mutiny occurred in one of the Swahili companies stationed there in July, 1900. The British officers could not speak the language, and the two Sudanese officers made no secret of their contempt for Swahilis, whom they considered fit only for porters. Finding themselves unable to secure proper attention to their grievances, 46 armed askaris broke out of their quarters at Lamogi, intending to march on Kampala and complain. At Masindi Wilson's influence and common sense averted bloodshed; the men were disarmed and submitted quietly.

During these years, while the memory of the mutiny was still fresh, any rumours of indiscipline, grievances or disaffection received immediate attention at high level. Sir Harry Johnston was impressed by the continued complaints of looting by the Sudanese, and particularly by the locust-like propensities of their women-folk. He suggested that men who were unable to control their families should be discharged, and asked Evatt whether such measures would be likely to cause trouble. Evatt thought that some husbands would be glad of such an excuse to get rid of their wives, but that others would desert if their wives were sent away. Gradual replacement of the Sudanese by local enlistments appeared to be the only solution, though it was obvious that this must be a long-term policy.

On the other hand, the Sudanese still had many grievances that were well founded. Clothing issues were constantly in arrear, and no allowance was authorized in lieu. The policy of settling ex-askaris in colonies was generally unpopular, especially among men discharged through old age or ill-health. But the chief grievance lay in the method of payment. In outlying provinces a high percentage of the troops' pay, sometimes even the whole, was still issued in the form of trade goods. In the Nile Province a contract had been made with an Indian trader at rates greatly to the disadvantage of the troops when the approach of the railway brought an influx of traders and a fall in prices. Only money or certain articles in particular demand, such as brass wire or beads of the colour then fashionable,[1] would purchase food from the local tribes, and as the troops were inclined to be lazy in raising their own crops and improvident in their consumption, they often went hungry. On changing station each askari was entitled to a porter to carry his household goods, but in practice porters were often unobtainable and the askari had to leave many of his possessions behind. Another grievance lay in the fact that only officers commanding districts could impose sentences exceeding

---

[1] Beads were a very convenient currency, as they could be separated into small units. They were known according to colour, e.g., *maziwa* (milk) for white. *punda milia* (zebra) for striped, etc. *Masango*, or brass wire, though coiled in bundles, could likewise be measured and cut into varying lengths. Strings of cowrie shells were carried up from the coast to be used as currency.

seven days' imprisonment, so that prisoners in small garrisons who were accused of serious offences sometimes waited for over a year on remand.

A collectorate was established at Nimule in 1899, and the post set up by Martyr at Affuddu was transferred there, to a station on a small plateau overlooking the Nile. Captain C. Delmé-Radcliffe (Connaught Rangers) assumed command of the Nile Military District, and the work of pacifying the Lango country and rooting out the last parties of the Sudanese mutineers, who were exercising a baneful influence on the tribes north and east of the Nile, fell to him. The distances he covered during the night marches of his military patrols earned him locally the name of Langa-Langa ('were-lion'), as the tribesmen thought it impossible for a mere human to traverse the bush so quickly under cover of darkness.

Early in 1901 Delmé-Radcliffe discovered through friendly chiefs that the principal cause of the trouble was a band of mutineers at Modo, about twenty miles north of Foweira. Headquarters had provided him with a nominal roll of 103 Sudanese known to be in the Lango and Acholi districts, and before beginning operations he issued a call to the mutineers to submit. Only three responded.

The area of operations lay between the Nile and the Aswa, a country of thick forest and tall grass six to nine feet high, where visibility was often nil. Though the native population was numerous, tracks through the forest were few, and the best road found in the whole campaign was a route beaten out by elephant on seasonal migration. The Lango Field Force set out in April, 1901, and remained in the field until August. These were the rainy months, and all the river valleys were filled with papyrus swamp, through which the troops often waded up to their necks. Many went sick with pneumonia or severe bronchitis, and the tropical sores caused by cuts from the sharp reeds.

The mutineers had built their station on the European model. They were organized as a company, and well officered by capable leaders who maintained strict discipline. Ammunition and supplies were plentiful, so that when pressed the men could vanish into the bush, living for weeks on game and the tubers of a creeping plant known to the natives as *ruk*. The Lango, who called the mutineers 'Black Turks,' were impressed by their assurance that Kabarega would shortly return and oust the British, and agreed to co-operate and to enter into blood-brotherhood. Even when the hopelessness of their resistance became apparent and they were ready to make peace, they first had to be absolved from the obligations imposed by this ceremony. Dr. Bagshawe, the medical officer attached to the expedition, injected apomorphia into the cicatrix of the incision, which made the subject violently sick and convinced him that the obligation was discharged.

The Field Force consisted of Nos. 1, 3, 5 and 8 Companies Uganda Rifles, totalling six Europeans and 405 native officers, N.C.Os. and men. There was also a Baganda levy of 100 men under a European instructor, and a body of Acholi, Madi and Bari tribesmen that grew to a thousand strong before the operations were over. Before the end of April the mutineers' stronghold was entered, and their company driven out. Throughout the succeeding weeks the Lango country was combed by flying columns. A base camp was built to accommodate prisoners and cattle, and later a hospital to deal with a serious outbreak of small-pox that added greatly to Delmé-Radcliffe's difficulties. Moving always by forced marches, sleeping in water and mud, continually searching the dense bush, in which every advantage lay with the enemy, feeding precariously on captured cattle and sweet potatoes grubbed from the shambas, ambushed unexpectedly by hostile natives, and on one occasion scattered and cruelly stung by swarms of wild bees, the flying columns steadily reduced the mutineers until by 20th August only seven remained at large. The Field Force then withdrew, having captured 1,485 prisoners, nearly 10,000 cattle, goats and sheep, 3,000 spears, 88 firearms and seven tusks of ivory. Including porters and native allies, the casualties numbered only 21 killed and 16 wounded.

With the completion of Delmé-Radcliffe's operations, the mutiny of the Sudanese could be considered at an end. Perhaps it is fitting to close this account of their grievances, their intractability, their ruthlessness and their bravery with the opinion of one who knew them well and who ultimately suffered death at their hands:

'Possibly they are not heroes—heroes are not required; but in endurance, subordination, patience and cheerfulness, they are a model to be admired and imitated by every army in the world. They would march twenty miles a day, or more, through long tangled grass reaching over their heads, through swamps and jungles, and at the end go foraging, sometimes for many miles, to fetch food. Crime and punishment were almost unknown; they worked at parade, at agriculture, or at housebuilding, from sunrise to sunset, and they did so cheerfully and well for their monthly payment of some four shillings' worth of white calico.'[1]

(vi) *The Third Expedition against the Nandi, 1900.* Map II (a).

In spite of the two punitive expeditions that had invaded their country, the attitude of the Nandi and Kamasya showed little improvement. Raids on the Uasin Gishu Masai and other nearby tribes were frequent; mail-runners and isolated stragglers from caravans were still attacked and murdered, and as military concentration on the mutiny operations allowed these depredations to go unpunished, the Nandi became ever more daring. Constant reports reached the Ravine of purposeless murders on the roads. Several askaris of the Uganda Rifles were killed and their rifles stolen. Late in 1899 Colonel Coles carried out brief retaliatory measures and took a number of sheep and goats. Few cattle could be found, however, and tracks showed that the herds were being driven into Lumbwa for safety, always an ominous sign. No reasons for the Nandi hostility were apparent, other than a general dislike of Europeans, which was sedulously fostered by the old men of the tribe. 'The Wanandi,' wrote C. W. Hobley, the sub-commissioner of the district 'with the exception of a few in the vicinity of the station, have all along viewed our presence in the country with veiled repugnance . . . We were unwittingly living on the edge of a volcano.'[2]

[1] Thruston, *African Incidents*, p. 235.
[2] Hobley to Johnston, 24.viii.1900. F.O.2. 556.

The situation was greatly aggravated by the approach of the railway. During 1899, while the track crept across the forty-mile floor of the Rift Valley, the survey parties worked ahead, running trial lines up the slopes of the Mau escarpment and through the forests, more than 8,000 feet above sea level. Behind them came the telegraph, which reached Eldama Ravine in March and Kisumu in December of that year. By April, 1900, the survey had been completed,[1] and the construction parties were at work in the area bordered by the Nandi on the north and the Kipsikis on the south.

At first the construction camps and store dumps were unguarded. The tribesmen were not slow in seizing the opportunity thus presented for stealing ironwork, telegraph wire and stores of all description. The success of their raids increased their daring. The worst area was in the Nyando Valley, between Molo and Kisumu. In March, 1900, the telegraph line was cut. In May the telegraph office at Kitoto's was raided. The Indian operator fled just in time, hid in the long grass and sought sanctuary in the village, while the Nandi looted his kit. In June a number of attacks was made on bridge-building parties, on caravans and even on military patrols, and the sub-commissioner appealed for more troops.

Nandi was garrisoned at that time by Nos. 7 and 14 Companies. Captain A. Parkin (Northants R.), who commanded the Eastern Military District, organized a small expedition early in June of 25 rifles and some Masai spearmen, killed 31 of the Nandi responsible for the raids and captured 229 cattle and about 1,800 sheep and goats. He was closely followed back to his base and lost two men killed and one severely wounded. But the situation was beyond the compass of the normal garrison, which was hardly able to maintain its small posts along the mail route and to meet the demand for escorts. Evatt therefore responded promptly to the sub-commissioner's request. On 3rd July a company of the Indian Contingent and No. 13 Company Uganda Rifles reached Kisumu. As the scale of the operations grew, these troops were joined on 14th August by No. 15 Company from Lubwa's; on 23rd August by about 300 Masai auxiliaries; on 25th September by half No. 10 Company from Fort Portal; on 13th October by half No. 4 Company from Masindi; and on 17th October by half No. 3 Company from Buddu. The Uganda Rifles had no reserves, and punitive expeditions of any size could only be carried out by withdrawing garrisons from other parts of the Protectorate.

Evatt entered Nandi with his troops on 5th July. The tribesmen pursued their usual tactics, refusing battle but lurking unseen in the long grass, ready to spear stragglers or isolated parties. Almost immediately Evatt's porters were attacked while watering at a stream; on 7th July five askaris from Bushiri post were killed while escorting the mails, and next day a transport convoy was attacked and seven askaris, a policeman, a clerk and several boys were killed. At Bushiri the situation was critical when the post was relieved on 9th July. Early in August an

---

[1] M. F. Hill, *Permanent Way*, p. 193. In 1900 Kisumu became provincial headquarters in place of Mumia's.

escort of 20 Sudanese was annihilated while accompanying the down mail to Fort Ternan, a new military post established by Coles in 1898. Evatt had been inclined to think that carelessness on safari and the neglect of standing orders by Parkin's troops, many of whom were Somalis who despised the Nandi, had led to these constant minor reverses that so greatly encouraged the tribesmen, but for weeks after his own operations began the Nandi raiders still continued their attacks on convoys.

After the Masai auxiliaries joined his force, Evatt adopted the plan of concentrating a column at Nandi Fort or some central camp while carrying out cattle raids of two or three days' duration. During September the wooded hills and valleys of the Nandi country were traversed from east to west in a series of raids by small mobile columns of about 40 rifles, assisted by 100 spearmen who acted as a screen and often surprised the Nandi by their skilful approach. The Masai did particularly well in attacking the cave strongholds near the western escarpment, some of which were large enough to hold two or three hundred cattle. Without their skill the entrance to these caves would have been hard to find, and they usually led the initial assault to remove the barricades, protecting their bodies from flights of arrows with their hide shields, and full of confidence so long as they were supported by rifle fire. After the capture of the second cave, the Nandi evacuated the remainder, leaving behind them large stores of grain. Evatt then worked the country from west to east, with columns operating from the main body, and reached Nandi station again on 24th September.

By this time another five officers and 296 men had become available as escorts. Evatt detached some of his own troops for this purpose and went south with the remainder, totalling 145 rifles and 300 Masai. Receiving news of the whereabouts of Kipeles and Koitalel, the two Nandi leaders primarily responsible for the trouble, he decided to attack before they could escape. On the night of 12th October two columns left the camp. The first, under Colour-Sergeant James Ellison, R.M.L.I., marched east over the Nyando river, attacked one of the bomas early on the following day, inflicted severe losses on the Nandi and returned to camp before nightfall. Owing to sickness among officers, this was not the first time Ellison had held independent command and conducted operations with ability and success. At 4 a.m. on the 13th the second column, commanded by Evatt, surrounded and captured Kipeles' boma, killing six Nandi. At 1 p.m. that day Evatt camped with his captures, 700-800 cattle and about 3,000 sheep and goats. His troops were tired and apparently did not complete their boma,[1] though Evatt was well aware of the risk of attack. About 9.30 p.m., on making his rounds, he ordered all camp fires to be extinguished. Shortly afterwards one of these smouldering fires was blown suddenly into a blaze, and simultaneously the Nandi attacked the camp in three parties, one of which broke through the Masai spearmen and entered the cattle enclosure. The night was dark and it was difficult to distinguish Masai from Nandi.

---

[1] Hobley, *ibid.*, p. 113, says that there was not enough bush available.

The cattle stampeded and about half of them escaped. No entrance was effected through the troops, however, and after the maxim gun got into action the Nandi withdrew. Unfortunately the medical officer, Dr. J. L. Sherlock, was wounded in the abdomen by a spear and died soon afterwards. Ten askaris were killed, and one officer and 18 others wounded. The operations of the two columns cost the Nandi 74 men killed, 1,039 head of cattle and 3,100 sheep and goats.

After this action Evatt returned to Fort Ternan. Some criticism was levied against him for the inconclusive nature of his operations, but his comparatively small expedition, raised from such troops as could be spared from escort and guard duties in the area, had covered 1,600 square miles of undulating, broken and precipitous country, varying from open grassland on top of the escarpment to thick forests in the north and east, where cattle could easily be hidden. The weather was wet and the nights cold, and the troops could carry only one blanket besides their food.

The total casualties of the operations, including police and auxiliaries, were 103 killed, four died of wounds and 111 wounded, of whom 44 killed and 38 wounded came from the military forces engaged. The medical report of the expedition described the arrow wounds as the only ones of surgical interest. Beyond thirty yards the Nandi marksmanship was poor, but by using a high trajectory they could inflict casualties from three times that distance. Some of the arrow-heads carried iron barbs fitted into sockets, and had considerable penetrative power. One fractured an askari's shoulder-blade, another penetrated an ankle bone, and several passed right through limbs or deep into soft parts of the body, causing severe hæmorrhage. Nearly all these arrows were poisoned, but of sixty arrow wound cases only two developed poison, and neither proved fatal.

At the Foreign Office criticism was expressed on the ground that some regular forces in the Nandi area had been replaced by Masai irregulars. Johnston admitted that he had withdrawn about 100 troops, but defended his action by asserting that their replacement by armed police provided a better means of 'keeping the ordinary robbers of the country in order'. He considered that the question of subduing the Nandi was bound to arise when the introduction of the railway opened up their country, that former administrators and commandants had shirked this issue, and that great credit was due to Evatt for the dogged way he had stuck to his task despite reverses. Sir Clement Hill reached East Africa on a tour of inspection on 4th October, and a few days later proceeded up-country, where he was met at the railhead by an escort of 80 men. Summing up the Nandi crisis as the culmination of a growing dislike for Europeans, Hill thought it unfortunate that this should have coincided with the moment when the railway was about to enter their territory. He began negotiations intended to maintain the peace for at least two years, and brought Evatt's operations to a premature close.

The station at Kipture was abandoned and transferred to Kaptumo, though without any improvement in relations with the tribe. Johnston journeyed through the district in January, 1901. Wire-cutting was still occurring, as the telegraph line was so badly constructed between the Kedong valley and Kavirondo Bay, 'simply slung from stick to stick, the sticks often being trivial little posts only seven or eight feet above ground,' that it offered a standing temptation, within the reach of any passing native.[1]

Colonel Coles and Lieutenant-Colonel Evatt put forward a proposal of their own to solve the difficulty. One company of the regiment was composed mostly of Somalis, who had in general proved themselves satisfactory soldiers. Coles suggested that they should be formed into a mounted company 124 strong, dressed in a distinctive uniform of tarbush and grey shirt instead of field cap and blue jersey, and be used in patrolling the Nyando valley section of the line. But a proposal to transfer the Eastern Province of Uganda to East Africa in order to place the railway within the jurisdiction of a single administration was already under discussion, and it was expected that responsibility for defence of the line would soon cease to be a commitment of the Uganda forces.

(vii) *The Affair at Ribo Post, 1900-01.* Map I (a).

> 'DEAR BAGNALL,
>
> 'I am having a bad time, fever bad, and having to fight all the time. The natives are one too many for us, bad rifles and too few men. Hope to hold out.
>
> 'Yours urgently,
>
> 'H. HYDE BAKER.'

This brief message, scribbled on a scrap of paper by an administrative officer, sick, surrounded and ignorant of the fate that had befallen most of his men, was the occasion of the only expedition undertaken by the Uganda Rifles against the Suk and Turkana. Set within the march of events in Uganda, the trouble at Ribo Post was a minor affair, but as a symbol of the determination that so often maintained small isolated stations in those early days, the story deserves to be extracted from its place among the files.

The Eastern Province of Uganda reached from the River Sio to Lake Naivasha and northward to the arid, inhospitable shores of Lake Rudolf. Sir Harry Johnston, whose arrangements tended to increase rather than curtail the limits of the Protectorate, considered that the treaties made during Macdonald's recent expedition had given to the Uganda administration 'control over all the waste and uncultivated land in the Protectorate'.[2] He was disturbed at 'a disagreeable little nucleus of enmity,' north of Mount Elgon, due chiefly to a settlement of Arabs and Swahilis at Marich, who were reported to be practising slavery and exporting illicit ivory. Moreover, certain Abyssinian claims had been preferred to the western shores of Lake Rudolf. Believing therefore that it would be advisable to demonstrate effective occupation in this area,

---

[1] Johnston to F.O., 6.ii.1901. F.O.2, 461.

[2] *Preliminary Report by H.M. Special Commissioner on the Protectorate of Uganda, 1900.* Africa No. 6 (1900) (Cd. 256), pp. 13-14, LVI, 865.

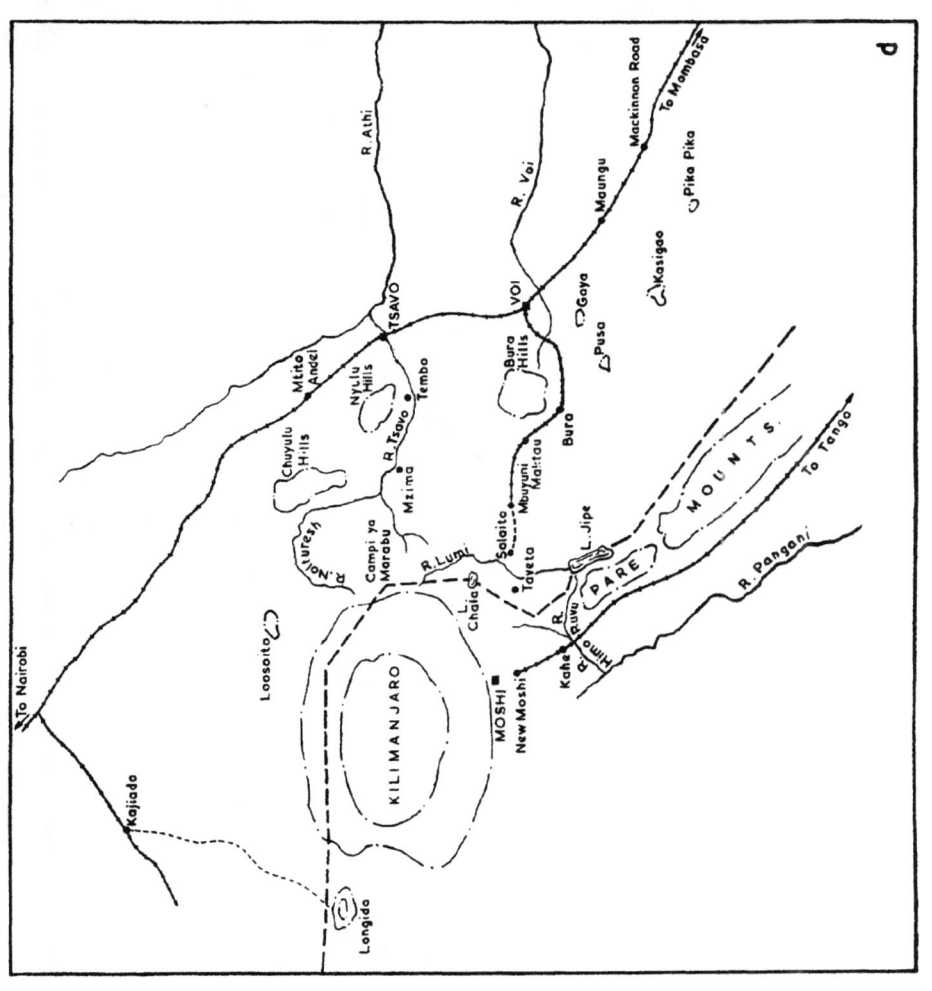

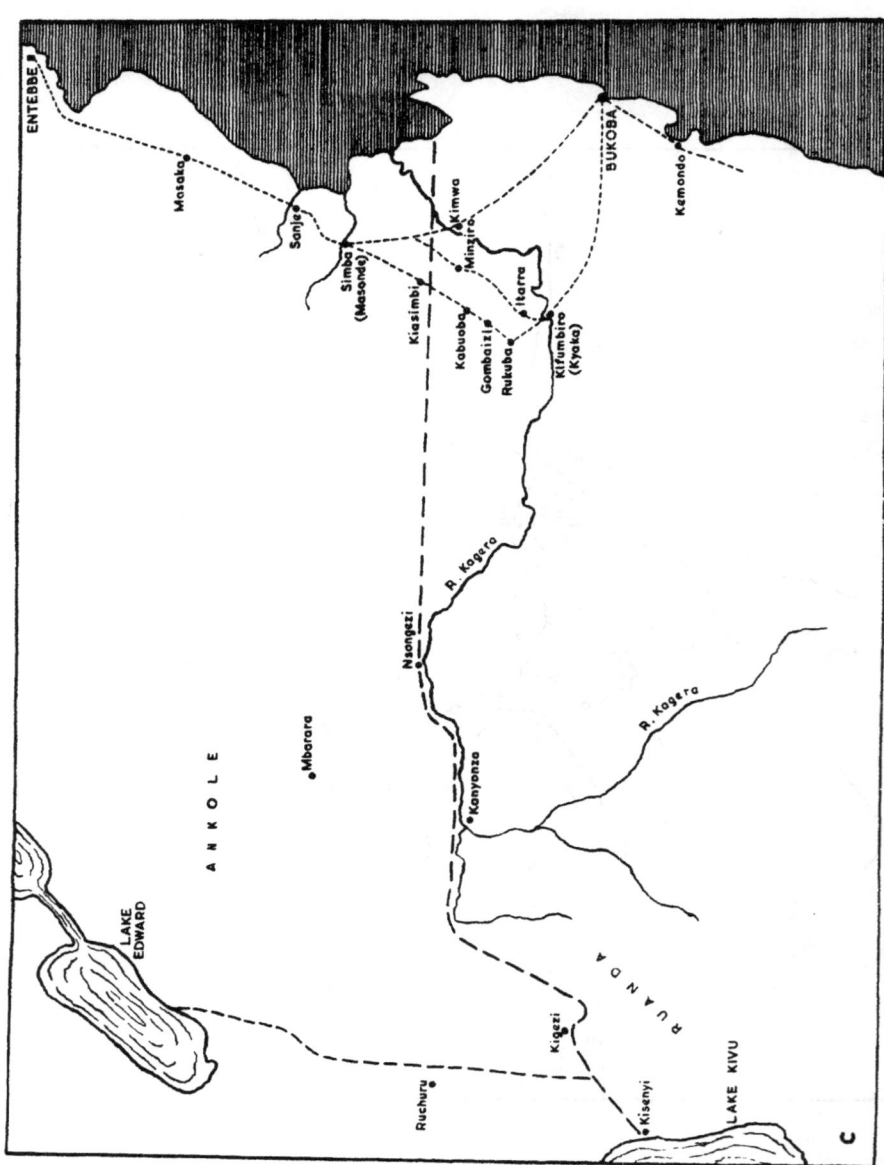

Johnston ordered the establishment of a station in the Ribo Hills, 140 miles north of Eldama Ravine.

There was no proper track to Ribo, and transport had to be by porterage or donkey caravan. Such convoys consume a high proportion of the food they carry, and the general shortage of all kinds of transport meant that a post so far afield had to rely mainly on local resources. The Enjamusi tribe near Lake Baringo had a long tradition of friendship with the British, but the tribes farther north were covertly hostile. Hyde Baker, who was appointed to command the post with a garrison of about 50 armed police, was from the start in constant difficulty over supplies.

In May, 1900, Captain C. E. Bagnall, the Acting Collector, Baringo District, was obliged to march from Eldama and punish the people of the Cheptulel section for their persistent refusal to co-operate with Baker. Silabui, their chief, then promised better behaviour and agreed to supply food in future. But when after Bagnall's departure Baker made several trips to Silabui's village he was met with fresh excuses, though grain was plentiful in the shambas and the crops were being reaped.

Silabui continued nevertheless to protest his friendship. One day a present of honey arrived at the post. Fortunately Baker ate only a little, for it caused him intense agony and vomiting for an hour. A native woman who found and ate the remainder nearly died. This treacherous attempt at poisoning could not be ignored, and Baker, despite his illness, set out with a strong party to arrest the chief. Silabui, guessing his purpose, retired discreetly to the hills behind the village, and sent a conciliatory message, saying that Baker was welcome to cut any of the grain still standing.

As the party had not come equipped for reaping, Baker returned to the fort, where he collapsed that night with a bad attack of fever and dysentery that undoubtedly saved his life. Unable to go himself, he dispatched his sergeant-major next day with 42 police, nearly the entire garrison of the post, armed with rifles, sacks and knives. The men failed to return, and the exact details of their fate have never been discovered. The shamba was found later to have been cut, but no sign of a fight was apparent anywhere near it.

Two days later, while Baker was still in bed, about 700 tribesmen surrounded the post and began driving the cattle from the boma. Baker rushed out to assist his police, and was wounded in the hand by a poisoned arrow. While he was attacking the thieves, others broke into his quarters and looted the store. After that he was virtually besieged, and could only reach his water supply under constant attack.

The garrison was now reduced to ten police and nine porters, with food for fourteen days at the most. Deciding that he could hold out for this period, though there was every sign that the besiegers were well organized and determined, Baker scribbled the appeal quoted above and smuggled two Enjamusi out of the fort by night. A police askari and three Masai brought the message into Eldama on 7th July.

Captain Bagnall, who had only taken up his appointment at Eldama in the previous April, was in no position to assist. He had already warned his superiors that Baker's force was far too small for its purpose and that his rifles were practically useless. Fortunately the situation at Ribo was saved by the timely arrival of a large body of Enjamusi. Meanwhile a series of curt telegrams was passing to and fro between Kampala and the Ravine, responsibility being disclaimed at both ends for Baker's predicament. Bagnall then wrote to Evatt, who had recently arrived in the province for the Nandi expedition, asking for a detachment of Sudanese to relieve Ribo. Evatt replied that he had no troops to spare, but would send some police and Sudanese settlers to Eldama, to be armed there with the rifles of a half-company that had recently been disbanded. Bagnall answered tersely that apart from two Martini-Henrys the only arms in his store were 'old iron, prehistoric Remingtons and Sniders to match . . . relics facetiously termed rifles'. The correspondence was fast becoming acrimonious, but Evatt sent a civil reply and gave orders for the dispatch of arms, ammunition and equipment.

On his recovery Baker was able to visit Eldama for fresh supplies. Bagnall reinforced him with 20 picked men and told him to remain strictly on the defensive for the time being. Baker went back determined to hold his own until a punitive expedition could reach him. He visited Eldama again in September and December, enrolling on the last occasion 29 Sudanese settlers as police for Ribo.

While the third Nandi expedition was in progress, accounts of hostile raids by the Suk and Turkana continued to reach the Ravine. Some reports asserted that the tribesmen were massing in thousands. Late in December Baker sent another urgent appeal for help, saying that the Turkana were preparing to attack the Enjamusi. Jackson, who was then at Eldama, was inclined to think the reports exaggerated, though he admitted that Baker was 'not the man to cry wolf'. It was evident, however, that operations would have to be extended far beyond Silabui's village. The Suk hills are intersected by pleasant streams running through glades of trees to join the Kerio and Weiwei (Kerut) rivers. Though the tribesmen often sow considerable areas with grain they are mainly a pastoral people, living in villages far up the hillsides, and bringing their herds down daily to graze along the river banks.

Rumours of the trouble at Ribo had by this time brought inquiries from home. Johnston replied that he would already have withdrawn the post, but for the 'great value of the countryside', and the entreaties of tribesmen for protection against the turbulent Arab and Swahili settlements. This did not altogether satisfy his superiors at Whitehall, where a minute was attached to the despatch describing the policy as a mistake, and 'one of the results of this constant pushing on'.

The military expedition at last left the Ravine on 9th January, 1901, under the command of Captain E. H. Gorges (Manchester R.) with a strength of five officers, No. 15 Company and a half-company each of Nos. 10 and 12 Companies: 145 rifles in all, with about 500 Masai and 100 Enjamusi auxiliaries. Finding his way through country new to him along the shores of Lake Baringo, Gorges reached Ribo Post by forced marches in eight days, arriving with many of his troops footsore owing to an issue of new boots. His first action was to send back a convoy of

75 donkeys to Eldama for flour, as 1,100 natives were now assembled at Ribo with food reserves barely sufficient for one day. Johnston was expected to visit the area while on tour in the Eastern Province, and Gorges and Baker were anxious to pacify all the tribes between Baringo and the Turkana country before his arrival.

Operations had first to be directed towards obtaining a supply of food. On 19th January the column marched across the River Kerio and dividing into two parties, attacked the Cheptulel on the surrounding heights. After a hard day clambering over the hills, 50 villages had been raided, but the only captures were 700 goats, as the cattle had all been removed to the grazing grounds down the river. Next day the column returned to Ribo, cutting ripe *mtama* from the shambas on the way. Enough food was thus collected for ten days' supply, and more was secured by a smaller raiding party on the following day.

The next move was made in two columns towards the River Weiwei (Kerut). This time resistance stiffened. Each night the tribesmen circled the heights above the boma in the hope of recovering the captured stock, and the need for guards reduced the number of troops available for operations. Baker pushed on to the river with a small party, but again found that the cattle had been moved far out on the plains.

Operations were next extended to the Kivas (Kapas) valley, where more stock was captured. The country was difficult; progress was slow and strongly contested. Several men were wounded by flights of poisoned arrows, fired by unseen marksmen among the rocks and bushes. The column then retired to Ribo, cutting more ripe *mtama* on the way.

In spite of these operations, the Cheptulel were unsubdued and made no overtures for peace. Gorges thought they were afraid to approach for fear of his Masai auxiliaries. During the first two weeks of February he turned his attention to the Suk villages on the eastern slopes of the Elgeyo escarpment, covering a large area where water was scarce and the terrain difficult and rough.

While the expedition was in progress news reached Uganda that a convention was to be made with Abyssinia, securing to the Protectorate all the west and part of the northern shores of Lake Rudolf. Johnston arrived at Eldama in February, and after discussing the matter with Jackson, decided to withdraw from the post at Ribo. Orders were accordingly issued that as soon as exemplary punishment had been inflicted on the Cheptulel, Ribo was to be abandoned and a station established instead near Lake Baringo, to protect the Enjamusi from reprisals. By the time he was informed of this Gorges had accounted for 130 tribesmen and captured 520 head of cattle, 80 donkeys and about 10,000 sheep and goats. He and Baker agreed that this punishment was sufficient. Ribo Post was abandoned and set on fire, and the expedition marched back to Lake Baringo, where the Masai and Enjamusi were allotted their share of the spoils. While the distribution was proceeding a deputation of Suk chiefs arrived. They were escorted back to the Ravine, which was reached again on 5th March. Johnston then made a ten-day trip to Baringo and followed this with a tour of the Elgon district before returning to Eldama in May *en route* for England.

The history of the Uganda Rifles is closely bound up with that of the Sudanese refugees. These trained and able soldiers were the foundation on which the Uganda Rifles (and to some extent the East Africa Rifles) was built. Faced by ten stormy years of incessant campaigning within their own territory, the armed forces of Uganda were never called upon for service abroad. They had the best recruiting material ready to hand, and as local commitments were the heaviest, the Uganda Rifles became the largest of the original units. During the next twelve years the regiment's successor, the 4th Battalion of the King's African Rifles, was called upon to continue the work of establishing and maintaining order in the remoter provinces of the Protectorate.

CHAPTER 4

The East Africa Rifles

(i) *The Armed Forces of the Imperial British East Africa Company, 1888-95.* Map 4.

THROUGHOUT its existence, the Imperial British East Africa Company made no comprehensive effort to organize proper forces for the maintenance of its authority. At the end of the Company's rule, it was described by the official who inherited its responsibilities in East Africa as 'an European administration . . . with no visible force at its back'.[1] The Company was formed primarily as a trading venture, but became vested through the turn of events with political and administrative functions that were beyond its capacity and too great for its financial resources. Sir William Mackinnon was aware from the start of the need for troops or armed police, but the scale on which they would be required seems never to have been realized. The Company's armed forces therefore developed into a curious hotch-potch derived from a number of sources, differing widely in quality, with no common status, and no central control.

The rulers of Zanzibar had relied in the past on mercenaries drawn from the Persian and Baluchi coasts. At the end of Majid's reign they numbered some 2,750 men, of whom about 2,000 were stationed at Zanzibar and the rest at Lamu and Mombasa. Small reliance could be placed upon these men, whose main duty was the provision of palace guards. When Sir John Kirk secured the co-operation of Sultan Barghash in the suppression of the slave trade, he realized that the new regulations could not be enforced without the help of land forces under European control to supplement the British naval patrols. In 1877 Lieutenant Lloyd Mathews, R.N.,[2] who was serving in H.M.S. *London* on the anti-slavery patrol, raised about 300 Zanzibaris for this purpose, and in 1878 was given leave to serve under the Sultan as Brigadier-General in command of the new army. Within another year Mathews' force numbered 500 men, armed with Snider rifles[3] and bayonets. By 1880 he had 1,300 men under his command. In 1882 these troops saw action on the mainland

---

[1] Sir A. Hardinge, *A Diplomatist in the East,* p. 164.

[2] Later Sir Lloyd Mathews, First Minister to the Sultan, 1891-1901.

[3] The Snider rifle had been in use in the British Army since 1867. Four years later it was superseded by the Martini-Henry, which was followed in its turn in 1888 by the bolt-action .303 Lee-Metford. The Lee-Enfield, employing an improved system of rifling to counteract the erosive effects of cordite charges, was introduced in 1893. A considerable time-lag elapsed in each case before the general introduction of these rifles to eastern Africa. The single loading .303 Martini-Metford rifle was still in use by the K.A.R. in Nyasaland in 1911.

against the chief Mbaruk of Gasi, who had defied the Sultan's authority. Mbaruk's stronghold at Mwele, situated on a wooded ridge 1,500 feet high, was stormed and 400 prisoners were captured.

So long as these troops were properly led they proved fairly efficient, but discipline suffered heavily when Mathews went to England on long leave. After the reorganization of the Zanzibar Government in 1891 he was appointed First Minister to the Sultan and his place as 'General' was taken by Captain G. P. Hatch (Wilts. R.), an officer who had previously seen service in Afghanistan and Egypt. The force then numbered 860 men, organized in 12 companies each of 63 all ranks with a band and drums in addition.

Before leaving on his mission to Uganda, Portal wrote in glowing terms of the improvement effected by Hatch, who had then been in command of the troops and police for fourteen months. Hatch had converted them from 'a slipshod, half-clothed and half-drilled collection of so-called "soldiers" into a well-disciplined, well-dressed and trustworthy force . . . able to place 200 drilled and disciplined men at the service of Her Majesty's Government for the purpose of the Uganda Commission'.[1] Once the expedition started, however, Portal rapidly revised his opinion, and was glad enough to return most of the Zanzibaris to the coast as soon as he had recruited Sudanese in Uganda to replace them.

The Company frequently sought the assistance of the Sultan's mercenaries for maintaining order in the coastal strip. These Arab troops were known to the Swahili as 'Viroboto' (fleas), supposedly on account of their strange antics when dancing. Their reputation was not high, for without European supervision, which the Company was rarely able to provide, they proved arrogant and indisciplined. At Zanzibar, however, they could give a spectacular display, marching off parade with a peculiar trick of imparting a glittering quiver to the edges of their double-bladed swords that no other troops seemed able to imitate.

At first Sir William Mackinnon considered seriously the possibility of recruiting outside East Africa. All available information indicated that local enlistment would be impossible in the early stages of the Company's rule, and it was suggested that suitable troops might be found in Sierra Leone or Zululand. Mackinnon thought that the cost of transporting men from West Africa was too high, and that the employment of Zulus was impracticable and undesirable. He therefore sought permission through the Foreign Office to recruit instead 'volunteers from the Punjab for police purposes'. The Secretary of State for India was opposed to recruitment in the Punjab, but raised no objection to it elsewhere in India. Permission was restricted later to the neighbourhood of Delhi. This police force was in effect the first Indian Contingent to be raised for East Africa.

When serious trouble occurred in areas accessible from the coast, the Company always sought naval assistance. The Anglo-German Agreement of 1890 had hardly been signed before need arose for a punitive expedition. Ahmad bin Fumo Luti, the Sultan of Witu, of whom previous

---

[1] Portal to Rosebery, 28.xii.92.

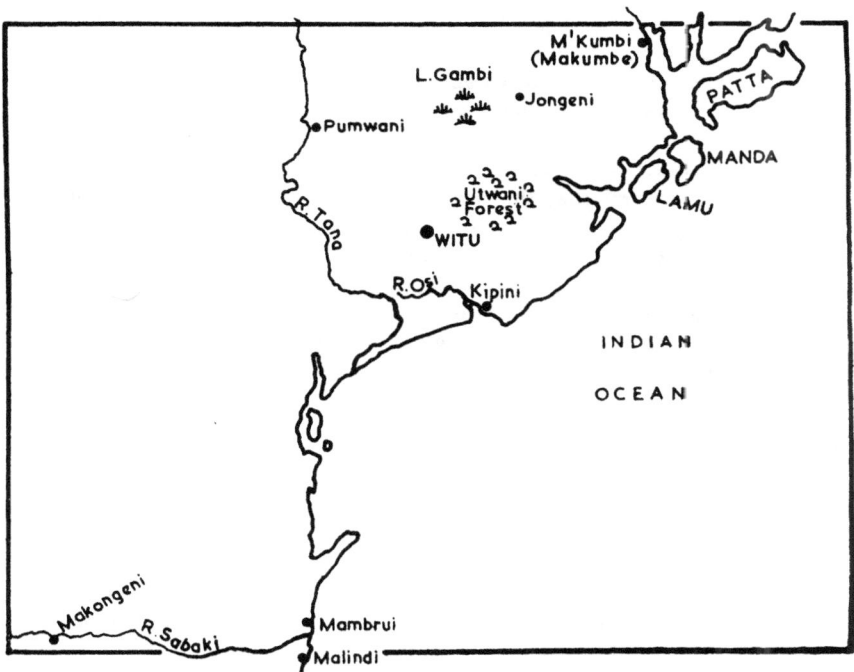

4. The Witu District

mention has been made, was succeeded in 1887 by Fumo Bakari. A German syndicate was bent on opening a timber concession in the Witu forests, and in August, 1890, Herr Kuntzel and ten mechanics arrived to begin operations. Fumo Bakari considered that the Germans had abandoned him to British domination, and refused Kuntzel permission. The latter was a man of violent temper, and within a few hours of his arrival at Witu had provoked an attack that resulted in the death of all but one of the party. The German Government held Britain responsible, and demanded that the outrage should be avenged. Such a task was quite beyond the Company's own resources.

Late in October Admiral E. R. Fremantle landed several field guns and a naval force of 800 men, which was joined by 150 of the Company's armed Indian police under Captain A. F. Eric Smith (Life Gds.). On the march to Witu the force was attacked, but Fumo Bakari's men were easily routed. Witu was bombarded and set on fire, and the rebels withdrew into the forests to the north. Had it been realized in Europe that the place was merely a stockaded native village situated in a dense forest, the matter might never have been treated so seriously.

In March, 1891, the Company took over the administration of Witu and garrisoned the area with Indian police. Their three years' contract was due to expire on 1st June, 1893, and none of the men was willing to renew his service. A. S. Rogers, who administered the district north of the Tana and after the declaration of the protectorate became sub-commissioner and resident at Witu, had the highest opinion of these men and said that 100 sepoys would be of more value to him than three or four times the number of Swahilis. The police finally agreed to remain until the end of July, and Rogers estimated that 400 men would be needed to replace them at Witu and the coastal ports: 100 at Mombasa, 100 at Kismayu, 60 at Witu, 60 at Makumbe, 40 at Lamu, 18 at Malindi, and the remainder to act as reliefs.

The Company felt that the drain on its military resources caused by the need to garrison the Protectorate of Witu was an obligation that should be borne by H.M. Government. Berkeley, who was then Acting Secretary of the Company in London, accordingly informed the Foreign Office that when the Indian police were withdrawn the Company did not propose to replace them. Owing to the depredations of Fumo Amari, who had succeeded his brother at Witu, the Company had been obliged to employ, in addition to the police, 100 Viroboto from Zanzibar, 50 irregulars from Mombasa, 20 locally enlisted askaris, and 117 troops from Kismayu and Gobwen, where, owing to the attitude of the Somalis, a larger garrison was urgently needed. The Foreign Office replied that the Indian police had been raised for service in the Company's territories generally and not specifically for Witu, but the Company adhered to its decision and withdrew from administration of the coast between the River Tana and Jubaland on 31st July, 1893. It was announced that the Sultan of Zanzibar had accepted responsibility, though the district was not to be incorporated in his dominions.

The declaration of the Sultan's authority over Witu was followed immediately by an expedition against Fumo Amari, who was now openly defiant and refused to meet the British Consul-General and General Mathews when they visited Witu to proclaim the new order. Rogers had already issued a warning that Amari's soldiery would overrun the district unless troops were sent to replace the Indian police, and Hatch arrived with 125 Zanzibar troops and 50 Sudanese, enlisted at Mombasa. Amari possessed two large fortified villages, Pumwani and Jongeni, situated at the forest edge. Rogers had already tried and failed to enter these strongholds with the Company's police. On the 6th August a naval force of four companies of seamen and one of marines, with 40 Sudanese and 20 Zanzibaris under Hatch, attacked Pumwani with a field gun and war rockets, blowing up the huge gate of timber piles interlocked with cross-beams, and burning the town.

Similar action was taken against Jongeni, and a few weeks later, following renewed activity by the rebels, a further expedition once more destroyed Pumwani, which had been partially rebuilt, and several other villages.

A force of 115 Zanzibaris and 50 Sudanese, with a few Arab irregulars, was left to garrison the district. In October, when Captain Hatch put forward a scheme for raising the Zanzibar police to 250 men and reducing the troops to the same figure, reorganized in five companies of 50 each, he was reminded by the First Minister that his scheme took no account of Witu, where 'at least 100 good troops' would be needed, to say nothing of the garrisons of the ports. The Sultan's responsibility lasted until the flag of the East Africa Protectorate was raised in July,

1895. Omar bin Hamid, a loyal member of the same dynasty, was then installed as ruler of Witu, and the presence of a garrison at Lamu was sufficient to ensure the tranquillity of a region formerly the most turbulent on the entire coast.

Overshadowed by the course of events in Uganda, East Africa west of the coastal strip lay practically untouched throughout the early years of the Company's administration. There were stations at Ndi, Machakos and Fort Smith, and the country was divided into districts, each under a district superintendent responsible to the Chief Administrator, but for practical purposes the whole vast area was simply the territory crossed by the 'English Road'. For 820 miles between the coast and Kampala the caravan track twisted inland, sometimes a thorny tunnel through the high, colourless bush; sometimes a beaten footway over the great grass plains; occasionally a cleared, straight earth road in the neighbourhood of a settled station; crossing the foodless valley of the Rift, where all supplies had to be carried; and at last climbing into the cold mists of the rain forests along the Mau escarpment to descend through Kabaras to the Kavirondo villages and the fertile country bordering the Lake. Along this route the caravans crept continually to and fro, averaging ninety days for the single journey,[1] while the Wakamba and Masai mail-runners passed and repassed on their fast stages between Mombasa and the busy station at Eldama Ravine, where they linked with the Baganda runners from Kampala.

For the protection of these caravans the Company relied mainly on undrilled, armed Swahilis, usually porters considered more reliable than their fellows. These askaris received an extra two rupees per month and were allotted at the rate of one for every 10-15 porters. At first the Company possessed no rifles, and the men carried old-fashioned muzzle-loading cap guns. Jackson pressed for Snider carbines when organizing his first expedition to the interior, on the ground that they were less wasteful of ammunition, as powder and caps were often spoilt by damp. Desertions on safari were numerous and sometimes wholesale. When this happened the firearms always vanished with the men, and this fact, coupled with the arms traffic of the Arab and Swahili traders, whose operations were actually encouraged by the Company in the early stages,[2] helped to maintain a widespread distribution of arms that later cost the K.A.R. many a toilsome punitive expedition, even up to the time of the 1914-18 war.

The natural routes to the interior appeared to lie along the courses of the rivers Tana and Sabaki. Lugard's first task in East Africa was to explore the Sabaki and establish a series of posts, manned by Viroboto, on the way to Machako's, then the Company's farthest station inland. But the unhealthiness of the river valley soon caused it to be abandoned in favour of the more direct route from Mombasa, even though this meant crossing the Taru Desert. In 1890 the post at Machako's was manned by one European and a dozen men. Lugard built another post beyond it at Dagoretti, where he left George Wilson and 40 men. The

[1] Caravan Table of Times and Distances. Mombasa to Mengo, 2.ii.93. F.O.2, 57.
[2] Jackson, *Early Days in East Africa*. p. 159.

Kikuyu proved hostile and Wilson had to fight his way out. A second fort, on a spur about nine miles outside the forest, was then built by Captain Smith. Fort Smith was of much stronger construction, with a stockade, deep ditch and barbed wire boma, and contained the first two buildings in the country to be made of burnt brick. During the next few years the garrison of Fort Smith was besieged on several occasions, and took part in a number of retaliatory raids against the Kikuyu.

With the exception of the well-run station at Machako's, Portal was surprised and horrified at the condition of the Company's posts at the time of his visit to Uganda in 1893; the mud house at Tsavo, run by a half-bred Portuguese youth who was more hindered than helped by his dozen Arab irregulars; the hut at Nzoi, where an old Swahili and a boy protected the stores of food; and the precarious existence maintained by the troops at Fort Smith. Even before he completed the journey he wrote home in scathing terms of the Company's administration in East Africa, saying that it was 'difficult to be too severe' over their failure to make roads and organize transport. In due course the Company replied with a long and vehement rejection of Portal's criticisms, but in his report and recommendations to the Government Portal made it clear that he saw no future for the Company as the administrative authority in East Africa, though he paid some tribute to the work it had accomplished in other ways.

The earliest record preserved at Eldama Ravine was a camp diary written by de Silva, a well-known caravan leader in the days when traffic along the English Road, as yet unrelieved by the railway, was rapidly growing. The diary begins with the assembly on the mainland near Mombasa:

> 'Camp Bandarini, 16 October, 1894. Drums beat at 6 a.m. Mustered men and called role [sic]. Gave posho for 12 days, the Porters getting one kebaba each, askaris $1\frac{1}{2}$ and headman 2 kebabas . . . Distributed suits to porters and askaris, together with Snider carbines and 10 rounds ammunition each. The headmen and Nubian askaris received each a Martini Henri rifle and 20 rounds ammunition. Put all Government loads in a gunney bag sewed up and roped outside and began making lots of 15 each and numbering them. . . . Finished numbering loads, called askaris and set watch for the night. Dressed a man's ulcer.'

The caravan started next day, carrying four Hotchkiss guns for Colvile's operations in Bunyoro. These weapons were so heavy that several of the porters were ruptured, and the difficulty was not solved until the guns were mounted on wheels with improvised wooden axles. As the caravan proceeded the diary records a daily toll of dysentery, fever, 'strained chests', and ulcerated feet, treated at the end of each day's march with lavish doses of chlorodyne, laudanum, quinine, cough mixture, and sulphate of zinc. At places where food was purchasable strings of coloured beads were issued to the men—two strings to a porter, three to an askari or personal boy, four to a headman and six to the chief headman. When the caravan reached the Rift Valley the rains had flooded the rivers and the poles and ropes had to be taken from the improvised gun-carriages to bridge the swollen streams. By now sickness and death had so depleted the porters that 24 Wanyamwezi were commandeered from a coast-bound caravan to get the guns forward. They reached Kampala covered with rust and dirt, but were cleaned and used by Ternan on his first operations against Kabarega. Ternan had them carried to Mruli in parts slung on poles; when afterwards they were assembled, it took 200 men to drag each gun through the swamps.

For the protection of each caravan, *ad hoc* arrangements were the rule; similarly the defence of up-country stations was often arranged locally. John Ainsworth, the Company's representative at Machako's, was much troubled during the early years with attacks on caravans, and undertook many little expeditions with his own resources. In March, 1894, he asked permission to form a native militia of his own from the Wakamba as a protection against the hostility of the Masai and Kikuyu, which had made the situation at Machako's 'a very near thing'.[1] The Company agreed, provided Ainsworth refrained from joining in purely tribal wars. Three months later he sent a good account of his volunteers, who had been armed with rifles and bayonets.

Excellent as were many of the pioneers in its employ, the Company was neither equipped nor financed for so difficult an undertaking as had fallen to its lot, and it became clear that its administration must be brought to a close. In June, 1894, the Directors intimated their willingness to negotiate the surrender of their rights. The Foreign Office put forward its proposals for compensation in the following November. After prolonged negotiations it was agreed that on termination of the Charter the Company's rights should be acquired for £250,000.

Arthur Hardinge,[2] the British Agent and Consul-General at Zanzibar, notified the Foreign Office early in March, 1895, that he was prepared to take over East Africa at an early date, and that he would retain most of the Company's employees. On 15th June it was announced that a British Protectorate would be declared over the area from which the Company was about to withdraw. The transfer was made effective from 1st July, 1895. Hardinge made the announcement at a special baraza in the presence of the Liwali and other Arab and Swahili notables summoned at Mombasa on that date. Similar declarations were made later at Kismayu and Witu.

The coastal strip did not revert to the Sultan. On payment of £11,000 annual rent, plus interest on the sum of £200,000 (which had been paid by the German Government in 1890 for the Sultan's possessions south of the Umba, and was now made over to the Company for the surrender of its concessions), the coastal strip was incorporated in the new Protectorate, which included all East African territory under British influence with the exception of Zanzibar, Pemba and Uganda. The new Protectorate was divided into four provinces, each under a sub-commissioner, and each province was subdivided into districts administered by district

---

[1] Ainsworth to Administrator, Mombasa, 31.iii.94. F.O.2, 74.
[2] Later Sir Arthur Hardinge, Commissioner and Consul-General, East Africa Protectorate, 1896-1900.

officers and their assistants. In addition to his existing appointment, Hardinge assumed also that of H.M. Commissioner for the East Africa Protectorate. From then until he relinquished his appointment in October, 1900, he was obliged to spend most of his time on the mainland, leaving affairs at Zanzibar to the Consul, Basil Cave.[1]

(ii) *The Organization of the East Africa Rifles, 1895-1901.* Maps 5 and 6.

In 1895 the Imperial British East Africa Company's miscellaneous collection of troops numbered 866 men, disposed as follows: 415 at Mombasa and in the coastal province of Seyyidieh; 176 in Ukamba; 180 in Tanaland, and 95 in Jubaland. Of these troops, 255 were Sudanese. Hardinge thought that about 1,000 men would be needed to garrison the new Protectorate, and suggested Captain Hatch as Commandant, to be assisted by two other English officers, one to command at Kismayu and one in Ukamba. From a military viewpoint the transfer of authority was made at an awkward moment, for the Mazrui Rebellion, the course of which is described in the following section, was in progress and full reorganization had to be postponed for some time. It was decided, however, to create at last a single unit, to be known as the East Africa Rifles, with headquarters at Mombasa, where Fort Jesus was converted to a barracks, military store and central gaol.[2]

Hatch was appointed Commandant of the new regiment on 11th September, 1895. The second-in-command was Captain F. E. Lawrence (Rifle Brigade), who was killed soon afterwards in the Mazrui operations and succeeded by Captain E. G. Harrison (West Yorks. R.). Hatch, who at the time of his appointment was in England on leave, suggested that in view of the troubled state of the coast 300 trained troops from a Punjabi regiment should be sent to East Africa. In August, 1895, the Treasury sanctioned an establishment of two British officers, 300 Punjabis, 100 Sudanese (raised later to 250), 300 Swahilis and a 'mixed force' of 200 men. The Government of India was asked to provide temporarily 15 trained gunners and a few hospital attendants.

The Protectorate was divided into three military districts. The first comprised the administrative provinces of Seyyidieh and Tanaland, and was commanded by Hatch in person. It was garrisoned by the Indian Contingent under Captain W. C. Barratt (1st Sikh Inf.) and Lieutenant T. E. Scott (3rd Sikh Inf.), and by about 400 Swahili and Sudanese. About 350 of these troops were stationed at Mombasa and the rest on or near the coast, with a few up the River Tana and an Indian garrison at Taveta.

The Second Military District, comprising the Province of Ukamba, was the scene of several minor expeditions during the time of the East

[1] Later Sir Basil Cave, K.C.M.G., C.B.
[2] The haphazard methods of the I.B.E.A. military policy dogged the new battalion for many years. As late as 1910 the Inspector-General wrote in his Report on 3 K.A.R.: 'This Battalion has never had a fair chance of being thoroughly trained and organized. From the time of its formation in 1895 it has constantly been experimented on. It was formed originally of ready-made but really untrained soldiers.' (C.O. 534. 12.)

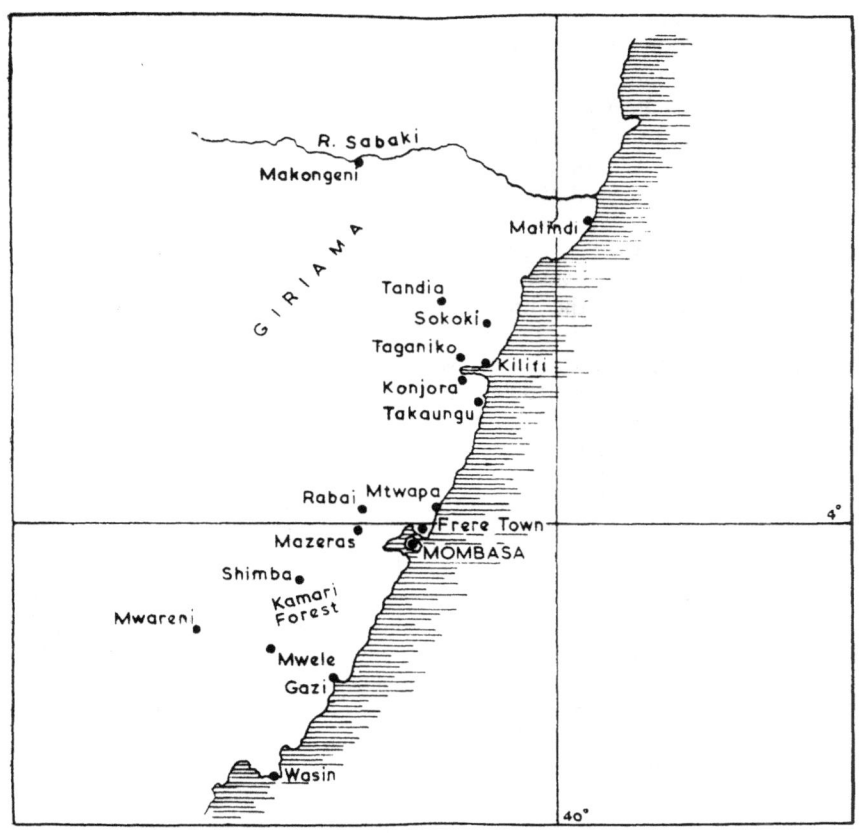

5. British East Africa, Coastal Area

Africa Rifles. In May, 1896, Captain Harrison was ordered to Machako's in command, with a company of 125 Sudanese. To check the Wakamba propensity for acquiring slaves, police posts had been set up in the Ulu area in July, 1895. In November the Wakamba attacked them and killed a number of police. Ainsworth, who admitted that this piece of treachery had taken him by surprise, organized an expedition of 130 Swahili askaris and porters, 20 of his new Wakamba recruits, and 800 Masai. Over 500 cattle and 1,000 goats were taken, and the rebel villages were burnt. Harrison's company settled soon afterwards into temporary quarters on the site of the old police fort at Kanjalu until barracks could be built at Machako's. The mere presence of his troops was sufficient to exact a fine from the Wakamba chiefs, though further expeditions against the tribe were needed during the next year or so, in the course of which the garrison lost five men killed and 14 wounded.

The civil province of Jubaland formed the Third Military District. Until a European officer became available the garrison of nearly 300 Sudanese, Somalis and Wagosha was commanded by Mr. C. de C. Middleton, the Assistant District Officer at Kismayu, who had a Sudanese officer to assist him. With the exception of a few men in the Gosha district, all troops were stationed near the coast.

Sir Arthur Hardinge submitted his first report on the condition and progress of the Protectorate on 20th July, 1897, i.e. two months before the outbreak of the Sudanese mutiny in Uganda. His forces then numbered 289 Indians (nominally a contingent of 300), 256 Sudanese, 368 Swahilis, 16 Arabs and 191 Somalis and Wagosha, totalling 1,120 men, with four British officers and three retired officers engaged in whole or part-time duty with the regiment. Regular barrack accommodation was available at Mombasa and Lamu forts for African troops; the Indian Contingent occupied the lines built by the 24th Bombay Infantry on Mombasa Island during the Mazrui Rebellion, hutted accommodation existed at Witu, Port Durnford, Kismayu, Machako's and Kikuyu, and new barracks were constructed at Malindi, Wasin and Ngongo Bagas (Fort Elvira). The pay of the Indian sepoys was Rs18 per month, and of the African askaris Rs16. Hardinge found the Sudanese 'born soldiers', but inclined to drunkenness, which sometimes resulted in violence. The Swahilis, on the other hand, though 'remarkably sober', he thought deficient in military instinct and spirit, though improving daily.[1]

There is no doubt that conditions of service, pay and accommodation made life much easier in the East Africa Rifles than in the Uganda Rifles. After the Mazrui Rebellion the Protectorate, with the exception of the Jubaland Province, was comparatively peaceful, while in Uganda campaigning was practically continuous. The Sudanese Mutiny therefore struck no answering spark in East Africa. The part played by the East Africa Rifles in the mutiny has already been described. Once the serious nature of the situation in Uganda was realized, the regiment was not long in responding. In November, 1897, Hardinge went up to Eldama Ravine. Feeling that the loyalty of the half-company of Uganda Rifles at Naivasha was doubtful, he transferred it to Machako's and sent Harrison to Uganda with 135 men. After a march of 380 miles, covered in nineteen days, Harrison reached the scene of action with 80 men. By the end of January, 1898, four officers and nearly 400 Indian and Sudanese troops from East Africa were in Uganda, and more troops were on the way. Transport difficulties made movement slow, but the partly built railway assisted to capacity and carried nearly 29,000 troops and porters to points beyond Voi during 1898.[2] The regiment lost one officer and 17 native officers and men killed, and one officer and 16 other ranks wounded during the operations in Uganda.

After the suppression of the Mutiny the East Africa Rifles, like the Uganda Rifles, underwent reorganization. The War Office, always anxious to avoid commitment in the military affairs of the African protectorates, confined itself to commenting in guarded terms on the schemes put forward. In these circumstances reconstruction came from within the regiment, and did not always originate with the Comman-

---

[1] *Report by Sir A. Hardinge on the E.A.P. from Establishment to 20th July, 1897.* Africa No. 7 (1897) (C. 8683), p. 33, LX, 199.

[2] M. F. Hill, *Permanent Way,* p. 189.

dant. Before embarking for England on leave, Harrison forwarded a report and recommendations regarding the regiment's future. His chief point was the difficulty of training African troops who were always split into a number of widely-separated garrisons, most of them under native officers and N.C.Os. He proposed that there should be one British officer to every 100 men; that the regiment should become a battalion 1,000 strong, with six companies of Sudanese and four of Swahilis, each of 100 rank and file; and that troops should be stationed only at Mombasa, Machako's, Tanaland and Kismayu, leaving all other stations to be manned by police. The police force at that time consisted only of two British officers and 77 N.C.Os. and men, stationed on Mombasa Island and the adjacent mainland. In the rest of the territory, police work was performed by African 'station askaris', who wore a khaki uniform not unlike that of the East Africa Rifles, instead of the ordinary police uniform of blue. Provided these police and station askaris took over all stations other than those listed above, Harrison thought that with a proper establishment of British officers the East Africa Rifles could dispense with the Indian Contingent. Hardinge approved these proposals and forwarded them to the Foreign Office, adding that some of the Sudanese troops in Uganda might be better employed in Jubaland, away from their old associations.

The revised establishment authorized at the end of 1898 comprised five Sudanese and three Swahili companies, rather less than Harrison's proposal. The strength of the companies was 110 rank and file, making a battalion 880 strong, with 19 British officers. Jubaland, garrisoned by three Sudanese companies, was an important and practically independent commitment and became a major's command. Two companies were based on Mombasa, two were stationed in Ukamba, and one in Tanaland. When the term of the Indian Contingent expired in October, 1900, it was not replaced, though Hardinge wrote in the highest terms of the exemplary conduct of these troops throughout their service in East Africa. A fourth Swahili company of 120 men was authorized instead, raising the strength of the regiment to 1,000 rifles.

From time to time further trouble had been experienced with the Kikuyu, and in September, 1901, an expedition was sent against the Maruka section, who had murdered a party of mail-runners and stolen their weapons. Captain Harrison was in command, with a force of one officer and 88 askaris, including 20 newly-enlisted Masai. A fine of 55 head of cattle and 500 sheep and goats was levied, and the Maruka were ordered to provide 100 men for a month's work on the roads. The Mbirri area was then coming under effective administration, and during the expedition Harrison reconnoitred a road route which he recommended for permanent adoption.

After the Ogaden campaign of 1901, Hatch pressed for an increase in establishment to 1,500 men, on the ground that such sudden emergencies showed the need for a mobile reserve. The provincial civil and military headquarters of the Ukamba Province had moved to Nairobi on the railway in 1899, and Hatch thought this a suitable location for such a reserve. His request for an increase was not granted, but the garrison of Ukamba was raised to four companies, two Sudanese and two mixed Swahili and Masai, with outstations at Machako's, Mbirri and Taveta. Fifty Masai had been recruited to form a Masai company. Death, desertion and sickness rapidly thinned the number to 18, but Captain A. G. G Sharp, who now commanded the Ukamba garrison, thought the Masai intelligent, generally well behaved and braver than the Swahili, and obtained leave for fresh enlistments. Slit and distended ears were not allowed with military uniform, so the Masai recruits tucked up their trailing lobes and twisted them round their ears. Hardinge thought the enlistment of Masai an interesting experiment, though they could hardly be used in their own country and were prone to home-sickness elsewhere. But some drawback attached to every race: the Indian troops needed a special diet; the large families of the Sudanese were a perpetual nuisance; and the Swahili were but moderate soldiers, though they showed some promise as policemen.

During its brief history of six and a half years the East Africa Rifles, besides service in Uganda during the Mutiny, took part in three campaigns. The first was against the rebel Mbaruk of Takaungu, and the others against the Ogaden Somali in Jubaland.

(iii) *The Mazrui Rebellion, 1895-96.* Map 5.

The most prominent Arab tribe in East Africa, paramount on the coast for very many years, was the Mazrui. When Mombasa finally capitulated to the Muscat Arabs in 1837, the tribe had split into two divisions, the senior or Beni Othman line at Gasi, and the younger or Beni Zaher branch at Takaungu, respectively thirty miles south and north of Mombasa. The suzerainty exercised by the Sultan of Zanzibar had perforce been light, and the Imperial British East Africa Company's policy was directed to securing the co-operation of influential Arab families. This policy was not wholly successful, as it was often interpreted as weakness, but old Mbaruk of Gasi, the head of the Mazrui, who had given the Sultan a great deal of trouble in the past, was now becoming reconciled to a peaceful old age. He received a subsidy from the Company and in return was under the obligation to furnish armed men on request, a commitment that he had been required to honour on two occasions.[1]

The anti-slavery laws, passed at Zanzibar under British pressure, did not increase Arab confidence in the Company's intentions. When Sheikh Salim of Takaungu died in February, 1895, and a dispute arose over his successor, the Company recognized his son Rashid instead of his nephew Mbaruk, as being the better disposed towards Europeans. This action may not have been wise, though Mbaruk and his friends at first agreed to recognize Rashid. Soon afterwards Mbaruk retired a few miles inland to Konjora, where he seized a stock of arms and ammunition left by the late Sheikh, and gathered together some 1,500 armed followers.

[1] The Company's lack of armed forces did much to weaken its authority with the Arab element on the coast. See C. W. Hobley, *Kenya from Chartered Company to Crown Colony,* p. 71.

Sir Arthur Hardinge, then preparing to take over the mainland in addition to his responsibilities at Zanzibar, advised the Foreign Office on 1st May, 1895, that trouble was brewing at Takaungu. After consulting Mathews and the Senior Naval Officer he gave his opinion that the means at his disposal were quite sufficient to deal with the situation. This premature opinion showed small realization of the difficulties likely to arise if the trouble were not promptly settled. The Company's troops were few and scattered, and the Zanzibar forces, the only ones of which Hardinge could have had much first-hand knowledge, were neither sufficiently large nor well enough trained in field operations to be of much value. At this time the Sultan's 'army' numbered two European officers, 29 native officers, and 513 rank and file, organized in a battalion of eight companies. As there were no proper barracks at Zanzibar the troops were allowed to live in the town, and their principal duties consisted of a drill parade lasting two hours every morning except Thursdays (when they washed their best white uniforms), and Fridays, when they marched to the Palace in the mornings to form a guard of honour for the Sultan's baraza, and again in the afternoon to salute His Highness and drill for half an hour in the square.

At the request of the Company's Administrator a warship was dispatched to Kilifi and Sir Arthur Hardinge prepared to negotiate. He reached Takaungu on 13th June, but Mbaruk refused to meet him. A display of force seemed necessary, so Hardinge marched on Konjora with 310 seamen, 50 marines, 54 Sudanese troops and 160 Zanzibari regulars. Mbaruk retired to the hills nearby. Two of his armed retainers passed through the village, and in an effort to stop them a rifle went off accidentally. Mbaruk's men then opened fire from the surrounding hillsides, thus committing an act of open rebellion and ending all hope of immediate settlement.

On 18th June Mbaruk fled north to the Sokoki forest, while his brother Aziz looted the village of Tanganiko. Hardinge's expedition reached the village two days later and built a strong stockade nearby, manned by 100 Zanzibaris under Captain A. E. Raikes (Wilts. R.). Mbaruk was outlawed, and escaped south to join his kinsman, old Mbaruk of Gasi. This was the situation when the Company surrendered its Charter and Hardinge went to Mombasa to assume control on behalf of the British Government. He was determined to take effective steps to destroy 'once for all the independent position of the chiefs of the Mazrui tribe in the district of Takaungu'. As the naval forces at his disposal could not be employed permanently on land, he began recruiting a 'native troop' of 300 men to stamp out all disturbances, intending to incorporate them later in the general forces of the new Protectorate.[1]

Hardinge now approached Mbaruk of Gasi to demand the surrender of his relative. The old Sheikh was in an embarrassing position and tried to temporize. Hardinge told Mbaruk that if he could not effect the arrest himself, he would send government troops to assist.

On 8th July Aziz made a night attack on Takaungu and the military

---

[1] Hardinge to F.O., 13.vi.95.

cantonments with over 300 rebels. Raikes defended the post with 138 Zanzibaris, who fought surprisingly well. Aziz was repelled and fled south to join his brother at Gasi. Old Mbaruk promised Hardinge not to oppose the arrest of the rebels, which was as far as he would go. The latter, however, decided not to wait and fled inland to Mwele. Mbaruk of Gasi, forced to make a decision, elected to go with them.

Towards the end of July Hardinge and Admiral H. H. Rawson marched to Gasi with a naval force of 309 men, accompanied by 70 Sudanese. Gasi was found deserted and a Sudanese garrison was left in occupation. On learning this news old Mbaruk ordered an attack on the frontier town of Vanga, which was sacked and burnt by his men. Rawson telegraphed home to recommend strong action, and on obtaining sanction set out from Kilindini with a naval force in two divisions (220 seamen and 84 marines), 60 Sudanese, and 50 Zanzibaris, with a long train of porters carrying ammunition, gunpowder, four maxim guns and a supply of war rockets. While these troops were marching on Mwele, Gasi was reinforced by sea with 100 Zanzibaris under Raikes, who was instructed to make a demonstration against Mwele. The main column was ambushed on the march, but the Sudanese drove the attackers off in confusion, and on 17th August the force came in sight of Mwele. Fire was opened on the northern stockade with a 7-pounder gun and the war rockets. The enemy made no reply, and an attack was then launched by the Sudanese and seamen on the left flank, supported by the marines and Zanzibaris. Mbaruk's men opened fire at close range, but the stockade was rushed after an engagement lasting two hours. The rebels escaped into the thick forest nearby.

Forty-eight stockades were destroyed around Mwele during the next few days, and it was hoped that the capture of Mbaruk's main stronghold would have a salutary effect throughout the coast, for to follow the rebels indefinitely was beyond Hardinge's power. 'That we can actually capture the Chiefs,' he wrote to Lord Salisbury from Zanzibar on 28th September, 'and stamp out the last remains of the rebellion with our existing forces is too much to hope; but I trust that when the Indian troops arrive we may succeed in doing so. My idea has from the first been to form a line of forts, in a sort of semi-circle, from Malindi to a point south of Mombasa at short distances from one another, and to patrol the country between them; but until we have men enough to do this we must be content to exhaust the rebels by constant attacks from the coast towns, and by preventing them from ever settling in one spot.'

A request for Indian troops to garrison the coast towns had first been made in July, when Hardinge first realized the magnitude of his task. Pending their arrival, little more could be done in the way of offensive operations. For the next four months Mbaruk of Takaungu and his brother held the initiative and carried out a successful guerrilla campaign. On 16th October Captain Lawrence, who had rushed a rebel boma at Mgobani with his raw Swahili recruits, was shot dead as he pursued on horseback after one of the rebel chiefs. Early in November rebel attacks were made on Mazeras and Rabai, only a few miles from Mombasa. Caravans were raided, and for a time British control in the coastal area was practically limited to the ports, for Hamis bin Kombo, the chief of Mtwapa, seven miles north of Mombasa, who had about 300 armed men, and other chiefs nearby and in the Giriama district joined the rebels.

The first Indian Contingent raised for service with the East Africa Rifles, numbering 299 men,[1] reached Mombasa on 30th December, 1895. Operations began without delay. Mtwapa's village was attacked from the sea and 18 rebels were killed. Next day the Indian troops followed in pursuit, but were deliberately misled by their guide Songoro, a slave of the Wali of Takaungu, and marched through the bush for twenty-two hours without water. The situation was saved by the discovery of a coconut plantation with the fruit in full milk, but the pursuit had to be abandoned and the troops returned exhausted. The rebels attacked Freretown on 21st January with 300 men, but were repulsed by a mixed force of Indians and Sudanese.

Faced with a mobile enemy operating over so great an area, the only effective strategy was constant pursuit and the occupation of all food centres. Two flying columns were organized, one to operate in the north and the other in the south. The rebels eluded the northern column, attacked Malindi, burnt 400 houses and looted the Indian *dukas*. A new fort was built at Tandia, three miles west of the Sokoki forest, and garrisoned by a force under Captain Harrison. During February the southern column, consisting of the naval brigade, 110 rifles of the Indian Contingent and 55 Zanzibaris, made a reconnaissance in force of Mbaruk's new position at Mwareni. A station was also set up on the Shimba range under Lieutenant Scott, who patrolled the district south of Mombasa and on 8th March repelled an attack by the rebels on his fort.

Most of Hardinge's troops were still swallowed up in the defence of numerous small stations and missions, and only 200 could be found for mobile operations. In February he appealed for more Indian troops to relieve the rest of his force for offensive tasks. The India Office complained that the continual demands from Africa on Indian troops and recruiting areas were prejudicial to the efficiency of the Indian Army. To this the Foreign Office replied that every effort would in future be made gradually to organize the local forces of the Protectorate. It was a task long overdue.

On 15th March Lieutenant-Colonel A. A. Pearson reached Mombasa in command of the 24th Bombay Infantry (Baluchis), with a strength of 12 European officers and 737 native officers and men. Lord Salisbury had ruled that the regiment was to be used for field operations and not garrison duty, and as senior officer Pearson took command of the Field Force, though not without protest from Hatch. At that time the Indian Contingent was stationed mainly in and around Mombasa,

[1] The Contingent was nominally 300, but one man died at Bombay before sailing.

and the Sudanese and Zanzibari troops mainly in Mombasa and the district to the north. The Sudanese were increased by 106 men recruited in Egypt by Raikes, who were sent to garrison the Malindi district. A line of posts was established along the Uganda road and on the southern frontier, and the Field Force began systematic operations against the rebel villages. By the beginning of April all was ready for the advance against Mbaruk. The main column, consisting of 112 rifles of the 24th Bombay Infantry and 40 rifles of the Indian Contingent, advanced into the Kamari forest. After a cautious approach, Mwele was found to be deserted. Operations were proceeding in the area, when news came that Mbaruk and about 3,000 rebels had crossed into German territory. On 20th April 1,100 of them, of whom 600 were armed, surrendered to Major von Wissmann, who had sent Mbaruk a stern ultimatum.

Though most of the forces employed were seamen, marines or Indian sepoys, Mbaruk's rebellion cost the East Africa Rifles one officer and 21 other ranks killed and one officer and seven other ranks wounded. Desultory operations continued for several weeks. In May Pearson suggested to the Foreign Office that his regiment should remain for another three months, to give Hatch a chance to reorganize his command, but in view of the attitude of the Government of India and the expense of maintaining the Indian troops, Lord Salisbury did not feel justified in retaining Pearson's regiment beyond the end of June.

In Hardinge's opinion this trial of strength with the Arab potentates of the coast was inevitable. He thought it as well that the matter had been decided 'in the infancy of the Protectorate'. It was better that the struggle should come over an issue like the Takaungu succession than over the question of slavery. The rebellion marked the end of the Arab predominance on the coast, and its replacement by the growing influence of Europeans. It was inevitable therefore that some repercussion should be felt at Zanzibar, where the use of the Sultan's troops against Muslims on the mainland was naturally unpopular. While Hardinge was engaged elsewhere the Sultan, Hamed bin Thwain, had been steadily increasing the size of his palace guard, the only troops whose allegiance was personal to himself. A brush with the police occurred in December, 1895, when 18 of the guard and 23 government troops were wounded. Hardinge threatened strong action, and the Sultan agreed to dismiss some of his men.

On 25th August, 1896, while Hardinge was on leave, the Sultan died suddenly. Seyyid Khaled bin Barghash at once occupied the palace, won over the guard of 800 men, and was joined by about a thousand others. The British Government had intended to recognize Seyyid Hamoud bin Mohammed, and refused to submit to this *coup d'état*. Naval assistance was summoned, the palace was bombarded and Khaled took refuge in the German Consulate. Hamoud was then declared Sultan. For a time it was thought advisable to strengthen the Zanzibar forces serving under Captain Raikes, and a part of the Indian Contingent was sent to Zanzibar. On its return to Mombasa Captain Barratt was complimented by the Consul-General on the excellent behaviour and reliability of his troops. It was the first occasion on which a garrison from the mainland was provided for Zanzibar.

(iv) *Punitive Expeditions in Jubaland, 1893-1901.* Map IV.

From the time when the administration of Kismayu was taken over by the Imperial British East Africa Company in August, 1891, to its conquest from the Italians fifty years later, Jubaland was the scene of frequent campaigns by the K.A.R. and its predecessors. The western boundaries of the province, ill-defined and largely unexplored at the period now under review, lay over 400 miles from the coast, though effective control inland was exercised only over a small area. Headquarters were at Kismayu, some twelve miles south of Gobwen, which lies on the right bank of the Juba. Kismayu has an excellent harbour, accessible to shipping at all seasons, and as the land route south crosses many miles of waterless bush, direct communication by sea with Mombasa was the normal means of reinforcing the garrison.

The River Juba was the boundary between British and Italian territory. Villages lay along the right bank, but most of the country was inhabited, as it is today, only by scattered nomad tribes. Much of it is covered with bush, sometimes sparse but often of a high, prickly density very difficult to penetrate. Between the coast and the group of wells, traditionally 114 in number, that are known as Afmadu ('Blacklips'), there lies an irregular system of swamp and shallow water-pans called Lake Deshek Wama. Most of the water-holes around which the tribal pastures lie dry up soon after the end of the rains. The tribes and their flocks are then confined to the few areas where water still remains and their location can be determined with certainty, but at other periods of the year punitive expeditions are particularly difficult against such mobile enemies, who use tracks known only to themselves through country where the visibility is often nil.

The first administrators found difficulty in handling the Herti section of the coastal tribes, who were estimated to number about 2,000 people. Berkeley, the Administrator at Mombasa, felt obliged to remove the Sultan's troops from Kismayu, even though this meant reducing the garrison, for they were practically useless and greatly disliked. To conciliate the Somali he settled a number of outstanding claims for blood-money against the Sultan. This was a false move, for inter-tribal claims and counter-claims made the division of this money very complicated, and led at once to disaffection and unrest. When they realized the dangers of this policy the Directors reversed it, but by that time the damage had been done. The attitude of the Herti grew increasingly insolent; parties of young warriors constantly entered the town fully armed, intent on creating trouble, and the slightest punishment of one of their number gave offence to the whole section. In February, 1893, the situation grew so threatening that J. Ross Todd, the Acting Superintendent at Kismayu, appealed for naval support. H.M.S. *Widgeon* was sent; a riot developed in one of Todd's barazas, in the course of which he was wounded in the head, and a number of Somalis were killed.

On receipt of this news the Company decided to increase the garrison to 300 men, and requested that the warship should remain at Kismayu meanwhile. Preparations were put in hand for the accommodation of a larger garrison. The troops were to be under the control of W. G. Hamilton, whose appointment was described rather vaguely as 'Superintendent in charge of askaris'. Hamilton was a stern martinet who had served in the Franco-German War and acquired a taste for German military methods. He had previously been at Taveta, where the Company had had cause to complain of his handling of the natives. In April he reconnoitred a site for a fort at Turki Hill, an eminence situated within a bend of the Juba close to Gobwen, overlooking two long stretches of the river and a shelving beach suitable for careening the Company's river steamer *Kenia*. Such a fort would assist in preventing the slave traffic by dhow and would also command the main route inland to Yonte. Authority was given for its construction, and it was agreed that Hamilton should command it in person.

By May the garrison of Jubaland had risen to 423 irregular and 46 of the Company's 'regular' troops. Experience had revealed no good reason for thinking highly of the Viroboto, but the first reports from Kismayu stated that they were proving better than expected. The shock was therefore all the greater when on 22nd August the Directors were advised by cable that the Viroboto had mutinied, captured the fort at Turki Hill, murdered Hamilton and disappeared into the bush with a quantity of ammunition and two cannon.

This outrage took place on 11th August, but despatches from R. G. Farrant, the Acting Administrator at Kismayu, showed that signs of disaffection had become apparent long before this date. There were about 110 Viroboto at Kismayu and another detachment at Gobwen who had previously refused to garrison the fort on Turki Hill. Hoping to replace them with less expensive troops, Farrant had begun local recruitment from freed slaves. Rumours began to reach him that the Viroboto intended to desert and join the Somali. On 8th August he was informed that 40 Viroboto had disappeared with their arms and ammunition. Two days later the number of absentees had risen to 54, and Farrant appealed for a warship and 100 askaris. But his action was too late to avert the tragedy. Though situated in a strong position, the new boma at Turki Hill consisted of little more than the thorn bush known locally as *ulimbi*, which would in time have grown into an impenetrable hedge. At 4.30 a.m. on the morning of 11th August the deserters and a number of Somalis broke through these defences with ease, overcame the garrison of 30 men and shot Hamilton through the heart. The affair was over in a few minutes.

The deserters followed up their success with an attack on the Residency at Kismayu, which was beaten off. H.M.S. *Blanche* reached the port and a naval expedition went up the Juba. Some villages within reach of the river were destroyed, and the Somalis vanished into the interior. For some time all communication with them was severed

After the proclamation of the Protectorate in 1895 the coastal Somalis were forbidden to enter Kismayu armed, and their chief, Sherwa

Ismail, became reconciled to British rule. Jubaland, now organized as the Third Military District, was garrisoned by three companies of the East Africa Rifles. The fort at Turki Hill had been rebuilt in stone, and a stockaded post was set up ten miles to the north at Yonte, on the bank of the Juba. At first effective control inland was limited to the Gosha region, a strip of forest country about 100 miles long bordering the river, inhabited by runaway slaves of mixed origin, including Yao and other tribes from Nyasaland. These people were known collectively as the Wagosha, and generally proved peaceful. But the attitude of the Ogaden group[1] of Somalis, whose country lay between Lake Deshek Wama and Afmadu, was very truculent, though their Sultan, Marghan bin Yusuf, had recognized the Company's authority, and his son Ahmad, who succeeded him in 1896, had visited Kismayu to swear allegiance to the Queen. In the far interior were the Boran Galla, a tribe of whom little was known, though extraordinary tales of their wealth in cattle and ivory were current.

The Ogaden were a fierce and warlike tribe estimated to muster about 6,000 warriors. They carried small round shields of giraffe hide and fought in pairs with stabbing spear and knife, one man seizing his adversary while the other stabbed him. As they possessed few firearms their tactical preference was for ambushes and close fighting in thick country of their own choosing, through which they could spread with unusual speed.

In 1897, in spite of a stern warning by A. C. W. Jenner, the sub-commissioner of the Province, the Ogaden made an unprovoked attack on the Boran Galla in the hope of securing cattle and slaves. As the Boran gave a good account of themselves, the matter was allowed to drop. A few months later two Ogaden spies captured near Mfudu killed their escort of native police and escaped. Ahmad bin Marghan was warned that Kismayu and the coast would be closed to his people unless the murderers were surrendered or blood money paid. Ahmad was pacifically inclined and paid an instalment of the fine, but his young warriors, anxious to 'wash their spears', were disgusted at such weakness and difficult to control. In April, 1898, a Galla slave who had obtained British protection was found by his Somali master and killed. Police action followed in the Afmadu area, where the murderer's cattle and some of his relatives were seized. The Somali promptly retaliated by raiding towards Kismayu and killing two Arab traders close to the town. The time had clearly come for decisive measures, and a military expedition was authorized.

The expedition of 1898 was commanded by Major W. Quentin, of the 4th Bombay Rifles, who in consequence of the Sudanese Mutiny had reached Mombasa with a wing of his regiment early in March. The force assembled during the course of the operations included, in addition to the three companies of the East Africa Rifles already in Jubaland, two companies of the 27th Bombay Infantry and four companies of the Uganda Indian Contingent, totalling 1,060 men.

[1] 'Ogaden' is not really a tribal name, but a term applied collectively to a group of tribes.

The expedition assembled in Jubaland during April and May. On 7th April the first company of the Bombay Rifles reached Turki Hill. A few days previously a detachment of the East Africa Rifles had been ambushed along the road to Yonte. A reconnaissance on 13th April found that the post there had been captured by Somalis, who had killed 15 of the police askaris before retiring into the bush. A few days later Quentin reached Kismayu with the second company, and took ammunition and rations for two months to his base at Turki Hill.

The enemy was reported in force near Lake Deshek Wama, but a column sent out to reconnoitre the lake found that the Somalis had withdrawn with their cattle towards Afmadu. On 17th May, when most of the force had reached the province, headquarters were transferred to Yonte, where the stockade was rebuilt. On 30th May a large party of Ogaden approached and attacked the cattle boma, but was driven off with loss.

Quentin now established an advanced post at Helished near the lake, manned by 150 rifles. On 22nd June an Indian officer and 41 men were out on patrol from this camp when they were ambushed by about 400 Somalis as they passed through thick bush in single file. The officer and 27 of his men were killed, and the enemy took their rifles and 1,640 rounds of ammunition. Quentin redisposed his troops, reinforcing Helished to a total of 168 rifles, garrisoning Yonte with 151, and leaving only 91 rifles at Turki Hill. Two companies of Sudanese were in the Gosha district, and 100 Sudanese and Swahili at Kismayu. On 14th July the Somali carried out a daring raid on Government cattle close to Kismayu. The Uganda Indian Contingent reached the port a fortnight afterwards, to occupy the base and so relieve Quentin's entire force for operations.

On 3rd August the main punitive column about 300 strong marched from Helished, forded the shallow lake and surprised the Ogaden camp at daybreak, inflicting heavy casualties and capturing 450 head of stock. Ten days later Quentin made a second large capture in the same locality. This brought the Ogaden to their senses and the Sultan and his chiefs sued for peace, surrendering all captured arms and agreeing to a fine of 500 cattle, which was paid very reluctantly and with the worst beasts that could be collected. A garrison of three companies E.A.R. was authorized for Jubaland, with headquarters at Yonte, where lines of grass huts were built and the whole camp, including officers' quarters and stores, was surrounded by a fence of barbed wire. Gobwen remained as a small post to protect the landing-stage used by the steam launch. Jenner toured the Ogaden country and met with a friendly reception; Sultan Ahmad paid several visits to Kismayu, and for a time all remained quiet.

In 1900 Jenner decided to explore the country in the direction of the Lorian Swamp. He was confident that friendship with the Ogaden was now established, and took with him only a small escort of 40 Herti police. 'A few police posts,' he wrote to Ternan, who was now at Mombasa as Acting Commissioner pending the arrival of a successor to Sir Arthur Hardinge, 'and a safari or two in the year should be

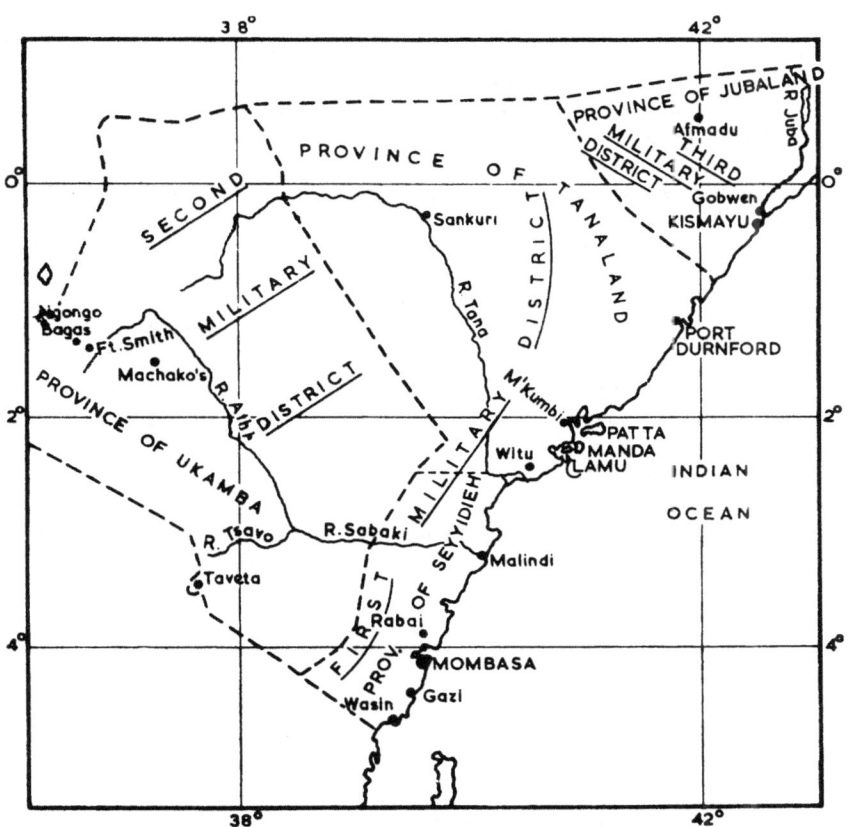

6. British East Africa: Civil and Military Districts, 1897

enough. . . . The pacification of the Ogadens was the result of the expedition of 1898. . . . I have never met natives of Africa who show higher qualities than they do.' But the loose organization of the tribe made it difficult for the Sultan to enforce agreements, especially when motives of personal vengeance were at stake. Unknown to Jenner, a chief named Hasan Yera, whom he had once imprisoned for failing to arrest the murderers of some Wagosha, had plotted his death with several other disgruntled chiefs, and was now determined to seize his opportunity.

In the early morning darkness of 16th November, Jenner's sleeping camp, which was unprotected by a boma, was suddenly attacked by about 300 Somalis. The policemen's rifles were unloaded, and before resistance could be organized, Jenner was speared to death and all but nine of his escort suffered the same fate. When the news reached Yonte 100 men of the garrison were dispatched under Captain H. W. Rattigan (K.O.S.B.), but heavy rain had made the tracks impassable and the expedition was obliged to return.

Further unrest was caused at this time by the murder of eight Boran traders returning up-country from the coast, and an Arab sheikh who was killed by the Ogaden near Gobwen. Ternan had heard rumours of the trouble, and accompanied by Hatch reached Kismayu on 25th November, followed by some 200 men drawn from the Depôt Company at Mombasa and the garrison at Nairobi. Omar bin Marghan, the Sultan's brother, who had visited Jenner's camp twice before the attack, was summoned to Kismayu to answer a charge of complicity in the murder, but failed to appear.

Ternan proposed no half measures. Informing the Foreign Office that Jenner had been 'a great admirer of the local Somalis, whom he unfortunately credited with high qualities quite foreign to their real character', he advised that the number of troops in Jubaland should be raised to 1,000, one company each to be stationed at Kismayu, Turki Hill and Yonte; one company at Kumbi, north-west of Lake Wama, where an advanced depôt was to be established; and the remainder to be employed as a punitive column to attack Afmadu, with himself in command. To this the Foreign Office agreed.

In January, 1901, Lieutenant-Colonel Hatch was pronounced by the medical authorities to be unfit to take part in the expedition. He handed over his command to Major T. Souter (Cam. High.) and returned to Nairobi for 'change of air'. Meanwhile a large body of troops was concentrating at Kismayu. There were already in the province five companies of the E.A.R., totalling nine officers and 475 native officers, N.C.Os. and men. The rest of the force consisted of a wing (eight officers and 445 native ranks) of the 16th Bombay Infantry, 52 rifles of the Aden Camel Corps, a section of No. 9 Mountain Battery, a company of Somali police, and two companies of armed porters, 1,404 men in all, plus about 100 Somali scouts. Nearly 600 camels and 900 porters were engaged to form the transport column. A base was made at Yonte, and after providing garrisons on the line of communication, a punitive column of 19 officers and 603 other ranks, including three companies of the E.A.R., left Yonte with a large train of camels, donkeys, cattle and goats on 28th January and reached Kumbi on 1st February. Unusually heavy rains had flooded the country, filling the wells and enabling the Ogaden to distribute their cattle. Ternan acted quickly: by 5th February he had occupied Afmadu with a light column, and a few days later with the remainder of his force. The Sultan surrendered and was sent to the coast under escort, on the ground that he was privy to Jenner's murder—an action of Ternan's with which the sub-commissioner at Kismayu did not agree.

A strong post was set up at Afmadu as a base for further operations. The chiefs responsible for Jenner's murder were reported to be in Jiro, about thirty miles north-west of Afmadu. On 12th February, leaving Souter in command at Afmadu, Ternan led a flying column of three companies E.A.R., one company Bombay Infantry, the Camel Corps and one gun of the Mountain Battery into unknown country that was practically waterless and covered with high, thick bush.

On the first day out the Camel Corps captured a small herd of cattle, which stampeded and was lost. On the 15th the column reached

Ghulime, the last water-hole on the Boran road, beyond which the guides said no water existed for 200 miles. Ternan decided to continue, and on the 16th, dispatching in the early morning his usual advance guard of 40 camelry, each with a Sudanese rifleman mounted behind, he followed with the main column for about ten miles. By that time he was in the neighbourhood of Samasa, some fifty-seven miles from Afmadu. Fresh tracks all around showed that the enemy was nearby in force, and Ternan decided to form a square[1] in the dense bush, with the Bombay Infantry on the front face and the East Africa Rifles on the other three. The rearguard had barely taken up position when the Ogaden attacked on three sides and tried to rush the camp.

Action at Samasa, 16th February, 1901.—The brunt of the attack at Samasa fell upon the rear face of the square, defended by No. 7 Company, E.A.R. The company turned and ran; some of the men stopped and fired, and then ran again to the right, leaving the field hospital exposed. For a time great confusion resulted; 17 Somalis got into the square and the medical officer, Lieutenant-Colonel Maitland, was killed. Eventually the company commander rallied some of his men; the rest of the square stood firm, and after ten minutes' hard fighting the Somalis drew off, all who had broken into the square having been killed.[2] Ternan's losses were 17 killed and 20 wounded, of whom four died. He estimated the Somali casualties at 150, though later on they gave the figure themselves as about 400, among whom were the murderers of Jenner.

The Camel Corps reconnaissance reported on its return that the bush ahead was too dense for passage except on foot, and as he was short of water and food Ternan returned to Afmadu. The Somali hung around his flanks and frequent volleys were needed to drive them off. On one occasion the gun exterminated with case shot a group of 12 who incautiously showed themselves in an open space.

[1] The square was the offensive and defensive battle formation often adopted by regular troops against uncivilized opponents. At this period its use had been tested on numerous occasions in the Sudan and on the North-West Frontier of India, and it was regarded as the typical product of small wars. (See C. E. Callwell, *Small Wars: Their Principles and Practice.* H.M.S.O., 1899. Chap. XIX.)

In essence the square was simply a formation showing extra fronts to flanks and rear, and was not necessarily four-sided. It arose from the necessity of protecting large convoys of supplies, and sometimes also wounded men and artillery. When on the move in proximity to the enemy, a modification known as the 'elastic square' was often adopted, especially in bush warfare. To march actually in square formation, particularly if this meant crowding a mass of animals into a small space, was very difficult, so unless the danger of attack was extremely sudden, it was often sufficient to march with a strong, compact rearguard capable of closing up very quickly, and with units in parallel columns on either flank, ready detailed to close into position and deploy at a given signal.

The square was a fighting formation well suited to native troops. As British officers were usually few, it was easy for such troops to get out of hand when dispersed, but the square made control easy and gave the confidence and cohesion of a compact group.

[2] Ternan to Eliot, 4.v.1901. F.O.2, 448. Ternan's official account of the engagement, which was published later in Parliamentary Papers (Africa No. 3 of 1901), made no mention of the defection of No. 7 Company, which was witnessed by himself and three other officers. It was only when wholly unjustified accusations of cowardice were levelled against the company commander concerned that Ternan felt obliged to inform Eliot of the true circumstances.

Ternan now sent two companies E.A.R. back to Yonte to escort stores to Afmadu. In his opinion to occupy the wells permanently would require 500 troops at Afmadu alone, and lack of water would make supply posts and convoys difficult. He therefore proposed as an alternative, 'almost equivalent to holding Afmadu', that a military post should be established about forty miles away on the River Juba at Mfudu, which could be supplied by boat. At this juncture some confusion arose over the intentions of the Foreign Office, where Ternan's indent to ration his troops till June was queried on the ground that the operations should be concluded with the least delay and the Indian troops released. Ternan accordingly returned to Kismayu, where he learnt that his proposals for a post at Mfudu had been approved. On 28th March he left Yonte with four companies of the E.A.R. and one company of sepoys. Stores were sent up-river by canoe, escorted by a sergeant and 20 men of the E.A.R.

Jenner had established a small post at Bura, in charge of a native agent and manned by a party of irregulars. Certain Wagosha chiefs, aided by the Ogaden, had attacked and captured this station, killing the agent and carrying off the flag. On 5th April these rebels kept up a running fight with the column until they were driven off with loss and several of their villages burnt. Mfudu was reached on 7th April and a strong post was built on the river bank. Captain H. W. R. Millais (Hamps. R.) was left in command with two combatant officers, a medical officer and 120 rifles of the E.A.R., and Ternan marched back to Yonte with the rest of the expedition, re-establishing the post at Bura on the way. Full intelligence and topographical reports were compiled during the expedition and distances measured by a cyclometer attached to a bicycle wheel.

The question of the future garrison of the province had now to be settled. On reconsideration, Ternan thought this should be confined to two companies of the East Africa Rifles at Kismayu, giving up Gobwen and Yonte, arming the Wagosha for their own protection and leaving the Ogaden to themselves. Sir Charles Eliot, the new Commissioner, who had reached Mombasa while the Jubaland expedition was preparing, did not agree with this view, though he was in favour of abandoning Mfudu and 'leaving the deserts alone', after the place had been occupied for six months as a demonstration of military force. When Hatch visited the province later in the year he gave his opinion that the occupation of Mfudu was useless, and ordered the withdrawal of the garrison. Yonte and Gobwen were retained, as the Government felt some responsibility towards the Italian frontier. In the event of operations arising it was intended to use a steam launch on the Juba, and it was therefore thought best to retain stations on the river bank.

In April the E.A.R. resumed sole responsibility for Jubaland, as the Indian troops were preparing to depart. The five weak companies in the Province were reorganized into three infantry companies, one to garrison Yonte and Gobwen, another Mfudu and the third Kismayu. In addition it was decided on Ternan's special recommendation to form a camel company with an establishment of 100 men. Mobility, in his opinion, was the keynote to effective control of the Ogaden Somali, and he thought that the Aden Camel Corps had amply proved its usefulness in the recent campaign. Under existing conditions the tribesmen were practically inaccessible for nine months of the year; lack of topographical knowledge seriously hampered every expedition, and to collect intelligence of this kind in time of peace was impossible unless one travelled with a slow and expensive infantry escort. But a camel corps, able to send out patrols strong enough to take care of themselves, could march fifty miles a day and cover double that distance without water.

Formation of the camel company took place at Gobwen. In the initial stages lack of experience caused a number of difficulties. The first camels drafted to the company had been employed on the campaign, and many of them were in a deplorable condition, weak, thin, and covered with sores. The rainy season was in progress and Gobwen proved an unsuitable station. Within two months 47 of the 100 camels had died, and by July only 33 were fit for riding. Lieutenant L. R. H. Pope-Hennessey (Oxf. Lt. Inf.), who commanded the company, appealed urgently for the construction of proper lines, the provision of medicines, and above all for the supply of suitable rations. After this matters improved and by October there were 109 fit camels on the strength. But the recruitment of suitable troops still remained a problem. A suggestion was made that Somalis should be recruited from British Somaliland, but neither Manning (now the Inspector-General designate of the K.A.R.), Swayne, who had been appointed to British Somaliland, nor Hatch approved this idea, partly because the need was for trained soldiers rather than recruits, and partly because experience had shown that Somalis did not mix well with Sudanese and Swahilis. The ranks of the company therefore filled slowly, and six months after formation it was still 17 men under strength. Other difficulties were the selection of the right type of arms and equipment. Considerable delay was experienced over this, especially in the provision of saddles.

A draft of 300 Sudanese had been recruited in Egypt by Major Harrison and Captain P. B. Osborn (Oxf. Lt. Inf.) in 1899. These men were due for discharge in 1902. Ternan, who had hoped to secure from them enough volunteers to fill the new camel company, found that few of the Sudanese were willing to re-enlist. A reaction appears to have set in after the Ogaden campaign, which in spite of the money and effort so freely expended had not met with spectacular success, and the morale of the troops who remained in Jubaland languished. Some of the Sudanese were unfit; many were homesick and asked that their families should join them from Ukamba. Ternan, who after the Uganda mutiny was particularly sensitive to disaffection among Sudanese troops, investigated these grievances personally and wrote in strong terms of the neglect that the Protectorate showed towards its native soldiers, complaining of the 'old perennial trouble' that nothing existed 'between the white officer and the black private, whatever his so-called rank'. This despatch produced a demand from the Foreign Office for explanations, especially in view of statements by Ternan and Souter that previous representations had produced no effect, and was to have further repercussions later when Ternan, having resigned his appointment as Deputy Commissioner to apply for special employment in South Africa, was able to voice his opinions in Whitehall.

At the beginning of June, 1901, however, when Ternan handed over the Jubaland command to Captain J. E. D. Ward (Middx. R.), he was able to report that the behaviour of the troops was satisfactory. To some extent the trouble had been caused by the difficulty of prompt investigation of minor grievances, as most of the officers in the E.A.R. spoke Swahili instead of Arabic. Regulations were accordingly drawn up to ensure that officers made themselves proficient in local languages, and to encourage them to study those of troops from outside East Africa who were serving in the protectorates. Within a year of secondment, officers were required to satisfy the Commissioner that they possessed 'a fair colloquial knowledge' of Kiswahili, Luganda, or some other relevant language, and failure to do so without reasonable excuse was to 'act detrimentally on the officer's prospects of promotion'. A bonus of £50 was awarded for passing within two years an examination in Arabic or Hindustani.

Sir Charles Eliot brought a new outlook to bear on East African affairs, and did not hesitate to make his views known to his superiors at home. Writing to Lord Cranborne some five months after his arrival, he drew attention to the changed conditions that had rapidly overtaken the country since the Mazrui Rebellion. East Africa was fast developing into a colony, in fact though not in name, and was hampered by still continuing under the old consular régime. The rapid but haphazard extension of governmental responsibility meant that the Commissioner's time was absorbed by constant attention to petty detail; at one moment the ordering of saddles for camels; at another, new boilers for a river steamer. Of all departments, Eliot complained that the military gave him the most trouble; no rules seemed to exist, and the pay, rank and promotion of every officer were occasions for prolonged correspondence and argument. There was more than a little truth in this contention. For a number of reasons, the time was ripe for major reorganization. When it came, all the protectorates on the mainland were equally affected.

PART II

THE CONSOLIDATION OF THE REGIMENT, 1901–1914

During the first decade of British rule in East and Central Africa, integration between the political and military aspects of government had been complete. The commander of the armed forces was the accepted deputy of the head of the administration. But the turn of the century witnessed a great change in African affairs, particularly in East Africa, where the balance of interest was shifting from the coast to the highlands. Plans for reorganization and economic development were everywhere under discussion. Many officials considered that local conflicts on any scale were already things of the past. Military matters were therefore no longer pre-eminent in the general scale of African affairs, but were directed instead towards the performance of a more specialized rôle.

CHAPTER 5

Formation and Organization, 1901-02

IN West Africa the local forces had undergone centralization as the West African Frontier Force, and early in 1901 the War Office pointed out the advantages of a similar system for East and Central Africa. The main object was to make the protectorates militarily independent as a whole, while at the same time ensuring the internal security of each. Neither East Africa nor Uganda was yet sufficiently strong to cope with serious trouble single-handed. The old policy of strengthening local defence by calling on troops from India had proved very expensive, and was increasingly unpopular with the Government of India. After the Ashanti campaign the capabilities of African soldiers were much more widely recognized. On the other hand, the Sudanese mutiny had shown the need for caution. It was felt that some Indian garrisons must be retained for a time, but that African troops might solve the important question of an emergency reserve, the need for which had been repeatedly demonstrated during the past few years. Such a reserve must be stationed centrally, and if possible consist of askaris with no local affinities in the areas where they might be called upon to operate. The Uganda Railway and the existence of the 2nd Battalion of the Central Africa Regiment seemed the answer to both these requirements.

It was natural that in seeking for a military officer to plan the details of the reorganization, the Secretary of State should turn to Lieutenant-Colonel W. H. Manning. He was the senior of the commandants then in the African protectorates; he had the longest unbroken service with African troops, having been seconded to the Central Africa forces since 4th July, 1893; had just received the sanction of the Government of India for another five-year renewal of his secondment, and by virtue of his civil appointment as Deputy Commissioner had also gained a wide experience of native affairs. Manning was due to return to England on leave, and in April, 1901, the Foreign Office instructed him by cable to break his journey at Zanzibar, where he was to call on Eliot and make certain inquiries into military matters. Eliot had been advised that a scheme was under consideration to create a military reserve in the African protectorates; that it would probably involve the maintenance of a battalion of the Central Africa Regiment 'at some place on the Uganda Railway within the East Africa Protectorate'; and that Manning would communicate with him on his way home, as he would be required to give an opinion on the best situation on the railway with regard to climate and suitable food, and also to what extent troops from the Nyasa region were 'likely to assimilate in habits, drill and equipment with the men of the East Africa Regiment'.[1]

[1] F.O. to Eliot, 19.iv.1901. F.O.2, 442.

Meanwhile suggestions for reorganization were being evolved independently within the protectorates. In Central Africa the future of 2 C.A.R., due shortly to return from Ashanti, was under discussion. At first Manning was firmly convinced that the battalion should be disbanded, on the ground that it would be impossible to recruit it to full strength again. He therefore forwarded proposals for concentrating the protectorate forces and ensuring economy of manpower. Assuming that the Administrator of the British South Africa Chartered Company no longer needed three companies of troops in North-East Rhodesia for police work, Manning proposed to withdraw these troops and by maintaining 1 C.A.R. at its full strength of nine companies to guarantee an expeditionary force for North-East Rhodesia if need arose, and a contingent of 350 men, with officers and Sikhs, for service abroad under the War Office whenever called upon. By the time the Foreign Office received these proposals, however, a scheme had already been drafted along different lines.

Manning left Central Africa for Zanzibar on 13th May. The first indication of the nature of the reforms being planned in London reached Sharpe early in June. He was instructed to recruit 1 C.A.R. to full strength and to reduce 2 C.A.R. to six companies, each 100 strong, for employment in Uganda, East Africa or Somaliland, with liability for three years' service abroad. Sharpe at once forwarded this news to Manning at Zanzibar, telling him that Cobbe had sounded the few men of 2 C.A.R. who had reached Zomba in advance of the main body, and had found none willing to re-enlist. Another term of one year was the most that could be expected of them, and in any case it was essential that Manning on reaching London should press for immediate increases in pay. This still stood at the original figure of 5/- a month for a private, but following representations by Sharpe and Manning was doubled when the reorganization came into effect, and increased still further for troops on foreign service.

A Foreign Office memorandum dealing with the proposed reorganization of military forces was forwarded to all three protectorates early in August. It stated that His Majesty's Government had decided on certain changes in view of 'the proved inadequacy of the present forces to meet the military needs of the protectorates', and the expense of getting help from India when trouble arose. The main objects were therefore two: the fusion of the existing forces into a single body, and the employment of a reserve battalion that could be sent wherever needed at short notice. Further details were given of the steps proposed to achieve these objects. The designation of the force was to be 'The King's African Rifles', to which His Majesty had already signified his assent. The present territorial designations would, however, be retained in addition to numbering five battalions. Officers were to be interchangeable, though those now serving would only be transferred with their own consent. A committee was to meet in England to discuss the various military ordinances and to prepare a draft for a new K.A.R. Ordinance,[1] and another committee of officers

---

[1] Lord Cranborne, Colonel Manning and a War Office representative were appointed for this purpose.

would draw up regulations for a common uniform. An inspecting officer was to be appointed, and the officer strength of battalions was to be increased to two and a half per company. 2 C.A.R. was to be taken over by the Foreign Office and formed into a Reserve Battalion, chargeable on the funds of all three protectorates. No steps were to be taken to form a permanent force in Somaliland until the operations then in progress against the Mullah were concluded.

On Manning's departure for home, Major F. B. Pearce, who had been Assistant Deputy Commissioner of Central Africa since 1897 and had led the British forces in the combined Anglo-Portuguese operations in 1899, became Acting Deputy Commissioner and also Acting Commandant of the Armed Forces. On orders from home, Pearce reopened recruiting, enlisting men on condition that they must serve in any of the African protectorates if operations were needed. Further inquiry convinced him that another spell of foreign duty would be very distasteful to the men of 2 C.A.R. Sharpe forwarded this opinion to Whitehall, as a warning that recruits might not be forthcoming, though he was careful at the same time to assure the home authorities that if men for 'active', as apart from merely 'foreign' service were needed, they could always be recruited for either battalion.

A sharp difference of opinion arose in the Protectorate soon after the arrival of Lieutenant-Colonel Brake and the main body of 2 C.A.R. from West Africa, the first detachment of which reached Zomba on 8th July. Partly on account of his campaigning experience during the past three years, and partly because his battalion was a War Office unit, Brake brought a different outlook to bear on the question of reorganization. He thought that with re-enlisted men and new recruits the strength of his battalion could be raised to the required figure of 600 within a few months. By the end of September he had enlisted 120 men, and the Administrator of North-East Rhodesia had promised to raise another 100. On the advice of the War Office, Brake had been appointed Acting Commandant of the Protectorate Forces in place of Major Pearce, though Pearce's civil appointment would make him Acting Commissioner if Sharpe left the Protectorate. This was an example of the complications that sometimes arose from coupling important civil and military posts, and in this case had some unfortunate consequences. The headquarters of 2 C.A.R. had been established temporarily at Fort Lister, two days' journey from the headquarters of the Armed Forces of the Protectorate and of 1 C.A.R. at Zomba. A very few weeks sufficed to show the disadvantages of this divided military control, and Sharpe wrote home in strong terms to point out that the commanding officer of 2 C.A.R. was by the nature of his appointment 'really a temporary visitor to British Central Africa' and that his men were being recruited by different methods from those of the Protectorate forces. It was the practice of 1 C.A.R. to keep garrison companies at the same stations for considerable periods. Their strength was maintained by local recruitment, the O.C. notifying village headmen when he needed recruits, who then came to enlist of their own accord. But Brake, anxious to justify his views and obliged therefore to recruit quickly on a large scale, sent recruiting parties on tour under officers who knew neither the language nor local conditions, and were forced to rely on interpreters. The approach of these parties convinced the natives that forcible recruitment was intended, and whole villages were sometimes found deserted. The civil collectors and the officers of 1 C.A.R. resented this procedure, and Sharpe was anxious for a decision on the permanent situation of 2 C.A.R. headquarters, which he would have preferred to be at Zomba, under more immediate control.

Brake had already commented in some detail on the proposed plans for reorganization. His main contention concerned the situation of the Reserve Battalion, which he held strongly should not be based in British Central Africa, on the ground that the establishment proposed for 1 C.A.R. was higher than would ever be needed for operations within the Protectorate, and that the troops would be too remote if a sudden emergency arose elsewhere, with a two-day journey from the Shiré Highlands to the river, a river journey that might take a week in the dry season, and an exit port at Chinde that could only be entered by sea-going steamers twice a month. He also thought that it would be difficult to find a station in Central Africa where so large a body of troops could be fed, and that the men would become efficient soldiers more quickly by serving abroad. Brake was in England on leave at the time Sharpe's letter, criticizing his recruiting methods and asking for a decision on the question of the Reserve Battalion's permanent headquarters, reached the Foreign Office. So strongly did he feel on the matter that he offered to resign if 2 C.A.R. were to remain in British Central Africa. As Manning had decided against East Africa as a permanent station for Central African troops, he recommended that Brake's resignation should be accepted,[1] and that Sharpe should be instructed by cable to select a permanent headquarters for the Reserve Battalion at once, in conjunction with his military authorities. Sharpe had originally suggested Zomba, Chiradzulu or Blantyre, and the choice ultimately fell on Zomba.

By October the number of recruits for the Reserve Battalion had risen to 170, and Sharpe expected the full 600 to be reached by the end of the year. The Foreign Office had originally given 1st October, 1901, as the date on which the reorganization was to take effect, but so many questions were then unsettled that the date had to be postponed. It was late in November before Manning wrote his final comments on the criticisms and suggestions offered by Brake. He estimated that only fourteen days would be needed to transport the Reserve Battalion to East Africa in case of emergency, even if it proved impossible to concentrate the battalion at one station. Sir Clement Hill agreed that the scheme as already settled should stand, and a telegram was sent to Sharpe telling him not to recruit beyond 820 men for 1 C.A.R. and 600 for 2 C.A.R. Sharpe replied that the strength of 1 C.A.R. then stood at 974, but that discharges would soon reduce it to the required figure, with which he was perfectly in agreement as he had repeatedly said that the Central

---

[1] Brake was afterwards appointed Commandant Local Forces and Inspector-General of Police, Trinidad.

Africa armed forces were now much larger than the Protectorate required.

The fact that Central Africa was to provide two battalions and that the functions of the second involved service abroad caused more negotiation and discussion with this Protectorate than with the others. East Africa, however, also had ideas to put forward, especially for the internal reorganization of its own forces. Before the Ogaden expedition Ternan had pointed out that East Africa would be left for the time being without reserves, and in fact with very few troops at all. Somewhat disturbed at this prospect, the authorities at the Foreign Office informed the War Office of the need for a reserve to be stationed temporarily at Mombasa, and inquired whether the troops of the Central Africa Regiment then on their way home from the Gold Coast could be diverted there. The War Office telegraphed the British Consul at Beira to inquire whether the men would volunteer, but when the message reached Beira the troops had already transhipped for Chinde. There seemed no other solution but to appeal once more to the Government of India, who agreed to hold another battalion in readiness for service in Africa if required. The Mhairwara Battalion was accordingly directed to stand by, though complaints were made of the difficulty of relieving it from its normal duties. 'I think,' Lord Cranborne telegraphed to Sir Charles Eliot, 'recent demand for extra troops from India for expeditions in Protectorates is uneconomical: am considering reorganization of Protectorate forces to avoid this in future.' He went on to request a report of the cost of the special assistance rendered by India to the East Africa Protectorate since 1895. Eliot replied that this had amounted to £105,000, including £53,000 for the cost of the two Indian contingents that had served in East Africa between 1896 and 1900. It was during this discussion on reserves that Sir John Ardagh, the Director of Military Intelligence, first made the suggestion that the best long-term policy would be to enlist men in both the C.A.R. battalions with the obligation to serve abroad, and that the battalions should then relieve one another periodically. Ardagh thought that if this were done it would be possible to reduce the E.A.R. to 600 men and to station the whole battalion permanently in Jubaland.

After the Ogaden expedition was over, Lieutenant-Colonel Hatch again raised the matter of reserves. Though agreeing to dispense with an Indian Contingent, he considered the indigenous tribes of the Protectorate as of very limited value, and was still inclined to rely upon Sudanese. Hatch asked for permission to recruit again in Egypt or the Sudan, but was informed that this could not be allowed, as the Egyptian authorities had made it clear that if they permitted any further enlistments the recruits would only be of a 'comparatively worthless class'. Hatch accordingly obtained permission to offer a bonus of one month's pay to any of his Sudanese willing to re-engage for another three years. Eliot sympathized with Hatch's desire for a reserve stationed on the railway, and for an increase in establishment to allow for emergencies, though he preferred police to soldiers. He inquired whether any Sudanese could be recruited in Uganda, but was told that the Commandant of the Uganda Rifles could not get enough for his own battalion.

Ternan wrote of the East Africa Rifles that 'much remained to be done towards organizing the corps on a sound basis'. Hatch protested strongly against some of his criticisms, but Eliot agreed that there was a great lack of system and endless delays. 'I do not feel competent,' he wrote to the Marquess of Lansdowne, 'to indicate any method of imposing a more methodical and businesslike spirit into the corps. Probably Your Lordship has already taken the most efficacious step possible in naming an inspector of the military forces in the African Protectorates.'[1] Reorganization was unlikely to be effective unless accompanied by reform.

In Uganda the situation was clearer than in the other two protectorates. The tour recently completed by Sir Clement Hill, and the return of Sir Harry Johnston to England, provided the Foreign Office with a great deal of valuable information and obviated the need for prolonged correspondence. The question was coupled with the decision to place the whole course of the railway under the supervision of one administration by transferring the Eastern Province of Uganda to the East Africa Protectorate. This entailed as well the transfer of the garrison of the Eastern Military District, which at the time was larger than usual on account of the recent operations in Nandi. After some discussion it was agreed that two companies of the Uganda Indian Contingent might be stationed permanently in the district, which was healthier for Indian troops than Uganda. These companies would remain under the administrative control of Uganda but be available for operations if called upon by East Africa. It was thought also that two companies of local troops would be needed in the Nyando valley. Apart from making this adjustment, the absorption of the Uganda Rifles into the new scheme was comparatively straightforward.

During the last quarter of the year the three regiments proceeded to revise their establishments to fit those of the new force. The nine companies of 1 C.A.R. (four at Zomba, three at Fort Manning, and one each at Mangoche and Mlangeni) were to be reduced to eight. The Yao were fast becoming the chief military tribe, numbering at that time 480 men, as against 309 Atonga (who were 286 under tribal strength) and 117 others. The issue of the Africa General Service Medal had favourably affected recruiting, and the Yao were usually ready to re-engage. The Atonga appear to have discovered that more money could be earned in civil life. The establishment of the Indian Contingent in Central Africa was 215, but the strength was only 163, of whom 26 were serving with 2 C.A.R. Captain Godfrey went to India in May to recruit a new Contingent, but found the task more difficult than before and was forced to return short of gunners, signallers and buglers. The reduction of 2 C.A.R. to six companies was carried out at Fort Lister in September, and at the end of the year the headquarters of the regiment moved with four companies to Zomba, leaving two companies of recruits to continue their training at Fort Lister. The East Africa Rifles, with three companies in Ukamba, three (including the new camel

---

[1] Eliot to Lansdowne, 31.x.1901. F.O.2, 451.

company) in Jubaland, and one each at Mombasa and in Tanaland, numbered 12 officers and 996 men, with six guns. The tribal distribution was nearly equal, being 514 Swahili and 482 Sudanese, though the Swahili companies included a small mixture of other tribes. In Uganda the Indian Contingent, newly recruited at the beginning of the year, was alone large enough to justify its formation into a separate battalion.

On 5th November the Foreign Office followed its despatch of 8th August with more specific information. The commissioners were informed that 'the definite constitution of the armed forces of the four African protectorates administered under this Department as one regiment, to be styled the King's African Rifles, will take effect from 1st January next'. Manning was nominated as first Inspector-General of the combined forces, with the rank of brigadier-general. His appointment dated from 1st October, 1901, and was for a period of one year, with a prospect of renewal for another three. If operations should occur in which more troops of the K.A.R. were involved than were normally stationed in a protectorate, it was proposed to employ the Inspector-General in command; in time of peace his duties were to be those of inspection, with authority to issue directions, though commanding officers continued to be responsible for the battalions under their command. The report of the committee on uniforms was enclosed, with a request that it should be transmitted to officers commanding troops for action. At the end of December this despatch was followed by another enclosing a provisional statement of conditions of service for officers. Secondments were to be for three years, the first being on probation, with a possible extension to five years. Though company commanders' postings might be made on occasion, appointments were generally to be made in the grade of subaltern, with rank according to the date of appointment or promotion in the K.A.R.

On 1st January, 1902, the King's African Rifles came into being, with the original forces of the protectorates incorporated as follows:

> 1st (Central Africa) Battalion, eight companies. (Formerly 1 C.A.R.)
> 2nd (Central Africa) Battalion, six companies. (Formerly 2 C.A.R.)
> 3rd (East Africa) Battalion, seven companies and one camel company. (Formerly the E.A.R.)
> 4th (Uganda) Battalion, nine companies. (Formerly the African Companies of the U.R.)
> 5th (Uganda) Battalion, four companies. (Formerly the Indian Contingent of the U.R.)
> 6th (Somaliland) Battalion. (To be formed later from three infantry companies, the camel corps, militia and mounted infantry of the local forces in British Somaliland.)

The new regiment was designated 'Rifles' because all the original regiments had at some time been so called, but the men drilled as infantry, most of the officers and all the Indian troops being infantry. Shortly after formation the total strength of the regiment was returned as 104 officers and 4,579 native officers and men. The two companies of the

Indian Contingent in Central Africa were to be attached to whichever battalion was on garrison duty in the Protectorate, and the camel company of 3 K.A.R. was intended for service in Jubaland only.

The first (provisional) edition of *Regulations for the King's African Rifles* did not appear until 1905, when some experience of the functioning of the regiment had been gained, but the general policy and most of the detailed regulations then published were in operation from the date of formation. 5 K.A.R. and the Indian Contingent of Central Africa were given precedence over the other battalions, which ranked then in order of number. The separation of civil and military authority and the subordination of the latter were emphasized. As commanders-in-chief, H.M. Commissioners were responsible for defining the object and scope of military operations, but not for undertaking their immediate direction. Military authority was never to be exercised in opposition to, or in competition with, that of the civil power; nor were military officers to enter into any discussion of the merits of measures proposed, or to exercise any discretion in granting or withholding military aid, though except in emergency civil officers were to obtain the sanction of higher authority before calling out troops.[1] It was conceded that when officers of the regular army were not available for secondment, officers of the Militia, Imperial Yeomanry and Reserve of Officers could be appointed instead. Within a year of arrival officers were expected to satisfy the Commissioner by examination that they possessed 'a fair colloquial knowledge' of the language spoken by their troops. The chief function of the Inspector-General was defined as the maintenance of a 'satisfactory and uniform standard' of efficiency and training, and the lines that this must follow were laid down in some detail. In view of the criticisms of lack of foresight made when war broke out in 1914, it is interesting to note that the provisional *Regulations* contained a warning that battalions of the K.A.R. could be called upon to serve anywhere, and might meet an enemy 'able to use arms of precision in open country', as well as opponents employing the usual native tactics at comparatively close quarters in the bush. The training of the K.A.R., therefore, was not to be limited to tactics suitable to local conditions, though each section of a company was to have at least one trained scout, found, it was suggested, from the hunters of a pagan tribe. Care was enjoined to preserve the natural mobility and marching power of the African soldier, and boots were to be discouraged for general use, though locally-made sandals were permitted for operations and long marches.[2]

The next edition of the *Regulations*, published in 1908, paid some attention to the exploratory work being done by K.A.R. officers in the remoter parts of the protectorates, and gave more detailed instructions for the compilation of route records and of traverses. For the first time

---

[1] Interpretation of this clause was needed later in the remote provinces of Uganda, though three and a half years before the formation of the K.A.R. the Commissioner of the Protectorate had laid down the principle that the civil official in charge of a district 'must alone determine the scope and objects of any local military operations'. (Berkeley's Circular No. 17, dated 5.vii.98, paras. 8-9. F.O.2, 592.)

[2] *Regulations for the King's African Rifles*, Provisional Edition, 1905.

guidance was given on the recruitment of men for service in the Indian Contingents. A significant amendment to the provisional edition was the rule that nominal rolls of all officers, showing whether they had passed a language test or not, were to be submitted to the Inspector-General at each annual inspection.

So the new regiment was at last established, though campaigns in British Somaliland, Nandi and elsewhere followed so quickly that in practice some parts of the scheme, such as the formation of 6 K.A.R., had to be postponed for a time. But the main object had been achieved. When instructions were issued to Lieutenant-Colonel J. Hayes Sadler,[1] the new Commissioner of Uganda, he was assured of the presence at Zomba of a Reserve Battalion of 600 men, drawn from those tribes who had so recently distinguished themselves in Ashanti, 'for dispatch to any point within the Protectorates at which its services may be required. The military position is thus thoroughly secured in the event of any further troubles arising. . . .'

This echoed the confidence that Manning's reorganization had engendered in official circles. The regiment itself was new, but its component units had already been proved in the field.

---

[1] Later Lieutenant-Colonel Sir James Hayes Sadler, K.C.M.G., C.B.

CHAPTER 6

Dispositions and Establishments

(i) *Trial and Experience, 1902-04.*

BEFORE describing the operations in which the battalions of the King's African Rifles took part between the formation of the regiment and the outbreak of war in 1914, a brief outline of the regiment's development will provide the background against which these operations were set. Fluctuations in policy were the cause of frequent changes in establishments. They resulted partly from growing experience of military needs, and partly from efforts within the protectorates to become financially self-supporting, which brought about certain economies that soon proved to have been particularly ill-timed.

Having planned and completed the organization of the regiment during the autumn of 1901, Manning left London for Africa in the following spring to carry out his first inspection of the East Africa and Uganda battalions. He thought it unnecessary to visit British Central Africa so soon in view of his detailed knowledge of military affairs there, especially as the relationship between civil and military authorities was now on a very cordial footing. Despatches informed him of the progress made by both the new battalions in Central Africa. 'The 2nd Battalion are outstripping the 1st in real smart work,' Sharpe wrote in July. 'You will be pleased with both battalions, however, when you see them again. B.C.A. troops are a real credit to the country.'[1]

As a result of his first tour, Manning sought and obtained the authority to issue direct orders in relation to defects observed on inspection. Besides many details relating to training and types of equipment, he recorded his impressions of the quality of the troops and raised several important issues. In 3 K.A.R. he noted certain 'grave defects' in interior economy and spoke of the need for 'radical reform'. He recommended that the headquarters of the battalion should be transferred to Nairobi, that Mombasa should cease to be a military station, and that the depot company there should be abolished. Eliot agreed with these proposals, though not with Manning's suggestion that, in common with the other battalions, control of military expenditure should be in the hands of the commandant, as he had a poor opinion of his military officers' business capacity.

In Uganda, Manning was pleased with the condition of both battalions, but especially with the Indian troops of 5 K.A.R. He discussed the authority that should be vested in Colonel Coles in his capacity as O.C. Troops for the Protectorate as well as Commandant, 4 K.A.R., and

[1] Sharpe to Manning, 14.vii.02. F.O.2, 606.

[Photo: Lt.-Col. C. R. K. Bacon

Atonga Company, 1 K.A.R., 1902

[Photo: Lt.-Col. C. R. K. Bacon

Fort Mlangeni, 1902

recommended that Coles should only exercise general supervision over 5 K.A.R., and not interfere in the details of command and administration. Manning was greatly impressed by the excellent intelligence reports compiled by the military officers in Uganda, especially those of Major Gorges and Major H. B. Rattray (45th Sikhs), and instructed other battalions to follow their example. He discussed also the future of the native officers, and recommended that this grade should be allowed to die out, except in 5 K.A.R. and perhaps later in 6 K.A.R., when that battalion was formed.

The K.A.R. Ordinances were issued in 1902. They related only to the African units as the Indian troops continued to serve under an Indian Ordinance. Commissioners were empowered, at the direction of the Secretary of State, to order the employment of a battalion or any part thereof outside their own protectorates.

1 K.A.R., commanded by Lieutenant-Colonel A. S. Cobbe, returned on formation a strength of 10 officers and 819 other ranks, against an establishment of 18 officers and 820 other ranks. 2 K.A.R., still nominally commanded by Lieutenant-Colonel H. E. J. Brake, were nearer establishment with 18 out of 20 officers and 595 of their 600 other ranks. The Indian Contingent numbered two officers and 160 sepoys, organized in two companies. The distribution of the eight companies of 1 K.A.R., the home battalion, was four companies at Zomba, two in Central Angoniland (Fort Manning), one in Southern Angoniland (Fort Mlangeni), and one on the eastern frontier (Fort Mangoche). 2 K.A.R. was soon called upon for renewed operations in British Somaliland against the Mad Mullah, and was followed later by four companies of 1 K.A.R.[1]

Military service continued to be popular in British Central Africa, especially among the Yao and Atonga. When six askaris from each battalion were sent to England in 1902 for the coronation of King Edward VII, it was from these two tribes that the Nyasa representatives were chosen. In the following year the recruitment of the Angoni began as an experiment at Fort Mlangeni. The men showed promise, and within two years 124 Angoni were serving with 1 K.A.R., as against 369 Yao and 204 Atonga. An encouraging feature of the liking and aptitude of the Nyasa tribes for military service was the high rate of re-engagement of the N.C.Os., and the success of the policy of training them to replace the Sikhs as drill instructors. By the beginning of 1904 the Sikh instructors with 1 K.A.R. had been entirely superseded. Another sphere in which selected men showed unexpectedly rapid progress was signalling. Two N.C.Os. and 12 men began instruction in 1903; fresh classes were instituted as required, and the signallers of both battalions proved their worth in the Somaliland operations. Great importance was also attached to the training of officers in African languages. It was decided in 1902 that all officers must qualify in Chinyanja, and that a bonus would be awarded to those who also passed an examination in Swahili. The first examination in Chinyanja was held in August, 1903,

[1] See Chapter 7.

and the first in Swahili in October, 1905, when the Bishop of Zanzibar arranged for a member of his staff to act as examiner.

So pleased was Sharpe with the progress of his new recruits that he asked Manning to authorize a more difficult musketry course than that proposed for the K.A.R. as a whole, saying that it was child's play to the troops in British Central Africa. Manning devised a new course, which was shot for the first time in 1903. The issue of .303 Martini-Enfield rifles, with their comparatively slight recoil, and an increase in the number of rounds per man allowed for practice greatly stimulated interest in shooting, though some askaris were apt to excuse their failures by pretending that canvas targets did not deserve the same trouble as a real enemy. On the whole, the troops were better at controlled volleys than at independent marksmanship.

3 K.A.R. was made up to its full strength of 25 officers by May, 1902: headquarter staff, major and O.C. Camel Company for Jubaland; eight company commanders, and 12 subalterns. After the transfer of headquarters to Nairobi, the battalion was concentrated for a time at three stations only: 550 troops at Nairobi, 350 in Jubaland, and 100 at Witu. This was soon modified in consequence of the growing trouble along the Nyando valley section of the railway,[1] where the garrison of 4 K.A.R. and 5 K.A.R. had to be supplemented in April and May, 1902, by five officers and 300 men of 3 K.A.R., who were posted to Fort Ternan to assist in patrolling the line.

On formation, nearly half 3 K.A.R. still consisted of Sudanese,[2] but recruitment now had to be developed on a larger scale among the indigenous tribes of East Africa. Reports on the Masai company varied, but on the whole Hatch was satisfied, though he recognized that the Masai were useless for service on the coast. Most of the 201 recruits enlisted in the battalion during 1902 were Manyema, Wanyamwezi or Swahili. In March of that year an outbreak of bubonic plague occurred at Nairobi, and two cases were reported in the old military lines of wattle and daub huts that had been built originally for the Ukamba garrison north of the town. These lines were burnt, and new ones of corrugated iron were built on the higher ground to the west, popularly known as the 'Hill'.

On 1st April, 1902, the former Eastern Province of Uganda was transferred to the East Africa Protectorate. Troops from Uganda were still employed in the area during the two troubled years that followed, but in April, 1904, two companies (one Sudanese and one mixed), totalling five officers and 250 rank and file, were transferred from 4 K.A.R. to 3 K.A.R. in respect of this commitment. The establishment of 3 K.A.R. was thus raised to ten companies, with a total strength of 29 officers and 1,258 men. Distribution was three companies each at Nairobi

[1] See Chapter 8.
[2] Some of these men had fought against the British during the operations in the Sudan. On one occasion a native officer from Egypt arrived in East Africa wearing the Sudan medal. It is said that some of the Sudanese in 3 K.A.R. sent a deputation to their Commanding Officer, saying they also had served in the Sudan. When told that they had fought on the wrong side, they replied that this surely made them even more worthy of the medal, as they had had a much worse time than the British forces.

and in Jubaland, and one company each at Fort Hall, Nandi, Kericho, and Witu, which, though now politically unimportant, continued to be a military station until March, 1905. The Fort Hall detachment was transferred to Nyeri in June, 1904, and in July the Nairobi garrison moved out to Ngongo Bagas for three months, while 2 K.A.R. occupied their lines for a trial period on the way home from British Somaliland, to see whether the station was likely to prove suitable for Central African troops.

In Uganda the internal military commitments were heavier than in the other territories. The large and thickly populated Protectorate had been divided into five provinces: the Kingdom of Buganda, the Western Province (Bunyoro, Toro and Ankole), the Central Province (Busoga, Bukedi and adjacent territory), the Nile Province (where administration was confined to the line of the river), and the Rudolf Province. In the area between the Nile and Lake Rudolf no attempt had yet been made to establish stations.

The two battalions responsible for garrisoning this great tract of country, which included at first the old Eastern Province, were on formation stronger in personnel and experience than those in the other protectorates. Most of the 23 officers on the establishment of 4 K.A.R. had been in Uganda for several years. This was the result of the numerous postings that had followed the Mutiny. For the same reason 19 British N.C.Os. were still in the country, nine with 4 K.A.R. and ten serving as instructors with the police. African combatant ranks serving with the battalion numbered 1,116, which included 18 native officers. 5 K.A.R., totalling six officers, one medical officer, eight native officers and 403 sepoys, had been in the country since April, 1901. Partly for reasons of health and partly to facilitate food supply, it was the policy to keep this battalion concentrated so far as possible. Two of its companies ('B' and 'D') were serving alternately at Entebbe and Kampala; the other two ('A' and 'C') had remained at Fort Ternan and Muhoroni on their way up from the coast, as part of the garrison of the turbulent Eastern Military District. The companies at Entebbe and Kampala had to be reduced to half-companies while the Nandi operations were in progress. The troops in Uganda were supplemented by 1,060 armed constabulary, who were liable for military service if required and came under the control of O.C. Troops for enlistment and training. As in Central and East Africa, the obsolescent Martini-Henry .450 rifles, which had only recently replaced Remingtons, were withdrawn as soon as practicable after the formation of the K.A.R. and replaced by .303s. A 7-pounder gun, three Hotchkiss and eighteen maxim guns completed the armament of the Protectorate.

The main reason for the continued presence of Indian troops in Uganda was the feeling, as expressed by the Commissioner, that it 'would not be altogether safe to ignore the stock and traditions of the Sudanese', who numbered 736 of the askari strength of 4 K.A.R. on formation and supplied a further 95 recruits during the first year. Some of the Sudanese companies, such as No. 6, had so many civilian followers that they were able to provide their own recruits. Companies stationed in the Nile Province could sometimes recruit Sudanese locally, or at any rate men of very similar characteristics.

The Indian companies of 5 K.A.R. were responsible for the Kingdom of Buganda, but 4 K.A.R. had to be widely scattered in the remoter parts of the Protectorate. The disadvantages of this were recognized from the first, and it was always intended to select as soon as possible a healthy site where the battalion could set up its headquarters and concentrate as many companies as possible for drill, musketry and training on a more advanced level than was possible on detachment. On formation, however, 4 K.A.R. had two companies at Nimule, one at Gondokoro, two at Masindi, one in Ankole, and the rest in the Eastern Military District. In planning his reorganization Sir Harry Johnston had thought the Nile Province too large to be controlled by one man, and had divided it into two sub-commissionerships, the Acholi, or Upper Nile, and the Bari, or Lower Nile. The former was administered by a civilian officer, but the latter was under the control of O.C. Nile Military District, who acted also as sub-commissioner. This appointment, first held by Major Delmé-Radcliffe, had passed at the time of the formation of the K.A.R. to Captain J. A. Meldon (R. Dublin Fus.) at Nimule, assisted by Captain R. C. R. Owen (Oxf. Lt. Inf.), who commanded the company stationed at Gondokoro and was also in civil charge of that part of the district. K.A.R. officers were often complimented on the work they were called upon to do in a civil capacity, but in a remote province such as the Nile it was not to be expected that divided control would always prove happy. Owen took too high-handed a line over a Belgian raid upon an island in the Nile near Gondokoro early in 1902, but by that time Sadler had already decided to put the Nile administration entirely into civilian hands.

(ii) *Reorganization and Definition of Functions, 1904-08.*

The administration of British Central Africa passed on 1st April, 1904, from the Foreign Office to the Colonial Office. This introduced a further complication into the status and control of the Reserve Battalion. The Somaliland campaign of 1902-03 had shown that a single battalion of 600 men, most of whom had to be discharged, replaced and retrained at three-yearly intervals, was an insufficient reserve for East African needs, and that Brake had been right in thinking Zomba too remote a location for it. The short period spent by 2 K.A.R. in the East Africa Protectorate, which lasted from 17th July to 20th October, 1904, had shown the suitability of the Nairobi climate for Nyasa troops.[1] A major reorganization of the two Central African battalions was therefore decided upon in December. As suggested by Sir John Ardagh three years before, 1 K.A.R. and 2 K.A.R. were placed on an equal footing as regards foreign service, which they were to carry out alternately. Enlistments were to be for six years instead of three, with the obligation to serve for three years

---

[1] There was another reason for the decision to send 2 K.A.R. to Nairobi for a few months at the end of their tour of foreign service. It was thought that accounts given by discharged askaris of conditions in Somaliland would interfere with recruiting if the idea got abroad that foreign service was necessarily confined to that country. (C.O. 534, 2. Draft dated 9.vi.05.)

Fort Mangoche, 1904

Yao Sergeant, 1 K.A.R., 1905

[*Photos: Lt.-Col. C. R. K. Bacon*

abroad. The establishment of both battalions was to be six companies of 100 men each, with an officer strength of two and a half per company, plus regimental staff. Each battalion was to have a depôt company of 100 rank and file, stationed at Zomba. These changes were to become effective on 1st April, 1905. 2 K.A.R., which had reached Zomba on 11th November, 1904, and was now mainly on leave prior to discharge and recruitment, was to serve at home for the first three-year period under the new arrangement. The Indian Contingent, the band, and the depôt company of the battalion were all to be attached to the home battalion.

Recruiting for 2 K.A.R. began in January, 1905, in the Mlangeni, Fort Johnston, Mlanje, and Nkata Bay areas. As recruits came in, the companies were made up to strength on a tribal basis: three companies ('B', 'D' and 'F') of Yao, two ('A' and 'E') of Atonga and lake tribes, and one ('C') of Angoni. Owing to the attractions of employment in the South African mines the Atonga were becoming difficult to obtain, and 'A' Company consisted mostly of Bemba, enlisted by permission in North-East Rhodesia.

On 3rd July 1 K.A.R. left the Protectorate for three years' service in British East Africa, with an embarkation strength of 12 combatant officers, one British warrant officer, and 593 N.C.Os. and men. A site near Mazeras had been selected for the Reserve Battalion and approved by Manning in March. The water supply, which had been described as plentiful, proved quite inadequate during the dry season, when the river became a string of shallow pools swarming with mosquitoes. The site was condemned by a medical board, and on 19th August 1 K.A.R. was transferred to Nairobi.

Meanwhile 2 K.A.R. settled down to a spell as home battalion, with 'A' and 'C' Companies at Zomba, 'B' and 'F' Companies at Fort Manning, 'D' Company at Fort Mlangeni and 'E' Company at Fort Mangoche, which remained the distribution until April and May of the following year, when the Zomba companies were changed with the outstations. The strength of the battalion by tribes (including the depôt company) was 246 Yao, 126 Bemba, 121 Angoni, 75 Atonga, and 71 others. By the following year the number of Yao had markedly declined, and Manganja, Anguru, and Achewa were serving instead.

Other reductions in the Central African battalions soon followed. On 20th August, 1906, the two depôt companies were reduced to one, to serve both battalions. This measure was the forerunner of even more drastic reductions carried out in the regiment during 1906-07. After the end of the Nandi Expedition of 1905-06 it was decided that the 14 companies (six of the Reserve Battalion and eight of 3 K.A.R.) stationed in East Africa could be reduced to ten. In March, 1907, 2 K.A.R. was therefore reduced to four companies (450 men). 1 K.A.R. was to be correspondingly reduced on its return from East Africa in the following year.

The effect of this measure was to reduce the garrison at Fort Manning from two companies to one, and of Forts Mlangeni and Mangoche from one to a half-company each. 'B' Company (Yao) and 'E' Company (Atonga), which at the time happened to be the two weakest, and the combined depôt company were disbanded. In compensation the formation of a reserve of trained soldiers was authorized, planned originally to consist of two companies of Yao. The Indian Contingent had already been allowed to decline in strength, and the new one which reached Central Africa on 8th March, the eighth to serve in the Protectorate, consisted only of two native officers and 100 sepoys. During the first year of these military economies a saving was effected of £9,496.

Detachments of the Indian Contingent were dispatched to relieve the outstations in Nyasaland during March, 1908, while the companies of 2 K.A.R. concentrated at Zomba preparatory to departure on foreign service. The battalion embarked at Chinde on 4th June, headquarters going to Nairobi, 'C' and 'D' Companies to Zanzibar, 'A' Company to Kisii and 'F' Company to Meru. 1 K.A.R. returned to Nyasaland in three parties during the last week of June, when the battalion was reduced as previously arranged to four companies: 'A' (Atonga), 'B' and 'C' Companies (Yao), and 'E' (later 'D') Company (Angoni).

The scheme for a Reserve Force in Nyasaland was formally authorized by the K.A.R. Reserve Forces Ordinance of 1908, which made the men liable for service on recall within or without the Protectorate. When the reduction of the regular companies was carried out in 1907, only 26 discharged men agreed to enlist in this Reserve. Recruiting posters in three native languages were sent to all civil and military stations, in the hope of recruiting 400-500 men. Reserve headquarters and two companies were to be at Zomba, and one company each was to train at Forts Mangoche, Mlangeni and Manning. This organization on a company basis was intended to preserve the tribal system when the regular companies expanded to double companies on mobilization. To begin with, recruiting was slow, but the first batch of reservists was called up for training in August, 1908. The wisdom of forming this Reserve when reducing the strength of the two battalions was shown before the end of the year, as troops in Nyasaland were warned to stand by for British Somaliland in October. Of 160 reservists then called up, 149 reported for duty. A temporary improvement in the situation caused them to be dismissed a fortnight later, but at the end of November, 1908, they were called up again, and 142 men reported. This time their services were required, and they amply proved their value in Somaliland, where they stiffened the ranks of the younger recruits. On the strength of this success, the Colonial Office instructed East Africa and Uganda to draw up reserve schemes of their own and submit them for approval.[1]

The decision to quarter the Reserve Battalion in East Africa led to a substantial increase in the military expenditure of that Protectorate in the year 1905-06, amounting to over £53,000. Though partly the result of rearmament with .303 rifles, this was mainly due to arrears in connection with the visit of 2 K.A.R. and the erection of new barracks and cost of passages for 1 K.A.R. Expenditure was reduced by some £30,000 in the following year, owing to the decision to cut the number of companies

---

[1] The Regulations for the K.A.R. Reserve, as discussed and approved by the Inspector-General in consultation with all the protectorates, are in C.O. 534, 14.

in the Protectorate to ten. The controversial Masai Company was one of those chosen for disbandment in April, 1907, Manning having expressed his doubts of the usefulness of these men in his Report for 1906, when he commented on their poor physique. The establishment of 3 K.A.R. was thus reduced to 20 British officers, one British warrant officer, and 765 native officers, N.C.Os. and men. Rather less than half this number were Sudanese. The remainder were drawn from no fewer than fifteen different tribes, several of which were not indigenous to the East Africa Protectorate. Headquarters of the battalion and two companies were stationed at Nairobi, two companies were in Jubaland, one at Lumbwa, and one divided between Embu and Nyeri. The appointment of a major to command in Jubaland, which had been in existence for six years, was abolished on 16th October, 1907, as O.C. Troops there was no longer *ex-officio* sub-commissioner of the Province, and the garrison had been reduced from its previous strength of three companies.

The reductions of 1907 were brought into effect in spite of the fact that the K.A.R. was by then responsible for the garrison of Zanzibar. On 19th September, 1906, a growing dissatisfaction among the Zanzibari troops and police at their rates of pay and conditions of service culminated in mutiny, and the troops refused to parade. Remembering past difficulties, the Acting Agent and Consul-General lost no time in telegraphing for a warship and asking East Africa for troops. Hearing that no British warships were immediately available, on his own initiative the Kaiser sent a German warship to Zanzibar. Fortunately there was no need for such assistance. Headquarters and 'A', 'B' and 'C' Companies, 1 K.A.R., left Kilindini on 21st September and landed at Zanzibar a few hours before the German vessel's arrival. The disarmament of the Zanzibar forces was effected, all guards were taken over, and the town was patrolled without any serious trouble arising.

The Zanzibar police force was reconstituted, but not the Zanzibar army. The British authorities there had at last become convinced, in the words of the Agent and Consul-General, that the men 'were not made of fighting material and could not be relied upon in time of need'.[1] The Foreign Secretary agreed that it was necessary to have 'an armed force at Zanzibar on which absolute reliance could be placed', and that the best course was to 'disband entirely the so-called army there' and replace it with a permanent garrison of the K.A.R. Application was therefore made to the Colonial Office, which in 1905 had taken over the administration of East Africa and Uganda, and arrangements were made for two companies of the K.A.R. from East Africa to be stationed at Zanzibar. When headquarters and 'C' Company, 1 K.A.R., returned to Nairobi, 'A' and 'B' Companies remained at Zanzibar. Lines were built for them near the town, and their efficiency, discipline and general behaviour made from the first a favourable impression. 'The force is certainly a fine one both in appearance and in discipline,' wrote Cave, 'and I am sure that if their active services were required they would prove of far greater service than the whole of the 1,600 men who were formerly

---

[1] Basil Cave, *Report on the Administration, Finance and General Condition of the Zanzibar Protectorate, 1890-1907.* Africa No. 4 (1909) (Cd. 4816), p. 9, LIX, 581.

under arms.' The Zanzibar Government agreed to contribute £10,000 annually in respect of this garrison.

In July, 1908, a new system for the distribution of troops came into operation in the East Africa Protectorate. Instead of the Nyasaland Battalion being regarded exclusively as a reserve battalion concentrated at Nairobi, it was agreed that the two battalions in the Protectorate should take it in turns, six months at a time, to find garrisons for the outstations or to remain as a complete unit at headquarters, except that 3 K.A.R. was always to garrison Jubaland. This system was the result of a recommendation by Colonel Gough, after his first visit to 3 K.A.R. as the new Inspector-General. The battalion had never yet trained as a unit, a handicap that Gough was anxious to overcome. During July, therefore, 3 K.A.R. concentrated at Nairobi, while 2 K.A.R. on reaching East Africa, took over the outstations and garrison duty at Zanzibar. This system allowed another reorganization to be carried out in 3 K.A.R. Gough was disturbed to find that out of 761 African ranks then serving with the battalion, 432 were Sudanese, who were becoming almost impossible to replace. At first sight he thought the Nandi 'the only decent soldierly material in East Africa'. A month after Gough's report was issued, however, Captain G. R. Breading (Worc. R.) returned from Abyssinia with 95 Amhara and Galla recruits.[1] More had been selected, but had deserted on the way or refused to board the steamer. Following the policy of utilizing to a more worthy purpose the warlike characteristics of former enemies, that had proved so successful with the Angoni, enough recruits (72) had now been enlisted among the Nandi to form a company by themselves, and the whole battalion was accordingly reorganized on a tribal basis: No. 1, Abyssinian; Nos. 2 and 3, Sudanese; No. 4, mixed Swahili, Manyema, Wanyamwezi, etc.; No. 5, Nandi; and No. 6 (the Camel Company), Sudanese. The new Abyssinian and Nandi companies had Sudanese N.C.Os.

Reorganization in Uganda began with the transfer of responsibility for the former Eastern Military District to East Africa in 1904, where two of the four sepoy companies of 5 K.A.R. had been stationed. Most of the Indian troops were then due for discharge, and as only two companies, one for Kampala and one for Entebbe, were required in replacement, 5 K.A.R. was disbanded as a separate battalion and the nine companies of 4 K.A.R. became seven African companies of 125 rifles,[2] and two Indian companies, each of 100 rifles. The new Indian companies were recruited from some of the best Sikh regiments, and the Commissioner was well pleased with their quality as a picked body of troops. This reduction in military forces helped to diminish expenditure for the year by nearly £33,000.

In spite of the principles laid down in the K.A.R. Regulations, it was not always clear what the policy in outlying parts of the Protectorate was intended to be. This was particularly the case in the Nile Province.

[1] Breading's interesting report on his experiences as a recruiting officer in Abyssinia, dated 10.ix.08, is in C.O. 534, 8.

[2] In 1906 the tribal distribution was 671 Sudanese and 185 'Swahilis', who included Baganda, Wanyamwezi, Kavirondo, and Manyema.

where the military objective was presumed to be the protection of the Nile route. But the zeal of administrative officers in extending their effective control was sometimes in advance of authority, as the Province was still officially considered 'too remote to raise the present hopes of extensive developments'.[1] One instance of this occurred in January, 1906, when the sub-commissioner for the Province and the O.C. Troops at Nimule had a difference of opinion regarding the proper function of the garrison. According to an instruction issued by the Commissioner in the previous October, the administrative head of the Province was only to call out troops under 'imperative necessity', except with prior sanction from headquarters. In spite of this the newly-appointed sub-commissioner showed a marked partiality for an escort of a whole company when investigating reports of minor tribal raids. Most of these reports proved to be gross exaggerations, and the troops thus broke their training to perform long and arduous marches for which no necessity was apparent. Matters came to a head when on the strength of an unconfirmed report of raiding by the Lokoya, the sub-commissioner tried to augment the company then with him by another half-company from Nimule and the company stationed at Gondokoro, thus converting an 'escort' into something approaching a punitive expedition, involving nearly the entire garrison of the Province. The key to all such expeditions was food supply, for the K.A.R. had no permanent carrier service. The troops rationed themselves, even on active operations, and without considerable preparation it was difficult to make long marches through little-known country where cash had no value for the purchase of food. Normally this helped to prevent a too-hasty use of force by the civil power.

The sub-commissioner was informed that the country through which he intended to march was difficult and largely denuded of grass. He replied that the expedition would be undertaken with police alone if the military garrison would assume their duties meanwhile. As there was ample time to seek and obtain the needed authority before his men could concentrate,[2] O.C. Troops referred the matter to headquarters, pointing out that the tribes in question were unadministered, and if expeditions of such a size were to be undertaken as a result of native reports in country where raiding was continual, 'not three companies but three times three would be needed in the Nile Province'. In reply a telegram from the Acting Commissioner cancelled all military movements pending the arrival of the Commandant to discuss the situation on the spot.

But the matter had a much wider significance than at first appeared. When Manning carried out his inspection of 4 K.A.R. that year, he discussed the general question of the distribution of troops in Uganda, partly for internal reasons of training and economy, and partly because attention in England had lately become focused on the dangers of foreign

[1] *'Report on the Uganda Protectorate for 1905-06.' Colonial Reports, Annual.* No. 525 (Cd. 3285-12), p. 31, LIV, 363.

[2] Extension of the telegraph line to H.Q., Nile District, at Nimule, was sanctioned in the estimates for 1905-06.

L

aggression in Africa. The distribution of the nine companies of 4 K.A.R. had been decided in 1902 with sole reference to the internal situation, and had not been materially altered since. The two Indian companies changed places between Entebbe and Kampala every nine months, but were not employed elsewhere. Two of the African companies were at Mbarara in the Western Province; two at Hoima in Bunyoro; and three in the Nile Province, two at Nimule and one at Gondokoro. The seat of government and in fact the whole Kingdom of Buganda was therefore held comparatively weakly, though with the most reliable troops, while the gradual extension of authority towards the west and north, that had been in progress ever since the Mutiny, had perpetuated the division of the battalion into a group of semi-independent companies. Manning had more than once drawn attention to this, recommending the concentration of four companies at Hoima. With the original distribution it was difficult for senior officers to exercise supervision, and unhealthy stations such as those in the Nile valley made the rate of wastage very high.

During the first three months of 1906 Whitehall issued successively the Colonial Defence Committee's *Memorandum on the Defence of Colonial Ports, Precautionary and War Stages of Defence Schemes*, and a document called *Notification of Preparations for War*. Maps of the Anglo-German boundary were also provided. In addition to local defence schemes against the possibility of native risings, Manning discussed the preparation of more general projects, though without making clear which nation was the potential enemy. As early as 1901 confidential information regarding those points on the railway most vulnerable to attack had been issued to the Commissioners of East Africa and Uganda, with an intimation that in the event of hostilities with 'certain Foreign Powers' it was 'not improbable the Railway would form one of the first objectives of the enemy's attack'.[1]

In 1906 the danger to Uganda, with more than one frontier facing a foreign power, loomed much larger than the danger to the railway. Instructions were issued to prepare defence plans at the northern and western stations. As O.C. Troops, Uganda, Major L. R. H. Pope-Hennessey (Oxf. Lt. Inf.) commented in detail on the general situation, and as an essential preliminary, pressed for a proper definition of functions. If defence were to be directed against foreign aggression, he recommended a concentration of all available troops at Hoima, to fall back upon the line of the Nile while awaiting reinforcements. If it were merely a question of internal danger, he thought the concentration might be either at Hoima or Kampala, though this would depend upon whether it was intended to administer the Nile Province. Pope-Hennessey recommended the disbandment of the expensive Indian Contingent, on the ground that Indian troops always remained susceptible to the climate and lacked mobility as they could not live on the country, so that special arrangements were needed to feed them. After the experience gained in eight years of campaigning in Nigeria, East Africa and Somaliland, his

---

[1] F.O. Despatches No. 237 to Eliot and 178 to Jackson, July, 1901. F.O.2. 443.

choice was for the Yao and Angoni tribes of 1 and 2 K.A.R., who he thought when well trained and well officered were as good as Sudanese and better than Sikhs.

George Wilson, who was temporarily in charge in Uganda after Hayes Sadler had gone as Commissioner and Commander-in-Chief, East Africa, in December, 1905, wrote a long despatch to the Secretary of State presenting what he termed the political, as apart from the military side. In his view the armed forces of the Protectorate were required to fulfil two functions: protection against foreign aggression, and the preservation of internal security, the second being subordinate, though at the same time a necessary prerequisite, to the first. 'Five years ago,' he wrote, 'any allusion to the possibility of foreign aggression was received with derision. . . . Now allusions to such a contingency, though very discreetly made, are sufficiently distinct.' Good relations with the natives were based on good administration, which could have 'no effective stability' without the presence of troops, at any rate in the early stages. For this reason Wilson recommended that so far from reducing the Nile garrison, it should be increased to four companies, three of them to tour the province as a preliminary to closer government, and one to remain on garrison duty at provincial headquarters. The rest of the armed forces could concentrate at Kampala, which was easy to supply and centrally situated.

Wilson had already made this proposal for a 'military promenade' in the Nile districts to Hayes Sadler, who had refused to sanction it. The authorities at the Colonial Office therefore decided to await the opinion of the new Commissioner, and in the meantime instructed Wilson that his troops were intended primarily for the preservation of internal peace, and that their strategic disposition for repelling foreign invasion should be subordinate to this.[1]

The new Commissioner of Uganda, H. H. Bell,[2] reached Entebbe on 23rd April, 1906. Shortly afterwards he left for a tour of the northern districts, and on his return recommended to the Secretary of State that the occupation of the Nile Province should be limited to a strip twenty miles wide, bordering both banks of the Nile, as he thought that the resources of the Protectorate were being wasted in the outlying provinces to little purpose. He proposed to guard this strip, intended merely to safeguard the Nile route, with police only, on the ground that a policeman cost Rs10 a month to pay, as against at least Rs19 for an askari, and that too much money in the Nile Province was 'detrimental' to the natives. The police had been given a distinctive uniform very shortly after the formation of the K.A.R. An Inspector-General of Police and

[1] An interesting minute written at the Colonial Office upon this correspondence explains the confusion that arose at this time in Uganda regarding the potential enemy: 'A few months ago the General Staff tried to frighten us into thinking that we were in serious danger of an attack from the Congo Free State. . . . We took the view . . . that if there were any trouble . . . the matter would soon be settled in Europe. . . . With regard to Germany, it seems probable that they will have enough to do for some time to come to keep their own natives in German East Africa in order, but in any case, with the troops in Uganda, the E.A.P., the B.C.A. Protectorate and Zanzibar . . . and with our white settlers and the railway, we ought to be able to dispose of any force which the Germans could send from their Protectorate.'
[2] Later Sir Hesketh Bell, G.C.M.G.

Prisons had been appointed in May, 1906, and the force was considered at last to have 'gained a distinct organization'.

The military evacuation of the Nile Province in 1907 brought about a reduction in the establishment of 4 K.A.R. by one company, but it also had the beneficial result of enabling some measure of concentration to be realized. Instead of Hoima, a number of alternative sites were examined closer to Lake Victoria, and one was eventually chosen at Bombo, about twenty-three miles from Kampala on a hill with good drainage and water, free from sleeping sickness, yet within easy marching distance of the lake. Arrangements were made to withdraw first the two companies from Nimule. The last details of 'B' Company had evacuated Gondokoro by May, 1908, and before the end of the year headquarters and four companies had concentrated at Bombo, one African company remaining at Hoima and one at Mbarara. At Bombo some sickness was experienced at first, probably contracted on the withdrawal down the Nile, but before long a marked improvement was noticeable among the troops. Serious offences declined and the men expressed themselves well content with their new station. But Colonel Gough, in his first report as Inspector-General, regretted the decline both in volume and in value of intelligence reports from the Nile Province after the withdrawal of 4 K.A.R.

Experimental recruiting among the less civilized Uganda tribes also began during this period.[1] It was often a delicate business, as the men were shy and their confidence usually had to be gained by an indirect approach. The kind of method that proved successful was that adopted by Captain C. R. Hall (R. Munster Fus.), who visited the Mbale district in June, 1906, to recruit 35 Bakedi for No. 3 Company. Hall was given special permission to shoot elephant in excess of his licence. He was therefore able to establish friendly relations with the chiefs by explaining that his armed escort was not intended for cattle-raiding or tax-collecting, and to attract the young men of the villages to his camp in the hope of securing presents of elephant meat. The question of government service could then be broached in an atmosphere free from suspicion. Inter-tribal raids sometimes made the men afraid of leaving their villages defenceless, but the commonest difficulty was their reluctance to leave their wives. Once they had been persuaded to try it, however, soldiering was not unpopular, and it was found that the best means of recruiting was to send askaris home to enlist their own relations. Some good Bakedi recruits were also secured in 1908 by the escort accompanying the railway extension survey.

Boundary commissions were constantly at work in East Africa and Uganda in the first decade of the century, involving the K.A.R. in escort duty for prolonged periods. The Anglo-German Boundary Commission began work in Uganda early in 1902, when Major Delmé-Radcliffe, second-in-command of 4 K.A.R., was appointed First Commissioner of the Survey. In April, 1904, two subalterns and 60 rifles 3 K.A.R.

---

[1] In February, 1908, the Sudanese serving with 4 K.A.R. numbered 595 out of a total strength of 774. Gough raised the question of a small reserve to be formed among the ex-askaris in the Sudanese settlements.

were detached for duty with the Commission at Karungu. This party was afterwards increased to 103 rank and file, and the duty lasted until July, 1905. Some friction occurred over the relative status of the officer commanding the Commission and the officer commanding the escort. Manning issued a memorandum in January, 1907, defining the responsibilities of O.C. Escort as the efficiency, economy and discipline of his troops, as cases had arisen of punishments awarded by survey officers outside the terms of the K.A.R. Ordinance. Boundary escorts were usually split into small, widely separated parties, employed as guards or on working parties to clear the bush and build beacons.

The German Commission was followed by another to demarcate the boundary between western Uganda and the Belgian Congo. Before his arrival in February, 1907, the head of the British Commission, Lieutenant-Colonel R. G. T. Bright, had asked for 14 Indian signallers equipped with helios and an escort of one and a half companies, including a machine-gun section. No. 6 Company and half No. 4 Company, 4 K.A.R., were detailed as escort, but the provision of signallers proved difficult. The total establishment was only eight; there was no spare equipment; helios were the most difficult instruments to handle; the training of African signallers in 4 K.A.R. had only just begun; the whole Indian Contingent was due for relief in March, and it was known that troops employed with the Commission would be lost to regimental duty for a considerable time. Bright was willing to accept partially trained African signallers, but the Inspector-General was anxious to keep them available as future instructors, so that eventually a naik and six sepoys were sent instead.

The rationing of troops on detached duty in Uganda was a difficulty to which the Inspector-General had more than once referred in his reports. All Uganda troops employed on the last Nandi expedition had been rationed free. While the German Commission was operating, the Colonial Office decided that the local administration should be responsible for feeding and transporting the escort. The maximum ration allowance at Mbarara, where Bright's party was assembling, amounted to Rs2/8 per month, and was probably regarded by most of the troops as a normal part of their pay. In static conditions the Sudanese of No. 6 Company always grew enough food for themselves and a surplus for disposal, but the more improvident Swahili and other races of No. 4 Company were not accustomed to grow any food at all. The matter was solved by calling on all troops to pay the cost of a local ration, five shells per day.

The work of the Commission lasted for nearly two years. By February, 1909, all parties of the escort had returned, even from the remote tip of the Protectorate where the British, Belgian and German frontiers met.[1]

---

[1] A dispute with the Belgians regarding the position of the meridian of 30° East, however, led to the despatch in March, 1909, of the 'Lake Kivu Mission', consisting of a political and four military officers, two Sudanese companies 4 K.A.R., 70 Sikhs, and some armed police. For several months these troops remained in a fortified position in the Mfumbiro hills, watching a force of Belgians, similarly entrenched, some three miles distant, while the question was investigated and agreement reached in Europe.

On Bright's recommendation the Secretary of State recognized the excellent service of Captains A. H. C. MacGregor (R. Irish Fus.) and S. M. L. Iredell (Middx. R.) and their troops in assisting the survey.

4 K.A.R. also supplied an escort of 80 askaris and six Sikh signallers to accompany Major E. M. Jack's party with the Uganda—German East Africa—Congo Boundary Commission in 1911; an escort of 61 rank and file under Captain W. T. Brooks (D.C.L.I.) for the Anglo-Belgian Boundary Commission (Mahagi Strip) in 1912-13, and another 75 men drawn from the Northern Garrison under Lieutenant H. A. Lilley (York R.) to accompany the Sudan—Uganda Boundary Commission during the first few months of 1913. Escorts for railway extension surveys and for caravans of specie were other military duties of this period.

Military reorganization on what was intended at the time to be a permanent footing was put in hand in British Somaliland after the fourth expedition against the Mullah in 1903-04. Two Indian regiments, the 101st Grenadiers and the 107th Pioneers (later replaced by the 33rd Pioneers), had been left with two Somali mounted infantry companies as a temporary garrison, and Swayne, who returned to the country with the local rank of brigadier-general in full civil and military control, was instructed to organize the tribes for their own defence. A start was then made in establishing 6 K.A.R. on a proper footing. As originally constituted the battalion comprised five companies of Somalis, all mounted: two on ponies, two on camels, and one on mules. In 1905 it was decided to recruit 6 K.A.R. entirely in India, with two mounted companies (one pony and one camel) and two infantry companies, each of 100 Punjabis. Six Somali companies (four mounted and two dismounted) were retained as a Standing Militia, and the whole force was supplemented by an auxiliary tribal militia of some 1,500 men, organized by the political officers in sections of 25 men each, to protect the grazing grounds. In 1907 it was decided to reduce the Indian element to two companies (one camel and one infantry) intended to supply fixed garrisons, and with effect from 1st April, 1908, four and a half companies (450 rifles) of the Standing Militia were drafted into 6 K.A.R. to form four Somali companies: 'A' and 'B' (Pony), 'C' (Mule), and 'D' (Camel), with the half-company as Depôt. Headquarters were at Sheikh; the Indian Contingent was stationed at Sheikh and Burao, and the Somali companies at Sheikh, Burao, Ber and Arialeh, though the pony and mule companies often had to move about the country in search of water.

Manning wrote in his report for 1906 that he was satisfied the Somali could 'attain to a high standard of efficiency in drill and training given sufficient opportunity, a point upon which I . . . was very sceptical'. He defined the functions of the armed forces in British Somaliland as the prevention of raids across the frontier by the Mullah's followers, but stressed the fact that they were not sufficient to give battle should the Mullah invade the Protectorate in force.[1] Colonel Gough, Manning's successor as Inspector-General, in his Report of June, 1908, also spoke

---

[1] *vide infra*, Chapter 7, Section (v).

of the great improvement in the Somaliland troops, and thought that if this continued, 6 K.A.R. would within twelve months be up to the standard of the other battalions.

The changes that took place in the establishments of the K.A.R. between 1904 and 1908 might well have terminated in the practical destruction of the regiment altogether. Early in 1906 the Commissioners of Uganda and East Africa were asked to consider a suggestion that all units in their territories should be amalgamated as a single force. This appears to have set far-reaching ideas in train, and in October, 1907, at the time when the status of Commissioner was changed to that of Governor and Commander-in-Chief, they both drew up proposals for widespread economies that actually included the disbandment of all K.A.R. battalions in their protectorates and their replacement by police. Fortunately this policy did not appeal to the British Government. Colonel Gough, asked for his opinion, deplored the suggestion that police would make an effective substitute for troops, urging that the African native required good officers, steady discipline and constant supervision to turn him into an efficient fighting man.

Soon afterwards Gough paid his first visit to East Africa as Inspector-General. On his return he wrote a memorandum summarizing the military situation, both internally and in relation to the Protectorate's German neighbours. It was an eloquent and reasoned plea for a 'larger outlook than a purely Protectorate point of view', and was favourably received at the Colonial Office. As the document that brought to an end this first movement for military retrenchment in East and Central Africa it is worth quoting at some length. After explaining that the King's African Rifles now consisted of five battalions, comprising five Indian and 24 African companies, with a total strength of 90 British officers, 500 sepoys and 2,700 askaris, maintained by funds allocated by each of the different Protectorates, Gough continued:

'I found during my inspection that the result of this system was that the Protectorates were naturally inclined to reduce their military expenditure to the lowest possible limit. It is quite sound that there should be no unnecessary expenditure on the Military Forces—but there is no doubt that reductions of the K.A.R. have been advocated by the Protectorates under the impression that military aid will, if required, be forthcoming from one of the other Protectorates. It is obvious that if the Protectorates all reduce their forces upon this principle there will be no margin left for mutual assistance. This requires guarding against, and the duty of ensuring that the Military Forces are kept up to the requisite strength must rest with the Home Government, who are the only authority in possession of sufficient general information to be able to form a really sound opinion. For example, in East Africa I was told that reductions could safely be effected as assistance would be forthcoming from Uganda or Nyasaland. In Uganda I was told that East Africa would supply reinforcements if required. This argument was even pushed so far, that a member of the Executive Council in East Africa advocated reducing the K.A.R. still further, on the grounds that if trouble broke out it would be cheaper to bring in outside Imperial troops to deal with the difficulty, than to pay for the upkeep of K.A.Rs. in peace. This might be called the extreme Protectorate point of view of the military requirements and of the manner in which it is proposed to deal with the question.

'I only mention the above arguments, in order to lay stress on the danger there is that the Protectorates, if left to themselves, would in all probability carry reductions far beyond the safety limit.'

Gough's views carried the day, and for the time being nothing more was heard of reducing the K.A.R.

(iii) *Concentration and Dispersal in British Somaliland, 1909-10.*

The wisdom of retaining enough troops to provide mutual support between the protectorates of eastern Africa was soon justified. In 1909 the situation in British Somaliland took a turn so serious that defensive measures were needed far beyond the military strength of the Protectorate.

Since 1904, when the fourth expedition against the Mullah came, like its predecessors, to an indecisive end, the Mullah had taken refuge in Italian territory. The comparative peace of the years that followed allowed the belated formation of 6 K.A.R. The battalion was dispersed in garrison stations intended to protect the coastal area and the routes inland from Berbera, and was too weak for operations on any but a very limited scale.

In 1908 renewed activity by the Mullah's agents caused serious disquiet in British Somaliland, and news reached Berbera that the Mullah was planning a return to British territory. Doubt, uncertainty and rumour were rife throughout the Protectorate, and the senior officers of 6 K.A.R. reported a 'moral deterioration' in the battalion that caused them some uneasiness. The Commissioner attributed this to 'the general feeling of apathy and disappointment' among the friendly tribes at the apparent inability of the British Government to protect them, and the troops in Somaliland were declared to be on active service. Though very loath to become involved in fresh operations, the Government eventually decided to reinforce Somaliland with 1,500 troops from Aden and East Africa. About 1,200 of these were to be drawn from the K.A.R. The result was the biggest concentration of the regiment yet to take place, involving in whole or in part four of the five battalions. Yet no serious fighting took place. Alarmed at the cost of transport, the Government sought other means of securing a settlement.

1 K.A.R. was called upon to contribute headquarters and three companies. As it was home service battalion at the time, Nyasaland was left with a garrison of 100 sepoys of the Indian Contingent and a single African company. The rest of the battalion, numbering six officers and 300 men (of whom 113 were reservists) under Lieutenant-Colonel H. A. Walker (R. Fus.), disembarked at Berbera on 6th January, 1909. On 25th January the troops reached Wadamago after a three-day march, where they remained for the greater part of the year, employed on escort

duty and fatigues. It was a period of trying monotony, but the health and behaviour of the troops was good and compared favourably with that of other battalions. On 17th December 1 K.A.R. left Wadamago for Burao, and on 6th January, 1910, for Berbera on relief by an Indian battalion. A fortnight later the men embarked for home, after a year and sixteen days in Somaliland without firing a shot or seeing a dervish. On arrival at Zomba the reserves were demobilized and the rest of the troops were sent on two months' leave. For a short while the Protectorate was left with practically no military forces at all, as the Indian Contingents were changing, the old one leaving for Bombay in January, 1910, and the new one under Lieutenant L. M. Heath (19th Punjabis) not arriving till March.

Most of the men serving in 1 K.A.R. had enlisted in 1904, and were now due for discharge. Recruiting again proved most popular among the Yao. More Atonga came forward than expected, however, owing to the co-operation of their chiefs. In September the reservists were called up for annual training, and again responded readily.

2 K.A.R. was the only battalion that did not participate in the concentration in Somaliland, as it was employed in manning outstations at Zanzibar and in East Africa. All four companies served in Zanzibar during 1909-10 and at Marsabit, Kerio, Meru, Embu and on patrols on the Tana and Athi rivers. A new garrison mess was formed at Nairobi for officers of both battalions stationed in East Africa.

While 'A' and 'D' Companies remained on duty in Jubaland and the Northern Frontier District, the remainder of 3 K.A.R. left for British Somaliland in February, 1909, under Lieutenant-Colonel J. D. MacKay (Middx. R.): nine officers, with 'F' (Camel) Company from Gobwen (86 rifles), 'B' Company (123 rifles plus a few men of 'A' and 'D' Companies), 'C' Company (123 rifles), and 'E' Company (118 rifles). On arrival in Somaliland 3 K.A.R. was also stationed at Wadamago. The battalion returned to East Africa in January, 1910, and during that year relieved the 2 K.A.R. detachments at Zanzibar.

The concentration at Bombo enabled 4 K.A.R. to respond promptly to the call from Somaliland, which reached Uganda in January, 1909. It was the first time that the battalion had been called upon for foreign service. Headquarters and four companies, totalling 11 officers, one warrant officer, and 460 rank and file under Lieutenant-Colonel B. R. Graham (Corps of Guides, I.A.), embarked at Mombasa in February. This left the defence of Uganda to the Indian Contingent and two African companies, a perilously small garrison, though the police force was now on a much better footing than formerly.

4 K.A.R. returned to Uganda in February, 1910. When the Inspector-General visited the battalion later in the year he found it again widely scattered, with 'A' Company at Hoima, 'B' and 'F' Companies on an expedition to Turkana,[1] 'C' Company at Mbarara, 'D' Company at Mbale on temporary police relief, and 'E' Company at Kigezi with the Boundary Commission. Besides Entebbe and Kampala, which were garrisoned

[1] See Chapter 9, Section (ii).

as usual by the Indian Contingent, only Bomba and Hoima were regular military stations. Five of the six African companies were still Sudanese, though many of these askaris came from the Nile districts south of Gondokoro and were not of the same quality as the original Sudanese troops.

The dispersal of the K.A.R. from British Somaliland at the beginning of 1910 was the result of a decision taken a few months previously to abandon the interior of the Protectorate and retain only Berbera, Zeila, Bulhar and a strip of the coast. This represented a complete reversal of the policy of the previous ten years. When all battalions from other territories had re-embarked, 6 K.A.R., which formed the rearguard, withdrew from the inland stations and marched down from the plateau to Berbera. The evacuation was completed by the end of March, and 6 K.A.R. was then disbanded. Most of the officers were transferred to the other battalions.

(iv) *The Second Period of Reorganization, 1910-14.*

In January, 1910, Sir William Manning was appointed Governor of Nyasaland. His long experience of African troops had stood the K.A.R in good stead during the regiment's formative years, when he had guided its development and co-ordinated its training as the first Inspector-General. There can, however, be no doubt that the fresh outlook brought to the military affairs of eastern Africa by his immediate successors, Colonel Gough and Colonel Thesiger, was of great value to the Colonial Office in guiding its decisions on the perpetual proposals for changes in establishment that arose in the African territories during the years prior to 1914. In practical matters, Gough and Thesiger were also responsible for a number of valuable and overdue reforms.

Thesiger's first inspection of 1 K.A.R. was carried out in Nyasaland towards the end of 1910. He reported very highly on the battalion, which he thought more suitable than any other for fighting in tropical countries, and 'a most valuable asset' in any military operation. As regards the internal situation of the Protectorate, Thesiger recommended that Fort Mlangeni should be abandoned as its usefulness for military purposes had passed. Fort Manning, first established with an eye to trouble in North-East Rhodesia, he was in favour of retaining for the time being. Fort Mangoche he considered strategically important, as the adjoining Portuguese territory was still practically unadministered. These views were accepted by the Acting Governor, who withdrew the garrison from Fort Mlangeni in December and dismantled the buildings.

The fact that the main strength of the K.A.R. had been concentrated in Somaliland during 1909 without dire consequences to the other territories did not pass unnoticed. Within eight years of its formation, the regiment had been reduced from six battalions to four. Yet so sanguine was the view now taken by the Governors and their Councils, many members of which thought it inconceivable that Europeans should fight one another in Africa, no matter what wars might arise at home, and that the growth of the police forces would meet all new commitments within their borders, that the K.A.R. battalions were hardly on their way back from Somaliland before further military economies were proposed.

This time the axe fell heavily upon the Nyasaland battalions. Manning had long been convinced that the military needs of the Protectorate were fast vanishing altogether. At the end of the financial year 1910-11 the grant made by Northern Rhodesia was due to cease, and Nyasaland was to be relieved of a potential commitment in that quarter. Manning accordingly advised the Colonial Office that in his opinion the requirements of Nyasaland could be met by a Native Armed Constabulary of 200 men, supported by a Native Reserve Force of 300 (enlisted from ex-K.A.R. askaris) and the European Volunteer Reserve which counted 140 members. He proposed to begin reducing 1 K.A.R. to these figures and that after the expiration of its tour of service in 1912, the Indian Contingent should not be replaced.

On reading this proposal, Colonel Thesiger pointed out the complete change of policy that had taken place with regard to the K.A.R. The Government of British East Africa, anxious to save the cost of transporting troops to and from Nyasaland every third year, had pressed for the abolition of the reserve battalion, provided the garrison of Zanzibar were reduced from two companies to one (plus extra police), and the establishment of 3 K.A.R. were increased by two extra companies to a total of eight. The acceptance of this scheme by the Colonial Office, which had now earmarked 2 K.A.R. for disbandment and 1 K.A.R. for reduction, meant that the former policy of settling the composition of the K.A.R. as a whole had been abandoned, at the instigation of the Governors, in favour of individual military establishments related only to the internal needs of each Protectorate. Though unable to alter this decision, Thesiger protested strongly against any attempt to substitute the name 'Armed Constabulary' for the K.A.R., which he insisted 'must be trained as regular troops available for service anywhere'.

In due course Manning was informed that the Secretary of State did not agree to any alteration in the charcter of his forces, which in name and training must continue as part of the K.A.R. He was asked whether two full companies, plus machine-gun sections, signallers and artificers, would meet his needs as a new establishment for 1 K.A.R. Manning cabled his agreement, but asked permission to find the machine-gunners and signallers from company strength, and to retain the band instead. In this, however, he was overruled by the Colonial Office.

On 20th February, 1911, the Commanding Officer of 1 K.A.R. was informed that he would not be required to relieve 2 K.A.R. in East Africa, as it had been decided that a reserve battalion was no longer needed. The order to disband two companies of 1 K.A.R. was issued in March. Manning selected the Atonga and Angoni companies, and they were discharged at Zomba on 3rd March and at Fort Manning on 15th April respectively, after which Fort Manning was handed over to the civil power.

The disappearance of the Atonga Company destroyed the last link with the original native levies in Nyasaland. One man, Sergeant-Major

Sumaili, had actually served under Lugard twenty-two years before. In his farewell address Manning commented on old associations and recalled that some of the men had served under him in the days of the Slavers' War.

A further boundary adjustment made in 1910 between Uganda and East Africa had again increased the territory to be administered by the latter. In Jubaland and the Northern Frontier District the Protectorate was also on the eve of a new 'forward policy' that could not fail to increase its military commitments. Yet in April, 1911, the Governor cabled his opinion that seven companies, instead of eight, would be a sufficient establishment for 3 K.A.R., five companies to be stationed in Jubaland and the N.F.D. and two at Nairobi. To justify this sacrifice of one company he advanced the curious reason that too large a force on the Abyssinian border 'might lead to collision with the Abyssinian Emperor'.[1] Thesiger, pointing out that the reductions already effected had been made 'largely in the financial interests of the East Africa Protectorate', ridiculed the idea that an extra company of 100 men strung out along a frontier 550 miles in extent could 'rouse the bellicose nature of Menelik', and the Governor was informed that the new establishment for 3 K.A.R. at a strength of eight companies must stand.

The hastiness of these ill-considered reductions grew apparent within a few weeks. Owing to restrictions in areas controlled by recognized native authorities, the police establishment in East Africa had also been reduced, and even so was not at full strength. It soon became evident that 3 K.A.R. could not cope with the rising military commitments of the Protectorate and of Zanzibar. In May instructions were cabled to Nyasaland to raise 1 K.A.R. once more to a strength of four companies, two to serve in Nyasaland and two abroad in East Africa and Zanzibar, changing with the home service companies every three years, i.e. the same system as before, but on an inter-company instead of a battalion basis. Fortunately recruits were still plentiful; 30 per cent. of those accepted were old soldiers, and with good N.C.O.s. two excellent Yao companies ('A' and 'D' Companies) were soon got together. On 1st October they sailed for East Africa under Major L. E. S. Ward (Oxf. & Bucks L.I.). The new company establishment of 1 K.A.R. was then fixed at one company commander and two subalterns, with 125 rank and file each for the home service, and 100 rank and file each for the foreign service companies. By a strange chance it was just at this juncture that a threat of disturbance—an unusual event in Nyasaland—led to a call for troops to aid the civil power in the Fort Johnston area. The Indian Contingent was dispatched from Zomba, and its presence was sufficient to forestall serious trouble.

In March, 1911, the news was broken to 2 K.A.R. that on return home the battalion would be disbanded. Headquarters and 'D' and 'F' Companies reached Zomba in June, and after their men had been sent

---

[1] 3 K.A.R. had carried out a prolonged reconnaissance of the N.F.D. and the Abyssinian frontier, involving an escort of 55 rifles of the Camel Company, in 1910. The result was an interesting and detailed intelligence report. C.O. 534, 14.

on leave prior to discharge, the officers were employed in recruiting the two new companies for 1 K.A.R. 'A' and 'C' Companies followed from Zanzibar in September. The official date for disbandment was 31st December, 1911, the date to which the N.C.Os. and men of the final detachment drew pay. In a farewell message the Secretary of State for the Colonies expressed his appreciation of the twelve years' arduous service performed by the battalion in Mauritius, Somaliland, West Africa and Zanzibar, as well as in its home territory of Nyasaland. Unfortunately few of these well-trained askaris were willing to enlist in the K.A.R. Reserve, partly because of the low retaining fee of Rs1 a month, and partly because service in the Reserve debarred them from joining the Police. Many therefore crossed the frontier and enlisted under the Germans. There was no disloyalty in this: Germans and British were on good terms and the men were anxious to continue in military service.

In writing his final report on 2 K.A.R., Colonel Thesiger placed on record his 'very high opinion' of its capabilities and efficiency, and continued: 'I am convinced that from an Imperial point of view it (i.e. the proposal to disband the battalion) would be poor economy and a mistake. We have got a Battalion not only suited for so-called savage warfare, but one that could hold its own in any form of fighting, and which is easily capable of expansion.'[1] None the less, in the interests of economy 2 K.A.R. had to go.

The key to the pre-war policy of H.M. Government in relation to defence of the colonies against external aggression is to be found in two decisions of the Committee of Imperial Defence. On 27th July, 1909, it was decided that defence schemes for African colonies should not include the use of native levies in the preliminary operations, though preparations should be made, in the provision of arms and ammunition, 'to make use of such levies at a later stage of the campaign if compelled to do so'. On 4th May, 1911, this policy was reaffirmed, when it was resolved to fix the strength of the military forces in the East and West African Protectorates at 'the minimum required to insure the maintenance of internal order and to deal with risings of the native population'.

The reductions of 1911 mark the lowest ebb ever reached by the regiment—three battalions, comprising altogether 17 companies. There were at the time a number of factors giving rise to a constant demand for the reduction of military establishments in eastern Africa: the successful pacification of the tribes, the increasing responsibility imposed upon colonial governments to balance their budgets; the desire of the Imperial Government to reduce its grants-in-aid, and in British East Africa the appointment to the Legislative Council of 'unofficial', or settler, members who were particularly interested in all matters affecting taxation. Some of these members unceasingly pressed the Government to curtail its military expenditure on the ground that the tribes were peaceable and the Northern Frontier District was sufficiently vast and desolate for protection against

[1] Thesiger's Report on 2 K.A.R., 1911, C.O. 534, 12.

the Abyssinians. It should, however, be recorded that there were others among the settlers who, while not perhaps foreseeing a major war, were mindful of the restraining effect exercised by the mere presence of disciplined troops, and remembering the propensities of the Abyssinians, thought that the word 'protectorate' implied a moral duty towards the northern tribes in British territory, however economically worthless the area in which they lived.[1] But the tendency for the K.A.R. to become the target of those who sought to reform colonial finance, and the bewildering changes in policy that resulted, were from the military viewpoint wholly bad, especially in their effect upon the attitude of the troops themselves. 'I need hardly point out,' wrote the Inspector-General when reporting on 1 K.A.R. in 1912, 'that the constant changes already mentioned have not had a good effect on the natives, and it is essential in the future to avoid any sudden disbandments which to the native mind look very like breaking faith.'[2]

Upon 3 K.A.R. the effect of the reductions of 1911 was nearly disastrous, in spite of the fact that they had been made primarily in the interests and at the instigation of East Africa. The Governor had given a 'personal guarantee' that no trouble would arise with the tribes in his territory, and that no difficulty would be experienced in recruiting two extra companies, and thereafter maintaining the strength of the battalion at eight companies. Yet in a very short time punitive operations were needed against the Marehan Somalis,[3] and the strength of 3 K.A.R. dwindled until the battalion became weaker than at any previous period in its history. News of the disbandment of 2 K.A.R. was not without its effect on the askaris serving in East Africa. During the next eighteen months very few time-expired men could be persuaded to re-engage with 3 K.A.R., and recruitment was so poor that the commanding officer had the greatest difficulty in relieving his detachments.

In May, 1911, Captain J. K. T. Whish (E. Surrey R.) recruited enough Kavirondo in the Nyanza Province to form 'G' Company, but to raise the second additional company proved quite impossible. When Thesiger inspected 3 K.A.R. early in 1912 he found the state of the battalion far from satisfactory. 'A' Company now consisted of 60 Abyssinians, whom Thesiger was anxious to replace as he considered them unreliable, and 40 Meru, who were in process of discharge as the trial of this tribe was adjudged a failure. 'B' and 'C' Companies (Sudanese) were under establishment, but together with 'D' (mixed) and 'E' (Nandi) Companies were the only ones Thesiger regarded as effective, since 'F' (the Camel) Company was only available in its own territory and 'G' Company was still raw and inexperienced. Even counting the establishment at seven companies, the battalion was 100 men under strength, and 140 if the Meru were included.

Thesiger regarded the question of recruitment as urgent and pressing. In unequivocal terms he stated that the battalion could in no sense be regarded as prepared for war. Since the last reductions, all troops in

[1] Lord Cranworth, *A Colony in the Making*, 1912, pp. 210-12.
[2] Thesiger's Report on 1 K.A.R., 12.x.12. C.O. 534, 15.
[3] See Chapter 8. Section (v).

East Africa had been fully committed, and there was 'not a single trained company that could . . . be sent out intact without having to be relieved by other troops'. In view of the proposals then being discussed for closer administration of the Marehan country, it was particularly important that 3 K.A.R. should be kept up to strength and properly trained.

Thesiger's report was forwarded to the Secretary of State with a covering letter from the Governor detailing his own comments and proposals. Some surprise was expressed at the Colonial Office that the Governor had passed these serious and emphatic paragraphs with the observation 'No remarks'.

In addition to his written report, Thesiger put forward his views at a meeting with the Governor, O.C. Troops and the Colonial Secretary, held at Nairobi. The Governor disagreed with many of his opinions and thought that matters should be more fully discussed in London. Thesiger then wrote a long memorandum reiterating his views. He described the military situation in East Africa as the worst ever known; advised strongly that three companies should always be held ready at Nairobi and that a minimum of five was needed for Jubaland and the Northern Frontier District, and concluded: 'I would ask for a full and careful consideration of our military situation in East Africa. Our position at the present time is, in my deliberate opinion, not only unsatisfactory but dangerous.'[1]

Fortunately Thesiger's opinions did not go unheeded for long. In 1913 a new Governor, H. C. Belfield,[2] was appointed to East Africa, and when Thesiger again inspected 3 K.A.R. he wrote at Belfield's request a long report that enumerated the tribal patrols and other operations carried out in the Protectorate since 1900, gave details of all the tribes so far enlisted as askaris, commented on the necessity for reserve forces situated on the railway, and summarized the whole position since the decision to disband 2 K.A.R. had been taken in 1911. Without mincing his words, Thesiger bluntly asserted that 3 K.A.R. had had a very rough deal, scattered in small detachments in places such as Marakwet and Mount Kulal for long periods without relief, despite frequent promises to replace them with police, and suffering 'all the disadvantages and none of the excitements of active service'. To this report Lieutenant-Colonel B. R. Graham, the new commanding officer, added his own appreciation of the situation. This contained a table showing the perpetual movements made to all parts of the Protectorate by the companies of 3 K.A.R. since 1910, and pointed out that the only striking force now available at Nairobi amounted to 75 men in all, including the band, headquarters staff and instructors.

The new Governor's letter to the Secretary of State, transmitting both these reports, revealed very different opinions from those of his predecessor. Belfield said that he regretted having to disagree entirely with the recently expressed views of the late Governor on the military needs

[1] Memo. by Thesiger on the Military Situation in East Africa and Uganda 17.iv.12. C.O. 534, 15.
[2] Later Sir Henry Belfield, K.C.M.G.

of East Africa, and concurred whole-heartedly in the Inspector-General's opinion that two more companies were needed, and that they could only be recruited in Nyasaland. This attitude was well received at the Colonial Office, where apprehension at the state of affairs in East Africa had been slowly maturing. On 17th April a conference was held in London under the chairmanship of Lord Emmott to discuss the question. No objection was made to increasing the permanent garrison, or to Thesiger's proposals for distribution of the troops. He took the opportunity to exact a promise that if any further reductions were made, they should not be at the expense of the Nyasaland companies, as they came from the best recruiting grounds, where already there had been too much discouragement.

Thus the immediate danger of a military collapse in East Africa was averted, but it had been very real while it lasted. A military unit is constantly dwindling: from the moment it is formed, the process of wastage sets in. Unsuitability, sickness, compassionate discharge, serious crime, and expiry of the time of service take constant toll, even in the best conditions of peace-time service. It was a measure of the difficulty of recruitment in East Africa that when Sudanese became unobtainable a long trip had to be made to a foreign country—Abyssinia—to find askaris. Though Thesiger's poor opinion of these men was by no means shared by all the officers under whom they served, it was inevitable that unless a depôt or agency were established in their country the Abyssinian company must in time become mixed, and evolve at last into a local company with a few Abyssinians, mostly N.C.Os., serving in it. This was the situation when war broke out in 1914.

The records of the time show very clearly the constant anxieties and difficulties that beset the junior officers who commanded the isolated posts along the northern frontier. Supplies were often precarious, and to supplement them by shooting game was a necessity and not merely a pleasure, as so often supposed. Month after month would pass among these semi-deserts of sand and rock beyond the time laid down for normal relief. A few weeks before Lord Emmott's conference met in London, this state of affairs culminated in a mutiny among the right half of 'D' Company, 1 K.A.R. After a long period on garrison duty at Ngabatok, whither their wives and families were not allowed to accompany them, the men were employed on the Kamasya Patrol. When it was over, instead of continuing their march towards Nairobi, as they had expected, they were ordered back along the same route to collect fines. Saying that they were tired out, and after being sent to Ngabatok for six months had been kept there for eighteen, the men refused to march, and had to be brought back to Nairobi, where a court-martial of the ringleaders was held. When the news of this affair reached Nyasaland the Acting Governor wrote to the Secretary of State expressing his concern at the conditions of military service in East Africa and asking for the appointment of an officer from 1 K.A.R. to act as second-in-command of the foreign service companies of the battalion. This request was granted, and the appointment was given to Captain L. H. Soames (E. Kent R.).

The military difficulties of East Africa were reflected at Zanzibar. After the reductions of 1911, the Committee of Imperial Defence ruled that the island could not be expected to provide more than one of the two companies required. The failure of 3 K.A.R. to recruit two new companies as promised by the Governor led to the raising of the two new foreign service companies in Nyasaland, almost immediately after the disbandment of 2 K.A.R. Meanwhile the Zanzibar Armed Constabulary came into being, and in due course Thesiger received an invitation to inspect it.

The new Zanzibar unit consisted of a company of infantry, with an establishment of three British officers, one native officer, and 99 rank and file. The company had no direct connection either with the K.A.R. or with the civil police. Thesiger found it well and efficiently administered, but in a letter accompanying his report he commented adversely on the principle involved. So small a body could offer no experience to officers with ambition, or to their men; some friction had arisen between the three elements into which the Zanzibar forces were now divided, and the arrangement seemed to Thesiger 'to combine the maximum of disorganization with the minimum of efficiency'. H.M. Agent and Consul-General did not dispute this view, though he pointed out that the cry for reducing the K.A.R. had not originated in Zanzibar, where the Government had been obliged to do the best it could in the circumstances. The Foreign Office asked for a return to the old system, and this was agreed, though for the next year or so the position was complicated by the unexpected need for extra troops to deal with the Marehan troubles in Jubaland.

On 1st June, 1913, the establishment of 1 K.A.R. was again raised by the addition of two more companies ('E' and 'F') of Atonga and Angoni respectively. Three companies of the battalion, each with an establishment of 100 rank and file, were for service in East Africa, and three, each with an establishment of 85 rank and file, for Nyasaland. The companies were formed in a very few days from reservists, 35 Angoni re-enlisting out of 39 under training and 64 out of 100 Atonga. In September yet another company ('G' Company, Angoni) was raised to replace 'C' Company, which had left for Nairobi on foreign service following the disbandment of the Zanzibar Armed Constabulary.

In Uganda local recruitment was satisfactory in the years immediately preceding the first world war. Early in 1912, Thesiger reported that 4 K.A.R. was only 16 men under establishment. Except in the matter of fire discipline, which was always the weak spot in the training of African troops, he found the battalion well trained, both on the square and in the field. Bombo was 'a model station', and Thesiger compared the running of the unit with that of 'a good English battalion'.

On his next inspection Thesiger found 4 K.A.R. up to strength. By that time the pacification of the northern frontier was absorbing an increasing number of troops, and although Thesiger deplored the renewed scattering of the battalion after all the efforts made to concentrate it at Bombo, he realized that for the time being this was inevitable, and hoped that a proper system of reliefs for the companies engaged would prevent much harm from resulting.

The last two years before the outbreak of war witnessed the final disappearance of the Indian Contingents and a consequent increase in the African establishments of the K.A.R., both regular and reserve. In Nyasaland, where nine Indian Contingents had been seconded for service, they had been the instrument of law and order from the time of the first administration. In Uganda they had been the means of restoring stability and confidence after the Mutiny. For several years, however, there had been a growing desire on the part of some senior officers, especially in Uganda, for the withdrawal of Indian troops, mainly on the ground of their expense and comparative immobility. Major Rigby drew attention to the matter soon after the new military headquarters were set up at Bombo, suggesting that the Sikhs should be replaced by Yaos, or even by Chinese. The Deputy Commissioner agreed with most of the points raised by Rigby. He admitted that the principal advantage of the Sikh troops was their fine appearance, which he thought 'must affect the indigenous native', though all the Sudanese officers denied this. He agreed that the Indian companies were immobile; that headquarters never thought of using them, 'so cumbersome does any inclusion of them in a general movement appear to be'; and that whenever they left Entebbe or Kampala they were like 'lost children in the wood'. Despite all this, however, he still advised their retention, and the Inspector-General agreed, thinking that Indian troops might yet be a factor in preventing any attempt at an African rising.

No further proposals for abolishing the Indian Contingents were put forward until the beginning of 1912, when the Governor of Uganda suggested that although the term of the Contingent then serving did not expire until March, 1913, they should be sent back in the previous September and replaced by an extra African company. Immediate approval was not given to this proposal, as the needs of East Africa made it essential to consider the military situation as a whole. But the growing confidence now placed in the reliability of African troops won the day, and the decision was taken at last to dispense with the safeguard so long felt necessary in eastern Africa. The last Contingent to serve in Nyasaland left Zomba for India on 19th December, 1912. The last Uganda Contingent left Entebbe on 24th February, 1913, and was replaced by a new company of Baganda. In the service of these contingents and their predecessors, in the response to the many emergency calls made in their early days, and in the campaign of 1914-18, the east and central African protectorates owe much to the troops of the Indian Army.

The Reserve Forces, having proved their value, continued to grow. In Nyasaland 251 reservists were registered in 1912, and of this number 217 reported for annual training. The retaining fee of 1/- per month during the eleven months of the year when they were not embodied was increased to 2/6. 'B' Company, 1 K.A.R., left for Jubaland in June, 1912, and as it had not returned when the Indian Contingent left the Protectorate in December, 'A' (Atonga) Company of the Reserve was mobilized. In East Africa, recruitment of time-expired askaris for the Reserve was regarded as satisfactory, with the number standing at about 350 men. In Uganda, however, owing mainly to the different circumstances obtaining among the askaris of 4 K.A.R., the Reserve had a much slower start. The Ordinance was not promulgated until 1912, and by the following year only 30 ex-askaris had joined. As so many men remained with the battalion practically for life, and were not discharged until they were really too old for further service, the Inspector-General recommended that 4 K.A.R. Reserve should be limited for the time being to 50 men, and in this the Governor concurred.

In 1913 the new policy of strengthening the K.A.R. led to further increases in the Nyasaland forces. Orders were issued for the reconstitution of the Depôt Company at Zomba, but in November this was cancelled in favour of another field company. The intention was to raise 1 K.A.R. to a strength of eight companies (four Yao, two Atonga and two Angoni), four of them, at 75 rank and file each, for service in Nyasaland, and four, at 100 rank and file each, for service in East Africa and Zanzibar. This doubling in size of the old establishment, which took effect from 1st April, 1914, virtually restored the cut made by the abolition of 2 K.A.R. By then the companies serving in Nyasaland were over strength, but this had been achieved mainly at the cost of the Reserve, which now numbered little more than half its proper complement of 300 men. There was no difficulty in recruiting for 1 K.A.R., particularly among the Yao, who were ever the keenest soldiers, though Nyasaland natives did not respond to the suggestion that they should engage for service in the new Camel Corps in British Somaliland.

A few weeks before the outbreak of war Colonel A. R. Hoskins, the new Inspector-General, put forward fresh proposals for a complete reorganization of the Regiment. Under this scheme battalion strengths would have become:

1 K.A.R.: Five companies (three in Nyasaland and two in Zanzibar).
3 K.A.R.: Five companies (in East Africa).
4 K.A.R.: Seven companies (in Uganda).
A new Nyasaland Battalion: Four companies (in East Africa).
Two flying columns (250 rifles each, in East Africa).

The scheme, very like a return to the original idea of a reserve drawn from Nyasaland for concentration on the Kenya—Uganda Railway, was approved, but the war prevented its being put into effect. In August, 1914, the crisis therefore had to be met with a regimental strength that stood as follows:

1 K.A.R.: Eight companies.
3 K.A.R.: Six companies ('C' Company not having been re-formed after an outbreak of beri-beri at Serenli[1]).
4 K.A.R.: Seven companies.

It was little enough.

---

[1] See Chapter 8, Section (v).

CHAPTER 7

Campaigns against the Mad Mullah of Somaliland

MAP III

(i) *The First Expedition, 1901.*

THROUGHOUT 1900 the Consul-General of British Somaliland was constantly pressed by the tribes living within reach of the Dulbahante for effective protection against the Mullah's raids. It was in answer to his urgent representations that the home Government first sanctioned active operations on a large scale. The difficulties of campaigning against so mobile an enemy, who roamed at will in a vast, arid, and largely unexplored country, were not at first fully appreciated, and for some time the idea persisted that the Mullah's régime was on the point of collapse, and needed but one more blow to send it toppling. The result of this belief was four campaigns in quick succession, involving in their course nearly all the battalions of the K.A.R. Severe punishment was inflicted upon the Mullah and his followers, who learnt at any rate that the tribes under British protection could not be raided with impunity. But the victories in action were by no means all one-sided; control of the eastern parts of the Protectorate continued uncertain; the Mullah himself remained at large; 'dervishism' (as his cause came to be known) was not stamped out, and the net result of these toilsome and expensive campaigns was merely an uneasy truce.

After the departure of 2 C.A.R. from Somaliland, Lieutenant-Colonel E. J. E. Swayne, aided by a new draft of British officers and later by 50 Punjabi havildars from India, pressed forward with his task of raising, equipping and training the new Somali Levy. Owing to the scarcity of water and the difficulty of transporting fodder, 1,000 men of the force were to be infantry, as against only 100 camelry and 400 mounted infantry. To raise the last-named proved particularly difficult, as the friendly tribes were unwilling to surrender their horsemen. By the end of February, 1901, though he had completed his camel corps and raised 954 infantry, Swayne had only 80 men mounted on ponies, and despite all his efforts could only double this figure before taking the field. To arm the force, 150 rifles had been obtained from 2 C.A.R., but the rest of Swayne's consignment of rifles was late in arriving from England, and training was correspondingly delayed. Two officers of 2 C.A.R., Lieutenants Byrne and Walshe, remained in Somaliland to assist Swayne, and were given command of the posts at Hargeisa and Adadleh, now taken over by the Somali Levy.

Threatened from the west by the Abyssinians, the Mullah had moved back to the Dulbahante country, on the confines of the Haud. The approach to this area lay through Burao and Ber, where ample water was known to exist. At this time the Mullah's force was reported to consist of some 1,200 horsemen and 6,000 foot, with about 300 rifles between them. As soon as the rains permitted, Swayne moved his advanced base from Adadleh to Burao, though the concentration of his force there had to be delayed until the last moment. It was impossible to move so many troops into the far interior until the rains had filled the wells and waterholes, and improved the grazing. That year the rains were late and fitful, and it was 22nd May before Swayne was able to advance.

The ostensible reason for employing a local levy in preference to regular troops was that the former could if necessary live on the country, and was expected to travel fast. Swayne's failure to raise more mounted men was a handicap, but even on foot the Somali can cover phenomenal distances on little or no food or water. Swayne meant to surprise his enemy, and to punish not only the Mullah, but all those sections of the Dulbahante who had given him support. The Levy was organized in three corps, one mounted and two infantry, but Swayne intended to operate in two columns: the larger as a mobile striking force, commanded by himself, and the smaller, under Captain M. McNeill (A. & S. H.) to guard the transport, stores and wounded when the expedition came within reach of the enemy.

The first day's march took the Force eighteen miles to Ber. Swayne marched by night to avoid advertising his presence by conspicuous clouds of dust. With the mounted troops scouting in advance, he reached Eil Dab on 28th May. While the main column continued its march, the mounted corps was then detached to the left flank to punish the Mahmud Gerad section of the Dulbahante and capture stock for the commissariat. Meanwhile Swayne reached a shallow pool of water at Samala, which offered a suitable site for his advanced position. Two zaribas reinforced with barbed wire were constructed to protect the transport camels and stock, and Captain McNeill was left with the second column to command the post.

On the morning of 1st June Swayne left Samala with the main body, driving his rations on the hoof. About 3.30 p.m. on the afternoon of the following day, McNeill noticed some horsemen on a range of low hills a mile to the south-east of his camp. They grew rapidly in number and began to descend on to the plain. McNeill hastily brought in the camels from grazing, and prepared to defend the post. He had with him 370 rifles, about 70 spearmen, a few horsemen, and a .450 maxim gun, mounted on a cairn of stones and commanding an excellent field of fire for 150 yards around the zaribas.

Action at Samala, 2nd-3rd June, 1901.—The dervishes appeared to number about 3,000 horse and foot. On approach they spread out and practically surrounded the camp, but all their attempts to rush it were checked by the maxim gun and controlled volleys from the troops. Two more attacks after dark reached the outside of the zaribas, but the dervishes were hampered by the wire and none succeeded in breaking in.

Next morning the attack was renewed by about 5,000 dervishes on foot, who advanced in a long line to envelop the zaribas. About 80 of them were armed with rifles, and opened fire at 400 yards, causing a few casualties. McNeill's troops stood firm and their fire prevented the enemy from getting within 150 yards, except at one corner of the camel zariba, which was the principal object of the attack. When the dervishes drew off at last, 180 dead were found outside the camp. McNeill lost nine killed and nine wounded, of whom one died.

As the Mullah's horsemen streamed southward in scattered parties through the hills, they were attacked from the flank by Swayne with the main column and split into demoralized groups. Leaving his transport under guard, Swayne continued the pursuit for several days, until the Mullah, with his followers scattered in all directions, fled over the frontier and into the semi-desert country of the south-eastern Haud, to seek sanctuary at the oasis of Mudug. With his ponies ridden to a standstill and his water supplies exhausted, Swayne then abandoned the chase and turned his attention to the punishment of the Ali Gheri and other sections of the Dulbahante, who had always been the Mullah's chief supporters.

As the Mullah was now in Italian territory, Swayne sought fresh instructions. The Foreign Secretary cabled that operations must cease, and requested Swayne's views on the suggestion that a mobile force should be stationed at Burao to prevent any further invasions of the Dulbahante country. When these instructions reached Swayne he was again in pursuit of the Mullah, who had broken back into British territory on account of the hostile attitude of the Sultan of Obbia, and as his force was now in the presence of the enemy, Swayne felt that it would be impolite to withdraw without first bringing the Mullah to action.

Battle of Ferdiddin, 17th July, 1901.—The dervishes were reported to be near Ferdiddin. Swayne halted fourteen miles away and built a camp for his transport and stores. There was no moon, so in order to make a surprise attack he decided upon a night march with 75 mounted troops and the rest on foot, accompanied only by 16 baggage camels to carry the maxim guns, hospital supplies and water tanks. At dawn on 17th July the column reached a shallow, bush-covered valley, where some prisoners reported that the Mullah's encampment was about three miles distant behind a spur. Swayne sent his mounted force in advance, with the first infantry corps following on the right to crown the hills, and the second on the left across the plain. Heavy firing soon showed that the horsemen were engaged, and the reserve company doubled up in support. This part of the force bore the brunt of the action until the outflanking movements on right and left brought sufficient fire to bear on the dervishes, and sent them scurrying into retreat. The Mullah's village was burnt and the enemy was followed in scattered parties for five miles through the dense bush. Over 60 dead dervishes were found on the scene of action. Swayne lost one officer and nine men killed, and one officer and 16 men wounded. Being short of water, he was forced to discontinue the pursuit, and once again the Mullah escaped into Italian territory.

The Field Force reached Burao on 28th-30th July, 1901. On the whole Swayne was well pleased with the performance of his Somali troops. No attempt had been made to teach them anything but to obey orders, to shoot, and to keep formation. Though excitable in action, the men had courage and at Ferdiddin extricated the maxim guns on their own initiative and brought them into action when the camels were shot in the opening stages of the fight. At least 1,200 casualties had been inflicted on the dervishes, and many thousand head of cattle had been captured. Unfortunately the expected co-operation by the Abyssinians came to nothing, as they were obliged to retire for want of food when they found it impossible to live on the country.

Swayne's operations led to a new realization of the strength of the dervish movement. The speed with which the Mullah was able to collect his following after the reverse at Samala, and even to increase it by a large number of well-armed supporters from the Mijertein, caused both Swayne and Sadler to revise their estimates of the permanent force needed to protect the friendly tribes, who if left to themselves were certain to become once more the Mullah's unwilling adherents. 'I was impressed,' wrote Swayne in his despatch of 13th July, 'with the danger of the Dervish movement. Until I actually saw the Mullah's men fighting, I had no idea that a Somali could be so influenced by fanaticism. . . . They have pass-words—wear a white turban, and a special breviary, and have sworn to throw up all worldly advantages . . . At Ferdiddin, after the others had fled, a number of these men remained behind to fight to the end, and were shot down as we advanced.'

The Somali Levy had only been raised as a temporary measure, but Swayne now proposed to retain 500 infantry and 100 camelry at Burao, with a reserve company at Berbera. The rest of the Levy (except the mounted infantry, who were disbanded) was to be organized as a militia to be called upon in emergency. But the Secretary of State, although permitting retention of this force as a provisional measure until the full effect of the recent operations could be assessed, would not agree to the permanent occupation of Burao or of any other post in the interior.

For a few months all remained quiet in British Somaliland. Then, on 16th December, a number of the Mullah's mounted riflemen suddenly surprised a large encampment of tribesmen at Idoweina. The Mullah announced his intention of punishing all tribes who had assisted the Government, of driving the English out of the country, and assuming the leadership of all Somalis himself. Captain H. E. S. Cordeaux, the Acting Consul-General, at once informed the Foreign Office that he was raising the Levy to its former strength, and appealed for more British officers.

This time a more serious view of the matter was taken in London, and prompt action followed. Instructions were cabled to British Central Africa to hold two Sikh maxim gun sections and 300 officers and men in readiness for active service in Somaliland. Swayne was asked to resume command in the Protectorate, and on Christmas Eve five officers of the K.A.R. who were on leave in England—Captains Cobbe, Rattigan, Osborn, and Barclay, and Lieutenant Fletcher—received telegrams ordering them to leave at three days' notice for Berbera. A further despatch from Cordeaux reported that the Mullah had raised his following to 12,000-15,000 men, at least 600 of them armed with rifles. In Cordeaux's opinion another expedition was imperative.

It was from the best troops of Swayne's Somali Levy that Manning had intended to form 6 K.A.R., with an establishment of ten British officers, eight native officers, and 1,037 other ranks. The battalion came nominally into existence in January, 1902, with the rest of the K.A.R., and three of the oldest companies of the Levy were selected to form the nucleus. But the continuous campaigning of the next two years prevented its formation as first intended. For the time being the Levy had to be perpetuated and increased, instead of reduced to the establishment authorized for the permanent regiment.

(ii) *The Second Expedition, 1902*

The instructions issued to Swayne on his resumption of command in Somaliland again emphasized the Government's defensive outlook. 'You should bear in mind,' he was informed, 'that His Majesty's Government do not wish to be drawn into a pursuit of the Mullah, and that operations should, so far as possible, be of a defensive nature.'[1] It was accepted, however, that the occupation of Burao must continue, and two 7-pounder guns were sent for the new fort. Cordeaux's view of the situation was more realistic. After obtaining an officer and 100 sepoys from Aden to take over garrison duty at Berbera, he began reinforcing the levies at Burao without further delay, and recommended that a new post should be established near the southern frontier, possibly at Bohotle. This would at any rate control the Ali Gheri, whom Cordeaux thought mainly responsible for the Mullah's return.

By the end of January, 1902, Swayne had restored the Levy to its former strength. By this time a new and disquieting feature had come to light: the rapid growth of the arms traffic that was springing up along the Somali coast. The dervishes were prepared to pay very dearly—as much as five or six camels per rifle—for arms and ammunition. The sources of this profitable traffic lay in Jibouti and Arabia, but especially in Jibouti, where Le Gras rifles of the 1874 pattern were to be had cheaply and in quantity. They reached the dervishes principally through Las Khorai (the chief town of the Warsangli) and the ports of the Mijertein. Until this traffic could be stopped Swayne saw little chance of peace among the tribes of eastern Somaliland, so the matter became the subject of strongly worded representations to the French and Italian Governments. H.M.S. *Cossack* and the Italian warship *Governolo* carried out joint patrols; many dhows were searched and several consignments were captured, but in the end Swayne attributed his failure to bring his enemy to account largely to the number of well-armed tribesmen from the Mijertein who joined the Mullah's following while the second expedition was in progress.

The dervish raid of December, 1901, had spread panic among the friendly tribes and filled Berbera with refugees. On 7th and 13th February the dervishes again made sudden swoops on the encampments in the neighbourhood of Burao, and escaped with a large number of

---

[1] F.O. to Swayne, 31.xii.01.

camels—the most valuable part of their loot—before their retreat could be cut off. This convinced Swayne that a counter-stroke was needed to restore confidence, and he asked, in addition to the old Levy, for a new force of 500 men, and for permission to mount another hundred of his infantry on camels. Manning, who visited Somaliland in February, 1902, *en route* for his first tour of inspection in East Africa and Uganda, supported this recommendation, and informed the Secretary of State that in his opinion also 'some counter-movement to endeavour to recover the loot taken in the last two raids must be undertaken'. He recommended the attachment of more officers, drawn from the 2nd, 4th and 5th battalions of the K.A.R. (which he thought best able to spare them), and the secondment of Indian signallers from 5 K.A.R. and the Indian Contingent of British Central Africa. The Foreign Office approved these proposals, but again sent a reminder that prolonged operations and unnecessary risks were to be avoided.

In April Swayne was appointed H.M. Commissioner, and Cordeaux reverted to his function as Vice-Consul. Swayne continued in active command of the Protectorate forces, with Cobbe as his chief of staff.

The importation of firearms had shown the Mullah the value to be attached to the possession of seaports, and he now began intriguing with the Warsangli at Las Khorai and in the eastern coastal areas of the Protectorate. Swayne thought it essential to deal with this potential threat to his left flank, and to deprive the Mullah of his communication with the Warsangli, before moving south. On 13th April he left Burao to concentrate a mobile column of 720 rifles. Marching into the Warsangli country, he captured two of the Mullah's emissaries and large numbers of stock. This helped to restore confidence among the friendly Ishaak tribes and to check the smuggling of arms. While the march was in progress Cordeaux made a voyage to Las Khorai in the *Cossack*. The Sultan and his principal advisers refused to visit the ship, so Cordeaux closed the port and summoned the Sultan to Berbera, where in due course he arrived to make his submission.

The way was now clear for the long-awaited offensive. On 26th May Swayne marched south from Burao with the largest force he could muster: 1,200 infantry, 50 mounted infantry, 20 camel corps, three maxims, two 7-pounder guns, and about a thousand burden and ration camels. A garrison of 150 men was left behind at Burao, and 100 men in a masonry blockhouse at Las Dureh. To defend these two posts Swayne asked for another six guns. Early in the year Sharpe had informed Sir Clement Hill that British Central Africa could, if need arose, send up to 950 men, drawn from both battalions, for service in Somaliland, and he was now asked by the Foreign Office to dispatch an officer and 60 Sikhs, with a maxim gun, and hospital stores, to garrison Berbera and other posts on the line of communication.

The Mullah was reported to be at Baran, watching through his scouts and spies the movements of the Field Force and waiting for a favourable opportunity to raid its communications with the coast. His livestock had been driven to Damot, where recent rain had filled the pools. After a brief stay at Wadamago, Swayne moved to Bohotle, where he intended to establish an advanced base from which to mount a swift attack either on Baran or Damot. A stockaded fort was constructed to command the wells and protect the reserve stores. Reports now showed that the Mullah had withdrawn with his livestock to Erego, still farther to the south, leaving 3,000 horsemen at Damot to watch the Field Force. This news was disappointing, for Erego was only one day's march north of the Mudug oasis, the Mullah's previous refuge, and could only be reached by crossing the waterless tract of the southern Haud. A garrison of more than 200 rifles would be needed to guard the post at Bohotle, which was practically isolated, as the dervish horsemen, operating from Halin in the eastern Nogal, frequently blocked the road, capturing caravans of supplies and preventing the mail-runners from getting through.

The strength of the Mullah's following was said to be increasing daily. The Dulbahante, terrified of the consequences if left again to fend for themselves after renewing their submission to the Government, besought Swayne to leave a permanent garrison at Bohotle for their protection. To free his force for mobile operations and to prevent the dervishes from raiding the Nogal valley while he was in the Haud, Swayne asked for 300 men of the K.A.R. Reserve Battalion to garrison another advanced post, probably at Wadamago. The Foreign Office agreed, and Major A. W. V. Plunkett left Zomba in July with five officers, one warrant officer, two Sikhs and 308 Africans of 'A', 'D', and 'F' Companies, 2 K.A.R. The speedy response made to this first call on the Reserve Battalion was highly commended in London.

Swayne had been accompanied by an Italian liaison officer, Captain Count Lovatelli, for the possibility of the Mullah again crossing the frontier had been foreseen. Attempts had been made to induce the Mijertein chief Yusuf Ali to occupy the Mudug oasis, but all he had done was to leave a weak garrison in a fort at Galkayu, on the southern edge of the oasis. Mudug was more accessible from the east coast than from the Haud, and the Foreign Office sought Italian permission to examine the coast near Illig with a view to landing a few hundred men.

Meanwhile Swayne's reconnaissance patrols had driven the Mullah's horsemen out of Damot and pursued them for twenty-five miles into the desert. But the Damot water was exhausted, and as he was temporarily unable to cross the Haud for lack of camels, Swayne moved east into the Nogal valley to check the raids from the Mijertein, detaching a column under Cobbe to attack Halin, where the existence of a stone fort had been reported. The fort was captured, and with it a number of Le Gras rifles and large quantities of stock. By the end of July the Field Force was hampered by 12,000 camels, 35,000 sheep, 500 cattle, and some 8,000 dispossessed tribesmen and their families. So large a concentration of people and animals could not be fed and watered for long in one place, and Swayne was constantly on the move between the Gaolo and Las Anod areas, where water and grazing were the most plentiful.[1]

---

[1] The small, black-headed, fat-tailed Somali sheep can do without water altogether when rain has made the grass lush and green. In the dry season they need water at least once a week. The Somali camel's ability to go without water

Reports by spies said that the Mudug oasis was now hopelessly overcrowded and that the Mullah's position there was rapidly becoming untenable, although he had overcome Yusuf Ali's garrison at Galkayu and gained undisputed possession of the wells. But the Mullah was well mounted, and Swayne wrote in August that he could only hope to bring him to account 'by a fortunate chance.' In the following month, however, Swayne wrote that he was confident that the break-up of the Mullah's power was 'only a question of time'. His object now was to collect transport and supplies while awaiting the reinforcements from Central Africa. Early in September he sent Cobbe back to Bohotle with the camel corps to meet 2 K.A.R. and bring them forward.

Great difficulty had been experienced in getting despatches through to the coast. Mail-runners frequently turned back on finding the route dangerous; attacks on caravans continued, and armed escorts were difficult to find. On 4th October Brigadier-General Manning was informed that the Secretary of State was sending him to Somaliland 'to organize a regular system of escorts moving between fixed posts, who will secure the ready passage of mails and stores'. Manning was instructed to confer with Swayne, assuring him that the Government was ready to reinforce him at once if need arose, though he was not to interfere in any way with Swayne's command of the operations. Swayne was informed of Manning's departure, and also that the Government would consider landing 600 men at Illig in the following April, if Swayne's expedition had not accounted for the Mullah before then.

On 2nd October Swayne wrote from Baran that he had been waiting for twenty-three days for 2 K.A.R. to reach him, and could now wait no longer as rain had recently fallen in the Haud and pools of water might be expected along the route. The latest information from scouts who had reconnoitred Mudug put the number of the Mullah's riflemen as high as 1,200, and reported the size of the encampment as twenty times that of Swayne's, packed with men and horses. That evening 2 K.A.R., some 250 rifles strong, reached Baran, having been delayed on the march by heavy rains, and so were just in time to join Swayne before he marched into the Haud. In their smart khaki uniforms they offered a striking contrast to Swayne's tattered Levy, who had been sketchily clothed in the first place, and had now been in the bush for many weeks.

The expedition left Baran on the evening of 3rd October, about 1,250 fighting troops accompanied by 4,000 camels, half as live rations and half carrying water, and entered the dense, dead thorn bush of the southern Haud, a country quite unknown to British officers. On the following day, mounted scouts in advance of the main column encountered and drove off a party of enemy horse. On the 5th the tracks of hostile scouts were seen near the camp and a brush took place with a party of 30 men, during which one was killed and one taken prisoner.

depends upon the amount of work required of it and the time available each day for grazing; two factors that seriously affected the mobility of military columns in this and subsequent expeditions. 'Las Anod' means 'Pools of Milk', *Las* meaning a shallow clay pan as opposed to the *eil* or *el*, which are permanent wells usually 50-80 feet deep.

On interrogation the prisoner said that the Mullah's main force was two days distant, approaching from the direction of Mudug. At 5 p.m. that afternoon, after forcing a passage through another area of close bush, the column halted for the night at a place called by the Somali Awan Erego.

Battle of Erego, 6th October, 1902.—The advance had hardly been resumed on 6th October when scouts from the front reported that the enemy was approaching in force. The bush was very dense, but realizing the danger of being obliged to fight when encumbered by his full train of transport animals in conditions that would make it almost impossible to draw up his troops in proper formation, Swayne continued to force his way through in the hope of reaching a clearing. Instead the bush grew even thicker, and at last he was obliged to halt and dispose his troops as best he could on three sides of a square around the camel transport, with one Yao and two Somali companies in reserve to close the rear. By that time the Mullah's scouts could be clearly seen, perched in the trees about 400 yards distant.

For some time the enemy made no move. Swayne resumed his advance very slowly and still in formation, with the guns in the front face of the square. The bush was so thick that it was impossible to see more than a few of his troops on either side. Then, as the transport camels began once more to lumber through the thorns, the dervishes attacked from all sides, 600 or more riflemen running in and out of the bushes and firing as they came, followed by others with spears and lances. On the right, two compnies of 2 K.A.R. and two companies of 6 K.A.R., comprising some of the best and most experienced of the Somali troops, held their ground and repelled the attack with rifle fire, but the more recently raised Somali levies on the left fell back in sudden panic on to the centre and rear companies, followed by a company and a half from the front. The situation was precarious. Captain J. N. Angus, R.A., was killed while serving the guns. Lieutenant-Colonel Cobbe continued to work a maxim gun though well out in front of the line, and ran out under hot fire to rescue a wounded orderly.[1] The front face of the square was restored by a half-company of Somalis under Swayne's direct command, who charged and drove the dervishes from the guns. Finding the rest of the square steady, confidence returned to the levies on the left, who resumed their old position and repulsed the attack on that side.

The sound of firing, which echoed loudly in the thick bush, had by now stampeded the camels, and a thousand or more rushed into the bush beyond the left rear of the square, jammed together in hopeless confusion and scattering their water-tins and ammunition boxes. Swayne led two companies 2 K.A.R. and two companies of Somalis to clear the ground, driving the enemy away from the scattered loads and recovering them all. That evening, finding that the dervishes did not renew the attack, he advanced two miles to his front with a company of Yaos and two of Somalis and rounded up about 1,800 of his missing camels. The Mullah's main force was located by scouts about four miles distant.

---

[1] For this action Cobbe was awarded the Victoria Cross.

Major G. E. Phillips, R.E., Swayne's second-in-command, had been killed while rallying his men. On the evening of the battle, Swayne buried his dead, who numbered nearly a hundred levies and spearmen. Early in the action one of the maxim guns had been dropped and lost in the bush. A long search failed to find it, though, as appeared later, the dervishes were more successful. Very little loot fell into the Mullah's hands, but he is said after the battle to have returned two cases of whisky, with a message to say that they were of no use to him.

According to Swayne's information, the wells at Mudug were forty miles away. His transport was thoroughly disorganized, and while so impeded he was anxious not to risk another engagement in the dense bush. On 7th October he accordingly moved to a pool of rain-water in a glade six miles off, at a place called Eil Garaf, where he entrenched his transport over the water and prepared to resume the offensive. The Mullah was encamped ten miles away, and the plan was to advance upon him next day with a mobile column consisting of all three companies 2 K.A.R. and five of the Somali companies. As he marched out on the morning of the 8th, however, Swayne's senior officers reported that they could no longer rely on the Somali troops, for the Mullah's growing prestige was beginning to impress all Muslims with a sense of his invincibility. Swayne cancelled his plans and returned to camp. Next day scouts reported that rifles and reinforcements were again reaching the Mullah. The way to Mudug led through thick bush; many of the water-tanks were damaged, and the pool at Eil Garaf was drying up. Swayne therefore decided to return to Bohotle, eighty-five miles away, the nearest water of which he had certain knowledge. The wounded and transport left on the night of 11th October. Swayne followed early next morning with a rearguard of three companies 2 K.A.R. and five companies of Somalis, and Bohotle was reached without incident on 17th October.

The news that an engagement had taken place at Erego with the Mullah's main force reached the Foreign Office on 18th October, in the form of two telegrams from Cordeaux. The first quoted a message from Swayne in which he reported that the enemy had been driven off with heavy loss and that he intended to renew his advance and attack the Mullah. The second stated that the fighting had been very severe; that the Somali levies were much shaken; that the Mullah was 'bringing up reinforcements from all sides'; and that Swayne was retiring immediately and wanted 600 reliable troops and the remainder of the Reserve Battalion to be dispatched to Berbera.

The tone of this message led the Government to believe that a serious situation had developed in Somaliland, and that Swayne's whole force was in immediate danger. This view was strengthened by a telegram from Manning, who was then at Aden, suggesting that Swayne should be supported with the least possible delay, and proposing the dispatch of 350 men from 1 K.A.R., the remaining half-battalion of 2 K.A.R., 100 Sudanese from 3 K.A.R., and 100 sepoys from 5 K.A.R. Sharpe had already been instructed to dispatch the rest of 2 K.A.R., and the India Office had been asked to warn an Indian battalion for immediate service in Somaliland. When informed of this, Manning replied that he preferred African troops to Indian as they would be more mobile in such a country as Somaliland. He was convinced that the time for suppressing the dervish movement with half-trained local levies was past, and that only operations carried out by regular forces could now hope to succeed.

No time was wasted in issuing the necessary instructions. On 21st October cables were sent to Central and East Africa ordering the troops detailed by Manning to embark for Somaliland as soon as possible. In Nyasaland the concentration of 1 K.A.R. and 2 K.A.R. was completed by forced marches. The company stationed at Fort Mlangeni completed the 200-mile march to Chiromo in four days. The river was low, and hasty measures had to be adopted to raise enough carriers, difficulties that induced Sharpe 'to think, after all, that perhaps the headquarters of the 2nd Battalion should be either on the coast or else on the East Africa Railway, where there would be no transport difficulties'.[1] But no time was lost, and the troops embarked in the German steamer *Bundesrath* at Chinde on 8th November: Lieutenant-Colonel E. C. Margesson (S. Wales Bord.) with seven officers and 360 rifles 1 K.A.R.; Captain H. E. Olivey (Suffolk R.) with six officers and 302 rifles 2 K.A.R.; and Captain C. Godfrey of the Indian Contingent, with 52 Sikhs. The Protectorate was left with only 35 Sikhs and 370 Africans of 1 K.A.R., under the command of Captain C. V. N. Percival, a very small force divided between Zomba and three outstations, but in Sharpe's opinion 'ample for anything which can possibly be expected to happen'.

Two officers and 100 rifles 3 K.A.R. and one officer and 103 rifles 5 K.A.R. sailed together in the *Bincoora* on 1st November and reached Berbera on the 9th, two days earlier than expected. Manning had decided to accept sepoys from India, and the troops of the Bombay Infantry regiment who had been standing by sailed accordingly before the end of October.

While all these troops were converging upon Somaliland, further reports showed that the situation had improved. Swayne's safe arrival at Bohotle relieved the necessity for emergency measures. By the end of October over a thousand troops were stationed in the interior at Bohotle, Wadamago, and Garrero, where a flying column under Lieutenant-Colonel Cobbe was held in readiness to protect the friendly tribes against raids. The Government was anxious to consult Swayne regarding future operations, and he was instructed to put Cordeaux in charge as Acting Commissioner, while Manning remained in command of troops. On 5th November Swayne left Berbera for England.

The campaign of 1902 cannot be accounted a complete failure. Headquarters of the Field Force covered 1,500 miles of incessant marching, and detached columns considerably more, scouring the Nogal valley and driving the dervishes southward and out of the Protectorate. Swayne estimated that he had inflicted 1,400 casualties, and his captures of stock included 25,000 camels, 1,500 cattle, 200 horses and a quarter of a million sheep. Moreover, it became known later that the Mullah regarded the action at Erego as a reverse.

[1] D.O. from Sharpe to Hill, 14.xi.02. F.O.2, 608.

But Swayne had learnt from his experience one lesson very thoroughly: the error of supposing that the friendly tribes could ever withstand the Mullah with the aid merely of half-trained levies and mounted *illalos*. In his last despatch before leaving Berbera he wrote of the superstitious awe that had sunk into the minds of all Somalis—'how deeply I did not know until the action of 6th October'. He was convinced that Somalis could no longer be relied upon for close fighting, and that no operations, even by regular troops, could be successful until the constant importation of arms had been stopped.

Two courses of action now appeared possible. The first was to remain strictly on the defensive, and confine all meaures to the protection of the tribes north of the Haud. The second was to carry out Swayne's previous recommendation for a converging attack on Mudug, now the Mullah's headquarters and the centre whence he drew his support. Not many years before, a defensive policy had been tried against the Mahdi in the Sudan. As a result his power and prestige so increased that at last operations on a large scale could no longer be avoided. The Government therefore chose the second alternative, and a still larger expedition was authorized against the Mullah.

(iii) *The Third Expedition, 1902-03.*

The third expedition against the Mullah, though more elaborately organized, accomplished less than any of the others. It was based on a strategy ill-suited to a desert terrain, where lines of advance and areas of concentration were limited by the position of water-holes well known to the enemy. The operational columns achieved some prodigious marches, suffered a tragic reverse that wiped out half the officers of 2 K.A.R. and practically two companies of troops, and in the end failed to prevent the Mullah from escaping through the line of communication into the comparative freedom of the Nogal valley. But there was no failure on the part of the troops themselves: K.A.R., Indian and Somali, all gave evidence of their endurance and fighting quality.

Brigadier-General Manning's first tasks were to strengthen his line of communication, to reinforce the flying column at Garrero, and to disband the greater part of the Somali Levy. He set about them with characteristic energy. On 4th November he took over command; on the 10th he left for Garrero; marched out to Bohotle on the 17th, relieved most of the Somali troops there with a company of the 1st Bombay Grenadiers, and returned to Berbera on the 23rd. With substantial reinforcements already arriving, Manning decided to retain only 750 rifles of the Levy: four infantry companies of 100 each (intended for garrison duty at Hargeisa, Burao and Garrero); 150 infantry to provide small detachments at Sheikh, Las Dureh and elsewhere; 150 mounted infantry, and 50 camelry. The two last-named were intended as a fresh nucleus for 6 K.A.R., but the recruitment of good material proved very difficult, especially for the camelry, whose establishment had originally been fixed at 150. A trial was even made of the Mullah's old adherents the Dulbahante, but they proved unreliable and many of them deserted during the course of the operations.

The troops from British Central Africa reached Berbera on 27th November, followed next day by a draft of 150 mounted infantry from the Punjab. Manning was now able to complete the dispositions he had planned for garrison troops and to form the operational column. The Somali levies at Hargeisa and Burao were stiffened with a half-company of Bombay Grenadiers. The recently arrived half-battalion 2 K.A.R. ('B', 'C' and 'E' Companies) was sent up-country to join the rest of the battalion at Garrero. The Indian Contingent from Central Africa was divided between Garrero and Bohotle. These troops were intended to form the backbone of the flying column of 600-700 rifles that was to operate southward from Bohotle. In selecting 2 K.A.R. for this task, Manning was influenced by the steady behaviour displayed by the Yao askaris at Erego, who in his opinion had 'alone prevented a disaster to the force'.[1] The flying column was further strengthened by two guns of a battery of 7-pounders loaned from Aden. As no other gun crews were available, this battery had at first been served by Somalis. They were now replaced by 21 Sikhs from the Indian Contingent, who soon proved themselves excellent gunners, and the unit was then known as the K.A.R. Camel Battery.

By this time Berbera had become the centre of a great tented city, a hive of excitement and activity that constantly increased as troops and stores continued to pour into the port. The presence of regular units went far towards restoring confidence among the Somali, an essential preliminary to the collection of camels for hire as transport. 'It was impossible,' wrote a newspaper correspondent, 'not to recognize the delight of the Yaos and the keenness of the Sudanese battalions of the K.A.R. in their work. They were ever ready for duty, soldierly in appearance, smart on parade, alert and determined. It was a matter for much congratulation that the Yaos had been mustered in such force.'[2]

The British Government had again opened negotiations with the Emperor Menelik for the movement of Abyssinian troops down the valley of the Tug Fafan to the Webi Shabelle, in order to seal the Mullah's escape route to the south. Menelik agreed, and two British liaison officers and a medical officer were sent to accompany his troops. A direct advance on Mudug was also to be made, with Italian consent, by the shortest practicable route from the east coast. In this way it was hoped to trap the Mullah between converging forces, or at any rate to cut him off from further withdrawal inland and drive him back into British territory, where the flying column would have a better chance of dealing with him. The plan might have succeeded had there been a tangible military objective instead of a highly mobile enemy who knew the country far better than his opponents.

During November another reconnaissance of Illig, Obbia and other points on the east coast was carried out by H.M.S. *Pomone* and the

---

[1] Manning to C.O., 2 K.A.R., 26.xi.02.
[2] Angus Hamilton, *Somaliland*, p. 122.

R.I.N. ship *Volturno*. An officer of the Bombay Rifles was on board the former to represent the military angle. The port recommended for disembarkation was Obbia, where the Sultan's son stated that up to 6,000 camels and drivers could be made available.

In December control of the expedition was taken over by the War Office. On the 19th Manning received orders from the Secretary of State for War to transport to Obbia the troops of 1 K.A.R. (three companies), 3 K.A.R. (one company), and 5 K.A.R. (one company), then concentrated near Berbera, together with 150 rifles of the Punjab Mounted Infantry, totalling some 700 men. Manning went to Aden and chartered an Indian-owned steamer, the s.s. *Haidari*. On the evening of 22nd December she left Berbera with the troops on board, with their guns, ammunition, stores, and rations for six months. Other troops were ordered to Obbia direct from India (the 2nd Sikhs, 200 rifles of the Bikanir Camel Corps, some Sappers and Miners and a section of mountain guns), and from South Africa (one company of British and one of Burgher Mounted Infantry). The whole Obbia column numbered 2,296 troops, and as it was cast for the principal rôle, Manning was ordered to command it in person.

The *Haidari* reached Obbia on 26th December. As the starting-point of a military expedition, the outlook was unpromising. Black reefs fringed the coast, and behind the town, rising gently from the sea towards a line of low, undulating hills, stretched a bleak prospect of rolling dunes and level sand devoid of a single tree or vestige of scrub. Heavy seas and a pounding surf made landing difficult. In the course of another four months the monsoon would make the use of the port impossible.

The troops of 1 K.A.R. were first over the side and at once went to work constructing a breakwater, wading all day into the sea to drag the incoming boats through the surf. By the evening of 2nd January, 1903, all troops and stores were ashore and in camp on sandy soil in the open country, a thousand yards from the beach.

Manning landed at Obbia on 5th January, to find the first of his problems awaiting him. In spite of their previous assurances, the attitude of the Sultan Yusuf Ali and his son proved most obstructive, and it soon became evident that their sole intention was to make money out of the expedition, while doing everything in their power to prevent it from moving into the interior. The tribesmen were forbidden to offer camels for sale except through the Sultan. Manning needed 3,500, but by the middle of January only four had been obtained, and those at an exorbitant price. Manning was hoping to get away by the end of January, and by taking a strong line secured another 150 camels, but the attitude of Yusuf Ali grew daily more defiant. Representations by Count Lovatelli led to the arrival of the Italian Consul-General in a warship, and Yusuf Ali and his son were deported. After that an open market was established, but the attitude of the local tribes was never co-operative, and desertions among the transport men were frequent.

While the troops from India and South Africa were assembling, Manning decided to reconnoitre the route towards Galkayu. Lieutenant-Colonel Cobbe, who had now arrived to take command of 1 K.A.R., left Obbia on 14th January with a strong column: 300 rifles 1 K.A.R., 75 rifles 3 K.A.R., 75 rifles 5 K.A.R., and 50 rifles 2nd Sikhs, with five maxim guns. Manning was taking no chances, and although the Mullah was reported to be far away to the north of Galkayu, ordered Cobbe to move only in square formation if he encountered thick bush, and never under any circumstances to allow his troops to pile arms. Cobbe examined the Kantor plain and selected a route via El Dibbir and Dibit. The wells along this route were cleaned and extra water collected in tanks. Other posts for stores were established along the route as far as Wargallo, beyond which reconnaissances were made to the west and north without encountering any sign of the enemy.

On 3rd February Cobbe was dispatched south towards El Hur, where Yusuf Ali's burden camels were said to be, with a company of 1 K.A.R. and a company of 5 K.A.R., 150 mounted infantry and 75 camelry. He got into touch with the Hawiya tribe and returned to Obbia on 21st February with about 400 camels.

The difficulties of landing camels, mules and stores at Obbia and of obtaining sufficient transport and reliable drivers on shore had already obliged Manning to postpone his date of departure. He now planned to begin his march on 22nd February, when a flying column was to leave for Galkayu, and to complete his concentration there by 13th March. Before moving he issued written instructions for closing down the base at Obbia, which had to be done by 15th April on account of the monsoon, and transferring it to Berbera. The posts remaining on the line of communication inland were then to close down in succession and move on the Field Force at Galkayu, which would in the meantime have opened up fresh communications via Bohotle. Instructions were also dispatched by sea to the officer commanding the Berbera-Bohotle force, describing the nature of the co-operation expected from him. The flying column was to move down from Bohotle to Damot, sinking wells or setting up tanks covered with sail-cloth, to be kept filled if necessary by regular camel convoys from Bohotle. The two columns at Damot and Galkayu were expected then to be about eighty miles apart, and every effort was to be made to gain touch by scouts, patrols, or wireless telegraphy. Little reliance could be placed on the last named, which had been tried between Obbia and one of the forward posts at Lodobal, but without success.

On 22nd February Manning left Obbia with the flying column to seize the wells at Galkayu. He took with him 275 mounted troops of the British, Burgher, and Punjabi Mounted Infantry and the Bikanir Camel Corps; 180 rifles 1 K.A.R., 75 rifles 3 K.A.R., and 270 rifles 2nd Sikhs. The column was joined on the march by other Indian troops from the garrisons of the forward supply points, to a total strength of 1,138 men. On 3rd March, while the main column was at Wargallo, a reconnaissance by mounted infantry showed that the wells at Galkayu were deserted. They were occupied forthwith; the rest of the mounted troops came forward in support, and by 5th March the whole column reached Galkayu, where a strong zariba was built.

The second column left Obbia on 6th March under the command of

Lieutenant-Colonel C. G. M. Fasken (2nd Sikhs). It included a company each of 1 K.A.R. and 5 K.A.R., and the balance of the mounted troops and Sikh infantry to a total of 807 men, with two guns of the Lahore Mountain Battery and a convoy of one month's rations. Water and transport difficulties delayed Fasken at Dibit and he had to divide his column into two, but by 24th March his troops had all reached Galkayu. The Field Force was therefore not ready to begin operations until very much later than originally intended.

News of the Mullah's whereabouts was difficult to obtain. Manning's Somali spies proved very unreliable and very timorous; the Mullah's spies, when taken prisoner, professed to have no recent information. The first object was to establish contact with the column from Bohotle. On 10th March Manning sent Cobbe north to reconnoitre Badwein, thirty miles along the track to Damot. There Cobbe met messengers who told him that Damot had been occupied by Plunkett on 3rd March. The line of communication was now continuous from Berbera to Obbia, a distance of over 500 miles, with troops distributed at fourteen posts along it. A telegraph section of the Royal Engineers, sent out from England, had constructed an airline from Berbera to Bohotle, with a cable extension for another forty-seven miles to Damot.

The object of this elaborate distribution of regular troops was to confine the Mullah to the west of the line, thus cutting him off from his allies and sources of supply in the Mijertein; and then, by advancing with the largest number of fighting troops that it was possible to concentrate, to crush him against the Abyssinian army approaching from the valley of the Webi Shabelle. Manning's first move therefore was to order Plunkett to join him from Damot with three companies ('A', 'C' and 'F') 2 K.A.R., 50 Somali Mounted Infantry, two guns of the Camel Battery (which he thought better suited to a country of waterless bush than the guns of the Mountain Battery), and a thousand transport camels. Plunkett performed this march, which he estimated at 105 miles (a greater distance than previously supposed) in four days.

Manning was now ready to advance with his striking force. The consensus of reports showed that the Mullah was in the neighbourhood of Galadi, with his stock scattered between there and Dudub. On 26th March Manning left Galkayu for Bera, which he had previously occupied as an advanced post along the Galadi road. His force consisted of 284 mounted troops, 278 men of the 2nd Sikhs, 149 rifles 1 K.A.R., 300 rifles 2 K.A.R., and 50 rifles 5 K.A.R. On 27th March mounted troops were sent ahead to occupy Dudub, and on the 28th Manning left Bera with the rest of his force, less a half-company each of 2 K.A.R. and 5 K.A.R., who were left behind to guard the wells. The strength of the column was then 867 rifles, including the men of the 2nd Sikhs who had previously formed the garrison at Bera.

It was soon necessary to reduce this number. Manning marched for eighteen miles through thick bush, and halted that evening on an open plain. At that point he thought it best to send back about 300 men of the 2nd Sikhs, as no news had reached him of the water situation at Dudub. This considerably relieved his transport, though on reaching Dudub

Manning found the water supply ample. On arrival at Galadi on 31st March he was relieved to discover that the wells numbered over 2,000, all of them well filled.

The mounted infantry had found Galadi occupied by a few enemy spearmen. Prisoners reported that the Mullah had left there when the Obbia column reached Galkayu, and had gone west towards Walwal, four or five marches away. His cattle and flocks were reported to be in the Gumburu Hills, some thirty to forty miles off. At 2 a.m. on 1st April Plunkett left camp with 60 rifles 1 K.A.R. and 170 rifles 2 K.A.R., marched to Gumburu, killed 40 of the Mullah's spearmen and captured 600 camels and 3,000 sheep and goats. On the following day Cobbe led a column of 120 rifles drawn from 1 K.A.R. and 2 K.A.R. on a mission to the south-west, where he achieved similar results. Mounted columns operating from Damot and Badwein also made captures of livestock. The camels taken in these raids were particularly valuable, though only a small proportion of them was suitable for use as transport animals.

Manning's information was that the wells at Walwal and Wardair, where water was said to be plentiful, lay about seventy-five miles to the west. It was there that he hoped to strike the final blow, or to tempt the Mullah to attack him in the thick bush as he approached. His intention was to amass a fortnight's supplies, establish a water-point to store two days' water for the entire force about twenty miles along the route, and then to bring up 3 K.A.R. and most of the 2nd Sikhs before advancing.

One essential point, however, still remained to be determined. Which was the route to Walwal and Wardair? The prisoners all professed ignorance; the Somali bush is intersected by a maze of tracks leading from one group of wells to another, often so tortuous that their initial direction gives no clue to their destination. Beyond a vague idea that the track passed somewhere to the north of Gumburu, nothing was known.

Eventually a guide was discovered who said he knew the route. Manning then detailed Cobbe and Plunkett, who had already been as far as Gumburu, to make a strong reconnaissance from Galadi while the rest of the troops and transport were awaited from Galkayu. A water-point had been established twenty miles out, garrisoned by 5 K.A.R. Cobbe was instructed to make every endeavour to set up another at Gumburu, and then, as the Mullah was believed to have withdrawn beyond Wardair, to reconnoitre the wells there and occupy them if possible.

Cobbe left Galadi on 10th April with five officers and 116 rifles 1 K.A.R.; ten officers, one warrant officer and 253 rifles 2 K.A.R.; one officer and ten mounted infantry 6 K.A.R.; two guns of the Camel Battery, four maxims and a transport column of 380 camels. He was joined at the water-point by one officer and 50 rifles 5 K.A.R. Manning expected to follow with the rest of his force on the 17th, when the 2nd Sikhs and 3 K.A.R. were due from Galkuyu. He realized that swift action was imperative, as he could not hope to maintain his force for much longer in the Haud, but was hopeful that one decisive victory would 'destroy the power of the Mullah for further hostile action'.[1]

By the time Cobbe reached the first water-point, a day's march from Galadi, he realized that he was too far to the south and on the wrong track for Wardair. Reporting this to Manning, he struck off through the bush to the north-west, hoping to reach the proper road, which the guide now said ran north from Galadi. Before long Cobbe crossed the track to Gumburu previously used by Plunkett. As his scouts could discover no sign of any tracks farther north, he decided to try the Gumburu route. The mounted infantry rode ahead, and were soon in touch with enemy scouts.

At four o'clock on the morning of 13th April, Cobbe's patrols reported the road clear in front. The column proceeded, though the guide was doubtful whether he was on the right road for Wardair. At the midday halt Cobbe was joined by two officers and 21 rifles of the British and one officer and 22 rifles of the Burgher Mounted Infantry, who had been sent to join him by Manning. Cobbe was then forty-nine miles west of Galadi, and still in the neighbourhood of Gumburu. After resting during the afternoon he sent all his mounted troops in advance and followed at 5 p.m. with the infantry, intending to march by moonlight. Four miles farther on the tracks of the mounted men were lost, and Cobbe halted until daylight on the 14th, when he resumed his efforts to get into touch with his scouts. The bush became thicker as the advance continued, intersecting paths seemed to disperse in several directions, and about midday Cobbe realized that the guide was lost, and decided to retire. Soon afterwards he was fired upon by enemy horsemen and some of his transport animals stampeded. Guided by the sound of firing, the mounted infantry regained touch with the main body and rode up in time to chase the Mullah's horsemen away.

Cobbe continued his retirement to a spot north of Gumburu Hill. He was then about forty-two miles from Galadi. A heavy thunder-storm broke on the 15th, and it rained hard for about an hour. Some pools were found, where the horses were watered and all empty tanks filled to form a water-point. Enemy horsemen were seen hovering around the camp. On the morning of the 16th Cobbe sent two half-companies to the west and south-west under Captains H. H. de B. Morris (E. Kent R.) and C. E. Luard (Norfolk R.) to prospect for water, and a mounted patrol to the north to search again for the route to Wardair. Morris found the enemy to his front and was soon in action; Luard's party was also heard firing and Cobbe sent another half-company to his support and more mounted infantry to occupy the enemy, who were evidently in some force to the west. The mounted infantry were soon in need of reinforcements, but Luard came up on their left and drove the enemy off. Lieutenant Chicester of 6 K.A.R. was killed in this action and one Burgher and two Somali mounted infantrymen were wounded.

Cobbe guessed that the Mullah's main forces were collecting in the thick bush ten or twelve miles away, and informed Manning that in the circumstances he would hold his post at Gumburu until the main column

---

[1] Manning to W.O., 12.iv.03. *Despatches relative to the Operation of the Somaliland Field Force,* 1903 (Cd. 1500), p. 21.

could reach him from Galadi. That afternoon he was reinforced by an officer and 48 rifles of the 2nd Sikhs, who had been sent forward with a water convoy. Major Margesson was sent out with a strong patrol and went four miles without seeing any sign of the enemy.

On 17th April, the day on which Manning was due to leave Galadi, Cobbe was preparing to send 150 camels back after storing their water supplies in his empty tanks. While thus engaged he dispatched Captain H. E. Olivey (Suffolk R.) with 'C' Company, 2 K.A.R., to reconnoitre three miles to the west, and Captain H. A. Walker[1] (R. Fus.) with a half-company 1 K.A.R. to a hill a mile and a half to the south-west, to see if the country were clear. Olivey left the camp just before daylight, and about three hours later sent back a message to say that he was then three or four miles out, had seen no sign of the enemy, and was returning. Soon afterwards Cobbe received another message from Olivey, timed 8.5 a.m., saying that the enemy was advancing upon him with horse and foot, that he was retiring slowly, and needed reinforcements. Cobbe ordered Plunkett out in support with 'A' Company, 2 K.A.R., 48 men of the 2nd Sikhs and two maxims. A slight delay occurred while the maxims were loaded and an extra 50 rounds per man were distributed. but at 9.15 a.m. Plunkett was ready to start. Just before he left a third message arrived from Olivey, saying that he was a mile and a half out, and not in action. Plunkett saw this message, and understood that his orders were only to bring Olivey back. After his departure Cobbe sent horsemen out to recall Walker, and continued to strengthen his zariba.

Battle of Gumburu, 17th April, 1903.—No European lived to describe the disastrous action that followed. The accounts of the African survivors show that after meeting Olivey about a mile from the camp, Plunkett joined forces with him and, instead of retiring, formed square with the Sikhs in the front face and marched west for about six miles to an open space surrounded by thick bush, where the dervishes had collected to await him. The troops were attacked by about 4,000 horsemen and 10,000 foot, apparently commanded by the Mullah in person. With the fanatical contempt for death that they always showed in his presence, the dervishes swept from all sides upon the square, first horsemen, then riflemen on foot, and finally hordes of spearmen who broke into the square with the weight of their headlong rush, heedless of the devastating fire of maxims and rifles. Plunkett was the first officer to be hit, wounded by bullet and spear. When his ammunition was nearly exhausted, he gave the order to break out with the bayonet and charge back to the zariba. By that time many of his men had been killed or wounded. The survivors rushed out upon their enemy, but few of them got very far. The maxim guns were broken up before they could be captured; then the little force was borne down and overwhelmed.

At 11.45 a.m. some of the Somalis at Cobbe's encampment reported that they had heard the sound of firing. It was scarcely audible, but Cobbe sent out some mounted troops to investigate. An hour later one of them returned carrying Plunkett's guide, wounded, upon his pony,

---

[1] Later Colonel H. A. Walker, C.B., C.M.G., D.S.O., Inspector-General of the K.A.R., 1927-31.

who said that 'the force had been cut up'. Cobbe sent back reports to Manning, and dispatched more mounted men for news, realizing that at least a hundred of the 250 men with him were needed to defend the camp, and that it was already too late to send out reinforcements. By now survivors from the battle were coming in, assisted by the mounted patrols. They were followed by dervish horsemen right up to the zariba, who had to be driven off with shrapnel, though their scouts remained closely on the watch.

Nine British officers lost their lives at Gumburu; one from the 2nd Sikhs, one medical officer, and no fewer than seven (Lieutenant-Colonel A. W. V. Plunkett; Captains J. Johnston-Stewart, H. E. Olivey, H. H. de B. Morris, and L. McKinnon; Lieutenants J. A. Gaynor and E. W. Bell) from 2 K.A.R. Two Indian officers and 185 sepoys and askaris were also killed, 'A' and 'C' Companies, 2 K.A.R., being practically wiped out. Of the 47 men who eventually straggled back to the zariba, all but six were wounded.

Cobbe regretted Plunkett's action in advancing against the enemy instead of retiring with Olivey as directed, both on account of the consequences to his troops and also because he thought an excellent opportunity of dealing with the Mullah had been lost by premature action.[1] But he had plenty of water, and was quite prepared to hold his zariba until Manning could reach him with the main body, when there was still a chance that the Mullah might be within reach.

On the evening of 17th April, the day of the battle, Manning received a message from Cobbe, saying that he feared Plunkett's party had met with some reverse. Though not at first suspecting anything serious, Manning dispatched Major P. A. Kenna and 100 mounted infantry with orders that Cobbe was to fall back upon the main body. At midnight Manning followed with 320 rifles 2nd Sikhs and 60 rifles 3 K.A.R. On the march further messages informed him that Plunkett had been overwhelmed and that the enemy was apparently still in the neighbourhood. At midday on the 19th Manning met Cobbe's force, returning as ordered with all transport and baggage intact. The fact that the dervishes did not attempt to interfere with the withdrawal was an indication of the heavy casualties they had suffered two days before.

Manning felt that for the time being a further advance was impossible. Nearly a quarter of his striking-force had been killed or wounded. Cobbe's camels were exhausted, and the ration stocks at Galadi would not permit a large concentration of troops there for long. Leaving Cobbe with 370 rifles at Galadi and Captain Phillips with 80 rifles at Dudub to cover the movement, he retired on Galkayu with the rest of his force. There seems no reason to doubt that Manning's decision was influenced partly by the evidence he now possessed of the dervishes' military spirit. In his despatch to the War Office he described the Adones from the Webi Shabelle valley, who were the Mullah's latest recruits, as 'men

---

[1] Cobbe's Report to the Chief Staff Officer, 21.iv.03. Though Plunkett's reasons for disobeying Cobbe's orders will never be known, it seems probable that the answer lay in his own character. Though a brave and capable officer he was choleric by nature, and may have tried impetuously to seize this opportunity of teaching the dervishes a lesson before he returned to camp.

who would come right up to the troops and take their rifles from their hands', and complained that 'the service ammunition, with the present rifle, has little stopping power, and in a fanatical rush of savages, a heavier bullet, or one with greater stopping power, is very requisite'.[1]

There was still a chance that the Abyssinian army, by approaching via Gerlogubi, might drive the Mullah back upon Galadi and again bring him to action. Manning's plan was to hold Galadi, Dudub, Bera, Galkayu and Badwein and so confine the Mullah's forces to their present area while he rolled up the Obbia line and based himself on Berbera. After that the possibility of further operations would depend on the number of fresh camels obtainable, and the Mullah's whereabouts at the time. It was not a very inspiring picture.

While Manning's withdrawal was in progress, the Bohotle column began its advance. In conjunction with his projected movement from Galadi on 17th April, Manning had ordered the flying column to move in a south-westerly direction, in the hope of attacking the Mullah from two sides. The immediate objective of this column was a large pool of water that had been reported at Danot. Major J. E. Gough (Rifle Brig.)[2] of 2 K.A.R. was in command, and his force consisted of eight officers and 260 rifles 2 K.A.R., four officers and 130 rifles (mounted infantry and camelry) 6 K.A.R., one officer and 85 rifles of the B.C.A. Indian Contingent, and two officers and 50 rifles of the Bikanir Camel Corps, with two maxim guns, hospital, and 406 camels carrying water for five days and rations for twelve.

Gough marched out with the infantry on 13th April, followed next day by the mounted troops, who had remained at Bohotle till the last moment to save water transport. A mounted column was sent ahead to Danot to report on the water supplies. The pool was reached on the 17th and a party of the Mullah's horsemen driven away. As the pool was shallower than expected, Gough decided to take forward from the infantry column only 100 rifles 2 K.A.R., 50 Sikhs and the two machine guns, and to send the rest back to Bohotle. At Danot a camp was set up and a strong zariba built to cover the water.

On 18th April Gough sent patrols of mounted infantry to the west and south-west. They returned with 400 camels and two prisoners, who said that three days' fighting had taken place between Galadi and Wardair, in which the Mullah had lost many of his men. During the next few days, while his column was assembling, Gough continued to send patrols in the direction of Wardair. More prisoners were taken on the 21st, who asserted that they had come from Daratoleh, about twenty-five miles to the south-east, where the Mullah had 50 mounted riflemen and 300 spearmen. These prisoners also reported that heavy fighting had taken place at Gumburu.

Gough was now ready to resume his march, and at 4.30 a.m. on the morning of 22nd April he set out from Danot with two officers and 30 rifles of 'E' Company, 2 K.A.R., four officers and 104 rifles 6 K.A.R.,

---

[1] Manning to W.O., 27.iv.03.
[2] Later Colonel J. E. Gough, V.C., Inspector-General of the K.A.R., 1907-09.

one officer and 12 Sikhs of the B.C.A. Indian Contingent, and two officers and 45 rifles of the Bikanir Camel Corps. The rest of the column remained at Danot under Captain F. B. Young (Cheshire R.) to protect the zariba.

Battle of Daratoleh, 22nd April, 1903.—The column had not far to march before meeting the enemy. By 7.30 a.m. the mounted patrols were in action against the Mullah's scouts. Another party was encountered some two hours later, and at 10.20 a.m. the mounted infantry reported a large enemy force in front. Gough at once dismounted his men and formed square with the camels in the centre. The ground was dead flat, with thornbush 15-20 feet high. A short period of extreme tension followed, and then the attack broke in a sudden uproar of rifle fire from the long grass and thornbush, at a range of 20-50 yards. Gough afterwards estimated the Mullah's force at 300 riflemen and about 500 spearmen. The attack continued for over three hours, while the square remained steady and the maxim guns were moved from point to point to counter each threat as it developed. By 2 p.m. ammunition was running short, and as the Mullah himself was reported to be present, which made it unlikely that the Obbia column could yet have approached Wardair, Gough decided to retire. Just then the dervishes were apparently reinforced, as their assault, which had gradually slackened, was suddenly renewed. To cover the retreat the Bikanir Camel Corps on the front face and 2 K.A.R. on the left charged for a hundred yards into the bush before the withdrawal began in the form of an 'elastic square'. Throughout the afternoon, as the retirement continued, the dervishes continually harassed the flanks and rear. They were driven off by repeated bayonet charges, most of them delivered by 2 K.A.R.

During the retreat, at a time when the rearguard had fallen some distance behind, Captain C. M. Bruce, R.F.A., Gough's staff officer, fell shot through the body. While Captain G. M. Rolland summoned help from the main body, Major W. G. Walker, Sergeant Nderamani and Corporal Surmoni of 2 K.A.R., Lance/Naik Maieya Singh of the B.C.A. Indian Contingent and Sowar Umar Ismail of 6 K.A.R. remained behind to fight off the dervishes pressing round them. Bruce was hit again and mortally wounded before help arrived. For the parts that they played in this incident, Rolland and Walker and later Gough were awarded the Victoria Cross, the men of the K.A.R. the African D.C.M., and the Sikh the Order of Merit.

At 1.15 a.m. on the morning of 23rd April, moving slowly with all the wounded and most of the dead carried on camels, the column reached Danot. Captain C. Godfrey of the B.C.A. Indian Contingent had been killed in the action; Major H. B. Rowlands (Suffolk R.) of 2 K.A.R. died of his wounds; and Major A. G. G. Sharp (Leins. R.), who commanded 6 K.A.R., Captain R. E. L. Townsend (Worcs. R.) of 2 K.A.R., and Captain E. M. Hughes of the Bikanir Camel Corps were also wounded. Of the rank and file 13 men were killed and 25 wounded. Gough was well pleased with the fighting qualities displayed by his troops. 'I cannot speak too highly of the behaviour of all ranks,' he wrote in his report of the action. 'It could not have been better, the Somalis surprising everyone by their steadiness and dash, the 2nd Bn. K.A.R. having both officers wounded and losing 11 men killed and wounded out of 30, and yet full of dash and fight.'

Gough had disbelieved the statements of his dervish prisoners that the British forces had been heavily defeated at Gumburu. At Daratoleh, however, he noticed with disquiet that some of his assailants wore British topees and the black fezes of 2 K.A.R. On 24th April official news reached him that Plunkett's force had been cut up at Gumburu and the Obbia column was probably withdrawing. Gough therefore issued orders to return to Bohotle, where he arrived on 28th April.

Manning was aware that the Mullah's main force was still in the Walwal—Wardair area, separated by about eighty miles of dense and waterless bush from Galadi, and by a hundred miles of similar country from Bohotle. During April and May the Abyssinian army, numbering about 5,000 men, had fought several small actions against the Mullah's followers, with some success. Manning now tried to communicate directly with Colonel A. N. Rochfort, R.A., the senior liaison officer, in the hope of persuading the Abyssinians to advance on Wardair via Gerlogubi. By the time the message got through it was nearly the end of May. But the Abyssinians lacked the transport needed to cross from the Webi Shabelle to Wardair. The opportunity for concerted action was thus lost at a critical period, though the Abyssinian army did succeed in again bringing the Mullah to action, and thus exerted a pressure from the south that may have dictated his subsequent movements.

By 25th May the Obbia line of communication had been closed up to Galkayu. Manning had been ordered to concentrate his force at Bohotle as a base for further operations. By 17th June he had concentrated all the garrisons from Galkayu, Galadi, Bera and Dudub at Badwein, ready to move in one body across the Haud. The total force numbered 1,480 fighting troops, 1,554 followers, 2,232 transport animals carrying four days' water, and a large quantity of livestock.

By this time certain indications of the Mullah's activities had come to light, the significance of which evidently eluded Manning at the time. Several deserters from the dervish camps asserted that the Mullah was preparing to move into the Nogal. Manning attached little importance to this since all the water-points were still in his hands. He apparently ignored the fact that the rains which fell in May and June could entirely change the situation for the time being. Early in June the telegraph line was cut north and east of Bohotle; strong parties of dervish horsemen were seen around the post, and also around Damot, which was still garrisoned as a half-way water-point for the crossing of the Haud. Then, just before Manning set out from Badwein with his main force, spies sent out by Major A. R. Hoskins (N. Staffs R.),[1] who was in command at Damot, brought news that the Mullah and all his fighting men, accompanied by their livestock, had passed right through the line of communication between Damot and Bohotle and escaped into the Nogal

---

[1] Later Colonel A. R. Hoskins, Inspector-General of the K.A.R., 1913-14.

valley, where he could resume contact with his friends in the Mijertein and so renew his stock of arms and ammunition.

It was an unfortunate termination to the campaign. Manning crossed the Haud in four days, uncertain whether the Mullah might attack him in the thick bush, but his concentration and movement appear to have been too rapid for news to have reached the Mullah in time.

By 26th June the whole column had concentrated at Bohotle, having captured 400 camels and 2,000 sheep and goats on the way, the tail end of the Mullah's vanishing herds. A strong column was then dispatched to bring in the Damot garrison. In view of the Mullah's presence in the Nogal, Manning decided to strengthen his principal posts along the line of communication. The troops of 3 K.A.R., 5 K.A.R., the B.C.A. Indian Contingent and the 1st Bombay Grenadiers were left at Bohotle, about 400 rifles all told. 2 K.A.R. and 50 Mounted Infantry of 6 K.A.R. were stationed at Garrero; 1 K.A.R. at Burao, and the 2nd Sikhs at Lower Sheikh.

The difficulties of disembarkation, transport and supply encountered on the third expedition were considerable, and subjected Manning's troops to a severe test under very trying conditions. From a study of his despatches, one cannot avoid the impression that his very success in leading and maintaining so large a force in the unknown interior of Italian Somaliland obscured to some extent the purpose that lay behind its presence. Bases were established, lines of communication laid out, roadways improved, supplies carried forward, strategic points occupied, and water-holes seized, all with the greatest efficiency and despatch. Yet at the end of all this effort the Mullah was still free; the only actions fought had been with far too few troops to affect the main issue; less stock had been secured than on the smaller, more mobile second expedition, and the dervish forces had escaped from the trap so laboriously set for them into their former haunts along the eastern borders of the Protectorate.

But by now the Government's prestige was at stake. It was decided to place the campaign on a divisional basis, with fresh reinforcements from India and Aden, and on 4th July Major-General Sir Charles Egerton reached Berbera to assume command.

(iv) *The Fourth Expedition, 1903-04.*

The part played by the K.A.R. in the fourth expedition against the Mullah was less prominent than before, partly on account of the continued growth of the Field Force, and partly because Egerton chose to rely for his striking-force on Indian troops. Yet the privations endured by the askaris on this expedition were greater than ever, and by the time it was over they had been reduced almost to extremity.

Manning's redistribution of troops along the line of communication was not completed until 16th July, so that Egerton's command only became effective on that date. From then until the end of October he was engaged in making roads, improving water supplies, and building up a new advanced base at Kirrit, which was protected by a small mobile column stationed first at Wadamago and afterwards at Eil Dab. All other troops were confined to their stations for the time being.

Egerton's reinforcements consisted of half the 1st Battalion Hampshire Regiment, the 27th Punjabis, some 700 strong, and about 300 Indian Mounted Infantry. The number of troops he now had to supply was so great that the advanced base at Kirrit grew but slowly. In the meantime a series of despatches and telegrams passed between him and the War Office, setting out alternative plans for the new expedition and discussing the advisability of again seeking Italian and Abyssinian aid. The British Government was averse from operations outside the Protectorate, and was anxious to avoid the risk of another expensive fiasco; on the other hand, sanction was refused for the protective administration of the Dulbahante, on the ground that no treaty existed with the tribe. But as all reports indicated that the Mullah's followers were demoralized, discredited and exhausted, so that only one final blow was needed to end "dervishism' for good, the Government decided not to let the opportunity slip. Unfortunately Egerton, with his front to a flank. was in no position to make a sudden dash with mounted troops.

The Mullah was said to have made his headquarters at Halin, with his *karias* occupying the triangle Halin—Gerrowei—Kallis. In October he seized and fortified the little port of Illig, which was difficult of approach from the landward side as it was protected by a wide tract of waterless bush. It was quite impossible to hide the movements of the Field Force from the Mullah's scouts, and if rain filled the wells there was nothing to prevent him from again escaping across the Haud, to foment a rebellion among the Ogaden. Egerton's strategy was therefore directed towards pinning the dervishes in the north, and the Emperor Menelik was asked once more to bar the route to the south by occupying Walwal, Wardair, and Galadi while the Field Force delivered its attack. Rochfort visited Sheikh and told Egerton that it was most unlikely that the Abyssinian army could reach Galadi before Christmas. Egerton thereupon decided to occupy Galadi himself, in the hope that this would encourage both the Abyssinians and Yusuf Ali, whom he wanted to reoccupy the wells at Galkayu.

Egerton had reorganized the Field Force into Divisional Troops (mounted troops, artillery, sappers and pioneers); the 1st Brigade, commanded by Brigadier-General Manning (the half-battalion 1 K.A.R., 2 K.A.R., the single companies of 3 K.A.R. and 5 K.A.R., the B.C.A. Indian Contingent and the K.A.R. Camel Battery); the 2nd Brigade, commanded by Brigadier-General Fasken (the 52nd Sikhs, 27th Punjabis, the half-battalion Hampshire Regiment and the 28th Mountain Battery); and line of communication troops (6 K.A.R. and the Bombay Grenadiers). To meet the needs of this Force, many thousands of camels were hired locally and imported from Aden, India and Abyssinia. No fewer than 26,000 were acquired before the end of 1903.

On 26th October General Egerton issued orders for the concentration of the 1st Brigade at Bohotle and the 2nd Brigade at Eil Dab. Manning was given sealed orders for the occupation of Galadi, and on 11th November left Bohotle with the 1st Brigade Headquarters. three companies of British Mounted Infantry, a company of Somali Mounted Infantry, the troops of 1, 2 and 3 K.A.R., 68 *illalos* and two guns of the Camel Battery. After a hot and trying march, Galadi was occupied without incident. Manning reconnoitred Damot (where he found the water insufficient for occupation), Dudub and Galkayu, and after three days marched back to Bohotle, leaving Major J. R. M. Marsh (Linc. R.) in command at Galadi with a garrison of one company British Mounted Infantry, 25 Somali Mounted Infantry, 250 rifles of the K.A.R., the two guns of the Camel Battery, and rations to the end of the year. On the way back Manning's mounted troops had a brush with a party of dervish raiders returning from the Ogaden, and after killing several of them, captured 385 camels and some sheep and goats.

While Manning was at Galadi a naval demonstration was taking place off Obbia to convince the Mullah that a second landing was projected to block his route south. The Sultan was given rifles and rations of rice and dates, to induce him to hold Galkayu. Other offers of help came from the Sultans of the Mijertein and the Warsangli, and from certain chiefs of the Ogaden.

Egerton did not place much reliance on local aid. Though he raised two irregular mounted corps to serve with the Field Force for three months, designated the Gadabursi Horse and the Tribal Horse, he considered them 'undisciplined, costly, unreliable, and troublesome' although he admitted that their local knowledge was useful. He had a poor opinion of the Somali as a fighting soldier, but paid tribute to the excellent intelligence work of the *illalos* and the Somali Mounted Infantry. The camelry of 6 K.A.R. had been disbanded in June and a second company of mounted infantry, 150 strong, was raised in their stead.

The occupation of Galadi diverted supplies from the advanced base at Kirrit, and Egerton decided to postpone operations until the end of the year. Meanwhile patrols were carried out in advance of Bohotle and Eil Dab, and to cover the latter an outpost was formed at Badwein. The Mullah's scouts were very active. Early in December news came that a dervish camp had been formed at Jidbali, about fifty miles east of Eil Dab, and that the position was constantly being reinforced. Believing that this might be intended to cover a withdrawal northward, Egerton ordered Lieutenant-Colonel Kenna to make a reconnaissance in force, hoping to induce the dervishes to reveal their strength.

Kenna left Badwein on the evening of 18th December with a mounted column of 442 British, Indian and Somali troops. He was followed in support by 100 men of the Hampshire Regiment and 150 men of the 27th Punjabis. Before daylight the column was close to Jidbali, which was lit by the glow of many camp fires. When it became light enough to see, Kenna opened fire in the hope of tempting the dervishes to leave their zariba. This he failed to do, and after three hours' desultory firing Kenna withdrew, as dervish reinforcements were arriving. He estimated the enemy at 1,500 foot and 200 horsemen, well armed with rifles, and thought that he had inflicted about 180 casualties.

Kenna's report reached Egerton at Kirrit just as a message from

Rochfort informed him that there was no immediate prospect of the Abyssinians reaching Galadi, owing to their usual difficulties with transport and water. As the Mullah appeared more likely to move north than south and the Galadi garrison was running short of supplies, Egerton decided to withdraw it, concentrate the 2nd Brigade and the mounted troops for a combined attack on Jidbali, and move the 1st Brigade into the southern Nogal to capture the Mullah's livestock and prevent him from breaking south. A column of Indian troops drawn from the 27th Punjabis, the Indian Contingent and 5 K.A.R., with a company of Somali Mounted Infantry, marched to Galadi, withdrew the garrison, returned to Bohotle, filled all water-tanks and reached Eil Dab on 15th January, 1904.

While this movement was in progress, Manning had been ordered to establish a post at Yaguri. Egerton now changed his plan, as scouts report that Jidbali was still being reinforced, and decided to attack the position with the biggest concentration of troops he could muster. On 9th January he assembled the Field Force at a rendezvous twenty miles east of Badwein: a mounted column of two British, two Indian and one Somali mounted infantry companies, the Bikanir Camel Company, the Gadabursi and the Tribal Horse; the 2nd Brigade with a section of the Mountain Battery; and 550 rifles of the K.A.R. from the 1st Brigade. Manning had been instructed to leave most of his supplies under guard at Yaguri.

Battle of Jidbali, 10th January, 1904.—Jidbali was the first engagement to be fought by the dervishes against regular troops in open country. In point of numbers it was also the largest, though owing, perhaps, to the fact that the Mullah was not present in person, it was by no means the fiercest nor the most hard fought. At dawn on 10th January, 1904, Egerton marched out of camp in double echelon, covered on front and flanks by the Somali Mounted Infantry and the Gadabursi and Tribal Horse. During the approach march the K.A.R. were stationed on the right flank. At 8.30 a.m. scouts reported that the dervishes, warned of the approach of the Field Force, were manning the edge of a wide, semicircular depression about two and a half miles in circumference in front of Jidbali. Sending Kenna with the mounted troops on a wide turning movement to threaten the enemy's right flank and block his retreat, Egerton marched to within 800 yards and halted in formation, with the 52nd Sikhs in front, 1 K.A.R. (275 rifles under Lieutenant-Colonel A. S. Cobbe) and 3 K.A.R. (75 rifles under Captain G. R. Breading) on the right face, and 2 K.A.R. (200 rifles of 'B' and 'F' Companies, and a section of 'D' Company under Major F. B. Young) in the right rear.

As the guns of the Mountain Battery came into action, shelling the main zariba and firing case into the bushes on the left front, the enemy opened a heavy but ill-directed fire. Egerton had ordered his troops to kneel or lie down, and casualties were slight. Within a few minutes the dervishes attempted to charge the Hampshires and Punjabis on the left of the square, rushing from cover to cover through the long grass. Unable to stand the intensity of fire directed upon them, they failed to cover more than half the distance, and the attack died away. It was followed by two attempts to rush the front and right. Egerton described the disciplined fire of the Sikhs and K.A.R. as 'terrific'. Notable was the work done by Sergeant Gibbs of 1 K.A.R., who fired a maxim from the right corner of the square at the groups of dervishes taking cover behind the scattered clumps of bushes. Except for the maxims and a section of 'B' Company, 2 K.A.R. on the right rear were never engaged, though they suffered casualties from the dervish fire, which passed over the front and right of the square. But within a few minutes the whole mass of the dervishes broke into full flight. The cavalry swept down to complete the rout, and maintained the pursuit for eighteen miles until both ammunition and horses were exhausted. The infantry action had only lasted for half an hour.

Egerton put the dervish strength at 3,000-6,000, but later estimates made the numbers much higher. There was reason to suppose that they represented the pick of the Mullah's forces. On the scene of the battle alone 668 bodies were counted. Owing to Egerton's precaution in making his troops lie down, casualties among the rank and file were few, though among the officers they were very high, three officers being killed and nine wounded out of a total casualty list of 27 killed and 37 wounded. Major Young and his adjutant, Captain E. H. Llewellyn, were severely wounded, and Captain Breading was slightly wounded.

The wells at Jidbali were choked with rubbish and dead dervishes. The Field Force halted about two miles beyond to await supplies from Yaguri and Badwein. On 12th and 13th January Manning marched to Damodleh with the K.A.R., preceded by the mounted troops. Hudin was reconnoitred on the following day. No sign of the enemy was found, but deserters said that the Mullah had gone to Halin. Seizing this opportunity to confine him to the north, Egerton occupied Dariali in the southern Nogal while Manning's brigade and the mounted troops proceeded to Adadero by forced marches.

The Field Force was now back in the territory covered by Swayne during the second expedition, with the 1st Brigade moving on Halin and the 2nd on Gaolo. Both centres were occupied on 25th January without opposition, though the signal fires of the dervishes were visible on the edge of the Sorl, the plateau that bounds the Nogal valley to the north. Further reconnaissance showed that the Mullah had escaped across the Anane Pass, in the direction either of Gebi or Jidali. For the moment he was out of reach, as communications were already stretched to the limit.

By 22nd February Egerton had re-orientated his Force. The 2nd Brigade was withdrawn via Eil Dab to Sheikh, ready to advance by the most direct route into the north-eastern parts of the Protectorate. A mobile column was formed at Eil Dab, and all posts in the southern Nogal were evacuated. The K.A.R., now brought up to strength by the troops from Galadi, who had covered 350 miles in a month's marching, remained in the field, and were based on Halin. Egerton, who had moved his headquarters back to Berbera, described these moves as completing the first part of his operations. He was well pleased with the result of the campaign so far, as the dervishes, after being decisively routed in the field, were now hemmed against the sea by the Field Force on the south and west, and by the professedly co-operative chiefs of the Mijertein on the east.

Operations were resumed on 10th March. While Manning maintained his watch in the Nogal valley, Fasken advanced from his forward base at Las Dureh with 500 mounted troops, 1,050 infantry and two guns of the Mountain Battery; and a mixed mounted column of 750 rifles moved simultaneously from Eil Dab. These columns met at El Afweina on 16th March. Next day it was reported that the Mullah had been at Danan, nearer than supposed, but was already in retreat. Fasken followed to Jidali, which he reached on 21st March, and continued east along the course of the Mullah's retreat, a trail well littered with the evidence of a hasty flight. But there were no signs of co-operation from the Mijertein chiefs, and at Ausaneh near the frontier the pursuit was called off. The mounted column was withdrawn and the infantry marched to Las Khorai to embark for Berbera.

On 7th April Egerton was instructed by the War Office to continue operations, and was told that he could enter Italian territory if necessary. Fasken's embarkation at Las Khorai was cancelled, and Manning was ordered to maintain his brigade for as long as possible in the Nogal. The dry season was now at its height; the K.A.R. were already living on half-rations, supplemented by captured stock; the transport camels were rapidly wasting away, and the officers were living largely on such game as they could shoot. The Brigade was not merely engaged in an idle blockade, but was carrying out a strenuous series of patrols, reconnaissances and raids, with a long line of difficult country to watch that stretched from Hudin on the west to Kallis on the east. Operational columns had always to be held ready. Seasoned as they were to campaigning in Somaliland, the K.A.R. reached the limit of endurance during the concluding phase of this expedition, and although he had placed his reliance primarily on Indian troops, Egerton was not slow to recognize the fact. 'I consider the steadfastness of the 1st Brigade,' he wrote at this period, 'consisting entirely of King's African Rifles troops, under these trying circumstances, was worthy of all praise.'[1]

Accounts by prisoners of the Mullah's intentions said that he was making for Illig, which was garrisoned by 200 riflemen and 500 spearmen. Deserters were leaving him in large numbers, and Egerton was convinced that the dervish following was widely scattered and no longer formidable. On 3rd April he placed Lieutenant-Colonel Kenna in command of a mounted column of 1,050 rifles, with orders to locate and attack the Mullah's headquarters. Soon after Kenna's departure Egerton telegraphed the War Office for permission to discontinue operations, on the ground that reports from both his brigade commanders showed the impossibility of maintaining their troops in such advanced positions once the rains set in. These opinions coincided with Egerton's own: 'The Mullah is a discredited refugee in the Mijjarten,' he wrote. '. . . His actual capture by the Field Force is, under present conditions, . . . im-

[1] Egerton to Army Council, 30.v.04.

practicable. There is now no enemy in arms against our authority in the Protectorate.'[1]

One necessary task remained before the operations of the fourth expedition could be closed: the capture of Illig. At Egerton's request 125 rank and file of the 1st Battalion Hampshire Regiment, commanded by Major S. C. F. Jackson, were embarked at Berbera in three warships. On 20th April the expedition anchored off the Gullule River, a few miles north of Illig. At dawn on the following day an advance party of seamen and marines landed on the beach, marched up the gully of the *tug* and seized the plateau on the south bank, a thousand yards from the beach. Within two hours the rest of the landing-party was ashore. Driving the dervish scouts before it, the force soon came in sight of the stone forts and towers of Illig. The troops were deployed with the Hampshires on the left and the seamen and marines on the right, and the attack was delivered against a brisk fire. With a single charge the dervishes were evicted from their zariba, and soon afterwards from the stone forts. The next few days were spent searching the cliffs, clearing the caves, and blowing up the fortifications. The troops then re-embarked, as the increasing swell made it impossible to maintain a garrison, and arrangements were made to hand the port back to the Isa Mahmud, from whom the Mullah had taken it. A significant feature of this operation was the nature of the fortifications. 'I was quite surprised,' reported the naval officer in command, 'at the natural strength which had been skilfully added to by works during the last S.W. monsoon by the Mullah and his Adviser, Haji Sudi, late interpreter of the *Ranger*.'[2]

Kenna led his mounted column over many weary miles, following false trails and encountering great difficulties, but without discovering the Mullah's whereabouts. Early in May Egerton recalled him, and on his arrival at Las Khorai on the 11th, all operations ceased. The 1st Brigade, relieved at last of its watch in the Nogal valley, arrived on 23rd May at Burao. The K.A.R. depôt was also transferred there from Garrero, where the post was abandoned. This movement was covered by a mobile column at Eil Dab under Major P. B. Osborn, who had done all the scouting that located the dervish position at Jidbali and won Egerton's commendation as 'an admirable leader of mounted troops'. Osborn's column consisted of 300 rifles 1 K.A.R., two guns of the K.A.R. Camel Battery, and two companies of Somali Mounted Infantry.

Egerton's total casualties were three officers and 31 British and African other ranks killed; ten officers and 54 other ranks wounded. He estimated that he had killed over 2,000 of the enemy. Nearly 500 rifles were captured, 24,000 camels and 36,000 other stock. In addition to the Abyssinian troops, who reached Wardair in January but were too remote from the scene of operations to help, about 6,000 regular and over 1,000 irregular troops were employed on the fourth expedition, at a cost of £2,500,000.

More effective co-operation by the Italians and the Mijertein Sultan

[1] Egerton to W.O., 12.iv.04.
[2] Rear-Admiral G. L. Atkinson-Willes to Admiralty, 23.iv.04.

might conceivably have resulted in the Mullah's capture on this occasion, but the chance was lost as soon as the rains set in, enabling him to exploit his extreme mobility and move freely beyond the range of the permanent wells. Egerton asserted that the actions at Jidbali and Illig, and the relentless pursuit to which the Mullah was afterwards subjected, had 'broken his power for a long time to come, and it will depend on the future of the Protectorate Administration whether it has not been broken finally and for all time. This, I take it, was the true object of the campaign'.

After the third expedition, it was counted an advantage to have driven the Mullah back into British territory, where he could be dealt with more effectively. After the fourth, it was claimed a victory to have driven him out. Somaliland was indeed a country where large armies starved and small ones were swallowed in the bush. Expeditions of both types had now been tried without success. The initiative was passed back the civil administration, and what has been termed the 'expeditionary period' came to an end.[1]

(v) *The Return of the Mullah and the Formation of the Somaliland Camel Corps, 1905-14.*

The strange situation that arose in British Somaliland during the years between the expeditionary period and the outbreak of war in 1914 may be described in a few pages. It involved the K.A.R. in a great deal of movement, but no fighting, and ended with the formation of a new Somali unit which became in due course an integral part of the regiment.

In October, 1904, the Italians opened negotiations with the Mullah, who had remained within their frontiers. An agreement was reached on 5th March, 1905, when the Mullah accepted Italian protection and was allotted an area on the Mijertein coast not far from Illig. This agreement was afterwards recognized by the British Government.

Though outwardly peaceable during the three years he spent in Italian Somaliland, the Mullah soon reopened intrigues with the Dulbahante and Warsangli tribes. Reports reached Berbera that his agents were constantly at work, seeking to undermine the loyalty of the tribes in British territory and to convince them that one day the Mullah would return and wreak vengeance on all traitors to his cause.

In 1908 the exhausted state of the grazing in the Mullah's sanctuary near Illig gave colour to a rumour that he was contemplating a return to British Somaliland. Under a reorganization that had taken place in 1906, 6 K.A.R. now consisted of four companies of Somalis and two of Indians, totalling about 650 rifles. One of the Indian companies was stationed in cantonments near the small blockhouse at Sheikh, and the other in a mud fort at Burao. The Somali companies were on garrison duty along the caravan routes. The fort at Bohotle had been dismantled; those at Shimber Berris and Kirrit were unoccupied, and the strong

---

[1] For a brief appreciation of political and military policy in relation to the Mad Mullah, see Chapter 14, Section (iii).

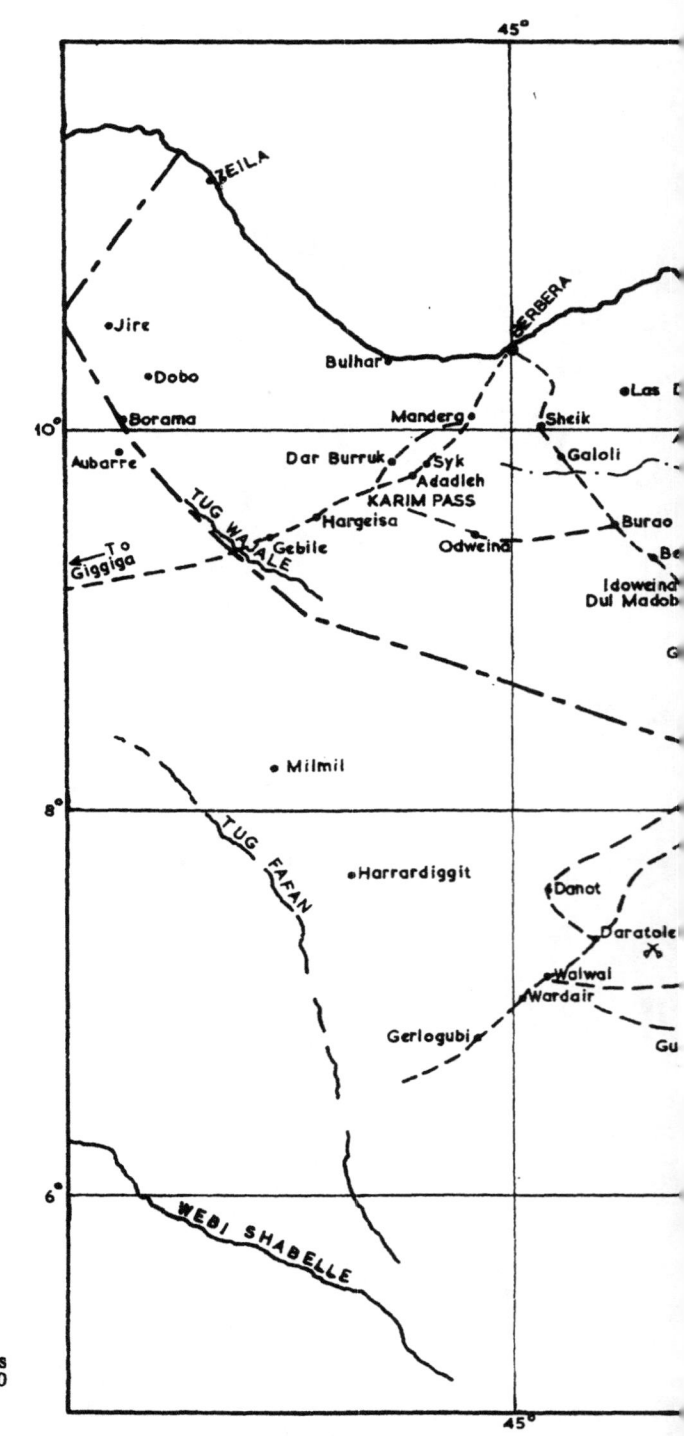

III. British Somaliland
To illustrate the Campaigns against the Mad Mullah, 1900-20

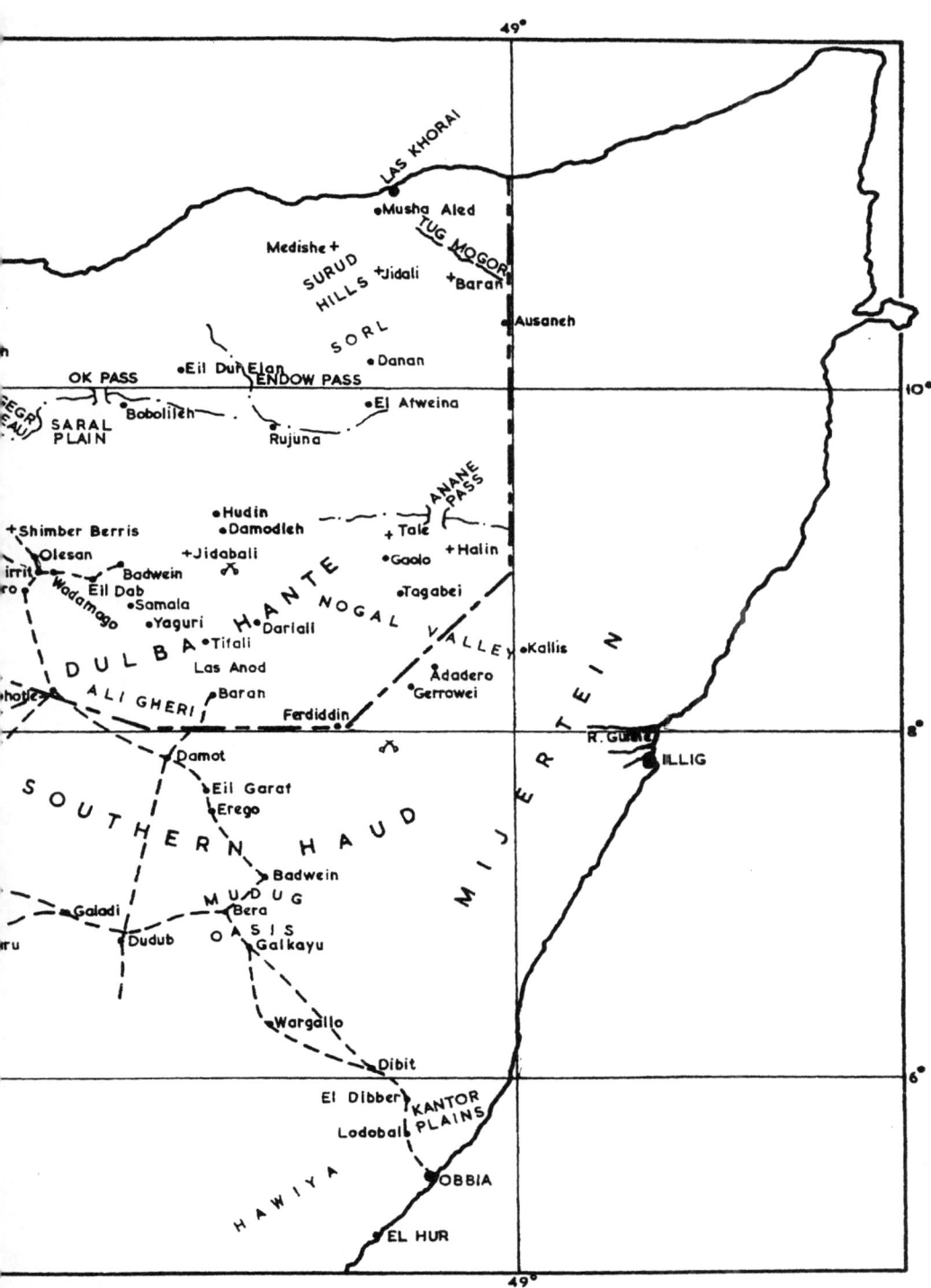

Face page 190

blockhouse at Las Dureh was garrisoned by a handful of tribal riflemen. The Standing Militia had been broken up, and so far from the armed forces of the Protectorate being able to take the field, it was doubtful whether even the garrison stations could be successfully defended.

The prospect of another expedition against the Mullah was viewed by the Government with great distaste. Control of the Protectorate had been transferred from the Foreign Office to the Colonial Office in 1905. Since that date the constant battery of complaint that the Mullah never ceased to levy against the authorities at Berbera showed clearly enough that his pretensions to be regarded as the ruler of all tribes in the interior were still alive. For a time the Government even considered the evacuation of the whole Protectorate, but fortunately saner counsels prevailed, and in 1908-09 the concentration of the K.A.R. in Somaliland, as described in the previous chapter, was ordered instead.

Although the Secretary of State had sanctioned this temporary military occupation of the interior, he decided that the cost of the camel transport needed for another expedition was prohibitive, and sent Lieutenant-General Sir Reginald Wingate to Somaliland to report upon the situation. Sir Reginald entered into lengthy negotiations with the Mullah that in the end proved quite fruitless. His recommendations were not published, but in November, 1909, instructions reached Berbera to abandon altogether the interior of the Protectorate and retain control only of the coast. It was hoped that the Mullah would be kept in check by the tribes themselves, who were to be issued with arms for their protection.

In January, 1910, General Manning reached Berbera as Commissioner and Commander-in-Chief, appointed to implement the new policy. He was certain that the Mullah's influence had so waned that the tribesmen would now be able to withstand him successfully. The task of withdrawing the inland garrisons did not take long. Movement began on 15th March, and within a fortnight, through the gloom and torrential downpour of the most violent thunder-storm ever experienced in Somaliland, the last companies of 6 K.A.R. marched down from the plateau by the winding track of the Sheikh Pass to Berbera, where the battalion was disbanded. The three coastal towns were again garrisoned by Indian infantry from Aden, and a few Somalis were retained as mounted police, allowed only to move within a three-mile radius of their stations. Arms, ammunition, ponies and mules were distributed among the tribes, who at once turned savagely upon one another to pay off old scores. This had been foreseen, but it was hoped that after the initial outburst the tribesmen would settle down and realize the need to combine against their common enemy.

The policy of coastal concentration proved from the start a complete failure. It was quite easy for the tribesmen to secure fresh ammunition and cheap rifles from Jibuti and Abyssinia, and instead of dying away, the orgy of raiding, quarrelling and fighting spread rapidly throughout the Protectorate. At the height of the anarchy, merchandise lay rotting in Berbera for want of caravans to risk the journey inland; looting went on almost up to the walls of the ports; even cases of cannibalism were reported, and a third of the male population perished. No such situation has been known before or since on British soil.[1]

In the midst of this shocking disorder the Mullah seized his chance. In July, 1910, he moved to Gerrowei on the frontier. During the succeeding months his followers steadily encroached on the Dulbahante country. In November, 1911, they attacked Bohotle, and it was realized that the Mullah's authority was again spreading all over eastern Somaliland, among tribes too disunited and too selfish to resist. The reign of terror grew, and at last, foreseeing that even the coastal towns might become besieged, H. A. Byatt, the new Commissioner, convinced the Government that something must be done. In June, 1912, authority was issued for a Camel Constabulary of 150 Somalis. The formation of this tiny force was in no sense a reversal of the coastal policy, for the Constabulary was forbidden to take action against the dervishes and was intended solely as a civilian police force, to keep the peace among the friendly tribes adjacent to the coast and patrol the caravan routes within a fifty-mile radius of Berbera. Many of the men recruited were ex-soldiers of 6 K.A.R. The Commandant was Richard Corfield, who was assisted by A. Gibb and C. de S. Dunn.

By the end of the year, the Camel Constabulary had begun its task of pacification and was operating in the Mandera area with excellent effect. Early in 1913 the Mullah was reported to be active in the Ain valley. With the help of Arab masons he eventually erected at Tale, his new headquarters, thirteen stone forts within an embrasured wall 12-14 feet thick at the base and 6 feet at the top. Outside this stronghold were three other forts 60 feet high. These permanent structures, which marked a new phase of the Mullah's activities, did not become military objectives until a much later period, but considerable uneasiness was felt over the presence of dervish horsemen not far from Burao, where the Camel Constabulary was now attempting to settle the quarrels of the local tribes. The Secretary of State made it clear that the Constabulary must not move into the Ain valley, but where exactly the line should be drawn was left for the Commissioner to decide.

In June Corfield, who had returned to Burao after spending some weeks settling disputes at Hargeisa, heard that the dervishes were raiding the friendly tribes near Idoweina. Fearing that in spite of the arms and exhortations that had been heaped upon them they would be too demoralized to resist, he moved out with his men, only to find that the tribesmen had withdrawn from their position. This forward move by Corfield produced a strongly-worded reminder from the Acting Commissioner, G. F. Archer,[2] that no discretion was allowed in the matter of taking up arms against the Mullah's followers.

For the next few weeks Corfield confined his activities to organizing the tribes for their own defence. On 6th August Archer reached Burao

---

[1] 'Berbera is now full of starving refugees, who are literally eating any filth they can pick up, and the unfortunate Byatt cannot feed them because, if he did, thousands more would flock in and it would become literally impossible to supply the country.' (Diary of the Inspector-General's Tour. 26th March, 1912.)

[2] Later Sir Geoffrey Archer, K.C.M.G.

with Captain G. H. Summers, Commandant of the Indian Contingent. Two days later an appeal for help came from the tribesmen, who reported that a big raid was in progress between Ber and Idoweina. Archer ordered a reconnaissance by 15 Constabulary mounted on ponies, and then at Corfield's request allowed him to follow with the rest of his available force, a total of 109 rifles. Summers was sent as military observer.

On the way out Corfield heard that the looted stock was being driven towards Idoweina. After nightfall he formed camp about five miles north-east of the village. The reconnaissance party returned with the news that the dervishes numbered some 150 horse and 2,000 foot. Their camp fires were plainly visible, and Corfield sought Summers' advice on whether to attack at once, or try to cut the dervish retreat at dawn. Summers strongly urged him to reconnoitre only, and prepare to withdraw on the following day.

Such a proceeding was too tame for Corfield. At 5.30 a.m. on 9th August, having issued ammunition to 300 Dulbahante who had offered to help recapture the stock, he moved off in the direction of Kirrit, travelling parallel to the dust cloud raised by the captured herds, which were moving out of sight behind a ridge. After an hour's riding Corfield dismounted his force and moved south to place himself across the dervish line of retreat. At Dul Madoba (Black Hill), in thick bush where visibility was limited to a hundred yards, he formed a skirmishing line so long that the flanks were invisible from the centre. Summers advised a square, but Corfield was unwilling to diminish the effectiveness of his fire.

In a few moments the dervishes appeared, firing as they came. The Dulbahante promptly vanished. Corfield's right flank was enveloped and began a disorderly retreat. The maxim gun was silenced by a bullet, and Corfield was shot dead. The Constabulary became very unsteady, continually retiring from the firing line, though when the first dervish attack died away they had to be restrained from rushing out in pursuit. When the attacks were resumed the nucleus of the force built a small zariba of dead ponies and camels. Rush after rush was made upon this barrier until about 11 a.m., when although their ultimate victory appeared certain, the dervishes unexpectedly withdrew in the tracks of the looted stock, which was now well clear of the battle area. It was learned afterwards that their ammunition had given out. In Dunn's opinion his men could not then have withstood even a determined charge by spearmen.

By this time only some 26 men fit for action were left in the zariba. Summers had been wounded and was weak from loss of blood, but Dunn took charge and extricated the force with great ability, including all the wounded. In the course of his retirement other men of the Constabulary rejoined him. In the middle of the night, while about eighteen miles from Burao, he was met by Archer with 20 sepoys and a number of armed tribesmen. On 10th August Burao was evacuated and the Camel Constabulary withdrew from the plateau, though Sheikh continued to be occupied by Indian troops. Archer deplored this retreat as 'politically disastrous'. The blow to British prestige was severe, as the dervishes soon followed up their advantage and in September sacked Burao for the first time since 1900.

The Mullah's armed following was now estimated at 6,000 men, many of them well supplied with rifles and ammunition. At Shimber Berris, fifty miles from Burao at the western outlet of the Ain valley, the Mullah built a series of stone forts which he claimed marked the frontier between his own and British territory.

For the protection of the coastal strip it was still essential to give effective support to the tribes. Berbera was reinforced by 300 Indian infantry, and the establishment of the Camel Constabulary was increased to 300 rifles. Proposals were made to recruit Yao and Sudanese, but had to be abandoned as insufficient men were forthcoming. In November command was given to Major A. S. Lawrance (1st County of London Yeomanry), who had previously served in 6 K.A.R. In the spring of 1914 the establishment was increased to 450, and in June Captain G. R. Breading was appointed second-in-command. The Constabulary then consisted of three Somali companies: 'A' and 'B' Companies, each of 100 men mounted on camels and 50 on ponies, and 'C' Company, with 100 on ponies and 50 on camels. There was also an Indian Contingent of 150 camelry, which operated as an integral part of the corps.

On 17th June the Constabulary moved to a training camp at Galoli, not far from Sheikh. At that time it was still under civil authority and was not under the jurisdiction of the Inspector-General of the K.A.R., who in fact considered its constitution thoroughly unmilitary and unsound, and deplored the fact that he had not been consulted in the first place. To all intents, however, the Corps was rapidly developing into a military force, capable of carrying out deep patrols and taking offensive action on a limited scale. To this force, aided by the Indian garrison, there fell the task of keeping the Mullah in check for the next five years, until the end of the 1914-18 war brought the K.A.R. back to Somaliland once more to participate in the closing scenes of the Mad Mullah's long career.

CHAPTER 8

Tribal Expeditions in East Africa

(i) *Internal Security in the Three Territories.*

BY African standards, the territory covered by British Central Africa was comparatively small. This greatly facilitated the extension of administrative control, and even before the turn of the century the tribes were settling down to a state of security hitherto inexperienced in their history. The standards of comfort and wealth steadily rose; labour was in demand, and men began to return from military service or from work in the Transvaal mines with surplus money that brought to the native villages many amenities previously unknown. For both activities there was no lack of men ready to volunteer.

A few minor disturbances were caused by the incidence of new taxation, some requiring a display of military force, but none military action. One such occasion arose among the Atonga of West Nyasa in March, 1902. Major Pearce visited Nkata Bay in his civil capacity, accompanied by Captain Margesson and 100 rifles 1 K.A.R., and explained the new tax satisfactorily. The K.A.R. company remained for a time to garrison a new station at Chintechi.

Even the Angoni had undergone a notable change of attitude. In Mombera's day the administration of Northern Angoniland could not have been established without the use of force, so he was left in possession during his declining years, on the understanding that he caused no trouble outside his own territory. After Mombera's death it was plain that the old authority had departed from the Angoni chiefs, and in September, 1904, Sharpe arranged to assume the full administration of their country. A few concessions were made, such as a promise to recruit the police force locally, and matters passed off with little trouble. No better example could be found of the new spirit in Central Africa than this agreement with the once intractable Angoni.

From time to time patrols were necessary along the eastern frontier to prevent raiding from Portuguese territory, but on the whole the Protectorate presented no military problem before the 1914-18 war. 'The Nyasaland Protectorate is a remarkably peaceful one, whose natives are the best in Africa and very well disposed towards the Europeans,' the intelligence officer reported to the War Office early in 1914, 'hence there is seldom anything of importance to mention in the quarterly intelligence reports, and they are poor things giving merely garrison returns, state of the weather and crops or progress of the railway.'[1] Pressure of other duties usually tied the K.A.R. intelligence officers closely to Zomba at

[1] Captain C. W. Barton to Captain H. E. Braine, the War Office, 13.iii.14. *C.A. Archives*, K.A.R., 8/1/2.

this period, particularly after the appointment was coupled with that of staff officer to the European Volunteer Reserve, and as the number of military outstations dwindled, they became increasingly dependent on the district residents for news. These civilian officers, though willing to help, were hampered by lack of time and transport, and perhaps by other matters. 'Some of us are getting old nowadays,' wrote one of them in response to a request for intelligence, while another replied that he spent his spare time entomologizing and found 'bounding after butterflies as hard as running after beagles'. Nevertheless, a great deal of useful intelligence regarding affairs in the adjacent German territory was collected as the years went on.

The internal situation in East Africa and Uganda was very different. The boundaries of both, now extended northward, included a vast unadministered area, practically unknown and largely unexplored. White settlement began in East Africa in 1903, and thereafter it was the highlands of the interior, served by the railway and stretching north and west of Nairobi, that dominated the country and its affairs instead of the coastal strip. The settlement policy itself involved some added military responsibility, but Sir Charles Eliot thought none of the tribes capable of causing serious trouble except perhaps the Masai and the Somali. In the main his opinion proved correct, with the addition of the Nandi, who were included in East Africa after the readjustment of the eastern boundary. But apart from the Nandi and the Marehan expeditions, the tribal problems of East Africa could not compare with the task that faced Uganda during the years prior to 1914. Most of the country north of Mount Elgon and the bend of the Nile as far as the frontiers of Abyssinia and the Sudan was found to consist of a vast fertile plain interspersed with isolated hills and ranges, well populated but in a state of continual unrest, caused by tribal raids, the illicit operations of Arab, Swahili and European ivory hunters, and at times by slave raids from the Maji district of Abyssinia. The administration of this great territory was gradually extended under cover of a series of protective operations carried out by 4 K.A.R., who performed during these years a function that was both exploratory and pioneering, as well as military. In East Africa and in Uganda, therefore, apart from some forces maintained centrally at their respective capitals, the tendency grew for the rest of the garrison to spread ever farther into the remote and unknown territories to the north.

A. C. W. Jenner, whose death at Somali hands was the occasion of the most expensive punitive expedition ever undertaken in the East Africa Protectorate, sometimes condemned these activities as mere unnecessary attempts by military officers to cover themselves with glory. In his opinion every officer on landing at Mombasa should have been presented with two medals, one to be withdrawn after his first punitive expedition, and the other after the second. No doubt some officers in the early regiments had volunteered for the African dependencies solely in the hope of seeing active service, and a few were not slow in pressing for official recognition of their campaigns. But the *Regulations* of the K.A.R. made it clear that the responsibility for punitive expeditions lay entirely with the civil power. Nevertheless, the theory that policemen were needed rather than troops continued to be argued until 1914, and even Sir Charles Eliot held the view that 'if there were no decorations, there would be fewer of these little wars'.[1] Whether or not he was justified may perhaps be gathered from the accounts of tribal expeditions that follow.

(ii) *The Defence of the Railway, 1902-06.* Map II (b).

Though the first railway rolling-stock got through to Kisumu in December, 1901, there were so many bridges and culverts to be completed, embankments to be strengthened and deviations to be straightened out that the permanent way was not properly completed until March, 1903. The third Nandi expedition, undertaken primarily in defence of the railway, had terminated before adequate punishment was inflicted on all sections of the tribe responsible, and the result was an early recrudescence of raids and thefts, directed from both sides of the Nyando valley.

This time it was the Kipsikis (or Lumbwa, as they were commonly called) who first threatened trouble. Like the Nandi, they were a warlike people possessing a well-developed military organization and the strong sense of discipline so often found in tribes who lived in close proximity to the Masai. Every male was born into one of four *puriosiek*, or regiments; raids were carefully planned, and the warriors were well led. Once the tribe became aware, therefore, of all the possibilities afforded by the new railway, defensive patrols alone were quite insufficient to protect the line. Owing to the temporary arrangement for dual occupation of the former Eastern Province of Uganda, the fourth series of operations against the Nandi group of tribes involved the 3rd, 4th and 5th battalions of the K.A.R.

The Province was officially transferred to East Africa on 1st April, 1902. Five days later the Nandi raided Kibigori station and stole thirty steel sleepers. It was the first time the tribe had attempted to carry off such a weight of metal, and Hobley, the Assistant Deputy Commissioner, after wiring O.C. Troops at Muhoroni to pursue the thieves, left for Nandi with 30 police. On arrival he heard that Captain Lindesay (Indian Staff Corps) of 5 K.A.R. had reached Kaptumo with 50 sepoys, and that the Nandi had just stolen another sixty sleepers. On 10th April Hobley left Kaptumo with an escort of 110 rifles for a meeting with several hundred Nandi warriors, including representatives of every section of the tribe. After a long palaver the Nandi admitted the thefts, saying that they were hungry and had taken the iron to cut up and sell for food. Hobley warned them that this was 'practically tantamount to an act of war, for the railway was as precious to us as their cattle was to them', and the missing sleepers were recovered.[2]

But this success was short-lived. Before the end of April a party of about 500 Kipsikis spearmen raided the construction camps, killed one

---

[1] Sir C. Eliot, *The East Africa Protectorate*, p. 200.
[2] Hobley to Eliot, 12.iv.1902. F.O.2, 571.

Indian coolie and wounded six others. Jackson, now Deputy Commissioner at Nairobi, telegraphed Uganda to inquire whether Coles could command a combined punitive expedition if such became necessary, and whether a Baganda and a Sudanese company, with 200 police and 300 auxiliary levies, could be sent to defend the line while the expedition was in progress. The Uganda Government agreed to spare a company and a half of regular troops, 100 police, and the Baganda levies. During April and May detachments of 3 K.A.R. totalling five officers and 300 men reached the district to reinforce Coles, who then reported himself able to protect the line against further threats. A special railway carriage was placed at the disposal of O.C. Troops, Eastern Military District, to facilitate control of his patrols along the permanent way.

The political situation in Lumbwa remained most unsatisfactory and it was decided at Manning's suggestion to establish a station there. A selection board composed of Hobley, Major Gorges, Captain Lindesay and a medical officer chose a site at Kericho, about fifteen miles south of Fort Ternan, as it was felt advisable not to go too far from the railway. A garrison of one Indian company was proposed, and as no civil officer was available, the East African Government applied for the services of Major Gorges to take military and civil charge for the first two or three months. Jackson had a high opinion of Gorges' capability in handling natives, and once, when reporting on an affair of theft and counter-theft between coolies and tribesmen, had described the matter as 'fairly typical of the troubles that Major Gorges and Captains Rumbold and Wortham of the 4th Bn. and Captain Lindesay of the 5th Bn. K.A.R. have had to deal with for a long time past. To them, and particularly to Major Gorges, I consider the greatest credit is due for having exercised so much patience and tact in their dealings with these naturally truculent and unruly people.'[1] Colonel Coles agreed to the appointment, as he also had a very high opinion of Gorges and thought that if anyone could, he would be able to avoid hostilities. The appointment proved typical of the excellent work sometimes done in a dual capacity by officers of the K.A.R., and Gorges remained with the Kipsikis until Coles, denuded of officers by the Somaliland operations, was obliged to make formal application for his relief in the following September.

The good behaviour of the tribes south of the line was thus secured without the need for a costly expedition, but a settlement with the Kamelilo or south-eastern sections of the Nandi was not reached so easily. 'The male sex,' Eliot wrote in his official report, 'are attracted by a particular kind of bolt which forms an ideal instrument for braining your enemy. . . .' In October Delmé-Radcliffe, who was at work with the Anglo-German Boundary Commission, was unable to use the telegraph as the tribesmen sometimes removed as much as 100 miles of wire at a time. During the last few weeks of the year, however, the thefts practically ceased, though heavy rains caused some uneasiness to the officer commanding, for the flooded rivers greatly restricted his movements. Moreover, the railway authorities complained of damage if their bridges were

---

[1] Jackson to Eliot, 29.v.02. F.O.2. 572.

used by troops, and in any case they were not negotiable by animal and wheeled transport, owing to the open spaces between the sleepers.

Early in 1903 the Kamelilo again became very restless and numerous thefts took place. As most of the construction camps were quite defenceless and at a distance from Fort Ternan and Muhoroni, where the troops were stationed, these thefts were often committed with great impudence. In January the Kamelilo made four trips to one camp and carried off a thousand dog-spikes at their leisure. From another camp they removed 800 rivets and a quantity of rope. These activities were combined with a number of cattle raids on the friendly western sections of the tribe. On 16th January Walter Mayes, Collector of the Nandi District, set out with a detachment of troops to visit the Kamelilo and endeavour to establish his authority. Two days later the Kamelilo spearmen again raided the railway in considerable force and removed thirty fish-plates in broad daylight. Patrols were dispatched twice daily from Fort Ternan to drive off any natives seen approaching the track, and a guard of one Indian officer and 50 sepoys 5 K.A.R. was mounted at the principal camp, with orders to patrol the vicinity. In spite of this, parties of armed natives constantly approached the line, and even attempted to raid the 5 K.A.R. cattle boma and regimental garden at Muhoroni.

Early in February Captain W. H. Nicolson (I.S.C.), the O.C. Troops at Muhoroni, accompanied Mayes on a second visit to the Kamelilo, with an escort of 30 rifles 4 K.A.R. and 30 rifles 5 K.A.R. with a maxim gun. The tribesmen promptly deserted their huts, hid the women and children and drove off their cattle, though Mayes succeeded in contacting their leader 'Taptongele'[1] and a few other influential elders. 'Taptongele' frankly acknowledged the thefts and the murder of two Indian coolies, and was given ten days to restore the material and surrender the murderers. Nicolson, who had undertaken the trip with an eye to punitive measures, noticed considerable cultivation and saw at a distance two large herds of cattle, though the country was difficult to traverse as it consisted entirely of deep valleys with steep sides and bottoms filled with dense bush. On return to Fort Ternan a conference took place with the Deputy Commissioner, who instructed Mayes to enlist the influence of a friendly Nandi leader known as 'Arab Sertoi' (Arap Sirtoi).[2] A project to settle Indian immigrants in the area was then under consideration, an added reason for strong measures against the Kamelilo, for the coolies were by now thoroughly terrorized.

The Kamelilo made no attempt to honour their promises, but before embarking on offensive operations it was necessary to make sure of the attitude of the Kipsikis. In March Nicolson therefore accompanied the Commissioner on a visit to Kericho. A suggestion had been made for employing 500 Kipsikis spearmen as auxiliaries, and the tribe seemed extremely friendly, men, women and children running from their villages to greet the party as it passed—an attitude very different from that shown

---

[1] Though so recorded at the time, this name would appear to indicate a woman.
[2] It was not realized until later that the Nandi were in the habit of giving their fathers' names, preceded by 'arap' (son of).

by the Kamelilo. Later inquiries showed, however, that although the Kipsikis were not harbouring Kamelilo cattle, the close bond between the tribes made it inadvisable to use them as auxiliaries.

Meanwhile the Kamelilo continued their thefts and attacked a Somali trader. Another visit by the civil authorities failed to obtain any reparation or guarantee of future good behaviour. The tribesmen were again entreated to listen to reason, but on this occasion met all accusations with flat denials. When their huts were searched almost every one of them was found to contain hoes, bolts, crowbars, steel keys and spikes in abundance. The rains were over and the rivers fordable, and all efforts at a peaceful settlement having failed, on 14th April Hobley formally instructed Nicolson to inflict upon the Kamelilo a compulsory fine of livestock and not to leave the country until the elders unanimously sued for peace. Special care was to be taken to prevent the Kamelilo from breaking south and involving the Kipsikis.

Nicolson had at his disposal the largest force yet employed in the district, comprising seven officers and some 580 regular troops, besides auxiliaries. The Field Force was made up of 120 rifles 3 K.A.R., 240 rifles 4 K.A.R., and 160 rifles 5 K.A.R., together with 50 Kavirondo levies armed with rifles and about 700 Nandi 'friendlies' under their own leaders. The Force possessed one Hotchkiss and five maxim guns.

Sending the Sudanese women and children of 4 K.A.R. to temporary quarters at Kericho and Nandi boma, Nicolson arranged guards of 3 K.A.R. for the railway, and organized the rest of his troops into three columns. The first, consisting of 70 rifles No. 4 Company, 4 K.A.R., commanded by Lieutenant F. J. E. Archer (Norfolk R.), was to march north from Fort Ternan to the Tindiret range and prevent the Kamelilo from driving their cattle east. The second, commanded by himself and consisting of 70 sepoys of 5 K.A.R., was to march north-east from Muhoroni. The third, Lieutenant N. E. Willoughby (Middx. R.), with 50 rifles No. 7 Company, 4 K.A.R., and 20 police, was to start from Nandi boma a day earlier than the other columns and march south-east. Each of the three columns was accompanied by two signallers of 5 K.A.R. equipped with helio, lamps and flags, as efficient communication was essential if the converging columns were to trap their enemy.

Nicolson's intention was to concentrate first on capturing cattle and prisoners, sending them back to Muhoroni under guard. He would then be free to continue burning huts and destroying crops until the Kamelilo sued for peace. Each column was ordered to camp not later than 1 p.m. daily, to give ample time for the construction of a strong boma. During daylight the guards were to be posted at least two yards inside the boma to avoid being speared through the branches, and at night auxiliaries were posted several hundred yards outside to give timely warning of an attack.

The fourth expedition against the Nandi set out on 28th April, and its operations lasted for five weeks over a tract of country bordering twenty miles of the railway line. The Kamelilo could not be tempted into open attack, but were constantly on the wait for stragglers and shot poisoned arrows into the camps by night. Rain fell daily and all streams were flooded, but the columns forced their way across steep mountains and through deep ravines, practically living on the country and destroying all the crops they did not consume. Long forced marches, often by night, were needed to effect surprise. At length, on 1st June, when 300 head of cattle and about 4,500 goats and sheep had been captured, and the Nandi had lost a hundred warriors, their envoys sued for peace. The expedition had cost two sepoys and two porters killed and one sepoy slightly wounded.

Sir Charles Eliot wrote to thank Nicolson for the ability and thoroughness with which he had carried out the orders issued to him by the Government. After this expedition an administrative sub-station under Hyde Baker was set up at Soba, about seven miles from Muhoroni. Although it was not yet possible to relax the vigilance of the railway patrols, Sir Donald Stewart, who was appointed Commissioner of East Africa in succession to Eliot in July, 1904, felt able in his first report to endorse his predecessor's opinion that for the time being the Nandi question was dead, and that a couple of years' uninterrupted peace in Lumbwa would remove the fear of serious trouble there as well.

Such optimism was not unusual when reporting the close of an expensive military expedition, but before the end of 1904 it was evident that the lesson inflicted on the Nandi was almost forgotten. Thefts of railway material continued, and a whole company had to be employed to guard the stretch of line between Muhoroni and Kibos. Within the next six months the tribesmen committed a new series of outrages. A Boer trader was attacked, beaten and killed; a missionary was killed because, the Nandi alleged, his mission guards had raided their cattle; stock was stolen from Boer settlers at Sergoit; the Kavirondo and Terik tribes were raided; murders continued along the railway and even the sub-station at Soba was attacked. In July, 1905, after more unsuccessful attempts to bring the Nandi to reason, the Commissioner delivered an ultimatum, and when this expired ordered an expedition on a scale that was intended to settle matters once for all.

The Nandi Field Force of 1905 was the largest punitive expedition ever to be assembled in the Protectorate, with the exception of the Jubaland expedition of 1901. Its composition was decided at a conference held at Nairobi on 26th September, 1905, when Lieutenant-Colonel E. G. Harrison was selected to command a force of six companies 1 K.A.R., six companies 3 K.A.R., and 200 armed police. As auxiliaries it was intended to raise about 1,000 Masai and Somalis, but few of the latter came forward and the Masai contribution was also less than expected. Orders for mobilization were issued on 28th September.[1]

The expedition was timed to begin during the third week of October. Harrison went to Kisumu to consult the local authorities. For the first stage of the operations he divided the Field Force into four columns. The intention was to march north and west from assembly points on the railway, separate the Nandi from their possible allies the Kipsikis, clear

---

[1] Nandi Field Force Diary, C.O. 534, 3. With the exception of small detachments at Nairobi and two companies in Jubaland, the whole of 3 K.A.R. was mobilized for these operations.

their hills and valleys of warriors and stock, and drive all those uncaptured into the Kapwareng forest. No. 1 column ('A', 'E' and 'F' Companies, 1 K.A.R., under Lieutenant-Colonel Gorges) marched north on 18th October from Londiani and traversed Sirikiu and the Ravine. Its operations were independent of those of the other three columns. No. 2 Column ('B', 'C' and 'D' Companies, 1 K.A.R., under Major H. A. Walker) left Lumbwa on 20th October and advanced via Tindiret and the Kamelilo country to Kaptumo. The third column (Nos. V and VI Companies, 3 K.A.R.) left Muhoroni on the same date under Captain F. W. O. Maycock for Kaptumo via the Soba Hills, continuing afterwards along the escarpment to the west. The fourth column (Nos. III and VII Companies, 3 K.A.R.) under Captain W. E. H. Barrett (Conn. Rang.) concentrated at Nandi Fort and marched north to Tobolwa, returning to Kaimosi along the escarpment that forms the boundary between the Nandi country and Kavirondo. Harrison disposed the remaining two companies of 3 K.A.R. along the line of communication and set up his headquarters at Muhoroni. With the consent of the Secretary of State and Brigadier-General Manning, some Sikh signallers from Uganda had been attached to the Field Force to ensure that the columns kept in touch.

So for the fifth occasion the long files of troops, flanked by the spearmen of the auxiliaries, toiled across the hillsides and ravines of Nandi, fighting sharp encounters with a courageous and mobile enemy and seeking to deprive him of his stock and so bring the operations to a speedy end. Though resistance was not well organized[1] and the Nandi possessed few firearms, they always merited respect, and stock driving by small parties was a perilous task. On 26th October one such party, consisting of twelve rifles of No. VI Company, 3 K.A.R., and 21 spearmen, was surrounded and cut to pieces near Kipture while driving cattle back to No. 3 Column. Two Masai alone survived, who escaped by lying in a stream until dark. According to their story the troops only had time to fire one volley before they were rushed.

By the end of October, reports indicated that Nandi proper was clear of tribesmen and herds. Scattered bands were, however, said to be concentrating in the Kapwareng forest. Harrison decided that the time had

---

[1] An unfortunate incident occurred at the start of the operations that appears greatly to have shaken the Nandi. An officer of 3 K.A.R., who had been ordered if possible to capture the Laibon Koitalel, arranged through his interpreter a meeting at Ket Parak Hill. The fact that the Laibon consented to appear at all was in itself suspicious, as he always refused to meet Europeans. The officer was accompanied by 80 rifles from Nandi Fort, but in accordance with the Laibon's wishes went forward to meet him with an escort of one native officer and four askaris only. The Laibon, however, was accompanied by about a dozen warriors, and many more could be seen lurking in the bush behind him. He refused to approach and shake hands, making the curious excuse that the sun was too hot for him to leave the shade of the tree under which he stood. At that moment the interpreter turned with his spear levelled, and the officer, now sure that treachery was intended, shot him dead. Spears and arrows at once flew at close range; the native officer shot the Laibon, the troops rushed to the rescue and altogether 23 Nandi were killed. Afterwards the tribe complained bitterly to Walter Mayes that their intentions had been honourable and that the treachery lay on the British side. Evidence taken at subsequent Courts of Inquiry did not wholly disprove these accusations, and Manning recorded his opinion that 'the reputation for fair dealing and honesty of the British Government had been called in question'. (C.O. 534, 3.)

come for the second stage of his operations. On 2nd November he moved his headquarters to Nandi Fort, in order to be closer to the western sector of operations, and planned a concentric movement by Columns 2, 3 and 4. Hearing that the Nandi concentration was larger than at first supposed, Harrison also formed a fifth column, to enter Kapwareng from the Kibos valley.

Soon afterwards news reached headquarters that No. 1 Column had reached the Ravine with 2,460 head of cattle and 3,150 sheep and goats. Small parties of tribesmen were still wandering through the forests and along the escarpments, but the main resistance had been broken and the Nandi were anxious for peace. On 14th November hostilities were suspended, and on the following day Harrison and the senior political officer began discussions with representatives of the tribe. Brigadier-General Manning paid a visit to Nandi Fort on 25th November, and laid great stress on the need for ensuring that Nandi truculence was at last effectively crushed. Experience had repeatedly proved that nothing could be more fatal than the half-hearted punishment of a warlike tribe, which always led to reprisals as soon as the punitive force was withdrawn. This lesson was pointed by an incident that occurred that very day, when Sergeant Milton and a cattle escort of 75 rifles had to fight their way home by firing volley after volley at the encircling Nandi tribesmen, expending no less than 70 rounds of ammunition per man.

The Nandi had lost to date some 600 men killed; the troops and auxiliaries a total of 90 killed and wounded. Over 10,000 cattle and 18,000 sheep and goats had been captured. With little difficulty, therefore, the Nandi agreed to move into a Reserve selected for them, comprising the Aldai and Kapwareng districts, west of the line Kapiyet—Kipsikak—Muhoroni. All murderers, rifles and spears were to be surrendered.

On 1st December the maintenance gangs were allowed to resume work on the railway, and the local settlers, who had gathered at Lumbwa while the operations were in progress, were returned under guard to their farms. A few days later, owing to the hostile attitude of the Nyang'ori people, operations had to be resumed. On 10th December Major Walker attacked the tribe at daylight, killing over 150 and taking some 1,200 head of cattle and 1,000 sheep and goats.

Harrison's method was now to cover the country with a network of military posts, each a company strong, well entrenched and in communication with one another by helio, while the Nandi were moved into their Reserve. Gorges, as O.C. Military District, was instructed to impress upon the tribesmen that those who moved of their own accord before 15th January, 1906, would get their stock returned in full; others would be moved by force. The Kamelilo had already shown signs of recalcitrance, and as it was evident that the Field Force would be fully employed, further help had been sought from Uganda to guard the railway. Captain Nicolson with two British officers, two native officers and 98 Sikhs of the Indian Contingent went to Muhoroni, and No. 4 Company, 4 K.A.R., having handed over its duties at Jinja to the police, was dispatched hurriedly to Fort Ternan.

Throughout January and February the work of moving the Nandi continued. On 27th February the Field Force was disbanded, though five companies remained to garrison the district. In June these troops, some 800 rifles with 100 armed police under the command of Major H. A. Walker, carried out a three weeks' drive of the whole area, to ensure that no Nandi remained outside the Reserve. On 1st August the troops were withdrawn, and within a comparatively short time Nandi askaris were proving their worth as disciplined troops in the K.A.R.[1]

(iii) *Punitive Expeditions in the Highlands, 1902-14.* Map 7.

There was no native kingdom in East Africa through which to exercise indirect rule. Recognizing from the first that the future of the country lay in the development of the thinly-peopled highlands, Eliot began to reorganize the civil administration in some detail, even before there was much to administer. Within a short time of its establishment at Nairobi, the Government of British East Africa consisted of fifteen different departments, and Eliot was ready to begin his policy of encouraging white settlement as the foundation of the country's economic future.

At first the offer of free grants of land failed to attract many settlers from the United Kingdom. The response from South Africa was greater, as many Boers were anxious to start life afresh after the end of the war. The arrival of these new settlers with their wives and families, and their occupation of widely-scattered farms, created new problems of internal security, and Eliot was quick to recognize that their presence would add considerably to his military commitments. By March, 1905, when the flow of British settlers was also beginning, the white population of East Africa numbered 1,464, of whom 233 were government or railway officials, a proportion much smaller than formerly and rapidly declining. Many of these settlers were retired army officers. They were not always easy to govern and did not hesitate to extend their perpetual criticism of authority to include military affairs as well.

So far as the highlands were concerned, the main task of the K.A.R. during the early years of the century lay in supporting the gradual extension of administration from Nairobi towards Mount Kenya. In June, 1901, Mbirri station was renamed Fort Hall, after the first district officer to be stationed there, who had died in the previous March. During the following year the Maruka section of the Kikuyu murdered five Indian traders and refused to submit to administrative control. On 4th September Captain F. W. O. Maycock led a punitive expedition of five British officers, 115 rifles 3 K.A.R., 60 police and 300 levies into the Maruka country, and by 25th October had covered it with patrols. Some resistance was met and the expedition lost one man killed and 13 wounded. About 300 cattle and 2,000 sheep and goats were taken. Twenty askaris were then detached from Fort Hall to garrison a new station at Nyeri.

[1] Manning wrote in his Report on 3 K.A.R. for 1906: 'Nandi have been lately enlisted experimentally and shape well.' The whole expedition was estimated to have cost the Nandi 1,117 killed; 16,213 cattle and 36,205 sheep and goats captured. The Government losses were 121 killed and wounded.

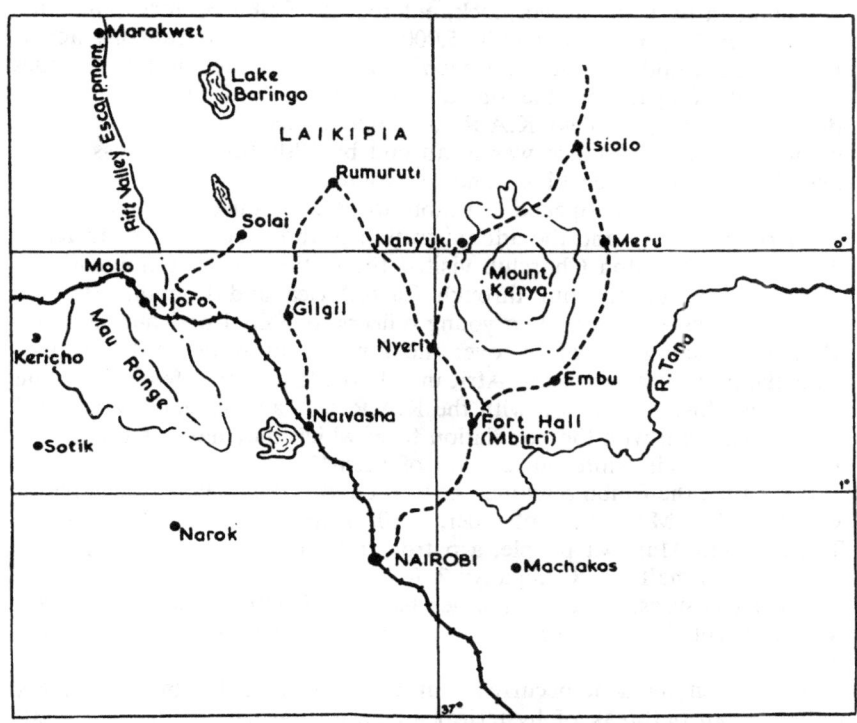

7. British East Africa: The Central Highlands

Sporadic outbreaks against friendly chiefs and attacks on mail runners occurred again early in 1903. For the first time a sub-section of the Embu was involved, the tribesmen raiding villages known to have paid hut-tax right up to the confines of the Fort Hall district. Punitive patrols were sent out in May and June. By the end of the year, unarmed caravans had become the rule in the area north and west of Nairobi as far as Nyeri and Naivasha, a risk that could not have been taken the year before.

In 1904, as a result of constant murders of friendly natives by the Iraini section of the Kikuyu, another expedition was authorized, under Captain F. A. Dickinson. The force comprised five officers, 135 rifles 3 K.A.R., 60 police and 300 levies. Between 13th February and 17th March, 1904, three patrols were engaged in capturing over 11,000 head of stock and securing the submission of recalcitrant chiefs. These operations again included the Embu, who put up a determined resistance that cost the patrols three men killed and 33 wounded. In June, 1904, Fort Hall ceased to be a military station and thereafter a whole K.A.R. company was stationed at Nyeri.

The Embu were still very restless, and showed unremitting hostility towards any tribe friendly to the British. Matters came to a head in 1906, when they massacred a deputation of their neighbours, who had sought government protection. On 18th June another expedition, again

P

commanded by Captain Maycock, entered the Embu country. The tribe was reported to possess 10,000-15,000 spearmen; the terrain lay across the broken, wooded ridges and deep marshy valleys of the lower slopes of Mount Kenya, and the operations were carried out in incessant downpours of rain. Two K.A.R. and one police column combed the country and all resistance was at an end by 19th July, at a loss to the expedition of two men killed and 14 wounded.

A new station was opened at Embu, to be garrisoned by the company formerly at Nyeri,[1] and the administration of the tribes across the River Tana began. Winston Churchill visited the station in the following year in the course of his tour through East Africa and Uganda. He was greatly impressed to find two young officers, one civil and one military, already presiding peacefully over the fortunes of some 75,000 natives with the help of a few score African askaris. 'Live for a few weeks,' he wrote, 'in close association with the K.A.R. . . . and it seems wonderful to contrast them with the population from which they have emerged. . . . How proud their white officers are of them!'[2]

For a time the Embu remained peaceful and in May, 1908, the garrison was moved to Meru. In September, 1910, owing to the truculence of the Tharaka and Mutejwa people, a patrol under Lieutenant L. H. Soames consisting of half 'A' Company, 2 K.A.R., was ordered to carry out punitive measures. A few casualties had to be inflicted, and the lesson was sufficient to restore order and ensure the future co-operation of the tribe.

In 1911 an incident occurred that was described in the Governor's report as 'an outbreak of hysterical mania on the part of the Akamba'. The trouble arose at Machakos, in an area where there were European women and children. The news reached Nairobi at six o'clock in the evening. The commanding officer, Lieutenant-Colonel G. R. Breading, was away in Jubaland with the Inspector-General, but Major L. E. S. Ward and two officers, a warrant officer and 112 askaris were on their way before midnight. The matter was settled without the use of force, a good example of the protective and preventive function exercised by the mere presence of disciplined troops, a factor that was all too often forgotten in a growing colony anxious to economize on 'non-productive' expenditure.

Perhaps the most unexpected aspect of the European settlement policy was the philosophic attitude adopted by the Masai elders towards the new situation. In June, 1901, Eliot wrote that he thought it would long be necessary to 'maintain an adequate military force' in the Masai districts. Within two years, though he still considered it 'unwise to irritate them', he reported that the Masai were 'no longer a formidable element' in East Africa. Some unrest occurred in 1902, when the *il murran* planned a raid that the elders were powerless to prevent, but the despatch of 180 troops to Naivasha soon checked the trouble. In September, 1904, Lieu-

---

[1] The whole company did not move at once to Embu. Manning in his Report dated 26.xii.06 recommended that the Nyeri detachment should either be raised again to a full company or replaced by police, as it was without a British officer.

[2] W S. Churchill, *My African Journey*, pp. 35-37 and 63-64.

tenant H. A. Wilson (Conn. Rang.) and 100 men visited the Loita Masai to recover cattle raided from the Kipsikis. In general, however, Masai auxiliaries were the allies rather than the opponents of governmental expeditions, until their employment in this capacity was discouraged by the Secretary of State in 1908, who was strongly opposed to the principle of setting one African tribe to control another, and only permitted auxiliaries to accompany the K.A.R. in a strictly non-combatant capacity.

Inter-tribal cattle raids and thefts from European farms, matters that today would call only for police action, were often dealt with before 1914 by small columns of the K.A.R., partly because the attitude of the tribes was still largely an unknown factor and partly because the first attempts to organize an efficient police force were not wholly successful. On a number of occasions such columns were required by the civil power to traverse the western parts of the Protectorate.

The people of Sotik were the first to give trouble in this region. In the spring of 1905 they raided the Masai and refused to release their captives or to restore the stolen cattle. The Secretary of State sanctioned an expedition and gave his permission for the country to be brought under control. A strong expedition was assembled under Major Pope-Hennessey and organized in two columns: No. 1 at Njoro (three companies of 3 K.A.R., a detachment of 1 K.A.R. and 600 Masai); and No. 2 at Kericho (one company 3 K.A.R., 30 police and 300 levies).

No. 1 Column left Njoro on 2nd June, 1905, and established an advanced base at Neilson's farm on the Mau escarpment. On 5th June, after dispersing the tribesmen who had assembled to bar their approach, the troops reached Sotik Post. A junction with No. 2 Column, commanded by Captain C. L. Barlow (W. York. R.), was made on 9th June, and Pope-Hennessey then decided to operate as a single force until more information was available. Reports indicated that the herds of stock were located on the borders of the neighbouring Buret tribe. Pope-Hennessey followed and captured large numbers. From his centre at Sotik he patrolled a wide area of forested and broken country. At the end of June he began to move his captures, in a column stretching over seven miles, across steep hills and deep gorges along the way to Molo, cutting a road thirty-five miles long as he went. The force was demobilized on 13th July, having released the Masai captives and taken over 5,000 head of stock.

The next expedition in this area was against the Kisii (Gusii). In September, 1905, Captain E. V. Jenkins (W. Rid. R.) left Kericho with No. 5 Company, 3 K.A.R., and some armed police to punish the tribe for murders committed in Kavirondo. The column was accompanied by a political officer, as it was intended after patrolling the area to select a site for an administrative station. The tribesmen, who were armed with long-shafted spears with small heads, attacked Jenkins' force on 28th September, sweeping right up to the bayonets of the askaris in a hand-to-hand fight which cost them 67 dead. On 4th October about 600 of them again attacked the patrol. On this occasion about 30 were killed and as many wounded, though the troops behaved with great restraint, firing at first over their heads. Jenkins gave the Kisii high marks for courage, but it was the first time their spears had been pitted against modern weapons, and some of them said later they had thought the askaris' rifles were only sticks.

In 1907-08 trouble was experienced in the Kitosh and Kabaras districts. Captain J. Bois (R. Lanc. R.) made a short patrol with 35 rifles of No. 1 Company, 3 K.A.R., towards the end of 1907, and Lieutenant R. C. Dobbs (R. Irish Fus.), with 50 rifles of 'A' Company, 2 K.A.R., spent five months in the area during the latter part of 1908, where he suppressed inter-tribal fighting and captured 550 firearms. Another and much larger expedition was dispatched against the Kisii in the same year. Angered at the hut-tax and other grievances, the Kisii went so far as to stick a spear into the back of their district officer, narrowly missing his spine. Though the wound was slight and the official concerned did not take a very serious view of the incident, at Nairobi the matter was regarded differently. Police from Kisumu and troops from Lumbwa were dispatched immediately. A punitive expedition was ordered under the command of Lieutenant-Colonel J. D. Mackay that consisted of nine British officers, a warrant officer, a native officer, and 323 N.C.Os. and men of 1 K.A.R. and 3 K.A.R., equipped with maxim guns and accompanied by a force of armed police and Nandi auxiliaries. As usual, exaggerated rumours were abroad, and strict precautions were taken as the column approached the Kisii country from Kongo Bay. But no serious fighting took place; small columns of half-companies were sent out to capture stock, about 150 Kisii lost their lives, and the miscreant who had caused the trouble was brought to trial. It is easy to blame the authorities for taking panic measures, but there seems little doubt that on this occasion an unduly serious view was taken of a comparatively trivial affair, and that the fact was recognized both by the K.A.R. officers engaged and by the civil officials on the spot. A temporary garrison of one company was left at Kisii boma.

In November, 1912, the Sotik people drove their stock out of the reserve and refused to return. Police were sent to round up the cattle, but the tribesmen attacked them, recaptured the animals, and drove them into the shelter of the Chepalungu forest. On 25th November an urgent call was made for troops. Lieutenant J. F. Edwards (S. Wales Bord.) was dispatched from Nairobi with 24 men and a maxim gun, and Lieutenant W. Lloyd Jones (Middx. R.) from Marakwet with 44 men of the Abyssinian company. Jones joined the patrol after covering fifty miles in thirty-six hours, a marching feat that earned the commendation of the Governor, but on arrival at Sotik the troops found the situation quiet. The political officer had imposed a fine of 130 heifers, and Edwards entered the forest to exact it. The tribesmen did not risk an action, though they did their best to impede the troops by felling trees across the tracks, digging pits, lining them with pointed stakes, and covering them with twigs and moss. Edwards then visited the Masai, who were on the move from Laikipia to the Solai plains, to impose a fine of 500 head of stock for stealing some of the Sotik cattle and for raiding and killing some Kipsikis.

Small punitive patrols were not always successful, as it was sometimes impossible to identify the offenders. In May, 1913, a patrol of 30 askaris from Marakwet and Nairobi assembled at Gilgil, where instructions were received from the civil authority at Naivasha to search the Laikipia Plateau and recover 290 cattle stolen from a party of Somalis near Rumuruti. A long search followed among the Masai and Samburu, but it was quite impossible to discover among their herds any cattle that could be identified with certainty as stolen.

On the whole, the East African tribes living in and around the highlands accepted their altered situation with very little trouble. During the first decade of the century they were brought suddenly into contact with Europeans arriving not to trade but to found permanent homes; found themselves moved from place to place or confined within restricted areas, and had to become used to the idea of taxation, however mild in degree and beneficent in intention. Their acceptance of this state of affairs was due to the attitude of their elders, which was generally reasonable, the patient handling of the political officers, and the prompt response—or sometimes the mere presence—of the disciplined askaris of the K.A.R.

(iv) *The Uganda Border and the Northern Frontier District, 1908-14.*
Maps I (a), IV.

As European settlement grew and the pacification of the highlands became an accomplished fact, the rôle of the K.A.R. became increasingly that of a frontier force. The presence of unadministered tribes near Lake Rudolf, in country where illicit ivory-hunting and gun-running still flourished, and of intractable Abyssinian neighbours beyond the Northern Frontier District, who rendered scant obedience to the control even of their own government, punctuated the monotony of service in those barren and little-known areas with unexpected incidents. There was also useful work for officers of the K.A.R. in collecting intelligence regarding the tribes and their country, with its rainfall, wells and resources.

The defeat of the Nandi in 1906 led naturally to the control of the tribes who lived beyond them, among the forested hills and well-watered valleys to the north. At one time it had been intended to leave control of all tribes inhabiting the Mount Elgon system to Uganda. During his commissionership Sir Charles Eliot informed the Foreign Office that he had no intention of administering his western frontier for some time to come, 'unless forced by unforeseen circumstances'. But in 1908 plans were made to open up this region, and after a patrol by a company of troops, administration was established in Kitosh. Though the concentration of the K.A.R. that took place in the following year in Somaliland left East Africa short of troops, it was decided to garrison a new station on the River Kerio. This post was first occupied by 'C' Company, 2 K.A.R., under the command of Captain F. H. Span (D.C.L.I.).

The different sections of the Suk, whose country had been the scene of Major Gorges' expedition some years before, were now well disposed towards the Government. But they were in frequent conflict with the Turkana, a numerous tribe of nomads living around and beyond the River Turkwel partly in East Africa and partly in Uganda. The Turkana were unfriendly and intractable, inveterate raiders and keen fighters.

They were armed with large, double-ended 'sword' spears, *simis* or short swords, annular wrist knives and curved finger knives for gouging out their opponents' eyes.

So far as East Africa was concerned, the chief offenders among the Turkana were the Neseto and Turkwel sections. Among the chiefs and headmen, Ebe, Abong and Lobwin were particularly troublesome. Span had not been long on the Kerio before he was ordered to punish the Turkana for a series of raids, in the course of which they had wiped out 55 of the 60 inhabitants of a single settlement. Lobwin's encampment was surprised, 30 Turkana were killed, and many head of cattle recaptured for return to their rightful owners. But the station on the Kerio was too far from the Turkana for speedy intelligence and prompt action, and as the site had not proved very healthy, the troops were transferred in September, 1910, to a new post at Ngabotok, near the junction of the Wei Wei and Turkwel.

The Government hoped that it had 'come to terms' with the Turkana, but their raids continued and many punitive patrols were needed in succeeding years. The most important of these was a protracted operation that began in November, 1912, and lasted for three months. It was commanded by Captain H. S. Filsell (R. Warwick. R.), who left Nairobi for Ngabotok with 60 rifles on 14th November. Other detachments joined him from the local stations, and Filsell began operations with a patrol numbering four officers, 63 rifles 1 K.A.R. and 42 rifles 3 K.A.R., with two machine guns. Marching first to the Loreu Hills, Filsell took many camels, donkeys and goats. On 31st December he came across a party of 30 Turkana at the mouth of the River Natomi. They fled in surprise, but soon returned and attacked the troops, who repulsed them with a loss of five tribesmen killed or wounded. Altogether about a thousand head of stock were captured. The political officer selected 200 as a fine, and then opened peace negotiations with the Loreu section.

Filsell next turned his attention to the Turkwel section of the Turkana. He marched his main column through Ngabotok, leaving a line of posts along the Kerio to prevent the herdsmen from breaking back towards the Loreu Hills. The impounding of stock then continued down the course of the Turkwel until 1st March, 1913, when the patrol returned to Ngabotok. Two officers and a half-company then left for the Kamasya country to exact a fine for certain raids upon European farms, and to arrest the murderers of some Kipsikis.

Filsell's patrol covered nearly a thousand miles of little-known country between the Sugota and a point north of the Turkwel mouth, and recorded a great deal of topographical and tribal intelligence. As a result of his operations the civil power exacted fines under the Collective Punishments Ordinance amounting to 250 cattle, 700 sheep, 175 camels and 275 donkeys. Serious opposition had been expected, but on this occasion the Turkana relied mainly on flight. After the patrol, many of the chiefs came in to make their submission, and the results were reported to be excellent. In August the military garrison moved from Ngabotok to a healthier and more central situation at Marich, within a deep gorge among the mountains, in sight and sound of running water all the year round. At the same time the Neseto section again became threatening, refusing to pay tax and adopting a hostile attitude. Captain A. C. Saunders (D.C.L.I.) was sent to Uganda to discuss plans for a combined expedition against the tribe, but the operations against the Marehan in Jubaland, and then the outbreak of war with Germany, prevented these plans from maturing.

Along the steep escarpments to the west of the Ndo valley lay the country inhabited by the Marakwet, a tribe estimated at 20,000 people, with a fighting strength of 3,000-4,000. In 1911 two members of this tribe were suspected of the murder of a white settler, van Breda, and in November a strong military patrol, consisting of three officers, 98 rifles 'D' Company, 1 K.A.R., and 53 rifles drawn from 'A', 'G' and the Depôt Company, 3 K.A.R., set out under the command of Major L. E. S. Ward to demand their surrender.

The Marakwet had no firearms, but fought with spears, swords and poisoned arrows. Their villages were scattered over the mountain slopes, with the lowest at least a hundred feet above the plain, and although it was unlikely that more than a hundred men would combine at a time, there was plenty of scope for ambushes among the thick bush covering the hillsides. Prolonged and patient negotiations took place, but as they failed to produce the murderers, punitive measures had to be undertaken. On two occasions the Marakwet offered armed resistance, severely wounding one askari. Eventually one of the murderers was given up and an Elgeyo chief promised to find the other, who was arrested later by the political officer at Nandi. The patrol was withdrawn on 6th January, 1912, Lieutenant W. Lloyd Jones remaining behind with 'A' Company, 3 K.A.R., as garrison.

In May, 1913, after many promises, the Marakwet post was at last taken over by police. Unrest followed immediately, the tribe refusing to pay hut-tax or obey the orders of the political officer. Between June and September Captain Saunders carried out patrols with half 'B' Company, 3 K.A.R., arresting the most recalcitrant chiefs. In October these patrols were extended to the Chepbleng or Endo, who lived on the escarpment to the north of the Marakwet. Though not previously hostile towards the Government, the Chepbleng were a wild people and difficult to control. Saunders' operations were the result of two plots to kill Adams, the political officer at Marakwet, for which Maburo, the headman at Sipo village, was considered responsible. While police manned the new station at Marich, Saunders and his askaris marched through the bush-covered gorges of the Chepbleng country. After refusing the first summons, Maburo gave himself up, but six days later slipped his handcuffs and escaped during the night. When Saunders returned to Sipo to demand his surrender, the tribesmen attacked the patrol, killing one askari. During a three-day armistice several hundred Chepbleng arrived to take the oath of allegiance, and soon afterwards produced the fugitive Maburo. For a time the troops were employed in cutting roads. They returned to Marich on 18th November, but were soon called out again to deal with mass desertions among Adams' porters. A few Chepbleng were killed during these operations, though Saunders forbade his troops to fire if it could be avoided.

The Northern Frontier District offered a different problem. The decision to administer it was taken in 1909, following a survey of the Anglo-Abyssinian frontier in the previous year. Archer, the political officer appointed to this task, set up a station on the mountain oasis of Marsabit, and Captain L. Aylmer (K.R.R.C.) a well-sited frontier post on the escarpment at Moyale, known at first as Fort Harrington. For a time these stations, each garrisoned by a half-company, were used only to gain information about the tribes, their habits and their country, no attempt being made at administration. In general the people of the Northern Frontier District were inoffensive, but the whole area was greatly unsettled by the incursions of Abyssinian raiders, and by the infiltration of Somali from the east, whose chief aim was the country's frugal resources in water and grazing. In 1909 some alarm was caused by the arrival on the Tana near Bura of a large number of Somali, estimated at 10,000, who had migrated with their herds in consequence of drought. A company of troops was sent to Sankuri, and with the support of this force the D.C. was able to prevent trouble until the rains broke and the Somali drove their cattle away.

In October, 1910, following reports of Abyssinian raids on the Samburu and Rendile near Lake Rudolf, the Marsabit garrison (half 'D' Company, 2 K.A.R.) was moved to a new post at Loiyangolani, near Mount Kulal. Communications were slow and supplies uncertain. Marsabit could be reached from Nairobi in thirteen days, but it took nearly as long again to get from there to Moyale. From Nairobi to Loiyangolani took approximately three weeks. Transport was almost entirely lacking, and for several years these small frontier detachments, which were often under strength through sickness, were required both to protect their stations and to carry out patrols on foot over some hundreds of miles of difficult and barren country, in sufficient strength to deal with highly mobile parties of well-armed marauders. In such conditions success was largely a matter of luck.

In April, 1911, the post at Loiyangolani was taken over by Lieutenant[1] A. C. Saunders with half 'E' (Nandi) Company, 3 K.A.R. The men had been recommended for a return to higher altitudes after a mild epidemic of fever and beri-beri while serving at Zanzibar. It is doubtful whether the station could from the point of view of health be regarded as an improvement, as it was very hot and the efforts of Saunders' predecessor, Lieutenant H. A. D. Bocket-Pugh (Glouc. R.) to grow vegetables had ended in failure, owing to the salt-impregnated soil. Two cows were kept to provide milk, and the Samburu and Rendile were responsible for providing sheep and camels for fresh meat and transport. This they were not over-anxious to do, as they much preferred possession of their stock to the americani, beads, axes and tobacco that they got in exchange.[2]

The station was built on a small rise about twenty miles west of Mount Kulal and a mile from the shore of the lake. It stood in the centre of an oasis, with palms and acacia trees surrounding the boma on three sides.

---

[1] Promoted Captain in November, 1911.

[2] One sheep (cost four hands of cloth, or about 1 rupee) rationed the detachment for a day; one camel (cost about 20 rupees) for nearly a week.

Several springs of fresh water bubbled out of the ground, but none ran for more than a quarter of a mile before disappearing in the thirsty soil. One of these springs was hot, and there the askaris took their baths, following them if they felt inclined by a cooling dip in one of the springs nearby. Beyond the oasis lay a wilderness of stones of all shapes and sizes; and towards Mount Kulal ridge after ridge covered with loose lava boulders, intersected by dry watercourses lined with thorn bushes and scrub, where camels could graze. The presence of gazelle, guineafowl, partridge, sand-grouse and innumerable ducks and geese on the lake helped to make the station self-supporting.[1]

Loiyangolani was swept for several hours each day by south-easterly gales. This interfered with Saunders' use of the lake, where he had a Berthon boat, but he used to fish and assist the El Molo to harpoon hippopotami, and began teaching his askaris to swim. The camp teemed with scorpions; the men were frequently sick, and the camels died, apparently from the effects of a poisonous shrub. Soon after his arrival Saunders tried an alternative site by moving one section five miles south-east to a bluff overlooking a deep gorge with a water supply at the bottom. The poisoning ceased, but the new station had to be abandoned as the camels soon exhausted the grazing and began dying of starvation instead. Saunders arranged for them to graze with the Samburu herds south of Mount Kulal.

Between the Turkana on the one hand and the Abyssinians on the other, the Samburu had suffered very greatly, losing most of their stock and being afraid to use their more accessible pastures. With troops at Loiyangolani their situation began to improve. Within a few months of his arrival, Saunders was informed that a political officer was to be posted to the district to assist him in administering the tribe. Much of his time was now taken up with settling disputes and doctoring sick tribesmen and their families. A native medical assistant was sent to join him, but before long went sick himself and had to be sent into the hills to recover.

Bocket-Pugh had had a camp on Mount Kulal, and had already sought permission to move his station to this healthier site. Loiyangolani was not even well placed to protect the Samburu, being too far south of the normal grazing areas. Early in November Saunders spent a week exploring Mount Kulal. After a long climb through the precipitous ravines that scored the sides, he reached a rolling plateau of excellent grassland, interspersed with forest. Buffalo and elephant abounded, and the devastation caused by the ivory-hunters who followed them was evident in the groups of burnt and broken Samburu huts, destroyed in the days before military protection had come within reach of the tribe. Kulal seemed to Saunders 'a country really worth looking after', and he decided to get permission to move his station there. Hidden within a precipitous ravine he found a small Samburu settlement. At first the people mistook Saunders' party for Abyssinians and fled, but were soon reassured and were evidently pleased at the prospect of closer protection.

As a result of Saunders' representations he was instructed to make a

[1] From a description of the post in Saunders' private correspondence.

more detailed reconnaissance and report the result. Various causes delayed his starting, but in March, 1912, he visited the mountain again. On the northern part of the plateau he discovered three permanent watering-places; at the southern end four, two of them in pleasant, park-like country with an excellent site for a boma. Saunders thought that transfer of the garrison there would bring the Samburu back to the mountain, where grazing was plentiful at all seasons, and enable them to raise their stock to its former level. The garrison moved accordingly, and within a short time had a skirmish with a party of Abyssinians, who refused to leave British territory and had to be driven off with a few bursts from a machine gun.

The decision of the Government to adopt 'a more vigorous policy' in administering the tribes of the Northern Frontier District resulted in a fourth station being opened at Wajir in January, 1912, where the local tribes were in some danger of being dispossessed of their wells. In a fight with the Yaben, the Garre, in collaboration with some Abyssinians, were reported to have taken 2,000 camels. Captain Aylmer, who had left the K.A.R. and was now political officer with the Garre, recovered about 300 of these, but the tribe protested that their allies had got away with the rest. The garrison at Moyale was endeavouring to stop the brisk trade in rifles along the border, and the whole country was infested with elephant hunters. In October Aylmer came across a party of six, and captured one of them.

Two incidents occurred during 1913 that occasioned some alarm at Nairobi. On 1st May Aylmer was on the way to Moyale, with an escort of ten men of 'D' Company, 3 K.A.R. A native had told him of the tracks of some Abyssinians, and at Gudderh Hill Aylmer came across thirteen of them, ensconced in a defensive position among the rocks. He called upon the party to surrender, and when they refused, opened fire at 200 yards. Within a few moments Aylmer had been shot through the right breast and killed; one of his askaris was killed and another wounded in the foot. Lance-Corporal Hamis bin Juma held his ground and finally drove the enemy off with a loss of several killed. For this exploit he was awarded the African D.C.M.

The second incident concerned a patrol operating from Kulal. Saunders' garrison of Nandi had been replaced by half 'D' Company, 1 K.A.R., which in May, 1913, was relieved in its turn by half 'A' Company, 3 K.A.R., under Lieutenant W. Lloyd Jones. On 3rd September, while patrolling along the eastern shore of Lake Rudolf about forty miles north of Mount Kulal with three Abyssinian and twelve Wakamba askaris, Jones discovered an Abyssinian boma, which had apparently been in regular use by hunters for some time. Jones' summons was answered by a volley that shattered the bone of his leg, killed one of his men and wounded another. The Wakamba, who were recruits in action for the first time, beat a hasty retreat on seeing their officer fall, but the three Abyssinians gallantly rushed the boma, killed all its occupants and carried Jones to safety. The Assistant D.C. from Marsabit was out surveying and tended Jones until medical assistance arrived.

These two incidents, coupled with the serious unrest along the frontier caused by arms being smuggled to the Marehan and the immigration of Boran tribesmen to avoid taxation in Abyssinia, made the presence of more troops for patrol work urgently necessary. Few could be spared, but in answer to an appeal from O.C. Northern Frontier District, Lieutenant A. K. D. Hall (Dorset R.) was dispatched with 60 rifles 'B' Company, 3 K.A.R. By the time he reached Marsabit in November the alarm had died down, and instead of reinforcing Moyale as originally intended he was diverted to Kulal. Later on the Marsabit station was closed and moved to Archer's Post.

(v) *Jubaland and the Marehan Expedition, 1902-14.* Map IV.

Outside Kismayu, the administration of Jubaland during the early years of the century remained exclusively military, with the officers of the K.A.R. exercising the necessary civil powers. For some time the garrison remained at two infantry companies and the camel company, nominally 350 troops, with headquarters at Yonte. Captain J. A. Hannyngton (Indian S.C.), who commanded the camel company, visited India for saddles and equipment, and Aden for remounts, where he secured a hundred young camels. On arrival in Jubaland they had to acclimatize and grow accustomed to the nature of the grazing. Before being used on patrol they were taught to stand firm against sudden rushes of men, and to ignore the sound of rifle fire under their noses.

After the expedition of 1901, £25,000 had been voted for the reorganization and establishment of the Jubaland permanent garrison. Much of this money was spent in building expensive barracks for the Sudanese on Ternan's recommendation, as he thought the question of accommodation one of their main grievances. These buildings were originally described as 'huts', and the Commissioner was called upon to explain later why they had cost a thousand pounds each. At Yonte an 'unfortunate site'[1] was chosen for headquarters, on a slight ridge about eighty yards from the river. There officers' quarters were built: wooden houses with felt-covered roofs and broad verandas, raised on iron pillars. The troops were accommodated in rows of *mahuti* huts, only a hundred yards distant. Though the country was fairly open on the British side, the Italian bank of the river was covered with palms and thick undergrowth, so that during the wet season the whole area swarmed with mosquitoes. A great deal of sickness continued among the camels. Only 30 were fit for riding at the beginning of 1902. In reporting on his first inspection of the K.A.R., General Manning expressed the opinion that the Somali might prove better recruits for the camel company than Sudanese, but in view of the uncertain loyalty of the tribes it was thought inadvisable to recruit them for service locally, and the idea was abandoned.

At the end of 1901 Major Harrison assumed command at Yonte. The main question then at issue was the payment of the fine that had been imposed some eight months before. To obtain the Somalis' agreement to a fine was one thing; to secure it by instalments after most of the troops

[1] Medical Report by authorities of the Malaria Control, 3.xi.01. F.O.2, 569.

had left the country was quite another. The British Government was anxious to avoid another costly expedition in Jubaland, and Eliot was instructed to see that his troops did not become embroiled in any operations that might lead to disaster. In October, 1901, Sultan Ahmad Marghan had escaped from custody through a breach made in a front window of his quarters. No action was taken to recover him, but as his section continued to pay their instalments, no great damage to British prestige appeared to have been done. On the whole, most sections appeared willing to complete their payments, though some were slow and others asked whether money could be accepted instead of cattle.

MacDougall, the sub-commissioner of the Province, was due to leave Kismayu in 1902, and Harrison had been told to take over his duties, which would absorb most of his time in civil affairs.[1] Before this happened both officers were very anxious to achieve a final settlement of the Somali fine. When the dry season was at its height, news reached MacDougall that all sections had collected with their cattle around the wells at Afmadu. Lack of water elsewhere would prevent their movement for some weeks. MacDougall and Harrison decided that when the moon became full at the end of February they would swoop on Afmadu with 200 men and see whether the sections who had paid the fine would help to bring pressure upon the rest. The plan was kept strictly secret, and by the time MacDougall informed Eliot it was too late to forbid it. Harrison wrote to Hatch in even stronger terms, saying that the Somali would 'either have to pay or fight for the water unless the rainy season commences earlier than usual. . . . I trust the authorities will on no account reduce the fine by a single head.'

The result was an escapade that caused considerable alarm in Whitehall, though it passed off without trouble. At 5 p.m. on 21st February, intending to begin with a night march, MacDougall and Harrison left Yonte with three officers, 115 rifles No. 1 Company, 60 rifles No. 6 Company, 35 rifles Camel Company, 50 baggage and 30 water camels. Their arrival at Afmadu completely surprised the Somalis, who had thought themselves out of reach until rain filled the intervening waterholes. Caught with all their cattle around them, and unable to drive the stock away from the wells, their attitude was perforce conciliatory. A strong stockade was constructed and Captain J. H. Bailey (Shrops. L.I.) was left with 80 men and a maxim gun. MacDougall and Harrison then marched back to Yonte, having given the tribesmen a week to pay the balance of the fine, and instructed Bailey to remain until it was done.

When Eliot heard this news he wrote a private reproof to both officers, and told Hatch to order an immediate withdrawal from Afmadu. The message was dispatched by telegraph to Lamu and thence by runner. Manning, who was in East Africa on his first tour of inspection, also expressed his disapproval, on the ground that the matter could easily have been referred to higher authority, though he was careful to point out that the power to act on his own initiative in an emergency must not be

---

[1] The F.O. authorized Eliot to appoint any officer acting as O.C. Troops, Jubaland, to be sub-commissioner of the Province. Major Ward had held this office on taking over from Colonel Ternan.

denied to a military officer. At home the despatches were minuted 'evidently a military expedition prepared to fight', and the Secretary of State described the affair as 'a very provocative measure', and 'one which should not have been resorted to without specific instructions'. Eliot was blamed for not making some effort to prevent it. In a long despatch dealing with native affairs in general that he forwarded to the Foreign Office a month later, he defended the expedition, saying that although 'somewhat irregular', measures of this type were 'far more efficacious than the costly and cumbrous methods of regular warfare'. But the most striking vindication of Harrison's action came from the Senior Naval Officer, Captain C. H. Coke, R.N., who visited Kismayu shortly after the event and was struck by the changed attitude of the Somali since he had last seen the port in June, 1901. 'I am strongly of the opinion,' he wrote to the Commissioner, 'that Major Harrison's recent march to Afmadu with two hundred men had a great deal to do with this satisfactory state of affairs. The Ogadens now clearly recognize that we are strong enough to go where we like in their country without summoning troops from elsewhere.'

After discussing with Manning the policy to be pursued towards the Ogaden sections, Eliot instructed Hatch to order constant mounted patrols within a radius of two or three days from Yonte. Movement was to be rapid, with a minimum of baggage, the object being to impress the Somali with the mobility of the force and accustom them to its presence. Any proposals involving a journey exceeding three days in duration were to be submitted to the Commissioner for authority. The troops were duly withdrawn from Afmadu before the balance of the fine was paid, and the defaulting sections of the Ogaden withdrew southwards towards Tanaland.

Although no longer able to act on his own initiative, Harrison had no intention of allowing matters to remain in such an unsatisfactory state. MacDougall was now at Lamu, and hearing that the Ogaden were in the Biscaya district, he and Harrison proposed a swift march to convince the tribesmen that they were not out of reach and to collect the unpaid fines. Jackson, the Deputy Commissioner, visited Lamu and Kismayu to discuss the matter, and, impressed both with Harrison's energy as a military commander and tact as an administrator, finally agreed.

Harrison set out from Kismayu on 16th August with a force of 130 rifles and 20 Somali police under the command of Captain H. F. Kirkpatrick (E. Kent R.). Seven riding and 50 baggage camels accompanied the force, which could make six marches between water. The first 300 miles of the route had never before been travelled by a European, but good camel tracks made the going fairly easy. Once again the Somali were surprised by the mobility of the troops, and Harrison had no difficulty in completing the collection of the fine. He also recovered several outstanding fines imposed for other offences, the balance of Jenner's kit, and most of the rifles captured from his police escort. Harrison was well satisfied with the result of his expedition, and expressed the hope that the three-day restriction would soon be removed, as he was certain that the only way to demonstrate possession of the country was to move frequently and freely about it with parties of troops. He also suggested that the money received from the sale of the cattle should be used for boring new wells and erecting windmills for pumping, but this proposal was vetoed by the Secretary of State on Eliot's recommendation, as savouring too strongly of a 'forward policy'.

Harrison suggested that Serenli would be a suitable site for a military post farther inland, to be maintained by river launch. Early in October the Italian Resident at Jumbo informed him that about two thousand of the Mullah's followers from British Somaliland were reported within a hundred miles of Bardera, and that the Italians had withdrawn their garrison from Lugh to reinforce the town. The Boran chiefs had already asked for protection, so Harrison renewed a former proposal that Boran levies should be raised and stationed at Wajir and Serenli, to prevent the wells at Wajir and El Wak being occupied by Ogaden Somali in league with the Mullah. This proposal was refused, though Harrison was instructed to place his posts at Gobwen, Yonte and Kismayu in a state of defence. Another of Harrison's ideas was to install Marconi wireless telegraph stations at Kismayu and Lamu, as the cost of extending the land telegraph north of Lamu had been considered too high, and intelligence regarding the Mullah's movements could only be sent by runner or by ship. The rumour that the Mullah's followers were coming so far south proved, however, to be unsubstantiated.

Rumours of the Mullah's intrigues continued to reach Nairobi in the Jubaland intelligence reports during successive years. Late in 1905 it was reported that a mullah named Ashgar, who had recently returned to Jubaland from the Mad Mullah's camp near Illig, was preaching sedition and had assembled a number of followers on the Ruga plain. Captain R. E. Salkeld (Oxf. Lt. Inf.), the acting sub-commissioner and O.C. Troops, went out with the Camel Company, some infantry and a few levies. On the morning of 29th December, 1905, he rode into Ashgar's camp with his advance guard. Ashgar attacked him at once; one of Salkeld's Sudanese orderlies was killed, and the other, who had been wounded, leapt at his assailant and in the course of a rough and tumble on the ground killed him with his own spear. The advance party then opened fire from the saddle and checked the rush of Somalis until the rest of the Camel Company came up, whereupon the tribesmen disappeared into the bush.

Although conditions in Jubaland remained fairly quiet during the next few years, Manning never regarded the attitude of the tribes as satisfactory, and from time to time drew attention in his reports to the probability that further military expeditions would be required. He thought the Somali, like the Nandi, were constitutionally incapable of settling down peaceably until they had proved for themselves that government orders could and would be enforced, and that a conflict might well come about if European planters were ever admitted to the fertile banks of the Juba.

In 1908 Jubaland was divided into two districts, Kismayu and Gosha. The Somali having now been quiet for some years, it was decided to open a trade route between the coast and the country of the Boran. Previously there had been no direct military connection between Jubaland and the rest of East Africa, the garrison being to all intents an isolated command reinforced by sea. Now a tenuous link was opened between Jubaland and the new frontier posts in the Northern Frontier District.

Increased knowledge of the inland tribes of Jubaland did not at first reveal any hostility towards the Government, but Major Gwynn, when reporting on his survey of the Anglo-Abyssinian frontier, drew attention to the possibility of future trouble with the Marehan, who lived upon and around the hilly Dilhara Plateau, the wedge of land lying between the Daua River and the upper reaches of the Juba. The Marehan were divided into two principal tribes, the Hassan and the Isaak. The Rer Talhe, a section of the latter, appeared comparatively peaceful, but the attitude of the other three sections, the Rer Farah Ugas, the Rer Ahmed Wet, and the Rer Ali Dera, known collectively as the 'Galti' (Strangers), was very different. They were said by the other Somalis to be recent arrivals from central Somaliland, who had come ready possessed of rifles and ponies and were now acquiring more from the Abyssinians.

Any mention of contact with the north, where the influence of the Mad Mullah was known to have spread to the Ali Gheri and sections living across the Webi Shabelle, was sufficient to awaken perturbation in Jubaland. Contact with the Galti showed them to be the typical intelligent, fighting Somali. West of the Dilhara Plateau the Garre tribe wandered at will across the undefined provincial boundary with the Northern Frontier District; south of the Plateau lay the country of the Aulyehan. The Galti were soon raiding both, with the natural result that they also sought to arm themselves with rifles, and gun-running across the frontier increased accordingly. Worst of the three sections was the Ahmed Wet under their chief Shirre, who was reported to be one of the Mullah's followers and consistently refused to meet a European.

In June, 1910, a new station was opened at Serenli, some 250 miles from Kismayu up the winding course of the Juba. The post was built on a small hill overlooking the river, four miles above the Italian station at Bardera. The outer zariba, provided with earthworks as emplacements for machine guns, was of a size suitable for defence by a company and a half; the inner defences of barbed wire with a small breastwork on one face could be manned by a half-company. The bush around was cleared to a distance of 50-200 yards, and a road cut through it to the ferry at Bardera. Tracks led north and west on to the Dilhara Plateau.

Serenli became the headquarters of a new sub-district. For about six months in the latter part of each year, communication was possible by steamer from Gobwen, a journey that took from fifteen to twenty days against the stream, but could be accomplished on the return in about half that time. By arrangement with the Italians, who had a wireless station at Bardera, communication could be maintained with the coast. The post was first garrisoned by three officers and 89 rank and file of 'F' Company, 3 K.A.R. Soon after its arrival at Serenli this company was required to provide also the garrison at Moyale.[1] The other two companies then

---

[1] Distribution was Serenli 30 rifles, Moyale 60 rifles. During the first year supplies for these garrisons were precarious. The garrison at Serenli was largely

serving in Jubaland ('B' and 'D' Companies, 3 K.A.R.) were at Yonte, with details at Gobwen. Kismayu had not been garrisoned for several years.

It was not as yet the intention of the Government to attempt direct administration of the tribes on the upper Juba. The policy in Jubaland, as in the Northern Frontier District, was described as one of 'observation', though interpretations of what this meant differed widely. But in April, 1911, Thesiger suggested that a stop should be put to the Marehan raids by disarming the tribesmen, and as the Aulyehan chiefs advised that a political officer with only a small escort would be useless, it was decided to increase the garrison of Serenli to a company and a half. Captain T. O. Fitzgerald (R. Lanc. R.) took over command of the post with two British officers, two native officers and 121 rank and file, and for a time was also Acting District Commissioner. Later in the year Thesiger himself went up the Juba to Serenli, and thence overland via Dolo, Moyale and Marsabit to Nairobi. The trip convinced him of the urgent necessity for a firm policy in dealing with the Marehan, and for the organization of a proper system of camel transport to supply the K.A.R. frontier garrisons and keep them mobile. In his opinion posts such as that at Serenli could fulfil no useful purpose. He advocated instead strong mobile forces that could accompany civil officers on safari, rather than the 'pepper-pot' method of dotting Jubaland and the N.F.D. with little static garrisons.

The increase in Serenli garrison was followed towards the end of 1911 by an outbreak of beri-beri, which raged among the askaris of 'C' Company and their families until April, 1912. Of 87 askaris, 25 women and 2 followers affected, 41 askaris and 3 women died. The disease was traced to a deficiency of mineral salts in the rice, and also to the general lack of variety in diet, the exceptionally hot climate of the station, and the fact that the troops were practically confined to their lines.[1] Other causes contributed to weaken the Jubaland garrison at the beginning of 1912. The Camel Company, which had been on detachment since June, 1910, shortly after its return from Somaliland, had long been without facilities for regular training, and had not fired a musketry course since 1907. One officer and 43 rifles were at Gobwen, but Thesiger thought it essential to withdraw the rest of the company from Moyale and Serenli forthwith. Sickness among camels had grown so serious that the greater part of the company was immobile.

The question of reliefs and reinforcements for Jubaland was urgent, but so low was the military strength of East Africa at the time that fresh troops did not reach the province for several months. In March Lieutenant-Colonel Breading informed the Inspector-General that owing to his increased commitments in the Marehan country he needed an extra company for six months, to 'give the 3rd Battalion time to get on its legs

---

dependent on what it could purchase from the Italians at Bardera, and at one time was even forced to use sacking for clothes. Throughout 1910 the Moyale garrison was usually on half, and sometimes on quarter, rations.

[1] Sudanese were said to be very susceptible to beri-beri. Fitzgerald received a warm tribute for the way in which he handled a very trying situation. Medical Board of Inquiry, C.O. 534, 15.

again'. Authority was therefore obtained to raise the garrison of Jubaland to four companies, and between May and August 'A' Company, 1 K.A.R., from Zanzibar, 'B' Company, 1 K.A.R., from Nyasaland, and 'E' Company, 3 K.A.R., from Nairobi disembarked at Kismayu. In July the remnants of 'C' Company, 3 K.A.R., returned to Nairobi, where they were posted to 'B' Company. For superstitious reasons 'C' Company was not re-formed, and the strength of 3 K.A.R. was thus reduced from a nominal seven companies to six.

The extra company for Jubaland was 'B' Company, 1 K.A.R., under Captain J. M. Mackenzie (R. Scots) and Lieutenant G. J. Giffard (The Queen's).[1] It had been sent specially from Nyasaland to take part in the Marehan patrol. It was not expected that this patrol would be required for longer than six months, for the idea that the Marehan were 'ready to welcome the advent of the Government' had yet to be disproved. At a baraza between Hope (the political officer) and most of the Marehan chiefs, no real hostility was apparent, and the chiefs generally expressed approval at the prospect of Government administration, agreeing to abide by Hope's ruling in an inter-tribal quarrel that had recently arisen between the Ahmed Wet and the Far Ugas. In October the Marehan Patrol set out from Serenli with a strength of four officers, 160 infantry and 30 camelry. The Marehan offered no opposition, but no attempt was made either to tax or to disarm them.

In the appreciation of the military situation which the Inspector-General drew up in 1912, he repeatedly stressed the dangers of military weakness in Jubaland and the Northern Frontier District. In his opinion five companies was the minimum garrison needed to ensure peace, with stations at Yonte, Serenli and Moyale in sufficient strength to provide escorts for the political officers administering the Marehan. With such a garrison a field force of two and a half to three companies could take the field in emergency. If the troops could be found in no other way, Thesiger suggested withdrawing all the garrisons from the Northern Frontier District, replacing them by police, and concentrating three infantry companies and two sections of the Camel Company at Serenli. With a proper transport service it should then be possible for a senior political officer to tour the district for at least a year, insisting that inter-tribal raiding and the importation of arms should stop. Thesiger thought the time was propitious, owing to the divisions that evidently existed between different sections of the Marehan.

Mackenzie's first patrol went as far as Lugh and Dolo. Afterwards the Marehan remained quiet for a time, and many of the former tribes, who had been driven away by constant raids, returned to the banks of the Juba. An advanced base was set up at Helomerera, but early in 1913, at the request of the political officer, was moved five miles north to Lolleshid. Hope had given judgment against the Ahmed Wet in their quarrel with the Far Ugas, imposing a fine of camels. They had been

---

[1] Later General Sir George Giffard, G.C.B., D.S.O., Inspector-General of the K.A.R. 1936-38; of African Colonial Forces 1938-39; and Colonel Commandant of the K.A.R., 1945-54.

told to produce this fine at Humbali,[1] whither the Patrol moved to receive it. As there was no sign of the Ahmed Wet on the appointed date the Patrol moved on to Arras, where the Ahmed Wet were then encamped, and at this threat of force the fine was paid without further delay.

From this time onward Mure, the officer now in political control, attempted to gain much closer contact with the Marehan chiefs. The results were not encouraging. No sooner had the troops departed than the Ahmed Wet sent threats and abuse. The Far Ugas were openly defiant. More serious still, rumours were current of an impending alliance between the Marehan and the Aulyehan, whose chief, Abdurrahman Mursaal, though a paid government agent, was suspected of being at the root of the trouble.

In March Mure wired to Nairobi for leave to take strong action against the Far Ugas. Permission was given, and on 3rd April Captain L. H. Soames, who was now O.C. Marehan Patrol, left Serenli with reinforcements of infantry for the new base at Lolleshid. He was followed next day by two sections of the Camel Company. On 10th April the Patrol left Lolleshid, with five officers, 45 camelry 'F' Company, 3 K.A.R., 68 rifles 'A' Company and 86 rifles 'B' Company, 1 K.A.R. Resistance was slight. Within ten days all the principal chiefs of the Far Ugas had submitted. Half their ponies and rifles were surrendered, and Mure imposed fines of baggage camels to form the nucleus of a military transport corps. The Patrol returned to Lolleshid on 28th April with 14 ponies, 25 rifles and 6 revolvers.

While this expedition was in progress, a conference took place in London to discuss the serious view taken by the Inspector-General of the military situation as a whole. Among the points raised at this conference was the question of the extra company loaned to the Jubaland garrison for the Marehan Patrol. It was agreed that the administration of the remoter areas of East Africa would greatly increase its military commitments, so on 1st May a cable was sent to the Governor authorizing him to retain 'B' Company, 1 K.A.R., as part of his permanent garrison.

The success of his action against the Far Ugas convinced Mure that the time was ripe for stronger action against the rest of the Marehan. Early in May he asked leave to disarm the other sections. O.C. Troops at Nairobi pointed out that this could have no permanent effect unless gun-running across the border could be stopped, and the Aulyehan and Garre were also disarmed. But the Governor wired his agreement, provided Mure was satisfied that protection from hostile raids could be given to all sections so disarmed.

Mure thought that the number of armed men among the Galti had been greatly over-estimated. He put the total at 700, of whom the Far Ugas numbered nearly half. O.C. Troops, Jubaland, thought the Marehan about 1,150 strong, and that the Ahmed Wet were about 200. Both agreed, however, that disarmament was possible with the Patrol at its present

---

[1] Three large hills—Humbali, Gohal and Madowa Ali—were prominent features of the Dilhara Plateau and were visible from practically any point upon it. From Humbali Hill helio communication could be maintained with the posts along the Juba.

strength. Mure saw no reason why it should not be followed by regular taxation and the levying of camels to provide transport for the garrison.

But the attitude of the Marehan, hitherto so quickly amenable at the sight of military force, underwent a marked change as soon as Mure attempted to enforce his new policy. His first order to the Ahmed Wet was issued on 19th May. No notice was taken, and encouraged by this the other sections, who like the Aulyehan had been waiting to see what would happen, grew sullen and unco-operative. The Ahmed Wet withdrew to the north, out of reach of the K.A.R. posts, and it was evident that if they were to be disarmed by force the whole country might flare into open revolt.

On 6th June Soames wired to Nairobi that all sections except the Far Ugas had combined to resist the disarmament order; that to enforce it he must be prepared to fight, and that he was in need of more mounted troops. Command of 3 K.A.R. had been taken over in the previous October by Lieutenant-Colonel B. R. Graham, who was now on his way to Jubaland to carry out his first inspection. The telegram was sent after him, with a message from the Governor saying that the Marehan must be made to obey orders and that it was up to Graham as O.C. Troops to settle the question of reinforcements.

Meanwhile preparations began at Serenli for a larger patrol, consisting of some camel sections and two companies of infantry armed with machine guns. This patrol was to follow Marehan and compel their submission. The rains were in progress and were expected to last until the end of July, which would greatly increase the mobility of the tribe. From June until November each year communication was possible with Gobwen by steamer, so that the best season for building up new bases in advance of Serenli was just beginning. Pending these preparations and Graham's report on the situation, the political officer left the province and his functions were taken over by Major L. H. Hickson, who was now in command of troops. On 22nd July he repeated the disarmament order. Again none of the sections obeyed, though the Ali Dera sent a reply questioning the right of the Government to issue such an order.

Graham reached Serenli in July, and early in August reported by telegram that the Ahmed Wet and Ali Dera were out of touch to the north-west, where they had withdrawn to avoid disarmament, and that he thought reinforcement by one more company was essential. Knowing that this was beyond the capacity of 3 K.A.R., he suggested that help should be sought from Uganda. To this the Secretary of State agreed, and 'F' Company, 4 K.A.R., was detailed for service in Jubaland. The company left Bombo on 20th September and reached Serenli on 31st October, under the command of Captain P. F. Carew (Suffolk R.).

Before the end of August Graham was back at Nairobi, where he wrote a detailed memorandum for the Governor. The Ahmed Wet and Ali Dera were reported to be on the River Daua, very much on the alert for any movement by the K.A.R. They had been given until 15th August to bring in their rifles, but Graham guessed correctly that there was little likelihood of their doing so. The country as a whole was fairly quiet, and he saw no pressing military reason for immediate disarmament, but the prestige of Government was at stake, and the order must ultimately be enforced.

In sanctioning the provision of yet another company for the Marehan Patrol, the authorities at the Colonial Office had foreseen the danger that with the tribesmen in their present mood, the injudicious action of some junior officer might provoke a general rising that would spread throughout all the tribes in Jubaland, and involve the country in another difficult and costly expedition like that of 1901. In the middle of September, therefore, when Hickson was informed that reinforcements were on the way from Uganda, he was told that on their arrival the Secretary of State authorized him to disarm further sections of the Marehan as opportunity offered, but that he would be held 'personally responsible' for 'any action that might aggravate the present situation or cause any considerable fighting, pending the arrival of the Inspector-General and consideration of his report'.[1] Since Hickson was quite unable to forecast what the reaction of the Marehan might be to any move on his part, he felt unable in the face of these rather minatory orders to take any offensive action at all for the time being, a view that Graham felt bound to support at Nairobi.

Hickson spent August and September building up his advanced base at Lolleshid ready to resume operations in October with about 200 askaris and followers. Meanwhile the inactivity of the troops greatly encouraged the Marehan. In early October, when water was becoming scarce, the Ahmed Wet moved towards the Juba near Lugh. On 21st October Hickson set up a semi-permanent camp at Garebahare, and as some unexpected rain fell at the same time, the Ahmed Wet once more retired. Only the Far Ugas remained in reach.

Colonel A. R. Hoskins, the new Inspector-General, reached Serenli on 1st November to find the general situation unchanged, though Hickson thought that the tribes possessed many more rifles than Mure and Soames had supposed. On 15th and 23rd November Hoskins summarized his opinion in two telegrams to Nairobi. Though agreeing that matters had gone too far to draw back without serious loss of prestige, he recommended that the immediate object should not be disarmament of the Marehan, which could not in any case be enforced completely, but the restoration of civil administration in the hope of regaining contact and eventually establishing some confidence between the Government and the tribe.

In the middle of December Hoskins returned to Mombasa, where he repeated his views in conference with the Governor, who gave his agreement and telegraphed the Secretary of State accordingly. It was on these lines that permission was given in London for the K.A.R. to undertake a punitive expedition against the Marehan. As the operations were to be on a larger scale than before, Graham left for Serenli to take command. Before he could arrive, however, the troops were again in action.

Major Hickson left Serenli on 21st November, and command of the garrison devolved temporarily upon Captain Mackenzie. Various posts

---

[1] Acting Governor to Hickson, 15.ix.13. C.O. 534, 16.

[Photo: Capt. A. C. Saunders
Askaris of 'F' Company, 3 K.A.R.

[Photo: Gen. Sir G. Giffard
Breaking up rifles during the Marehan Operations of 1912-14

and signal stations had been set up at strategic points along the river or on the plateau to the north of Serenli, and recently a new camp, well protected by a boma of thorns and barbed wire, had been established at Garba Harre, about eighteen miles from the Juba and eighty from Serenli. Two infantry companies were stationed there and one at Serenli, with detachments of the Camel Company. A much smaller force, amounting in all to about half a company, was at Lolleshid and Garebahare. The Ahmed Wet, Ali Dera and Rer Hassan were reported to be near Humbali and Arras.

The attitude of the Marehan towards the K.A.R. posts had become increasingly hostile. Bodies of tribesmen frequently collected and fired scattered shots into the camps. On 15th December the Rer Talhe attacked the signal station at Adalileh for over two hours, killing one askari. The tribesmen were driven off with a loss of at least eight men killed. Next day the enemy threatened to attack Garba Harre, and on 17th December Mackenzie, who was trying to concentrate his forces there, wired that he feared it would be necessary to fight in order to avoid a breakdown of the whole situation.[1] During the next few days bodies of the enemy were reported at Denli, Dabli and Humbali.

For the time being Mackenzie could only adopt a defensive attitude. Encouraged by this, the Mareham awaited a favourable chance to strike again. On 19th January, 1914, Captain W. G. Stonor (Middx. R.) left Serenli for Garebahare with a convoy, guarded by about 150 rifles of 1 K.A.R. and the Camel Company. As this meant crossing the country of the Rer Telhe, whose presence on the line of communication was a constant menace, Stonor hoped to teach them a lesson *en route*, in reprisal for the attack on Adalileh. Tempted by the prospect of looting the convoy, the Rer Talhe were quite ready to give battle, and on 21st January attacked the rearguard of the convoy at Bogalti, with a force estimated at 400 men, with 150 rifles. This figure was probably too high, but the morale of Stonor's men was shaken, and although the enemy were driven off, he was dissatisfied with the conduct of some of his troops. Lieutenant A. W. D. Bentinck (C. Gds.), a Sudanese officer, and two other ranks were wounded, and as Stonor had too few troops to escort them back to Serenli, he returned there with the whole of the convoy.

The news of this action and its consequences caused consternation at Nairobi. It was the first intimation that the troops on the spot were incapable of dealing with the situation, and unduly alarmist inferences were drawn. It was feared that Garebahare was cut off; that Serenli was surrounded and the troops confined to their boma; that an expensive relief expedition might have to fight its way north through a spreading revolt that would eventually reach the coast. The fear that major operations might be needed in Jubaland was further increased by another telegram from Serenli, asking what extra troops could be spared. A reply was sent that Uganda had promised three companies, and that a Yao company was ready at Nairobi.

Graham reached Serenli on 3rd February, to find a situation that bore

[1] 'If no action taken shall be up against all Marehan.' Mackenzie to Hickson, 17.xii.13. C.O. 534, 16.

signs of becoming serious. He at once telegraphed for the company from Nairobi, and asked that one of the companies at Zanzibar should be held ready to move. Soon afterwards he wired again, saying that a strong body of the enemy was between him and Garebahare and that he needed the three companies from Uganda. Lieutenant-Colonel Ward left Uganda at once with 'A', 'B' and 'C' Companies, 4 K.A.R., totalling 424 rifles. The company from Nairobi had already started.

Difficulties of communication made it impossible to reinforce Serenli at short notice, as it was the wrong time of year for use of the river. Three land routes ran from Gobwen to the north: the Gosha road, which followed the Juba as far as Mfudu; a military road that had been cut from Yonte across the Deshek Wama, and thence via Mfudu and Salagli; and the Somali track through Afmadu. The river route was infected by fly, and so only available to porters. The military route, which was about 200 miles in length, required one day's water and could be covered in fifteen to eighteen days by a camel convoy. The Afmadu route was thought to be about three days longer, and four days' water was needed for use between wells. As the local resources in camels were insufficient for the expedition, the Government of India was asked for three companies of camel transport. The infantry company from Nairobi reached Kismayu on 18th February, the three Uganda companies four days later, and the transport companies from India on 18th March. In view of the size of the forces now assembling, the Secretary of State had cabled his wish that the Inspector-General should take command, but Hoskins, who was still at Nairobi, deprecated the frequent changes that had already taken place at Serenli. He did not think the operations were likely to be serious, or that the reinforcements sent to the lower Juba would be needed. The Governor concurred, and Hoskins remained at Nairobi. To his mind the crux of the matter lay in improved communications. If that could be achieved, with an experienced senior political officer in control, supported by one or two military garrisons at Garebahare or elsewhere and a mobile column of 250 rifles for patrols, Hoskins considered that the country should be secure, without the need for complete disarmament of the tribes.

Meanwhile Graham had begun his operations. Garebahare could only be reached under strong escort, as he had insufficient troops to man the line of communication. Rumours were current that the Aboukir Jibrahil section of the Aulyehan was also hostile. If this section joined the Marehan, Graham thought that the danger of a rising by the rest of the Agaden Somali would be greatly increased. After some persuasion, he secured the assistance of 70 Jibrahil as *illalos* to act as scouts and drovers for captured stock. This co-operation with Government forces committed the Aulyehan in advance, and forestalled the danger of a combination with the Marehan.

On 17th February Graham advanced against the Rer Talhe, who put up some opposition but withdrew after suffering casualties, driving their cattle into the thick bush lining the Juba. The rains were soon due and might put an end to operations, so Graham decided to leave the Rer Talhe and attack the Ahmed Wet, who were reported to be near Gare-

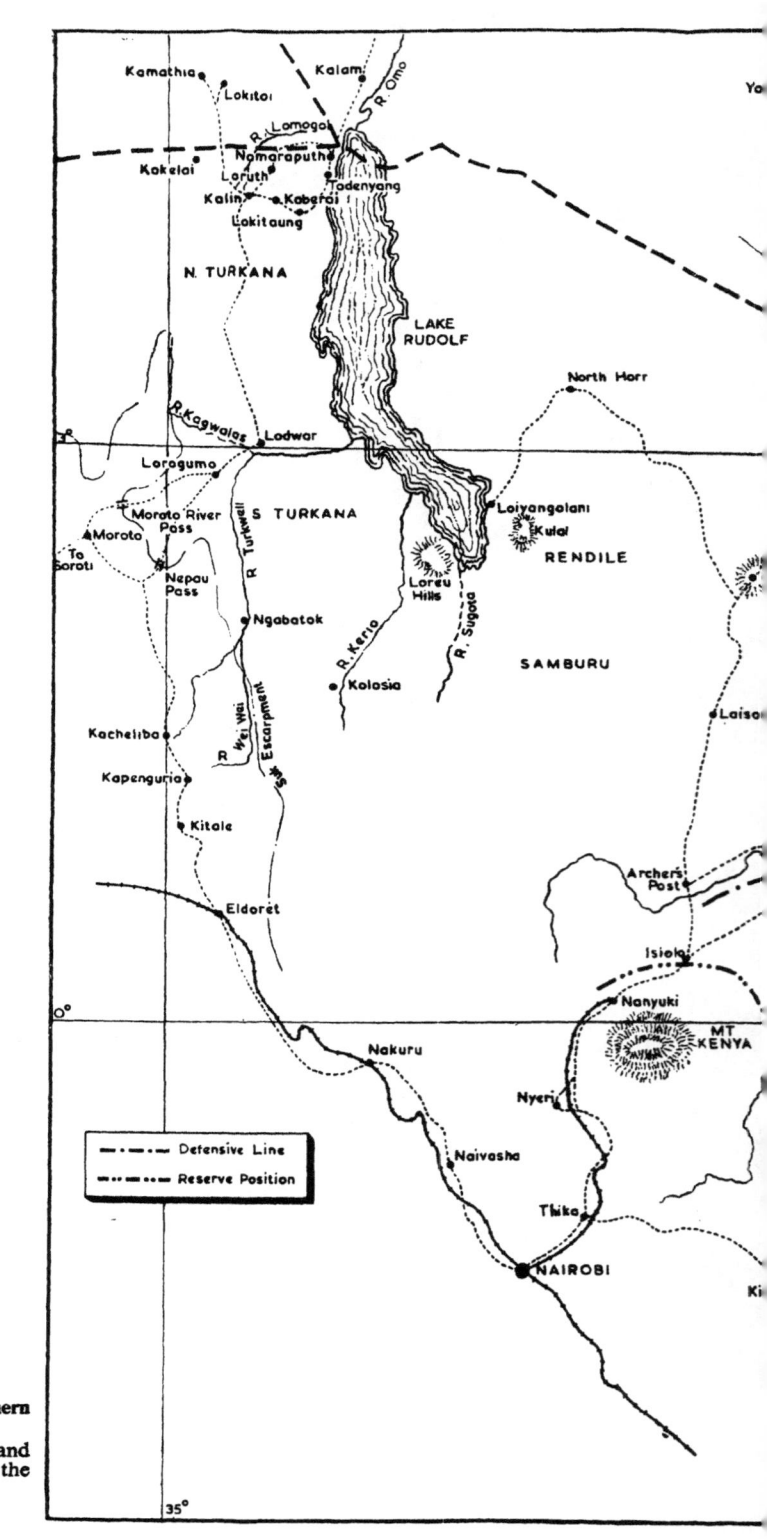

V. Jubaland and the Northern Frontier District

N.B. The Defensive Line and Reserve Position refer to the dispositions made in 1939)

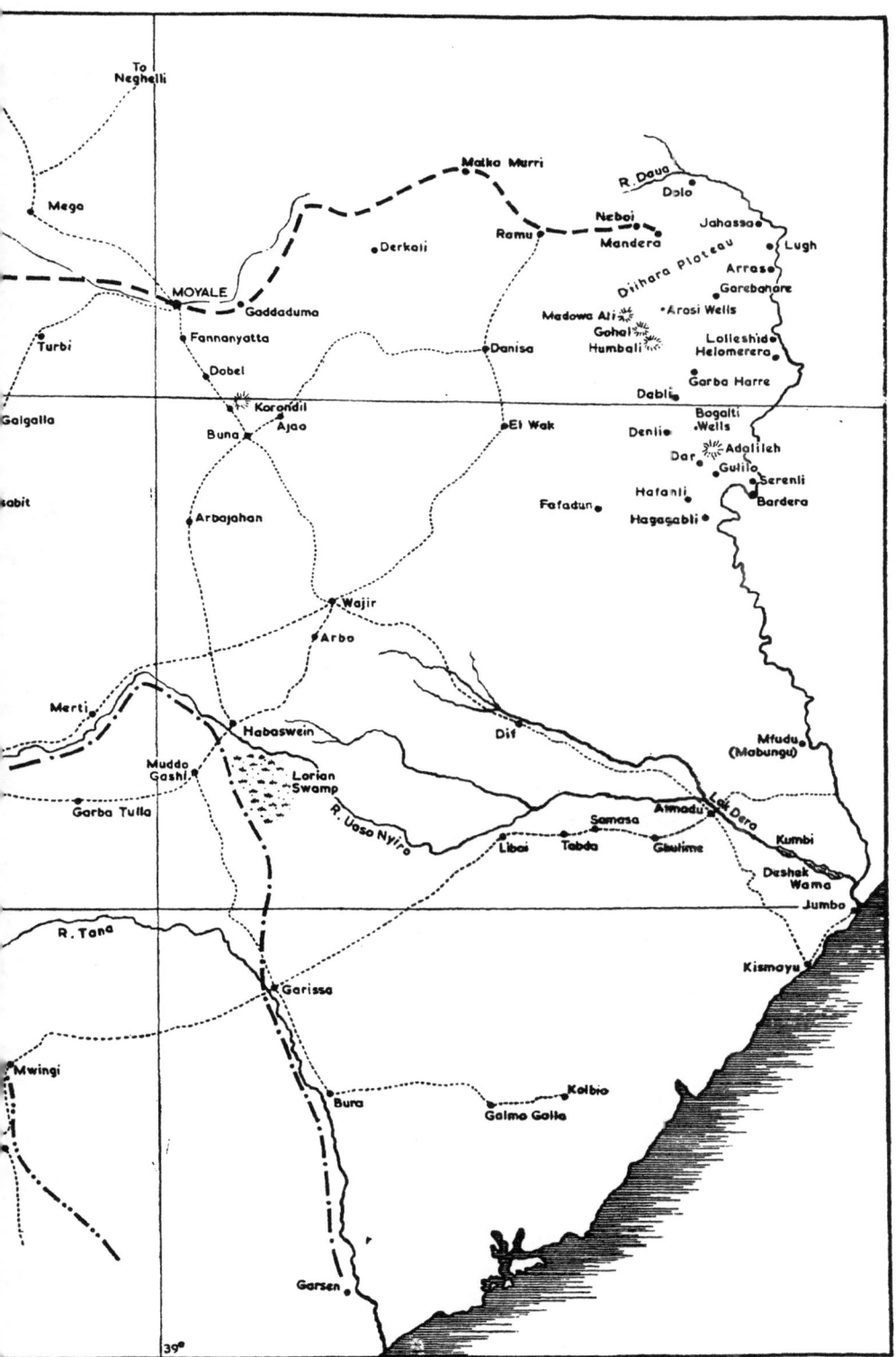

the tribes lay a mountain fastness honeycombed with hiding-places known only to themselves. To catch and punish them was not easy.

When Sir Harry Johnston visited Mount Elgon in 1901, the Gishu attacked his caravan and killed several porters. After the mutiny operations, the Bukedi district was administered for a time by the Kakunguru, a remarkable Muganda who was actually appointed for a short time Assistant District Officer and who continued, as he had done in the past, to take part in expeditions in command of local levies. The little Baganda 'colony' that grew up around him was expected to check Bakedi raids, which the Kakunguru and his men certainly did, though at the expense of reducing many of the local tribes to destitution by confiscating their land. His activities became 'a constant source of worry',[1] and his wholly illegal offers of free land gathered so many followers round him that his authority had to be brought to an end. A European political officer was established at Budaka, and the Kakunguru and his retainers then settled near Mbale. This was resented by the Gishu, who repeatedly raided the newcomers. Finding all complaints disregarded, the sub-commissioner at Jinja patrolled north from Mbale with half No. 3 Company, 4 K.A.R., under Lieutenant R. M. Tidmarsh (W. Rid. R.). The Kakunguru and his armed levies accompanied the force as auxiliaries. Opposition was not serious, and a good deal of stock was seized, but on the way back the patrol was attacked by chief Uguti at the Malawa River, and had to fight its way across.

In January, 1904, the administrative station was moved to Mbale, which had grown into a thriving centre. Six months later another and larger expedition had to be undertaken. At the end of August A. H. Watson, the Acting Collector, Bukedi District, reported to the sub-commissioner that two Indian traders had been killed on the Karamoja road not far from Mbai. Reports showed that this was the work of an unadministered tribe living to the north of the Jackson Falls. The Indians, accompanied by three porters, had slept for the night on a hill-top, and next morning, meeting a native, inquired the way to Mbai. This man summoned his companions, who at once attacked the party with spears, killing the Indians and capturing the loads. The news was taken to Watson at Mbale by one of the porters.

The tribesmen concerned had also been involved in the attacks on Johnston's caravan, and in 1903 had stolen some cattle that Grant was bringing from Karamoja. The Baganda accused them of raiding tribes weaker than themselves and continually watching the road to cut off stragglers from passing caravans, and suspected a combination between the Yobo, Alasi, Bosia, Hogo and Lamboli, all of whom were inclined to think that such depredations could be committed with impunity. The first two tribes had been particularly truculent, and A. G. Boyle, the acting sub-commissioner, hoped that a sharp lesson, coupled with an invitation to other recalcitrant chiefs to explain their misdemeanours while a military force was still at Mbale, might prevent an extension of the trouble.

Before Nos. 4 and 7 Companies, 4 K.A.R., were transferred to 3

---

[1] Jackson to F.O., 24.i.02. F.O. 2, 590.

K.A.R. on 1st April, 1904, No. 9 Company, the garrison of Jinja[1] in the Central Province, was brought up to strength, partly with men from Nos. 4 and 7 and partly with a half-company of Swahili raised at Entebbe in 1902. This became the nucleus of a new No. 4 Company, that was destined to be continually engaged in patrols and small expeditions during the next few years. Boyle now asked the Commissioner for permission to employ half this company on the proposed expedition, saying that Watson was inexperienced and might get into trouble if he visited the tribesmen alone. Colonel Hayes Sadler agreed that an expedition should be sent to impose an exemplary fine of cattle and to secure the murderers, but left the composition of the force to the commandant. The expedition as finally constituted by Colonel Coles numbered two officers, one medical officer, 81 rifles No. 4 Company, 4 K.A.R., 40 police and 16 maxim-gun porters, of whom seven were armed with rifles. This force left Jinja on 21st September under the command of Captain A. H. C. MacGregor. A week later, accompanied by Boyle as political officer and the Kakunguru with 150 armed followers, the expedition set out from Mbale.

MacGregor marched north-north-east and within three days found himself in an area of undulating country sloping upward towards Mount Elgon and covered with patches of bananas and long grass. The cultivated district was enclosed by two mountain spurs, one about six hundred and the other a thousand feet above the plain. To the south lay a dense, uninhabited forest. The hostile tribesmen were estimated to number about 1,000 warriors, armed with spears, bows and arrows. Few cattle bomas or tracks were visible, indicating that they were not rich in stock. This was a disadvantage, as the approach of the expedition could not be concealed and effective punishment of a tribe unhampered by cattle was a very difficult task. Three men from Mbai who visited the camp that evening reported that resistance could be expected, as war horns had been blown and groups of men had been seen assembling during the past few days.

On 30th September MacGregor left a section to guard his camp and with the rest of his troops climbed the lower of the two spurs to prospect. About 20 natives who had been visible on the top of the ridge disappeared before the askaris reached the summit, but a number of huts were found, all deserted and stripped. Some cattle were being herded up the second hill to the south. The Kakunguru was certain that they could not be driven out of the country, so MacGregor returned to camp. Next day he moved to the second spur and built a boma. Hampered by incessant rain, he burnt the huts, climbed the hill and again found the crest deserted. A mile or so beyond a crowd of 150 natives made a hostile demonstration, but were scattered by a few shots from the maxim gun. Most of the stock had been driven towards the forest, but the Kakunguru's Baganda worked round to the right flank and took some cattle and goats.

During the next few days, while the Baganda continued to round up

---

[1] Though garrisoned for some years, Jinja was not then regarded as a 'regular' military station.

what stock they could find, MacGregor marched his troops to the highest point in the country, searched the valleys, followed the course of the Simu River and traversed the edge of the forest from north to south. The tribesmen generally fled at his approach, but often returned to attack the rearguard of the cattle parties with poisoned arrows. On 4th October most of the local chiefs arrived at MacGregor's camp, complaining that 25 of their men had been killed and asking for peace. Although only 50 cattle and 692 sheep and goats had been taken, Boyle agreed to suspend operations. It appeared on investigation that the man mainly responsible was a drunken chief named Songoro, who was reported to be gradually losing his senses. To ensure better behaviour in future, the boma at Mbai was moved along the road to a point nearer the disaffected area.

Before the troops left Mbale for Jinja, Boyle was anxious to teach the troublesome Yobo people a lesson as well. The Commissioner telegraphed authority, and on 18th October MacGregor marched out again with a column 381 strong, of whom 78 were askaris of No. 4 Company, 4 K.A.R., 61 armed police, and the remainder maxim gun porters and Baganda. These tribesmen were expected to be a much tougher proposition, as they were reported to have 5,000 fighting men, some with firearms, and to possess 3,000 cattle and as many goats. Two minor chiefs who came to make peace beforehand said that most of the tribesmen were determined to fight and had boasted that they would kill one European at least. One of these chiefs acted as guide to the expedition.

The area of operations was extensive and very enclosed, and it was fortunate that the tribesmen did not combine to offer resistance. The eastern boundary was shut in by steep cliffs impracticable for cattle, and MacGregor sent a hundred Baganda to close the route south into the Tuta country. To the north lay the Alasi, who inhabited more open country where refugees could easily be followed.

The track was difficult owing to the recent rains and the deep valleys that cut across it. On the day after leaving Mbale the troops reached the country of the chiefs who had surrendered, where they found dense bush interspersed with banana shambas. These people stayed within their huts, but parties of natives assembled in the hills to the left and along a high ridge beyond a deep valley in front. A few rounds from the maxim cleared this ridge and MacGregor built a boma. As another chief came voluntarily to make peace, operations were not begun immediately in the hope that the rest would follow his example.

MacGregor wanted to avoid many miles of toilsome marching by outflanking and surrounding the tribesmen and their cattle in the early stages of the operations, while they were still prepared to resist. He sent the Kakunguru and a hundred of his men round the right flank while he made a frontal advance on the ridge facing the camp. By the time the troops reached the crest the few scouts watching this movement had disappeared. Sloping away on the far side lay an enormous banana shamba, and as the troops advanced towards it about a hundred natives charged them from the left, waving spears and shouting war cries. Two volleys were sufficient to disperse this attack, and another volley a second attack that came a few minutes later, as the troops were entering the shamba. As they advanced through the banana groves in extended order, firing was heard from the front. The Kakunguru had worked around the flank, bringing in a hundred cattle.

The rest of the day was spent collecting stock. While the Baganda explored the Siroko River, small parties of troops searched the country to the south. Some determined resistance was met and in one deep valley two askaris were wounded. On 21st October the captured cattle was driven under escort to Mbale, while the Baganda and police went out to discover in which direction the rest had gone. Next day three columns searched the country to the east, between the camp and the Siroko. One of the police parties came under constant attack, but captured a herd of 48 head.

So far there was no sign that resistance was slackening. Scouts reported that the tribesmen intended to drive their remaining cattle east, and MacGregor decided to repeat his former tactics. At 4 a.m. on 23rd October he sent the Kakunguru with 150 Baganda, and 30 police under a sergeant, to make a surprise attack. Two hours later Lieutenant S. W. H. Rawlins, R.A., left with half a company of troops to support the first detachment and pick up strays. Each party of the enemy resisted the capture of its cattle, on one occasion at such close quarters that three cows were wounded and had to be killed. Rawlins then heard heavy firing from the direction of the Baugo spur, and found the police party retiring in good order with a haul of 110 cattle, pursued by their owners, who constantly pressed the attack. When they heard the sound of the K.A.R. bugles the police were running short of ammunition, and were already in an awkward situation. It was not often that the tribesmen came to such close quarters, for their usual tactics were to stand well back under cover of the long grass and shoot arrows into the air in the hope that they would strike the columns on the bush paths.

During the next few days all the cattle was driven in and MacGregor marched back to Mbale. He estimated that about a hundred casualties had been inflicted, and his total captures of stock amounted to 1,027 cattle and 1,604 goats. These expeditions brought useful experience of the new K.A.R. equipment. MacGregor recorded that the bayonet frogs were so long that they tripped the men, so that when running the bayonet and scabbard had to be taken out of the frog and stuck through the belt.

In the latter part of 1905, besides a reconnaissance on Mount Elgon to prevent the Nandi moving that way during the operations of the fifth expedition, No. 4 Company, 4 K.A.R., carried out another punitive expedition, this time in the Budama district. The chief Bwino Kiko was the leading spirit of a rising that had culminated in the destruction of the boma at Peta and the massacre of 40 Baganda.

The expedition assembled on 13th September, under the command of Captain L. E. S. Ward. It consisted of two officers, two political officers, a medical officer, a European police instructor, 87 rifles No. 4 Company, 71 police, three sepoys with a maxim gun and 40 Basoga levies. On moving into Budama a base camp was formed at Peta, where the tribesmen proved decidedly unfriendly and the attitude of the few chiefs who arrived to parley convinced the political officers that operations must proceed.

Ward's tactics were to make daily expeditions into the disaffected areas with two columns of troops. Each column split into three parties, two to round up cattle while the other stood by in support. Ward had been told to expect strong opposition, but the tribesmen's primitive weapons and lack of organization prevented them from standing up to his troops for long. The columns moved through Mulanda and the neighbouring villages, destroying shambas and huts and capturing cattle and sheep. Bwino Kiko surrendered on 24th September, after the destruction of his own village. About 70 tribesmen were killed, at a cost of one Basoga wounded.

While troops were still in the district, the political officers decided to break the power of Chief Eseme, who had long disturbed the area around Kileu. On 4th October Ward accordingly set out again. Eseme's people were reputed to be armed with 300 rifles, so an attempt was made to surprise them by a night march. This failed owing to the unreliability of the guides. Ward then concentrated his force, as he found the native attitude so threatening that the vicinity of the camp had to be cleared with the maxim gun. Eseme's boma was of course deserted, but the huts were burnt and some cattle collected. While these operations were in progress a small party of police was attacked by Eseme with a Mauser rifle and about 15 of his followers armed with Martini-Henrys. The police were hard pressed until a detachment of No. 4 Company, guided by the sound of firing, arrived in supoprt, whereupon Eseme's party split into small groups and fled, leaving one man dead. But the chief did not submit, and when the expedition withdrew the tribesmen still presented a bold front.

A great change, however, was taking place in the native attitude in the Central Province, where the political officers were now treated with respect. This was due in large measure to the work of No. 4 Company, 4 K.A.R., which for the past three years had been on active service for several months of each year, operating in difficult and often unknown and roadless country, making forced marches in torrents of rain, with the troops often on half rations as they clambered from dawn to long after dark across the hills and valleys to ensure that the area of operations was always thoroughly searched. Expeditions of this kind cost the Government very little in terms of money, and were a necessary preliminary to closer administration. Raiding and the occasional murder of government agents and others still continued in succeeding years among the Mount Elgon tribes, but the small expeditions to which they gave rise were usually within the compass of the armed constabulary.

(ii) *The Turkana Mission, 1910-11*. Maps I (a), (b), (c).

Although the disarming of turbulent elements among the tribes became a police function as soon as a new district was brought properly under administration, 4 K.A.R. was not infrequently called upon to assist. One such occasion arose in the Mbale district towards the end of 1910, when the police were temporarily under establishment and hardly able to perform their gaol guards, bazaar patrols, escorts of treasure and the ever-present duty of suppressing the virulent brand of liquor brewed by the Gishu.

A disquieting state of affairs had become apparent in the closed area between Mount Elgon and the northern frontier,[1] which was crossed by a route from Mbale to Maji on the western plateau of Abyssinia. Late in 1910 Captain Tanner led a police patrol through Karamoja and the surrounding districts to Tshudi-Tshudi, the site of an illegal Abyssinian trading-post where firearms were sold to the tribes in exchange for ivory. Rumour said that the Governor of Maji had an army of 60,000 men and was planning to extend his territory at the expense of the unadministered areas in Northern Uganda, but the immediate object of Tanner's journey was the arrest of Dasta, a notorious Abyssinian leader, who was caught together with some of his men. Tanner also secured 388 tusks of ivory and a number of Snider and Le Gras rifles from the Abyssinian camps. On his return he wrote an interesting report on the state of affairs among the Kamchuro, Bokora, Moroto, Turkana, Jiwe and Dodos tribes.

So long as gun-running remained an easy and profitable venture, there was no chance of pacifying and administering the area. The Traders' Regulations of 1900 had absolutely prohibited the sale or gift of firearms, gunpowder or ammunition to any native of the Uganda Protectorate, but north of Mount Elgon this had never been enforced.[2] Tanner found that the Kamchuro had been well supplied with rifles for many years, and that the Dodos were steadily acquiring them, either by trade or by capturing stragglers from caravans. Swahili traders were wandering about at will, and their safaris, though ostensibly licensed, were usually well armed with unregistered rifles. Tanner thought the whole area lawless and unsettled. Every man who could obtain a rifle had at his mercy the cattle and possessions of each neighbour armed only with a spear. This situation was exploited to the full by the Abyssinians and Swahili, whose method was to play one tribe off against another. The price of a rifle with 40 rounds of ammunition varied from 35 to 50 pounds of ivory. Ammunition alone was sold at three rounds per

---

[1] Few Europeans had visited this area since the days of Macdonald's expedition, but at the end of 1907 Lieutenant C. E. Fishbourne and S. Ormsby (Collector) made a journey from Nimule via Manimani to Mbale. Fishbourne reported: 'From near Mount Elgon to Debosa on the Abyssinian border, the country is without running water; everywhere digging has to be resorted to, and in places the natives excavate to depths of 30 feet in sand, no mean feat considering the primitive implements used. . . . The natives and herds migrate according to the season of the year in order to find sufficient water to supply the needs of their huge herds of cattle. . . . They raid neighbouring tribes and each other quite impartially. They have a quarrel of long standing with the Turkana, another nomad tribe to the north and east of their country. . . . The only article that is traded in this district is ivory, which they exchange for cattle. . . . All the country lying west of Lake Rudolph and for some distance south of it is continuously swept by raiding bands of Abyssinians and any post would have to be well garrisoned and protected.' (Military Intelligence Report No. 33, May, 1908. C.O. 534, 9.)

[2] Reports of gun-running to the Bakedi and Karamojong were frequently referred to in the Uganda Intelligence Reports, e.g. Nos. 27 (March) and 28 (August) of 1906. C.O. 534, 3.

pound of ivory. Calculating on this basis, Tanner estimated that a quarter of a million rupees' worth of ivory must have passed through Tshudi-Tshudi into Abyssinia during the previous three years.[1]

In 1910 the Government of East Africa began administering those sections of the Turkana within its borders, and complained to Uganda that the tribe was being raided from Karamoja. 4 K.A.R. was accordingly instructed to provide an escort for Thomas Grant, the political officer appointed to investigate, and £1,000 was authorized to meet the cost. So little was known of the approach to the Turkana country from Jinja via Mbale, Marich and the Muroni valley that it was decided to send the expedition via Nakuru and Baringo. The result was a prolonged struggle to procure and transport food throughout the course of a lengthy safari that culminated as a punitive patrol in Karamoja.

The Turkana Mission of 1910 was commanded by Captain R. F. B. Knox (R. Dub. Fus.) and comprised two officers, Lieutenants W. P. Baldock (York & Lanc. R.) and E. G. M. Thorneycroft (R. Lancs. R.), a medical officer (Dr. Cobbe), a composite company of 103 rifles drawn mainly from 'B' and 'F' Companies, 4 K.A.R., and a maxim gun detachment. The troops left Bombo for Kampala on 14th November, 1910, whence they travelled by steamer to Kisumu and by rail to Nakuru. There an ox train of supplies was arranged before marching north. On 21st November the K.A.R. left Nakuru, accompanied by 300 porters. Grant followed next day with 153 more.

The column marched daily before dawn, while the officers went ahead to shoot game in the cool of the morning to secure meat and skins for sandals. The boma at Lake Baringo was reached in a week. Here a prolonged and irritating halt occurred while awaiting the waggons from Nakuru. Bruce, the A.D.C., was away collecting taxes, but on his return arranged for the hire of donkeys, as the contractors at Nakuru would not allow their ox-waggons to proceed farther than Baringo. Over a hundred donkeys were collected, but less than half could be equipped with pack saddles, so the askaris were set to work improvising panniers from empty sacks to protect the bags of food from thornbush. Between Baringo and the station on the River Kerio water was reported to be available at ten paces, either from holes or by digging. Beyond the Kerio was a fly belt without game or food of any kind, so Knox intended to use porters for the next four days' march to Ngabotok, where the D.C. Mbale had been asked to form a dump of supplies from Uganda.

The waggon loads of flour, salt, sugar and rice began arriving from Nakuru on 11th December. Grant left for the Kerio two days later with the first safari of 350 porters. While waiting to move, the askaris practised loading and unloading the donkeys and soon became expert at tackling escaping animals low. The porters were practically useless at such unfamiliar work and many were already suffering from dysentery. It was not until 28th December that the donkey column got away under Lieutenant Baldock. It was expected to move slowly, but

---

[1] Tanner's Report, November, 1910. *Uganda Govt. Records.*

although the troops marched early next day, three days elapsed before Baldock was overtaken.

On 2nd January, 1911, Knox reached the River Kerio, a clear running stream twenty yards wide surrounded by thick groves of large trees. Here he camped for the night. The Suk brought in bullocks and sheep for purchase. Kerio post, a group of small grass huts standing on a rocky hill, was reached on 5th January, and contact made with H. B. Kittermaster,[1] the D.C. Turkana District.

Meanwhile Captain A. E. Newland, R.A., who commanded half 'D' Company and 12 signallers at Mbale, where he was assisting the police and recruiting at the same time, unaware of the long delay that had overtaken the Turkana Mission, was trying to get into touch with Knox at Kerio, which he failed to reach with a small party of his men owing to shortage of food. The D.C. at Mbale had, however, found little difficulty in depositing 800 loads of flour at Kilimi, where they were guarded by a detachment of Newland's men. Knox was informed of this by letter, passed from village to village among the Suk, which made him wonder why he had been sent via Nakuru, with a month's wait for supplies at Baringo. Moving without delay towards Ngabotok, he was met by Newland, who had been told of his approach by the officer commanding the detachment of 2 K.A.R. there. On Newland's advice Knox decided not to march his men any farther north into an area where they could not be maintained for long and where it was unlikely that anything useful could be accomplished. Grant was also impressed by Newland's report that the Turkana had carried out the first raid and killed a number of the Karamojong.

Kittermaster agreed to take over the surplus stores at Kerio, and the Turkana Mission set out via the Muroni valley for the Swahili trader's boma near Kilimi. Newland's men blazed a trail beforehand, but the going was rocky and difficult. Porters continued to collapse with dysentery; the medical officer himself contracted it; elephant and rhino were numerous and on one occasion stampeded the donkey column. But at last the column reached the Turkwel boma, where food was plentiful and cheap.

So far the Turkana Mission had accomplished nothing but a very long, painful and expensive march that had swallowed up all the money authorized. It was only after arrival on the Turkwel that Grant could begin his investigation into the trouble. The baraza began on 17th January, when the Turkana gave an account of six raids on their settlements. Next day the Suk and other tribes were heard. The Suk were cautious and said they knew of these raids only by hearsay; the Karamojong laid the blame on the Jiwe, Bokora and Manimani people. While Grant was at work sifting the evidence, Newland returned to his company and Knox set up signal stations on hills near Kilimi, Save and Mbale, opening up communication by runner as well. As the baraza proceeded, Grant became convinced that the Turkana were themselves partly to blame, but it seemed useless to fine them as all their cattle

---

[1] Later Sir Harold Kittermaster, K.C.M.G., Governor of British Somaliland, 1926-31, and of Nyasaland 1934-39.

were diseased. He therefore obtained permission for the expenditure of another fifty pounds to enable him to march farther north with an escort of 50 askaris.

On 4th February Knox was recalled to Bombo, and Lieutenant Thorneycroft took over command. The Mission proceeded towards Mount Debasien, and it was apparent that the presence of troops in the country was having a salutary effect. Grant continued his conversations with the tribesmen, imposing fines of cattle if he found them guilty of raiding. The Bokora and the people of Manimani did not at first obey the summons, but later all came in and were questioned. The raid on Lobwin's section of the Turkana was admitted, no excuses being offered except that raiding had been an immemorial custom. Grant imposed a fine of 300 head of cattle, intending to send them to Lobwin as compensation. Only 62 were brought in, and finding the villages deserted Thorneycroft went in pursuit, overtook the herds, fired a few shots and captured about 800 head. These were handed back except for 201, which were delivered in compensation to a delighted party of Turkana sent by Kittermaster to receive them. The troops were then free to return by the short route home, thus completing a total march of 780 miles. The unfortunate Baldock did very much more, as he had to retrace his steps to Baringo to return the donkeys.

So ended the Turkana Mission of 1910-11, hardly an occasion for military enterprise, but a typical example of the semi-police work that had now become one of the normal commitments of 4 K.A.R. In his despatch to the Secretary of State the Acting Governor expressed his satisfaction at finding the officers and men of the regiment so ready to respond to any call made upon them. Grant had strongly urged greater control in Karamoja and the Rudolf Province, with frequent tours and visits by police officers to prevent traders from buying ivory and to warn the natives that the slaughter of elephants must cease. A police tour was ordered in Karamoja, and in consequence the K.A.R. half-company at Mbale had to remain till the end of July.

(iii) *Operations of the Northern Patrol, 1911.* Maps I (a), (c).

As in British East Africa, after 1910 the rôle of the K.A.R. in Uganda became largely that of a frontier force. From then until the outbreak of war in 1914 a dozen expeditions, involving altogether four and a half companies, took place in the lawless, unadministered tract of country between the meridian of 33° E. and Lake Rudolf. Much of this area was mountainous and covered with thick bush and long grass, in which the hill tribes were particularly difficult to catch. The main purpose of these military expeditions was the suppression of the illicit arms traffic. Determined resistance was sometimes experienced, but in general tribal organization was so elementary that large combinations of warriors were rarely met. The work was begun by the Northern Patrol, which was instituted in 1911, and continued by the Northern Garrison, which came into being in the following year. The general pacification of this area cost 4 K.A.R. 15 askaris killed, 17 wounded, and the death by sickness and exposure of 17 followers. In the course of the operations the tribes suffered about 300 casualties, surrendered large numbers of rifles, and were fined about 7,000 cattle, besides sheep and goats.

The Northern Patrol may be said to have originated in July, 1911, when Lieutenant W. I. Webb-Bowen (Middx. R.) and Lieutenant Baldock were sent from Hoima to Nimule with 'A' Company, 4 K.A.R. The P.C. of the Nile Province had asked for an officer and 50 askaris to enforce the Collective Punishments Ordinance of 1909 against two hill tribes, the Eiyerri and Gimorreh, who lived on the southern edge of the Latuka country about fifty miles north-north-east of Nimule and were continually raiding along the Acholi border. It was thought both safer and administratively easier to send a whole company for this purpose, and Webb-Bowen accordingly embarked in the Nile flotilla at Butiaba on 10th July with one maxim gun, five porters, and 80 askaris in full marching order, carrying 100 rounds per man. This was the maximum number that could be rationed at Nimule at the time, but 35 reinforcements were to be brought on later from Hoima by Captain Tanner.

The force reached Nimule on 13th July, and Webb-Bowen reported to the D.C. to receive the latest news and discuss the plan of campaign. Very little was known of these hill tribes as they lay outside the old administrative area, but it was plain that they would be very difficult to surprise. Their villages were placed on the tops and sides of scarped and difficult hills, natural fortresses covered with dense bush and enormous boulders and riddled with caves. As raiding was a normal feature of their existence, the tribesmen were constantly on the watch from well-placed observation posts. From these positions great distances could be seen, and the slightest unusual movement or the smallest column of smoke rising from the plain was unlikely to be missed. On the approach of a superior force the tribesmen would play hide-and-seek among the hills and caves, and on more than one occasion Webb-Bowen laboriously pursued his foes to the top of a hill, only to see them moving away down the valley from which he had just come.

The approach of the rains made it necessary to start at once, before the rivers Aswa, Nyimur and Ateppi came down in flood. The best method appeared to be an indirect approach through the friendly villages of Lokai and Parajok. The expedition left Nimule on 15th July and marching in great heat covered the ten miles to Lokai on the first day. Next day Webb-Bowen crossed the Aswa and the Nyimur, streams thirty to forty yards wide and about three feet deep, with swift currents that would make both rivers impassable in the rains. All natives seen were armed with Snider or Le Gras rifles. On 17th July the column passed through Parajok and met with a friendly reception from the chiefs. The Ateppi was crossed on the 18th, and the troops passed into a foodless country where water was scarce and long grass made the going difficult.

Another day's march brought the K.A.R. close to the foot of the hill where the Eiyerri villages were situated. Webb-Bowen posted his sentries in trees, for the grass was twelve feet high. The maxim gun was mounted on a convenient ant-hill, a boma was built around the camp, and the grass cleared for two hundred yards outside it. Unfortunately the chance of surprise by a night march was lost, as the Acholi guides were unreliable and the patrols sent out after darkness reported a non-existent swamp at the base of the hill.

Early on 20th July the column reached the hill. which appeared to be nearly 2,000 feet high and was covered with huge boulders, thick bush and long grass. Putting out an advanced screen, Webb-Bowen began the climb with his main body. About half-way up the alarm was given and the tribesmen withdrew in orderly fashion. About ten of them were shot, and on reaching the village Webb-Bowen burnt all the huts, cut the standing grain, and drove off a hundred sheep and goats. As he retired the Eiyerri reoccupied the hill, but were scattered again by a few shots from the maxim gun, as a timely hint not to attack the camp that night.

Next day the troops climbed another hill and burnt the village on top, but found that all stock and possessions had been removed. On 22nd July Webb-Bowen resumed his march towards the country of the Gimorreh. He camped that night in a bamboo brake overlooked by towering hills, determined this time to achieve surprise by marching well before dawn. Camp was broken at four o'clock and the foothills were reached at daylight. Again the alarm was given and the first bomas, standing on a large ledge about a quarter of the way up the hill, were found deserted. Food was stored in the caves behind and the sound of natives talking could be plainly heard. The rocks and caves were searched for two hours without much success, and the maxim was turned on parties of the enemy who could be seen stalking the porters below. Next day Webb-Bowen led a section and a half to the top of the hill, a somewhat hazardous climb that involved the barefoot crossing of a great slab of rock tilted at a steep angle over a thousand-foot drop to the plain. Another party sent to approach from the east reached the top first, and found the chief's boma deserted. A day was spent burning huts and searching all the caves, and the expedition then withdrew with difficulty, as the paths were treacherous and the terrain well adapted for ambushes.

The return march was hampered by rain, though Webb-Bowen was able to make use of elephant paths through the long grass and bush. He had inflicted about 20 casualties for the loss of four porters severely wounded. Neither Eiyerri nor Gimorreh had offered organized resistance, both tribes confining themselves to harassing tactics, creeping up among the grass and boulders to throw their spears at short range before vanishing. Perhaps the best result of the expedition was its effect on the Lokoya tribes, who lived on the plateaux of a long mountain range where their villages were approached by narrow passes and surrounded by bare hills and granite bluffs. They now proposed of their own accord to pay a fine in compensation for their depredations.

Within a few weeks the Northern Patrol was again on the move, in co-operation with Tanner and the police. This time the objective was the tribes of the Opei and Nangiya hills, the intention being to clear this area of illicit traders, to punish all tribesmen who harboured them and acquired arms to raid their neighbours, and to select sites for a line of permanent camps.

On 7th September Webb-Bowen left Nimule with 'A' Company, 107 rifles strong, and ten armed police. The Aswa was crossed in flood and three days later the expedition reached the village of Ajok, one of the principal Acholi chiefs. Here a section had to be left to guard some of the stores, for the Acholi were not used to carrying. Owing to their elaborate hair-styles two porters were needed for each load, which had to be slung on a pole between them.

Webb-Bowen reached the foot of Mount Opei, a heavily-wooded mountain which he estimated at 2,500 feet, on 15th September, and camped a mile from the Madi village there. Reports came in that the Okuti people, who lived in the Nangiya range, had murdered 14 Swahili traders. The march was resumed, and two days later, after an exhausting safari in great heat with little water or food, Kiteng Hill was reached, where it was intended to establish the first post. There Webb-Bowen received a note from Tanner to say that while confiscating cattle from the Madi he had been attacked, and that one of the K.A.R. askaris with him had been killed and another wounded. Help was needed if the tribe was to be punished effectively.

Lack of porters hampered Webb-Bowen's movements. Sending for Akowo, the local chief, he demanded 200 men by five o'clock the following morning. Akowo did well to produce half that number, and moving his stores to the site chosen for them and detailing a guard of 20 rifles, Webb-Bowen set out with the rest of his men for Akol Hill, where he found Tanner and the police guarding 211 head of cattle. Contact was established by helio with the camp at Kiteng, where all was reported to be well, and Lieutenant Baldock was sent in advance with 35 men to Opei. The rest of the company followed next day, less a small party left in charge of the cattle.

The Madi villages ran for three-quarters of a mile round the base of the mountain, protected on the open side by a high natural hedge lined with palisades. Baldock camped overnight within shelter of a boma, and when he began next morning to burn the huts encountered fierce opposition. On the arrival of the rest of the company a covering party took up position on the hillside above, where it was assailed with rifle fire, spears and rocks. The hill was covered with thick bush and honeycombed with caves, so that nothing was seen of the enemy but the brief movement of a hand or arm over the top of a rock. The Madi had at least one good rifleman, who shot an askari through the chest. That night Webb-Bowen attacked their camp fires with maxim-gun fire and war rockets, with spectacular effect.

On 21st September the chief Aluru and one of his headmen arrived at the camp to sue for peace. Tanner demanded the surrender of all firearms. Aluru replied that the tribe was scattered and the rifles would take some time to collect. Only three old muskets were produced, so that night the maxim and war rockets were used again. The destruction of huts and crops continued, and some casualties were inflicted by a guard mounted over the water-hole. Aluru, who had been detained, said that his people were particularly afraid of the war rockets, which had killed three men sitting round a camp fire, but he seemed unable to bring about their surrender.

The company reached Kiteng again on 27th September. A few days later news came that seven Swahilis were trading rifles to the tribes in the Nangiya range. On 30th September the company again marched out, 100 rifles strong, and reached Ukuti in heavy rain. Before dawn next morning Webb-Bowen left his camp, hoping to surprise the traders, who were reported to be on the opposite side of the valley. The way was rough; the night was very dark, and progress was difficult, so that the askaris' approach was heard and the traders' camp (which proved to be Abyssinian) was found deserted. Although voices could be heard in the distance, no sign of a track was discovered, and Webb-Bowen was obliged to abandon the pursuit and return to Kiteng.

A site for the permanent camp was found on an eminence overlooking the water-hole, and given the name of Post Hill. The work of construction began, but was constantly interrupted by the need for further patrols. On 6th October, leaving Baldock in charge at Kiteng, Webb-Bowen set out to visit the notorious Abyssinian base at Tshudi-Tshudi, via the Nangiya and Rom mountains. On reaching Lokuta he found Captain H. M. Tufnell,[1] the D.C. Turkana district, with a police patrol of 30 men. Tufnell had had a short skirmish with the Abyssinians, and captured four of them. He thought the area was now free of illicit traders, though some of those whose licences had expired were believed to be across the frontier at Maji, waiting until the coast was clear.

On 11th October Tanner and Tufnell left for the Jiwe country. Webb-Bowen tried unsuccessfully to get in touch with Baldock by helio and then resumed his patrol, making notes of topographical features, water-holes and food supplies in his diary as he went, in case military operations on a large scale should ever be needed. He found the country rather barren and thinly covered with thornbush growing in a stony soil. On one occasion he dug up 76 tusks of female elephant ivory, reported to have been hidden there by two white hunters. Tshudi-Tshudi was reached on 26th October. The camp was deserted, but the walls of the huts were still standing. A few days later the patrol attacked the tribes near Ukuti, who replied with rifle fire. Webb-Bowen cleared the hill, burnt five villages, and recorded his opinion that some of the enemy's rifles were better than his own.

Napori Peak was climbed and more villages were destroyed and food collected without opposition. For the next two days the men rested and were employed in making sandals. On 4th/5th November a night march was made to the Killari Peaks, but all cattle had been driven away. Another long march brought the troops to Mount Rom. The tribes there were caught unprepared, but having some months previously succeeded in massacring a well-armed party of Acholi who had accompanied Tanner and the D.C. on a tour of the area, they attacked the patrol with confidence. The maxim gun gave the tribesmen a surprise, but as their positions were strong and they possessed accurate breech-loading rifles it took two days to disperse them into the deep, thickly-wooded ravines. After this Webb-Bowen climbed Mening Hill, where the huts were scat-

---

[1] Tufnell was a militia officer who took a civil appointment in 1908, after five years' service with 4 K.A.R.

tered in almost inaccessible positions, some on impregnable peaks approachable only by a single path. Six villages were burnt and much food destroyed at a cost of one askari killed and one wounded. Webb-Bowen thought that to be properly effective, operations against the Nangiya tribes should be carried out by at least three companies, manœuvring in half-companies to surround the villages and achieve surprise.

The post at Kiteng was left to a garrison of ten askaris, and by the end of November another post, manned by 10 askaris and 20 police, was set up at Lokuta. The rest of 'A' Company continued constantly in the field, though the process of converting the Northern Patrol into a settled garrison had already begun.

(iv) *The Lango Detachment, 1911-12*. Map I (a).

The Lango district consisted of the low, undulating country lying in the bend of the Nile between Foweira, Mruli and Lake Kwania, drained by the rivers Toshi, Koli and Parossa. The tribes were related to their neighbours the Acholi and Bakedi. Never yet subjected to control, and amenable to their own chiefs only for so long as they continued to lead them in inter-tribal raids, they were expected to be difficult to administer. The first attempts to open up the district were made in February, 1909.

To support the authority of the D.C. Eastern Province, it was decided in 1911 to station a whole company of 4 K.A.R. near Olett's village on the banks of the River Koli. 'B' Company was chosen, under the command of Captain R. H. Johnston (Lincoln R.). On 12th September the company, 125 rifles strong, arrived after a march of 200 miles. Johnston selected a healthy site for the new post on the side of Ngetta Hill, a thousand yards from the river bank. Grass-roofed bandas with mud walls were constructed for accommodation and stores, and the troops built a mosque in their spare time. An Indian trader appeared from nowhere, and set up a *duka* below the camp to sell salt, tobacco and cloth.

A semi-permanent move of this nature entailed considerable difficulty and hardship for the askaris, as it involved the transplanting of a complete little colony of 300 people. Besides the troops and porters, a number of women and children also had to make the long march, all but the smallest *totos* carrying loads. It was therefore disappointing to meet with a somewhat frigid reception from the D.C., who was horrified at such an invasion of his territory, complained that food could not be found throughout the year for so many people, and proposed that half the company should return forthwith to Bombo with Lieutenant Thorneycroft, who had been ordered back to assume the adjutancy. Finding the local tribes friendly, Johnston had expected to tour farther north in the unadministered gun-running areas, thus connecting up with the work of the Northern Patrol, but he was curtly forbidden to enter any unadministered area without permission, or even to tour the settled parts of Lango without prior consultation, and then only with a small personal escort of 12 men. At a loss to understand why the movement of his company had ever been ordered, Johnston sought instructions from higher authority and asked permission to return. He was informed that the company was at the D.C.'s disposal, and that he should not make patrols unless requested.

For the next two months Johnston only moved from his camp on a few short journeys to purchase supplies. Half the company was sent back in October as requested by the D.C., leaving Johnston with 67 rifles, 40 porters and women and children to a total population of 189. For the time being his weekly reports were concerned almost wholly with food. The countryside seemed to him the most fertile in the Protectorate, with plentiful water and grass growing from six to nine feet high. Vegetable gardens were started; several acres were marked out for grain shambas, and a request sent for jembies, and for beads to use as currency. Large quantities of *wimbi* were purchased to build up a reserve before the heavy rains made movement difficult. Meanwhile the troops were kept busy with daily parades, hut building, and the construction of a 450-yard rifle range.

On 12th November, at the D.C.'s request, Johnston began a short tour in the unadministered country around Eruti and Alito. He was interested chiefly in the possibilities of helio communication between these hills and his station at Ngetta. A month later he made another safari past Eruti to Omali's on the Aswa River. At this time of year it was a swift, deep but narrow stream, and the askaris bridged it before returning. On 30th December Johnston was interested to hear that the Northern Patrol was occupying Tshudi-Tshudi east of the Nangiya Hills, and wondered whether communication by helio might be possible via the intervening peaks, if the D.C. would agree to a safari through the Lira country to find out. On 17th January, 1912, he wrote to the Adjutant 4 K.A.R. that a Lira native had reached him in twelve days with a letter from Baldock at Tshudi-Tshudi, and pressed for a policy of joint patrolling, with helio stations on the hills at Napono and Eruti, to exchange news quickly of the gun-runners' movements.

The decision to open up the country west of Lake Rudolf made operations on an extended scale very probable, and military headquarters in Uganda became interested in topographical and general intelligence reports of the area. Johnston was informed that 'D' Company was under orders for the north, half under Captain R. H. Leeke (Rifle Brig.) to escort Captain Tufnell on a tour of Karamoja, and half to relieve him at Ngetta. He was again reminded that every opportunity must be taken to assist and advise the D.C., and was asked to discover the best routes north via Mount Parabong. Early in February another runner came through with despatches from Webb-Bowen, who was then fifteen miles south of Tshudi-Tshudi. Johnston therefore informed headquarters that the route via his own camp was the best way north, especially as he had heard that there was no water on the track from Mbale.

On 8th February Lieutenant H. A. Lilley relieved the Lango Detachment with 58 rifles 'D' Company, and Johnston marched out next day. For the first fortnight Lilley concentrated on short tours to purchase food. The rains were not due for some weeks, but it was already pouring heavily, and Lilley determined to visit the Aswa River to inspect Johnston's bridge of logs, as there was only one deep ford usable when the river was in flood. Early in March he began his safari, but was forced to return as a tribal squabble had broken out near Ngetta over a stolen cow. Another message arrived from Webb-Bowen at Lokuta who said there were no gun-runners among the Lira people, as the tribe had very little ivory. On 13th March Lilley went to Nabiessu, where the D.C. had made a temporary station. He was requested to tour the administered villages to stop outbreaks of fighting. Among other villages punished was that near the store at Eruti, where the tribesmen had burnt the huts. This was small loss, as all the grass huts built by Johnston had now grown very untidy in the high winds and were full of *dudus*. Lilley began building mud ones to replace them.

In the latter part of April, Lilley made his safari through Lira to Mount Parabong. This route had never previously been crossed by a European. For the first twenty miles beyond the Aswa, Lilley found an uninhabited country of *gubba*, thick and woody, with plentiful water and game, including elephant and giraffe. The tribesmen proved very friendly and brought in food of their own accord, as they were rich in cattle and goats and cultivated large shambas of *mtama*. Lilley made corrections to the map as he went, finding some of the places marked upon it as far as thirty miles out of position. At Parabong he estimated that he was only three days' march from the headquarters of the Northern Garrison at Kiteng. In forwarding the report to the Chief Secretary, the Commanding Officer, Lieutenant-Colonel L. E. S. Ward, suggested that this route north might prove a better means of reinforcement than the river journey to Nimule. There were now two and a half companies in the Northern and Lango districts, split into four detachments, and Ward was finding it difficult to arrange leave for the officers. The Lango detachment was ordered to concentrate at Kiteng, but this had to be cancelled as its presence was required in Lango until August.

Sleeping sickness was now spreading along the north bank of the Nile, and the Government decided to clear the affected villages.[1] In May, owing to the untimely death of Captain Tanner, this work was in abeyance, and the P.C. Northern Province requested Lilley to second 25 men to assist the A.D.C. at Gulu. The work was expected to take three or four months, as all the Bachopi were to be cleared from the north bank, and their crops, shambas and huts burnt. The unfortunate tribesmen took refuge on the islands and hid their canoes, but offered no resistance.

In August the P.C. appealed for a second A.D.C. and a police officer for the Lango district. Until these officers could be sent, he requested that the K.A.R. detachment should remain, as the Lango were now accustomed to troops and their sudden withdrawal might lead to a renewal of lawless behaviour. After returning from the Nile, Lilley concentrated on smartening his troops, resuming drill parades and practising for sporting events in conjunction with the police, a new departure in

---

[1] Sleeping sickness was first reported in Uganda in 1901. It occurred along the margins of lakes and rivers. The preventive measures adopted were to cut down the vegetation that harboured the tsetse fly and to depopulate the affected areas.

which the men showed keen interest. A Coronation grant of fifteen rupees had been allotted to the detachment, and as this did not go far between 65 men, Lilley set it aside as prize money for the tug-of-war.

Communication continued with the Northern Patrol, though the runners were sometimes attacked by the Acholi. On this account and at the D.C.'s request Lilley undertook one or two minor punitive expeditions. The rains were again filling the rivers and swamps, making safaris difficult, and the troops often waded for long periods through water breast high, with their rifles and equipment on their heads. Towards the end of August two askaris of 'A' Company got through from Madial in four days, a distance of a hundred miles. Lilley was anxious to join the Northern Patrol, for it had now been definitely decided that the K.A.R. detachment should leave the Lango district at the end of October.

In reporting on 4 K.A.R. at the beginning of 1912, the Inspector-General had deplored the renewed scattering of the battalion brought about by the extension of control in the north and west. 'A' Company and half 'D' Company were then on the Northern Patrol; 'B' Company was in Lango, and with two other companies in the Western Province, only one and a half were in training at Bombo. Reports indicated that the northern tribes had several thousand modern weapons in their possession so there appeared to be no immediate prospect of altering this distribution. But the Northern Patrol was now asking for a minimum of three companies and even for artillery to blast the more inaccessible mountain strongholds, and Thesiger recommended that the situation should be examined forthwith and a policy laid down. After consulting O.C. Troops the Governor decided to send a senior officer to undertake this task, and Major J. K. Clothier (W. Yorks R.) was selected.

Travelling north by the land route via Lango, Clothier reached Ngetta on 21st August, where he remained for several days to meet Spire, the P.C. Eastern Province, Jervoise, the D.C. Lango, and Tufnell, the D.C. Rudolf, who had been accompanying the Northern Patrol as political officer. Tufnell described his experiences since he began touring the area in June, 1911, and a general discussion took place. It was agreed that for the next year or so the Karamoja district should be closed while Tufnell continued his work with the patrol farther north. The best distribution of troops seemed to be a company at Madial (which replaced Kiteng as the base camp), a half-company at Morongole, and the transfer of the half-company at Ngetta to Magosi as soon as the new political officers reached Lango. This distribution would, it was hoped, stop the inter-tribal raids, especially between the people of Manimani, Jiwe, Suk and Turkana; prevent the hill tribes of the Nangiya range from attacking the Dodos, and check arms smuggling from Abyssinia.

The passage of Clothier's safari north was virtually the opening of this new route. Lilley detailed eight men to escort him. Johnston's bridge over the Aswa had been washed away, and the river was now too swift to ford. An attempt to cross by raft failed, and Clothier eventually got over some fourteen miles upstream by a native bridge of tree trunks lashed together. But in spite of the difficulties caused by the rains, the route was used again in September by the Commanding Officer 4 K.A.R. on his way north to Madial on inspection. By that time the Aswa was fordable, though breast high.

Before marching north from Ngetta, Lilley sent the women and children back to Bombo. Clothier ordered him to start on 30th October, and sent 50 porters to carry the company stores and kit. A hundred more had to be provided locally by the D.C. The removal of the old headquarters of the Nile District from Nimule to a more central position at Gulu, the opening of another station at Kitgum, and the gradual extension of the administration of the Acholi to include the Lango and contiguous tribes, had all been achieved by the presence rather than the use of military force. The Governor recorded his satisfaction at this in his report to the Secretary of State, though he coupled it with a warning that the same rate of progress could not be expected in the Rudolf Province, where the hill tribes were not easy of access and the proximity of the Abyssinian border demanded constant vigilance.

(v) *Operations of the Northern Garrison, 1912-14.* Maps I (a), (c), 8.

'One company and two half-companies have been engaged in operations among the native tribes of the Nile hinterland and on patrol duty.' In his annual report the Acting Governor devoted no more attention than this to the work of pacifying the northern frontier, which was still proceeding in 1912. In March of that year a half-company had moved against the Morongole, and though meeting strong resistance captured 2,000 cattle. In April and May operations were undertaken against the Nakwai, who like the Morongole possessed a number of rifles. Sixteen villages were destroyed and a quantity of stock was captured. In May the Northern Garrison marched against the Lokoya, and in June and July Captain Leeke carried out another series of operations in the Nangiya and Teretenia hills. As each group of villages was disarmed, it had to be brought under protection from its warlike neighbours. The best way to effect this was by disarming the raiders themselves, and so the area of operations steadily expanded and the commitments of the Northern Garrison increased.

The new base camp at Madial was about twenty miles from the Logire Mountains. The tribes who lived on the lower slopes of the main mountain peak and its spurs were armed with spears and shields, but also possessed a number of rifles and muskets, with which they frequently raided the plains near Morongole. Their settlements were difficult of access, so it was decided to begin with a night march against the group of villages situated on the most easterly spur of the range. The operations lasted from 21st to 29th October and were carried out by 'A' Company, who surrounded a number of villages and captured many cattle and goats for the loss of two askaris, killed with spears. The troops then climbed the mountain, meeting little resistance until they were suddenly and fiercely attacked by the Dongotono, a tribe living on the crest, of whose existence they had been completely unaware. Though armed only with spears and poisoned arrows, this tribe pressed the two sections of 'A' Company so hard that they only got back to the plain

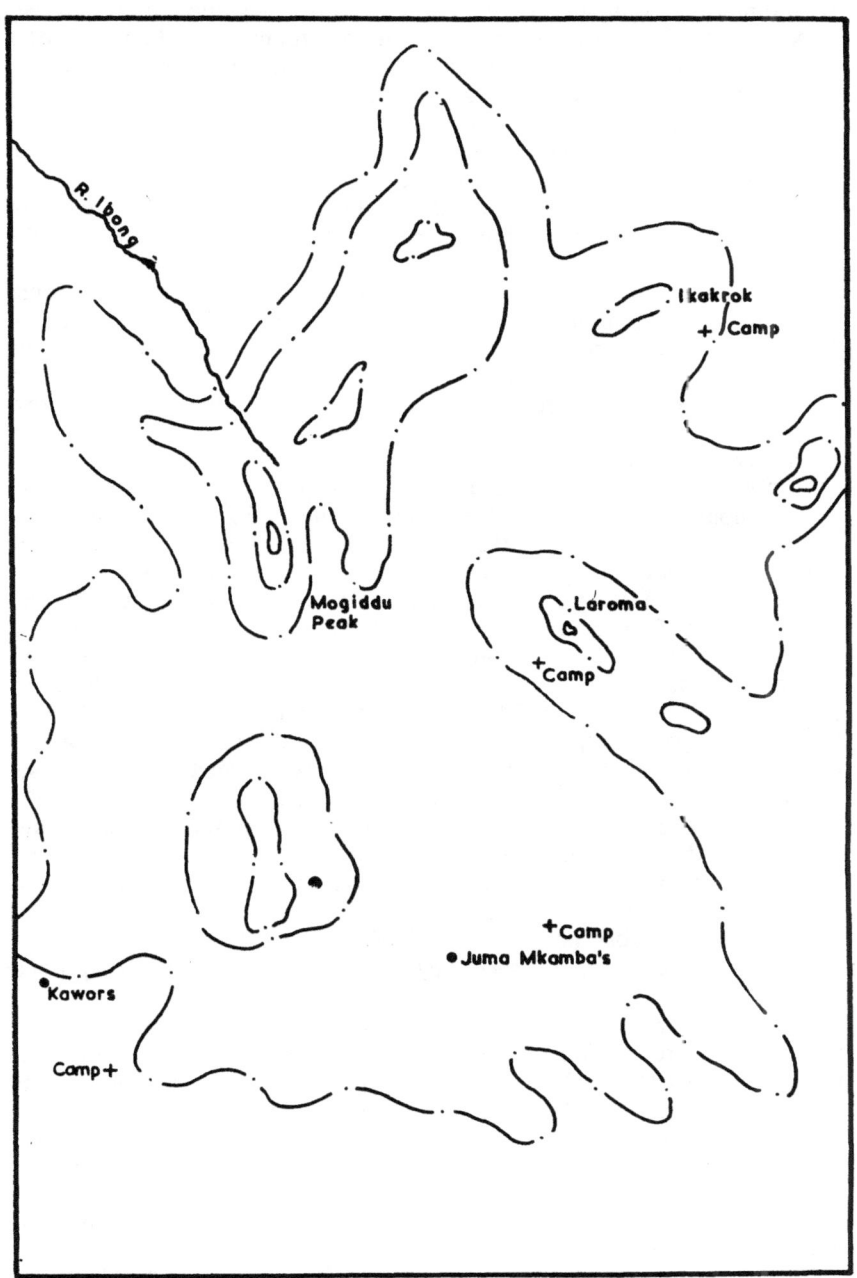

8. Military Camps in the Logire Hills, December, 1912
(From a sketch by Lieutenant M. G. B. Copeman)

with difficulty, losing another man killed and two wounded in the process.

After Lilley's arrival at Madial with the troops from Lango, Major Clothier felt strong enough to resume these operations against the Logire. The centre of the mountain was covered with dense uninhabited forest, and it was expected that when attacked the tribe would drive their cattle there, or upward to the Dongotono, though the two tribes were not supposed to be on friendly terms. The Logire sections near Kawors had now submitted, and also some of the Dongotono from the southern heights, but the sections of both tribes on the north-eastern part of the mountain were still hostile.

Early in December 'A' and 'D' Companies concentrated at Juma Mkamba's, and marched thence to the Laroma valley, where a few hostile shots were fired. On 10th December 'A' Company climbed the spur above Ikakrok, with half 'D' Company under Lilley working round the right flank, and the rest of the troops guarding the baggage below. The tribesmen rolled down large boulders and fired a few shots, but were soon driven from the crest. 'A' Company spent the following day rounding up stock, while the tribesmen were held off by rifle fire. Meanwhile 'D' Company was clearing the neighbouring hills. Operations were suspended on the 12th as the chiefs of both sides showed signs of surrender. Though the patrol was resumed, no more resistance was met. Ten days later a telegram reached Clothier with orders to proceed to Gulu to meet Tufnell and to detail half 'D' Company as escort to the Sudan—Uganda Boundary Commission. The operations were therefore broken off and Clothier returned to Madial with 72 firearms and the captured stock. Lieutenant M. G. B. Copeman (Leic. R.) was left with half 'D' Company to patrol the lower slopes of the mountain and maintain the peace. As several food depôts had to be guarded he set up posts at Kawors, Juma Mkamba's, Laroma and Ikakrok.

In January, 1913, Colonel Thesiger visited the posts at Madial and Logire. He thought that if, after the boundary had been redrawn, the Sudan undertook the administration of this area, all detachments of 4 K.A.R. could be withdrawn. If not, some posts would have to be retained, perhaps those at Madial and Morongole. The Didinga, as yet untouched, would certainly seize any opportunity to begin raiding on a large scale.

Operations against the Dongotono were continued in March. In spite of its fighting reputation, which had perhaps been too easily gained in the previous October, the tribe offered little resistance. Copeman continued to reconnoitre the Logire hills and valleys, and to send back interesting reports on the tribes. He met occasional trouble and continued steadily to confiscate firearms. By October pacification of the eastern slopes of Logire was felt to be complete, though a small post of 15 men was left at Juma Mkamba's, as Leeke thought it inadvisable to withdraw from the whole area at once.

Early in 1913 'A' Company, which had had a long and exhausting period in the field, was ordered back to Bombo. The march was made via Acholi, to assist the police in disarming that tribe. The Acholi district was divided into three sections, of which the police covered two and 'A' Company one. Slight resistance was met and many guns were smuggled across the Nile into Belgian territory, but by 18th March a total of 1,409 firearms had been taken, of which 566 were found to be unregistered.

'A' Company was relieved by 'E' Company, part of which had been employed as escort to the Anglo-Belgian Boundary Commission under the command of Captain W. T. Brooks, who now succeeded Major Clothier as O.C. Northern Garrison. In May, 1913, the escort provided by 'D' Company for the Sudan Boundary Commission returned to duty with the Garrison. The two companies were divided between Madial and Logire. All the tribes between Nimule and the Karamoja escarpment had now been brought under control and an administrative officer was functioning at Kitgum. Most of the Nangiya tribesmen were working peacefully for the Government, though some of them, mainly those who wanted to avoid confiscation of their firearms, had gone north to join the Didinga, whose country was said to be 'the home of every malcontent and gun-owner in the district'.

The Didinga were a little-known tribe inhabiting a deep range of mountains a day's march north of Nangiya. So far as was known, no trader, European or native, had ever visited these mountains, so the tribe was thought to be without firearms. In general they were hostile to their neighbours, who held them in great fear with the exception of the warlike Toposa, who lived on the plains to the east. The Morongole tribes, who were now under British protection, suffered greatly from the Didinga, especially since they had been disarmed. Strong warnings were issued on several occasions from headquarters at Madial, but they were met by taunts and ridicule. The new boundary demarcation had placed the Didinga country north of the frontier, but the Government of the Sudan was unable to administer the country immediately. Permission was therefore given for the Northern Garrison to undertake operations.

The expedition was led by Captain Brooks. It took place during June and July, 1913, and its immediate object was to exact compensation for five recent raids on the Dodos. The force consisted of 190 rifles 'D' and 'E' Companies, divided into three columns: No. 1: Lieutenant M. G. B. Copeman with 60 rifles; No. 2: Captain Leeke with 60 rifles; and No. 3: Captain Brooks with 70 rifles. Columns 1 and 3 each had a maxim gun; all men carried a hundred rounds of ammunition and six days' rations, and an equal quantity of ammunition was carried in reserve.

Nothing was known of the Didinga country beyond the Laroma valley, which lay about twenty-eight miles from Madial, and any attempt at reconnaissance would have destroyed all chances of surprise. Only a general plan could be drawn up in advance. The first column was to block the Didinga escape, while the second and third columns drove the range from different directions. No. 1 column therefore left Madial first, marched to the north bank of the Kidepo River and thence under cover of darkness took up a position east and west, facing south. The other two columns followed a day later and entered the Laroma valley the same night, whence No. 2 struck north and No. 3 north-east, in roughly parallel directions. Communication was by helio.

The initial stages of the operation were carried out as planned. On 19th June No. 1 column took the first group of villages by surprise. Though many of the Didinga escaped owing to the difficult approaches, eight were killed and four captured, with 400 head of cattle, many donkeys and goats and three tusks of ivory. The other columns, though not achieving such complete surprise, attacked several villages along their lines of march, killed 12 tribesmen and captured respectively 63 and 160 head of cattle, besides a number of goats.

On 20th June all three columns began driving the hills. The Didinga range proved to be about twenty-four miles square, well populated and very fertile, with scattered villages built on hill-tops and approached only by steep, narrow paths running through closely-wooded country, well suited for ambushes and guerrilla tactics. At first, thrown off their balance by invasion from three directions, the tribesmen offered little resistance, but after the first ten days their methods became very effective. Watchers on the hill-tops gave warning that a column was approaching. The tribesmen, each carrying from three to six spears, would then descend, lay an ambush, stab their victims from close quarters and depart silently through the undergrowth. On one occasion the advance guard of No. 1 column was ambushed at five yards' range in a deep gully filled with dense bush. The attackers were estimated at 100-200 strong, and only the coolness of the askaris averted disaster. One young recruit, Private Sanane, courageously stood over a wounded comrade though himself suffering from a spear wound. Three askaris were killed and four wounded in this action.

Tactics such as these, carried out by a plucky and persistent enemy and combined with frequent night attacks on the cattle bomas, considerably slowed operations. Sometimes in thick country the columns could move no faster than half a mile an hour, while the bush was patrolled to front and flanks. The work went on until 7th July, when the country had been cleared as far as the Morongole Hills and Brooks decided that he had taken enough cattle to compensate the Dodos.

In spite of the punishment they had suffered, the Didinga were still unsubdued, and Brooks found the task of extricating his force, hampered by some 2,000 cattle and 11 badly wounded men, the most difficult part of the operations. The going was so rough that in some places eight bearers were needed for each stretcher, and eventually it was found easier to carry the wounded in blankets. The evacuation was carried out by stages. All columns first converged upon a base camp, where the cattle were collected in a large boma. Brooks then detailed No. 3 column to escort them to Madial. Free of the cattle, he then moved his wounded to a new camp in the Laroma valley, where the remainder of the expedition concentrated by 28th July. These moves were carried out under constant attacks that increased the number of wounded and so hampered the columns still more. On one occasion the advance guard of No. 1 column ran into a determined ambush as it passed along the crest of a narrow ridge, where deep bush-filled clefts scored the hillside to within six feet of the path. The whole column came into action before the attack could be driven off.

The force was back at Madial by 7th August, with 2,037 head of cattle, 1,660 goats, 62 donkeys and seven tusks of ivory. Three askaris of 'D' Company had been killed, and eight of 'D' and two of 'E' Company wounded. Several followers were also wounded. The expedition had been particularly exhausting and uncomfortable for the troops, and Brooks recommended in his report the provision of a new type of sandal, designed to protect the toes, and of waterproof sheets. The casualties inflicted on the Didinga were known to be high. Brooks saw and warned three of the five principal chiefs. One of them had come in voluntarily with an offer of peace, but his people still continued their attacks and boasted that they would repel the invaders by force. Though he thought the lesson sufficiently sharp to keep the tribe quiet for so long as troops were stationed near Madial, Brooks felt certain that if the garrison went south the Didinga would try to recapture their cattle.

As a result of the operations carried out over the past two and a half years, the administered area of Uganda now extended over the whole Protectorate with the exception of the Rudolf Province and a small portion of the northern part of the Eastern Province. In 1913 attention therefore became focused on the Turkana, and particularly on the northern sections of the tribe, who were receiving arms and encouragement from Abyssinia. It was clear that there could be no peace in the Rudolf Province until the refractory elements among the Turkana had been taught a sharp lesson.

A difficult tract of country lay between the Turkana escarpment and Lake Rudolf: much of it foodless, waterless and unknown. The only map of the area available at the time was vague and misleading. Its blank spaces were filled with imaginative and amateurish legends, such as 'Nomad tribes, treacherous', or unhelpful reiterations of the obvious, such as 'rolling hills, dry except during rains'. During the dry season prolonged operations were only practicable by way of the Turkwel River or within reach of Lake Rudolf, unless accompanied by camel transport, for which the animals were available but not the equipment. After the rains suitable grazing could be found for donkeys. Porters were extremely scarce, for the Banyoro who had accompanied the troops north were not of much use in such country, and the recently subdued indigenous tribes were too untrustworthy. The Mbale area was the most likely source for obtaining followers, but the D.C. there had his own troubles, and asserted that porters could not be provided.

The Turkana country extended south of Lake Rudolf into the Northern Frontier District of East Africa. In May, 1912, the provincial commissioners of Naivasha and the Eastern Province of Uganda had met to discuss the best means of controlling the tribe as a whole, and had agreed that as the Turkana were more closely allied to the Karamojong than to the Suk, they could be best administered from Uganda. To assist the political officer appointed for this task, it was considered that a military force of at least 75 rifles with 100 camels would be required. Higher authority, however, decided not to extend its administration for the time being, and it was agreed instead that officers of the two protectorates should meet twice a year to discuss and settle tribal disputes.

After his visit to the Northern Garrison in January, 1913, Thesiger advised that if operations were to be undertaken against the Turkana, two new posts, one at Magosi and one at Lokuta, should be established as forward bases for a mobile patrol. He recommended a company at the former and a half-company at the latter place, provided the water proved sufficient. The post at Magosi would also act as a check on the large number of undesirable Swahilis who still infested the area west of Lake Rudolf, smuggling arms and seeking illicit ivory. It was evident that the establishment of authority over the whole of the northern districts of Uganda could not be longer delayed, and in due course authority was given.

In August, 1913, Captains Brooks and Leeke made a tour from Madial via Tshudi-Tshudi, Lokuta, Magosi, and Manimani to Kelim, to investigate the suitability of Lokuta and Magosi as military posts and to visit the Karamojong. They found Lokuta well sited to defend the Dodos from Turkana raids and as a centre for the collection of food. Lieutenant J. S. Wilkinson (Notts & Derby R.) was instructed to establish a post there and another at Morongole, each to be garrisoned by a half-company. Magosi, however, was found to be deficient in water, and Brooks was inclined to think Manimani would prove a better site. Eventually, following a further recommendation by Leeke, Moroto was selected, as situated on an easier supply route communicating with the River Turkwel, and better placed for the protection of the Karamojong.

Captain Leeke, now in command of the Northern Garrison, discussed the question of large-scale punitive measures against the Turkana in his monthly report for August, 1913. The Garrison still consisted of 'D' and 'E' Companies, maintaining four posts at Madial, Lokuta, Morongole, and Logire. (The Logire garrison was not finally withdrawn to Madial until December.) Lieutenant-Colonel Ward agreed that operations were inevitable before administration could become effective, but thought that they should be postponed until the following year, when 'C' Company was to be posted north on relief and would raise the strength of the garrison temporarily to three companies. In the meantime Leeke began collecting donkeys and accumulating supplies. He set up a depôt at Kiteng, which was five days from Lokuta and two from Madial, to store food from the Nangiya tribes, and another at Tarash, as a collecting centre for the villages of Karamoja. Leeke also asked that 'C' Company should be equipped with a supply of sacks for donkey panniers, all the water-bottles that could be spared, and as many drums or other receptacles capable of holding water as could be collected.

Not all sections of the Turkana were troublesome: those near Tarash were on good terms with their neighbours the Magosi and Dodos. Egyot, the chief of these friendly sections, was a useful source of information and warned Leeke of the large number of Le Gras rifles being purchased from the Abyssinians by Lolel, a chief who lived between Mount Pelegech and the Lake. Wilkinson, who was commanding the Morongole garrison (half 'E' Company), was attacked when on a reconnaissance about sixteen miles south-west of Mount Zingote, when the Turkana tried to capture his baggage, which he had left in a boma while searching for water. Leeke thought that the greed for rifles displayed by this section was sufficient proof of their aggressive intentions.

Ebe, the hostile chief of the section who grazed their cattle farther south, was also inclined to be treacherous and was given to raiding the Karamojong. Recently all the Turkana and Suk had shown a tendency to move north and west away from the Turkwel, possibly to avoid taxation by officials at the new stations set up in the East Africa Protectorate. They were apparently convinced that the area west of Lake Rudolf belonged to the Abyssinians, who still roamed there practically at will, poaching elephant in large numbers. In the course of two short tours Leeke had counted over twenty elephant skulls bleaching in the sun, and secured the buried tusks of one male and five females. Abyssinian poachers, Swahili gun-runners, and hostile Turkana, all of whom knew the country well, combined from time to time in raiding the weaker and more peaceful tribes and were very difficult to catch.

Leeke's plan was for an attack in two columns directed on Mount Pelegech, one from Morongole and the other from Lokuta. In January, 1914, reports reached him that the Abyssinians and Turkana were raiding in concert, and it seemed likely that when attacked, Lolel and his people would break to the north. A tour in Karamoja to purchase food showed the tension that existed there owing to the pressure exerted by the Suk and Turkana. Leeke could do no more than inform the D.C. across the frontier at Ngabotok, as his plans for operations farther north were already far advanced and he was about to concentrate his troops well forward at Tarash.

Early in March Lieutenant E. B. B. Hawkins (W. Yorks R.)[1] carried out a fortnight's reconnaissance from Lokuta up the Tarash River into the valley between Mounts Pelegech and Longolechum. The object was to discover where Lolel's people were grazing, and the whereabouts of the rivers and water-holes. On 20th March, just as the concentration of 'D' and 'E' Companies at Tarash was completed, news reached Leeke that the Turkana were raiding the Toposa near Mount Zingote. Friendly chiefs had already warned Leeke of the dangers of inaction in the face of such raids, and he at once dispatched Captain S. W. H. Silver (Suffolk R.) with half 'E' Company, who located the raiders, killed 19, and recaptured the stolen stock.

Leeke set out with the main expedition from Tarash on 2nd April, with Captain Silver, Lieutenants Hawkins and H. S. Pinder (Leic. R.), 99 rifles 'D' Company and 101 rifles 'E' Company. Dodos levies accompanied the force to drive cattle. Reports stated that the tribesmen were grazing their animals along the Tarash River about twenty-four miles north of the camp. In spite of a night march no tribesmen were discovered, though many tracks could be seen leading in the direction of Mount Pelegech. Leeke decided to follow. Reaching the mountain late next day, he saw through a telescope a string of camels near the topmost peak, about 2,000 feet above his camp. The top of the mountain is formed by the ring crater of an extinct volcano, with the wall broken down on the western side. At four o'clock next morning two columns of

---

[1] Later Major-General E. B. B. Hawkins, O.B.E., D.S.O.

troops began the climb from opposite directions. Hawkins, commanding the advance guard of the largest column, reached the lip of the crater at 9 a.m., in time to see a mass of cattle, protected by a rearguard of warriors, disappearing hastily up the opposite slope and over the crater wall.

A sharp engagement followed. The Turkana were driven off with many casualties, and by evening the whole herd, numbering nearly 5,000 cattle, camels, donkeys, sheep and goats had been overtaken. Leeke was particularly pleased to learn later that 600 of the cattle came from Lolel's private herd.

Next day Leeke and Hawkins ascended the peak, which they calculated to be 5,500 feet above sea-level. The captured stock was driven down the mountain, to be sent back to Tarash while the expedition continued eastward in search of Lolel, who was believed to be near the Lake. On 8th April, however, Leeke received a letter from headquarters with an enclosure from the Chief Secretary forbidding him to extend his operations, as the expedition against the Marehan Somalis in Jubaland was in progress and 4 K.A.R. might be required to send reinforcements. Leeke and his officers were bitterly disappointed as they feared the effect of a withdrawal on the attitude of the friendly tribes, who had spent so many months assisting their preparations. The Turkana could now obtain rifles in exchange even for goats, and it seemed unlikely that anything less than vigorous operations directed against the source of supply could stop the traffic. But for the moment Leeke had to be content with patrols in the unknown area around Mount Zingote, where a brush occurred with a party of Abyssinians and Swahili who were discovered in the act of driving away the proceeds of their illicit trade.

On 2nd May the expedition returned to Tarash. Leeke did his best to explain the situation at a baraza of Turkana chiefs, all of whom promised good behaviour and co-operation in the future. Altogether about 8,000 stock had been captured during these operations, and distributed mainly among the Dodos and Karamojong in compensation for past Turkana raids. The K.A.R. had one armed porter killed and one askari wounded; slight losses as the country was open and offered little chance of ambush or surprise. But the southern sections of the Turkana were still untouched in the country nearer to the Lake.

The withdrawal of Leeke's force to Morongole and Lokuta encouraged the Turkana to risk another raid. On 8th May, Captain Lilley, commanding the detachment of 'E' Company at Morongole, was told that a big raid was in progress against the Dodos villages on Lotim Hill. Owing to faulty information he set out in the wrong direction and the raiders got away. A second raid was attempted on 7th June. This time Lilley was determined there should be no escape. In twenty minutes his men were on the march, carrying three days' rations. A mile out of camp another report confirmed that the raiders were Turkana armed with rifles, and that they were driving the stolen cattle towards Mount Oropoi. Lilley followed for another five miles, and then heard shots in front. The raiders were again at work on a hill two miles north-east of Lotim. Lilley divided his force for a converging attack. On reaching the top of the hill his column came under fire from a hidden enemy about two hundred yards distant across a deep valley filled with bush. The askaris replied, killing at least six Turkana, but the bush was too close to penetrate in the face of a well-concealed enemy and Lilley moved his men to the right. In doing so he was suddenly ambushed at five yards' range by a small party of Turkana riflemen, whose first volley killed the guide. The troops scattered for cover, and after twenty minutes' firing killed all but one of the enemy. This man was left to the Dodos auxiliaries, who ran away as soon as the troops had left and let him escape.

Lilley now pushed ahead after the cattle, which was escorted by about 300 Turkana. The raiders were well organized and in no hurry to retreat, with a rearguard of riflemen who stood up confidently to attack. The tribesmen were not all in one party, and while Lilley was pursuing the main body, Lieutenant Pinder with the second column brought another group to action at long range. An excellent little operation was also carried out by Corporal Adam Abdulla, who had been left in charge of the baggage. Hearing of a party that had so far escaped attention, he correctly deduced their line of withdrawal, laid an ambush with 12 of his men, attacked the raiders at point-blank range and recaptured all the cattle.

Darkness forced Lilley to camp for the night, and though he continued next day as far as Oropoi, contact was not regained. The raid had been the biggest for some years. Between four and five hundred Turkana were engaged, of whom at least 50 were armed with rifles. They had surrounded several villages, killed 14 men and massacred 96 women and children in cold blood. Owing to Lilley's prompt action they did not on this occasion escape unscathed, for about 150 were killed and a part of their gains was recaptured.

Another good example of initiative in the absence of a British officer occurred at Morongole on 13th-14th June, while Lilley and Pinder were away from the post. Reports came of a large raid in progress south of the station. Colour-Sergeant Murjan Effendi pursued at once, caught the Turkana as they passed through a deep defile, killed 57 and recaptured all the stock. After that the Turkana left the Morongole area alone for a time and began raiding the Toposa across the frontier instead.

A tour carried out by the D.C. Marich in May and June convinced him that only joint operations on both sides of the border could be completely effective. The Turkana were extremely mobile and would have to be chased all over the area for many weeks, until water and grazing gave out or their cattle died of exhaustion. As well as the half-company of 3 K.A.R. already at Marich, he thought another 150 troops would be needed, operating in three columns with levies from the Suk and friendly sections of the Turkana. To the north, Leeke was still seeking permission to resume operations as soon as 'C' Company reached him, and had sent a detachment of 'D' Company to build a new advanced post at Moroto. His plan now was for an attack on Mount Lobur, marching by way of the Turkwel and Lake Rudolf, as he was not certain of its precise location or whether he had enough camels for a water convoy. He would have preferred to attack from the north, but this seemed impossible, though Pinder with half 'E' Company from Tarash could patrol among the mountains and act as a stop while the drive from the south was in progress.

In due course news reached Uganda of the successful conclusion of the Marehan operations, and sanction was given for the largest expedition yet to take the field against the Turkana. It was estimated that troops drawn from four companies of 4 K.A.R. would be needed, in addition to half 'B' Company, 3 K.A.R., which was then stationed at Marich and would come temporarily under the orders of the O.C. Turkana Patrol. In July 'C' Company, 4 K.A.R., began the move north via Jinja and Mbale to relieve 'D' Company at Moroto, while 'B' and 'F' Companies moved into East Africa to concentrate on the River Turkwel.

But Leeke's carefully planned expedition was not to take place after all. The news that Britain was at war with Germany led to the hasty recall of all these troops to deal with a far more dangerous enemy elsewhere, and for the time being the task of controlling the Turkana fell to the Sudanese forces, who assumed temporary responsibility for northern Uganda and took over the post at Morongole.

PART III

THE EAST AFRICA CAMPAIGN, 1914-1918

'*The K.A.R. . . . hardly ever lose a rifle. . . . The conclusion is the same that every thinking soldier in the force has arrived at after a year in British East Africa, namely that only the best and most highly trained troops, British or Indian, are or can hope to be a match for the trained Africans of a fighting tribe in the bush.*'—LT.-COL. S. H. SHEPPARD, G.S.O.1, *September, 1915.*

CHAPTER 10

The Defence of the Uganda Railway
AUGUST, 1914-FEBRUARY, 1916

(i) *The Opposing Forces and the Theatre of War.*

TWELVE years of constant marching, patrolling and fighting lay behind most of the 21 companies of the King's African Rifles in the summer of 1914. The maintenance of internal security had been their primary duty, and the tactics of bush warfare their principal training. In Somaliland the troops had found a campaigning-ground upon a larger scale, but in general it was only the Reserve Battalion that had ever acted, or even been quartered together as a unit. In their rôle of garrison troops the companies had operated under the authority of the governors of their respective territories. Though the three battalions of which they formed a part acknowledged a common policy in administration and training, exerted through the co-ordinating and advisory functions of the Inspector-General, there was no staff, no central organization for supply, transport and medical services, no artillery, and a system of reserves that was still incomplete. The regiment was neither designed nor prepared for a major war.

The campaign that now fell so suddenly upon the K.A.R. represented only a subsidiary phase of the world-wide conflict occasioned, though not caused, by an unexpected turn of political events in Europe. It was one of several satellite wars in the colonial field. Though the largest, longest, and most determined of these campaigns, it was overshadowed by the unprecedented stress of the great military operations elsewhere. The story of that struggle with the Germans for the possession of what is now called Tanganyika is little known. It was a local war with problems of its own, totally different from those of the blood-soaked strip of territory that twisted its tortuous barrier across Europe from the Alps to the sea; a tropical war of forced marches in the cool, long-shadowed hours that surround the African dawn; and of actions fought by tattered, hungry men in heat and dust, or rain and mud.

It has sometimes been asserted[1] that the security of the East African territories had never, prior to 1914, been considered from any but an internal aspect. In fact, as we have seen, the protection of the Railway from foreign aggression was raised at the time of its completion,[2] and

---

[1] E.g., in Appendix IV (ii), p. 559, of *Military Operations in East Africa*, Vol. I.

[2] *Vide supra*, p. 142. In 1912 the political officer at Taveta also drew attention in a confidential memorandum to the ease with which the Germans, operating from Moshi in two columns via Taveta and the German police post at Rombo, could reach the railway at two points and then combine with other forces to attack Nairobi.

during the years 1905-07 considerable thought was given to the safety of the British colonial possessions in general. At that time Major Pope-Hennessey specifically drew attention to the presence of 140 German troops at Tsavo, and the German garrison of 62 rifles known to be at Shirati on Lake Victoria, within reach of the terminus and port of Kisumu. But no one imagined that East Africa could be defended solely, or even primarily, by African troops. Even Pope-Hennessey thought that the time taken by the Germans to concentrate their main forces would allow help to arrive from India and South Africa, and that 'in a few months German East Africa would be British, should that consummation be desired.'[1] Many bitter lessons had to be learnt before the principle of depending chiefly upon East Africa's own resources in manpower was accepted.

The end of July, 1914, when the Marehan operations had barely concluded and a new expedition against the Turkana was in preparation, found the K.A.R. as usual widely scattered. 1 K.A.R. was equally divided between its home territory and Jubaland. Headquarters and four companies of 75 rifles each (of which two were on leave) were stationed in Nyasaland, south of the lake and far from the German frontier. Of the other four companies, each nominally 100 rifles strong, two were at Yonte and two at Serenli. The six companies of 3 K.A.R., each 125 rifles strong, were even more widely scattered. In Jubaland the camel company was at Gobwen, and an infantry company at Serenli. 'G' Company formed the sole garrison of Zanzibar, within a few miles of the hostile German coast. An attempt to supplement the troops at Zanzibar with armed police had not proved a success, but as the cable and telegraph station was recognized in London as an imperial commitment, the cost of raising the garrison again to two K.A.R. companies had been admitted as a charge upon army funds. The requirements of the Marehan operations and the injudicious reductions that had taken place in the K.A.R. establishments during 1911 had temporarily left Zanzibar with a single company for its defence. The rest of 3 K.A.R. was strung out in half-companies towards the northern frontier, at Marich, Mount Kulal, and Moyale, with two half-companies at Nairobi, one of which was in training as mounted infantry.[2] Of the seven companies of 4 K.A.R., which also numbered 125 rifles each, three were employed with the Northern Garrison (one at Morongole, one at Moroto, and one *en route* to the latter station); two were in East Africa *en route* for the Turkana operations; one was at Bombo, and one at Entebbe. Meanwhile the long, vulnerable line of railway that paralleled the German frontier, and at one point actually approached it within a distance of seventy miles, remained to all intents unguarded and unpatrolled.

But for the moment, the Germans were little better prepared. Despite the initial friction with the Imperial East Africa Company over Witu and similar questions, they had received on the whole considerable

---

[1] L. R. H. Pope-Hennessey, 'Memorandum on the Distribution of Troops in the Uganda Protectorate', 12.v.06. *Uganda Govt. Records*.

[2] The Inspector-General had called attention to the need for a mounted company in East Africa during the reorganization of 1911. C.O. 534, 14.

encouragement and understanding from the British in their East African undertaking. Neither the arbitrary line of their northern boundary, diverted at their own desire to enclose in German territory the slopes of the Kilimanjaro massif, nor the 250-mile stretch in the south between Lakes Tanganyika and Nyasa, had been drawn with regard to strategical requirements. Much of German East Africa was uninhabited bush, and the elevated regions that were sufficiently well watered and healthy for European settlement were by no means all situated in the most defensible positions. This was particularly true of the settlements in the Pare and Usambara ranges, that ran roughly parallel to the frontier from Kilimanjaro to the sea. Farther south, rising from the eastern edge of the inland plateau, lay two other mountain systems, the Nguru and the Uluguru, both of which exerted a significant influence on the course of the campaign. Another settled area lay in the south-western highlands, between Iringa and Lake Nyasa.

The Germans had built two railways inland from the coast. One ran from Tanga between the mountain range and the River Pangani to Moshi on the southern slopes of Kilimanjaro, a distance of 218 miles. The other, known as the Central Railway, ran from Dar-es-Salaam via Morogoro and Tabora to Lake Tanganyika, and had reached its terminus at Kigoma, nearly 800 miles from the coast, only a few weeks before the declaration of war. As the British invasion of the country took place from north to south these railways were only of limited value, and in view of the unexpected strategy adopted by the German commander, their possession did not prove decisive.

The native population controlled by the Germans numbered nearly seven millions, only about one million less than the combined populations of British East Africa, Uganda, Nyasaland and Northern Rhodesia. Under German administration there had been several risings, at first in the early years of their occupation, and again in the serious Maji-Maji rebellion in the southern part of the colony in 1905-07. Since then the country had been fairly quiet, and as in the British territories, military forces had been reduced in favour of an increase in police. At the outbreak of war the available field force consisted of 14 independent companies, each of 16-20 German officers and N.C.Os. and about 200 askaris. Attached to each company were some 250 carriers and a varying number of auxiliaries or *ruga-ruga,* armed sometimes with firearms, though more often with spears. Each company had from two to four machine guns, as against one per company in the K.A.R., but the German forces suffered at the outset from a serious deficiency in modern rifles. Eight of their companies were still armed with rifles of the 1871 pattern, and the black powder used by this weapon frequently gave away the position of German troops in the bush and instilled in the askaris a depressing sense of inferiority.

With the advent of more peaceful conditions, a civilian Governor, Dr. Schnee, had been appointed to German East Africa. His military commander was Lieutenant-Colonel von Lettow-Vorbeck, an officer of outstanding energy and capacity who had previously served in South-West Africa. At the beginning of the campaign his resources totalled 260

Germans and 2,472 askaris. From the first, the Germans had always employed a high proportion of white N.C.Os. and non-combatants with their native troops, and this represented a considerable initial advantage, for the K.A.R. establishment could only show 73 British to 2,325 askaris in its three battalions. Moreover, at the outbreak of war the K.A.R. was 150 rifles under strength.

There were other foes to be encountered, even more insidious and far harder to combat. German East Africa was essentially a country in which disease was always waiting to attack the unwary. In 1914 medical knowledge and equipment were quite inadequate to cope with the situation that arose when men were poured by the thousand into low-lying river valleys and kept there, sometimes marooned and often half fed, throughout the rains that broke in the first few months of each year. At the beginning of the war, however, operations were mostly confined to the great tracts of thornbush that lay between the Uganda Railway and the frontier. There it was a case of too little water rather than too much.

The framers of the Berlin Act of 1885, concerned at the possibility of conflict between the small handful of Europeans of different nationalities who were charged with the control of so many millions of Africans, and anxious to safeguard the rights of the signatory parties, inserted clauses to provide for neutrality in Africa in the event of war elsewhere.[1] But these clauses were only to become operative if the powers concerned so proclaimed the fact, and fulfilled 'the duties which neutrality requires'. Belated attempts to invoke these clauses proved ineffective, as by the time they were made acts of hostility had already taken place.

(ii) *The Concentration and Deployment of the K.A.R., August, 1914*

It is not intended to give in this and succeeding chapters a full account of the campaign of 1914-18 in East Africa. But an outline of the operations as a whole will be essential if the part played by the K.A.R. is to be seen in proper perspective, or even made intelligible. With the major forces of the British Empire gripped for four years in the stranglehold of static warfare, it was inevitable that the East African theatre should find it difficult to secure or retain any troops suitable for employment in Europe. Yet the need for a major expansion of the local forces was long in gaining recognition. In 1914, while practically alone in the field, the K.A.R. began the campaign, and in 1918 was called upon to finish it. In the period between, the regiment formed part of a polyglot army more varied in race, language, training and experience than was grouped elsewhere under British command in any theatre of the war.

One reason for the failure to embark from the outset upon a long-term policy of African recruitment can be recognized from the start. The European expectation of an early peace, so frequently expressed at home during the first few weeks of the war, had its counterpart abroad, and perhaps with better reason. Events soon showed that the campaigns in all the other German colonies were of comparatively short duration, and having regard to the scantiness of von Lettow's resources, and the un-

Berlin Act, Chapter III, Arts. X-XII.

likelihood of any material assistance reaching him from Europe, there seemed good reason to believe that once the country was seriously attacked, German East Africa must also rapidly succumb. Due credit was not at first given to the skill and determination of the German commander, nor did anyone in authority foresee the nature of the protracted campaign he intended to wage, nor the use he would make of the vast difficulties inherent in such a climate and so difficult a terrain.

The frontiers of German East Africa were half as long again as all the battle-fronts of Europe. To state this without qualification, however, would be to give a false impression of the situation that confronted the opposing forces, for the possible lines of attack were comparatively few. The vital sector, from the viewpoint of either belligerent, lay on the northern boundary of German territory, between Mount Kilimanjaro and the sea: partly because it was close to the main area of German settlement, but mainly because it was flanked on both sides by a railway. The existence of the German line from Tanga did much to convert the well-watered mountain salient of Kilimanjaro into a threat directed towards the Uganda Railway. British East Africa was no longer merely the territory crossed by 'The Road', whether caravan or rail. Not only did the railway form Uganda's main communication with the world, but the changes brought about by colonization had placed the White Highlands also in economic dependence upon it. Moreover, those sectors of the line that approached most closely to the German frontier were found to be particularly vulnerable, as they ran through uncultivated and uninhabited bush country that afforded excellent cover for military movements. On the other hand, the German line, though nearer to the frontier, was protected by the Pare and Usambara ranges and was beyond the reach of small parties of raiders. Apart, therefore, from the ill-fated Tanga expedition, in which the K.A.R. had no part, and one or two unsuccessful attempts at operations elsewhere, British strategy in the north centred for the first year and a half on the defence of the Uganda Railway. During this phase the three regular battalions of the K.A.R. proved beyond doubt their skill in patrolling and bush warfare.

Three urgent measures had to be undertaken during the first month of the war: the provision of increased military strength, either from local resources or by reinforcement from elsewhere; the concentration and redeployment of the troops already available; and the immediate defence of the railway, with its bridges and culverts, against the attempts that would certainly be made to destroy it.

The first of these tasks was carried out on a wave of enthusiasm. As soon as the news of the declaration of war reached Nairobi, the Governor proclaimed the formation of a Volunteer Reserve. The European response was immediate, at first greatly in excess of the Government's capacity to organize and equip. Nearly 1,800 recruits were accepted, and enlisted in the East Africa Mounted Rifles, the East Africa Regiment (which also raised an Indian company), the Railway Pioneers, and various other units. About 100 ex-askaris of the K.A.R. reported for service, and two Reserve Companies were formed in British East Africa: No. 1 of ex-askaris, and No. 2 of Arabs, the latter under an influential leader who knew them well,

Lieutenant A. J. B. Wavell (late Welch R.). Both these companies were employed in the coastal area. Meanwhile Uganda also had its European Volunteer Reserve, and a Reserve Company, about 90 strong, of 4 K.A.R. With the help of these and various auxiliary levies, such as the Masai Scouts and a few local units in southern Uganda who were organized later into a useful force known as the Baganda Rifles, the regiment prepared to defend its home territories against attack.

Meanwhile the Colonial Office was taking parallel steps at home. Once again the long tradition was invoked of seeking help from India. War had hardly been declared before the Secretary of State for the Colonies filed his request for a brigade of Indian infantry. This was referred to the appropriate sub-committee of the Committee of Imperial Defence, who viewed the problem primarily from a naval angle, and recommended the dispatch of an expedition from India to attack Dar-es-Salaam. To this was added later a recommendation that three battalions should be sent from India to reinforce the K.A.R. Steps were immediately taken in India to select and dispatch the latter force (known as Indian Expeditionary Force 'C'), and the first transport left Karachi in the third week of August.

While these measures were in progress, the redeployment of the 17 scattered companies of the K.A.R. in the northern theatre was rapidly proceeding. Command was assumed by the senior officer then serving with the regiment, Lieutenant-Colonel L. E. S. Ward, commanding officer of 4 K.A.R. and O.C. Troops, Uganda. Ward reached East Africa and was replaced in command in Uganda by Major L. H. Hickson of 3 K.A.R.

4 K.A.R. was the battalion with the greatest number of troops readily available. 'B' and 'F' Companies, which were at Mumia's and Baringo respectively, *en route* for Turkana, were summoned to Nairobi. Two other companies, 'A' and 'G', were sent from Bombo and Entebbe to Kisumu, whence one of them was dispatched to Nairobi a little later. The risk involved in thus temporarily denuding western Uganda of troops was justified by the difficult nature of the country that bordered the German frontier west of Lake Victoria, and the imperative need to mass troops at all costs within reach of the railway. To replace them two of the three companies forming the Northern Garrison were recalled. They were concentrated, together with a number of armed police, at Masaka with an advanced post nearer to the frontier at Sanje. So far from threatening an offensive, however, the Germans had withdrawn their troops from Bukoba to Mwanza, and all remained quiet on the western shores of the lake.

The first troops actually to assume war stations were drawn from 3 K.A.R. Five days before the outbreak of war, the handful of troops then in Nairobi had been sent down the line to defend the bridges at Tsavo and Voi, and to patrol that sector of the railway in conjunction with two hastily improvised 'armoured' trains. These troops consisted of half 'D' Company (Captain T. O. Fitzgerald with one officer and 84 rifles), followed soon afterwards by Lieutenant H. Home Davies (R. Welch Fus.) with 21 rank and file of the half-trained K.A.R. Mounted Infantry, who were stationed at Voi with a small post at Bura, near a group of hills some twenty-two miles out along the old caravan route to Taveta, close to the German frontier.

Six companies were still in Jubaland: 'A', 'B', 'C' and 'E' Companies, 1 K.A.R., and 'E' and 'F' Companies, 3 K.A.R. Whether to withdraw some or all of these companies at once, and if so by what means, offered a problem. Past experience did not encourage the belief that the Marehan would remain quiet for long if the country were left without a proper garrison. Half the troops were at Serenli and half at Yonte or Gobwen, and only one small steamer was available to transport them by sea. Though the Governor of British East Africa was at first reluctant to drain Jubaland of troops, 'B' Company, 1 K.A.R. (Captain G. J. Giffard), one of the two companies then guarding the base, left Kismayu on 7th August for Voi, and thence shortly afterwards for Nairobi. Meanwhile local concentration was proceeding in Jubaland by forced marches, as a preliminary to withdrawal. Within the space of a week, a half-company of 3 K.A.R. which had been stationed at Dolo covered the 175 miles back to Serenli. On 18th August Major L. H. Soames, the officer commanding the latter station, took matters into his own hands and marched away with most of his troops, leaving at Serenli a garrison amounting to about one company in strength. The decision to withdraw most of the troops from Jubaland was thus taken, though some weeks elapsed before they could reach the railway.

Nyasaland was no better prepared for war than her sister territories in the north, though at the instigation of the War Office a great deal of information regarding the composition and distribution of the German armed forces had been collected during the preceding five years. Even before 1911, when the unfortunate disbandment of 2 K.A.R. led to so many well-trained askaris taking service under the German flag, it was known that the German garrison at Neu Langenburg was recruited largely in British territory. So many ex-K.A.R. askaris were serving there that English bugle-calls and words of command were in regular use.[1] The frontier ran from a point near the southern end of Lake Tanganyika between Abercorn and Bismarckburg to the mouth of the River Songwe, near the northern tip of Lake Nyasa. It was far distant from the main centres of British settlement, which were south of the lake, and the country that bordered it on either side was difficult and sparsely inhabited, with few roads or tracks. Nominally the Stevenson Road ran from Karonga to Abercorn, but some sections of it were still uncompleted, and parts had been allowed to fall into disrepair.

When war broke out 'D' and 'F' Companies, 1 K.A.R., were on leave. 'G' Company at Mangoche and 'H' Company at Zomba were 70 and 50 rifles strong respectively, mostly recruits. The Reserve was called out, and 158 ex-askaris rejoined the colours. Within five days all available troops had been concentrated with four guns at Fort Johnston as the Nyasaland Field Force, under the command of Captain C. W. Barton (Northants R.). Only ten regular officers were present with the Force, which Barton organized in three double-companies: 'D' and 'F'; 'G' and 'A' (Reserve); 'H' and 'B' (Reserve). Other military resources were

---

[1] 'Notes on Neu Langenburg', 23.xii.08. *Central African Archives, K.A.R. 3/1/1.* In 1911 and again in 1913 very complete notes appear in this file showing the detailed composition and distribution of the German armed forces.

the European Volunteer Reserve, and the well-armed and efficient police forces of Northern Rhodesia. but it was impossible to count on any troops other than the K.A.R. for prolonged service in the field.

By mid-August the concentration and redeployment of the K.A.R. along both frontiers was well advanced. On the western side the frontiers were tenuously joined by a line of Belgian posts along the lakes of the Rift Valley. At Nairobi an improvised headquarters staff was beginning to function, and the organization of a Carrier Corps for supply and transport had begun.

(iii) *Initial Operations in the Northern Area, August-October, 1914.* Maps 9, 10, 12, II (c), II (d).

It was a fortunate circumstance that the British dispositions had been made without loss of time, weak and scattered though the available forces were. Both sides at this stage of the war were inclined to exaggerate the numbers and resources of their opponents, and when the Germans found all their initial advances met, they failed to press any of them. The result was that the enemy achieved no success important enough to follow up.

Von Lettow, hampered during the first few weeks of the war by Dr Schnee's hope that conflict might somehow be avoided, well realized that time was on the side of his enemy, and strongly urged an offensive policy. Though he did not reach the Moshi area himself until early September. it was here that he saw the greatest opportunity and he began at once to press his local commander to attack and destroy the Uganda Railway. There were three possible approach routes across British territory, and their existence made the most likely points of contact plain to both sides. One lay to the west, and two to the east of Mount Kilimanjaro. Northwest of the mountain a branch line runs from the Uganda Railway through Kajiado to Lake Magadi in the Rift Valley depression. By striking west of the mountain from their railhead at New Moshi, the Germans could find water for an advanced base on Longido Hill that would enable them to cross the waterless stretch of bush and strike the branch line at Kajiado. Or choosing the eastern side of the mountain (which was felt to be the more likely approach, as the railway ran here at its shortest distance from the frontier), an attempt could be made to disrupt the main line. Here there were alternative routes across the plains. One lay down the course of the River Tsavo from its source in the Kilimanjaro foothills to the important bridge where the railway crosses the river not far from its junction with the Athi; the other, through the gap between Mount Kilimanjaro and the Pare range, where a deep bulge in the German frontier was occupied by the British police post at Taveta. west of the Lumi River. Between the Lumi and Voi, the nearest point on the railway, lay sixty-five miles of practically waterless bush, but it was crossed by an ancient caravan route, and in the circumstances was the most easily negotiable and the likeliest line of approach between British and German territory. It was for this reason that Bura had been selected as an outpost for the protection of the Voi sector.

It was recognized that for the time being the Taveta salient was quite indefensible. The expected German attack began on the night of 14th/15th August, when fire was opened on the frontier police picquet. Early next morning a force of about 300 troops advanced upon Taveta. In accordance with instructions, the Assistant District Commissioner withdrew his police in good order and retired to Voi. The Germans followed as far as the Lumi, where they destroyed the bridge.

There was no question of any counter-attack in the foreseeable future, but it was plain that this line of approach must be carefully watched. 'F' Company, 4 K.A.R., which had now reached Nairobi from Baringo, was sent forthwith to Bura. The company had hardly arrived when an unexpected difficulty led to its despatch on a punitive expedition against the Giriama, a primitive tribe inhabiting the River Sabaki area. The tribesmen had shown some restlessness in the previous year, and now, apparently influenced by propaganda from German sources, suddenly attacked the Assistant District Commissioner's camp in the Mangea Hills and the mission station at Jilori. Prompt action was taken. 'F' Company, 4 K.A.R., marched north from the railway and joined No. 1 Reserve Company, 3 K.A.R., which had gone by sea from Mombasa to Kilifi Creek. On 28th August the combined force encountered about a thousand Giriama and dispersed them for the loss of two men wounded. This was sufficient to settle the matter, though precautionary patrolling followed for several weeks with troops that could ill be spared, and a regrettable delay occurred in the transfer of 'E' Company, 1 K.A.R., from Jubuland, as the company was landed unnecessarily at the Tana River and delayed there for lack of shipping until the end of September.

While the Giriama affair was in progress, the Germans began their first raids upon the permanent way. One party, consisting of two Europeans, three askaris and a few porters well loaded with dynamite, was tracked by a detachment of 3 K.A.R. and captured near Maungu on 25th August. No damage had been done as the Germans were looking for the Voi bridge, and complained that the British map they were using had misled them.[1] On the same day the K.A.R. detachment at Maktau, posted there when 'B' Company, 1 K.A.R., took over the position at Bura, repelled the attack of a small German patrol. A few days later, when it became evident that the enemy was active on the upper reaches of the Tsavo, 'B' Company was ordered to watch this line of approach also, and a section was sent to establish a post at Campi ya Marabu. On 3rd September one of 'B' Company's patrols was in action near Maungu, where a party of raiders was charged with the bayonet. One askari was killed and two were captured, the rest being chased into the bush with the loss of their weapons and kit. To wander lost through the bush without water-bottle and rifle, where waterholes were few and lion and rhinoceras plentiful, was enough to make the security of a high barbed-wire fence eminently desirable, and five days afterwards the German commander of this party, alone and exhausted, walked into Bura and surrendered.

[1] A German rifle taken from this party, claimed to be the first captured in the campaign, was preserved in 3 K.A.R. Mess at Nairobi.

While the K.A.R. was watching the approaches east of Mount Kilimanjaro, other troops had been sent from Nairobi to patrol the western route, where the enemy was reported to have occupied the water at Longido and to be moving troops towards the frontier. This assignment fell to the East Africa Mounted Rifles, who had a stiff skirmish with the enemy late in September. To enable a larger force to be maintained in this area, water was piped to the forward base at Kajiado and improvements were made to the railway line.

The Tsavo River route was the first of the three lines of approach to become really active, and the lower reaches of the river, where the bush grew thick, became the scene of the first engagement of the campaign worth describing as a military operation. By the end of August the Germans had concentrated most of their forces in the Kilimanjaro district. On 1st September Brigadier-General J. M. Stewart reached Mombasa with the 29th Punjabis, the first contingent of Indian Expeditionary Force 'C', and half this regiment was sent to the Tsavo—Voi sector. Its arrival coincided with the appearance on the upper Tsavo of a strong German force, totalling 11 officers and some 200 askaris with four machine guns, intent on carrying out a deep reconnaissance and if possible attacking the railway. The detachment at Campi ya Marabu was obliged to retreat, and on receiving news of this a scheme for surrounding the enemy and bringing him to battle was hastily devised by the newly-arrived senior officer of the Punjabis, Major A. A. James, who had had no time to examine the nature of the ground.

Action in the Tsavo Valley, 5th-6th September, 1914.—The greater part of 'B' Company, 1 K.A.R., and about half 'D' Company, 3 K.A.R., were already in the Tsavo valley, where the Punjabis now concentrated. 'A' Company, 4 K.A.R., was sent down the line from Nairobi, and 'B' Company was switched up the line to Mtito Andei, with orders to march thence to Killakuni. Thus using the mobility afforded by the railway as a base-line, James hoped to lure the enemy down the course of the Tsavo and into the embrace of a ring of troops closing in simultaneously from Killakuni, Tsavo, Maktau and Bura. This somewhat optimistic scheme might have succeeded but for the difficulties of the country and the total lack of any means of rapid communication between the various components of the British force.

On 5th September Captain H. T. Skinner with two companies of the 29th Punjabis and 45 rifles of 1 and 3 K.A.R. advanced up the Tsavo valley to meet the enemy. At the same time orders to close in upon the river were sent to the detachments at Killakuni, Maktau and Bura. Skinner met the section of 1 K.A.R. retreating from Campi ya Marabu, but by nightfall had seen no sign of the enemy. Early on 6th September Major James moved a few miles up the valley with the rest of the troops from Tsavo, and hearing from Skinner that the Germans had apparently slipped past him in the bush, ordered him to march back towards Tsavo and take them in the rear. But the enemy was not inside the trap, and as soon as Skinner reversed direction, neatly turned the tables by following up and unexpectedly opening fire upon his rearguard. Finding the Germans in position on some rising ground behind him, Skinner turned to attack.[1] Fortunately the enemy commander, now conscious that he was far from his base, had little wish to become involved in a serious fight. Outflanked on the right by the Punjabis and on the left by the K.A.R., he soon abandoned his position and withdrew. As news reached him that British reinforcements were approaching, he continued his retreat with all speed, and a patrol sent to follow him next day was unable to regain touch.

The plans for intercepting the German retreat miscarried completely. 'B' Company, 4 K.A.R., which should have advanced through the gap between the Chyulu and Nyulu Hills, never received their orders; the Germans retreated so fast that the troops from Bura arrived too late to intercept them; and the K.A.R. Mounted Infantry from Maktau, though they gained contact with the enemy, were too few to affect the issue. The whole affair proved a salutary lesson in the difficulties of bush warfare.

The result of such operations as this had an important influence on local tribes in the no man's land between the railway and the frontier. German propagandists were active, and many of the tribesmen were beginning to doubt whether the British Government would win the war. Valuable information regarding the enemy's movements could be obtained through retaining the friendship and confidence of these tribes, and this was an added reason for maintaining posts on the upper reaches of the Tsavo. Captain A. C. Saunders, who was now sent to command the Tsavo River area, envisaged a line of defended posts along the course of the river, capable of development into supply points for an advance into German territory.

On 19th September Captain C. de S. Isaacson (Spec. List) and Lieutenant A. C. H. Foster (Hamps. R.), who had reoccupied Campi ya Marabu with a detachment of Mounted Infantry and of 4 K.A.R., attacked and drove off an enemy raiding party about a hundred strong. In this action Foster and six of his men lost their lives, and Saunders decided to withdraw the post to a situation where it could be more quickly supported. An intelligence scout, H. E. Frost, had been sent to select a site near the junction of the Mzima and Tsavo, as a suitable position for patrolling up the courses of both these rivers. The site selected lay about half a mile west of the Mzima, on a small hill within a bend of the Tsavo. Here the river and the track that ran beside it were flanked on one side by hills and on the other by a stretch of nearly impenetrable thorn, about eight feet high, that reduced visibility to fifty yards. An entrenched camp was built to accommodate a garrison of one company and a machine gun. Saunders called it 'Frost's Castle' and sent Captain Isaacson with 'B' Company, 4 K.A.R., a section of the Mounted Infantry and some Somali scouts to occupy it.

Attack on Mzima Post, 25th September, 1914.—On 25th September the advance guard of an enemy force, estimated at about three companies, appeared on the River Nolturesh. Next day, shortly before 1 p.m., Saunders reached Mzima with a machine gun and 20 men. The post was

[1] George Williams, an African signal sergeant of 3 K.A.R., was awarded the D.C.M. for his bravery during this action in twice reconnoitring the enemy position and returning with information at great personal risk.

attacked a few minutes later. Owing to the thick bush it was difficult for the enemy to see the position, and also for Saunders to gain any idea of his opponents' strength. For four hours the Germans maintained their fire, while they attempted to close on the British trenches. Several of the six enemy machine guns were silenced and abandoned in the bush. When the attack was broken off Saunders thought it unwise to leave his trenches, but reconnaissance next day showed that the enemy had withdrawn in several parties and recrossed the frontier. A blood-stained satchel belonging to Lieutenant-Colonel von Bock was found in the bush, containing papers with details of the German force.

For some time thereafter the Tsavo River remained quiet, as the German commander had reported after the last attack that this line of approach was too difficult and too well-defended for penetration. Small raiding parties continued their attacks on the Tsavo—Voi—Maungu sector of the line, but by the end of September the worst danger had passed. In view of the waterless nature of the country, 'F' (Camel) Company, 3 K.A.R., was tried in the Voi area, but so many camels died from tsetse that the company had to be employed on the Giriama patrol instead.

By this time a new line of operations had developed in the coastal area. At the start of the war great anxiety was felt for the safety of Mombasa, the sole British port of supply. From there the coast road ran southward for twenty-five miles to Gazi. Beyond that a bush track continued for another thirty miles to Vanga, on the south bank of the Umba estuary. The German frontier post of Jasin was only two miles south of Vanga, and no rivers or other natural barriers lay between. The whole district was covered with thick, swampy bush, and was extremely unhealthy.

Vanga was a civil station, and like Taveta was considered to be too remote for defence. About the middle of August reports said that the enemy was assembling at Kiberule, a few miles south of Jasin, and it was decided, rather than wait for the attack, to make a demonstration and then withdraw. On 21st August half the K.A.R. Reserve Company at Mombasa was sent to Vanga by sea. These troops were followed a few days later by the Arab Company. With this force, on 30th August Wavell attacked the German outpost at Jasin, followed his retreating enemy, and fired into the camp at Kiberule. Vanga was then evacuated, and a post was set up ten miles to the north at Majoreni, defending the crossing of the River Mwena.

Action at Majoreni, 22nd September, 1914.—For the next three weeks all remained quiet in the coastal area. Then the Germans advanced in their turn to reconnoitre the British position, and on 22nd September crossed the Mwena and attacked Majoreni. The assault was successfully resisted, though Wavell was badly wounded. News had now reached Mombasa that the German cruiser *Königsberg* had entered Zanzibar harbour on 20th September and destroyed H.M.S. *Pegasus*, the only British warship then in East African waters. It appeared that Mombasa was now in danger of attack by land and sea, and if therefore the defence of the port had to be undertaken in earnest it was essential to occupy positions that could be easily reinforced and supplied. Majoreni was

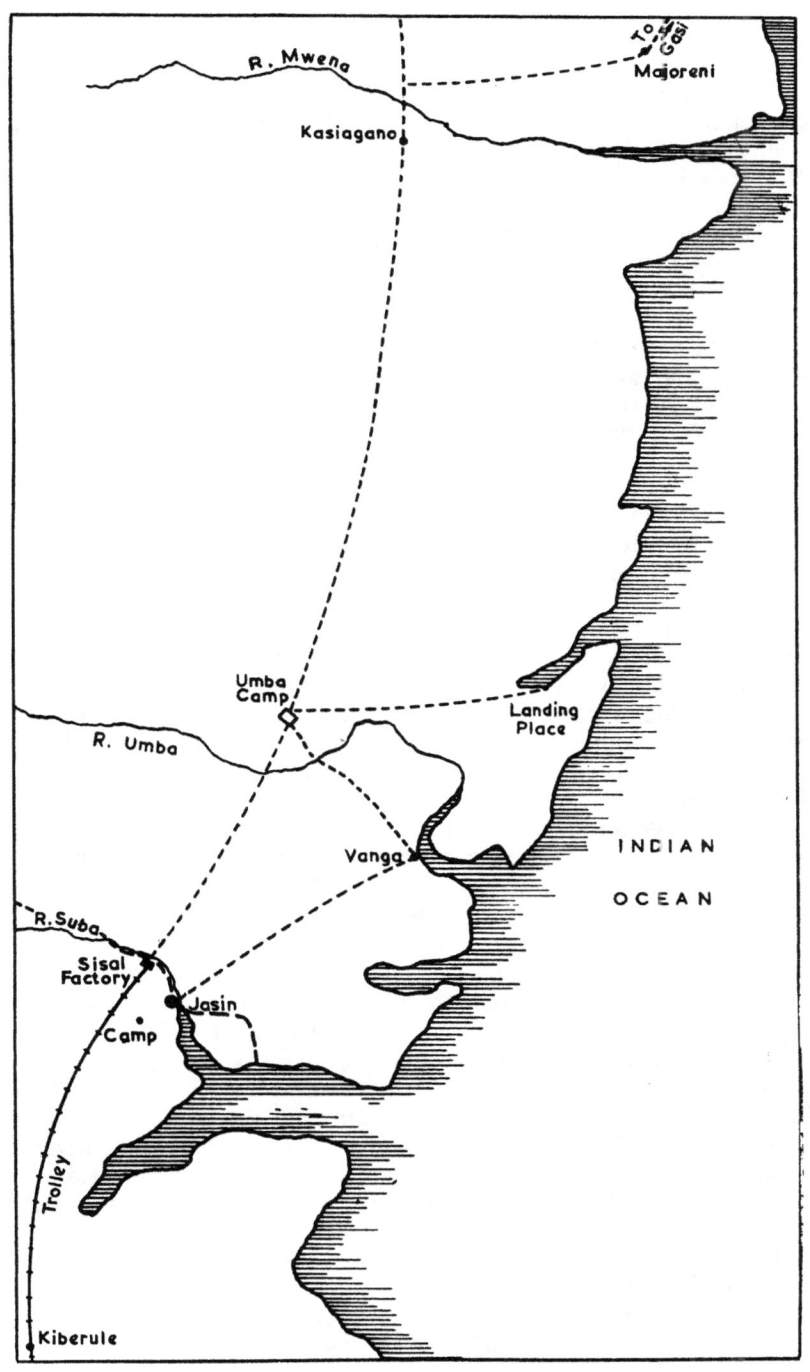

9. The Coastal Frontier Area

accordingly evacuated and a new post was built at the end of the motor road at Gazi, where the Reserve Company and the Arabs were reinforced by 'C' Company, 1 K.A.R. (Captain W. G. Stonor, Middx. R.), a company of the 29th Punjabis, and other Indian troops who had arrived at Mombasa with Indian Expeditionary Force 'C'. By 6th October some 850 troops, including six officers and 182 other ranks of the K.A.R., were at Gazi under the command of Major G. M. P. Hawthorn (Liverpool R.).

Action at Gazi, 7th October, 1914.—As matters turned out, the *Königsberg* failed completely to take advantage of her victory and was not seen or heard of again until she entered the mouth of the Rufigi nearly six weeks later. But dispositions to protect the land route had been taken none too soon. The Germans had lost no time in occupying Majoreni, and were now ready to resume their advance. Early on the morning of 7th October two German columns, one about 300 and the other 180 rifles strong, converged upon Gazi by the tracks running from Kikoreni and Kidimu. Confused fighting resulted in the bush all round the British position. A counter-attack by Captain Stonor with 'C' Company, a half-company of reservists and a company of Punjabis, halted the advance of the Kikoreni column for a time, and allowed Hawthorn to withdraw his troops within the main defences. At 3.30 p.m. 'C' Company was called upon to attack again. All four officers taking part were wounded, and command devolved upon Colour-Sergeant Sumani, who continued to press the assault. The Jhind Infantry came to his support, and the main attack was driven off. Other German attacks from the south and west failed to penetrate, and towards nightfall the enemy broke off the action and withdrew, though not without considerable difficulty. In this action the K.A.R. played a conspicuous part, and suffered most of the casualties.

As in the Tsavo valley, the Germans were now convinced that no quick victory was possible in the coastal area. To ease their supply problems they withdrew once more across the frontier, leaving only two small patrol posts to watch the bush tracks in British territory.

Action at Kisii, 12th September, 1914.—By this time operations had begun around Lake Victoria. The first clash took place on the eastern side of the lake, and with a little more enterprise on the part of the enemy might have had serious consequences, as by von Lettow's orders it was specially directed against the railway viaducts. Early in September a force of about 400 Germans, askaris and *ruga-ruga*, with a 3.7-cm. gun, crossed the frontier and, operating in conjunction with the German armed tug *Muansa,* occupied the little port of Karungu. From there they advanced to the civil station at Kisii, whence the District Commissioner and his police withdrew. 'G' Company, 4 K.A.R., was at Kisumu, and set out at once for Kisii, followed by 'C' and 'D' Companies, dispatched hastily from Uganda, and a small party of armed police. Under the command of Captain E. G. M. Thorneycroft (R. Lan. R.), this force reached the environs of Kisii on the morning of 12th September, and occupied the high ground above the village. The Germans were holding a parade of their troops below.

Thorneycroft's arrival took the enemy by surprise. Quickly deploying his troops, he led the attack on the right and was almost instantly killed. Meanwhile the Germans were attacking the opposite flank. Little progress was made by either side, though by nightfall the whole of the British left flank, now very short of ammunition, had been forced to retire.[1] The action was broken off, and the K.A.R. withdrew to the north, to be reinforced by the Reserve Company from Uganda. But the enemy, although left in possession of the field, had lost more than half his Europeans; the carriers had panicked, and realizing that the way to Kisumu was now barred, the German commander withdrew his force across the frontier. Karungu was evacuated a few days later.

The affair at Kisii drained all troops from the area west of Lake Victoria, leaving the southern frontier of Uganda to be watched only by a few hundred police and native levies. As the presence of enemy detachments was reported, it was decided to display a bold front, and as a precautionary measure the frontier was crossed and the bend of the River Kagera occupied to secure possession of the most important crossings. The enemy made no move, and as soon as the threat to Kisumu was over, the Reserve Company, 4 K.A.R., returned from the eastern side of the lake. On the northern frontier of Uganda the Sudan Government had agreed to relieve 4 K.A.R., and 'E' Company (Captain R. H. Leeke), the last of the former Northern Garrison, reached Bombo in the middle of October.

In Nyasaland the month of August passed uneventfully. Though German bases lay much nearer to the frontier than British, news of the outbreak of war did not reach them until the middle of the month. By that time the only German steamer on the lake had been surprised and disabled, and a small British flotilla consisting of all the Government trading and mission vessels had been assembled to transport the Field Force, about 500 strong with four 7-pounder and two 9-pounder guns, to the head of the lake. By 22nd August the Force had concentrated at Karonga, to be met by the news that the Germans had already crossed the frontier and occupied Kapora. Unaware that British troops were within reach, the Germans unwittingly gave Barton another fortnight's grace to collect information and complete his preparations. Reports then came that their main force, consisting of some 300 askaris and *ruga-ruga*, with two 3.7-cm. guns and a mob of spearmen, was approaching the frontier.

Action at Karonga, 9th September, 1914.—Barton had always intended to take the offensive, and the news that German troops were on the move twenty miles north of Karonga did not deter him. Leaving Lieutenant P. D. Bishop (K.A.R. Reserve) with ten British ranks, 43 askaris and some police at Karonga, on 8th September he marched inland with the rest of his force towards Mambande, intending to surprise the detachment at Kapora early on the following morning. But the main German force was closer than he thought. Hidden by the thick bush that borders the north-western shores of the lake to a depth of several miles, Barton marched right between two columns of the enemy

---

[1] Sergeant Miydiyo of 4 K.A.R. was awarded the D.C.M. for the great bravery he displayed while fighting at close quarters, in spite of being twice wounded.

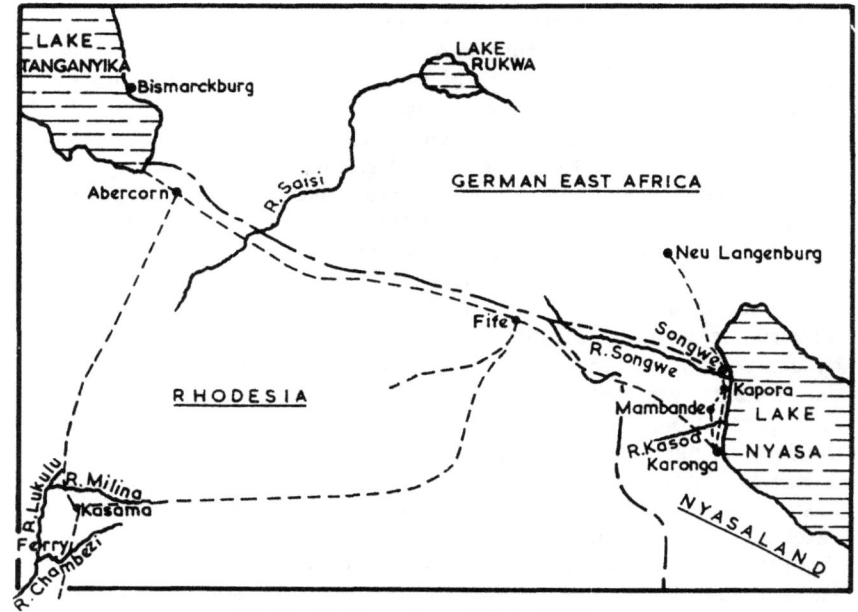

10. The Southern Area of Operations

coming south from Kapora and Mambande to attack Karonga.

Fortunately Barton was the first to discover what had happened. Hearing that a party of German askaris had occupied Mambande, he had just planned an encircling movement to cut off their retreat when his patrols reported enemy troops on the lakeside track leading from Kapora to Karonga. As the main German force was thought to be still on the Songwe, Barton concluded that these men were patrols, and having sent back news of their presence to Karonga, he camped late that night in the bush.

Early on 9th September Barton crossed the Lufira and had gained contact with the enemy when he heard that Karonga was being heavily attacked. Deciding to seize the opportunity thus offered, he abandoned his movement against Kapora, sent one of his companies back to Karonga, and moved with the remainder of his troops across the Kapora—Karonga track, hoping within a few hours to ambush a retreating enemy.

The compound at Karonga was surrounded by a loopholed wall. Behind its protection Bishop put up a gallant defence that took the Germans completely by surprise. The arrival of the relief company completed the rout. Within a few minutes, with both their machine guns out of action, the Germans were streaming northward in full retreat. Barton was waiting for them near the River Kasoa, and as the enemy came up a fierce fight developed in the thick bush that lasted for two hours. Bayonet charges by the K.A.R. were followed by German counter-attacks in which severe casualties were suffered by both sides, until towards the middle of the afternoon the scattered remnants of the German force disappeared into the bush for good.

On the southern front von Lettow, while urging offensive action, had been obliged to leave matters largely to the discretion of his local commander. The result of the latter's attempt to carry out this policy at Karonga was sufficient to stabilize matters in the southern theatre until the period of immediate danger ended with the coming of the rains in December. The successful defence of Karonga by 1 K.A.R. was a creditable victory and a most encouraging start to the campaign. For so small a force the cost of the engagement was high: three officers and eight askaris killed; three officers[1] and 42 askaris wounded. But the enemy losses were very much higher, and all their guns and machine guns were captured. The Germans withdrew beyond the Songwe, and Karonga, easily supplied by water and situated in comparatively healthy country where food was obtainable, became for the second time in its history a base for military operations in the north of the Protectorate.

Early in September the Germans became active along the Rhodesian sector of the frontier. A movement against Abercorn was repelled by the Northern Rhodesia Police, but sporadic raids continued along the border and by water down Lake Tanganyika. To meet these threats while the newly-raised Rhodesian volunteer units were still in process of formation, the assistance of Belgian troops was obtained in garrisoning Abercorn and patrolling the adjacent frontier.

'Prompt action promises quick results,' von Lettow had telegraphed to his commander at Moshi on 7th August. This policy was urged upon his commanders everywhere, and it was only the equally prompt response of a handful of K.A.R. companies that saved the British protectorates from invasion. By October, however, their action had gained the necessary breathing-space; on both fronts the Germans had been taught that easy victory was impossible, and some 5,000 British, Indian and African troops had assembled for the defence of the Uganda Railway.

(iv) *The Tanga Expedition and its Consequences, November-December, 1914.*

The expedition against Tanga that took place early in November, 1914, was the first attempt at a major operation in East Africa. It was planned and directed from overseas and the K.A.R. played no part in it. The fate of that luckless enterprise greatly modified the official attitude towards the East African theatre of war, affected the whole plan of subsequent operations, and made inevitable a campaign on a scale not previously contemplated. This in its turn indirectly brought about an expansion of the K.A.R. from three battalions to 22.

At the time when the Tanga expedition was conceived, the control of the sea against German raiders still loomed largely in the grand strategy of the war, for seven enemy cruisers were upon the high seas and mass movements of troops were already in progress from India to other theatres of war. The capture of German overseas ports was therefore an important object, as the means of depriving sea-raiders of their refuge. There was also another purpose involved in such expeditions:

---

[1] Barton was among those wounded, and command of the Field Force passed to Captain H. W. Stevens (Res. of Officers).

the isolation of German land forces from outside supplies. If this could be effected in East Africa, it was assumed that it would be comparatively easy to advance along the railways, and having secured the European settled areas, to enforce a general surrender.

The original intention had been to attack Dar-es-Salaam. One Indian brigade was considered sufficient for this purpose, and preparations for its dispatch had already begun when the situation was changed unexpectedly by the entry of Turkey into the war. The brigade selected was sent to the Persian Gulf, and another brigade, the 27th, was prepared for East Africa in its place. This brigade included a British battalion, the 2nd Battalion Loyal North Lancashire Regiment,[1] but for a variety of reasons the quality of the Indian battalions was not high. Several other units from the Indian States were formed into an Imperial Service Brigade, and with Sappers and Pioneers the whole force, known as Indian Expeditionary Force 'B,' came to about 8,000 men. Brigadier-General A. E. Aitken was given command with the temporary rank of major-general.

It was not the intention of the home authorities to direct operations from Whitehall.[2] The first paragraph of Aitken's instructions read, 'The object of the expedition under your command is to bring the whole of German East Africa under British authority . . . ,' and his terms of reference were widely phrased. But they included the suggestion that as the threat to the Uganda Railway constituted the main danger to East Africa, and co-operation could presumably be expected from the British forces already poised on both sides of Kilimanjaro, a simultaneous attack on both ends of the Tanga Railway should be the first step. Unfortunately these suggestions reached India in such a form as to imply that they were definite instructions to occupy Tanga as a preliminary move, and that Aitken's discretion was confined, after consultation with those on the spot, to devising the course of subsequent operations.[3]

Owing to changes in the original plans, Aitken's force was hastily assembled. Some of its units had to be brought up to strength by drafts from others, and many of the officers were posted at short notice. While naval escort was awaited the troops were confined on board for some time before sailing. The transports were small, and the voyage slow. Aitken went ahead of the convoy to confer at Mombasa with the Governor, Brigadier-General Stewart and Lieutenant-Colonel Ward. There the dispositions of the German forces were explained to him, and as Tanga was thought to be practically unprotected, no great difficulty was foreseen in the projected occupation of the port. Little importance appears to have been attached to the fact that the railway offered a rapid means of reinforcement from the main area of German concentration at Moshi. Lieutenant-Colonel B. R. Graham (3 K.A.R.), realizing the difficulties that must arise in the initial stages, offered to provide

---

[1] Now the Loyal Regiment, and referred to hereafter in the text as 'The Loyals'.

[2] It should be noted that the War Office was not involved in the planning of this expedition.

[3] *Military Operations in East Africa*, Vol. I, p. 67.

troops from his battalion to cover the landing. Aitken thought this unnecessary, and declined.

Tanga stands on the southern shore of the bay, protected to seaward by the headland of Ras Kasone. Approaching from the south-west, the railway encircles the town on the seaward side, running through a deep cutting before curving round to reach the shore of the bay. Between this cutting and the coastline south of Ras Kasone lay several miles of plantations and bush. Unless the transports could enter the bay it would be necessary to land somewhere on the coast and approach the town across country. Only a couple of rough and inaccurate sketch-maps were available.

The need for reconnaissance might in any case have prevented surprise, but as matters fell out, von Lettow got sufficient warning to rush from Moshi to the rescue. Early in the war the Royal Navy had arranged a truce with Dar-es-Salaam and Tanga, and it was now thought necessary to give at least an hour's warning of its termination. As the convoy approached Tanga, H.M.S. *Fox* steamed ahead to warn the German District Commissioner. Considerable delay followed in bringing the convoy up, choosing a suitable beach among the thick mangroves for the first landing party, concerting arrangements, and sweeping for mines. It was 10 p.m. that night (2nd November) before the first boat-loads of troops made for the shore. By then von Lettow was well on his way with reinforcements.

They arrived just in time. By dawn on 3rd November the beach south of Ras Kasone was filling up with troops and stores, and the original landing party under Brigadier-General M. J. Tighe was approaching the outskirts of the town. It was held up by a German company sited behind the railway cutting. Von Lettow's first troops were meanwhile detraining a few miles short of the town, and, entering the bush, began a wide flanking attack on the British left. The Indian troops, much exhausted after their recent experiences and shaken by casualties, particularly among their British officers, had to retire. Reinforcements came forward from the beach to check the German pursuit, and von Lettow was then left alone for the rest of the day to arrange his defences, while the British disembarkation continued.

It was noon on 4th November before Aitken's troops were deployed for the attack, with the Imperial Service Brigade on the right and the 27th Brigade on the left. While the former made a frontal advance against the railway cutting and the town beyond, the latter was to envelop the German right, and by cutting the railway prevent the enemy from getting his forces away. As the hottest hours of the day approached, the troops pressed slowly forward through the thick plantations of sisal and rubber and the unaccustomed tangle of bush, striving to maintain touch as they progressed. With no adequate guiding line but the shore of the estuary, a tendency soon developed for some units to close to the right, thus opening up a gap and leaving the troops on the extreme left dangerously isolated. It was in these circumstances that von Lettow's troops suddenly attacked the Indian battalion on the British left, which despite a gallant resistance became split into small groups. Stragglers then began to drift back to the rear, to the dismay of the troops in reserve.

Meanwhile the 2nd Loyals and the Kashmir Rifles had forced the railway cutting and entered the town. There the fight continued, but the situation was confused and it soon became plain that the enemy resistance had not collapsed. When the effect of the German counter-attack was felt on the British left, the Loyals and Kashmiris were obliged to withdraw to the railway cutting. In response to an appeal, H.M.S. *Fox* then bombarded the town, and this apparently prevented the Germans from pressing their advantage. Before nightfall the bush was full of disorganized parties of Indian troops making for the beach, where their arrival threw the mass of carriers into confusion.

In spite of this set-back, General Aitken's first intention was to regroup his forces and renew the attack by moonlight. But the grave reports on the state of some of the Indian units received from both brigadiers and the conditions developing on the beach dissuaded him. There seemed no prospect of immediate success, and to prolong the operation was impossible, if only because the Ras Kasone peninsula had no water supply, apart from that at the German hospital. Unfortunately the necessity for re-embarkation was so completely unforeseen and the urgency so great that all heavy stores, including ten machine guns and a quantity of ammunition and signal equipment, had to be abandoned. On 5th November, while the troops were crowding back into the transports, the Loyals and Kashmiris covered the embarkation with perfect steadiness, though the morale of the other units was badly shaken. The total casualties numbered over 800, of whom no fewer than 20 British officers and 340 other ranks had been killed or died later of their wounds.

Had Aitken known it, von Lettow was convinced that Tanga could not be further defended, and was already formulating plans to withdraw from the port and take up a position inland. The re-embarkation of the British expedition and the acquisition of so much valuable war material took him by surprise. He was credited with the victory, none the less. 'Tanga,' he wrote afterwards, 'was the birthday of the soldierly spirit in our troops.'[1] Thereafter his askaris faced the war with confidence, and the German colonists, who had been inclined to distrust his judgment as that of a comparative newcomer, now gave him their whole-hearted support.

Meanwhile Indian Expeditionary Force 'B' crept northward to Mombasa, where the re-training of the weakest Indian units was put in hand. The rest of the force was sent to Nairobi or posted along the railway. Aitken took a very pessimistic view of the situation that faced him in his new command. Knowing that further reinforcements from Europe or India were unobtainable, imbued with a most unfavourable opinion of many of his troops, and convinced that the enemy was in much greater strength than originally supposed, he could only propose that the old defensive rôle should be resumed. With this the home authorities

---

[1] Von Lettow, *War mir die Engländer über Ostafrika erzählten*, p. 31.

agreed, and on 22nd November the War Office assumed responsibility for the East African theatre of war. In December Aitken was succeeded in command by Brigadier-General (afterwards Major-General) R. Wapshare, and in the same month the appointment of Inspector-General of the K.A.R. was suspended.

The redistribution of the new troops from India was effected by the end of November. The K.A.R. was then no longer the largest element in the command. Plans for concentrating each of the three battalions for unit training had already been discussed, but for the time being this was impossible. Three of the four companies of 1 K.A.R. in the northern area were now in the Voi—Tsavo sector, and one near Magadi. 3 K.A.R. was even more widely scattered, with two companies on the coast, two still in the Giriama country, one and a half on the Voi—Tsavo sector, one near Magadi, one and a half on the northern frontier, and one at Zanzibar. Apart from a company in the Voi—Tsavo sector, 4 K.A.R. was stationed around Lake Victoria, with two companies in Uganda and two east of the lake. The whole of that area was now under the command of O.C. Troops, Uganda.

A few minor actions were fought by 4 K.A.R. near Lake Victoria in November and December. On the eastern side Major R. F. B. Knox, commanding 'E' Company, set up a main camp at Suna with defended outposts, and in conjunction with a troop of the East Africa Mounted Rifles patrolled the border. West of the lake the Kagera was crossed, Kyaka Fort occupied and posts set up elsewhere along the river. These positions were not far from Bukoba, which had now been reoccupied by the Germans in considerable force. In November 'D' Company, 4 K.A.R., was accordingly switched from east to west of the lake, and the 13th Rajputs were brought up by rail from Mombasa.

The expectation of a German attack on the Kagera was soon fulfilled. On 20th November the enemy attacked Kyaka Fort. After a stout defence the garrison withdrew across the river, hoping that the enemy would follow and expose his rear to an attack from Kimwa. Unfortunately no attack materialized, as other German forces were containing the British outposts between Kyaka and the lake, so that the enemy was able to penetrate in some force as far as Kabuoba. Though the Germans were still on their own side of the frontier, Lieutenant-Colonel Hickson had no intention of allowing matters to remain as they were. Concentrating 'D' Company, two companies of the Rajputs, 150 Police and a section of the Mountain Battery at Kiasimbi, he advanced on the night of 5th/6th December and surprised the main body of the enemy at Gombaizi while the K.A.R. Reserve Company moved from Minziro on to the German flank at Itarra. The enemy was taken off balance and was soon in rapid retreat across the Kagera and into the stone fort at Kyaka. Without more artillery Hickson was unable to reduce it, and withdrew his troops into the area around Rukuba. For some time all remained quiet in southern Uganda.

On the railway vigilance could never be relaxed. German raids continued without ceasing, and in fact became more active and daring. Small patrols played a perpetual game of hide-and-seek with Germans and rhinoceros alike through the thick bush of the Tsavo valley. Farther south, where the open plain was sprinkled with hills covered to their summits with undergrowth that sometimes betokened the presence of springs of fresh water, it was possible to site additional outposts, such as that at Kasigao, to watch for enemy patrols and prevent them from approaching the line. From time to time, however, parties of raiders got through, planted their explosives upon the permanent way, and caused damage to the railway rolling-stock. So long as the initiative remained with the enemy such damage was inevitable. Though many expedients were tried, troops well trained in bushcraft were the only effective answer, and to bring the whole force up to the standard of the K.A.R. regular battalions would take some time. Nor was this the only problem to be faced: British, Colonial, Indian and African troops were all differently administered, rationed and supplied, and this gave rise to so many difficulties that even at the end of the war some of them were still unsolved.

Thus along the greater part of the frontier, the year 1914 closed quietly, in spite of the tremendous encouragement given to the Germans by the news of the British failure at Tanga. In Europe also the immediate crisis was past, though no hope could yet be entertained in East Africa of reinforcements from home in sufficient strength to enable the offensive to be resumed. Only one indication of a more hopeful future was apparent. The Taveta gap was recognized as the gateway through which the invasion of German East Africa must eventually be made, and authority was given for the construction of a branch railway from Voi. With its aid a sufficient concentration of troops might in time be assembled within striking distance of von Lettow's advanced base at Moshi.

(v) *Operations in the Coastal Area, December, 1914-January, 1915.* Maps 9, 11.

One more offensive operation was undertaken before the East Africa Command settled down to a prolonged period of preparation. Though better conceived and more efficiently carried out, it proved in the long run no more successful than the affair at Tanga. Four companies of 1 K.A.R. and two of 3 K.A.R. took part. Their bushcraft and record of health compared favourably with that of the Indian units employed in the low-lying and thickly-forested coastal belt.[1]

The enemy occupaion of British territory beyond the Umba had sent some thousands of natives flying northward. This circumstance, in conjunction with the news of the Tanga disaster, helped to spread doubt and dismay among the British tribes. Wapshare therefore decided to reoccupy this area, which was known to be very thinly held by the Germans. Command of the operation was given to Brigadier-General Tighe. 'B' and 'D' Companies, 3 K.A.R., had been sent by sea to Gazi

[1] The unsuitability of Indian troops for employment in tropical Africa had been pointed out by officers serving with the K.A.R. in pre-war years. Major Rigby once suggested West African troops as a better source of reinforcement in case of need. [Rigby to Commissioner, Uganda, 1.vii.07. C.O. 534, 5.] This policy was adopted in the later stages of the East Africa Campaign.

after the failure at Tanga. Since then they had been engaged in daily patrols and were constantly in touch with the enemy. They were now reinforced by the 101st Grenadiers, the 2nd Kashmir Rifles, and half a battalion of the Jhind Infantry, which together with the Arab Company, some scouts and two machine-gun sections made a total force of 1,800 men. Over 5,000 carriers were assembled for the supply column, so that the project was by far the most important yet to be undertaken by land.

Tighe disposed a part of his force on the landward side to guard the flank of his advance. On 17th December the remainder marched south by the coast road, with the two companies of 3 K.A.R. leading. They were soon in contact with German patrols on the River Mwena. While the main body closed up, the K.A.R. began reconnoitring the Umba valley ahead. Tighe paid tribute to their work, and described them in his report as an invaluable 'substitute for light cavalry'. On 20th December a camp was formed near the Umba, overlooking the flat, unhealthy plain of mud and mangrove swamp through which the river wandered. Next day the advance guard crossed the river and found that the Germans had abandoned Vanga. K.A.R. patrols then pushed on and attacked Jasin on the higher ground beyond, but the enemy reoccupied the post after the patrols withdrew.

At six o'clock on the morning of Christmas Day, Captain T. O. Fitzgerald attacked Jasin again with one of his K.A.R. companies and a company of the 101st Grenadiers. The Germans were taken entirely by surprise, one of them being killed in his pyjamas. The enemy trenches were captured with the bayonet; by 8.30 a.m. Jasin was in British hands, and Fitzgerald retired, laden with his opponents' Christmas dinner.[1]

The Germans made no attempt to reoccupy Jasin. Tighe set up a defended camp close by and posts to watch the frontier. A new base was opened, and the rest of the troops were distributed behind the Umba, ready to deal with an enemy counter-attack.

The Germans had taken up a position on rising ground a few miles south of Jasin. On 5th January, 1915, this position was reconnoitred, but appeared to be too strong for attack. A few days later the enemy in their turn tested the position at Jasin, which was held by the Jhind Infantry. A company of 3 K.A.R. went to their support, and the attack was repulsed. Another German attack, made on 12th January, was likewise driven off. It was then hoped that the position on this part of the frontier would stabilize, but the Germans soon showed that they had no intention of allowing the occupation of Jasin to remain unchallenged.

While these operations were in progress, the four companies of 1 K.A.R. serving in the northern area took part in a small expedition to Mafia Island, off the delta of the Rufigi. The *Königsberg* had taken refuge up one of the river channels, and the naval authorities sought military help in capturing the island as a base from which to attack her.

[1] T. O. Fitzgerald, Typescript *Record of 3 K.A.R. during the Great War in East Africa*.

The German garrison was reported to be negligible, but no chances were taken. Early in January Lieutenant-Colonel L. E. S. Ward embarked with 'A', 'B', 'C' and 'E' Companies, 1 K.A.R., and a company of the 101st Grenadiers. On the 10th the force landed on Mafia, and by the end of the next day had driven the enemy from his entrenchments at Ngombeni. Major L. H. Soames, commanding the four companies of 1 K.A.R., was severely wounded and Captain G. J. Giffard assumed command of the detachment. The surrender of the island followed soon afterwards.[1] On the way back the transport *Barjora* was ordered into Vanga, as the troops of 1 K.A.R. were to relieve the two companies of 3 K.A.R. in the Umba valley.

Meanwhile von Lettow had been moving troops rapidly down the Tanga Railway, to build a concentration of nine companies not far south of Jasin. The enemy's preliminary attacks had been in the nature of reconnaissances in force, but now, at dawn on the morning of 18th January, when the reinforcements brought by the *Barjora* were about to land, he suddenly attacked Jasin in considerable strength.

The post was defended by two companies of the Kashmir Rifles, one of the Grenadiers, and a K.A.R. machine-gun section. A little way to the north, at the crossing of the River Suba, an outpost garrisoned by 40 Kashmiris had been stationed at the sisal factory. In siting these posts it was hoped that the prickly thickness of the sisal plantation in which they were situated would afford some natural protection, but the plantation also limited the field of fire and provided cover for the enemy's approach. 'B' and 'D' Companies, 3 K.A.R., had already played their part in defending these posts, but had now been withdrawn to the Umba camp to await embarkation.

Action at Jasin, 18th-19th January, 1915.—Rockets fired at Jasin gave prompt warning of the attack. So far only 'B' Company, 1 K.A.R., had got ashore. This company and the two companies of 3 K.A.R. were sent forward at once under the command of Captain G. J. Giffard. By the time they reached the Suba the Germans had occupied rising ground overlooking the banks, with their right flank protected by a bend in the river and the left by a patch of dense bush. The three companies were held up by heavy fire on attempting to cross.[2]

Giffard now divided his force, sending the two companies of 3 K.A.R. to make a frontal attack on the river, and moving west with his own company to relieve the garrison at the sisal factory. With 'D' Company on the left and 'B' Company on the right, 3 K.A.R. got across the Suba and gained the ridge on the southern bank. But no further progress could be made, as the enemy was in far greater strength and had dug in on the edge of the sisal plantation. After maintaining the position for some

---

[1] The *Königsberg* was finally destroyed on 11th July, 1915, but most of her crew escaped to join von Lettow's forces, taking the cruiser's ten 4.1-inch and two 3.5-inch guns with them.

[2] 'In order to engage the enemy while hurrying from his places of assembly to the assistance of the advanced post, in favourable tactical conditions, I intended to place my troops in readiness on his probable lines of advance, in such a manner that he would have to run up against them.'—Von Lettow, *My Reminiscences of East Africa*, p. 57.

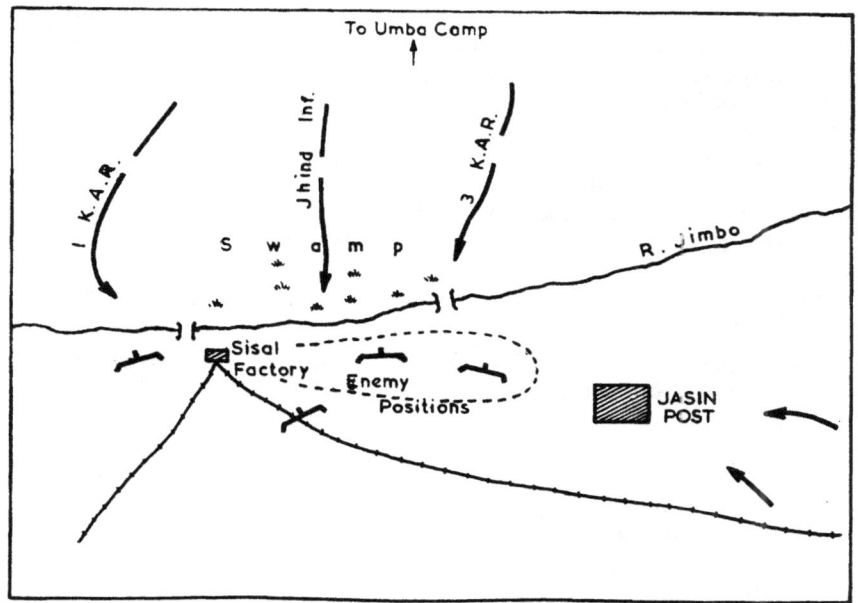

11. Action at Jasin, 18th-19th January, 1915

time, 3 K.A.R. was obliged by shortage of ammunition to withdraw across the river.[1]

The attempt to relieve the sisal factory was also unsuccessful. By eleven o'clock the Kashmiris had exhausted their ammunition, and fixing bayonets charged out of the factory and scattered. Most of them eventually got back to Umba camp. Meanwhile Captain Giffard had called for reinforcements. By this time the other three companies of 1 K.A.R. were ashore. 'A' and 'C' Companies came forward, with 'E' Company in reserve, and a fresh attack was mounted, with 1 K.A.R. on the right, two companies of Jhind Infantry in the centre, and 3 K.A.R. on the left, while a section of the Mountain Battery engaged the German machine guns.

Deployed invisibly in the dense bush, in positions of his own choosing, the enemy had all the advantage. Only 3 K.A.R. got across the river, but nothing further could be accomplished. Not realizing that Jasin was in immediate danger, Tighe decided to concentrate his troops before renewing the attack and to ask for a naval demonstration. Early on the following morning, however, it was discovered that the garrison at Jasin, attacked again soon after dawn and with its ammunition nearly gone, had surrendered.

When the news of this reverse reached England, Lord Kitchener sharply criticized Wapshare's attempt to take the offensive without adequate information and with insufficient reserves. No substantial advantage had been gained by provoking a fight in the unhealthy valley

[1] Sergeant Juma Gubanda was awarded the D.C.M. for swimming to and fro across the river with information, under heavy fire.

of the Umba, where the objectives were limited and the result, however successful, could not be a prelude to a full-scale invasion. As it was, out of nearly 500 casualties, 276 men, including eight of the K.A.R. machine-gun section, had been taken prisoner.[1] Orders were issued to withdraw once more to the area around Gazi, which was to be garrisoned by four companies of 3 K.A.R. and four of Kashmiris.

By 8th February the evacuation of the Umba valley had been completed for the second time. The affair was a gloomy beginning to a new year that as yet bore no prospect of brighter things.

(vi) *Defensive and Preparatory Operations in the West and South, 1915.* Maps 12, II (c).

While the operations in the Umba valley were in progress, Brigadier-General J. M. Stewart had gone to the eastern shores of Lake Victoria, where the enemy was again reported to be active, with reinforcements from the Loyals and the 28th Mountain Battery. In retaliation for frontier raids, the little German port of Shirati was shelled and occupied, and 'E' and 'G' Companies, 4 K.A.R., joined the Loyals there.

Action at Gurribe, 16th January, 1915.—For the time being Shirati was used as a base to patrol the area, in the hope of striking at the main German forces. In the course of these operations, on 16th January Captain R. F. B. Knox was returning from a reconnaissance with 'E' Company when he heard that about 100 German troops were on Gurribe Hill, close to the frontier. The ground was difficult, but Knox attacked next day at dawn. He took the hill, and with it a gun and all the German baggage, but the victory was tempered by the discovery that he had lost all his own, which the Germans had found in the bush. Soon after this the Loyals were recalled to Nairobi, and 4 K.A.R. resumed its former defensive rôle.

Although major operations were forbidden, it was neither possible nor desirable to avoid action altogether in the lake area during 1915. Offensive patrols were essential, if only to maintain the morale of the troops, and as the German commanders thought the same, these patrols culminated from time to time in actions that were usually followed by periods of quiet.

By the end of February renewed enemy activity had again made it necessary to reinforce the eastern side of the lake. The Reserve Company, 3 K.A.R., and the Mounted Infantry, now 80 strong, were sent with a section of the Mountain Battery and some scouts to join the two companies of 4 K.A.R., and by 2nd March the whole column had concentrated under Lieutenant-Colonel Hickson at Niasoku, a prominent hill a few miles north of the border.

On 4th March Hickson invaded German territory on a night march to Ikoma. This hill was found to be occupied by a small force of the enemy, who were driven off by 4 K.A.R. Next day the Reserve Company, 3 K.A.R., carried out a similar operation against Susuni Hill. These minor actions were followed by an encounter with the main German

---

[1] 1 K.A.R. lost one officer and 10 other ranks wounded; 3 K.A.R. 15 other ranks killed, one officer and 38 other ranks wounded.

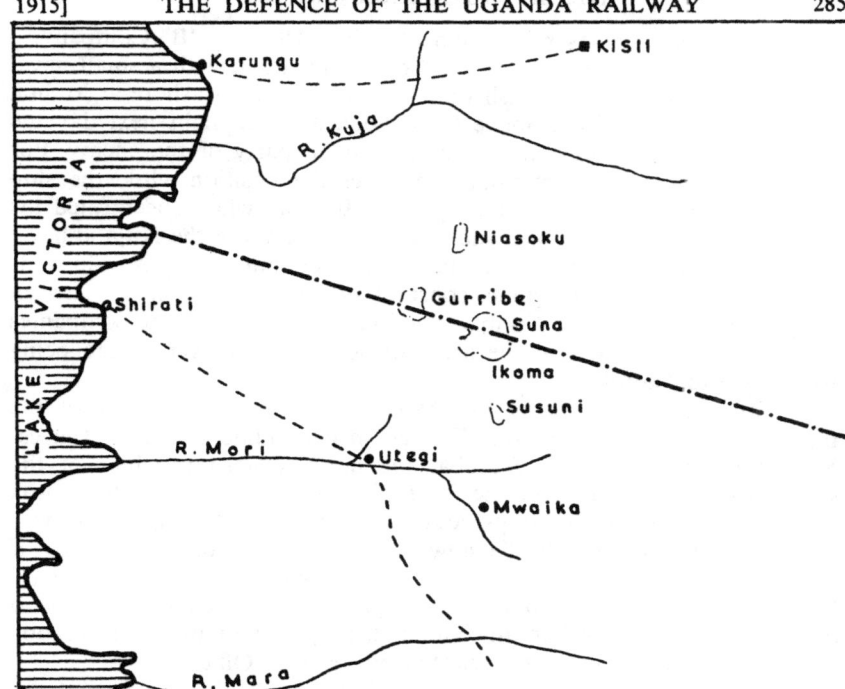

12. Lake Victoria: Eastern Area

forces on 9th March. Early that morning, at a place called Mwaika, the Mounted Infantry were moving in advance when they found the enemy approaching from the south.

Action at Mwaika, 9th March, 1915.—Hickson at once deployed his force on the nearer of two parallel ridges, while the enemy rushed to occupy the other. By galloping forward at once, the Mounted Infantry secured the right flank; 3 K.A.R. Reserve Company and the guns took the centre, and 4 K.A.R. the left. A lively fight ensued, with both sides attempting to move around the flanks: the Mounted Infantry at one end of the line and the Germans at the other. Neither movement succeeded, and at nightfall both sides were still in position. Next morning it was discovered that the enemy had retired across the Mara. The K.A.R. lost three officers, a British N.C.O. and nine askaris killed in this action, but the German losses were much heavier.

Hickson was now far from his base and expected that at any moment the Germans would renew the attack. Withdrawing to Utegi, he called for reinforcements. One company of the Loyals and 'A' Company, 4 K.A.R., were sent up by rail, but all remained quiet, and by 22nd March Hickson had withdrawn unmolested to Niasoku.

By the beginning of May a large German force, which report put as high as 1,000 men, was again over the Mara and raiding the frontier. 'B' Company, the Reserve Company, and later 'D' and 'E' Companies,

3 K.A.R., were sent as reinforcements. On 11th May 'B' Company, 3 K.A.R., with two companies of the Loyals embarked with a small naval expedition to rescue the British vessel *Sybil,* which was ashore at Majita, a few miles north of the Speke Gulf. Soon after daylight next day the troops were put ashore and drove off a small party of the enemy. For the next few days they remained to cover the position while the ship was salvaged. 'B' Company then joined Hickson, who concentrated his forces once more at Niasoku and began to reconnoitre the Kuja valley.

For the next few weeks, in a countryside depopulated by hostile raids and now swarming with game, constant skirmishes took place between the patrols of both sides. No major action took place, but the companies of 3 K.A.R. were kept in the area for some time longer before being withdrawn to Nairobi.

So far, the British forces had had on the whole the better of the fighting around Lake Victoria. Though in communication with Dar-es-Salaam by wireless from Bukoba, the north-western province of the German colony was too remote for rapid reinforcement, and there was no railway along which troops could be moved, as at Tanga. A newly-organized British naval flotilla now controlled the lake, and the idea of some spectacular stroke to keep the enemy quiet and help to maintain the spirits of the British troops was tempting. Major-General Tighe, who had now replaced Wapshare in command, proposed an attack on Bukoba or Mwanza, but the idea was rejected by the War Office.

West of the lake, the Germans continued to be active around the Kagera. The importance of this theatre was now increasing with the growing prospect of Anglo-Belgian co-operation. At first the Belgians had been content to leave the initiative to their allies. In January, 1915, they agreed to take over the defence of the frontier in the remote, mountainous corner of Uganda where British, German and Belgian territory met. In the same month Brigadier-General W. Malleson went from Nairobi to Ruchuru to discuss the possibility of further co-operation. He found the Belgians very short of transport and ammunition. It was agreed that supplies of the latter should be forwarded via Mombasa, and in March a detachment of two officers and 50 men of 4 K.A.R. was stationed at Fort Portal to escort the consignments that came up country during the ensuing weeks via Kisumu and Kampala.

Attack on Bukoba, 22nd-23rd June, 1915.—In June Tighe at last obtained the agreement of the War Office to a combined operation on the lake. Bukoba was chosen for attack, and as the Germans had considerable forces in the vicinity, intensive patrol activity was arranged along the Kagera to pin them down while the raid was in progress. Brigadier-General Stewart was appointed to conduct the operation and a large mixed force, nearly 2,000 strong, drawn mainly from the two English battalions, the Punjabis and 3 K.A.R. (three companies), concentrated at Kisumu. The force embarked on 20th June, and late on the following evening approached the coast a few miles north of Bukoba. The alarm was given at once by a German look-out post.

Bukoba was a small port lying in a saucer-shaped depression surrounded by hills. The church, wireless station and custom house near the landing-stage were conspicuous landmarks. Along the shore and at the foot of the hills near the spot selected for landing were thick patches of reeds, high grass and swamp, and most of the hills near the town were covered with plantations of bananas. All this became visible at daylight on 22nd June, as the first boats, carrying the Royal Fusiliers, made for the shore.

Stewart had intended to land 3 K.A.R. south of the town, but the activities of a German field gun sited near the church caused him to change his mind, and soon after 11 a.m. the three companies waded ashore to a beach not far from the first landing, though nearer to the town. They then occupied a nearby hill, with the Fusiliers and Loyals on other hills to their right. The enemy was facing them on the high ridges concealing the town, with his field gun and several machine guns in position. Stewart brought the mountain guns into action as a preliminary to the infantry advance, which then progressed slowly across the hills and valleys until nightfall. Enemy patrols were active during the night, but were all driven off.

Next morning the Fusiliers were ordered to take the town, while the Loyals moved round the enemy's inland flank. Progress was slow at first, but the Germans were outnumbered and had to abandon their field gun.[1] By mid-morning the Fusiliers were able to get along the shore, with the K.A.R. and Punjabis in reserve. The enemy then withdrew to the hills west of the town, broke off the action and retreated. A number of rifles and 32,000 rounds of ammunition were taken, the wireless station was destroyed, and the whole force, greatly elated, re-embarked the same evening for Kisumu. Casualties had been slight.

Although the attack on Bukoba had been an all-British effort, the plans for Anglo-Belgian co-operation which had been under discussion since the beginning of the year did eventually crystallize into concrete proposals. The Belgian Government had given control of operations to the Acting Governor of the Katanga Province, M. Tombeur, who was later commissioned and promoted to the rank of major-general. Lieutenant-Colonel Molitor became his chief of staff. The Belgians were anxious for a combined offensive. They recognized the necessity of first gaining control of Lake Tanganyika, which had become a German military highway flanking their frontier, and after that hoped, in conjunction with forces from Uganda, to capture Ruanda as a preliminary to an advance upon Tabora. The insistence of the War Office that no offensive could be contemplated for the present caused these plans to be postponed, but towards the end of the year the Belgians asked for a demonstration from southern Uganda to prevent the Germans from concentrating in the Ruanda district.

In November Lieutenant E. B. B. Hawkins of 4 K.A.R. made a deep reconnaissance south of the Kagera to ascertain the whereabouts and strength of the German positions. He found their forward posts well supported. Early in December three companies of 4 K.A.R., 250 men of the Police Service Battalion, and two guns of the Mountain Battery assembled near Nsongezi, where the Kagera runs between high banks

[1] This gun rolled into the lake during shipment and was lost.

and is about eighty yards wide. While feint attacks were made at Kanyonza and along the shore of the lake, a light floating bridge was thrown across the river near Nsongezi. The Germans having abandoned their post, the bridgehead was consolidated without opposition, and a British outpost was established a little way to the south to guard the approach to the river. The way was thus prepared for an invasion of German territory in force, and meanwhile patrols could operate across the river with much greater freedom than before.

On the southern front, very little happened during the year 1915, at any rate so far as the K.A.R. was concerned. In December, 1914, command in Nyasaland was taken over by Lieutenant-Colonel G. M. P. Hawthorn. Soon afterwards 1 K.A.R. was called upon to deal with a native rising in the Shiré Highlands, brought about by a certain John Chilembwe of the 'Watch Tower' sect.[1] The matter appears to have been regarded more seriously than it deserved, for the rebels were easily scattered by Captain L. E. L. Triscott (K.A.R. Reserve), with 100 recruits from the Zomba depôt, aided by about 40 European volunteers. Meanwhile, in answer to an urgent summons, Captain H. G. Collins (R.F.A.) was hurrying south from Karonga with a double company ('F' and 'H') of 1 K.A.R. By lake steamer and forced marches he covered eighty-six miles in forty-seven hours and reached the scene of action in time to deal with the remnants of Chilembwe's followers. Their leader was killed by the police while attempting to escape.

Before returning to Karonga, these troops took part with the lake flotilla in a small combined operation at Sphinxhaven, where the enemy was reported to be repairing the small vessel disabled there in August, 1914.[2] Before dawn on 30th May the K.A.R. landed on a beach about a mile from the harbour. At daylight the troops advanced in the face of hostile fire to attack the German defences, which consisted of a small stone fort armed with a machine gun. As they approached, the fort was bombarded from the lake, after which the askaris charged with the bayonet, only to find that their enemy had fled. The German steamer was further disabled, and the K.A.R. re-embarked under fire, carrying the German flag and some 7,000 rounds of ammunition.

Except for patrols, all continued quiet on the northern frontier of Nyasaland. German activity was practically confined to the Rhodesian sector, where for a time Belgian troops remained to assist the Northern Rhodesia Police. A stone fort was built on the Saisi River as a base for patrols. The Germans attacked it in June and again in July, but were unable to breach the walls with their artillery.

In accordance with their plans for an offensive farther north, during the course of the year the Belgians withdrew most of their troops from Rhodesia, and the fort at Saisi had to be abandoned. For a time the British defences in this area were dangerously weak, but the situation improved at the end of the year with the arrival on Lake Tanganyika of two motor-boats, the *Mimi* and *Toutou*, sent from England to the Cape

[1] A religious sect stemming from 'Jehovah's Witnesses', into whose teachings a racial significance had been woven.

[2] *vide supra*, p. 273.

and thence overland via the Belgian Congo to be assembled on the lake. The *Toutou* sank in a storm, but as the first of the German vessels to be captured was repaired and brought into British service, command of the lake was very soon gained. It was now the Germans who had to guard their shores for fear of hostile landings.

Towards the end of the year, when the invasion of German East Africa was pending from the main theatre of war in the north, simultaneous operations were planned to take place along the Rhodesia—Nyasaland frontier. To command them Brigadier-General E. Northey[1] was sent out from England. He reached Zomba at the end of January, 1916, and without delay began a lengthy tour of the whole frontier from lake to lake, reorganizing the defences and planning roads, carrier services and supplies for the forthcoming advance. Meanwhile various Rhodesian and South African units, released by the collapse of German resistance in South-West Africa, were moving north to this new theatre of war.

(vii) *Defence and Preparation for the Offensive in the North, January, 1915-February, 1916.* Map II (d).

In January, 1915, the War Office issued orders for a defensive policy along the whole of the northern front. With the coming of static conditions and the resultant apathy that affected some military units, the ravages produced by sickness grew more apparent. European and Indian troops alike were especially prone to fever in districts such as southern Uganda and the Tsavo valley. The African troops also suffered, but in general their healthier record stood out in marked contrast. It was noteworthy that officers serving with the K.A.R. had a much lower rate of sickness than those with other units.

The year 1915 was the most depressing period of the whole campaign in East Africa. The initial outburst of enthusiasm had evaporated. One by one the settlers obtained permission to return to their farms, until the strength of the newly-raised white units was halved.[2] The chief military command, now almost in disgrace at home, was influenced by local expressions of opinion that reinforced the cautious outlook following the two unsuccessful operations in the coastal area. One example of this was the view that military movement would become completely impossible during the rains. The result was the recall of all forward posts from the vicinity of Mount Kilimanjaro, on the ground that they could not be maintained.

Action at Salaita, 29th March, 1915.—To cover this withdrawal in the Voi—Tsavo area, a company of 1 K.A.R. and two companies of Baluchis made a vigorous demonstration on 29th March against the German

---

[1] Afterwards Major-General Sir Edward Northey, G.C.M.G., C.B., Governor and Commander-in-Chief, Kenya Colony, 1918-22.

[2] It was argued that East Africa was no longer in danger of being overrun, and that in view of the large numbers of troops from abroad who had to be fed and maintained, the settlers could best serve the war effort by returning to their farms. Yet in the 1939-45 war, when no policy of early release was possible, the situation on the Kenya farmlands was met and handled with success, mainly owing to the devotion and capability of the womenfolk.

position on Salaita Hill. By pushing the attack to close range the operation succeeded in drawing all the surrounding enemy forces into that sector. The British column then withdrew, rather more hastily than intended owing to a heavy concentration of fire against its right flank. On the other side of the mountain the post at Longido was also withdrawn, with the result that the Germans promptly reoccupied the site and began a series of raids against the Magadi branch line.

It was during this time of stagnation that the possibility of raising new battalions of the K.A.R. was first considered seriously. The newly-organized intelligence service in East Africa was beginning to collect unmistakable evidence of a steady increase in the German forces.[1] Since reinforcement from overseas was impossible, this could only be the result of local recruitment. On the British side, it was known that the European and Mesopotamian theatres of war were likely to absorb all the troops that could be spared from England and India for some time to come. Two battalions, however, did reach East Africa during the first part of the year: the 2nd Rhodesia Regiment and the 25th (Service) Battalion Royal Fusiliers, formed from members of the Legion of Frontiersmen. This battalion was untrained, but in view of the previous campaigning or pioneering service of its members was considered fit for service in East Africa, where it was expected to gain the necessary experience in the field.

In January Major-General Wapshare proposed, in view of the long period of inaction now forced upon him, that authority should be granted for the raising of two more battalions of the K.A.R., which he thought would take eight months to enlist and train. The Governor thought that not more than 600 suitable men could be obtained, and suggested that they should be absorbed into the existing battalions. Colonel H. E. C. Kitchener (Lord Kitchener's brother) was then on his way to East Africa to examine local resources as a whole.

The emphasis in the discussions that followed seems to have been placed mainly upon the possibility of raising fresh units of Europeans. For various reasons the civil authorities in East Africa were not anxious to recruit Africans on a large scale, nor was it thought that they could be trained in time to influence the course of the campaign. Climatic conditions in German East Africa, and their effect on white troops if an invasion of German territory lasted beyond the dry season, were not properly considered. Many officers whose experience of East Africa was limited held a poor opinion of the value of Africans as fighting troops, and thought that suitable officers would be hard to find. Doubt was cast on the wisdom of training large numbers of askari in the use of modern arms. Lord Cranworth, who was serving on Colonel Kitchener's staff, and the senior officers of the K.A.R. battalions did not agree with these

---

[1] Von Lettow's new troops were armed from the cargo of a successful blockade runner, the S.S. *Rubens*. She was chased into Manza Bay and left on fire by a British warship, but her crew extinguished the flames and landed 1,800 rifles, $4\frac{1}{2}$ million rounds of small-arms ammunition, several thousand rounds of artillery ammunition, and a quantity of other war material. Von Lettow afterwards described the failure to destroy this vessel as the greatest mistake made by the British in the whole campaign.

views, but Kitchener came to the conclusion that the value to be derived from African troops would not justify the increased expenditure. For the time being no more was heard of expanding the K.A.R.

When Major-General M. J. Tighe took command on the northern front in April, 1915, he put forward proposals for offensive operations on a limited scale. Permission was refused, and in fact, as events proved, Tighe was hard pressed during the next few months even to carry out his essential task of defending the railway. The minor operations now to be described must be imagined against a constant background of patrol activity and raids, while fever decimated the troops, rhino charged them unexpectedly in the bush, elephant attacked the railway gangs, and giraffe snapped the new telegraph routes. In theory, 1915 was a stagnant year; to the men on the spot it rarely lacked excitement.[1] Through it all the new railway crept steadily forward from Voi, accompanied by a pipe-line that tapped the water of the Bura Hills, and by the end of June had reached Maktau.

The Germans well knew what was happening. Raids upon the new line were frequent. Salaita had been their most advanced post in this area, but they now built a strong, entrenched position on a ridge of high ground astride the Taveta road at Mbuyuni. This was too close for comfort, and Brigadier-General Malleson, who commanded the area between Kilimanjaro and the coast, assembled a force at Maktau to attack it.

Attack on Mbuyuni, 14th July, 1915.—The German position was defended by 45 Europeans and 600 askaris with six machine guns. Malleson's composite force consisted of English, Rhodesian, Indian and African troops, and was about double the German strength. He divided it into two columns: one, which included two companies of 1 K.A.R. and a troop of the K.A.R. Mounted Infantry, to deliver a frontal attack; and the other, which included two companies of 4 K.A.R., to turn the enemy's left. Early on 14th July the main column reached the open valley facing the German position, with the K.A.R. leading. The force deployed, but before long all progress was held up by small arms and machine-gun fire from the concealed German trenches. Meanwhile the flanking column, led by Cole's Scouts and the two companies of 4 K.A.R., had approached the position under cover of darkness. The troops worked forward for some distance, but were then likewise halted by enemy fire.

This was all that the attack achieved. The Germans had been forewarned by a patrol that bumped the forward camp on the previous evening. Malleson's plan was simple, but there was no proper system of communication between the two columns. The attack was therefore ill-co-ordinated and lacked the flexibility needed to effect a change of plan after the troops were committed. Even so, a panic developed among the German carriers, and as the threatened left flank was weakly held their situation might soon have grown precarious. Malleson was unaware

---

[1] The part played by the K.A.R. at this time was recognized by the nickname 'Suicide Club' bestowed upon its officers by those of other units. R. V. Dolbey, *Sketches of the East Africa Campaign*, p. 6.

of this, however, and decided to withdraw. Then it was the turn of the British porters to panic. The K.A.R. companies, who had already played a major part in the battle, showed up well in the retreat. While the Punjabis lost some of their ammunition and the Loyals one of their machine guns, the two companies of 1 K.A.R. covered the main withdrawal under heavy fire, and eventually marched into camp with all their equipment and carrying their dead.[1]

From Mbuyuni and elsewhere German raiding continued unabated. At the end of July the railway was blown up no fewer than five times in a single week. Actions were fought from time to time between parties of troops from the opposing camps at Maktau and Mbuyuni. Later in the year rivalry developed for possession of Kasigao, an isolated hill that rose from the plain not far from Mackinnon Road station, and possessed the only natural water supply between that part of the line and the frontier. The enemy overwhelmed the Baluchi garrison, but later evacuated the hill, which was then reoccupied by a detachment of 3 K.A.R. under Lieutenant N. A. Kenyon-Slaney (Spec. List). In December this garrison, about half a company strong with some irregulars, was besieged by 250 of the enemy. An enemy Abyssinian N.C.O. arrived with a message demanding surrender, found some of his countrymen among the K.A.R., and in the course of conversation gave away the dispositions of the attackers. Surrender was refused and resistance continued until all ammunition was expended. Knowledge of the enemy's whereabouts then enabled the detachment to scramble down the precipitous slopes of the hill and escape. After that the Germans occupied Kasigao with a strong garrison of some 650 troops. In this advanced situation, well placed for attacks both on the main line and on the new extension, their presence constituted so dangerous a threat that some 5,000 British troops were distributed around Kasigao in a defensive semi-circle, including three companies of 3 K.A.R. along the Voi—Mackinnon Road sector, another operating from Pika Pika, a company of 1 K.A.R. from Pusa and a company of 4 K.A.R. from Goya.[2]

Until the middle of 1915 the K.A.R. were not employed in the Magadi area. By then the Germans had occupied the abandoned British post at Longido West in some strength, and as they showed signs of activity, it was decided in August to increase the British troops at Bissil. 'A' and 'B' Companies, 3 K.A.R., were among those selected.

Attack on Longido West, 20th September, 1915.—In September a column assembled under the command of Lieutenant-Colonel Jollie (28th Cavalry, I.A.) to attack the enemy position at Longido. In addition to 'A' and 'B' Companies and the Mounted Infantry of 3 K.A.R., Jollie had 135 men of the E.A.M.R. and a squadron of the 17th Cavalry. His plan was to attack from three directions with the K.A.R. and E.A.M.R., and to drive the enemy out of his position in the only direction left open,

---

[1] A description of this action from a personal viewpoint is given in Wynn E. Wynn's *Ambush*, Chapter XXX, 'The Battle of the Baobab'.

[2] Kasigao was evacuated by the enemy in January, 1916, when the advance of the railway to Mbuyuni and beyond made the position untenable.

whereupon they were to be mopped up by the cavalry, hidden out of sight upon the plain.

Jollie left Bissil Camp on 16th September. Next day, while the main column halted at Ol Doinyo Orok, the E.A.M.R. reconnoitred the German camp, which lay along a spur projecting from the southern side of the mountain. Not much information was gained, but the troops moved off after dark, to be in position at dawn. 'A' Company, 3 K.A.R., was to get above the spur and attack downhill with the bayonet. 'B' Company was to assemble below the German camp and attack uphill as soon as 'A' Company's assault materialized or, failing that, as soon as it was light enough to see. The E.A.M.R. and Mounted Infantry were to bring fire to bear from the east, i.e. the direction opposite 'B' Company.

The German camp was well sited among the rocks, covering the water supply, and more strongly defended than had been supposed. 'A' Company had a difficult climb and was not in position by daylight. 'B' Company therefore began the battle, but was soon split into groups by an unexpected maze of thorn bomas, and on reaching the crest of the ridge came under heavy fire, part of it from the E.A.M.R. and Mounted Infantry on the opposite side of the camp. At this juncture 'A' Company delivered the bayonet charge, but swung right-handed and instead of reaching the enemy came down on 'B' Company. The attack then languished, and little further progress was made. As at Mbuyuni, once the force had separated lack of communication made it impossible to change the plan. For an hour or so the firing continued, until Lieutenant-Colonel Jollie sent forward the order to retire. The affair was an unfortunate experience in which 3 K.A.R. lost 41 men killed and wounded, marched thirty-six miles and fought for several hours with very little water.[1] Some result was obtained, however, for the Germans evacuated Longido that night.

The nadir of the campaign was reached during the latter part of 1915. In spite of all the white and Indian troops that had arrived since the first few weeks when K.A.R. and settlers stood alone, sickness had taken such toll that a year after the outbreak of war Tighe informed the War Office that he had no more than 4,000 infantry fully fit. Two companies of 1 K.A.R., made up of men who had exceeded their normal period of service by more than a year, had to be sent back to Nyasaland, where all those eligible for discharge were allowed to take it. A recruiting campaign was then started to raise 500 askaris for service with 1 K.A.R. in the northern theatre. Meanwhile, as the British effectives dwindled, the German forces grew. The Europeans in East Africa demanded conscription, but it was found that only 99 of their number were not covered by the numerous exemption rules. In spite of everything, the lesson that should have been drawn from these facts, that African troops could provide the answer to the manpower problem, still remained unlearnt.

Tighe even doubted whether the railway could be safeguarded for

---

[1] This was the last occasion on which 3 K.A.R. carried unfurled flags into action. Three askaris lost their lives in succession carrying 'B' Company flag. T. O. Fitzgerald, *ibid*.

much longer. As the year drew to a close, the enemy became increasingly active. Raids took place nightly; explosions were frequent; the damage to engines, which were limited in number, grew serious. 3 K.A.R., charged with the defence of the vulnerable stretch between Samburu and Voi, had an especially anxious time. The German mines were simple, home-made affairs, consisting of tin boxes fired by springs released when trains passed over them. At night, when lights were forbidden, it was impossible to see where the ground had been disturbed, and many derailments occurred. Battalion headquarters were at Samburu, where 'A' Company was also stationed, less a detachment at Pika Pika. 'B' Company was at Maungu, and 'D', 'E' and 'G' Companies were distributed along the line. Officers cycled up and down the permanent way to visit their patrols. Life was full of exciting incidents, false alarms, and disappointments. The thick bush bordering the line was a dangerous region on more accounts than one. Lion were plentiful, and took unwary sentries from time to time. Members of patrols were sometimes known to kill one another, for at night it was difficult to prevent the troops from shooting at anything that moved. On one occasion an askari's random shot brought down an owl, neatly drilled through the neck. A multiplication of such incidents kept the railway patrols constantly upon their toes.[1]

But time was on the British side, and von Lettow was well aware of the fact. German resistance in South-West Africa had collapsed in the previous July, and after prolonged negotiations East Africa was about to be reinforced from the Union of South Africa. In London, as the autumn merged into winter and brought a lull in the operations in France and Flanders, the War Office turned its attention to the long-delayed conquest of German East Africa. The question was discussed in November at an inter-departmental conference, and then in a special sub-committee of the Committee of Imperial Defence. Sir Horace Smith-Dorrien was appointed Commander-in-Chief, and while assembling his staff in London drew up an appreciation of the position. He viewed the campaign he was to conduct solely as a conflict between two European races who happened to be on African soil. A converging attack from either side of Kilimanjaro was proposed, followed by a landing in the south, preferably at Dar-es-Salaam. The whole situation was thought out in terms of guns, aeroplanes and lorries, instead of bushcraft, carriers and quinine.

On Christmas Eve, 1915, the new Commander-in-Chief and his staff sailed for South Africa. At the start of the voyage he contracted pneumonia, and soon after his arrival at the Cape was obliged to resign. On 6th February, 1916, he was succeeded by Lieutenant-General J. C. Smuts, who lost no time in setting out for his new command.

Meanwhile Major-General Tighe was re-disposing his troops in readiness for the coming offensive. There was nothing new about the plan to attack on both sides of Kilimanjaro. Hitherto the troops had been administered and commanded in two areas, Mombasa and Nairobi. Those west of Kilimanjaro were now designated the 1st Division, while

[1] Diary of Lieutenant W. G. Edwards, 'E' Company, 3 K.A.R., January, 1916.

those in the Voi—Tsavo district became the nucleus of the 2nd Division. The area around Lake Victoria was a separate command.

This organization provided the framework into which the South African units were fitted as they began to arrive early in the new year. By February a mounted brigade, three infantry brigades and a number of artillery units had reached East Africa or were on the way. Two more Indian battalions, some artillery from England and a detachment of the Royal Naval Air Service brought the total of combatant troops to over 27,000, with 71 guns and 123 machine guns. Late in January the railway reached Mbuyuni, which had been evacuated by the enemy.[1] The plain around became a vast military camp, though lack of water forbade full concentration until operations were due to begin. The line meanwhile was pushed forward to within three miles of the German advanced position at Salaita Hill. Hoping to capture this outpost at once and so free the way for the general advance, Tighe attacked it with two brigades on 12th February, but they were repulsed in an action that showed the new South African troops that German-trained askaris were more formidable than they had supposed.[2]

Numerically, the three battalions of the K.A.R. formed but a small part of the force now assembled in East Africa. For the coming operations it was at last possible to effect some concentration of their scattered companies. 1 K.A.R. (four companies) was in the Longido area. 3 K.A.R. (five companies) concentrated at Voi and on 16th February left for Serengeti to join the 1st East African Brigade. 4 K.A.R. (four companies) was in the Tsavo—Mzima area. The question of raising new African units still remained in abeyance, for no one doubted that the coming campaign would be a short one.

So the long period of preparation, with its complicated patchwork of little actions and limited expeditions, drew to a close. On 19th February General Smuts reached Mombasa. The rains were almost due, but with characteristic energy he paid flying visits to the advanced positions at Mbuyuni and Longido and cabled to London for permission to attack forthwith. Agreement came back promptly, and by the beginning of March all was ready.

---

[1] Von Lettow, *My Reminiscences of East Africa*, p. 79, says that shortage of water was the reason for this.

[2] The K.A.R. was not engaged in this action.

CHAPTER 11

The Invasion of German East Africa
MARCH-SEPTEMBER, 1916

(i) *The Encirclement of Kilimanjaro, March-April.* Maps II (d), 13.

THE double approach around the great mountain mass of Kilimanjaro was retained by Smuts as the basis of his plan, though he changed the method of carrying it into effect. The eastern route, supplied and watered by the new railway and pipe-line, was to be the scene of the main attack, though it was here that the enemy was ready to offer the strongest resistance. There were three defensible positions on this route into German territory: Salaita Hill, the Lumi River, and the twin ridges of Latema and Reata, which stood behind the frontier village of Taveta. These two hills lay just south of the Moshi road, and the track to Kahe, the first station on the Tanga Railway south of the terminus at New Moshi, ran between them. To advance by the eastern route therefore meant driving the enemy through a bottle-neck, with the foothills of Kilimanjaro to the north, and the thick mass of bush, marsh and swamp that lay around Lake Jipe and the River Ruvu to the south. On the other hand, to encircle the mountain via Longido from the north and west meant crossing long, waterless stretches and then traversing the little-known areas of forest and ravine that lay beyond.

The 1st Division, under Major-General J. M. Stewart, was to advance from Longido. Its cavalry included the K.A.R. Mounted Infantry, and its infantry the four companies of 1 K.A.R., under Captain G. J. Giffard, attached to the 2nd East African Brigade. The rôle of this Division was to threaten von Lettow's line of retreat by crossing the River Sanya, attacking Moshi and Kahe, and so cutting the railway. Meanwhile the enemy's prepared positions on the eastern route were to be outflanked by South African mounted troops and infantry under Major-General J. L. van Deventer, who was to execute a turning movement and seize the Chala heights. The main attack on these positions was then to be driven home by the 2nd Division, commanded by Major-General M. J. Tighe. The five companies of 3 K.A.R. were included in this Division, as part of the 1st East African Brigade. 4 K.A.R. (with the exception of one company at Mwele, near the coast) was now back in Uganda, with headquarters and two companies on the Kagera Line and the other five companies in reserve.

The 1st Division, which had the longest way to go, set out from Longido on 5th March. The column advanced through the gap between Mounts Kilimanjaro and Meru, and entered the difficult country of desert, bush and forest that flanked the lower slopes of the mountain. Heavy rain made the tracks difficult and progress was slow. Stewart sent his cavalry ahead, but they were unable to cope with the bush and had

1 K.A.R. entering Longido Camp, 1916

[Crown Copyright

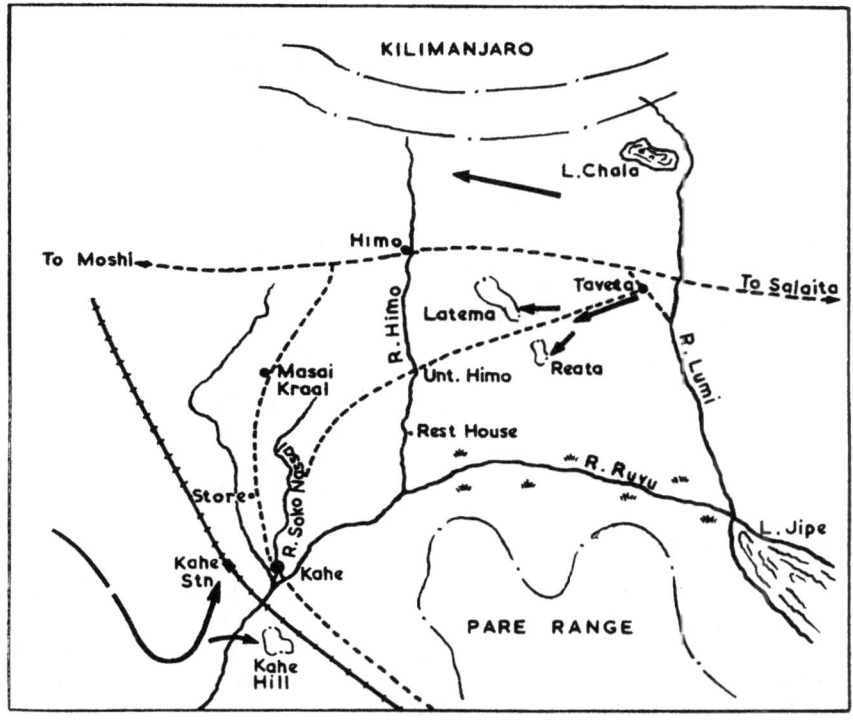

13. The Taveta—Kahe Area

to be withdrawn.[1] A company of 1 K.A.R., supported by Punjabis and artillery, was then detailed as advance guard and reached the Sanya River without sighting the enemy. While the advance continued a party of the enemy located the cavalry, now well in the rear with the transport, and fought a short action, though in the general obscurity neither side realized the true state of affairs. After this the cavalry had to be guided forward to join the infantry. In spite of messages from Smuts urging him to hurry, Stewart found the going so difficult for his baggage train that he failed to reach the railway in time to block the German retreat, and the chance of achieving a decisive effect was lost. When at last his troops did approach the line, with 1 K.A.R. still in the lead, they found themselves under fire from van Deventer's South Africans, who had not yet learnt to distinguish between the British and German askari uniforms.[2]

On 7th March, two days after the advance from Longido began, van Deventer's troops set out to turn the left flank of the enemy, followed by the Force Reserve. The Lumi was crossed and the heights of Chala occupied. Meanwhile the 1st East African Brigade was holding the divi-

---

[1] Cavalry were not a success in the East African campaign. Thick bush, uncertain water supplies, and the presence of tsetse fly rendered conditions most unsuitable for this arm.

[2] The advance guard point was carrying a Union Jack 3 ft. x 6 ft. in size. One askari was slightly wounded, and three porters and a mule were killed.

sional front, with 3 K.A.R. on outpost duty at Nyoro Drift, about 4,000 yards short of Salaita Hill. Under this cover the artillery deployed and on the morning of 8th March carried out a long bombardment of the German position.

Smuts began his main advance on 9th March. The artillery bombardment reopened and continued for several hours. Soon after noon Smuts ordered his forward troops to take the hill, and the infantry advanced across the open, with 3 K.A.R. in the lead. But the flanking movement had had the desired effect. Salaita was deserted, and by four o'clock the position that had previously proved so formidable was occupied unopposed. As Salaita had been evacuated several hours before, the enemy got across the Lumi before the bridge could be seized, leaving behind his field telegraph cable, slung at giraffe height on 20-foot poles, with empty beer-bottles as insulators.

On 10th March the advance was resumed, and the Division crossed the Lumi. 3 K.A.R. left Salaita at 8.15 a.m. and marched through thick bush to the river. The Lumi was only about two feet deep, but the approaches were steep and difficult, and while a new bridge was being built to get the guns and transport over, 3 K.A.R. held the farther bank to cover the crossing.

Battle of Latema Nek, 11th-12th March, 1916.—The enemy now stood in strength[1] on the Latema—Reata ridge, and here the first serious action was fought. Owing to the position of these two hills and the nature of the country, flank attacks were impracticable. On 11th March three battalions of the 1st East African Brigade (2 Rhodesia Regiment, 130 Baluchis and 3 K.A.R.) were ordered to carry the hills by direct assault. The troops took up position with the K.A.R. on the left, the Baluchis on the right, and the Rhodesians in reserve. Latema was the first engagement ever fought by 3 K.A.R. as a unit. Lieutenant-Colonel Graham deployed his battalion with 'B' and 'G' Companies in the line, 'A' and 'D' in reserve.[2] The attack moved forward across a wide stretch of open country and entered the thick scrub lining the base of the hills. At 1,000 yards from the enemy position the troops were halted by heavy rifle and machine-gun fire. A long pause ensued while the artillery opened up in support. About 2 p.m. the advance was resumed. Graham had come forward himself with 'D' Company, and some further progress was made during the next hour. The higher command was not at this time anxious to push the assault too vigorously as van Deventer, well out on the right, was moving towards Moshi and it was thought that the Germans would give way on finding that their position had been turned. Before daylight faded, however, Major-General Tighe, who was now directing the battle in person, sent forward the Rhodesians, who, joining the K.A.R., dashed at the double up the steep, bush-covered slope of the ridge. Graham was killed at the head of his troops, but isolated parties reached the top, where they maintained themselves in the gathering dark-

---

[1] About 1,000 rifles with three guns and eight machine guns.

[2] 'E' Company was on garrison duty at Taveta, with some platoons employed on picquets and patrols.

ness until the Germans counter-attacked and drove most of them off. 'A' Company on the left flank was attacked from Reata and also retired.

An attack was now made by two battalions of South African infantry. Once again several parties gained the top of the ridge, though most of the troops were driven back. Smuts refused further reinforcements, and the attacking force was then withdrawn. At daylight British troops were seen on the ridge, which was then occupied. The Germans had long since withdrawn, and were out of sight in the thick forest below. The great chase across mountain, bush and swamp, that was only to be terminated by the signing of the Armistice in Europe, was about to begin.

3 K.A.R. lost more heavily than any other unit at Latema. Three officers (including a medical officer) were killed and one died later of wounds; 11 other ranks were killed, and with wounded and missing the total casualties came to 81. The loss of Graham, a gallant and well-loved officer of long experience in East Africa, was felt very keenly.[1] His death was apparently caused by a German machine-gunner, who called out in English to deceive him, and then shot him through the neck.[2] On 12th March the battalion concentrated at Taveta, and two days later Major (afterwards Lieutenant-Colonel) T. O. Fitzgerald took command.

Van Deventer's mounted troops, now able to move unimpeded into Moshi, reached the terminus of the Tanga Railway on 14th March and joined forces with the 1st Division. But the trap had failed to close in time. Von Lettow had extricated his force and withdrawn some way down the line.

The task now before the Force was to clear the whole Kilimanjaro area up to the River Ruvu, before the rains brought operations to a temporary standstill. From Lake Jipe the Ruvu flowed west through a maze of swamp and forest to form with the Himo, Soko Nassai, and other tributaries the headwaters of the Pangani. The river was deep and full of crocodiles, and the banks of the network of streams that intersected the area were covered with bush, often impenetrable. The enemy had now deployed in a wide arc covering the Ruvu, particularly strong on the left flank, where his escape route lay down the Tanga Railway and the road that ran parallel to it.

Once again General Smuts planned to cut the railway in rear of the German position while delivering a frontal attack in strength. A patrol of 1 K.A.R. reconnoitred the enemy positions at Kahe, which were to be attacked by the South African Mounted Infantry, moving in a wide sweep through the bush to cross the Pangani and cut the railway below the station. While this was in progress the 1st Division was to attack down the road from Moshi, the 2nd Division to operate from Taveta, and the South African Infantry between the two. The bush was thick everywhere, with outlying hills, many of them occupied by German

---

[1] 'Walked up to see the Colonel's grave and to pay my respects to a really fine human man whose loss to us all cannot be replaced.' (From the diary of a 3 K.A.R. subaltern, 13.iii.16.)

[2] J. H. V. Crowe, *General Smuts' Campaign in East Africa*, p. 80.

outposts, rising here and there above the sea of brown and green.

In the action that followed, the K.A.R. played only a minor part. The advance began on 18th March. The 1st Division met strong resistance and had to withdraw. The South African brigades in the centre carried some of the outlying hills. Next day the 1st Division drove the enemy down the road and advanced as far as Store,[1] but the South African infantry were recalled from their attempt to force a passage down the banks of the Himo, and Smuts decided to concentrate on Kahe. Van Deventer therefore set out from New Moshi on his turning movement. While he was negotiating the twenty-five miles of bush that lay between him and the Pangani, the enemy delivered a series of determined night attacks on the troops who had dug in around Store, but were finally beaten off with loss.

On reaching the Pangani, van Deventer could find no place to cross. Turning up-river towards the railway, he saw enemy troops occupying Kahe Hill on the farther bank. In spite of the depth and speed of the river, two squadrons got across and seized the hill. By now the alarm had been given, and the enemy moved out of Kahe to meet the column. Retreating slowly, they evacuated the railway station and blew up the bridge. Meanwhile the 1st Division had renewed its drive down the road from the direction of Store. When the attack met the German positions hidden in the dense bush lining the banks of the Soko Nassai, it came to a halt and the troops dug in for the night. Next morning the Germans were miles away and out of touch. Von Lettow had once again extricated his force, and gone twenty miles down the line to Lembeni, where the track could be enfiladed as it swept in a wide curve into the hills.

During this action 1 K.A.R. had been held in reserve, but was now brought forward to establish a bridgehead on the south bank of the Ruvu. On the British left flank patrols of 3 K.A.R. had been out in the forest, destroying log bridges over the Lumi and searching for scattered parties of the enemy who were still reported in the area. Detached companies were sent to picquet the hills near Unterer Himo and the bridge at the German Rest House, in support of the forward troops. On 29th March the battalion was ordered back to Taveta, and from there to Mbuyuni to rest and train. With the enemy driven off the flank of the British advance the first phase of the operations was complete, and the way was clear for the railway extension to be brought forward and linked with the Tanga line, ready for a resumption of the offensive when the slackening of the rains allowed. Meanwhile most of the troops moved back from the Ruvu to higher and healthier localities.

In preparation for the next move, Smuts reorganized his force into three divisions: the 1st Division (Major-General A. R. Hoskins), to consist of the 1st East African Brigade (Brigadier-General S. H. Sheppard) and the 2nd East African Brigade (Brigadier-General J. A. Hannyngton); and the 2nd and 3rd Divisions, under Major-General van Deventer and Major-General C. J. Brits respectively, each to consist of one South African mounted and one infantry brigade. In spite of the

---

[1] An Indian *duka*, so marked on the German maps, that became an advanced depôt of some importance.

experiences of the past few weeks, Smuts still thought that cavalry would justify its employment once von Lettow was on the run. Arrangements were also made for the provision of troops from West Africa.

But the most far-reaching decision was Smuts' acceptance of a scheme for expanding the K.A.R.[1] The old objection that the campaign would be over before fresh units could be trained was met by the argument that in any case a much larger garrison than three K.A.R. battalions would be needed in East Africa in future. Hoskins held a conference of senior K.A.R. officers at Nairobi on 6th April, when it was suggested that several new battalions should be raised. The Colonial Secretary agreed to a joint proposal by the Governor and the Commander-in-Chief that the K.A.R. should be regarded as Imperial troops for the rest of the war. With the exception of certain reservations in Nyasaland, unified command was thus achieved.

Recruiting for the northern theatre had opened in Nyasaland at the end of 1915. Military service was popular, and over a thousand men reached East Africa early in the new year. Before the general decision to expand the K.A.R. was taken, the War Office had agreed to the formation of a new battalion with these Nyasaland recruits and former askaris, and on 1st April, 1916, 2 K.A.R. was reconstituted at Nairobi.

Recruits for the other battalions now came forward in large numbers. No more Sudanese or Abyssinians could be obtained, so in East Africa other tribes—Wakamba, Meru, Kipsikis—were enlisted instead. In Nyasaland and North-East Rhodesia recruiting was particularly good, and during July and August nearly 1,800 men were obtained for 1/2 and 2/2 K.A.R. As the regiment was now committed to major operations, irregular levies such as the Nandi Scouts and Baganda Rifles were used increasingly for guard and patrol duties, especially around Lake Victoria.

Now that the German armed forces were fully occupied on the mainland, the danger to Zanzibar receded. Soon after the declaration of war all able-bodied Europeans had been enrolled in a Town Guard to assist the K.A.R. company. In November, 1914, the British Resident asked for a whole battalion. Four companies of the Gwalior Rifles were sent. The Town Guard was then reorganized as the Zanzibar Volunteer Defence Force, which was later increased by a company of native police At the end of April, 1915, the K.A.R. garrison was withdrawn. The Gwalior Rifles followed in October, and Zanzibar was left to defend herself. The result was the formation of two local levies, the Zanzibar African Rifles and the Mafia Armed Constabulary.[2]

(ii) *The Advance to the Msiha River, May-June.* Maps V (b), 14.

The second stage of Smuts' invasion involved a march down the Pangani, the clearing of the Tanga Railway line, and an advance on to the central plateau. In all these operations 3 K.A.R. and the Mounted Infantry played an active part.

[1] Lieutenant-Colonel C. Hordern, *Military Operations, East Africa*, Vol. I, App. IV, pp. 561-63.

[2] Further details of the expansion of the K.A.R. are given in Chapter 12, section (i).

The rains were late in 1916. When at last they broke they were unduly heavy, swamping the branch railway from Voi, flooding the rivers and streams, and converting the bush tracks and earth roads into quagmires sometimes as difficult for men and animals as for wheeled traffic.

Rain exercised an important influence over the operations ahead. During the lull that followed in the Kilimanjaro area it would have been possible to effect a major switch of forces, with the object of advancing from Lake Victoria to the German supply centre at Tabora, or of organizing a new invasion by sea to strike inland up the river valleys. The latter seemed the more likely strategy, since it offered the chance of capturing the railways as main arteries of supply and at the same time depriving the enemy of their use. There were, however, many practical difficulties, and Smuts rejected the idea in favour of a direct invasion of the country 'across the grain' from north to south, supplied from the advanced base that he had already acquired and was in process of building up.[1]

About two hundred miles of difficult country lay between the two German railways at their nearest point of approach, which lay far south of the Ruvu down the Tanga line. A renewed attack along this railway, in the valley between the Pare range and the Pangani, was clearly what von Lettow expected and was prepared to resist, knowing that his presence was still a threat to the Uganda Railway.[2] Such an approach, with the Pangani on one side and the mountains on the other, would be very difficult as long as the rains continued. Smuts decided, therefore, to begin his advance from another direction altogether, in the hope that this would cause von Lettow to detach some of his troops to meet the unexpected threat, and so weaken the opposition to be faced in the Pangani valley.

There were only two practicable lines of advance: through Handeni and the Nguru Mountains to Morogoro, or from Arusha to Kondoa Irangi and thence by several tracks to Dodoma or other places on the Central Line. The latter route was thought likely to be the drier of the two, and as it was known to be lightly defended Smuts decided to seize Kondoa Irangi before von Lettow could reinforce it. The task was allotted to the 2nd Division.

The enemy had a strong outpost on a large, isolated hill that rose above the plain at Lokisale, thirty-five miles from Arusha. On 1st April the 1st South African Mounted Brigade captured the position, and the rest of the Division was then able to follow the Mounted Brigade south. The rains proved far worse than expected. Horse sickness depleted the cavalry; the tracks became morasses; men and animals were continually soaked and could never be properly fed. When the Mounted Brigade drove the German forces from the hills before Kondoa Irangi their limit had been reached. The infantry struggled through a fortnight later. But the purpose had been achieved. Von Lettow detached the greater part

---

[1] Smuts' Despatch, 27.x.16.

[2] German raids on the Uganda Railway still continued during April and May, 1916.

of his troops from the Pangani area, and with these and other forces, numbering about 4,000 men all told, he attacked van Deventer at Kondoa Irangi on 9th May. By that time the South Africans were strong enough to repel the assault. An inconclusive engagement ended in stalemate, a state of affairs that lasted throughout May and most of June.

Now that the defenders of the Tanga Railway had been weakened, Smuts decided on a rapid advance to Handeni before the enemy forces sent to Kondoa Irangi could be recalled to oppose him. If this succeeded, the Germans still left in the Usambara region would be effectively isolated, and it would then be unlikely that von Lettow could concentrate enough troops to bar both approach routes to the Central Railway simultaneously.

Speed was essential. By the middle of May the rains were slackening. Major Kraut, commanding the Usambara forces, was believed to have not more than 2,000 rifles and some artillery. Reconnaissance showed several defensive positions along the railway, and as the Germans retired, their demolitions would no doubt be thorough. Smuts therefore decided to outflank the railway on both sides, and make a threefold advance on Bwiko to clear the enemy from the Pare Mountains and the upper reaches of the Pangani. With this in view he regrouped the 1st and 3rd Divisions into three columns. The largest, or River Column, under the command of Brigadier-General Sheppard, was to move as rapidly as possible down the left bank of the Pangani, where the bush was reported to be sufficiently open to permit its passage. The Centre Column, commanded by Brigadier-General Hannyngton, was to force the Germans out of their prepared positions along the railway. The Eastern Column was to approach the Pare from Mbuyuni, enter the hills by way of the valley through which the River Ngulu flows north to Lake Jipe, and continue along the eastern slopes to join the railway at Mkomazi. This column was commanded by Lieutenant-Colonel T. O. Fitzgerald, and its combatant units consisted of a company of the K.A.R. Mounted Infantry, 3 K.A.R., and a section of 27 Mountain Battery.

Throughout April and the first three weeks of May, 3 K.A.R. had been in camp at Mbuyuni, splashing around in the rain, holding frequent parades, practising night marching, performing fatigues, playing football, and taking part in brigade exercises. There were no regrets when the news came that Smuts was about to resume the advance. Owing to its distant starting-point and the hilly nature of the ground, Fitzgerald's column started first. 'A' Company, the advance guard, left Mbuyuni for the Ngulu Gap on 18th May. At 10.30 p.m. on the 20th the rest of the column, extended over two miles by a long line of transport carts, began its march. The night was dry but cool, and by the time camp was made at dawn on the 21st, the column was close to the Pare Mountains.

On the night of the 22nd Fitzgerald resumed his march. At half-past nine next morning the small German post at Nyata, near the head of the Ngulu valley, was taken by surprise. After firing at the Mounted Infantry the German in charge departed hurriedly with his handful of askaris, leaving his breakfast, a freshly killed goat, behind him on the table. With access thus gained to the mountain range, the column rested for a day while the Mounted Infantry patrolled to the south and news was collected from natives visiting the camp.

By now the River and Centre Columns had also begun their advance. Patrols reported that the defensive positions on the railway at Kisangire and Lembeni had been abandoned. Along the river bank grass plains and sandy nullahs alternated with patches of thick forest. The heat was exhausting, especially during the early stages of the march, when the leading troops often had to cut a path for the rest of the column.

On 26th May Fitzgerald continued. Another small post was surprised and captured in the hills. That evening, when the Column camped at the pleasant water-hole of Maji ya Njuu, Fitzgerald heard that the Centre Column, now at Same, was leaving the railway and turning east through the hills to join him at Mandi. Smuts no longer expected serious opposition until he reached the point farther south, near Mikocheni, where road, rail and river run close together below the escarpment, and he therefore intended to strengthen the eastern arm of his advance, hoping to take the enemy in rear by approaching down the valley of the River Mkomazi. The junction of the two columns took place on 27th May, Brigadier-General Hannyngton assuming command of both.

Hannyngton's combined column continued its march on the 28th. The track, now a road of some importance serving the German rubber plantations, was splendidly aligned around the curves of the hills; no obstructions were met, and all bridges were intact. But beyond Gonya, which was reached in the early afternoon of the 29th, it was a different story. The bridge had been smashed, and 3 K.A.R. worked all night to repair it. Thereafter a succession of blown bridges and felled trees faced the column throughout its long, dusty march down the Mkomazi valley, and eventually forced Hannyngton to diverge eastwards and march through the hills. On the 31st he was approaching the railway. Two gaps appeared on the crest in front. 'A' and 'D' Companies, 3 K.A.R., and the Mounted Infantry were sent ahead to one of them, and the E.A.M.R. to the other. Both parties came under fire and were ordered to dig in. Mkomazi station lay six miles ahead, and the shelling came from a 4.1 inch *Königsberg* gun, mounted on a railway truck.[1]

Meanwhile, after a march of 112 miles, the River Column had reached Mabirioni, where a short halt was made while Hannyngton's column got into position. The Rhodesians then attacked the enemy at Mikocheni, while the Baluchis climbed into the hills on the flank. The Germans were driven out of their trenches and were already retiring through Bwiko when Hannyngton reached the hills overlooking the railway. On 1st June the two columns gained touch at Mkomazi.

When Smuts' headquarters reached Bwiko a halt was ordered, as supplies were well to the rear and all troops were on half rations. Some German civilians at Moshi had been heard to boast that it would take two years to turn their forces out of the Pare and Usambara Mountains, but the first stage had been accomplished in less than a fortnight. For

---

[1] The *Königsberg's* armour-piercing shells did little damage unless they registered a direct hit, but the arrival of the blockade-runner (p. 290, f.n.) provided them with more suitable ammunition.

the moment, however, the invasion had reached its limit. The railway was not yet functioning; the overburdened road transport needed overhaul; repairs and improvements were urgently needed along the rough tracks carved out by the River Column, and the troops were going sick with fever in large numbers. While work began on a half-finished trestle bridge that the Germans had started over the Pangani, Smuts paid a brief visit to the 2nd Division at Kondoa Irangi, instructing Hoskins to resume the advance as soon as possible.

Smuts hoped to bring von Lettow to a decisive battle and so end the campaign somewhere on the Central Railway. With this in view, his intention was to gain Handeni, a German administrative boma where several roads converged upon the new military highway, and so drive a wedge between von Lettow and Kraut's 'Northern Army', which could be defeated in detail. A dual advance from Handeni and Kondoa Irangi would then cut the Central Railway at two points and perhaps trap the main German force between. Kraut was now at Mombo, whence a trolley line ran to Mkalamo, crossed the Pangani, and continued to Endarema, just beyond Handeni. This line and the road farther south from Korogwe offered Kraut two possible escape routes. Smuts' plan was therefore to cross the Pangani with Sheppard's column and find a way down the right bank, while Hannyngton pressed forward along the road and railway that ran parallel to the Usambara range.

3 K.A.R. got little rest at Mkomazi. On 4th June the Mounted Infantry went ahead and found the enemy strongly entrenched at the Ngoha River, seven miles down the line. 'B' and 'D' Companies, 3 K.A.R., and a detachment of Baluchis followed, and on 7th June the rest of Hannyngton's column, with two K.A.R. companies in the lead. The way led through cultivated shambas, where the askaris were permitted to help themselves to sugar-cane, and enjoyed that night the luxury of roasted mealies. At dawn on the 8th the march continued through European plantations and native shambas. Mazinde was reached and a hold-up occurred for some hours while bridge repairs were undertaken. Next day the enemy was found in position before Mombo. The 40th Pathans, who were then in the lead, deployed for the attack, while 3 K.A.R. moved round through the rubber plantations at the foot of the hills. After two hours' fighting the enemy retired, leaving the station and railway bridge completely wrecked, and at 2 p.m. the column entered the town. Next day the German District Commissioner came to surrender the civilian headquarters at Wilhelmstal, where large numbers of women and children had collected. Troops of the K.A.R. Mounted Infantry were sent to take over the town.

On 11th June the march along road and railway was resumed to the sound of distant explosions. For the next two days progress was slow as repairs were effected to demolished bridges and culverts. Resistance was stiffening, and the Mounted Infantry, who had been constantly in the lead, ran into an ambush that cost them half a dozen casualties and nine of their mounts. At 10 a.m. on 14th June the column entered Mauri and so reached once more the banks of the Pangani, to find that the railway bridge over the river had been destroyed.

By this time it was evident that Hannyngton's column was opposed by the German rearguard. Kraut, with the rest of the 'Northern Army', had concentrated about Mkalamo in the path of Sheppard's column, which was now advancing through thick and swampy bush down the right bank of the Pangani. The two forces came into action on 9th June. After a confused fight in very dense bush west of Mkalamo, Kraut withdrew under cover of darkness towards Handeni.

Hannyngton's column was still north of the Pangani. When the time came to rejoin the main advance, the only feasible route, now that the railway bridge at Mauri had gone, would be by means of the Zuganatto bridge just short of Korogwe, whence an excellent military road crossed the river and ran via Kwamhere to Handeni.[1] The possession of this bridge was therefore a matter of the highest importance. To press the frontal attack would be fatal, and Lieutenant-Colonel Fitzgerald was ordered to take his battalion over the Pangani by means of a native crossing near Mauri, march along the south bank under cover of darkness, and seize the Zuganatto bridge at dawn. It was the kind of operation for which 3 K.A.R. was well fitted.

Action at the Zuganatto Bridge, 15th June, 1916.—Fitzgerald moved out of Mauri at 10 p.m. on 14th June. The Pangani ran through a deep gorge, and the 'native crossing' proved to be a rickety swinging bridge and a succession of tree trunks thrown across the different arms of the river, which was broken at that spot into swirling torrents. To negotiate such obstacles in the dark was not easy, and by 3 a.m. on the 15th only two companies were over. As daylight was due in three hours' time, Fitzgerald decided to march at once, leaving the rest of the battalion to follow.

It was about nine miles from Mauri to the bridge, and dawn was breaking when the leading platoon gained touch with the enemy at 1,000 yards' distance. As quickly as possible the two companies deployed, seized a hill commanding the German trenches, and brought machine-gun fire to bear on the bridge, which was defended by strong positions at either end. Across practically open country Lieutenant B. C. E. von Otter (Spec. List) worked his platoon forward and with a maxim silenced two enemy machine guns.[2] By 7 a.m. another company had joined the attack. At nine o'clock the Germans fell back over the bridge to the north bank, and soon afterwards broke off the action and withdrew towards Korogwe, leaving the bridge intact. It was found that preparations had been made to burn it.

3 K.A.R. marched back to Mauri, arriving late the same evening. While their action was in progress Hannyngton had moved with his main column down the roadway towards Korogwe, which he entered at 11 a.m. after slight resistance. Though the railway station was wrecked, it was possible to purchase a few articles in the town, such as cigarettes, soap and coffee, that were particularly welcome supplements to the rations.

---

[1] This road had been specially constructed to supply the German army in the north, and at least 8,000 carriers had been continuously employed upon it. Von Lettow, *op. cit.*, p. 52.

[2] Von Otter was awarded the M.C. for his part in this action.

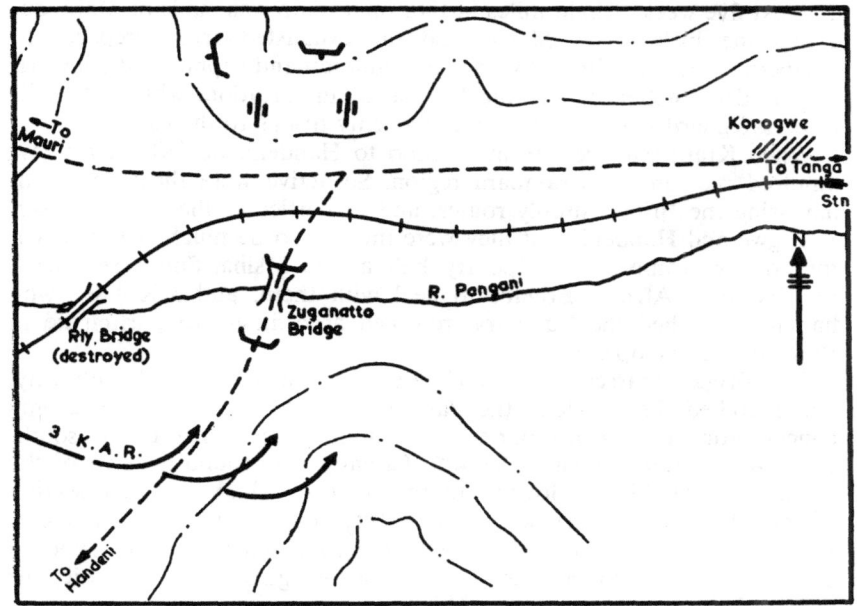

14. Attack on Zuganatto Bridge, 15th June, 1916

At Korogwe Hannyngton received the expected order to rejoin the main advance. Leaving some Indian troops to guard the town against the remnant of the German forces that had now disappeared down the railway, he crossed the Zuganatto Bridge with his column, and advancing by forced marches along the military road, gained touch with the rest of the force near Handeni on 19th June. After the engagement at Mkalamo, Smuts had returned from Kondoa Irangi and leaving the Pangani at Luchomo had crossed the waterless tract to the south,[1] found the enemy in position before Handeni, and dislodged him by a wide flanking movement to the west, combined with a frontal attack.

By this time the difficulties of further pursuit were severe. Shortage of water, however, made it impossible to halt long at Handeni; the chance of a decisive action on the Central Railway seemed at hand, and Smuts decided to push on at all cost. Apart from some scouting by the Mounted Infantry, 3 K.A.R. was not much concerned in the operations of the next two or three weeks, and had time to construct a camp of grass bandas on the hill opposite the German boma. Meanwhile the enemy was steadily driven south until he turned to resist on the high ground beyond the River Lukigura. On 24th June Smuts turned the left of this position with a mobile column that approached through the bush and surprised the defenders with a sudden bayonet charge. For the first time the German troops were completely routed in battle, and lost all their machine guns and one of their field guns.

The action at the Lukigura marked the end of the main advance for

[1] The agonies of this march are described by F. Brett Young in *Marching on Tanga*, pp. 177-82.

the next five weeks. Eight miles farther on a camp was made at Makindu, across the little River Msiha, and the exhausted army prepared to recuperate, refit, and bring forward ammunition and supplies. Much work was needed on the lengthening line of communication, which had still to be safeguarded from the threat of enemy troops to the east.

When Kraut withdrew from Mombo to Handeni, he left only a few hundred men in the Usambara region. So active were these forces in harassing the British supply routes, and in particular the road between Korogwe and Handeni, that they were thought to be much larger. When the advance came to a temporary halt at the Msiha, Smuts sent back the 2nd East African Brigade to deal with them, and 3 K.A.R., who had now reached the Lukigura, returned accordingly to participate in these subsidiary operations.

The Brigade passed through Handeni on the morning of 14th July, and marched thence along the Pangani road to Makanya. An enemy concentration had been reported at Mzundu, a few miles to the southeast. Hannyngton detached the 40th Pathans, who found no sign of the enemy. On the 17th, following another report, 3 K.A.R. and a section of the Mountain Battery were sent twenty miles south to Kwa Konje. Enemy picquets were contacted and driven in, and Fitzgerald detached part of his force to cut the Kwa Konje—Ruguzi road, by which he expected the enemy to retire. This manœuvre succeeded in capturing a German baggage train, but when at 1.30 p.m. the K.A.R. marched into Kwa Konje they found that the enemy had escaped by another route.

Next day 3 K.A.R. rejoined the Brigade at Mzundu. The elusive enemy was also being attacked by line of communication troops from the north, and to co-operate in this movement Hannyngton sent a column consisting of the Kashmir Rifles, a company of 3 K.A.R. and a section of the Mountain Battery to Mgambo Kadodo, where the enemy was reported in force. As the column did not arrive until after nightfall, the attack was postponed until next morning, when, as usual, the enemy position was found deserted.

At the end of July the Brigade was ordered back to Handeni, after two exhausting weeks of incessant marching for little result. 3 K.A.R. found some consolation in the arrival of their second-line transport. For the first time since leaving Mbuyuni the men had blankets as well as groundsheets.

Eventually the enemy forces east of the Korogwe—Handeni road were driven south. The Navy was operating along the coast, and Tanga and the Umba valley were occupied by Indian units. The nights spent on the fever-laden banks of the Pangani now bore their inevitable fruit, and sickness took an increasing toll of men and animals.[1] But the morale of the army was good; the Nguru mountains were in sight across the southern horizon, and beyond them lay the country traversed by the Central Railway.

---

[1] The Indian units suffered particularly from lack of suitable food, and a kind of dysentery spread rapidly until they learnt that mealie husks must be removed before cooking the grain.

(iii) *The Advance to the Central Railway*.[1] Maps V (a), V (d), 15, 16.

The 2nd Division moved first.

By the end of June, Smuts' advance beyond Handeni had forced von Lettow to recall most of his troops from Kondoa Irangi, and by the third week in July, van Deventer was ready to resume his advance. Several routes led towards the Central Railway, and on Smuts' instructions the main thrust took place along the most easterly of these, the intention being to close up towards Morogoro, the objective of the Handeni column, in the hope of surrounding the enemy's main force. Unfortunately, as events soon showed, von Lettow had no intention of being caught.

Van Deventer began his march south on 19th July. At Haneti the main column divided, the cavalry proceeding south-east to Nyangalo, and the infantry south, following the German rearguard directly towards the railway. Meanwhile two smaller columns were clearing the right flank along the tracks to Mponde and Singida. Dodoma was reached on 29th July; the cavalry, after fighting an action at Nyangalo, sent one regiment on to Kikombo, and the smaller columns cut the line at Saranda. The enemy had eluded van Deventer's grasp and retired eastward in good order, but by mid-August he had secured a considerable sector of the railway and concentrated the bulk of his force at Nyangalo, ready for the next move.

There was no likelihood that the 1st and 3rd Divisions, which constituted the main advance and were commanded by General Smuts in person, could reach the Central Railway so easily. South of the River Msiha the road skirted the eastern flank of the Nguru Mountains, from which many streams flowed to join the Lukigura and the Wami. Throughout July the Germans had been preparing their defences, which now barred the route in considerable strength where it ran below the Ruhungu spur, protected on one side by the steep slopes of the mountain and on the other by the dense bush, high grass and swamp of the Lukigura valley. The road itself was mined and blocked by fallen trees.

The Germans apparently thought that the Nguru range was too difficult for troops to cross in strength. But reconnaissance showed that the great mountain mass was split by the valleys of two rivers, the Mjonga and the

---

[1] Abridged Order of Battle, 5th August, 1916:

1ST DIVISION (Hoskins)

1st E.A. Bde. (Sheppard)	*2nd E.A. Bde.* (Hannyngton)	*Div. Troops*
29 Punjabis	3 Kashmir Rifles	E.A.M.R.
130 Baluchis	57 Wilde's Rifles	25 R. Fus.
2 Kashmir Rifles	3 K.A.R.	2 Rhodesia R.
		Cape Corps Bn.

Attached: K.A.R.M.I.

3RD DIVISION (Brits)

2nd S.A. Mtd. Bde. (Enslin)	*2nd S.A. Inf. Bde.* (Beves)
5 S.A. Horse	5 S.A. Inf.
6 ,, ,,	6 ,, ,,
7 ,, ,,	
8 ,, ,,	

Lwale, which flowed from north to south to join the Wami. Scouts reported that it would be possible to reach the head of these valleys, in which small bodies of enemy troops were stationed, and by following their course to converge on Turiani, where the main road crossed the Lwale as it debouched from the hills. If this movement could be started in secret and carried out in conjunction with a holding attack on the main German position, there was a good chance of forestalling the customary retreat.

Throughout the period of inactivity the enemy had been pounding Msiha Camp with his long-range naval guns, to which the British forces could make no effective reply. All movements in this area were in clear view of the German look-out posts in the hills. Smuts therefore assembled the troops for the turning movement out of sight along the Lukigura. The 3rd Division, led by the 2nd South African Mounted Brigade, was to follow the valley of the Lwale and seize Turiani, while the 2nd East African Brigade advanced down the course of the Mjonga. The attack on the main German defences at Ruhungu was to be delivered by the 1st East African Brigade.

The concentration on the Lukigura was carried out during the first few days of August. As part of the 2nd East African Brigade, 3 K.A.R. left Handeni early on 2nd August and completed the forty-four-mile march before 1 p.m. on the 3rd.[1] By the following day the concentration was complete, and on 5th August the 3rd Division, which had to cover the greater distance, moved into the hills. On the 6th the 2nd East African Brigade began its march, with the 57th Wilde's Rifles in advance. The way was difficult and progress slow, but that evening the Brigade reached Mahasi, where it was to enter the Mjonga valley.

Next day the 2nd Brigade began its march down the valley, with 3 K.A.R. leading. Obstacles were encountered every few miles and enemy picquets were met and driven off. Diverging into the hills to the right of the valley, Kwa Chengo was reached at noon, the German occupation troops retiring when the Brigade deployed. Meanwhile in the Lwale valley the going had proved so difficult that most of the column had been ordered back to the Lukigura, leaving the advance to continue with light forces only.

The transport of the 2nd East African Brigade was likewise unable to proceed beyond Mahasi. While the Kashmiris occupied the former German position at Kwa Chengo, Hannyngton withdrew the rest of his Brigade for several miles while all porters and mules returned to bring forward the rations. To the enemy this delay was invaluable. On 9th August the Brigade, which had been joined during the night by a column of South African Horse, advanced laboriously for another five miles to Matamondo, where the enemy was found in position on high ground, waiting to dispute the passage of the River Mjonga. Here the road defiled through the hills. 3 K.A.R. and Wilde's Rifles deployed before darkness fell and exchanged a few shots with enemy snipers.

[1] The divisional commander took Colonel Fitzgerald to General Smuts to report his arrival. Smuts remarked that the K.A.R. could march faster than the South African cavalry. On several occasions this proved to be true.

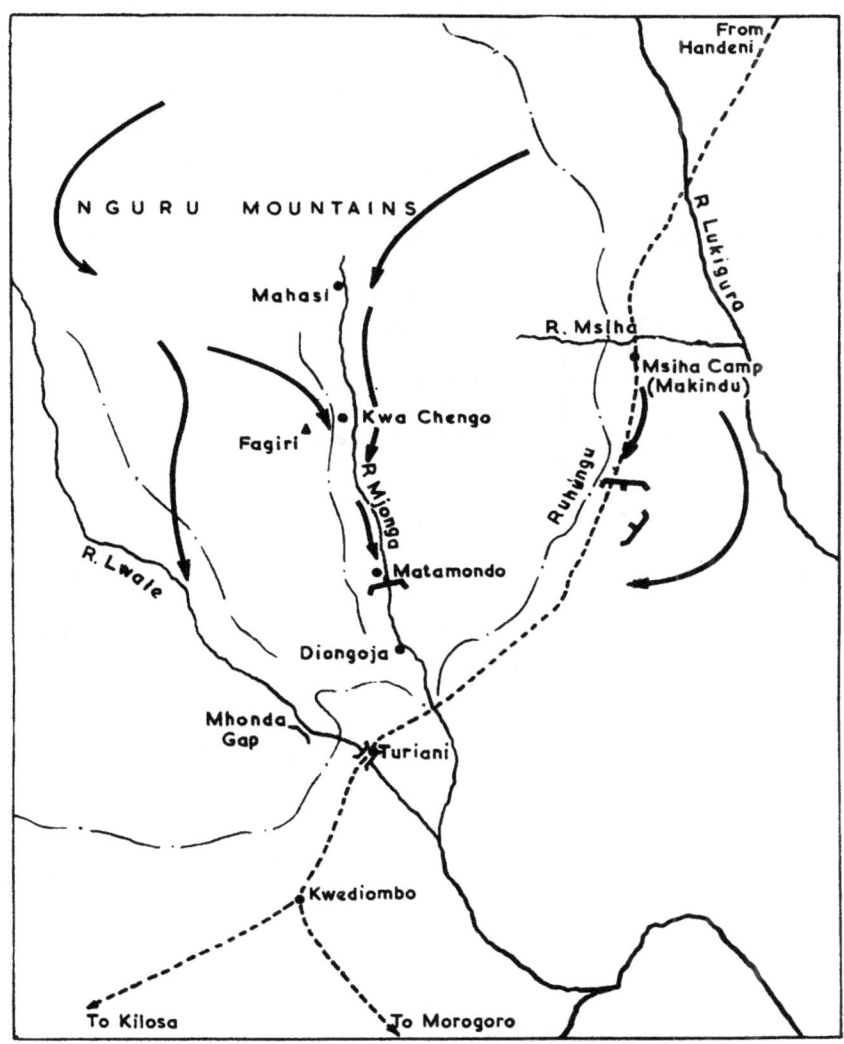

15. Outflanking Movement through the Nguru Mountains

Action at Matamondo, 10th August, 1916.—At dawn on 10th August, patrols from 'B' Company, 3 K.A.R., went forward to probe the enemy defences.[1] Hannyngton began his attack immediately afterwards, with the K.A.R. on the left and the 57th on the right. Both battalions were pinned down and then forced to retire. In the late afternoon two South African Infantry battalions came forward and attacked on the left flank, where they continued to fight until darkness put an end to the action. By that time the enemy's right had been driven in, and, as usual, the

---

[1] Lieutenant R. G. Glenday (Spec. List) charged three enemy machine guns and had a revolver duel with a German officer. He was wounded and subsequently lost an arm. Glenday was awarded the M.C. for his part in this action.

position was evacuated during the night. Three K.A.R. officers were wounded in this action, of whom one died later.

Since 7th August the 2nd South African Mounted Brigade had been held up by the enemy at the Mhonda Gap, where the track down the Lwale reaches the plain, not far from the Turiani bridge. This position was vital to the Germans as it covered their main withdrawal. After the action at Matamondo the 2nd East African Brigade pushed forward towards Mhonda, but the way lay through thick bush and elephant grass, and by the night of the 11th Hannyngton had only reached Diongoja, eight miles farther on. It was not until early on the 12th that the Brigade joined the South African cavalry at Mhonda. By that time there was no further need for haste, as the enemy had passed through Turiani and burnt the bridge. Two attempts by the 1st East African Brigade to pin the enemy down by engaging his main defences at Ruhungu had completely failed, so once again Kraut[1] escaped in good order. Smuts could only regroup his scattered forces, secure the crossing of the Wami, and try to discover whether the enemy had retreated south towards Morogoro or south-west to Kilosa.

The 2nd East African Brigade moved to Turiani on 13th August, where fatigue parties of 3 K.A.R. were employed in repairing the river crossing. The Lwale flowed between high, steep banks, which had to be cut away to form ramps. 3 K.A.R. crossed to the south bank, where a causeway had to be built over three miles of papyrus swamp before the wheeled transport could move forward.

The roads to Kilosa and Morogoro diverged at Kwediombo, a junction which the enemy was expected to defend. Hannyngton's Brigade marched off early on 14th August, with 'E' Company, 3 K.A.R., leading the advance. The enemy was found on a ridge overlooking the little River Mkindu. Hannyngton deployed two of his battalions, with the K.A.R. on the right. The attack was impeded by tall grass, but by nightfall 'D' Company had worked round the enemy's left flank. Daylight showed that the position was deserted, and 3 K.A.R. crossed the river and camped.

By 16th August the Brigade had reached Mwomero on the Kilosa road. A quantity of German ammunition was captured and destroyed. Orders then reached Hannyngton to halt his advance, as it was now plain that the main German withdrawal had followed the Morogoro road. The enemy was disputing the passage of the Wami at Dakawa, where the river was thirty yards wide and four or five feet deep. Smuts supported his frontal attack by a threat to both flanks, carried out by the 1st East African Brigade down the south bank of the Wami on the German right, and by South African cavalry on the left. After prolonging their defence throughout the 17th, the Germans withdrew in the night towards Morogoro. The 2nd East African Brigade was then recalled from the Kilosa road and reached Dakawa on the morning of the 20th. The next two days were spent in rebuilding the bridge over the Wami.

By this time van Deventer's 2nd Division, after marching and fighting

[1] At this time von Lettow was at Morogoro.

THE INVASION OF GERMAN EAST AFRICA

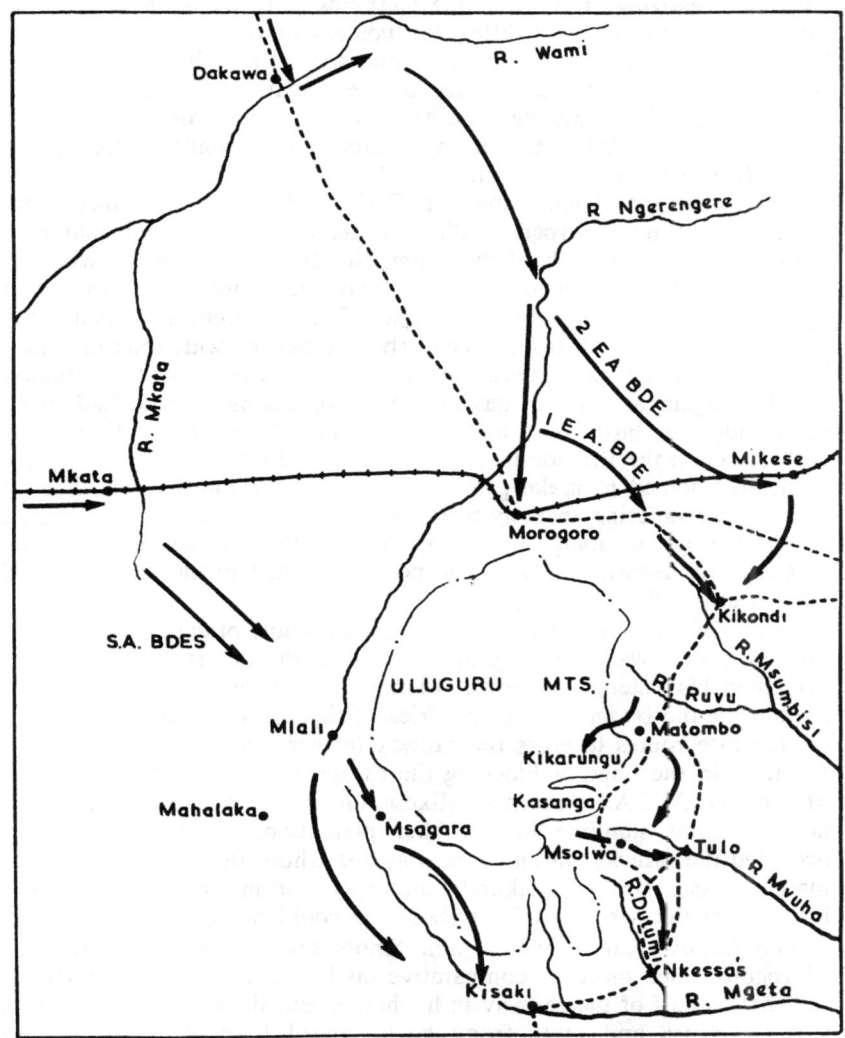

16. Advance round the Uluguru Mountains

for ninety miles across some of the wildest and most broken country encountered during the campaign, had reached Kilosa, with transport far behind and men and animals in a state of complete exhaustion. But Smuts, about to resume his main advance from the Wami, was still convinced that he faced a demoralized enemy and was determined that the pursuit should continue without pause. South of the Central Railway lay the Uluguru Mountains, across which no practicable route existed. Von Lettow had no intention of allowing himself to be trapped with his back against this mountain mass. After the war was over he expressed his astonishment that Smuts could ever have imagined he would stand and allow himself to be squeezed between the two prongs of the British advance. Realizing at last that the Germans were planning to continue their retreat instead of fighting for possession of the railway, Smuts hoped to bring them to battle by cutting simultaneously the tracks that ran west and east of the Uluguru to meet again at Kisaki. With this purpose in mind he directed the Mounted Brigades from the 2nd and 3rd Divisions on Mlali to cut the western route, while deflecting his own advance towards the east.

Early on 23rd August the 1st Division began its advance from Dakawa, not by the road south towards the railway, but marching eastward down the bank of the Wami. By 10 a.m. 3 K.A.R., with the 2nd East African Brigade, had reached the point where the river approaches most nearly to the course of the Ngerengere. Thence the Division was to march from river to river across the wide tract of waterless thornbush that lay between. After rest and refreshment the battalion marched again at 3 p.m., making slow progress as a route had to be cut through the bush. At 6 a.m. next morning the march continued. By mid-afternoon the Brigade had lost the way and had to retrace its steps. Bush fires helped to make progress more difficult, and by this time all troops were suffering severely from thirst. After one of the most painful marches in the campaign, 3 K.A.R. reached the Ngerengere at sunset. Not a single askari, and only one porter attached to the battalion, had fallen out.

As the Division approached Morogoro, the sound of explosions showed that the enemy was preparing to leave. On 26th August the Rhodesians and Baluchis entered the town, to find it occupied only by civilians. Meanwhile the 1st and 2nd East African Brigades were hurrying forward by separate routes to cross the railway farther east and converge upon Kikundi, in the hope of blocking the escape route east of the Uluguru Mountains. 3 K.A.R. reached Mikese on the 27th and camped at a large hospital standing in a rubber plantation, while one company occupied the railway station. Next day the whole Brigade continued its march, passed through Kikundi, and was just in time to secure the bridge over the Msumbisi River before it could be destroyed.

Von Lettow had escaped again. Smuts set up his headquarters at Morogoro, once more in comparative civilization, and with nearly all the eastern half of the railway in his hands. But the British supply lines still ran north and south from the advanced base at Handeni, over routes that might well became impassable in the rains. Already the artillery and other front-line transport was being requisitioned to bring forward supplies from the rear, and it was evident that the limit of movement had nearly been reached.

Since the force had left the Ruvu, the King's African Rifles had been represented only by the Mounted Infantry and 3 K.A.R., serving for most of the time with the 2nd East African Brigade. Early in August the first of the new battalions, 1/2 K.A.R., left Nairobi for the front with a strength of 21 officers, two warrant officers, and 511 African ranks. At the end of the month the battalion reached Morogoro, but almost immediately was sent back to Tanga, with orders to embark there for Kilwa Kisiwani.

(iv) *From the Central Railway to the River Mgeta.* Maps 16, V (d).

Despite all difficulties, General Smuts was determined to continue his dual advance round both sides of the Uluguru Mountains in the hope of trapping the enemy by a converging attack on Kisaki. The result was a new series of operations in wet and mountainous country that lasted for six weeks. 3 K.A.R. was actively engaged throughout.

The British force now faced one of the most difficult operational areas of the whole campaign. Fast pursuit around Uluguru was impossible. On the west, many tracks shown on the maps could not be found, and all heavy transport had to return to Morogoro while the South Africans forced their way south, deprived of blankets, greatcoats, food, porters and even information. On the east, along the track that became the main line of advance, miles of foothills, rivers, precipices, streams, bridges, culverts, demolitions and road-blocks flanked the massive side of the mountain range. The rains broke, and fell in persistent torrents. Motor transport was stretched beyond all limit; animals died in a few weeks.

The painful story of the South African advance beyond Mlali can be told in a few words. It was made in two columns. One was intended to follow the valley of the Mgeta, but finding this impossible struck through the hills farther east. Neither column was in touch with the other, nor with headquarters, and on approaching the German boma west of Kisaki, each engaged the enemy independently. The columns thus failed to support one another, and as they were too depleted and exhausted to press home their attacks, for the first time in the campaign the enemy saw British troops retire. Fortunately von Lettow was too much occupied with the threat from the opposite side of the mountain to follow them up.

Action at Pugu, 29th-30th August, 1916.—The 1st Division, with the 2nd East African Brigade in the lead, resumed its march down the eastern route to Kisaki early on 29th August. The 3rd Kashmir Rifles formed the advance guard, and 3 K.A.R. marched at the head of the main body. At 9.30 a.m., when the Brigade, strung out in column of route, was entering a narrow gorge surrounded by high hills, a shell fell on the track among the leading company of 3 K.A.R., cutting a few men with flying stones but failing to explode. A *Königsberg* gun and several others had the range to a nicety, and before long shells were coming thick and fast from the German emplacements on a ridge some 1,500 yards to the front.

Deployment was not easy in such broken country, but Hannyngton sent 3 K.A.R. into the hills, two companies going forward to gain the ridge. The movement was spotted by the German gunners, who began to shell every hill they saw occupied. The guns of the Mountain Battery came forward to reply, but had nothing like the range and fire-power of the enemy. It was an awkward and nerve-racking situation, and to make matters more uncomfortable, heavy rain began to fall and the porters were afraid to carry up the rations.[1]

[1] 'Colonel furious, I furious, all of us wet and filthy.' (Diary of a 3 K.A.R. subaltern.)

The two K.A.R. companies gained a footing on the ridge. The ground was steep and rain continued throughout the night. The rest of the battalion now came forward, and by daylight, with 'D' Company in the lead, the ridge was secured at a cost of four men killed and 19 wounded.[1] The enemy retired towards the River Ruvu and 3 K.A.R. occupied his camp, sending a half-company forward to regain touch. The pursuit was then taken up by the 57th Wilde's Rifles, who forced the crossing of the river late on 31st August and next day attacked the German rearguard on the heights beyond. 3 K.A.R. arrived in support, waded across the broad but shallow river, and deployed to the right of the road. The two battalions worked slowly forward over the hills to Matombo Mission, which was surrounded by 'A' Company, 3 K.A.R., and found to contain 24 Europeans and four askaris. A brief halt was made while the rest of the Brigade came forward.

Attack on Kikarungu, 4th-6th September, 1916.—A few miles farther on the enemy was securely entrenched on high ground at Kikarungu, occupying a position two miles in extent. The Gold Coast Regiment, newly arrived, up to strength, and well armed with machine and mountain guns, went forward to attack Kikarungu on 4th September. Next day the whole Brigade came into action, with Wilde's Rifles and the Royal Fusiliers, now reduced in strength to about one company, extending the line to the east and 3 K.A.R., with a section of the Mountain Battery, moving well out to the right to occupy Lusangalale Hill and turn the left flank of the German position. The going was hard and it was late afternoon before 3 K.A.R. came into action. After dark the turning movement was resumed, and dawn found the battalion in an excellent position overlooking the German left. Under cover of the guns, the askaris attacked down the ridge, and the enemy, pressed in front and flank and bombarded by artillery, began to retire. It was none too soon, as 3 K.A.R. and the mountain guns already commanded the road in rear of their position.

No respite was given. Early on the morning of 7th September 3 K.A.R. concentrated on the Kikarungu nek and, accompanied by the Mountain Battery, pursued the enemy up and down steep hillsides and over swollen streams to Kasanga, five miles farther on. At nightfall the guns opened fire on the enemy rearguard, and 3 K.A.R. occupied the position. On the 8th the march was resumed towards Tulo, whither the rest of the Brigade was converging by another track to the east. On approaching Msolwa a short engagement was fought by 'D' Company, which resulted in the death of one German and the capture of three askaris and a pom-pom gun carriage, with 150 rounds of ammunition.

At noon on 9th September 3 K.A.R. surprised a German Field Company cooking food at a drift. After a short action two Germans, 26 askaris, some ammunition and all the baggage were taken, and the food gratefully consumed. Without the thick cover of the surrounding bush none of the enemy would have escaped. Tulo was reached that after-

---

[1] A farewell message, signed by Captain Stemmermann, who commanded the German forces retiring by the eastern route, was found in an empty champagne bottle, saying the Germans had left at six o'clock.

noon, where the battalion rejoined the Brigade and received Hannyngton's commendation for its long march through the hills, which had successfully cleared his right flank of the enemy.

Action at the Dutumi River, 10th-12th September, 1916.—By this time both British and Germans were very near exhaustion. But the claws of the pincer were nearly closed, and Smuts, hearing of the check to the South Africans before Kisaki, ordered the 1st Division to press forward. At 4 a.m. on 10th September the 2nd East African Brigade left Tulo, and marched for four hours in the cool of the morning before the first halt. At ten o'clock the Brigade reached a wide plain across which the road ran towards the village of Nkessa's and the River Dutumi, which flowed south from the Uluguru to join the Mgeta. There the enemy was posted in strength,[1] concealed in the thick growth of elephant grass and bush that covered most of the plain and the banks of the river, ready to dispute the crossing.

The 3rd Kashmir Rifles were leading. Hannyngton sent forward a company of the Loyals and part of the Mountain Battery, but the bush was so dense that the frontal attack made little progress. Meanwhile the 57th Wilde's Rifles was ordered to secure Kitoho Hill, which overlooked the position on the right of the road. These movements developed slowly, and it was 2 p.m. before 3 K.A.R. got orders to turn the enemy's right by making a wide sweep round Kitoho Hill, crossing the Dutumi, and moving down-river to threaten the enemy's retreat.

The going was hard, and it was nearly nightfall before Fitzgerald reached the summit of a ridge near Kitoho Hill. There he saw a small stream, and sending a half-company to occupy the high ground beyond it, secured a water-point for the whole Brigade. Without this Hannyngton might have been obliged to break off the action next day.

At dawn on 11th September Fitzgerald crossed the stream with the rest of his battalion, and in a short while was overlooking the banks of the Dutumi. Two companies crossed and moved down the right bank; one company moved down the left, with another following in support. The 57th had not yet driven the enemy from the lower slopes of Kitoho, and about noon the advance of 3 K.A.R. was held up by machine-gun fire from an emplacement on a spur of the hill. During the afternoon enemy reinforcements from Kisaki moved up the right bank of the Dutumi, attacked the two companies that had crossed and drove them back over the river. The company on the left bank was obliged to conform. As darkness fell the battalion concentrated and was reinforced by two companies of the Gold Coast Regiment and a section of the mountain guns.

The advance was resumed at daylight on the 12th. One K.A.R. and one Gold Coast company crossed the river and moved down the right bank and into the hills beyond. They were followed later by the other Gold Coast company, while the rest of 3 K.A.R. moved in a parallel column down the left bank. This time there was no opposition, and finding that the lower part of Kitoho had been abandoned, the 57th were also moving on Nkessa's. At 1 p.m. 3 K.A.R. were in a position

---

[1] About 2,200 men and 24 machine guns.

on a ridge overlooking the village and the road. The action in the thick country south of the road was still proceeding. Towards evening news reached Fitzgerald that the enemy was beginning a general retreat. Two companies 3 K.A.R. then got round the German left and maintained the action until well after dark. The askaris could do no more, for it was the culmination of three days' continuous marching and fighting through very difficult country.

Once again von Lettow slipped from his opponent's grasp. The morning of 13th September found Nkessa's evacuated, and next day when the South Africans, approaching once more from the western side of the mountain, made a wide sweep around Kisaki to isolate the town, they found the German forces already south of the River Mgeta and preparing to defend the crossing. The 7th South African Horse and the 5th and 6th South African Infantry got across the river and established a bridgehead, but were in no condition to make any further progress.

In spite of his failure to trap the supposedly demoralized remnant of von Lettow's troops in the Uluguru range, General Smuts still adhered to his opinion that one more supreme effort might end the war before the rains bogged down his forces in the Mgeta valley or forced them to retire. The enemy had vanished into a maze of tropical jungle, a fever-ridden, steaming swamp of intolerable, sticky heat. No one knew his exact position, but there was every sign that he intended to remain and challenge his pursuers to evict him. If action were to be taken, it must be quick.

In these circumstances the 2nd East African Brigade was ordered to probe south from Nkessa's down the course of the Dutumi to its junction with the Mgeta near Msogera, cross the latter river and move up the right bank until the whereabouts of the enemy's right flank were discovered. This task, which was understood by the troops to be a 'demonstration' in aid of a South African attack from the west, was allotted to 3 K.A.R.

Shortly after 8 p.m. on 18th September the battalion left Nkessa's. The night was misty and dark, though a glimmer of moonlight shone after midnight. The guides were poor and on several occasions led the troops in circles around the native paths that intersected the banks of the Dutumi. The Mgeta was reached shortly after dawn on the 19th, and although in flood could be waded waist deep across a ford. By eight o'clock 3 K.A.R. was moving through thick bush up the right bank of the river. An hour later the first enemy picquets were driven in, and at 11.30 a.m. the main position was reached. In heavy bush, where enemy scouts could be detected in trees directing the fire, the battalion progressed to the edge of a clearing and there dug in, unable to go farther. For some time it was practically impossible to move, and only the invariable askari habit of firing high saved 3 K.A.R. from heavy casualties.

Towards mid-afternoon the firing died down and it was possible to consolidate the position. Scouts located the enemy in a deep nullah running down to the Mgeta, only 200 yards distant. At five o'clock the attack was renewed, the enemy creeping up towards the K.A.R. trenches, but retiring again at nightfall. During the night Lieutenant-Colonel Fitzgerald constructed a perimeter camp with its ends resting on the river, and so secured his bridgehead. A casualty check showed that Captain R. M. T. Rose (York and Lanc. R.), Adam Effendi (a Sudanese officer of twenty-four years' service), and 19 other ranks had been killed or wounded during the day.

Within that camp 3 K.A.R. remained for the next five days, unable to move. On the 20th the Gold Coast Regiment arrived in support, camping on the opposite side of the river and sending one company to join the K.A.R. Patrols were sent out to reconnoitre a small village that was being used as cover for snipers, and to search for the enemy flanks, though with little success. Rain fell in torrents, flooding the Mgeta and nearly rendering the camp untenable. From time to time the German artillery put over a few shells, notably on the morning of the 23rd, but without causing much damage. On the 25th the position was taken over by the Gold Coast Regiment and 3 K.A.R. marched back to the brigade camp at Nkessa's.

The rains continued. Flour, meat, some coffee, sugar, and native tobacco, but little else, came forward across the sodden tracks to the north, now rapidly becoming impassable. The South Africans were shooting hippopotami for meat. For medical as well as for military reasons, Smuts realized that he must withdraw his forward troops and turn the enemy out of the Mgeta position by a strategical threat to his rear. Operations were accordingly broken off, and on 28th September 3 K.A.R. marched back to Tulo.

While the advance from the River Msiha and the pursuit around the Uluguru were in progress, other forces were occupying the ports along the German coast. The Royal Navy, assisted by a detachment of the Zanzibar Rifles, occupied Sadani and Bagamoyo during the first fortnight of August. These moves were preliminary to an attack on Dar-es-Salaam. A column supported by the Navy marched south from Bagamoyo along the coast, while two flying columns moved inland in the vain hope of saving the railway bridges at Ngerengere and Ruvu. On 4th September, as the coastal columns closed on Dar-es-Salaam, the Navy sent a ship into the harbour to demand surrender. This was granted by the Deputy Burgomaster and the troops marched in, to find all the enemy gone except hospital patients and non-combatants.

G.H.Q., previously stationed at Korogwe and Tanga, opened at Dar-es-Salaam on 12th September. Advanced G.H.Q. remained at Morogoro, and work began at once to establish the railway link between them. Practically every bridge and culvert had been destroyed, but the first load of supplies left Dar-es-Salaam for Ruvu on 4th October, and the first train got through to Morogoro on 24th November.

In March, 1916, Portugal had declared war on Germany. The local forces in Portuguese East Africa occupied the coast up to the mouth of the Rovuma and made an unsuccessful attempt to cross the river into German territory. A few months later some poorly-trained and unacclimatized reinforcements reached the colony from Portugal under the command of Major-General Gil. After considerable delay Gil crossed the Rovuma unopposed and established himself on the northern bank.

Despite Smuts' representations, however, he was afraid to move inland to close the German line of retreat for lack of proper roads, transport and supplies. Apart from a line of scattered posts the Portuguese frontier therefore remained practically open.

It was evident that von Lettow was unlikely to be caught by frontal attacks from the north. An Anglo-Belgian advance from the west and Northey's attack from the south had penetrated far into German territory.[1] Smuts now determined to place himself on the flank of the German line of retreat by establishing new bases at several ports south of Dar-es-Salaam, from which columns could strike inland towards the German rear. On 7th September Kilwa was captured after slight resistance, and Kilwa Kisiwani, about twenty miles to the south, was occupied at the same time. Mikindani, Sudi, Lindi, and Kiswere were occupied during the next ten days.

To form these columns new battalions of the K.A.R. were beginning to take the field. Though unrealized at the time, the limit of Smuts' achievement, closing the second phase of the campaign, had already been reached. The greater part of the German colony, including the most important areas, was now in British hands. But von Lettow was still undefeated; the cost of the operations in men, animals and material had been greater than expected, and the South African troops were at the end of their endurance. A new stage had begun in which the future prosecution of the war passed wholly to the African battalions.[2]

There was no longer any lack of confidence in the askari's fighting qualities. They had been amply proved by the four depleted companies of 3 K.A.R., now resting, training and road-building at the 2nd East African Brigade camp near Tulo.

(v) *Invasion from the West: Operations of the Lake Force.* Maps V (c), 17.

While 3 K.A.R. was serving with the main invading force, 4 K.A.R., with all companies withdrawn from the railway area to Uganda, was preparing to assist the Belgians in driving the enemy from the territory lying between the southern frontier of Uganda and the Central Railway. At the beginning of 1916 the German troops in this area numbered some 4,000 men under the command of Major-General Wahle,[3] though this force was weakened when von Lettow became hard pressed by Smuts.

On 19th February, 1916, the Lake Force was constituted as a separate command under Lieutenant-Colonel D. R. Adye (98th Infantry, I.A.), embodying the troops east and west of Lake Victoria. On the Kagera River, holding a number of posts from Kamwezi to the Lake, were some 1,500 rifles, with four guns and six machine guns, comprising

---

[1] See Sections (v) and (vi).

[2] 'Already, as one of the main lessons of the campaign, it was indisputable that for warfare in tropical Africa troops other than native Africans had proved in general unsuited.' (Hordern, *Military Operations in E.A.*, I, p. 393.)

[3] Wahle was a retired officer caught by the war in East Africa while on a visit to his son. He had previously commanded the German 1. of c.

Landing party from Mafia at mouth of Saimba, Uranga entrance, River Rufigi, 5th May, 1916

[Crown Copyright

Patrol of 2 K.A.R. at Schaedel's Farm, July, 1917

[Photo: Lieut. W. G. E. Longworth

four companies (10 officers and about 300 men) of 4 K.A.R.; two companies of the 98th Infantry; the Uganda Police Service Battalion; the Baganda Rifles, and some Nandi Scouts. East of the Lake were the remainder of the 98th Infantry, based on Karungu with forward posts to the south-east, and a picturesque body of native refugees from German territory, known unofficially as the 'Skin Corps'. These men, who were serving for private motives rather than pay, went practically naked except for a head-dress of lion skin, and were employed as scouts.

With the help of a transport and carrier service organized by the British Command, the Belgians were ready by the beginning of 1916 to take the field with over 11,000 troops. In April Brigadier-General Sir Charles Crewe, formerly Director of Recruiting in South Africa, reached the Belgian headquarters as representative of General Smuts.

The Belgians' immediate objective was the conquest of Ruanda and Urundi, and their plan was for a dual advance with two brigades. On 25th April the Northern Brigade under Colonel Molitor set out in two columns from the area north of Lake Kivu, and advancing into Ruanda reached Kigali on 6th May. Meanwhile the Southern Brigade under Lieutenant-Colonel Olsen made a demonstration from south of Lake Kivu towards Nyanza, which was occupied on 19th May. The Germans withdrew without offering serious opposition; the Belgian columns linked forces, and the occupation of Ruanda was soon complete.

Smuts was not anxious to become too actively involved in these operations, as he considered the transport services he had organized for the Belgians as much assistance as he could afford. It was with some reluctance, therefore, that he agreed to let Adye take advantage of his undisputed command of the lake to seize Ukerewe Island at the entrance to the Speke Gulf. This was intended as a preliminary move for attacking Mwanza, and so securing a starting-point for an advance on Tabora in conjunction with the Belgian forces.

Capture of Ukerewe Island, 9th-10th June, 1916.—Ukerewe is an island only by virtue of a very narrow channel between a tongue of land at its eastern extremity (known as the Igongo Neck) and the mainland. The centre and west of the island were covered with wooded hills; on the east and at places round the coast the cultivation of rice was of great importance to the Germans. The operation was therefore timed to take place shortly before the crops ripened. Though the German garrison was small, it was capable of rapid reinforcement from the mainland. Adye therefore planned a double landing: at Nanso Bay, situated in the south-east corner of the island, and at Igongo Neck.

The troops embarked during the first week of June, and were transported to an assembly point on the uninhabited island of Bukerebe. The force comprised about half 4 K.A.R. (some 450 rifles) under Lieutenant-Colonel W. G. Stonor, 200 men of the Baganda Rifles, 140 of the Skin Corps, and an Indian machine-gun section, totalling (with ancillary troops) about 900 men. At dawn on 9th June the expedition approached the selected landing-places on Ukerewe. 4 K.A.R. landed a mile west of Nanso and occupied the village, while the Skin Corps, landing farther to the east, fought a fierce little action that quickly routed the advance guard of a German force about to cross from the mainland. Next day 4 K.A.R. moved inland to Buramba, where a camp was set up. Small columns then searched the island and within a few days the occupation was complete. Eight Germans and two field guns were captured; the askari garrison unofficially demobilized and disappeared among the native population.

While this operation was in progress the Belgian columns continued their advance into Urundi. Little resistance was met, and at the end of June they had reached Nyamirembe, forcing the Germans to withdraw from the Karagwe district between the bend of the River Kagera and the Lake. Finding that Kyaka and other German posts south of the Kagera had been evacuated, the British Lake Force, now under the command of Brigadier-General Crewe, lost no time in following, in the hope of bringing them to action. A flying column of 190 rifles 4 K.A.R., with some Baganda Rifles and Nandi Scouts, marched on Bukoba while a detachment of Indian Infantry and Baganda Rifles prepared to make a landing from the Lake. Bukoba was deserted, and the combined force sailed for Nyamirembe. Meanwhile two other columns, one consisting of a company of 4 K.A.R. and auxiliaries and the other of troops of the Police Service Battalion, were on their way southward through Karagwe. The German forces moved too rapidly to be caught, and by 9th July practically all Crewe's troops from southern Uganda, numbering some 1,200 rifles with seven machine guns and one Hotchkiss gun, had concentrated at Nyamirembe. A further 700, with eight machine guns, were on Ukerewe Island.

By this time Smuts, whose own troops had temporarily reached the limit of their advance at the River Msiha, was prepared to authorize a movement by the Lake Force towards the Central Railway, directed against the important food-producing centre at Tabora. For this purpose Nyamirembe, which proved to be practically waterless, foodless, and infected with tsetse fly, was quite unsuited, and Crewe determined to capture Mwanza without delay.

Mwanza lies a little way up the long and narrow Mwanza Gulf. As the Germans had prepared defences along that part of the coast, Crewe decided to make his assault from the land by disembarking his troops at Kongoro Point on the other side of the promontory. From there a dual advance was to be made on Mwanza: 'A' Force, consisting of 4 K.A.R. (seven companies, with seven machine guns) and some scouts, moving directly on the town via Mwamba Hill, and 'B' Force, which consisted mainly of the Police Service Battalion with a detachment of 4 K.A.R., following the line of the coast.

The Attack on Mwanza, 11th-14th July, 1916.—The landing of 'A' Force began after dark on 11th July. The Skin Corps went ashore first, fanning out inland to cover the landing of the remainder. Force 'B' went ashore at daylight on the 12th. By then 4 K.A.R. was well on the way to Mwamba, which was occupied before nightfall. On the 13th, after a successful engagement against the enemy, who had become aware of the approach of 'A' Force, 4 K.A.R. was near Muhanga, while 'B' Force, which had been in action against the coast defences, was at Hale. The

THE INVASION OF GERMAN EAST AFRICA

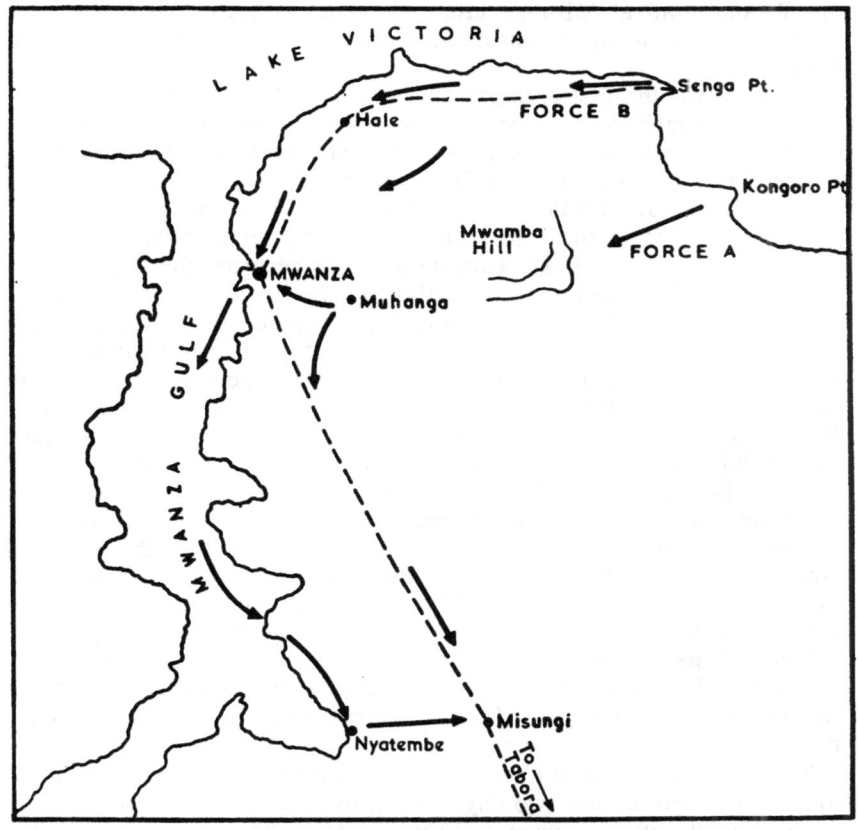

17. Attack on Mwanza, 11th-14th July, 1916

two arms of the invasion were therefore within striking distance of Mwanza, though the Germans appear to have been unaware of the situation of 'B' Force.

Next afternoon the two columns, converging on Mwanza, got into communication by helio. The Germans, apprised at last of the threat to the town, withdrew in haste, their rearguard putting up a brief fight and eluding an attempt by 40 rifles of 4 K.A.R. and some Nandi Scouts to cut off their retreat.

The European population had escaped in small vessels up the Mwanza Gulf. Crewe decided to follow in person, accompanied by two companies 4 K.A.R. and 50 Scouts under Captain R. B. L. Harvey. He hoped not only to overtake the European party but to intercept also the askari companies retreating down the Tabora road.

Harvey's troops, in two ships of the Lake Flotilla, spent the afternoon of 15th July moving slowly up the shallow waters of the Gulf. As darkness fell they struggled ashore through the reeds at a point several miles short of the head of the Gulf. The German vessels were captured a few hours later, but the enemy had already gone. Harvey followed, and struck the Tabora road at Misungi, after marching all night. There he was attacked by the enemy in considerable strength and withdrew by road to Mwanza.

Mwanza was the first occasion on which 4 K.A.R. was in action as a battalion. Though the fighting was not severe, it was an excellent start to offensive operations by the Lake Force, which was now provided with a secure and accessible base in German territory.

Throughout July the Belgians continued to advance and the Germans to withdraw. Before the end of the month the Belgians had occupied Ujiji and Kigoma on Lake Tanganyika, thus securing the terminus of the railway, which was also cut farther up the line at Ruchugi. Crewe, determined that British forces should participate in the forthcoming advance on Tabora, held a conference with Major-General Tombeur at Entebbe. Meanwhile a forward depôt was established at Nyatembe on the southern tip of the Mwanza Gulf, and Misungi was occupied by the Police Battalion. Great efforts were made to organize a proper carrier service, without which the barren and inhospitable country between the lake and the railway could not be crossed.

As the largest British unit involved, 4 K.A.R. formed the mainstay of the advance. On 20th July the battalion was conveyed up the Mwanza Gulf and landed at Nyatembe. Followed by the Police from Misungi, the K.A.R. then advanced through Mabuki to Runere, driving away German patrols. On 25th July the German rearguard was routed in a sharp, short action at Ilola. There for a time Crewe halted to organize his line of communication and resume negotiations with Molitor's Northern Brigade, which was supposed to be marching on the Central Railway by a parallel route to the west.

News had now reached Crewe that the enemy was massing in strength to bar his progress some two days' march to the south. Many of his men were already suffering from sickness, and in these circumstances he sought the direct support of Belgian troops before resuming his advance. But after prolonged negotiations General Tombeur decided that Molitor's march must continue by an independent route, and on 26th August Crewe gave the order to resume his advance.

Two companies 4 K.A.R. were reconnoitring on the left flank towards Gumali. The rest of the battalion marched to Ugalo. German forces were known to be in the Seke Hills, but withdrew when the K.A.R. reached Mwasimba on the 27th. Two days later the Germans were driven out of Shinyanga, where another halt was called.

On 6th September Crewe moved his headquarters forward to Shinyanga. Lack of proper communications made it difficult to discover what was happening elsewhere, but the Belgian Southern Brigade was progressing along the railway and advancing from the south to attack Tabora. The pressure created by these movements weakened the resistance encountered by the Lake Force, but there were many other difficulties to make progress hazardous. Along a rough track through the barren and sterile country flanking the Tindo Hills the Force moved slowly forward, with 4 K.A.R. and a battery of naval guns forming the main body, and halted once more at Kigahumo. The heat was excessive;

there were no local supplies, and as the line of communication lengthened, belts of fly country were crossed that made the use of pack animals impossible. On 10th September 300 rifles of 4 K.A.R. with six machine guns under Captain W. J. T. Shorthose (S. Staffs. R.) went ahead to Nzega and had a brief fight with about 100 of the enemy, losing one man killed and one wounded. Crewe then resumed his march, to halt again at Ngalia's while the column closed up. On 25th September he was in position at Ndala, ready for his final thrust to cut the railway east of Tabora and co-operate with the Belgians in attacking the town. That afternoon news reached him that Tabora had fallen six days before.

The news that they had been forestalled was a great disappointment to 4 K.A.R., who had had the worst route to traverse and could have moved very much faster had the carriers and supplies allotted to the Belgians been available. But one important task still remained. The main enemy force, under Captain Wintgens, had withdrawn due south via Sikonge. Another column, estimated at 400 rifles, under Captain von Langenn-Steinkeller, had gone eastward along the railway. With the capture of Tabora the Belgians regarded their objective as achieved, and were not prepared to go farther. Crewe therefore proposed to Smuts that the Lake Force should clear the remainder of the Central Railway. Van Deventer, whose extreme right was then at Kilimatinde, was instructed by Smuts to patrol west, and Major H. A. Lilley, with 450 rifles 4 K.A.R., six machine guns and a field gun, struck the railway at Igalula on 28th September and moved east. On 4th October Lilley overtook the German rearguard outside Malongwe station and forced it to retreat. The enemy left the railway and went south to rejoin Wintgens at Iringa. Two days later van Deventer's patrols reached Malongwe, and the whole course of the railway was in Allied hands.[1]

The rôle of the Lake Force was over. Brigadier-General Crewe returned to South Africa; the Police Service Battalion, Baganda Rifles and Nandi Scouts returned to Uganda, where they were disbanded, and on 12th October 4 K.A.R. left Malongwe to march east along the railway to join van Deventer's 2nd Division.

(vi) *Invasion from the South: Brigadier-General Northey's Operations.*
Map VI (b).

North of Lake Nyasa lies the high region of the Poroto and Ukinga mountains. Overlooking the western slopes the Germans had built their district headquarters, called Neu Langenburg, and now known as Tukuyu. The town was connected by earth roads with other upland centres to the north and east: Iringa, Mahenge and Songea, all of them in food-producing areas that became increasingly important as the German forces withdrew towards the south. It was into this region that Brigadier-General Northey thrust his invasion during 1916. His force thus became the anvil to Smuts' hammer descending from the north, a perilous rôle for so few troops in the face of a determined enemy.

The Nyasaland-Rhodesia Field Force, as it was now called, numbered

[1] Many stories were told of the cannibalism of the Belgian troops. Lilley was shown the remains of a fire on one of the station platforms, at which it was alleged that three Belgian askaris had cooked a victim.

fewer than 3,000 men. 1 K.A.R., over 800 rifles strong, under the command of Lieutenant-Colonel G. M. P. Hawthorn, was the only regular battalion. Other units were the South African Rifles, the British South Africa Police, and the native Northern Rhodesia Police. The artillery numbered 14 guns.

The rains were heavier than usual in the first few months of 1916. Reports by patrols and spies during this period showed that the Germans were in three defended posts near the eastern sector of the frontier, at Ipiana, Igamba and Luwiwa; and in a fourth, Namema, on the west. Northey planned to attack all four simultaneously from the nearest bases on the British side, i.e. Karonga, Fort Hill, Fife and Abercorn. On 15th May, a week before Smuts began his march down the Pangani, Northey set up his headquarters at Fife.

Command of the column to operate from Karonga was given to Hawthorn, who concentrated his troops (four companies 1 K.A.R. and 200 men of the South African Rifles) behind the River Songwe at Ngaramu. On 20th May the march began. Enemy outposts were known to be watching the river at Kasimulo and Nsessi. Detaching a party to deal with the former, Hawthorn got a company of 1 K.A.R. across by boat near Nsessi, overwhelmed the German picquet and covered the construction of a pontoon ferry. During the night of 21st/22nd May the rest of the column crossed, and the invasion of German territory began. On the 23rd Hawthorn reached Ipiana to find that the enemy had already withdrawn towards Neu Langenburg.

The march of the second column began on 24th May, when Major R. L. Flindt (2nd South African Rifles) left Fort Hill with a company of his own regiment and two companies of 1 K.A.R. He also found his objective at Igamba evacuated, and on instructions from Northey pressed on to Neu Langenburg. The town was entered on 29th May, and quantities of supplies and ammunition were taken. Hawthorn had continued his march, first to the east and then to the north of Neu Langenburg in the hope of cutting the German retreat, and on 31st May was at Mwakaleli.

During these operations the third and fourth columns had encircled the German posts at Luwiwa and Namema. The enemy escaped from both places during the hours of darkness. Northey had hoped to trap the German forces at Neu Langenburg by bringing the third column into the hills in a wide sweep to approach the town from the north, but the column reached Rungwe too late for this. The fourth column, after pursuing its retreating enemy for some distance, turned west to occupy Bismarckburg on Lake Tanganyika and was then ordered to join the third column at Rungwe. Thus ended the first phase of the operations, with all columns of the Field Force far into the mountains and the German forces in full retreat.

It was now the beginning of June. The border was clear; Northey moved his headquarters to Neu Langenburg; and supply columns were organized from a new base at Mwaya, on the head of the Lake, for Smuts was anxious that the enemy should be followed and denied access to Iringa and the surrounding country.

V. **German East Africa. Northern Sheet**
   (a) The Arusha—Dodoma Area
   (b) The Pare—Usambara Area
   (c) The Advance of the Lake Force
   (d) The Area of the Central Railway
   (e) The Pursuit of Wintgens and Naumann

Face page 325

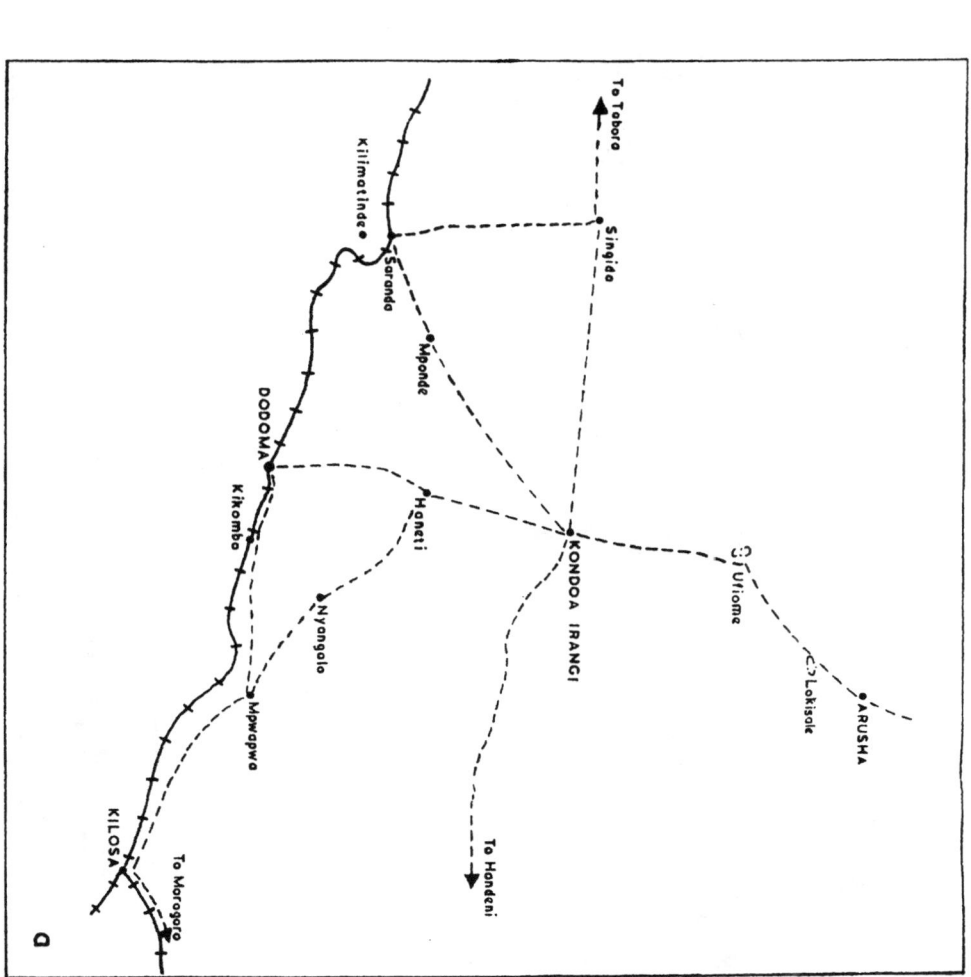

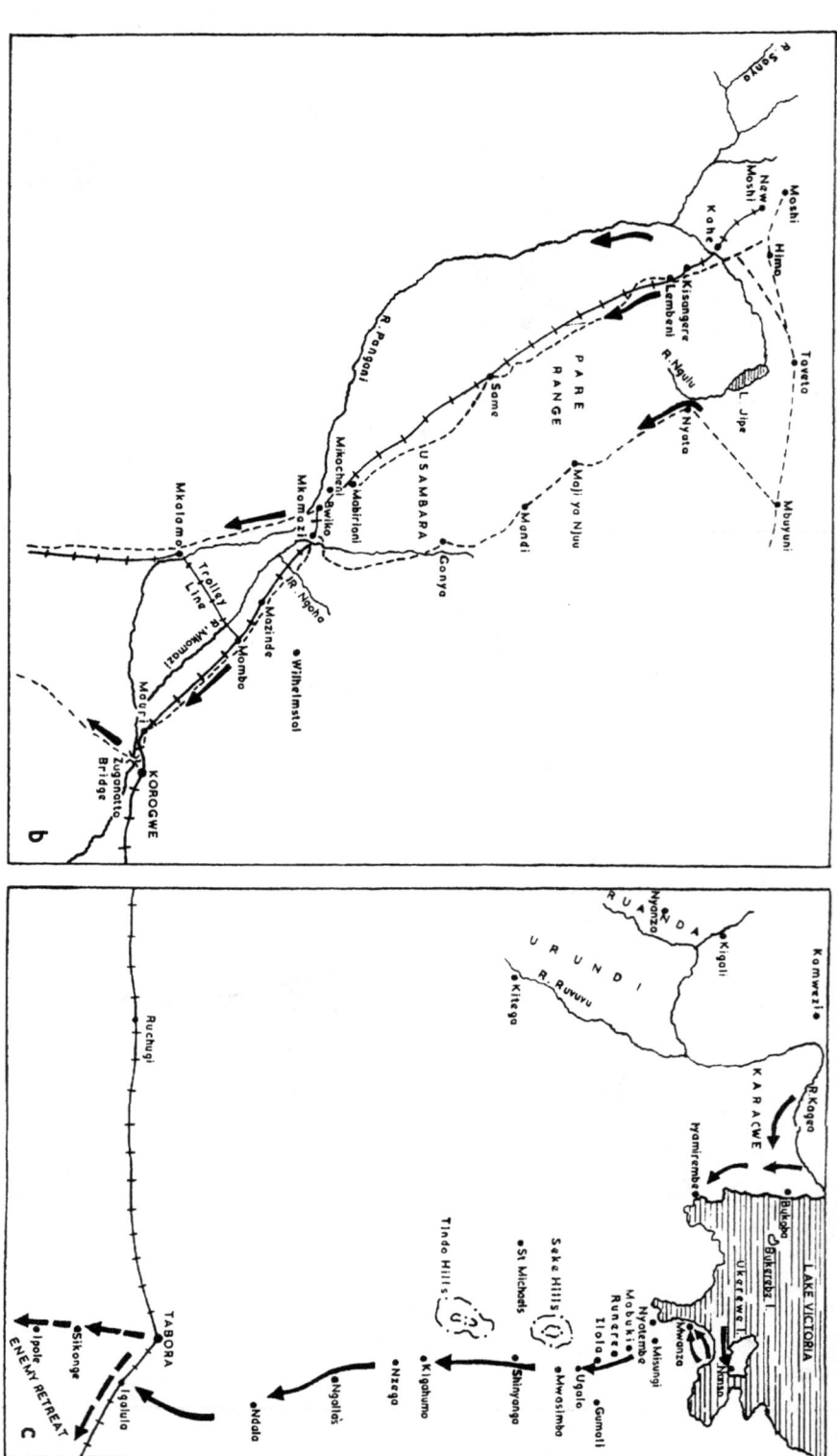

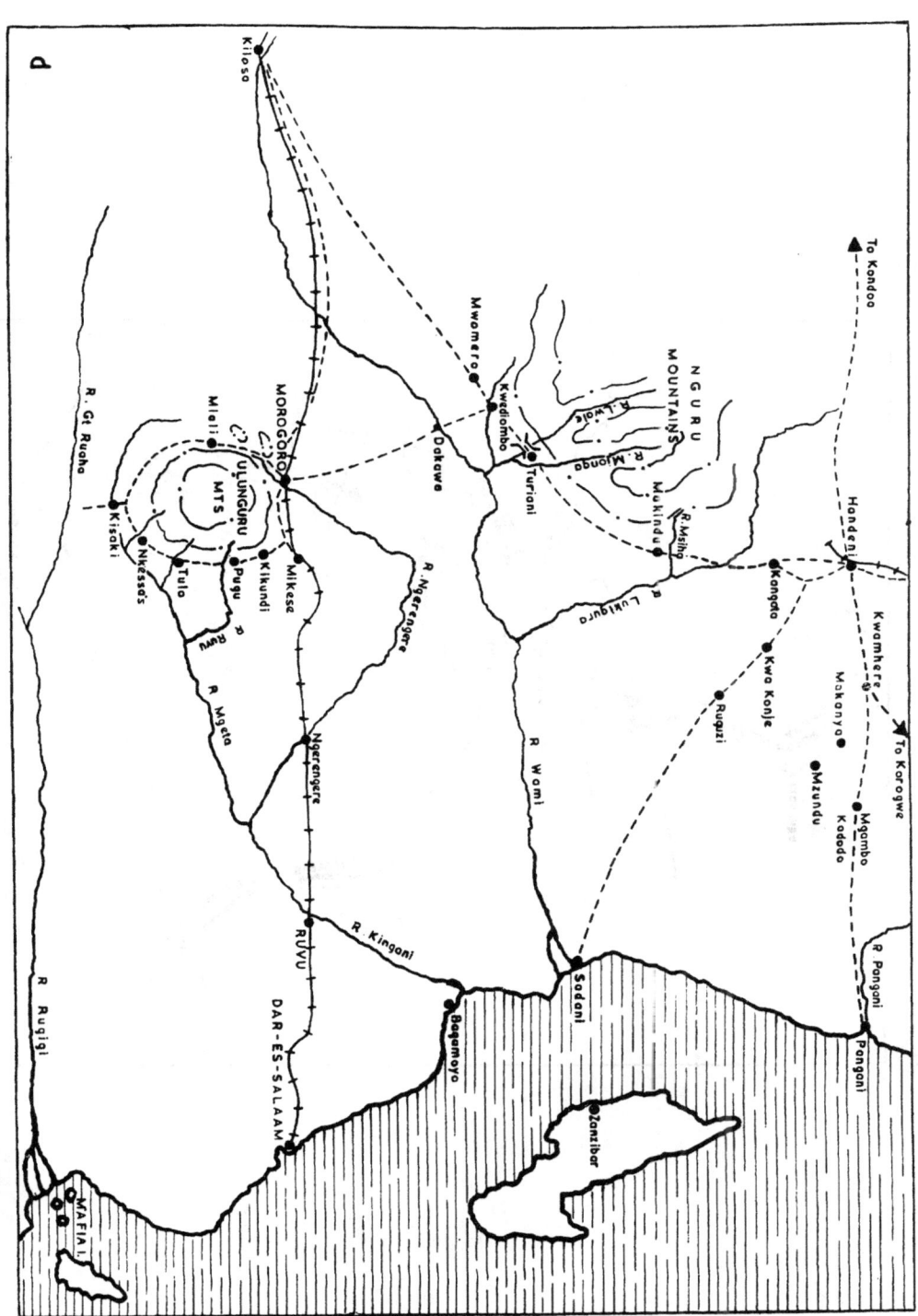

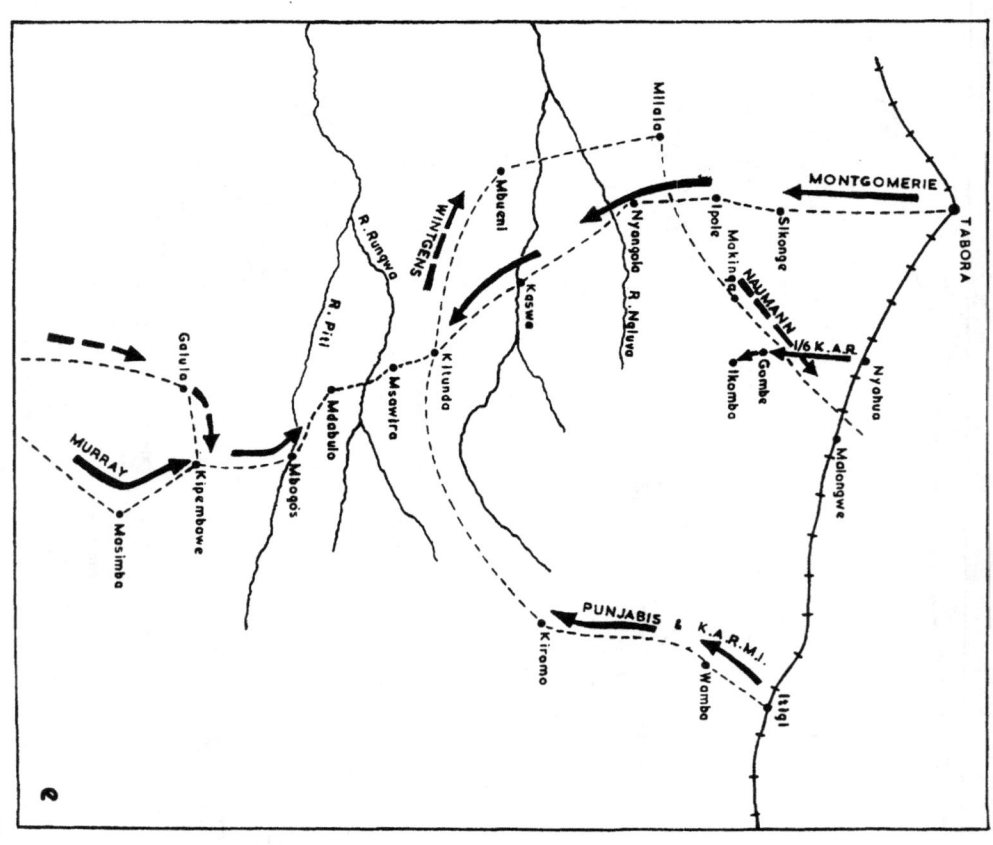

From Neu Langenburg a track ran eastward across the mountains, through Ulongwe to Njombe (Mdandu), where it was joined by a track from Songea. The enemy was reported to be preparing to defend this route. The direct way to Iringa lay north-east through Magoje, and along this track Hawthorn set out with 1 K.A.R. to pursue the retreating Germans.

It was a hard and difficult march. Cold, windswept plateaux alternated with scorching, sheltered valleys. The battalion made long and exhausting marches, capturing the baggage of the German rearguard at Magoje and picking up straggling porters and abandoned stores *en route*. But the enemy was not caught. On 6th June Hawthorn reached Buhora, a day's march beyond Brandt. Rain had made the track impassable, and turning west through New Utengule he overtook and fought the rearguard of another retreating column near Masanga. Though his pursuit had been carried out with commendable speed across very difficult country, supply troubles had become acute and he was ordered to occupy New Utengule, with garrisons along the line of communication.

Not all of 1 K.A.R. took part in Hawthorn's thrust to the north-east. Two companies, one at Mwakaleli and one near Ulongwe, were guarding the approaches to the eastern route. In the middle of June they were embodied in a column under Major R. L. Flindt, formed to pursue the enemy along the route to the east. Suffering considerable privation from lack of food and blankets, Flindt's column marched across the mountains to Njombe, whither Hawthorn had also been directed from New Utengule. Neither column encountered serious resistance. The enemy withdrew in good order north towards Iringa and east towards Mahenge. This marked the end of the second stage of the operations, as reports came that enemy forces were collecting at Malangali, north-east of the British positions, and Northey thought it advisable to build up supplies before attempting a further move.

By the beginning of July the first real battle was pending. Two routes ran north-east from Neu Langenburg towards Iringa, one via Madibira and one via Malangali. Both places were now occupied by the Germans in considerable strength, their retreating forces having been reinforced by a detachment of over 100 officers and men from the *Königsberg*. Fortunately, although the transport service still left much to be desired, local supplies were fairly plentiful, and Northey was soon ready to attack. His plan was to contain the enemy at Madibira while Hawthorn marched north from Njombe to Malangali, supported by a column from Buhora under Lieutenant-Colonel E. Rodger (2nd South African Rifles).

Hawthorn left Njombe with 1 K.A.R., several squadrons of the South African Rifles and some artillery on 4th July and marched to Soliwaya. A German outpost retired before him. A smaller force sent via Emmaberg had a brief encounter with the enemy, and advancing in parallel, the two parts of the column then reunited at Idunda. There a pause ensued while supplies were brought up and the enemy positions before Malangali were reconnoitred. During these patrols 1 K.A.R. rounded up several parties of the *Königsberg's* crew, the sailors proving easy game for the K.A.R. in the bush.

The main track through Malangali to Iringa ran down the length of a broad ridge that lay between two small rivers. Here the Germans had built their main position, strongly fortifying a rocky outcrop at the eastern end of the ridge that covered the approach along the road below. The enemy possessed a 10.5-cm. howitzer, which was more effective than any of Hawthorn's artillery. His column and Rodger's totalled about 1,200 rifles, which was believed to be slightly stronger than the enemy. Unknown to Hawthorn, however, the Germans had begun to withdraw towards Iringa shortly before the action began.

Action at Malangali, 24th July, 1916.—On 23rd July Hawthorn left Idunda, intending to make a night march that would bring him on to the left and rear of the German position early next day. The column consisted of five companies 1 K.A.R., three squadrons of the South African Rifles, six guns and 11 machine guns. The country was broken and the going was difficult. Hawthorn's troops struggled on in the darkness across a series of alternating ridges and ravines. At eight o'clock on the following morning, when Rodger, advancing from Igawiro with a company of 1 K.A.R. and two squadrons of South African Horse, gained the western edge of the ridge and began his attack, Hawthorn's advance guard was still some distance from the Iringa road.

The volume of enemy fire from the rocky outcrop was so intense that Rodger's troops were unable to cross the open ground before it. While they were thus at a standstill, two of Hawthorn's K.A.R. companies and one of his squadrons got astride the Iringa road at the eastern end of the ridge, and by midday had established a position facing in both directions, with 'A' (R) Company, 1 K.A.R., watching the route from Iringa.

As Hawthorn's troops came into action against the main enemy position, pushing in the outlying posts, two of his guns engaged the German howitzer but were knocked out almost immediately. Soon afterwards some enemy troops who had already withdrawn towards Iringa returned and entered the battle, engaging 'A' (R) Company in a hot little action in which nearly all the officers were killed or wounded.[1] For a time the situation was precarious, but reinforcements were spared from the main battle and the enemy was driven off. At the western end of the ridge, Rodger's K.A.R. company had at last effected a lodgment, but the issue was still in doubt when darkness put an end to the engagement. Abandoning the roadway and with it their 10.5-cm. howitzer, the Germans made off across country during the night. Thus the outcome of this inconclusive battle favoured the British, no doubt partly owing to the advance on Madibira that was carried out simultaneously.

By now Northey's little force had gone so far into enemy territory that the right flank was dangerously exposed. Van Deventer had begun his advance from Kondoa Irangi to the railway, and as the area in German hands continued to shrink, Northey's awareness of his danger grew. Lupembe lay at the edge of a food-producing area that helped to supply

---

[1] Lieutenant E. K. Borthwick (Spec. List) was awarded the M.C. for his prompt action in destroying two German machine-gunners who had got into the K.A.R. position, and capturing their gun.

the Mahenge plateau. Ten days before the action at Malangali Lieutenant E. G. Cooper (L'pool R.), patrolling from the outpost at Njombe on the extreme right of the British area, had found a party of the enemy at Lupembe and after a brief skirmish captured Dr. Stier, the Governor of Neu Langenburg. Since then reports had arrived of German movements from Iringa and Mahenge towards Lupembe.

Of all the columns invading German territory, Northey's was the only one that had any real cause to fear a counter-offensive. Suspending his advance beyond Malangali, he lost no time in investigating this threat to his right flank. On 26th July he dispatched Captain A. C. Masters (S. Wales Bord.) with a company of 1 K.A.R. and four 7-pounder guns to carry out a reconnaissance. Masters found the reports well founded. Moving down the Lupembe road he encountered on 4th August an enemy force that outnumbered his own by at least two to one, and before he could withdraw lost Lieutenant Cooper and six other ranks killed. Masters and 21 other ranks were wounded.

On receipt of this news, Northey at once ordered Hawthorn with 1 K.A.R. (five companies), a detachment of South African Rifles and supporting artillery to Njombe. On 12th August Hawthorn began his march down the Lupembe road. The enemy retreated before his approach, evacuating Lupembe and Mfirika, the last village on the edge of the plateau. Below lay the green carpet of forest and bush into which the German troops had disappeared. The whole area was intersected by the streams and rivers that form the headwaters of the great system that feeds the River Rufigi. Across the horizon, a hundred miles away to the north-east, lay the blue outlines of Mahenge.[1]

Hawthorn established his troops on the edge of the plateau, and his patrols began searching the country below. A large draft of recruits had reached him from Nyasaland, whom Hawthorn used to guard his line of communication while they continued their training. For the time being the right flank was secure.

As Smuts approached Morogoro, all indications of the enemy's line of retreat showed that it would lie towards Mahenge rather than Iringa. With Smuts' approval, therefore, Northey resumed his interrupted march from Malangali during the latter part of August. On the 29th Iringa was entered by the Northern Rhodesia Police, the Germans withdrawing towards Mahenge before their retreat could be intercepted.

In pushing his advance to Iringa, Northey had made effective contribution to the course of the invasion from the north. The Nyasaland Field Force was now distributed in two main groups, around Iringa and Lupembe. Smuts was convinced that it would still be possible for some of these troops to cross the headstreams of the Kilombero and reach Mahenge, at any rate for a brief raid on the crops, before the enemy could occupy the plateau in strength. The result for 1 K.A.R. was

---

[1] 'I can picture now the grandeur of this scene, its enormity and splendour. Far below trees dot, like little figures, the green carpets of the mighty plain; whilst the Kilombero, like a streak of silver, reflects the rays of a sun which brings the Mahenge hills close and in bold relief.' (Shorthose: *Sport and Adventure in Africa*, p. 127.)

several weeks of adventurous operations in thick forest, very different from those that had gone before.

Early in September a complicated series of movements began around the eastern escarpments, descending thence into the dense country bordering the rivers below. The plan was for a double advance, from Iringa and Lupembe, down the escarpments at Muhanga and Mfirika respectively, followed by a linking of forces at Makua, and then a joint advance on Mahenge.

From Iringa two columns set out through steep, broken country to follow the German retreat south-east. 'D' Company, 1 K.A.R., was included in this force. As the advance progressed the enemy rearguard had to be continually prised out of positions of great natural strength, though it soon became obvious that the Germans had no intention of making a stand. The edge of the plateau at Muhanga, where the hills fall away abruptly to the plain, was reached on 11th September. Before descending, the Germans had left their sick and wounded behind and destroyed all the ammunition and food they were unable to carry.

Muhanga was occupied, with forward posts in the valleys below, but here the pursuit from Iringa came to an end, owing to supply problems and the proximity of enemy columns retreating before van Deventer to the north. 'D' Company, 1 K.A.R., and a detachment of Rhodesians were then ordered south through the foothills to contact Hawthorn at Makua. It was a particularly arduous march, with the cool of the mountains suddenly changed for the heat of the plains. Marching at first on quarter rations and then for nearly a week on no rations at all, 'D' Company reached Makua on 20th September and gained touch with Hawthorn, who was near Kisingo, fifteen miles farther south.

Hawthorn's column had begun its eastward advance from Lupembe on 6th September. At Smuts' headquarters the idea still persisted that Mahenge could be raided quickly before the Germans assembled there in force. Inadequate maps caused some confusion in the attempt to co-ordinate Hawthorn's movement with the advance from Iringa, but his patrols ascertained that the Germans were across the Ruhuje, thus clearing the way for the junction of the two British columns. Cattle could not be driven on foot into the forest belt, and 1 K.A.R. had to depend partly on elephant meat and other game.

Descending into the valley of the Nyama and Mnyera rivers, Hawthorn reached their junction on 15th September, where he halted for supplies. Two companies of 1 K.A.R. were then sent ahead to Kisingo, and contact was established with the column from Iringa.

By this time the situation had become so obscure, both to Northey and to his column commanders, that the latter, who realized the hopelessness of attempting to reach Mahenge before the enemy could arrive, were obliged to act on their own initiative. Reports indicated that the enemy forces across the Ruhuje, who were in the neighbourhood of Mkapira, were being reinforced. On 20th September Hawthorn therefore led his column in that direction, and 1 K.A.R. began an extensive reconnaissance.

The Ruhuje was found to be a wide river infested with crocodiles, and some days elapsed before a way across was discovered. On 25th September a company of 1 K.A.R. reached the east bank and occupied the high ground beyond. The rest of the column followed two days later.

So far no opposition had been met. On the 28th, however, a force of the enemy with a light field gun suddenly opened a concentrated fire on the centre and right of Hawthorn's position. In the tangle of long grass and bush it was difficult to estimate the weight of the attack, which seemed in the confusion and noise to be heavier than was really the case. The field gun was soon put out of action, but the enemy continued to fire until darkness fell.

The supply situation was now so precarious that the advance towards Mahenge could no longer be pressed in the face of growing opposition. Hawthorn therefore withdrew from his exposed position across the Ruhuje and concentrated with the Iringa column in the area about Mkapira, while the work of organizing the line of communication went forward.

By September Northey's advanced troops were over 200 miles from their base on Lake Nyasa. As there appeared to be no prospect of the Portuguese linking up with his right flank, a detachment of the Rhodesia Native Regiment had been sent to occupy Songea. Van Deventer's right flank had reached the River Ruaha south of Kilosa, thus completing a tenuous line of posts that stretched right across German East Africa from Lake Nyasa to Dar-es-Salaam. All the German forces now lay to the south-east with the exception of von Wahle's, whose retreat from Tabora was in full progress towards the British line. In four months' campaigning the Nyasaland Field Force had made a notable contribution to the course of the campaign, though the dispersal of the troops over so great an area, where supply difficulties made rapid movement impossible, had placed many of the garrisons in positions of dangerous isolation.

So far, the brunt of these operations had fallen upon 1 K.A.R. Augmented by the draft of 500 recruits who had reached Lupembe in August, the battalion now numbered 35 officers and 1,286 African ranks, nearly half the total of Northey's entire force.

CHAPTER 12

The Expulsion of the Enemy from German Territory
OCTOBER, 1916-NOVEMBER, 1917

(i) *The Expansion of the K.A.R.*

TOWARDS the end of 1916, during the lull that came with the onset of the rains, General Smuts took stock of the situation and was obliged to recognize that most of his white troops were no longer fit for service. Medical boards were set up to investigate and as a result of their recommendations over 12,000 South African troops were on their way home, or earmarked for return, by the end of the year. The two English battalions were given recuperative spells in South Africa, but on their return the incidence of sickness proved as great as before, and they were posted to other theatres during 1917.[1] The health record of the Rhodesians was little better. Most of the Indian units continued to show a sick-rate of at least 20 per cent., and as supply problems mounted, became very difficult to feed. They also were withdrawn at the end of 1917.[2]

The task of driving von Lettow's forces from the southern half of the colony thus fell increasingly to the K.A.R. and the units from West Africa. Recognition of the principle that African campaigns are best conducted by African troops, so belatedly reached at the beginning of 1916, now began to bear fruit. Some of the highland tribes who enlisted in the new battalions suffered on transit to lowland or coastal areas, but otherwise sickness was comparatively slight, despite continued hardship and irregular supplies. It was noticeable that the experienced K.A.R.

---

[1] The Loyals went to Egypt and the Fusiliers were sent home.

[2] 'The valour and steadfast endurance of the troops from the United Kingdom and the British dependencies elsewhere were of no avail to keep them in the field. Only the African soldier could stand the East African climate indefinitely.' (Hordern, *Mil. Ops. in E. Africa*, I, 513.) W. W. Campbell in *East Africa by Motor Lorry* (p. 124) has told what campaigning in the lowlands of the coastal area meant to the European: 'I am perfectly certain the sun's power caused many of the extraordinary vacillations that trebled the difficulties of our unenviable experiences in this dark land.

'Distressed and depressed beyond measure, we felt that death and ugliness lurked everywhere. It was in the air we breathed, the water we drank, the sun that warmed our bodies; it crawled on the ground. dripped heavily from rain-sodden trees, hung suspended in the humid, reeking atmosphere. Every living thing went in fear of its life, or turned upon another in self-preservation. Human life itself was an embodiment of ignorance and suspicion. It permeated our very souls, turned bright thoughts into dark, and made one long for the fate that he feared.'

Hoskins in his despatch dated 30th May, 1917 (pp. 161-62) recognized that the inability of white troops to stand the climate had put an additional strain on the Indian, and especially the African units: 'The hardships of the campaign and the brunt of the fighting since 1914 had been borne by some Indian units and by the King's African Rifles. These had also suffered severely from sickness, especially the Indians; but units were so weak as to make it impossible to withdraw any of the King's African Rifles, and only certain of the Indians were able to be sent to healthier ground to recuperate.'

officer, unlike his colleagues in the white regiments, proved nearly as healthy as his men.

While the three regular battalions were serving in the field under Northey, Smuts and Crewe, the training of new units went forward. The officer responsible was Colonel E. H. Llewellyn, who in due course was appointed Commandant of the K.A.R. with the rank of Brigadier-General. He was aided by an Assistant Commandant (Colonel G. F. Phillips) and a headquarters staff. Recruiting was centralized; differences of pay and conditions were smoothed out, and authority was obtained to include a number of British N.C.Os. on establishment.[1] Before proceeding further with the military operations of the campaign, it will be appropriate to summarize here the expansion and complete reorganization of the K.A.R. that took place towards the end of 1916 and during the first half of 1917.

When Smuts began his invasion of German East Africa, the Nyasaland forces were still under the Colonial Office, and the companies of 1 K.A.R. serving with Northey drew their reinforcement drafts direct from home territory. The rest of the K.A.R. reinforcement and training was carried out at Mbagathi near Nairobi, where from very small beginnings a large training depôt grew up, for officers as well as men. Officers were supplied largely from the ranks of the East Africa Mounted Rifles and the Rhodesia Regiment, with a few from South African units.[2]

On 22nd January, 1917, 1 K.A.R. was divided into two battalions, each of four companies. 1/1 K.A.R., serving in the Lupembe area, was formed from 'A'(R), 'B'(R), 'H' and 'D' Companies, and 2/1 K.A.R., first employed in the Songea area, from 'C'(R) and 'F' Companies, plus recruits in each case. The latter battalion, under strength at first, was not brought up to establishment until later in the year, when another company was added.

It will have been noticed that the four companies of 1 K.A.R. serving in the northern theatre disappeared from Smuts' invasion force after taking part in the encirclement of Kilimanjaro. They were withdrawn to form the nucleus of the new 2 K.A.R., which came into being at Nairobi on 1st April, 1916, with 31 officers and 333 other ranks, to whom were added the first draft of recruits from Nyasaland. In May it was decided to form two battalions, and during the next few weeks this reorganization was carried out, 1/2 K.A.R. being primarily a Yao battalion, and 2/2 K.A.R. predominantly Atonga and Angoni. As already noted, 1/2 K.A.R., under command of Lieutenant-Colonel L. H. Soames, who afterwards commanded the depôt battalion of this regiment, was the first new unit to take the field, and reached Smuts' advanced headquarters at Morogoro on 28th August, 1916. 2/2 K.A.R., also on the way south,

---

[1] At the beginning of the war there were two B.N.C.Os. serving with the regiment. Shortly after it ended there were nearly 3,000. But the proportion of B.N.C.Os. to African ranks was at its lowest (1:35½) during the first half of 1917. See Appendix E.

[2] Lack of *experienced* officers, though the number of officers increased proportionately towards the end of the campaign, was a great handicap to the new K.A.R. units. It was no unusual thing for officers to lead their troops in battle without being able to say a word to them in their own language.

got as far as Handeni by 8th September. Both these battalions returned to Korogwe and thence to Tanga, where they embarked to join a new force then assembling down the coast at Kilwa.

In September, 1916, Smuts was beginning to regroup his forces. It was now plain that von Lettow would withdraw slowly on to the Mahenge plateau and then probably into Portuguese East Africa, where he would gain more room for manœuvre. For the moment, however, the German forces were still divided, those near Mahenge or withdrawing in that direction from Tabora being separated from von Lettow's position on the Mgeta by the formidable barrier of the Rufigi. To drive the enemy south across this river by a frontal attack would be an arduous task, as the rains would convert large tracts of the Rufigi basin into impassable swamp. Smuts estimated that his advance from the Mgeta position would therefore be confined to the vicinity of Kimbambawe and Mroka, where the river flowed through higher ground. His plan was to combine this advance with a thrust inland from the port of Kilwa, which would threaten the German rear while he endeavoured to separate von Lettow's troops from those about Mahenge and drive them towards the coast. Van Deventer and Northey were to attack the Mahenge position simultaneously.

During the last few months of 1916 the regrouping of the British forces went forward accordingly. Command of the Kilwa force was given to Brigadier-General Hannyngton, whose infantry was formed into a 3rd East African Infantry Brigade (1/2 and 2/2 K.A.R., two Indian battalions, and the 2nd Loyals). The 2nd East African Infantry Brigade, now commanded by Colonel H. de C. O'Grady, left Tulo on 7th November for Dar-es-Salaam, where 3 K.A.R. embarked on the 21st and reached Kilwa a week later, together with a large batch of recruits. It was intended that 3 K.A.R. should be given some six weeks in the Kilwa area, to form two battalions and complete the absorption and training of the new draft.

A few days were spent establishing the camp, and the work of reorganization began. 3 K.A.R. had served under Smuts as a battalion of four companies: 'A', 'B', 'D' and 'E'.[1] 'B' and 'D' Companies now became the nucleus of the new 1/3 K.A.R., and 'A' and 'E' Companies of 2/3 K.A.R. Each of these companies was then divided into two, 'B' Company becoming Nos. 1 and 2 and 'D' Company Nos. 3 and 4 of 1/3 K.A.R. The company cadres so formed were then brought up to establishment by drafts from the depôt recruits, N.C.Os. were made up, and a new organization by platoons instead of sections was adopted.

After the disbandment of the Lake Force, 4 K.A.R. was incorporated in the 3rd South African Infantry Brigade, which formed part of van Deventer's 2nd Division. In view of the coming expansion, its eight companies ('A' to 'H') were regrouped during October and November, 1916, into four numbered companies. 2/4 K.A.R., a new recruit battalion, reached Dar-es-Salaam by sea on 1st February, 1917, and went

---

[1] 'C' Company had not been re-formed after the beri-beri outbreak; 'F' (Camel) Company was in Jubaland; part of 'G' Company was still in the N.F.D., and the rest of it had been drafted to the other companies.

to the Dodoma area to complete its training. The reorganization involved splitting the original 4 K.A.R., 1/4 K.A.R. retaining Nos. 2, 3 and half No. 4 Company, and posting No. 1 and the other half of No. 4 Company to 2/4 K.A.R. The former battalion went to join Northey in March, 1917, leaving behind with the Iringa column the company and a half that were eventually absorbed into 2/4 K.A.R. In May, 1917, 1/4 K.A.R. was brought up to strength at Njombe by a new draft of 10 officers and 384 other ranks.

The early part of 1917 thus found the original battalions and 2 K.A.R. divided into two, while the training of a third battalion for each was in progress. A new 5 K.A.R., with eight companies of 100 men and two Mounted Infantry Sections of 50 men each, had been formed out of the companies of 3 K.A.R. still on the northern frontier ('F' and 'G' Companies), the Turkana Service Company, 'D' Company of the disbanded Police Service Battalion, the Jubaland Constabulary, and some 800 Somali, Giriama and other recruits. The task of this battalion was to garrison Jubaland and patrol the Abyssinian border. At this stage of the expansion, therefore, the K.A.R. consisted of five regiments, each with its own depôt, and comprising altogether 13 battalions.

Prior to June, 1916, a K.A.R. battalion was organized in eight single companies, each commanded by a captain. Afterwards the organization of those intended for German East Africa was changed to four companies, and the senior captain in the battalion was given the rank of Temporary Major. On 28th June, 1917, the War Office sanctioned the formation of a half machine-gun company for each battalion. The title 'Commandant' as applied to the officer commanding a battalion was abolished.

In February, 1917, it was decided to increase the K.A.R. to 20 battalions, partly because the possibility of employment in the middle eastern theatre of war was under discussion. In addition to a fourth battalion for 1, 2 and 3 K.A.R., and fourth, fifth and sixth battalions for 4 K.A.R., two new regiments were also raised.

The formation of 6 K.A.R. began in April, 1917, at Morogoro, partly from experienced ex-enemy askaris in the prisoner-of-war camps, and partly from recruits originally intended for the extra battalions of 3 K.A.R. Two battalions of this regiment were raised.

The Zanzibar African Rifles and the Mafia Armed Constabulary had been amalgamated in October, 1916, the intention being to include them in the K.A.R. under the title 'King's African Coastal Rifles'. After some discussion and examination of alternative proposals, it was finally decided that this force should be one of the new battalions authorized by the War Office, and 7 K.A.R. accordingly came into being at Zanzibar on 1st May, 1917. The depôt was also at Zanzibar, and recruiting went on there and in the coastal areas of the mainland. In July the battalion moved to Voi for service as line-of-communication and coastal-garrison troops.

The final strength, therefore, reached by the K.A.R. during this campaign was seven regiments, totalling 22 battalions. Some of these were training and garrison units, but about half served in the field during the operations now to be described. At first the quality of these new units was very different from that of the three battalions that had participated in the campaign to date, and the superiority of the seasoned enemy askari over the young K.A.R. recruit was very marked. So much the greater, therefore, was the achievement of those officers, N.C.Os. and experienced soldiers who carried the new battalions through the disasters that befell some of them during their first few months on active service.

(ii) *The Advance from Kilwa: Operations around Kibata, October, 1916-January, 1917.* Maps VI (a), 18, 19.

During the last quarter of 1916, as the water rose in the Rufigi basin, German supply troubles on the swampy Mgeta front steadily multiplied. Their troops were fed by boat from the fertile areas surrounding the lower reaches of the river, and soon after the position on the Mgeta stabilized, von Lettow began a steady withdrawal of his forces towards these centres of supply. Reports reached General Smuts of the regrouping of the enemy's main strength near Utete, and of the establishment of food depôts in the south, at Madaba and Liwale. Kilwa was the best base from which to attack the latter, and to assist in a fresh encircling movement to pin von Lettow against the sea.

Though at that time quite undeveloped, the harbour at Kilwa Kisiwani, unlike that at Kilwa Kivinje, where ships had to lie several miles from the beaches, had deep water close to the shore. The first troops dispatched there in September, 1916, took up defensive positions on the heights around, while the construction of landing-piers and other works began. By the end of September the equivalent of four infantry battalions had arrived, and many technical units. Headquarters of the 3rd Infantry Brigade (Brigadier-General J. A. Hannyngton) landed on 6th October; of the 1st Division (Major-General A. R. Hoskins) on 13th November; and of the 2nd Infantry Brigade (Brigadier-General H. de C. O'Grady) on 29th November. The fighting troops of these formations included two new battalions, 1/2 and 2/2 K.A.R., and two reorganized battalions, 1/3 and 2/3 K.A.R. Other units were the Loyals, the 2nd West India Regiment, the 40th Pathans and the 129th Baluchis.

The first K.A.R. unit to reach Kilwa was 2/2 K.A.R., on 29th September. The battalion was soon in action. The country was wild and there were no proper maps, so that reports on the direction and condition of roads and tracks depended on native sources. Eight miles west of Kilwa, at the ford over the River Matandu, a defensive post had been set up. On 2nd October the enemy attacked this and occupied some heights nearby. 2/2 K.A.R. was sent up to reinforce the fort, but the Germans broke off the action and retired towards Kimbarambara.

The natural route inland lay up the valley of the Matandu to Njinjo, a distance of forty-two miles. Beyond there, other tracks branched north to Utete, west to Madaba, and south-west to Liwale. But there was another route from Kilwa to Utete, that ran direct to the north-west over the Mtumbei Hills, a great mass of uplands, cooler and healthier than the steaming districts bordering the Matandu valley and the coast. In the centre of these hills the Germans had constructed a strong fort at Kibata.

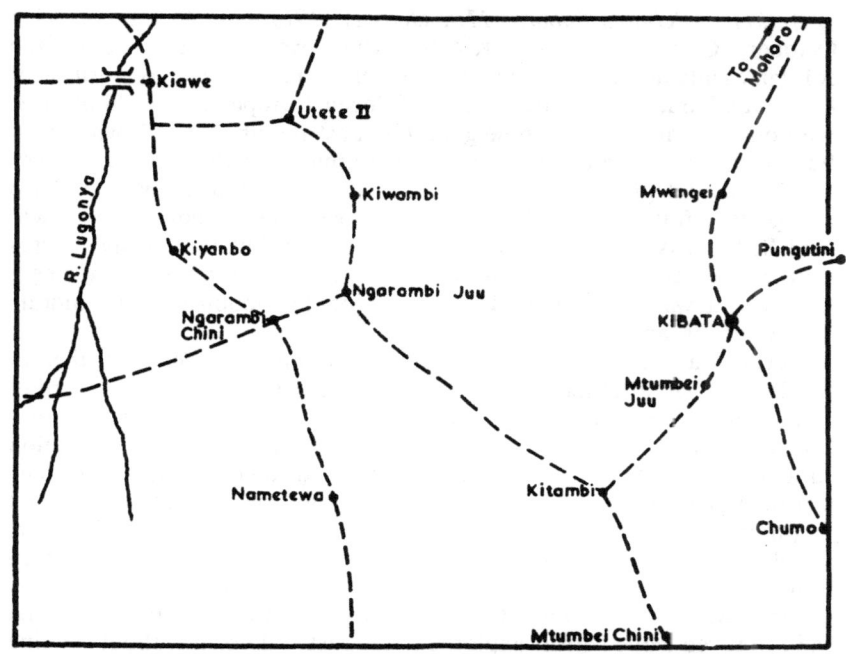

18. The Environs of Kibata

Action at Njinjo, 9th October, 1916.—Smuts had given instructions that the Kilwa Force should push inland as soon as possible. On 4th October 2/2 K.A.R. under Lieutenant-Colonel H. S. Filsell (R. War. R.) therefore marched west up the river valley to occupy Njinjo. On arrival Filsell went into camp beyond the village. His presence was at first unsuspected, and on 8th October the German District Commissioner, complete with staff and treasure chest, was taken prisoner. On the following day a German detachment 60 strong arrived from the direction of Kibata. 2/2 K.A.R. took it by surprise and for a loss of two men killed and six wounded killed the German commander, two other Europeans and 15 askaris, wounded two and captured 16 others and a machine gun. It was a dashing little action that acted as a tonic on the new soldiers, and particularly on those in No. 4 Company, who were chiefly responsible for the success.

Reconnaissance from Njinjo revealed the presence of weak enemy detachments at Ndende, Mtumbei Chini and Nambanje to the north, and at Mpotora to the west. There was no sign of any large concentration of the enemy. After a few weeks 2/2 K.A.R. was relieved and withdrawn to Mitole for a rest that proved to be short-lived.

To co-operate directly with the main British forces in the north, and to prevent his troops from going sick in the coastal area, Hannyngton had decided on a simultaneous advance into the Mtumbei Hills. On 7th October 1/2 K.A.R. disembarked at Kilwa Kisiwani, and went into camp near Kilwa Kivinje. Three days later the battalion, about 650 rifles strong, accompanied by 250 rifles of the 129th Baluchis, set out for Kibata.

Action at Kimbarambara, 11th October, 1916.—At 8 a.m. on 11th October, 'C' Company, 1/2 K.A.R., which was marching before the column as advance guard, came upon a well-entrenched enemy position at Kimbarambara, manned by some half-dozen Europeans and 70 askaris, with one gun and one machine gun. The post lay upon a hill, with thick bush to the east and comparatively open ground on the south and west. 'B' Company deployed to the right and 'A' Company to the left. A sharp engagement followed as all three companies pressed home the attack. One British askari was killed and two wounded, but the enemy's losses were greater and he soon withdrew northward into thick country where fast pursuit was impossible. The success of this action sent the morale of the new askaris soaring.

Next day a similar action was fought by the Baluchis, who were then in the lead. That afternoon the column reached Chumo without further contact with the enemy. Many of the young troops were suffering from exhaustion through lack of water, and coco-nuts from a nearby plantation supplied the deficiency. Kibata was reached on 14th October. The Germans had evacuated the stone fort the night before, leaving a white flag flying above it, and retired along the road towards Utete.[1] The fort stood in a prominent position on top of a large, cleared hill with steep slopes to north and east, and was dominated by a number of other hills covered with trenches and defensive works. These were now enlarged and improved while patrols explored to the east and north without sighting the enemy. The Baluchis then returned to Kilwa.

Lieutenant-Colonel Soames left Kibata for Kilwa on 24th October, and Lieutenant-Colonel G. J. Giffard took command of 1/2 K.A.R. During the month a small German detachment was driven from Ndende. The Njinjo garrison (which early in November transferred most of its strength to a new position on a hill at Mchemera, four miles to the west) had established an outpost at Nambanje on the Utete road, and the western flank of the Kibata position was further secured by the occupation of a strong position first at Mtumbei Chini and then at Kitambi. The only garrison then left at the fort consisted of two platoons and a machine-gun section.

Early in November news reached the headquarters of 1/2 K.A.R. at Kitambi that the enemy was advancing against Kibata, with a force of about 400 rifles and two machine guns. Giffard hurried to the rescue by forced marches, to find the enemy occupying positions that already threatened the fort. On 8th November 'A' and 'C' Companies, going into action immediately on arrival, dug themselves in under a heavy fire. The enemy withdrew that night. Patrols followed, while the battalion set to work improving the defences around Kibata.

The main enemy forces were now concentrating around Utete and Mohoro. Von Lettow, after reacting to a minor British movement southward from Dar-es-Salaam, had discovered that the real threat was likely to come from Kibata. The result was a series of determined attempts to retake the position that began early in December and lasted

---

[1] A copy of a letter found in the fort described the position as untenable, and said the intention was to withdraw if attacked.

with intervals until the middle of January. Kibata was the real baptism of fire of the K.A.R. New Army, and its defence was a grim affair, involving concentrations of fire hitherto unknown in East Africa.

At the end of October Smuts visited Kilwa, and it was then that the decision was taken to send Hoskins with the headquarters of the 1st Division and a second infantry brigade. By the beginning of December Kibata had been reinforced by the Baluchis. The 40th Pathans were at Ngarambi and 2/2 K.A.R. in reserve at Mitole, where Hannyngton had his headquarters. The newly-arrived 2nd Infantry Brigade had taken over the line westward, ready for an advance on Liwale, with the Gold Coast Regiment at Mchemera and Nambanje. 1/3 and 2/3 K.A.R. were in camp at Mpara near Kilwa, carrying out the reorganization into two battalions. For this and the field training so necessary for the recruits, they had been led to expect a six weeks' interval.

On 17th November Lieutenant-Colonel Hulseberg of the 129th Baluchis took command at Kibata. The post now formed the key to all the northern dispositions of the 1st Division, with roads radiating north via Mwengei to Utete and Mohoro, west to Kitambi, and back through Chumo village to the base at Kilwa. The narrow, cleared valley that surrounded the fort was protected by defence works on the other hills. The most important of these were two redoubts on Picquet Hill, which lay to the left of the road down which attack might be expected, and overlooked the fort. To the right of the position lay a wide ridge of high ground that circled round past Coco-nut Village to terminate at Mbirikia Hill. Another ridge extended through Ambush Hill to the north, where the road was flanked by an eminence, later occupied by the German Headquarters, that came to be known as the Kommando Berg. The positions constructed by the Germans on these heights near the Utete road were particularly strong, with well-concealed defences made of fallen trees with pointed branches, faced by deep pits covered with brushwood and grass.

The garrison of Kibata was now about 800 strong, including 18 officers and 563 African ranks of 1/2 K.A.R. Part of the battalion was holding outposts at Coco-nut Village and on Ambush Hill. By the first week of December patrols were in contact with the enemy, who was approaching from the north with gangs of natives dragging heavy artillery behind him.

Action at Kibata, 6th-9th December, 1916.—About 1 p.m. on 6th December the German columns came in sight of Kibata, advancing in extended order across the Kommando Berg and on to Ambush Hill. The K.A.R. outposts were forced back and Coco-nut Village went up in flames. Rifle and machine-gun fire continued till nightfall.

At daylight next morning the enemy extended their attack to the position at Palm Village. Shortly afterwards a determined onslaught was made upon Picquet Hill, the key to the whole system. The redoubts were garrisoned by two companies of the Baluchis, who were bombarded at close range by a 4.1-inch *Königsberg* gun, a 4.1-inch howitzer and a field gun. Of 272 shells that fell upon the British defences during this bombardment, over 100 fell upon No. 2 Redoubt, which was nearly destroyed. Strenuous efforts were made to repair the damage. At 6 p.m., after another bombardment lasting half an hour, the enemy again attacked in force. The Baluchis held on, though they could not prevent the enemy from gaining a footing on the western side of the hill.

When darkness fell the Baluchis were withdrawn from Picquet Hill and replaced by 'C' Company, 1/2 K.A.R., under Captain R. C. Hardingham (Middx. R.). A projected night attack had to be called off, as the young askaris had been too shaken by the bombardment. On the morning of the 8th the enemy guns again opened fire, and the assault on the redoubts was renewed. After initial hesitation the men of 'C' Company stood firm, and had already repulsed the attack by their rifle fire before the arrival of 60 Baluchis, sent up to reinforce them. Firing was kept up throughout the day while the enemy tried to work around the flanks of the British position.

By this time reinforcements were on the way. On 7th December 2/2 K.A.R. and two guns of 27 Mountain Battery were ordered to Kibata from the reserve force at Mitole. In pouring rain Lieutenant-Colonel H. S. Filsell made a forced march of thirty-six miles in thirty-four hours over a series of razor-backed ridges separated by deep gullies, across which the track ran in a straight line. Troops, mules, stores, ammunition and guns reached Kibata at two o'clock on the morning of 9th December. As senior officer present Filsell took command and at once reinforced Picquet Hill. The rest of his battalion camped in the depression between Mango Hill and the fort, known to the officers as 'Happy Valley', until forced into the shelter of Fort Hill next day after twelve hours' continuous shelling.[1]

At 10 p.m. on the 9th a counter-attack was made on the German trenches on Picquet Hill by a company of Baluchis, supported by two platoons of 1/2 K.A.R. The effort failed, and for some days nothing further was attempted. Intermittent shelling continued, and the fort slowly disintegrated, though the Union Flag still flew from its staff above the ruins.

In the middle of December Brigadier-General O'Grady took command. The Gold Coast Regiment, 40th Pathans, more mountain guns and a badly-needed convoy of grenades and ammunition arrived. Casualties were now 31 killed, 88 wounded and eight missing, mostly from the two K.A.R. battalions. An attempt to relieve the pressure by threatening the German emplacements along the Mwengei road was made by the Gold Coast Regiment at Banda Hill. Progress was soon stopped by artillery fire, which left the British troops pinned down in positions on the rocky hills where cover was difficult, and the attempt was abandoned.

On 15th December the enemy was at last dislodged from Picquet Hill. The Mills grenade, like the Stokes mortar, was a new weapon in the East African theatre, and it was decided to make use of its surprise effect. The enemy's trenches were protected by stakes and thorn bomas, and the intention was to stun him into inactivity with the bombs while these obstacles were torn away. The attack was made after dark by the Baluchis; the enemy was driven out with loss, and the ground so gained

---

[1] As late as the following July some askaris of 2/2 K.A.R. were using this hurried move at Kibata as an excuse for lost kit!

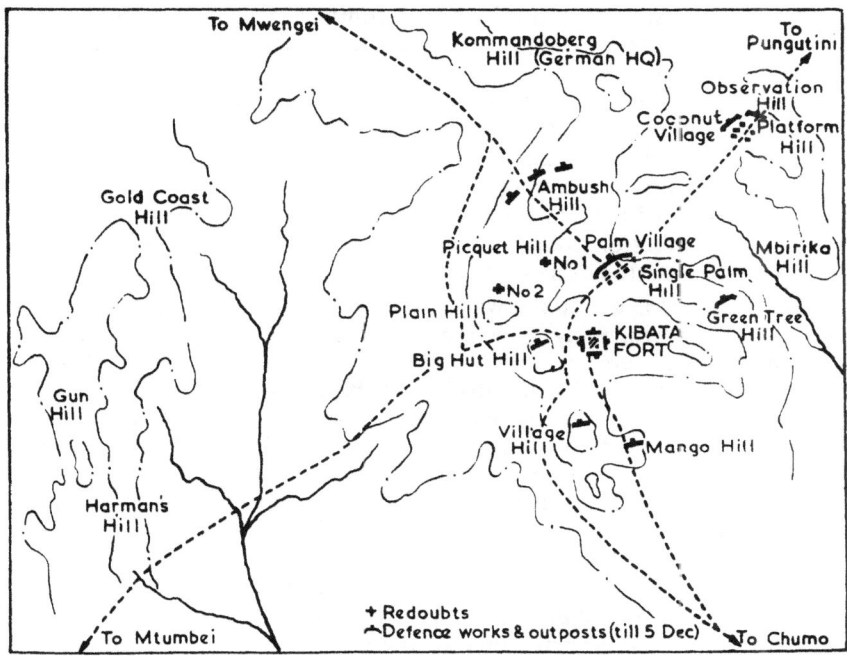

19. The Kibata Positions

was then occupied by 'A' Company, 1/2 K.A.R., who were subjected to a severe bombardment throughout the following day.

On 18th December 1/3 K.A.R. reached Kibata. Ten days before, less than a week after the reorganization of 3 K.A.R. into two battalions, 1/3 K.A.R. had been ordered to Matandu, a difficult move carried out in pouring rain with the aid of sick and broken-down mule transport. Two days later the long, muddy march to Chumo began. On arrival two companies essayed an attack on the German left flank, but heavy rain prevented this and the whole battalion marched to Kibata. 1/3 K.A.R. then relieved the troops in some of the outposts, and 2/2 K.A.R. was withdrawn to Mchemera. 2/3 K.A.R., moving inland from Kilwa, went into reserve at Mitole.

Except for patrol actions and intermittent shelling, a lull now succeeded at Kibata. With most of the Kilwa Force committed to positions in the Mtumbei Hills, the projected advance to the west had been postponed. Pressed by Smuts to attack the important enemy supply centre at Liwale, the Portuguese had occupied Newala, but late in November they were invested there and forced to scatter into the bush with the loss of much valuable equipment. The German escape route to the south therefore still remained open.

By this time (mid-December) comparatively few enemy troops remained on the Mgeta front. Hoskins was convinced that von Lettow could not turn him out of Kibata, and Smuts thought that if he could cross the Mgeta and the Rufigi before the floods rose, he might join hands with the Kilwa Force at Ngarambi, and so complete the encirclement of the enemy on the Lower Rufigi. Crossing the Mgeta with four columns at the end of December, Smuts drove the enemy over the Rufigi. The Germans then stood to defend the approach to Mibaba, possession of which was essential for the safety of their main forces, then waiting to harvest the crops near Lake Utenge. Hoskins had been ordered to hold a battalion ready to move to Ngarambi, but the tsetse fly, heavy rains and soft roads of the Matandu valley had made supply so difficult that any large number of troops at Ngarambi might be in a dangerous position so long as strong enemy forces remained in the Mtumbei Hills.

The next step, therefore, was a renewal of the British offensive at Kibata. The German right having already proved unapproachable and a frontal attack being considered too costly, it remained to explore the German left, and a series of patrols took place over the turn of the year. Volunteers were also called upon to locate the exact position of the enemy guns. On 31st December Brigadier-General O'Grady and Lieutenant-Colonel Giffard carried out a daring reconnaissance of Mbirikia Hill. A machine gun that for three weeks had menaced the cross-roads below the fort was silenced, and Lieutenant C. G. W. Anderson (Spec. List) of 1/3 K.A.R. went off on a four-day patrol to reconnoitre an approach to the heavier artillery. On 1st January, 1917, two companies 1/3 K.A.R. and a section of mountain guns marched six miles eastward to Pungutini, where they ejected a small force of the enemy.

Action at Kibata, 7th-9th January, 1917.—The flank attack via Mbirikia, Platform Hill and Coco-nut Village was entrusted to 1/2 K.A.R. The approach by tracks through the thick bush of the intervening valley was reconnoitred, and on the night of 6th/7th January Lieutenant-Colonel Giffard with 'A' and 'B' Companies, 1/2 K.A.R., and four machine guns crossed the floor of the valley and gained a commanding position at the top of Mbirikia Hill, about 1,200 yards from the enemy outpost on Platform Hill. At dawn 'A' Company moved forward, drove in the enemy picquets, threw smoke bombs to indicate the position to the gunners at Kibata, and after the bombardment had lifted, rushed the hill. From there Giffard pushed on without pause to Observation Hill, seized it almost at once, repelled a counter-attack and before midday had the satisfaction of seeing the enemy retreating from Coco-nut Village, which was occupied by 1/3 K.A.R. and the Baluchis.

On 8th January the outflanking movement was resumed. At Coco-nut Village Giffard's column was joined by another company of 1/2 K.A.R., 100 Baluchis, four machine guns of the Loyals and a section of mountain guns. By 11.30 a.m. he had captured Single Palm Hill, which at two o'clock was taken over by 1/3 K.A.R. Meanwhile the advance continued against Ambush Hill, which the enemy evacuated after a short resistance. Giffard's troops dug in under artillery fire, not far from the Kommando Berg.

The final stage of the action took place next day, when a general attack was ordered on the Kommando Berg up the four steep spurs on the south and east faces. Little resistance was encountered, as the main body of the enemy had already withdrawn. On the 11th the Baluchis took up the pursuit and drove the German rearguard out of Mwengei. There roads branched north to Utete and north-east to Mohoro. 'A' and 'B' Companies, 1/2 K.A.R., and the Baluchis followed the former. On 13th January the German rearguard made another stand. While the Baluchis attacked, a detachment of 1/2 K.A.R. marched round the western flank, and finding themselves thus threatened the enemy withdrew that night, after destroying the *Königsberg* gun. This was the last action fought by the Germans before finally evacuating the Mtumbei Hills.

So ended the Kibata campaign, the first set battle in which the new K.A.R. units took part. It was fought in conditions nearer to those in Flanders than any other engagement during the whole East Africa Campaign: incessant rain, opposing trenches approaching to within eighty yards, sapping, periscopes, sniping, and grenades. On the whole, after becoming inured to gun fire, the recruits stood the test with credit. 1/2 K.A.R. bore a large share of the fighting, and lost three officers killed and died of wounds, two officers wounded, 17 other ranks killed, 46 wounded and one missing, besides casualties among the porters.

(iii) *The Advance from Kilwa: Operations around Utete, January, 1917.* Maps VI (a), 20, 21.

In January, 1917, Lieutenant-General Smuts relinquished his command in East Africa to attend the Imperial Conference in London as representative of the South African Government. The unbounded energy and enthusiasm with which he had conducted the campaign had deprived the enemy of nearly every important geographical and economic factor in the colony. But this circumstance, however fortunate in itself, tended to obscure the important fact that von Lettow and his army were still in the field, experienced, unbeaten, and full of fight. Smuts left Dar-es-Salaam on 20th January and was succeeded in command by Hoskins.

The attack from the north across the Rufigi was now being pressed, and the 1st Division prepared to co-operate by continuing its advance to the north and west over as wide a front as possible. West of Kibata the 3rd Brigade, led by the 40th Pathans, went forward to Ngarambi, which was reached on 11th January. 2/2 K.A.R. moved up from Mchemera by companies, headquarters of the battalion reaching Ngarambi on the 22nd. Brigade Headquarters, some artillery and the Gold Coast Regiment followed soon afterwards, and patrols were dispatched towards Lake Utunge and Madaba. On 27th January Filsell advanced to Kiwambi with a column consisting of 150 rifles 2/2 K.A.R., 250 Pathans and a section of mountain guns. The enemy retired about two miles to the north-west, where he took up position on 'Sugar Loaf Hill'. Filsell dug in, as for the time being shortage of water and food prevented him from following. It was not until 5th February that he was ready to attack, only to find that the enemy had already retired.

The advance of the 3rd Brigade had exposed the western flank of the Kilwa area. This brought 2/3 K.A.R. into active service for the first time. On 7th January the battalion left Mitole, where it had been held in reserve, and marched to Mchemera. Patrols were sent to Mpotora and

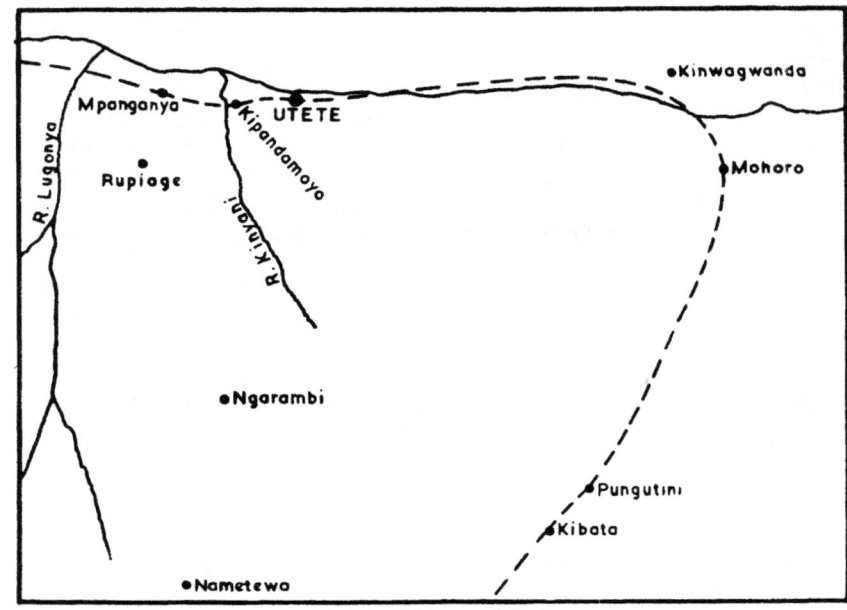

20. The Environs of Utete

Nambanje, to investigate enemy activities reported at both places. It was soon discovered that six Germans and about 100 askaris were entrenched near Mpotora.

Action at Mpotora, 22nd January, 1917.—On 22nd January Major H. C. Dickinson (Somerset L.I.) set out to attack this position with a force of 125 askaris and four machine guns. Making a wide circle along the bank of the Matandu, Dickinson came round to the west of Mpotora, reached the Liwale road, and almost at once sighted the enemy position among some high rocks about 300 yards north of the track. Though realizing its strength he decided to attack, but as little progress had been made at the end of an hour, ordered a general retirement. This was the signal for a counter-attack pressed with such determination that Dickinson had some difficulty in getting away with his wounded. He estimated the enemy strength at 150 rifles and three machine guns.

Mpotora was again reconnoitred on 1st February by Lieutenant L. A. Pickerell (Spec. List). A few days later the same officer, when patrolling with a dozen askaris, attacked an enemy detachment without first discovering its strength. As this proved to be five Europeans and 60 askaris he was obliged to make a hasty retreat.

After the expulsion of the Germans from Kibata, 1/3 K.A.R. was ordered eastward through Pungutini on the road towards Mohoro, to clear the whole of the divisional right flank as far as the sea. Fighting frequent small actions against rearguards and patrols, Lieutenant-Colonel Fitzgerald advanced to Mohoro, which he reached on 16th January. A few days' patrolling showed that the enemy had evacuated the coastal area and gone towards Utete. On 22nd January Captain von Otter took a section across the Rufigi in boats, marched north for five miles to

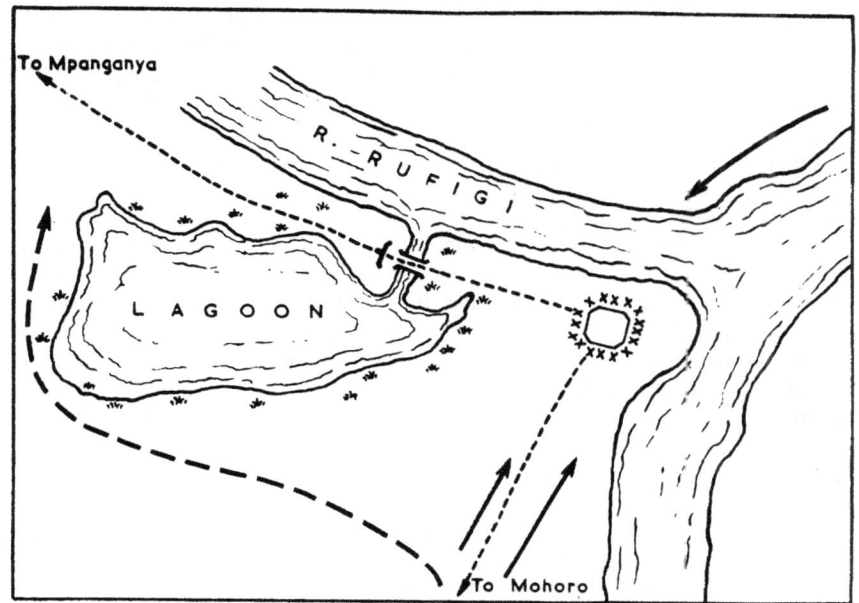

21. Investment of Utete Fort, January, 1917

Kinwagwanda and captured six out of a party of seven Europeans, with most of their followers and baggage. A patrol under Lieutenant E. Tarlton (Spec. List) achieved a similar success at Utunge a few days later.

Orders were now issued for an attack on the German fort at Utete. Fitzgerald set out with his battalion from Mohoro, and Major Hardingham with 'A' and 'B' Companies, 1/2 K.A.R., marched north from the Mtumbei Hills. Hardingham arrived on 27th January, and detaching a small picquet to watch the fort, camped at a water-hole two miles to the rear. The enemy then sallied out and drove the picquet back to the camp, and only withdrew when the advance guard of 1/3 K.A.R. arrived to take part in the action. By the evening of the 28th both columns had concentrated for the attack.

Attack at Utete, 29th-31st January, 1917.—Fitzgerald planned to invest Utete on all sides to prevent reinforcement or escape. The fort was an elaborate and well-equipped building of solid stone two storeys high, built around a stone-flagged courtyard. It stood on a small hill in a bend of the Rufigi, protected by a system of trenches and obstacles. Reports put the garrison, which was commanded by the veteran Lieutenant-Colonel von Bock, at from one to three companies. On the south the position was protected by a swampy area surrounding a shallow lagoon. The north bank of the river was also swampy, but to complete his cordon Fitzgerald decided to send a half-company across. As the enemy had collected all the boats this detachment had to march back to Utunge, causing several days' delay.

In the meantime reconnaissance of the fort and its surroundings continued. A road was discovered running west between the lagoon and the river, in the direction of Mpanganya, crossing the swamp by a causeway. About 400 yards from the fort this causeway was broken by a bridge over a small stream. The point was protected by a German outpost with two machine guns, and the whole causeway could be swept by fire from the fort.

On the evening of 29th January the German outpost was attacked by two companies of 1/3 K.A.R. under Captain W. G. Edwards (Spec. List). That day a British aeroplane, sent to bomb the fort, had landed seven bombs in the British trenches instead. This did not improve the morale of the K.A.R. recruits, and Edwards met with so intense a concentration of fire that he felt unable to press the attack. Next day the aeroplane returned, and this time delivered eight bombs upon and around the British trenches. A mountain gun arrived and shelled the fort. Fitzgerald decided before renewing the attack to try an approach to the causeway from the direction of Mpanganya. A half-company was detailed for this purpose under Captain von Otter, but its progress was slow as the area surrounding the lagoon proved very difficult to cross.

Heavy rain fell during the night of 30th/31st January. Under cover of darkness the enemy silently evacuated the fort and withdrew across the causeway. At daylight von Otter's little force was brushed aside. A detachment sent to cut the road farther west and pin the enemy between the lagoon and the river fared no better. Further reinforcements were brought forward by Captain Edwards from the fort in an effort to bring the retreating enemy to action, but the result was merely to confuse the situation in the thick bush, and despite due precautions the K.A.R. detachments were soon fighting a lively little engagement on their own while the enemy drew clear. Fortunately casualties were very slight, though the expenditure of ammunition was high.

Eventually the pursuit was resumed, and at 10 a.m. on 2nd February the enemy rearguard was met, entrenched across the track near Kipandamoyo. The two K.A.R. companies attacked, but were in turn counter-attacked and driven back with serious loss. The pursuit was then abandoned and the companies returned to Utete Fort, having lost out of their combined strength of about 160 men two officers wounded and 60 other ranks killed or wounded. A fresh company was sent west to establish an outpost along the road.

1/2 K.A.R. was withdrawn to Kilwa for rest and re-equipment pending transfer to the Lindi area. 1/3 K.A.R. remained in position around Utete. On 7th February the enemy rearguard withdrew from Kipandamoyo across the River Kinyani, which was beginning to flood. No. 3 Company took up position covering the crossing, facing an enemy post on the opposite bank. As the waters widened between them, the K.A.R. had continually to move their camp on to higher ground. The Germans were in still worse plight, and at last the officer in command, marooned without food on top of some native huts, was obliged to appeal for rescue.

Patrolling continued, but larger operations were no longer possible. On 25th February Rupiage was occupied, and after an unsuccessful attempt to recapture it next day, the enemy retired over the River Lugonya. 1/3 K.A.R. was now distributed with one company at Rupiage, one at Kipandamoyo, one in detachments along the Rufigi watching the enemy at Mpanganya, and one in reserve at Utete.

From January onwards the rains descended with abnormal violence. The floods rose, roads vanished under water or turned into sticky morasses, animal transport died, carriers went sick. All hope of striking the final blow to end the campaign gradually vanished. The enemy had evacuated the Rufigi delta, so light-draft vessels were able to use the river, supplying Utete with food and reinforcements. Many of the other British units, less conveniently placed, had to be withdrawn from the forward areas. Between the advanced troops of the Nigerian Brigade at Mkindu and the outpost manned by 2/2 K.A.R. at Kiwambi lay the German escape route, no more than fifty miles wide, but a gap that it proved impossible to bridge.

(iv) *Operations in the South, September, 1916-February, 1917.* Maps VI (b), VI (c), VI (d), 22.

In September, 1916, Northey's combatant troops, numbering over 2,000 rifles, were scattered along a front 200 miles in extent. 1 K.A.R., now in the river valleys east of the escarpment, was 35 officers and 807 African ranks strong. Nearly 500 recruits were under training at the advanced depôt. Van Deventer's 2nd Division was too exhausted and too deficient in transport and supplies to advance far south of the railway. In this situation Northey learnt with growing concern of the approach of von Wahle's 'Tabora Force', which was marching eastward in three columns under Captain Wintgens, Captain von Langenn, and Lieutenant Zingel.

British intelligence put von Wahle's men at about 1,200 rifles, and considered them a demoralized force. Actually they were nearly double that figure, and as they were still undefeated in battle their morale was high. When it became plain that the enemy intended to keep well south of the railway and make for Mahenge, van Deventer withdrew the bulk of his troops from Kilimatinde to Dodoma and sent a small force to occupy the crossing over the Ruaha. With this and Smuts' permission to withdraw his advanced detachments if necessary, Northey had to be content.

The columns commanded by Hawthorn and Murray on the Mnyera were faced by considerable forces of the enemy, and were too far away for quick recall. On 11th October German detachments were seen approaching Neu Utengule from the west. During the next fortnight these columns broke right across the line of communication between Iringa and the Lake. Iringa was besieged, and the large supply depôt at Ngominyi was overwhelmed after a gallant defence. The position was serious, as for the time being the initiative lay entirely in von Wahle's hands. Fortunately lack of communication between his columns and the independent attitude adopted by some of his subordinate commanders prevented him from exploiting his advantage.

While these events were in progress Hawthorn and Murray were also under attack. After withdrawing the K.A.R. across the Ruhuje on 28th September, Hawthorn had occupied a low, flat-topped hill between the Ruhuje and the Mnyera, a dry and advantageous position, though surrounded on all sides by swampy bush. 'D' Company under Captain J. E. E. Galbraith (R. Fus.) was detailed to guard communications with Lupembe, and the rest of 1 K.A.R., with the Rhodesian column under Murray, who reached the position a few days later, manned defensive posts upon the plateau, with an outpost at Picquet Hill, some 2,500 yards to the west.

Operations at Mkapira, 21st-30th October, 1916.—The enemy force, commanded by Major Kraut, was eight miles downstream on the opposite bank of the Ruhuje. On 21st October British patrols and picquets north and south of Mkapira reported that the Germans were advancing. During the night the enemy advance guard made its way along the banks of the Mnyera to the west, and at dawn rushed Picquet Hill. There a field gun was mounted which opened fire on the main British defences. Meanwhile other enemy forces worked around to the south-east and began to penetrate along the road to Lupembe. Though no general assault was made, it was evident that Kraut intended to invest the position and cut off supplies.

Hawthorn was in touch with Lupembe by wireless, and so heard of von Wahle's approach from the west. The rains had nearly ceased and the swamps were drying. Patrols discovered lines of approach through the bush, and on 29th October Hawthorn issued orders for an attack on both flanks of the German line through Picquet Hill.

During the night of 29th/30th October Major G. L. Baxter (Cameron High.) with 'A'(R) and 'C'(R) Companies, 1 K.A.R., found his way through the swamps bordering the Mnyera. Unsuspected by the enemy, Baxter got his force around the far side of Picquet Hill and deployed within 4,000 yards of the German positions. At daylight, led by Baxter and Captain A. H. D. Griffiths (D.C.L.I.), the K.A.R. rushed the Hill with the bayonet, captured the gun and put the enemy to flight. The Rhodesians attacked the other end of the German line with similar success. For a time the centre held out. A converging attack was organized by Baxter with 'C'(R) Company from the northern flank, Lieutenant P. E. Mitchell[1] (Spec. List) with 'H' Company from the front, and Galbraith with 'D' Company and a 7-pounder gun from the direction of Lupembe. Under this combined assault the enemy resistance collapsed, and before 9 a.m. they had scattered in small parties into the bush, making for the crossings over the Ruhuje. Five Germans and 37 askaris had been killed, six Germans and 76 askaris captured. For the time being it seemed unlikely that Kraut would resume the offensive.

On learning of the success achieved by Hawthorn and Murray at Mkapira, Northey recalled the latter to assist in the defence of Malangali, where an important depôt was guarded solely by a raw company of the Rhodesia Native Regiment. For various reasons von Wahle's designs against Iringa had miscarried, and his columns were now attempting to reach the Mahenge plateau by the southern route, past Njombe and Lupembe. After Murray's arrival the attack on Malangali was abandoned and the enemy resumed his march. The strength and determination

---

[1] Later Major-General Sir Philip Mitchell, G.C.M.G., M.C., Governor and Commander-in-Chief, Uganda, 1935-40, and Kenya, 1944-52.

of his forces were now only too well appreciated, and Northey could do no more with his scattered columns than adopt a defensive attitude to guard the main camp and supply depôts. The most important of those threatened was Lupembe.

Lieutenant A. H. L. Wyatt (Spec. List), who commanded the garrison at Lupembe, had a force of 250 rifles with four machine guns and three muzzle-loading 7-pounders. Most of these troops were Bemba recruits in training for 1 K.A.R., and they had with them in the camp about 300 women and children. The post, built originally by the Germans, was well entrenched along the summit of a high ridge, with steep slopes to north and south and a deep gully on the west. The weak point was on the east, where the slope was gradual.

Investment of Lupembe, 12th-15th November, 1916.—On 12th November Wintgens' column invested Lupembe. Before dawn on the 13th the enemy attacked. Five askaris were actually bayoneted inside the British trenches, but the recruits did not give way, though the enemy captured an outpost and manned it with snipers. Firing continued throughout the day, bringing down the wireless masts and so cutting off communications.

Next day the steadiness of the Bemba recruits again saved Lupembe. At four o'clock in the morning the enemy attacked along the eastern slope, but was halted by intense fire from the trenches. Soon afterwards a determined attack on the north face brought the Germans right up to the wire, but again heavy casualties prevented them from pressing the assault. They withdrew at dawn, removing their wounded under a white flag.

During the night of 14th/15th November and again on the 15th, fire was maintained by machine guns and snipers, but only to cover the passage of the main German columns, which could be seen throughout the next few days moving in long lines with their carriers and herds of cattle across the hills about five miles to the north. Hawthorn, who had been ordered to withdraw from Mkapira on 9th November, reached Lupembe unopposed and joined the garrison. Von Wahle's rearguard of 300 men with a 4.1-inch howitzer was surrounded and surrendered on 26th November, but the rest of his force, about half the number who had left Tabora, descended the escarpment and joined Kraut on the Ruhuje, where von Wahle took command. A German outpost was left on the crest of the escarpment at Mfirika.

In conjunction with his advance across the Mgeta at the end of December, Smuts had ordered two simultaneous thrusts from the west: by van Deventer from Iringa and by Northey from Lupembe, where most of the Nyasaland forces were now concentrated. If the enemy troops under Wahle and Kraut, estimated at five or six companies, could be driven behind the Kilombero, Smuts then intended to hold the line of that river with outposts and withdraw the rest of his troops until the rains were over.

The immediate object of van Deventer's attack was a force of about 500 rifles under Captain Lincke, who occupied a position in the hills east of Dabaga. By this time van Deventer's South Africans were greatly

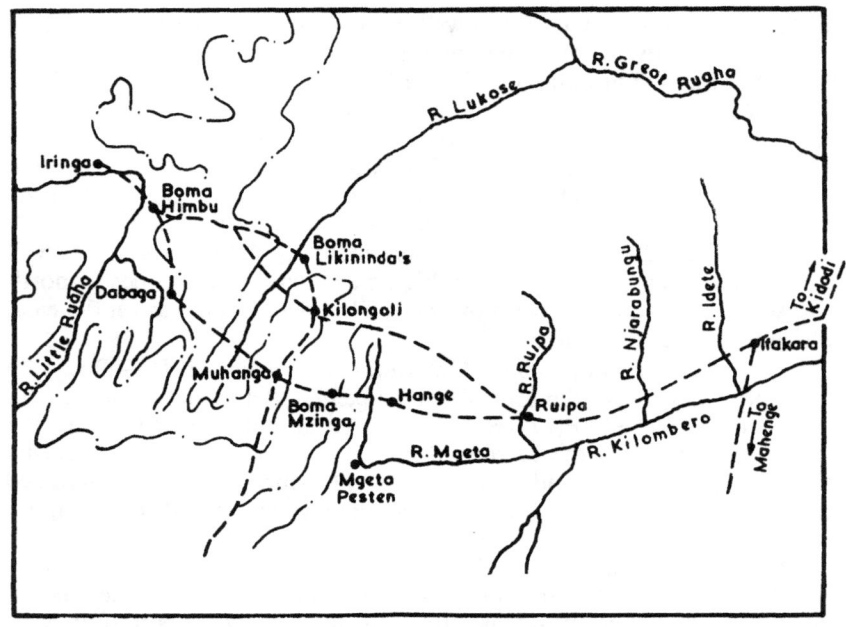

22. Operations against Lineke

reduced in numbers and nearly all his cavalry had been dismounted, but he had also under his command the 17th (Indian) Infantry and 4 K.A.R. The plan was to advance with three columns to outflank and surround Lincke before he could withdraw.

Operations against Lincke, 23rd-29th December, 1916.—The rôle allotted to 'A' Column (S.A. Mounted Brigade) was to make a wide turning movement round Lincke's southern flank. 'B' Column was to hold him by a frontal attack from Dabaga, and 'C' Column to march by way of Boma Himbu round the northern flank. The last-named column, commanded by Colonel Taylor, consisted of the 8th South African Infantry (about 290 rifles and four machine guns), 4 K.A.R. (about 500 rifles and four machine guns), and a section of the 28th Mountain Battery. The frontal attack was timed for 25th December, and the two outflanking columns were to begin their march a day or two before.

The country to be crossed was mountainous, the maps were poor and unreliable, and before starting the troops were informed that only half rations could be expected. 'C' Column assembled at Boma Himbu and on the morning of 22nd December marched into the hills in a ceaseless downpour of rain. Kit was cut to a minimum as carriers were difficult to obtain, and the locally impressed natives, unused to such work, were soon ill with discomfort and cold. The River Lukose was crossed and on the 24th the column reached Boma Likininda's. Beyond this village the track dwindled to a narrow footpath leading into the mountains. Through sheets of driving rain the column toiled in single file up and down the steep slopes crossed by the muddy track, a treacherous way that caused the death of some pack animals and carriers unable to cope with their loads in such conditions. At length Taylor reached the crossroads at Kilongoli, and having secured the position sent back word for the rest of the column to bivouac along the route.

Taking with him three companies of 4 K.A.R., Taylor continued on Christmas Day to Muhanga, where he drove off a small detachment of the enemy and took up a position on the heights commanding the road from Dabaga. The rest of 'C' Column closed up during the day, thus, in spite of all difficulties, severing Lincke's main escape route at the time planned for 'B' Column to deliver the frontal attack.

'A' Column had started to advance round the southern flank on the afternoon of 23rd December, and by the time 'B' Column attacked was in position due south of Lincke. But although touch was gained with 'C' Column at Muhanga, the South African Brigade was strung out over a difficult and almost unknown tract of river, swamp and hilly forest. With useless maps, incompetent guides and the difficulty of maintaining communications, the Brigade was unable to prevent Lincke from slipping away southward and making a wide detour to reach Hange. At dawn on 27th December the attacking troops of 'B' Column found Lincke's position evacuated, and by the 29th it was realized by the other columns that the enemy had escaped.

The difficulties of supply were too great for anything further to be attempted. While the South African troops were withdrawn to the railway to recuperate before being sent home, 4 K.A.R. and the 17th Infantry occupied Boma Mzinga and Mgeta Pesten, with outposts along the river. Before long it was discovered that the enemy troops facing them were being withdrawn to the south.

Simultaneously with van Deventer's advance from Iringa, Northey began his forward move from Lupembe, seeking under conditions of equal difficulty and with no better success to surround and destroy the forces opposed to him under von Langenn. His command was still grouped in two main columns: 1 S.A. Rifles and 1 K.A.R. (less the Bemba recruit company) under Hawthorn, amounting to about 1,000 rifles, with two guns of the Mountain Battery; and the B.S.A. Police and the Northern Rhodesia Police, totalling some 900 rifles, under Murray. The Bemba recruits, 2 S.A. Rifles and four mountain guns were in reserve.

Northey's supply route lay across mountain passes rising to 9,000 feet near the head of the Lake, and the accumulation of reserves was a lengthy process. On 23rd December all was ready and headquarters was transferred to Lupembe. The enemy had been at work improving his defences on top of the escarpment at Mfirika, and Northey's plan was to demonstrate against this position while it was outflanked by Hawthorn's column on the south and Murray's on the north. No tracks led in these directions, and the two columns spent 24th December and the following night in forcing their way through the wet bush. On Christmas morning they were both in position for the assault, only to find that the enemy had slipped away and was now in position on another ridge, about six miles to the east.

After a pause to bring up supplies, Northey repeated his manœuvre, switching his columns to the opposite flanks. Another difficult approach followed, but when Murray attacked on 2nd January, 1917, the enemy disappeared once more into the dense bush. Von Langenn was now reinforced by Kraut, and a third position on high ground was taken up. Again Northey's columns went forward, advancing cautiously through the dense and dripping bush of the river valley to locate the enemy's flanks and envelop them. Three days passed in this attempt, but by 7th January it was obvious that the Germans had again retired, and for some time it was impossible to locate them.

It was now that the first definite indications reached Northey of a general movement by the enemy towards the south. A captured message indicated that in future the detachments under Kraut, Langenn and Wintgens were to depend for supplies on the district north of Songea. Murray's column was therefore withdrawn and sent to Ifinga, ready to co-operate with the forces about Songea, which Northey had already reinforced after an attack on the garrison in November. For another week the askaris of 4 K.A.R. continued to advance slowly through the sodden forests of the valley, unable to cook their scanty supplies of food and in constant danger of ambush by the German rearguards. On 16th January Hawthorn reached his old site at Mkapira, where the advance was brought to a halt.

Northey's need to operate once more in separate areas, supplied from different bases at Alt Langenberg and Wiedhaven, caused some delay in the division of 1 K.A.R. into two battalions. His original intention was that 1/1 K.A.R., about 500 rifles strong, should operate along the route Mfirika—Mkapira, and that 2/1 K.A.R., together with a few other units in a column commanded by Hawthorn, should go to Songea. But on 25th January, when it became clear that Wintgens and Kraut were no longer facing his advanced positions and were in all probability already on their way south, Northey issued orders for Murray's Rhodesians to relieve 1/1 K.A.R., which was to concentrate at Mfirika ready to follow Hawthorn to Songea.

Hawthorn's column landed at Wiedhaven on 5th February. Two days later Kraut's vanguard reached the River Lumecha, marching south. He had joined forces with Wintgens at Gumbiro, and finding food supplies scarcer than they had expected, the two commanders had agreed on a daring and independent scheme that had no approval from Wahle, still less from Lettow, to raid the British supply depôts instead, Wintgens going north and Kraut south. Hawthorn's arrival at Wiedhaven was therefore timely, though at first he was immobile while strenuous efforts were made to raise carriers.

On the evening of 10th February Kraut's patrols attacked a small British outpost at Johannesbrücke, on the line of communication between Wiedhaven and Songea. Next day enemy patrols attacked the post at Nyamasi, only thirty-five miles from Wiedhaven. Hawthorn's column was already on the way, toiling up the steep mountain track. Marching to the sound of firing, the advance guard of 2/1 K.A.R. reached the vicinity of Nyamasi in time to drive off the attackers, killing one German and one askari, and wounding five others. But these enemy movements were merely covers for Kraut's main force, which was crossing the road on its way south. Hawthorn followed to Kigonzera and then, climbing through the mountains, fought a short action against the German rearguard on 19th February near Litembo. Kraut then made off towards the Portuguese border, where he roamed at will, raiding the villages for food. As Lincke's detachment had appeared near Likuyu and taken up an entrenched position, Hawthorn was recalled by Northey to take command at Songea, where 2/1 K.A.R. was able to rest and reorganize, the rains having started in earnest.

Meanwhile Wintgens' column had begun a fantastic march that was to carry it nearly to the borders of British East Africa and to cause consternation and alarm out of all proportion to its powers.

(v) *The Pursuit of Wintgens and Naumann, February-September, 1917.*
  Map V (e).

Wintgens left Gumbiro with about 500 combatant troops, 13 machine guns and three small guns. The operations that followed lasted for many months before the last remnants of this force were hunted down, and involved several units of the K.A.R.

It was 10th February before the unwelcome news reached Northey that Wintgens was apparently making for Tandala, a post held by about 100 troops, mostly details and convalescents. Patrols were sent out to get in touch with the enemy column, and Northey ordered 1/1 K.A.R. and Murray's column to reinforce Tandala with the utmost speed. Headquarters 1/1 K.A.R. were at Lupembe, with the three companies of the battalion distributed along the road to the east, but a half-company under Captain A. C. Masters was lifted by some light motor transport, and reached Tandala on the 18th. The rest of 1/1 K.A.R. followed by forced marches, while the lorries ran a shuttle service to hasten them forward.

Action near Tandala, 19th February, 1917.—On the evening of his arrival Masters took up a position in the hills a few miles south of Tandala. His presence was soon discovered by enemy scouts. In the early-morning darkness of 19th February the Germans tried to rush Masters' position, but were stopped by steady rifle fire. When daylight came Wintgens brought his machine guns into play, and concentrated his attack on Masters' two machine guns, which were posted on a small hill covering the right flank. By mid-afternoon this hill had fallen to a bayonet charge, and half the K.A.R. had become casualties. Though unable to bring away the guns, Corporal Stima and Private Saidi, the sole survivors of the detachment, remained to disable them before withdrawing. With considerable difficulty Masters then extricated his force, having lost two officers and seven other ranks killed, 18 wounded and eight missing.

Masters' gallant defence of the approach to Tandala undoubtedly saved the situation. During the time thus gained, two more companies 1/1 K.A.R. had arrived and entrenched themselves. After investigation by patrols, Wintgens moved west into the hills and camped. Major Baxter arrived on the 21st with the rest of his battalion, and then troops of Murray's column. After two days' hesitation Wintgens abandoned his designs and went off to the north-west. 1/1 K.A.R. and a detachment of the Northern Rhodesia Police pursued towards Magoje, but were soon recalled. Rhodesian and South African Police columns under Murray and Tomlinson were sent across the Lake to Mwaya, in an effort to head Wintgens off from the frontier of North-East Rhodesia, and if possible to intercept him.

Wintgens reached Magoje on 26th February, and continued his march through Brandt, Neu Utengule and Ruiwa. Foraging parties scoured the countryside along his flanks. Prisoners captured from these patrols said that Wintgens had promised to make for the Tabora district, where his troops had been recruited, and to disband the column there. There was nothing to impede his progress, and everything to hinder that of his pursuers, who were forced to follow his lead through the areas his troops had devastated. This was a foretaste of the much more serious chase that came during the following year.

Northey appealed for help, but all Hoskins could spare was a half-battalion of 1/4 K.A.R. from Iringa. These reinforcements reached Njombe in the middle of March, and Northey then ordered 1/1 K.A.R. forward to join Murray's column at the Igale Pass. The battalion reached Murray on the 28th, by which time Wintgens was at St. Moritz. One of his detachments raided the stores left by 1/1 K.A.R. at Utengule on the following day.

The threat to Northern Rhodesia had been averted, but Wintgens was heading north at speed, and it was unlikely Murray could catch him before he reached the Central Railway. The co-operation of Belgian troops on the western flank was promised, and Hoskins called upon his recruits and reserve troops, who were reorganizing within reach of the railway. This brought a new K.A.R. unit into the chase.

On 17th March Hoskins ordered Major H. G. Montgomerie (Spec. List), with a force of some 300 rifles, mostly ex-German askaris enlisted for the newly-formed 4/3 K.A.R., to leave Morogoro by rail for Tabora. These men, who later became the nucleus of 1/6 K.A.R., were ordered into the field so soon after enlistment that the officers had to learn German methods and words of command, and use them until the operations were over. Though it had never been intended to bring them into contact with enemy forces so soon, they did not appear to resent the situation, and as trained askaris were able to stand the rough conditions so unexpectedly thrust upon them.[1] At the same time about 200 *ruga-ruga*, who were at Iringa, were ordered to entrain at Kilosa and follow Montgomerie.

Montgomerie left Tabora on 23rd March. Though porters had joined him *en route*, no supplies could be organized and he was expected to follow Wintgens' example and live on the country. His immediate destination was Kitunda, 130 miles south of the line, where he arrived on 3rd April. Wintgens was then approaching Kipembawe, well ahead of Murray, whose difficulties over carriers and supplies were increasing at

---

[1] 'In spite of being in close contact with the Germans for this initial period their ex-askaris behaved splendidly. I lost only one deserter, a sergeant.' Major D. St. J. Clowes, formerly of 4 Company, 1/6 K.A.R., in a letter to the author, 24.x.52.

every step. It was not until 13th April that he was able to leave Iwungu, and 1st May before he reached Kipembawe, to find that the enemy had long since gone on.

It was evident that Montgomerie's little force could not resist Wintgens alone. On 14th April one of his patrols had thrown back an enemy flank guard on the River Piti at Mbogo's, but as the main column advanced Montgomerie retired before it as far as Sikonge, where the Belgian IVth Battalion had arrived in support. On the same day (1st May) Wintgens was honoured by the formation of a new British command formed especially to deal with him under Brigadier-General W. F. S. Edwards. EDFORCE consisted of 1/6 K.A.R. (which had been formed at the end of April from the ex-German askaris and other recruits, originally intended for the 4th, 5th and 6th Battalions of 3 K.A.R.); the *ruga-ruga*, 400 rifles of the Cape Corps; the 309th Punjabis at Itigi; the 130th Baluchis at Tabora, and 50 rifles of the K.A.R. Mounted Infantry, who were sent to watch Wintgens' right flank at Kiromo. The total force placed at Edwards' disposal was no less than 1,700 rifles and 14 machine guns.

Edwards set up his headquarters at Tabora on 8th May. Next day he learnt that Murray's column would probably be withdrawn. The latter struggled as far north as the River Ngluva, but Northey was threatened by new German movements in the south and could no longer spare troops for a pursuit that had long since passed beyond his territory. On 1st May the rest of 1/4 K.A.R. (four officers, one B.W.O. and 182 rank and file) had reached Njombe, and Northey now had the whole battalion in reserve. He ordered it south to Fort Johnston, intending to replace it at Njombe with 1/1 K.A.R. as soon as Murray's column returned. Meanwhile Edwards, acting on representations from Montgomerie, had withdrawn 1/6 K.A.R. into reserve at Tabora in order to give the new battalion a breathing-space for consolidation and training.

By the middle of May, Wintgens, worn down by fever and hardship, was a very sick man. On the 21st he handed over command to Ober-Leutnant Naumann and remained behind the column to surrender. The result of this change of command was a complete reversal of policy. There was no more talk of disbandment in the vicinity of Tabora, which had already been reached. Instead Naumann decided to strike northeast through the bush, cross the railway, and exploit his nuisance value to the full by devastating the country round Mkalama. At that time his column numbered 48 Europeans, 421 askaris, 12 machine guns, two 3.7-cm. guns, and 700-800 carriers.

Masking his movement by a feint against Ipole, Naumann marched towards Makinga. Though information regarding his intentions was scarce, this brought 1/6 K.A.R. back into the picture with a rapid movement that but for an unfortunate misapprehension might have ended Naumann's exploit there and then. Edwards ordered the battalion by rail from Tabora to Nyahua. On arrival, leaving 150 men on the railway in reserve, the rest of 1/6 K.A.R. was to march to Gombe. The K.A.R. Mounted Infantry were ordered from Kiromo to Makinga, and the Baluchis were also set in motion.

Marching right across the track that Naumann's column was so soon to follow, 1/6 K.A.R. reached Gombe in the late afternoon of 22nd May. Unfortunately Montgomerie decided not to stop there. It is possible that some confusion existed in his mind, or had been apparent in his orders, between the places marked Gombe and Ikomba on the maps. At any rate, finding no defensible position with command of a water supply at Gombe, he continued to Ikomba, where he arrived next day with his whole force. Patrolling during the next few days made contact with the enemy only once, the K.A.R. patrol being driven back after a brief skirmish. Two officers and 33 men of the K.A.R.M.I. arrived on the night of the 26th/27th, and then news came from Belgian sources that the enemy had already gone past to the north. Montgomerie returned to Nyahua by forced marches, and arrived on 29th May, only to learn that Naumann had crossed the railway some time before. About one o'clock on the afternoon of 26th May, covered by picquets up and down the track, he had led his force through a deep culvert where the line ran through wild bush country seven kilometres west of Malongwe station, and escaped to the north, leaving Edwards' converging columns with nothing in their grasp. The news was given by a wounded ganger who was found on the line the same afternoon.

Reinforced by the 4th Nigerian Battalion and more Belgian infantry, Edwards now withdrew all troops who were south of the railway and regrouped them in two mobile columns. Naumann appeared to be making for Mwanza. He was followed by the Eastern Column (Nigerians and Belgians) through Singida to Mkalama, where the small garrison under Captain M. J. Holland, the Assistant Political Officer, was relieved after a siege of three days. The Western Column, commanded by Lieutenant-Colonel P. H. Dyke of the 30th Punjabis, consisted of 173 rifles of that regiment and 1/6 K.A.R., with 18 officers and 511 African ranks. This column left Tabora on 2nd June to co-operate with Belgian forces moving in to cut Naumann off from the west.

Dyke reached Shikara on 6th June. Hearing that the enemy was at Mkalama he moved east, but was recalled by Edwards and sent north to Iwingo. By that time, unknown to his pursuers, Naumann was already at Shanwa, a good sixty miles ahead. Dyke was sent forward to Shinyanga, where Edwards moved his headquarters from Tabora. The Western Column then continued its march, and Naumann, perhaps realizing that he could not raid Mwanza without being trapped, continued to the north. At this point, after an inter-allied conference held by van Deventer, who had replaced Hoskins as Commander-in-Chief, it was decided to hand over the pursuit to the Belgians, operating with a smaller and more mobile force. 1/6 K.A.R., who had got as far as Mabuki, were therefore recalled to the Central Railway with the Punjabis, Nigerians and Cape Corps, and came again into general reserve.

The Belgian operations were short-lived, for after unsuccessfully attacking Naumann at Ikoma, where he had occupied the empty fort, supply difficulties prevented them from following when he withdrew to the east. It was the beginning of a new phase of the pursuit, that brought the old battle areas of 1916 once more into the campaign and revived the invasion scare in British East Africa. As soon as it was known for certain that the German column was heading east, Brigadier-General Llewellyn, Commandant of the K.A.R., was given executive command of all troops in East Africa. In practice this meant the new battalions *en route* to the main theatre, and recruits under training.

Defensive dispositions were soon made. 3/4 K.A.R. was at Kilindini awaiting transport for Lindi. Llewellyn removed Nos. 1 and 2 Companies to garrison Voi, where they remained for ten days before resuming their journey south. A detachment of 300 K.A.R. recruits was sent to establish a post near Lake Magadi, to block this line of approach to the Uganda Railway and Nairobi. On 19th July 7 K.A.R. (five officers, five B.N.C.Os. and 573 African ranks) landed at Kilindini and entrained for Voi, where the unit remained until the end of the month. Arusha was garrisoned by a detachment of the Cape Corps.

Abandoning all thought of invading British East Africa, Naumann had gone via Lake Manyara to Mbugwe. As this might imply a threat to Kondoa Irangi, 100 rifles of the K.A.R.M.I. were dispatched there from Dodoma on 24th July. At the same time two companies 7 K.A.R. were sent from Voi to reinforce Arusha, and half 1/6 K.A.R. at Tabora was ordered to stand by for emergencies.

Naumann marched south towards the Central Railway, while Nigerians and Cape Corps tried to hem him in. A mobile column was again formed to undertake the pursuit, with the Mounted Infantry and 50 *ruga-ruga* of 1/6 K.A.R. attached to it as scouts. Naumann took refuge in the hills and split his force into several detachments. As there was some danger of these raiding the main line of communication leading south from Korogwe, another call was made on Llewellyn to supply recruits as garrisons. On 12th August Major H. A. Lilley left Nairobi for Korogwe with 450 rifles and four machine guns of 4/4 K.A.R. Korogwe was reached two days later, and on the 18th part of the unit was sent ahead to garrison Handeni and patrol to the west.

By this time the situation was extremely confused. No one knew for certain which detachment was commanded by Naumann in person. At length proof was obtained that he had again turned north, and as he was reported to have charges of dynamite in his possession, fears were expressed for the vital railway bridge at Kahe.

On 28th August Naumann reached Arusha Chini. Captain G. R. King (Spec. List) was on the way there from Korogwe with 100 rifles 4/4 K.A.R. On the 29th he unexpectedly struck one of Naumann's picquets near Arusha, and returned in haste to Kahe. During his absence a party of enemy raiders, 50 strong, had spent two profitable hours at the station, looting stationary trains. Three British officers were captured, several native passengers killed, and a quantity of military stores was burnt. Fortunately the bridge, situated a mile distant, was left intact.

All the former apprehensions for the safety of East Africa were instantly revived. Another 200 K.A.R. recruits were sent from Nairobi to Taveta. The Governor expressed his grave fears by telegram to van Deventer, and the Secretary of State followed suit on behalf of the Colonial Office. But Africa is not a continent in which troops can be diverted from their bases at short notice to deal with unforeseen emergencies.

September came with Naumann still in the field. Lilley was now commanding in the Arusha—Moshi area, and Colonel H. C. Tytler the pursuing column. One of the enemy detachments had surrendered to the Cape Corps. Another, consisting of two Germans and 53 askaris, surrendered, at the end of its resources, to 7 K.A.R. at Mbulu on 2nd October. The rest, amounting to about one-third of the original force, were near the Kondoa Irangi—Handeni road.

Naumann was still actively raiding. Strong K.A.R. posts (75 rifles at Handeni and 110 rifles at Mgera) barred his way to the east. On 4th September Lieutenant-Colonel Lilley with more troops of 4/4 K.A.R. moved via Handeni towards Mgera, sending 75 rifles south to the Lukigura. On the 16th he moved to Merusi, with a column some 500 rifles strong that for the past week had marched an average of seventeen miles a day. The pursuing columns were steadily closing in upon some high ground where Naumann was entrenching a position. On 26th September Lilley's troops joined hands with the Cape Corps in completing a ring round the hills, about twenty-five miles in circumference. More troops, including artillery, were brought up for the final assault; telephonic communication was established right round the position, and the K.A.R. Mounted Infantry patrolled the perimeter.

On the evening of 30th September, before the general attack could be delivered, a letter arrived from Naumann requesting a conference. A meeting took place on the following morning, conditions were agreed, and on 2nd October Naumann formally surrendered, with 14 Europeans, 165 askaris and about 350 porters.

For close on eight months this detached column had kept the field. It represented a venture entirely unauthorized and as such von Lettow refused to admit its value to the main campaign.[1] But it involved British forces in a chase exceeding 1,600 miles, created disorganization far beyond its potentialities, and diverted many units that should have been employed elsewhere. Perhaps, so far as the K.A.R. was concerned, Naumann should have been thanked for providing active service conditions for training recruits.

(vi) *Operations of the Kilwa Force, February-August, 1917.* Maps VI (a), 23.

The last stage in the expansion of the K.A.R., authorizing the further increase that in due time raised the strength of the Regiment to 22 battalions, was the immediate outcome of the serious situation facing the Allies in the early part of 1917. Not only in Europe, but in the eastern Mediterranean, in Mesopotamia and at sea, the war was at a critical period. No longer was any doubt cast upon the askari's capacity to cope with operations of a more serious character than mere punitive expeditions. Smuts himself paid public tribute to the 'splendid infantry' of the African battalions, and the War Office was anxious for a speedy ending to the campaign in East Africa, not only on account of the constant drain

[1] Von Lettow, *My Reminiscences of East Africa*, p. 189.

of transport and supplies and the continued use of shipping so urgently needed elsewhere, but to release some of the K.A.R. battalions for service in Egypt. This notable reversal of opinion had come about in less than two years.

Few men knew the K.A.R. better than Lieutenant-General A. R. Hoskins, the new Commander-in-Chief. It was largely under his advice and guidance that the expansion of the regiment had begun in April of the preceding year. The Africanization of his fighting troops was by no means contrary to Hoskins' wishes, but he felt obliged to sound a note of warning.[1] In many of his speeches Smuts had given the impression that the war was practically over in East Africa. Hoskins stated plainly that a formidable fighting enemy was still in the field; that von Lettow had control of a vast tract of practically unknown country, where he would be particularly difficult to reach; that it might be impossible to prevent his escape into Portuguese East Africa, and that no quick or easy end to the campaign was to be expected. For this reason Hoskins asked that even if fresh South African troops were to be denied him, Indian units should for the time being continue to serve in East Africa. He also asked for more transport, more artillery, Stokes mortars and Lewis guns.

Patrols during the period of the rains confirmed accounts from native sources that von Lettow's main force was leaving the Rufigi valley. Hoskins' plan was to penetrate the enemy area from five directions and bring the Germans to bay or drive them south. To accomplish this the Nigerian Brigade was to advance from the Rufigi; the 1st Division, with its northern flank now secure, from Kilwa towards Liwale; O'Grady with a brigade of troops from Lindi towards Masasi; the Iringa column towards Mahenge, and Northey from Songea towards Liwale or Tunduru.

Hoskins' proposals reached Whitehall at the end of April. On 3rd May he was informed by the Secretary of State for War that after his prolonged service in a trying climate the War Cabinet had decided to relieve him.[2] He was succeeded in command by van Deventer, who reached Dar-es-Salaam from South Africa on 29th May.

While Hoskins had been busy with his plans for a new offensive, continued heavy rain had led to withdrawal of the 1st Division outposts. In April, instead of decreasing as usual, the rainstorms rose to fresh fury, postponing all prospects of serious operations. The Germans, however, occupying higher ground away from the coast where the flooding did not reach the same intensity as in the lower river valleys, were in general better placed and found movement feasible.

The fact that the enemy was engaged in a general withdrawal was not realized until later, though von Lettow's movement resulted in several small actions with patrols of 2/2 and 2/3 K.A.R., who were watching his eastern flank. Throughout March and early April the time was spent in vigorous patrolling in a countryside largely converted to swamp. It was useful training for the young askaris, who had on more than one occasion to fight their way out of ambushes. The shortage of officers in both

[1] Despatch dated 30th May, 1917. Lond. Gaz. Supp. No. 30447, 27.xii.17.
[2] Hoskins was later given command of the 3rd (Lahore) Division in Mesopotamia.

battalions was at this time so serious that a special appeal was made to Nairobi for reinforcements and British N.C.Os.

Action near Nambanje, 13th March, 1917.—The most important of these minor actions took place on 13th March. Reports were received of a concentration of enemy troops (actually a flanking force masking von Lettow's movement) near Nambanje, and the brigade commander ordered a concerted attack by 2/2 K.A.R. and 2/3 K.A.R. The German position was approached on the night of 12th March by Captain T. J. W. Weld (Lovat's Scouts) with 80 rifles of Nos. 3 and 4 Companies, 2/2 K.A.R., expecting to make contact with the patrol of 2/3 K.A.R. for an attack next morning. Unluckily the latter column bumped a German patrol and so put the enemy on guard. Contact between the two K.A.R. detachments was never established, and supposing that for some reason the patrol from 2/2 K.A.R. had not arrived, the company of 2/3 K.A.R. retired.

The result was an unpleasant experience for Weld's force, which was now left to face alone a greatly superior detachment of the enemy, who was fully alive to the situation. Weld's advance was stopped by heavy fire; he was attacked with determination on both flanks, and driven back with the loss of one machine gun and the whole gun team of another. In this engagement one officer was severely wounded and fell into enemy hands, where he died later; seven men were killed and ten wounded.

Von Lettow reached Mpotora on 15th March, and his presence there became known about a fortnight later. Numerous native reports revealed the growing strength of enemy forces in the area south-west of Kilwa. Redeployment of the 1st Division followed early in April, and for the time being the brigade organization was suspended, Lieutenant-Colonel H. F. L. Grant of the 2nd Brigade taking command of all troops north, and Lieutenant-Colonel Rose of the 3rd Brigade all troops south of the River Matandu. Rose set up his headquarters at Mnasi, twenty-two miles from Kilwa Kivinje, close to the Liwale road, where he entrenched a defensive position, established outposts and sent out patrols.

2/2 K.A.R. was relieved by the 129th Baluchis and sent to Mnasi, where the battalion arrived on 14th April. As by that time enemy patrols were active around Mnasi, new positions at Rumbo and at 'Beaumont's Post', covering the ford over the River Ngaura, had been hastily prepared. The Germans were encamped in the bush near Makangaga, and their total forces in the area were variously estimated at from eight to 13 companies. It was obvious that a major engagement was impending, and great hopes were placed on the outcome.

Action at Rumbo, 18th April, 1917.—Rose was ordered to attack the enemy camp at Makangaga. He entrusted this task to Lieutenant-Colonel Tyndall of the 40th Pathans with a column of 450 rifles drawn from the Pathans, the Gold Coast Regiment, and Nos. 1 and 3 Companies, 2/2 K.A.R. The column assembled at Rumbo on 17th April. Leaving a detachment of Pathans and Gold Coast to hold the position there, Tyndall marched next morning, crossed the Ngaura, and climbed the high ground beyond. There he drove off a German picquet and soon afterwards came under heavy fire from the direction of his left flank.

A force of about two enemy companies was well established upon a spur, 700 yards from the road. The intervening terrain was covered with tall elephant grass and thick bush, but Tyndall thought it essential to postpone his advance on Makangaga until this threat to Rumbo and his own retreat had been removed. Dispatching the K.A.R. into the bush to work around the German right, he began a frontal attack with the Pathans. Several hours of firing did little but reveal the enemy strength, and Tyndall, realizing that success was beyond his powers, ordered a general retirement. This was the signal for a determined counter-attack. The morale of the German askaris was high, and throughout the afternoon they pressed hard upon the rear and flanks of Tyndall's force. The two pack guns were saved, but the Germans captured three machine guns and a quantity of baggage and ammunition. The action had been fought in heavy rain, which since the morning had flooded the Ngaura. The Pathans lost another machine gun in getting across, and the K.A.R., who owing to their detached position made the crossing lower down, were obliged to swim for it, casting away a good deal of their equipment. In this reverse 2/2 K.A.R. lost four askaris killed and one officer and 12 African ranks wounded.

Three days later 2/2 K.A.R. moved to Rumbo and for the next two months was employed on incessant patrolling against enemy parties raiding the British supply dumps. This was the testing time when the battalion, after taking two severe knocks at Nambanje and Rumbo, outgrew the recruit stage and developed into an experienced and effective unit.

One more action was fought by 1/3 K.A.R. in the northern part of the 1st Division area before the district was evacuated and the battalion withdrawn. On 11th April, long before the floods had subsided, 1/3 K.A.R. was ordered from Utete Fort to the place known as Utete II, which lay about twenty-two miles to the south-west.[1] Utete II was reached on the 13th, and an enemy patrol was driven from the water-hole. The River Lugonya had become a fast, unfordable torrent, confining the enemy entirely to the left bank except for a bridgehead at Kiawe. There the road crossed the river by a bridge approached on either side by a causeway over the swampy ground. Not wishing to fight with their backs to such an obstacle, the Germans had constructed their main defences on the left or farther bank.

Action at Kiawe Bridge, 9th April, 1917.—Surprise could only be achieved by crossing the river elsewhere. By plaiting withies and covering them with the tarpaulin from a tent floor a serviceable coracle was made, capable of holding five men. The operation was carried out by Captain B. Francis (R. High.) with half No. 3 Company. Early on the morning of 29th April Francis got most of his men across the Lugonya a mile or so below the bridge. With the rest of his force he then made a feint against

[1] A few days before the move, No. 2 Company had gone on to Nyawanje, a village about half-way, where fires had had to be lit around the camp as a man-eating lion killed one of the sentries. When the battalion reached Utete II, lions again proved troublesome. One of them, believed to be the same animal, sprang upon Private Nugwe while on sentry duty and dragged him off. The picquet followed, whilst Nugwe shouted his whereabouts to direct their fire. After a hundred yards the lion dropped his prey, who died next day after losing his leg. The lion was found shot through the heart, and its head and skin were afterwards placed in 3 K.A.R. Mess at Nairobi.

the bridge, and another about a hundred yards upstream. When the attack developed on the flank and rear of the German position it proved decisive, and the enemy withdrew in haste, leaving most of his baggage.

After this action 1/3 K.A.R. formed a post on the left bank of the river, and began patrols towards Utunge and the west. Most of the enemy at Mpanganya had already surrendered on account of the floods, and the rest were disappearing towards the south, after a half-hearted attempt to retake the bridge on 11th May. 1/3 K.A.R. moved via Kitambi to Mchemera to join the newly-formed No. 2 Column. By the beginning of June the enemy was south of Mibaba and the whole of the right bank of the Rufigi was clear.

With the rains drying up and the enemy once more on the move, the campaign had entered a new and more difficult phase. There were no longer any fixed points of importance, such as ports or railways, awaiting capture. The sole objective was the enemy, roaming at large in a wilderness intersected by bush tracks and dotted with small villages and patches of cultivation. There was no line of communication that could be cut to starve the enemy into surrender. Instead his supply depôts, believed to lie mainly in the Liwale—Masasi area, were stocked and replenished locally and lay in the centre of his territory. Yet speed was essential if von Lettow was to be attacked before he was again reprieved by the rains. The War Office therefore promised several hundreds of light lorries, sought permission to recruit carriers in Portuguese East Africa, and told van Deventer that he was to bring the campaign to a speedy end.

Kilwa and Lindi were to be the main bases for the new offensive. The 1st Division was re-designated the Kilwa Force, and its two brigades became No. 1 Column under Colonel G. M. Orr, and No. 2 Column under Colonel H. F. L. Grant. No. 1 Column, which included 2/2 K.A.R., was dispersed along a line of posts covering Kilwa, the most important being Mnasi, Mgerigeri, Mitole, Rumbo and Beaumont's Post, where the Kilwa—Lindi road crossed the River Ngaura. At the end of May a company of 1/3 K.A.R. was sent from Mchemera to Kirongo to select a site for the headquarters of No. 2 Column, which began to concentrate there on 2nd June. This brought 1/3 K.A.R. and 2/3 K.A.R. together once more, and later on part of 3/3 K.A.R. also joined No. 2 Column.

For a time the position remained static, while van Deventer awaited the promised lorries and other reinforcements. The British forces held a line running from Kilwa along the Ngaura towards Liwale, with No. 2 Column occupying the western sector. A light railway had been built along the road from Kilwa as far as Mgerigeri. As it ran parallel to the enemy front it had to be constantly patrolled. The Germans were occupying high ground to the south, with their camps well concealed in the thick bush. Patrols identified their positions opposite Kirongo, Mnasi and Rumbo.

Brigadier-General Beves, who was temporarily in command at Kilwa, was anxious to attack the German forward positions before they could be withdrawn, but the experience gained at Rumbo in April had shown the futility of too hasty action. At the end of June he had also at his disposal a third column, formed temporarily from the 40th Pathans and two companies of 3/3 K.A.R.

Van Deventer had not as yet received sufficient transport to mount an offensive simultaneously from Kilwa and Lindi. During July the Lindi Force was therefore instructed to contain its opponents without attempting any large-scale operations, while a limited advance was made from Kilwa to drive the enemy out of the hills. This involved two severe actions in which all four battalions of the K.A.R. took part.

The main enemy force was well entrenched in a strong position near Mnindi. All three columns were to make a converging attack: No. 1 from Beaumont's Post against the north-east face, No. 2 from Kirongo against the west, and No. 3 from Wungwi on the shore of the harbour.

Affair at Mnindi, 6th July, 1917.—The advance began on 5th July. No. 1 Column left Beaumont's Post at 4 p.m. and bivouacked along the track. Next morning in the darkness shortly before dawn, 2/2 K.A.R. under Lieutenant-Colonel Filsell struck the first enemy picquets about four miles from Mnindi. No. 1 Company, the advance guard, drove them back through a field of cut *mtama*, where the long stalks prevented a bayonet charge.[1] Filsell sent No. 4 Company on a wide flanking movement round the enemy left, while No. 2 Company went forward to support No. 1. At noon No. 4 Company delivered a vigorous assault on the flank, and the enemy retired from his position, which was then occupied by the battalion. No. 4 Company had kept in touch by a field cable laid under heavy fire. For the first time the battalion had gone into action supported by the Stokes mortars, which greatly demoralized the enemy.[2]

Meanwhile the task of No. 2 Column was to deliver a flank attack and if possible to cut off the enemy's retreat. Reconnaissance showed that all approach routes were watched. At dusk on 5th July the column therefore halted some miles west of Mnindi, while 1/3 K.A.R. laboured throughout the night cutting a new track on a compass bearing through the bush.

At 5.30 a.m. on 6th July No. 2 Column moved forward with 2/3 K.A.R. (plus one company of 3/3 K.A.R. attached) as advance guard, under Lieutenant-Colonel J. Latham (R. Munster Fus.). The enemy position at Mnindi was sighted at 10 a.m. and the battalion deployed. The terrain was difficult, and crossed by a succession of ridges covered with thick elephant grass, with intervening hollows choked by bamboo thickets. About 11.30 a.m. the troops reached a point some two miles north-west of Mnindi. From there two low ridges stretched in parallel towards the enemy. While 2/3 K.A.R. maintained its position in the centre of the line, the company of 3/3 K.A.R. worked forward along the northern ridge, and a company of 1/3 K.A.R., brought up from reserve, along the southern.

Progress was slow, but the action continued until 2.30 p.m., when the firing died down. Two hours later, on discovering that his line of retreat was in danger, the enemy began a heavy counter-attack on the K.A.R. right flank. Fresh reinforcements from 1/3 K.A.R. came up in support,

[1] The askaris referred to this action afterwards as the 'Mtama battle'.

[2] A captured German complained that the mortars were 'unfair' because the discharge made insufficient noise to act as a warning.

but ammunition was short and before nightfall a good deal of the ground so hardly gained had been lost. During the retirement a company of 1/3 K.A.R. was surrounded on three sides, but maintained its position until darkness set in, when it was able to retire and rejoin the column. By means of this counter-attack the enemy kept the road open and withdrew along it that night. The brunt of the action at Mnindi, which was the first in which any troops of 3/3 K.A.R. took part, had fallen upon the K.A.R. battalions; in No. 2 Column alone they had lost three officers wounded, three other ranks killed and 27 wounded. After the action No. 2 Column returned to Kirongo, where command was taken over by Lieutenant-Colonel Ridgeway.

The Germans had retired to Mchakama, where they were expected to put up a strong defence, as at this point the road to Narungombe ran through a rocky defile piercing a long range of hills running east and west. No. 1 Column, which had occupied Mnindi on the day after the action, moved south to Kiwatama, five miles short of Mchakama, on 9th July. At the same time No. 2 Column advanced from Kirongo. Again a special track was cut through the bush, this time by 2/3 K.A.R. It was a task at which the askaris excelled, and in four hours the battalion had cleared a broad strip eight miles long, passable for artillery and motor transport. In this way the enemy, who had already begun his retirement, was surprised at Mtandawala on 14th July from an unexpected direction, and driven out after slight resistance. A post was formed there and garrisoned by 2/3 K.A.R. A combined attack by all three columns was then planned on Mchakama, but the Germans retreated before it could be delivered. A small rearguard of two Europeans and 30 askaris was left in the gorge, but failed to delay 2/2 K.A.R. for long.

On 17th July No. 1 Column continued the pursuit. The enemy was feverishly preparing to stand at Narungombe. On 18th July his rearguard stubbornly defended five separate positions against the advance of 2/2 K.A.R. That night camp was made a mile or two from Narungombe. Nos. 2 and 3 Columns had also closed up, and although little was known of the strength and dispositions of the German force, a combined attack was ordered for the following day.

Battle of Narungombe, 19th July, 1917.—The frontal assault was allotted to No. 1 Column, while Nos. 2 and 3 moved against the enemy's left and right flanks respectively. At daybreak on 19th July No. 1 Column advanced with the Gold Coast Regiment leading and 2/2 K.A.R. in reserve. The enemy's main position was reached before 7 a.m. It proved to be a series of breastworks and redoubts, occupying the upper slopes of two hills, one on either side of the road, and extending for a distance of two miles. The Germans had eight companies, two guns and 48 machine guns, and were evidently determined that this time there should be no rapid withdrawal. The three British columns totalled about 1,700 men with 20 machine guns.

The advance of No. 2 Column towards the German left flank had also begun at daybreak, led by two companies of 1/3 K.A.R. By 10.15 a.m. the column was ready to attack, with 1/3 K.A.R. on the extreme right. At noon touch was gained with the enemy, whose left flank was pro-

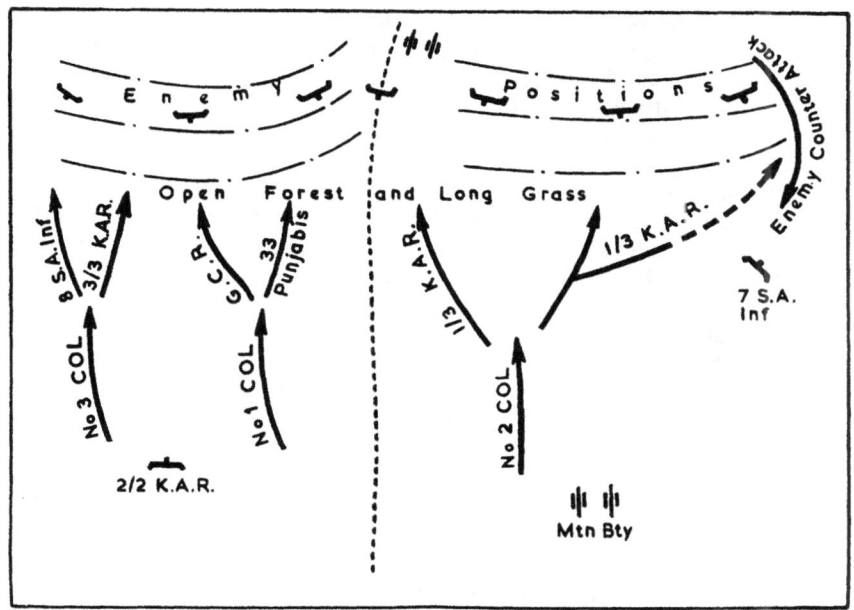

23. Battle of Narungombe, 19th July, 1917

tected by very thick bush. The right flank rested upon a swamp. Within a few minutes the advance was held up and little progress was made for an hour or more, until the pressure exerted by No. 1 Column made itself felt.

Meanwhile 3/3 K.A.R. and the Pathans of No. 3 Column were attempting to turn the enemy's right. About 200 yards from the German trenches both units were pinned down and suffered severe casualties. Most of the men serving in 3/3 K.A.R. were in action for the first time, and their difficulties were increased by the fires that raged across the long grass, the result of explosions from the Stokes mortars. Before long the battalion was obliged to give way, leaving many of the wounded behind, and seeing this the enemy counter-attacked at once, forcing the whole column back. Lieutenant-Colonel H. C. Dickinson was badly wounded in the face, and the raw askaris of 3/3 K.A.R. were greatly shaken.

By this time the Gold Coast Regiment and the Punjabis of No. 1 Column were hard pressed to maintain the frontal attack, and several companies of 2/2 K.A.R. were called up from reserve. At 2 p.m. No. 2 Company was sent forward to support the Punjabis in resisting an enemy counter-attack. At 4.30 p.m. No. 1 Company relieved the 8th S.A. Infantry. Night descended with the troops digging in upon the positions held, while water and food were brought forward from a point five miles to the rear.

Despite the severe fighting on all sides, little success had been achieved, but the action was now saved from complete failure by the courage and dash of 1/3 K.A.R. When No. 3 Column gave way on the left, the enemy mounted a fierce counter-attack, which he had been some time preparing, on the British right, charging the line to the accompaniment of much bugle-blowing and cheering. All available men of 1/3 K.A.R. were collected and the attack was held; and then, advancing at the charge under Major C. G. Durham (Spec. List), the askaris drove the enemy out of his trenches at the point of the bayonet The enemy scattered in all directions, abandoning a machine gun,[1] two tripods and a quantity of ammunition. The position thus gained was consolidated, and night fell with 1/3 K.A.R. in occupation of the trenches they had just captured.

The action of 1/3 K.A.R. on this occasion altered the whole situation. When daylight came on 20th July and the three columns prepared to renew the attack, they were found to be already in possession of the field. The enemy had evacuated the entire position and withdrawn to Mihambia, greatly to the annoyance of von Lettow, who was already hurrying north from the Lindi area with reinforcements. The German losses had been heavy, but so had the British. 1/3 K.A.R. alone losing six officers killed and 200 other ranks killed and wounded. Every officer with the battalion had either been hit or had bullet holes in his clothes.[2]

After the occupation of Narungombe, though patrolling was active, no major movements took place for the next eight weeks. Sickness and battle casualties had greatly reduced the strength of the Kilwa Force, and all units were in need of rest. Two companies 3/3 K.A.R. were drafted to 1/3 K.A.R. and the rest of the unit was distributed along the line of communication.

On 27th July No. 2 Column set out for Nanganachi, twelve miles to the south-west, 1/3 K.A.R. leading. About three miles from Nanganachi the advance guard was ambushed by a party of the enemy, who opened fire with a machine gun. Within a few moments the officer in command and six of his askaris had been killed and the rest wounded. The enemy vanished without trace into the bush.

Nanganachi was occupied, and 1/3 K.A.R. again went forward to clear the way to Mssindye. The rest of the column followed, and 3/3 K.A.R. took over the defence of Nanganachi. After a brief skirmish with an enemy picquet Mssindye was occupied on 29th July by a company under Captain G. H. de la Pasture (Spec. List). The rest of the column arrived and formed a defensive camp there next day. On 5th August the 129th Baluchis, with a company of 1/3 K.A.R. in reserve, fought an action against a German entrenched position at Nanyata, nine miles from the new camp, in which the K.A.R. had one British N.C.O. and five African ranks wounded. For the rest of that month and the first part of September, 1/3 and 2/3 K.A.R. were alternately engaged in outpost duties or patrols that brought them into constant touch with the enemy.

Throughout this period No. 1 Column remained at Narungombe. Patrols of 2/2 K.A.R. were constantly employed reconnoitring the enemy position at Mihambia, and an outpost was formed along the track, manned by two companies of the battalion.

The combined attack by the Kilwa and Lindi Forces, that was intended

---

[1] This gun was afterwards mounted at the K.A.R. Mess, Nairobi.
[2] This action at Narungombe is one of the battle honours borne by the K.A.R.

to bring von Lettow to bay or drive him out of German territory, was timed to begin in the middle of September. In the meantime the Kilwa Force was strengthened by the arrival of several Indian units, and preparations for an advance were pressed forward. An airfield was constructed, food dumps were built up, and the light railway was extended at the rate of a mile a day. General Hannyngton resumed command, and in September moved his headquarters from Kilwa to Mssindye, ready for the renewal of operations.

(vii) *The First Operations from Lindi, February-July, 1917.* Maps VI (a) and VI (e).

Lindi was the most important centre in the southern part of German East Africa. It possessed a stone fort, barracks, many other buildings along the foreshore, and behind them an extensive town of native huts. The coast is low-lying, with higher ground a short way inland. A number of European estates for the cultivation of rubber, sisal and other products had been laid out in the vicinity. The harbour, situated on the estuary of the River Lukuledi, was not so good as that at Kilwa and in 1917 was quite undeveloped.

Lindi was first garrisoned by two companies of the West India Regiment, who were watched by small enemy patrols from the heights inland. At the end of 1916 the German troops under Captain Looff of the *Königsberg*, who had driven the Portuguese from Newala, were ordered by von Lettow to the Lindi area. As soon therefore as the offensive on the Rufigi came to a standstill, Hoskins decided to strengthen the Lindi garrison and to place Brigadier-General O'Grady in command.

O'Grady's orders were to prepare for an advance to Masasi, where the enemy was collecting and storing great quantities of food. By the time he landed at Lindi (23rd February) the bulk of his force was already arriving or on the way: 1/2 K.A.R. under Lieutenant-Colonel Giffard; a detachment of the 5th (Indian) Light Infantry; the Arab Rifles (recently withdrawn from Jubaland), and some artillery. Reports said that the enemy forces in the vicinity now totalled about 600 troops.

1/2 K.A.R. disembarked at Lindi on 5th March, at the mouth of a creek fifteen miles long. The enemy was holding the line Mkwaya—Mingoyo—Schaedel's Farm—Schaeffer's Farm (near Ngurumahamba). During the month of March O'Grady pushed forward his outposts and patrolled widely to gain information. The rains were still heavy; the country was rough and broken, and covered with a thick growth of bush. Giffard made a flight inland by seaplane, but little could be seen.

On 9th March a detachment of 1/2 K.A.R. crossed the estuary and established an outpost on Nyanda Hill. Next day other forces turned the enemy out of Schaeffer's Farm. This position was retaken, however, and a British post was set up at Mtanga instead. On 24th March this post was taken over by 1/2 K.A.R.

As von Lettow's army came south, the pressure on Lindi grew. Fresh enemy camps were reported at Yangwani and Lutende. O'Grady was not the man to adopt a passive attitude and had been ordered if possible to divert some of the enemy from Kilwa. But the Germans were aggressive and enterprising, well led and with a high proportion of European officers and N.C.Os. In this respect the British troops were particularly weak, the proportion in 1/2 K.A.R. being 1 to 70, which made the young African recruit very difficult to handle in action. The Kilwa Force had learnt this lesson at Rumbo; it now remained for the Lindi Force to learn the same thing.

Actions at Yangwani and Lutende, 23rd-25th April, 1917.—As soon as he heard of the new enemy arrivals, O'Grady decided to attack. On 22nd April Lieutenant-Colonel Giffard marched out to Namembo with 1/2 K.A.R., 50 rifles of the 5th Light Infantry, some machine-gun sections, mortars and mountain guns. Yangwani was approached under cover of darkness, and at 10 a.m. on 23rd April the enemy was surprised and forced to make a hasty retreat. Giffard then sent out patrols to locate the camp at Lutende, but twenty-four hours elapsed before it could be found. By that time the enemy had been warned, and a second night march on 24th/25th April failed to take him by surprise. Though Giffard's attack at first drove the Germans back, it was met by a heavy concentration of fire and a counter-attack by forces estimated at 400 rifles with six machine guns. Fighting continued throughout the day, but casualties, especially among the officers, were serious, and at dusk the action was broken off. 1/2 K.A.R. had recently absorbed 180 young recruits, and 'A' Company had gone into the action without any officer at all. Through pouring rain the battalion marched wearily back through the darkness, having lost three officers out of eight (one died of wounds, one wounded, one missing), eight African ranks killed, 45 wounded, and six missing.

For several weeks a lull ensued on the Lindi front. Still more recruits, but this time with European officers and N.C.Os., arrived for 1/2 K.A.R. For many months a *Königsberg* 4.1-inch gun, hidden in the bush near Mingoyo, had at intervals shelled the port. Towards the middle of May the Germans moved this gun to a new position at Schaedel's Farm.

Soon after this, orders were issued for an attack in force on the German headquarters at Schaeffer's Farm. Three columns were organized: one consisting of the 5th Light Infantry and some mountain guns, to advance via the post at Mtanga; another of Arab Rifles with machine guns of the West India Regiment, to proceed by boat, land near the enemy position and join the first column; and a third, consisting of 1/2 K.A.R. (475 rifles and six machine guns), who were to concentrate at Namembo and march west-south-west across country to take the enemy by surprise with a simultaneous attack.

Action at Schaeffer's Farm, 18th-19th May, 1917.—While the attack of the other two columns was developing, 1/2 K.A.R. found progress difficult over broken country covered with thick bush and high grass. Weary after their long night march, the battalion did not reach the vicinity of Schaeffer's Farm until noon on 19th May, when the advance guard ('B' Company) was checked by fire from the German outposts on a ridge running north-west. 'A' Company came up; the rest of the battalion deployed, with one company in reserve, and the engagement became general. At 2.30 p.m. the enemy drove home a bayonet attack on the right flank. Some of the young recruits fell back in disorder for half a mile, and in spite of all that the handful of British officers could do, confusion spread and ended in a rout. The situation was saved from worse disaster by the steadiness of some of the N.C.Os. and older askaris, and by the reserve company under Captain R. G. H. Wilson (Spec. List), who made a counter-attack that checked the enemy. This enabled the troops to be reassembled about a mile to the rear, and prevented the reserve ammunition from falling into enemy hands. The battalion then marched back to the Mtanga post, covered by a steady rearguard of 60 rifles who eventually stopped the enemy pursuit. The battalion had lost 22 men killed, died of wounds or missing, and one officer and 36 African ranks wounded. Realizing that the attack had failed, O'Grady ordered the other columns to break off the action and retire.

At the beginning of June Lindi was reinforced by the newly-formed 3/2 K.A.R., 1,100 strong, and by the 25th R. Fusiliers, reduced to 250 men, back from a recuperative spell in South Africa. O'Grady was now able to plan his advance inland up the valley of the Lukuledi. Whatever may have been thought of the campaign in England, no one at Lindi was under any misapprehension as to the nature of the difficulties ahead, or the fighting spirit of the enemy to be overcome.

Attack on Enemy Positions near Lindi, 10th-12th June, 1917.—The German positions flanked the shallow waters of the creek, and the first movement was to be a combined operation designed to cut the trolley line above Mingoyo to prevent removal of the 4.1-inch gun, and to block the retreat of the enemy at Schaeffer's Farm. Naval craft were to cover a landing at Mkwaya by the Fusiliers, 520 rifles and eight machine guns of 3/2 K.A.R., and some artillery, towed up the creek in lighters. Meanwhile on the northern flank a column consisting of 687 rifles 1/2 K.A.R. and 100 rifles 5th Light Infantry, with guns and machine-gun sections attached, left Lindi at 1.30 p.m. on 10th June to march via Namembo to Lutende, ready to advance next day at dawn and cut off the retreat of the enemy at Schaeffer's Farm. The advance guard of this force was commanded by Lieutenant-Colonel Giffard.

The night of 10th/11th June had been chosen because high tide was at 7.30 p.m., so that the troops could be landed in darkness, and later have the benefit of the moon (which was due to rise an hour before midnight) for their advance inland. The enemy got warning of the approach and lit the water with star shells as the convoy went past, but apart from some sniping, the landing was made practically unopposed on the pier at Mkwaya.[1] Under the command of Lieutenant-Colonel C. G. Phillips (W. Yorks. R.) 3/2 K.A.R. set out at 11 p.m. to cut the trolley line near the Mandawa Hills. At dawn Phillips reached the hills near Tandamuti, where he halted to reconnoitre Schaedel's Farm and Mwreka. With the rest of his column O'Grady was advancing direct on Schaedel's, and sent instructions to Phillips to conform to his movements. The trolley line ran along a ridge flanking a swampy valley. Sensing the intention of the British commander, the Germans lost no time in manning this ridge

---

[1] The first tow landed at 7.30 p.m. and the last, which had stuck in the river, at 11 p.m.

and bringing their machine guns into action against the Fusiliers, who had occupied the parallel ridge across the valley.

It was past midday before Phillips got the order to advance on Schaedel's Farm. A wide stretch of bush-covered hills now separated him from O'Grady's force, and 3/2 K.A.R. could only make slow progress. O'Grady had postponed his attack, waiting for the K.A.R. to arrive, but about 2.30 p.m. Phillips' column was suddenly attacked by two companies under Captain Looff, approaching from the south-west. A bayonet charge by No. 3 Company and two platoons of No. 1 Company drove the enemy back, and at 4.30 p.m. the march was resumed. Just before dusk Looff attacked again, and a confused fight was in progress when darkness fell. The column became split; two machine guns were lost, and to reassemble his scattered companies Phillips decided to return to Mkwaya, where his column collected during the night.

Meanwhile the northern column had gained Naiwiti unopposed. Pushing ahead through difficult and exhausting country, Giffard's advance guard found the enemy about 100 strong in position before Mayani, and captured a convoy *en route* for Schaeffer's Farm. On 12th June Mayani was occupied and then Mingoyo, and the advance continued without opposition through Mwreka to Schaedel's Farm. That night enemy patrols were active around the camp, which was attacked next morning, but these movements were only intended to cover the general withdrawal of the Germans from their advanced positions. Avoiding envelopment, they escaped down the trolley line with the 4.1-inch gun.

O'Grady withdrew the bulk of his force to Lindi. 1/2 K.A.R. occupied Mingoyo, where the men were accommodated in huts and bandas and the village was put into a state of defence. The place was accessible to sea-going dhows and was a distributing centre for the area. On retirement the Germans had sacked it, and trade goods of all kinds—beads, glassware, compasses, typewriters and even perambulators—were scattered in the streets. Gum, rubber, beeswax and elephant tusks were found there awaiting export.

So far as could be ascertained by constant patrolling during the next two weeks, the German forward positions were near Mkwaya, at Tandamuti Hill and at Schaedel's Upper Farm, with reserves at Mtua. Schaedel's Lower Farm was now a British outpost, and the dense thornbush and rubber trees between the two were the scene of frequent encounters. On 21st June Major Hardingham with two companies 3/2 K.A.R. fought an engagement around the Upper Farm, turning the enemy out of his trenches and causing several casualties. On the same day the enemy's heavy guns, which could be easily moved on the trolley line, bombarded 1/2 K.A.R. at Mingoyo. After that the camp was moved to a new site on the left bank of the Mwreka River, where concealed trenches were dug.

Towards the end of June it became evident that the main body of the enemy was in the Lindi area, and an attack on Mkwaya was expected daily. On the afternoon of the 30th a whole German company with two machine guns suddenly attacked a ration escort of six Bemba recruits and 18 porters. Instead of retreating, Lance-Corporal Ndoya, the African

N.C.O. in command, kept his porters under control and returned the enemy's fire until he was joined by Sergeant Edward with another 20 askaris. Two volleys were fired and an advance was then made on the enemy. At this juncture the sound of firing was heard by Lance-Corporal Mwenyedawa with a patrol of four men of No. 3 Company, who promptly came into action on the flank, skilfully deceiving the enemy as to his numbers. By this time 100 rifles had been dispatched for a counter-attack, but by the time they arrived the enemy had withdrawn in some haste, routed by a party of 33 rifles commanded by African N.C.Os. alone.

Von Lettow was now reported to be at Lutende with a considerable force. Van Deventer, who visited Lindi on 9th July, decided that the Lutende position, which was situated on a hill, was too strong to attack. Plans were therefore laid for an outflanking movement up the valley of the Lukuledi, but before they could materialize von Lettow withdrew from Lutende and went north to assist in delaying actions against the main British advance from Kilwa.

On 14th July 1/2 K.A.R. took over from 3/2 K.A.R., with detachments at Lower Schaedel's and Mkwaya. Throughout that month intermittent shelling of the British positions continued. On one occasion an armour-piercing shell landed centrally on Lower Schaedel's farmhouse, exploding right in the centre of the K.A.R. camp but wounding only one man. Equipment and reinforcements from England now greatly increased the efficiency and fighting strength of the new K.A.R. units: new rifles, Lewis guns. British warrant officers and N.C.Os. who had fought in Europe on the western front. After their reverses at Lutende and Schaeffer's Farm the recruits in the Lindi Force were settling down, and their N.C.Os. were gaining experience. One patrol of 1/2 K.A.R., commanded by Corporal Kaisi, located and burnt an important enemy food store near Tandamuti. Another, under Lance-Corporal James of 'C' Company, was surrounded after bombing some enemy picquets, but hid for three days in an ant-bear hole and then bombed its way through the enemy posts by night.

At the end of July Lindi was reinforced by the 8th South African Infantry from Kilwa, by more Indian units and artillery, and by another recruit battalion, 3/4 K.A.R.

Action at Tandamuti, 3rd August, 1917.—During August, while the Kilwa front remained quiet, operations were resumed at Lindi in preparation for the combined advance in September. The main German positions now stretched from Mandawa to Tandamuti Hill. The outposts were attacked on 2nd August, ready for the main assault next day. For this the Lindi Force was organized in three columns. The main one, consisting of the 25th R. Fusiliers, 259 Machine Gun Company and 3/4 K.A.R., was to attack the enemy right flank on Tandamuti Hill; on the British right 3/2 K.A.R. was to advance from Schaedel's Farm, and between these two columns were the 30th Punjabis. 1/2 K.A.R., now brought up to a strength of 33 officers, 35 British N.C.Os. and 690 African ranks, with eight machine guns and eight Lewis guns, was in reserve at Mkwaya.

On 3rd August the main column was soon faced with a fierce and determined resistance, based upon a concealed redoubt on Tandamuti Hill, the existence of which had previously been unsuspected. The Fusiliers were weak in numbers, and 3/4 K.A.R. was in action for the first time, only a few days after arrival in the field. Attacks on the redoubt were all beaten off, and the column came to a standstill. The Punjabis in the centre were thus left unsupported, and when counter-attacked suffered a serious reverse.

At 2.15 p.m. 1/2 K.A.R. was ordered up to the Punjabis' support. 'B' Company engaged with the enemy about 4 p.m., and 'C' Company soon after. 1/2 K.A.R. followed up, but by this time the battle line was in some confusion and for a few minutes they found themselves in action against 3/4 K.A.R. By now it was evident that Tandamuti could not be taken before nightfall, and a general retirement was ordered.

Meanwhile the transport columns had been ambushed and most of the porters had scattered into the bush, throwing down their loads along the track. For some hours after darkness fell 'A' and 'D' Companies, 1/2 K.A.R., covered the collection of these abandoned loads and the evacuation of casualties. They regained their original position in the small hours of 4th August, after an exhausting and disheartening day, bringing in about 600 frightened porters.

Operations at Narunyu, 10th-19th August, 1917.—During the night of 3rd/4th August the enemy began his withdrawal, and after a few days spent in reorganization the British columns resumed their advance. 1/2 K.A.R. plus two companies of 3/4 K.A.R., the 8th S.A. Infantry, and some mountain guns left for Mkwaya on 9th August, crossed the Lukuledi and advanced round the right flank of the enemy, who now occupied a new position at Narunyu. Next day the column arrived unobserved at a point about a mile and a half to the east of the German position, where trenches were dug. 'C' Company reconnoitred Narunyu but became engaged and had to retire. The enemy followed and attacked the camp, but was repulsed by 'D' Company.

During the next few days the other columns pressed forward and patrol actions were frequent. Heavy rain flooded the valley, converting much of it to swamp, through which the transport columns floundered in the effort to maintain supplies. On 17th August 1/2 K.A.R. led the advance on a compass bearing through the bush. At 9.30 a.m. on the 18th the Mtua—Mingoyo road was reached and an enemy picquet was engaged. As the main position at Narunyu was approached, 1/2 K.A.R. changed to 'bush formation' to drive in the picquets, but the undergrowth was so dense that by noon the battalion had to change back to march order. Before long sniping came from the shambas to the right of the column, and three companies deployed to clear the area. The enemy tried to outflank first 'A' Company and then 'C' Company, maintaining his fire until dark though without pressing his attack. A perimeter camp was then made for the column, which included the Royal Fusiliers and a company of 3/2 K.A.R. who had joined shortly before nightfall.

The column was now practically isolated and in a dangerously advanced position very close to the enemy.[1] About ten o'clock that night the

---

[1] The K.A.R. and German askaris could call across to one another. On this

Germans suddenly opened fire and made a great deal of noise with bugles and shouting, but no attack materialized. Lieutenant-Colonel C. G. Phillips of 3/2 K.A.R. tried to get through to the camp with ammunition, but the company of his unit escorting it was ambushed and obliged to retire. On the 19th another company of 3/2 K.A.R. succeeded in reaching the camp, and 1/2 K.A.R. was ordered to dig in. Brigadier-General O'Grady and his staff got through and laid out the dispositions of a new defensive line. But the camp was still invested on three sides by the enemy, and it was impossible to reach the men with hot meals or drinks. As the food had to be prepared well to the rear and carried forward in water-proofed rice bags it was often mouldy.

For several days 1/2 K.A.R. and the Royal Fusiliers maintained themselves precariously in the perimeter camp, hungry, thirsty, tired and subjected to spasmodic attack. A sense of comradeship and mutual appreciation arose between the two units that perhaps had never been experienced before.[1] Both were prepared to renew the assault on the German position, but reconnaissance showed that the enemy had been heavily reinforced, and in view of this General van Deventer sent orders that the Lindi offensive should be pressed no further. On 27th August 1/2 K.A.R. was therefore withdrawn to rest at the main camp in rear, while the forward positions were taken over by 3/2 K.A.R.

(viii) *The Operations of the Western Columns, March-November, 1917.* Maps VI (a) and VI (b).

Despite the cold of the Livingstone Mountains and the rains of the river valleys below the eastern escarpments, the troops operating in the western area suffered less hardship during the abnormal rains of 1917 than those in the Rufigi valley and the coastal regions. None the less, exhaustion and the difficulties of supply resulted in a similar stagnation after the disappearance of Wintgens on his race to the north. The 2nd Division had been disbanded on the withdrawal of the South African troops, and the rest of what was now called the Iringa Column was for the time being immobile, with headquarters and two companies 1/4 K.A.R. at Boma Mzinga, and two companies at Mgwadia's. The troops were often on half rations, but training and reorganization continued, as well as patrols. Farther south, Northey's men were also at a standstill, grouped around two widely-separated areas at Njombe and Songea. Von Langenn faced them on the Ruhuje and Lincke at Likuyu. Kraut had disappeared towards the east.

In the latter part of April, 1917, Hawthorn moved east from Songea. After skirmishing with Lincke's outposts on the River Likuyu he crossed

---

occasion the latter inquired whether their opponents had fought at Kibata. Sometimes the K.A.R. askaris would taunt their enemy with 'fighting for nothing' and sing impromptu songs on the advantages of being British soldiers.

[1] A Fusilier officer, writing later of the engagement at Narunyu, gave expression to this as follows: 'It was here that one saw, and realized, the full fighting courage to which well-trained native African troops can rise. The first-second King's African Rifles was one of the original pre-war battalions, and magnificently they fought here; and we, who were an Imperial unit, felt that we could not have wished for a stouter, nor a more faithful regiment to fight alongside of.' (Captain A. Buchanan, *Three Years of War in East Africa*, p. 193.)

the stream on the 23rd with his main column, and four days later occupied the enemy's camp, which had been evacuated. While this movement was in progress a company of 2/1 K.A.R. was detached to the flank to hold Kitanda.

About this time reports reaching Northey showed that Kraut's column had broken into two, and that one of these, commanded by Major von Stuemer, was raiding in Portuguese territory well south of the Rovuma and not far from the eastern frontier of Nyasaland. Once again the centre of danger was shifting southward. Northey therefore transferred his headquarters from Njombe to Zomba, halted the projected advance beyond the Likuyu, recalled Hawthorn to command the troops in Nyasaland, and began to regroup his forces. 1/1 K.A.R. was recalled from the pursuit of Wintgens to garrison Njombe; Lieutenant-Colonel W. J. T. Shorthose with half 1/4 K.A.R. was ordered to Fort Johnston, and all available K.A.R. details in Nyasaland moved out to Mangoche with the 5th S.A. Infantry. Von Stuemer's patrols had already crossed the border, but now withdrew. The South Africans then occupied Namweras to watch the principal route into Nyasaland, with an outpost at Mtonia, sixty-five miles to the north.

On 25th May the rest of 1/4 K.A.R. reached Fort Johnston. Northey ordered one company of the battalion to Namweras and another to Mtonia, recalling all K.A.R. details to continue their training. Recruitment had reopened in March and the formation of 3/1 K.A.R. was in progress near Zomba.

It was van Deventer's intention that when the general offensive reopened, Northey should move eastward from Songea towards Liwale or Tunduru, in the hope of cutting the enemy off from Portuguese East Africa. To achieve this seemed to Northey impossible, but he advised van Deventer that by the beginning of July three columns would be ready to co-operate: the first (1/1 K.A.R. and other troops then at Songea) to advance on Liwale; the second (some troops of Murray's column, now on their way back from chasing Wintgens) to move on Tunduru; and the third (1/4 K.A.R.) to move north from Mtonia. This plan was agreed, and the columns began to concentrate accordingly.

During the first week of May the company and a half of 1/4 K.A.R. that had been left behind at Boma Mzinga when Shorthose took the rest of the battalion south were ordered back to Iringa in case Wintgens broke to the east. On 18th May headquarters and 580 rifles 2/4 K.A.R. reached Iringa from Morogoro and absorbed these troops into the battalion. By that time the danger from Wintgens was over.

The rôle allotted to the Iringa column in the scheme for a general offensive was to clear the enemy from the valley of the Kilombero by advancing on Ifakara. Belgian troops were to co-operate and afterwards to take over garrison duty in the area and release the British units for operations elsewhere. The Iringa column was commanded by Colonel H. C. Tytler, whose force consisted of 2/4 K.A.R. and the 17th (Indian) Infantry, totalling 1,053 rifles with 12 machine guns. One company 2/4 K.A.R. was left to garrison Iringa, and one company Mgwadia on the right flank of the advance.

Tytler's orders were to secure the river crossing at Ruipa by the end of June, and then the crossing of the Kilombero south of Ifakara. The difficulties of climate and terrain were likely to prove greater obstacles than enemy opposition, for beyond the concentration point at Boma Mzinga the track descended some 3,000 feet to the River Mgeta, with gradients in places as steep as one in three, impossible to negotiate with pack animals. In spite of this, Tytler had to be satisfied with fewer carriers than he needed. Nor could animals be used with success in the Mgeta valley, which was covered with tall elephant grass, had no grazing, and was thought to be infected by fly.

2/4 K.A.R., less those troops detailed for garrison duty, left Iringa on 19th June and reached Boma Mzinga five days later. Before the end of the month the whole column had concentrated there with its artillery. The advance began on the 30th, and two days later the forward troops were in touch with the enemy on the Ruipa river. By 7th July a bridgehead had been established, and pressing slowly forward against the enemy rearguard, Tytler successively occupied all the positions along the course of the river.

The Germans now fell back behind the River Njarabungu. Hampered by the appalling difficulties of his line of communication, it was the end of July before Tytler could reach the new position and attack again. After a brief action the Germans withdrew towards the River Idete. On 10th August the Iringa column was reinforced by the first of the Belgian troops, and the combined force then resumed the advance. The Idete was crossed on the 26th. Two days later the column entered Ifakara and joined a Belgian column from the north. 2/4 K.A.R. was then withdrawn and sent to join Hawthorn's column, while the Belgians continued against stiffening resistance to force their way on to the Mahenge Plateau.

Northey's first column concentrated at Likuyu at the beginning of July. Baxter had marched south from Njombe with 1/1 K.A.R., picking up the company at Kitanda *en route*. He joined 2/1 K.A.R. at Likuyu just too late to catch Lincke, who had made a tentative attack on the K.A.R. positions there with about five companies and a field gun. The column, commanded by Lieutenant-Colonel Hawthorn, was then completed by the addition of the 1st S.A. Rifles and a section of the Mountain Battery.

Hawthorn began his advance on 3rd July. Lincke had taken up a position covering the junction of the road fork leading to Mahenge and Liwale, and it had been supposed that the pursuit would lie in the direction of the latter. Hawthorn deployed and attacked, but when the enemy withdrew he unexpectedly took the Mahenge road. Across difficult and broken country, well suited to rearguard defence, the long pursuit began, driving the enemy laboriously from one position to another. As the German lines shortened, other forces joined them and resistance became stronger. Throughout the months of August and September Hawthorn with his two K.A.R. battalions fought a number of small actions among the difficult ravines and valleys of the country round Mponda's, and along the River Luwegu. Early in October he succeeded in crossing the river, and on the 16th, having been reinforced by 2/4 K.A.R., renewed his attack on the enemy, some six miles to the north. The Germans evaded action, destroyed and abandoned both their guns, and began a general withdrawal down the Luwegu. Hawthorn followed, and for the next two weeks pressed hard upon the rearguard. On the night of 1st/2nd November he attacked the enemy near Liganduka's, capturing 24 prisoners and a machine gun. After that the withdrawal continued towards the southeast, with Hawthorn following, while Murray's column pressed along the Songea—Liwale road.

Meanwhile, at the end of June Shorthose had begun his advance from Mtonia towards Mwembe. His column consisted of 1/4 K.A.R. (677 all ranks, with eight machine guns), two machine-gun sections of the 5th S.A. Infantry, and a section of the Mountain Battery. The rest of the South African Infantry remained to garrison Namweras and Mtonia. Apart from a rearguard action, von Stuemer offered little resistance, and by the end of the first week in July, 1/4 K.A.R. had occupied Mwembe and Likopolwe. A halt was made while companies watched the roads to Maziwa and Nanguare. On 14th July Shorthose received orders by air to occupy Tunduru, over a hundred miles to the north. On the 31st he crossed the Rovuma on rafts of grass packed into tents, and occupied Tunduru on 23rd August after slight opposition.

From Tunduru Shorthose sent a strong detachment north-east to the River Mohesi. In the middle of October he increased this to a strength of two companies, extending his advance to Abdullah kwa Nanga, about fifty miles south of Liwale. 1/4 K.A.R. had now penetrated the fertile area from which von Lettow drew much of his food, and was in an extremely isolated position between the main German army and Tafel's forces around Mahenge. Nevertheless Shorthose was ordered to continue his advance and a detachment of 250 rifles under Major E. B. B. Hawkins entered Liwale on 29th October, where 24 Europeans were taken prisoner.

Four days later Liwale was taken over by the Belgians, and Hawkins withdrew to Abdullah kwa Nanga, where he was soon threatened by Tafel's advancing troops. Leaving one company to garrison Tunduru, Shorthose now set out to reinforce him with headquarters and the remaining company of 1/4 K.A.R. (192 askaris, four machine guns and two Lewis guns). By this time the German western front was crumbling. The Belgians had entered Mahenge on 9th October and Tafel had begun a general withdrawal in the hope of rejoining von Lettow. Shorthose's scattered column lay right across his path.

On 13th November, the day that Shorthose left Tunduru, Tafel's advanced patrols were in the vicinity of Mandebe. Next day Hawkins advised Shorthose by runner that an action was impending. Hastening forward by forced marches, the latter reached the high ground south of Abdullah kwa Nanga at 5 a.m. on the 16th, when he heard the sound of heavy firing. At 7 a.m. Shorthose's advance guard was suddenly attacked and forced to retire upon the main body. The enemy followed in overwhelming force on centre and flanks, rushed and captured the machine guns and split the infantry into groups. Shorthose withdrew as best he could, with heavy loss.

Meanwhile Hawkins' projected attack had become a defensive action in hastily-prepared trenches. There he defended himself until nightfall, when the enemy withdrew, sweeping away in three columns, some 1,700 strong, towards the south-east.

For the time being the fighting on the western front was over. 1/4 K.A.R. and 2/4 K.A.R. withdrew to rest and refit. Both battalions were to come unexpectedly to the forefront in the following year, during the closing operations of the campaign.

(ix) *The Combined Offensive in the East, September-November, 1917.* Maps VI (a), 24.

Northey's columns had made some progress in their penetration from the west before the two forces based upon the coast were ready to begin their combined offensive. It was 10th September when van Deventer moved his Advanced Headquarters to the Kilwa area, ready to co-ordinate the southward thrust from there with the movement to the south-west from Lindi. This time there were to be no limited objectives, but a continuous advance that should link the Kilwa and Lindi forces in a common effort to bring the campaign to an end.

In the Kilwa area, the enemy still occupied his position at Mihambia, barring the road to the south. No. 1 Column (with which 2/2 K.A.R. was still serving) was to deliver the direct attack from Narungombe, while No. 2 Column (which included 1/3 and 2/3 K.A.R.) advanced from Mssindye to prevent escape to the south-west.

Action at Mihambia (Mnandi), 19th September, 1917.—On 18th September 2/2 K.A.R. began the advance on Mihambia, while most of the Gold Coast Regiment moved west to cut the retreat. On the morning of the 19th the column struck through the bush, while two detachments sent east and west diverted the enemy's attention. A general assault was then delivered on the western face of the German position. Once the picquets had been driven in, it was discovered that the enemy had cleared an extensive field of fire before his main defences and that the bush on either side was too thick for outflanking movements. In these circumstances the column was obliged to maintain a frontal attack that lasted all day, the enemy retiring at dusk and evacuating the position during the night. The action cost 2/2 K.A.R. heavier casualties than in any other single day's fighting: two officers killed, two wounded, two B.N.C.Os. wounded, and 103 other casualties among African ranks and porters.

Meanwhile, in order to block the enemy's retreat to the west, Colonel Ridgeway, commanding No. 2 Column, had ordered the construction of a boma of thorn and brushwood, five miles in length. Each unit of the column was allotted a section to build. The boma was then picqueted at intervals and the troops of the column were stationed in the rear, with reserves at the southern end.

The Nigerians had moved to the south; a small column of 2/3 K.A.R. under Lieutenant-Colonel J. C. Freeth (Transvaal R.) advanced from the north. During the night of 19th/20th September the enemy made several attempts to break through the boma. On the afternoon of the 20th he attacked the right of the line. 1/3 K.A.R. was in reserve, and about 3 p.m. was sent forward to support the 129th Baluchis. The attack was driven off, but the enemy, setting fire to the long grass, broke out southwards during the night. The Nigerians fought to stem the retreat, but as No. 2 Column was temporarily immobilized for want of food and water, the Germans were able to break away in scattered parties through the bush and to withdraw to the line of the River Mbemkuru.

On 20th September No. 1 Column continued its pursuit of the main enemy force. A stubborn rearguard action was fought beyond Mpingo. 2/2 K.A.R. suffered heavy casualties as the battalion was stationed on the right flank of the firing line, which was swept by machine-gun fire on open ground. On 24th September the advance was resumed. The enemy had now taken position about half-way up the large, saddle-backed hill that rose above the plain at Nahungu. No. 1 Column, with the Gold Coast Regiment in advance, approached on the 26th, driving the enemy rearguard along the road. The Nigerian Brigade was advancing along a parallel road to attack from the north-west.

Action at Nahungu, 27th September, 1917.—The German defences at Nahungu were conspicuous and exposed, with a poor field of fire. While 2/2 K.A.R. delivered the frontal attack the Mountain Battery silenced the German guns. At 6 p.m. the enemy made a violent counter-attack, the force of which fell mainly upon the Gold Coast Regiment on the left flank. This caused a panic among the porters, who ran back for several miles through the gathering darkness. During the night the Germans evacuated Nahungu and withdrew to the south-west, leaving a hospital and food store to fall into British hands.

No. 2 Column reached Nakiu and the River Mbemkuru without encountering further opposition. For a day or two the troops were occupied in cutting roads and patrolling the course of the river. On the 27th 1/3 K.A.R. was ordered to the support of No. 1 Column, then hotly engaged at Nahungu. The 129th Baluchis had received similar orders.

Action at Kihende, 30th September-1st October, 1917.—While the Nigerians went across country to join the Lindi Force, Hannyngton's two columns from Kilwa set out to cross the Mbemkuru. The enemy was reported to be entrenching a new position on Kihende Hill, a short distance up-river. 2/2 K.A.R. was ordered to cross the river higher up and get behind this position, while 1/3 K.A.R. and the Baluchis attacked. 1/3 K.A.R. crossed the Mbemkuru under fire on 30th September, and advancing under cover of the broken ground on the right bank, got within 500 yards of the enemy's trenches. Beyond that point further advance was impossible, though the mountain guns shelled the position and a hot fire was maintained with rifles and machine guns.

Meanwhile No. 1 Column was working through the bush towards the river. The Gold Coast Regiment got across on 1st October at Miteneno and the column then approached the enemy position down both banks. The Germans fought grimly to cover their withdrawal, and as the river was deep and the muddy banks were lined with high reeds, 2/2 K.A.R. had to go back to the crossing before support could be given to the Gold Coast Regiment. Next day 1/3 K.A.R. also crossed the Mbemkuru and joined No. 1 Column. Patrols gained touch with the enemy about four miles to the south.

The stalemate on the Lindi front lasted until late in September, when operations were resumed in conjunction with the advance from Kilwa. For some time 1/2 K.A.R. remained in reserve at the main camp, subjected morning and evening to regular bombardment by the enemy's armour-piercing naval shells, that did little damage on account of the sandy soil. Later on the battalion again took over the front line and resumed patrolling. It was now at a strength of 25 officers, 15 B.N.C.Os. and 540 African ranks.

Action at Mtua, 28th September, 1917.—The main part of the Lindi Force had been reorganized in two columns, called Nos. 3 and 4. The enemy was still in a position based on Narunyu and Mtua. On 24th September operations were reopened with a frontal attack upon the former, while 1/2 K.A.R. with the rest of No. 3 Column began a wide turning movement south of the Lukuledi, directed against Mtua. Four days later contact was gained with the enemy, and with 1/2 K.A.R. on the left flank, astride the main Mtua—Mingoyo road, the first enemy outposts were stormed and the action became general. The machine-gun officers and N.C.Os. were early casualties. The enemy retired, fighting rearguard actions as he went, and then stood and attacked the British left in strength. The defence of this flank fell upon 'D' Company, 1/2 K.A.R., which was reinforced towards dusk by two companies of 3/2 K.A.R. Soon afterwards the enemy withdrew, leaving a quantity of baggage in the abandoned camp. In this action 1/2 K.A.R. lost nine African ranks killed and 60 wounded, mostly from 'D' Company.

On 29th September the abandoned German positions were occupied, and the advance continued slowly, with 3/2 K.A.R. in the lead. The Lindi Force was awaiting the arrival of the Nigerian Brigade before pressing the next attack. 1/2 K.A.R. returned for a few days to the camp on the Lukuledi before relieving 3/2 K.A.R. in the new forward position astride the track near Mtama, with 'A' and 'B' Companies across a small river to the right. On 7th October Lieutenant-Colonel Giffard and his battalion stormed a ridge to the front, which was then occupied by 3/2 K.A.R.

During the first part of October the enemy continued to retire before the Kilwa Force, making for Ruponda. Hannyngton was ordered to move his main force up the Mbemkuru valley to reach Ruponda first, leaving only a detachment to press the German rearguard. After a few days' rest, No. 1 Column therefore resumed the advance from Miteneno, with 1/3 K.A.R. as advance guard.

Action on the Mbemba Road, 4th-6th October, 1917.—At 7.15 a.m. on 4th October 1/3 K.A.R. drove in the enemy picquets, and by eight o'clock had found the main position on a line of hills running south at right angles to the Mbemkuru, and parallel to the Mbemba—Mawa track. The battalion deployed but was held up by heavy fire. When the rest of the column came forward some progress was made under cover of fire from the Mountain Battery, but the intensity of fire from the German position and an enemy counter-attack against the Baluchis again brought the advance to a standstill, and the column dug in for the night. 1/3 K.A.R. had been without food for twenty-three hours, and when the transport arrived after midnight, many of the men were too tired to draw their rations.

On 5th October the attack was renewed, but again failed against heavy fire from well-sited positions. At nightfall the troops were withdrawn to the perimeter camp and plans were made to cross the hills towards the enemy's right. This movement began at dawn on the 6th, the column withdrawing to the south in parallel lines of battalions, with 1/3 K.A.R. on the left flank. After three miles the column wheeled to the right and came into contact with the enemy, who had discovered the threat to pin him against the river and was already escaping to the south. After an exchange of shots in the thick bush the German column extricated itself and withdrew towards Mawa, while the British, contrary to the expectation of the enemy, went west along the river to Mbemba, following the alternative route to Ruponda.

Mbemba was reached on 8th October. Next day the column left the river and struck south to Mnero Mission. The enemy was still unaware of the direction taken by the pursuit, which reached Ruponda from the west at dawn on 10th October. As the result of this successful strategy the enemy was hustled out of Ruponda after very slight resistance, and forced to resume his southward march towards the Lukuledi. Ruponda had been one of his principal magazines, and great stores of food and war material of all kinds fell into British hands. The enemy had set up repair workshops with fittings from the *Königsberg*, in which local timber was used to make new rifle stocks.

Ruponda was an important road centre, and its capture by No. 1 Column, which had marched over a hundred miles since 19th September, drove a deep wedge into the area between Tafel's forces around Mahenge and von Lettow's main army in the east. A camp was formed in preparation for a halt of several days, while fatigue parties began digging extra wells. Patrolling continued in all directions, and showed that large enemy forces still lay to the north-east of the column.

On the day that Ruponda was occupied, the Lindi Force resumed its advance towards Mtama. 1/2 K.A.R. followed patrols along the northern bank of the Lukuledi. During the afternoon halt a party of the enemy was seen to move round the perimeter and bring up a machine gun under cover of a large anthill. Sergeant Saiti, accompanied by an askari, crawled forward with grenades, disabled the gun and killed two of the crew.[1] The enemy then abandoned the attempt and withdrew.

Mtama was reported to be held by nine companies. Outflanking movements were attempted, but the enemy, aware perhaps of the approach of the Nigerian Brigade, evacuated the place on 15th October and retired towards Nyangao. No. 3 Column followed, with 1/2 and 3/2 K.A.R. astride the main road, fighting small rearguard actions all day. At dawn on the 16th the advance continued towards Nyangao, with 1/2 K.A.R. along a separate track to the north of the main column. No. 3 Column camped, and was joined that evening by No. 4 Column.

A great change had come over the operations in the Lindi area. Von Wahle had been forced out of a large and difficult stretch of country and

---

[1] Saiti and his askari were later awarded the Military Medal.

was now retiring rapidly. With no blankets and on short rations, the British columns were pursuing, well in advance of their baggage trains. The dense and tangled bush of the coastal region had given way to more open country of undulating hills, covered with short grass and patches of forest, where concealment was difficult. A major action was now impending, and von Lettow had hurried south with five companies to join von Wahle.

Battle of Nyangao (Mahiwa), 17th-18th October, 1917.—After withdrawing from Nyangao on 16th October, the main enemy force took up a position along a ridge about two miles to the south-west, behind the bed of a small stream. At daybreak on 17th October, No. 4 Column (Tytler) advanced from the Nyangao camp and gained contact with the enemy almost immediately. 3/4 K.A.R. attacked, and by one o'clock had carried part of the ridge. Meanwhile No. 3 Column (O'Grady), continuing its advance on the right or northern flank, had also gained contact. The Bharatpur Infantry attacked, supported by 1/2 K.A.R.

Few actions of the campaign exceeded in fury the fighting at Nyangao. Attack and counter-attack succeeded one another without respite and casualties mounted. Early in the action all the light machine guns of 1/2 K.A.R. were disabled, and practically all the gun teams were wiped out. 'C' Company dashed out to recover one gun that had apparently been abandoned in the open, and found the entire team lying dead around it. 'A' and 'B' Compnies had been the first committed to battle, and when they were forced to fall back 'C' Company went through them at the double, with bayonets fixed. Lieutenant-Colonel Giffard, who at great personal risk was rallying his troops in the forward line, brought up 'D' Company while 'A' and 'B' Companies re-formed. By early afternoon his whole battalion was again committed, and in answer to his representations the column commander sent forward two companies of 3/2 K.A.R. in support. The rest of that battalion arrived soon afterwards and began to dig in a little to the rear. Thrown back by the weight of the German assault, 1/2 K.A.R. dug in beside them, and the whole force remained upon the defensive until the enemy broke off the attack about 8 p.m. 1/2 K.A.R. had lost over half its European and over a third of its African personnel.[1]

The night of 17th/18th October was comparatively quiet, but the enemy attacked again in the morning, supported by the fire of howitzers and heavy guns. The attack was concentrated on the gap between the two columns, and in trying to stem it the last remnants of the 25th Royal Fusiliers, all that remained after two years' campaigning in Africa, were practically annihilated. 'B' and 'D' Companies, 1/2 K.A.R., were sent up in support, but were too late to prevent the disaster. With 3/2 K.A.R. leading, No. 3 Column attacked the enemy's left flank and gained some ground. The Punjabis of No. 4 Column likewise occupied some of the German trenches, with part of 3/4 K.A.R. on their left, but a strong counter-attack on this flank forced the column back to the river-bed,

---

[1] 1/2 K.A.R. went into action about 1 p.m., and the two companies of 3/2 K.A.R. entered the battle about 4.30 p.m. Attack and counter-attack went on all the afternoon, the ground changing hands four times. The action is commemorated in the K.A.R. battle honours.

where the position was maintained and all further attacks were beaten off. After its experiences on the previous day 1/2 K.A.R. remained in reserve on the 18th, having lost 44 per cent. of its fighting strength since the reopening of the Lindi offensive.

At nightfall the enemy broke off the action, and both sides withdrew. The battle had been fought to a standstill and neither side could continue without a pause for reorganization and supplies. As the engagement took the form of a pitched battle in open country, losses had been heavy. The greater part of von Lettow's forces had been engaged, under his own command,[1] and he claimed afterwards to have won the greatest victory since Tanga. But owing to his losses in men and ammunition, Nyangao really broke his offensive power. To some extent his prestige must also have suffered, as deserters came into the British camps for several days afterwards. For the next two weeks operations were confined to patrolling the front and flanks of the German position.

Simultaneously with the battle at Nyangao an action was fought on the Kilwa front that concluded operations there also for a time. On 12th October Lieutenant-Colonel Fitzgerald was ordered to Chingwea, fifteen miles south of Ruponda, with 1/3 K.A.R. and a squadron of the 25th Cavalry to seize the wells and some water-tanks nearby, on which the enemy depended for his retreat over the waterless stretch beyond. Fitzgerald approached Chingwea at dawn on the 13th. The cavalry reported that the village was unoccupied, whereupon 1/3 K.A.R. moved in, burnt the buildings and removed the tanks before retiring to Ruponda. Next day 1/3 K.A.R. was sent to occupy Mnero Mission. A garrison was left, and the rest of the battalion returned to Ruponda.

Action at Lukuledi Mission, 18th-21st October, 1917.—The enemy was reported to be holding Lukuledi Mission with a strength of about three companies, and on 17th October the whole of No. 1 Column left Ruponda to attack the post. Water supply was still a difficulty, and as the distance could not be covered in a single march, 2/2 K.A.R. went to Chingwea on the previous day to secure the water in advance. In spite of this, water was so scarce that 1/3 K.A.R. on arrival at Chingwea with the main column had to send fatigue parties to scoop rain-water from the holes in a large rock some two miles distant.

On 18th October No. 1 Column continued south along the direct route to Lukuledi to deliver the frontal attack, while 1/3 K.A.R. followed a track through the bush leading west of the Mission towards the enemy's left flank. Leaving camp at 5.30 a.m., before the march of the main column, 1/3 K.A.R. reached the Lukuledi at noon. There Fitzgerald remained hidden in the bush, waiting for the frontal attack to develop, as the guide said he was now within four miles of the Mission. A broken cable prevented orders from reaching him, and at 2.30 p.m. Fitzgerald decided to march. The distance proved much longer than expected; after an hour's march the sound of distant firing showed that the Mission was still some way off, and another hour elapsed before Fitzgerald deployed for the flank attack.

---

[1] Nyangao was said to be the only occasion on which von Lettow wore his full regimentals.

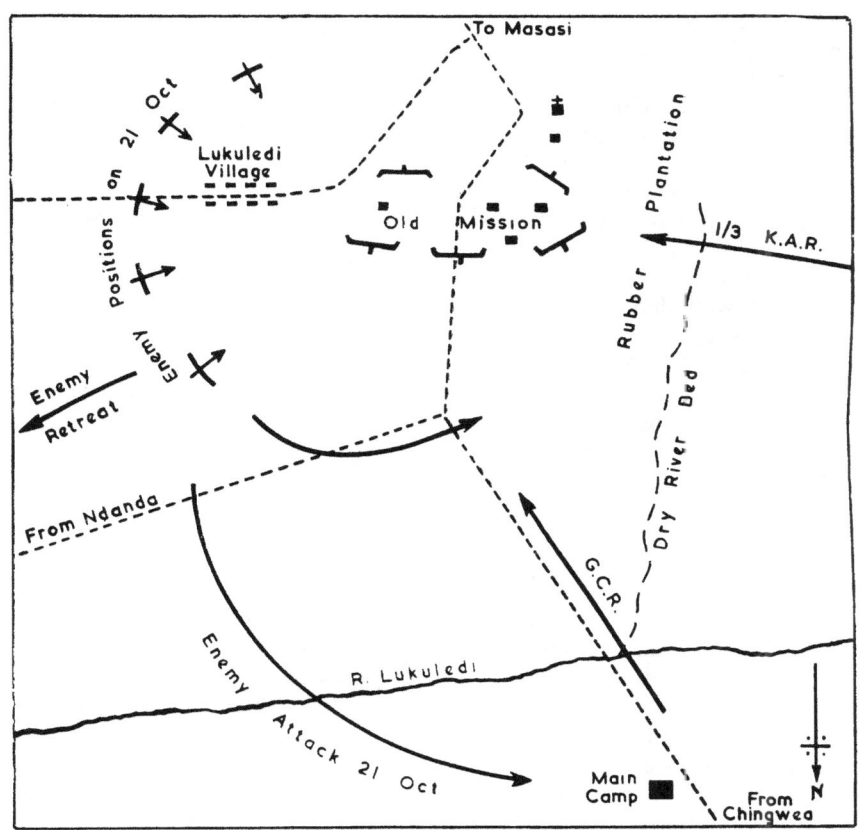

24. Action at Lukuledi Mission, 19th-21st October, 1917

The enemy was grouped around the buildings of the Old Mission. The Gold Coast Regiment, approaching down the road from Chingwea, had been counter-attacked on the right-flank. The unsuspected arrival of 1/3 K.A.R. on the right of the British column was therefore timely. The enemy was driven back, and by 8 p.m. 1/3 K.A.R., then within 200 yards of the German trenches, was in touch with the Gold Coast Regiment and digging in for the night.

Next morning it was discovered that the enemy had evacuated Lukuledi and retired towards Ndanda. 1/3 K.A.R. occupied the position while the rest of the column remained at its camp some two miles back along the Chingwea road. Extensive patrolling took place during the next two days. Governor Schnee and many other civilians were reported to be at Masasi, and on the evening of the 20th 1/3 K.A.R. was ordered to proceed in that direction to support a reconnaissance by the 25th Cavalry, leaving only 25 rifles to garrison Lukuledi. The rest of the column was to advance on Ndanda.

At dawn on 21st October the advance guard of 1/3 K.A.R. moved out of the camp. The troops had covered only a short distance when they came under heavy fire from the edge of the bush. The advance guard at once deployed between the church and the Old Mission, while the rest of the battalion manned the trenches. By this time the enemy's fire had increased, and a detachment of No. 2 Company, sent through the village to outflank the concealed attackers, came across a whole company of the enemy and was driven back. Great gallantry was displayed by a native officer of this detachment, Adam el Hashim. Finding himself isolated and surrounded by the enemy, he drew his revolver, shot three Europeans who were attempting to capture him, and managed to rejoin his men. But communication with the main column was cut, and three orderlies were killed or wounded trying to get through.

At 7.45 a.m. the enemy brought forward two guns and began shelling the camp. 1/3 K.A.R. did not possess even a Stokes gun with which to reply,[1] and the concentration of fire upon the centre of the position became so intense that movement was very difficult.[2] The enemy was now very close to the eastern face of the boma, but about 9.30 a.m. a message got through to the headquarters of the column. A detachment of the enemy, sent to mask the main camp, had done considerable destruction in the horse lines of the 25th Cavalry, and apprised at last of the true situation, the column commander sent forward the 129th Baluchis, while the mountain guns and howitzers opened fire on the enemy. By 11.30 a.m. the Germans realized that their attempt to wipe out the isolated K.A.R. position had failed, and breaking off the action withdrew towards Ndanda. Before withdrawing they fired six shells into the roof of the church, a beautiful building then nearing completion after seven years' work. Within a short while it was burnt to the ground.

Patrols discovered the enemy re-forming about two miles down the Ndanda road. In the late afternoon another attack was attempted but not pressed, and 1/3 K.A.R. easily repulsed it, capturing two machine guns and some prisoners. Altogether the day's fighting, one of the severest ever experienced by 1/3 K.A.R., cost the battalion one officer killed and six wounded; one British N.C.O. wounded; 11 African ranks killed and 36 wounded. In addition to this, the battalion lost six porters killed and 27 wounded.[3]

Lukuledi was too far from the Kilwa base to maintain a column there, and on 22nd October the troops marched back to Ruponda. 1/3 K.A.R. remained to form the rearguard, lighting fires to give the impression that the place was still occupied. 'A' Company was left on outpost duty at Chingwea, and the rest of the battalion reached Ruponda on the 23rd. By that time the enemy forces had been driven from Ruangwa by No. 2 Column, and had retired to Mnacho. A general pause then ensued along the whole Kilwa front, while supplies and reinforcements were brought forward.

[1] The gun had been withdrawn from the battalion to form a Stokes Gun Section.

[2] Fitzgerald afterwards paid tribute to the courage of his stretcher-bearers and ammunition porters, who carried on in spite of casualties among themselves.

[3] Captain W. G. Edwards was awarded the M.C. for his bravery and devotion to duty during this action, in rallying his men and re-occupying a line of trenches, vacated by mistake, just in time to forestall their capture by the enemy.

Von Lettow's main concentration, consisting of 12-13 companies, now lay between Nangoo and Lukuledi. A further seven companies were still about Mahiwa; one or two at Mnacho, and two at Newala. Van Deventer requested the Portuguese to take up dispositions along their frontier, and fixed 6th November as the date of his next advance.

After the battle of Nyangao the Lindi columns had formed a new camp about a thousand yards from the scene of the action. Casualties had been so heavy that for tactical purposes it was decided to combine 1/2 and 3/2 K.A.R. as a single unit under the command of Lieutenant-Colonel Giffard. This combined battalion was organized in four companies, Nos. 1 and 2 being formed out of the remnants of 1/2 K.A.R. and Nos. 3 and 4 out of 3/2 K.A.R. Towards the end of October the battalion was strengthened by a new draft of two British N.C.Os., with 105 Bemba recruits for 1/2 K.A.R. and 28 for 3/2 K.A.R.

On 6th November the Lindi Force advanced with the Nigerian Brigade on the right, No. 4 Column in the centre, and No. 3 Column on the left. Mahiwa was occupied by No. 4 Column, but the main opposition was met by No. 3 Column, which got across the Masasi road on the enemy's right rear. A detachment of No. 2 Company, followed by the whole of No. 1 Company of the combined K.A.R. battalion, went forward to support the Cape Corps in this action, and the enemy's counter-attacks were repulsed. They were only intended as delaying actions to allow the main force to withdraw over the waterless stretch of twenty miles that lay between Mahiwa and Nangoo. No. 3 Column, strengthened by 3/4 K.A.R. from No. 4 Column, was ordered to pursue.

The German rearguard was driven off by the Cape Corps and Nigerians on the 8th, and No. 3 Column took up the pursuit on the following day. Moving back from one position to another in the dense bush and bamboo forest, through which the bullets ricochetted with tremendous noise, the enemy contested every inch of the way and progress was slow. The K.A.R. led the advance, fighting one action after another. In the late afternoon the enemy was discovered posted upon a ridge overlooking the track. O'Grady and Giffard went forward to reconnoitre, and on their return the ridge was bombarded for over an hour by the howitzers. It was then assaulted successfully by No. 2 Company.

The K.A.R. again led the advance on the 10th, when resistance was less determined and progress faster. On the 11th, with the Cape Corps as advance guard, Nangoo was reached without further opposition. All along the route signs had been visible of the enemy's hasty retreat: graves and unburied bodies, European as well as African; abandoned material and, to the joy of all who saw it, the last remaining 4.1-inch gun from the *Königsberg*.[1] It was fortunate that the enemy did not defend the water at Nangoo, as supplies across the waterless tract to the rear could only be maintained by motor transport and porterage from the River Lukuledi near Mtama, a distance of about forty miles.

At Nangoo contact between the Kilwa and Lindi Forces was at last

---

[1] The enemy still retained some ammunition for this gun, which was used to improvise land mines. The gun sights, suitably mounted and inscribed, are now in 4 K.A.R. Mess at Jinja.

established by a patrol of No. 2 Company, 2/2 K.A.R., from Ndanda. 1/2 and 2/2 K.A.R. thus met for the first time since the operations at Kibata.

No. 3 Column marched again at dawn on 12th November, and soon afterwards crossed the cool waters of the Bwinji stream, which flows at the foot of the Makonde Plateau. The plateau is some thirty miles long by ten wide, and the ascent from the Bwinji is difficult and steep. While the column camped at the foot of the escarpment, patrols were sent out to discover the best way up without using the recognized tracks. No. 1 Company of the combined K.A.R. battalion then made the ascent, crossed the plateau, and dug in overlooking the large German encampment at Chiwata. After nightfall the rest of the column followed in the light of a rising moon, the troops crawling on hands and knees up the steepest slopes and the long files of porters struggling to get their loads to the top.

During the week that had elapsed since the Lindi Force resumed its offensive, the Kilwa Force had continued its movement to the south. On 7th November Nos. 1 and 2 Columns had resumed their advance. On the 10th Ndanda was entered after slight opposition. The large mission station had many good buildings and bandas, and the place was full of German civilians, as Ndanda was the last reception station that von Lettow organized. About to escape on the final, fugitive stage of his operations, he was abandoning all hindrances in advance.

The next few days were spent in clearing the hills south and east of Ndanda and effecting contact with the Lindi Force. To co-operate in the forthcoming attack on Chiwata, a column was meanwhile directed through Masasi towards Mwiti, where on 14th November an enemy force was contacted two miles west of the village.

Action at Mwiti, 14th November, 1917.—The Germans had chosen a position around a collection of mission buildings standing on an isolated hill in the centre of a valley overlooked on all sides by higher ranges. The north side of this hill was practically sheer, with a road cut out of the side along which 1/3 K.A.R. was ordered to attack. Instead of opposing the ascent of the hill, the Germans had taken up a position about a hundred yards beyond the crest, and the two leading companies of the battalion were thus able to scale the hill with very few casualties. On top they found an open patch of burnt ground, with a company of the enemy and two machine guns at the far side. 1/3 K.A.R. charged and drove the enemy off the crest, but came under heavy fire from another detachment. Supporting troops now arrived, and after a brief action the Germans retired. 1/3 K.A.R. had lost two officers and one B.N.C.O. killed, and two B.N.C.Os. and 27 African ranks wounded.

With the junction of the Kilwa and Lindi Forces the campaign in German East Africa reached its final phase. Van Deventer went to the Makonde Plateau, visited the camp set up by the K.A.R., and decided to attack Chiwata with both his Forces. The German position lay below at a range of about 1,500 yards, well protected by entrenchments.

Signs of impending evacuation had been apparent at Chiwata on the afternoon of 14th November. On the 15th, while No. 1 Company descended the escarpment and advanced directly on the position, the rest of Giffard's battalion moved forward across the Chiwata—Kitangari road, which was reached by Nos. 2 and 3 Companies in time to engage the German rearguard. Chiwata was occupied after slight opposition and many British prisoners, European, Indian and African, were released. Nearly a hundred enemy Europeans and 425 askaris were taken prisoner.

The enemy was retiring rapidly. Giffard's battalion followed, No. 3 Company and part of No. 4 Company fighting a spirited little action against the rearguard. Van Deventer was pressing the pursuit with Nos. 1 and 3 Columns and the Nigerian Brigade, while No. 2 Column remained in reserve at Mwiti and No. 4 was employed in cutting a motor-road from Mtama. Water was again proving a difficulty, and had to be carried forward by porters from Chiwata in chaguls. Mules proved useless for this purpose as they bumped together and burst the containers.

Action at Lutshemi, 17th November, 1917.—During 16th November the pursuit continued, with constant patrol and rearguard actions in the thick bush. Early on the 17th it was discovered that the enemy had occupied a high ridge, well entrenched and protected to the front by a deep cleft. 1/3 K.A.R. had been sent round the flank and was now in position overlooking the valley, though the precipitous hills and thick bush prevented contact by patrols. But helio communication was established at sunrise, and the battalion, reinforced later by two companies of 2/2 K.A.R., was ordered to attack.

A brisk encounter followed. On the frontal position the enemy used his howitzers and field guns, disabling two guns of the Mountain Battery. On the flank one company of 2/2 K.A.R. ambushed the enemy's watering-place at the foot of the ridge, and a company of 1/3 K.A.R., sent to support an attack along the valley by the Nigerians, became heavily engaged by about three companies of the enemy. Another company was sent forward in support and with the aid of covering gun fire from the rear the enemy was driven out. The action continued until after nightfall, the gun flashes stabbing the darkness along the hillsides.

On the 18th patrols sent out at dawn found no sign of the enemy. To the rear of the position a hospital was taken, with over 250 European and 700 African troops. No. 3 Column continued the pursuit; No. 2 prepared to receive Tafel's approaching force, and No. 1 moved to support the mounted troops at Lulindi.

On 20th November Giffard's battalion reached another enemy camp, where 52 Europeans and 75 askaris were waiting to surrender. Von Lettow was now forced to recognize that he could no longer maintain his troops in a defined area, where they could be fed from fixed supply dumps and where static hospitals could be maintained. He had also become very short of ammunition and realized that the time had come to make for Portuguese East Africa, where fresh supplies might be found. Accordingly the German retreat became very rapid, as all the sick, wounded and faint-hearted were left behind to surrender and much surplus baggage was discarded. No. 3 Column was therefore unable to regain contact although the pursuit was continued through Mwiti to Masasi.

Von Lettow had now reached Newala, where he carried out a final reorganization to rid himself of all doubtful or unwanted followers before crossing the frontier. Turning west in the hope of meeting Tafel, he marched up the Rovuma, crossed it on 25th/26th November at Ngomano, and escaped up the valley of the River Lugenda with about 300 Europeans, 1,700 askaris and 3,000 followers. He spoke afterwards of the sense of freedom with which he finally shed all fixed commitments and took to the bush with only the stoutest and most hardened of his troops.

Meanwhile reports showed that Tafel was moving down the River Mbangala towards its junction with the Rovuma. Van Deventer sent Nos. 1 and 2 Columns to intercept him. On 26th November further reports showed that Tafel's force was marching south-east and might cross the rear of the British columns. No. 1 Column was therefore directed on Luatala, and a camp was formed at the crossing of the River Mwiti.

On the evening of 27th November a detachment of 1/3 K.A.R. under Lieutenant A. R. Dallas (Spec. List), who had been sent that morning to the confluence of the Miesse with the Rovuma, was approached by a party of Tafel's troops under a white flag, bearing a letter addressed to 'The O.C. British Forces at Bangalla'. This was the preliminary to the surrender of some of Tafel's troops (37 Europeans, 178 askaris and about 1,100 followers) to the post at Luatala on the 27th, and of Tafel himself with 19 officers, 92 other Europeans, over 1,200 askaris and about 2,200 followers on the 28th. Tafel had been caught in uninhabited and foodless country a few days too late to join forces with his commander-in-chief. Von Lettow described it afterwards as his greatest disappointment of the whole campaign.

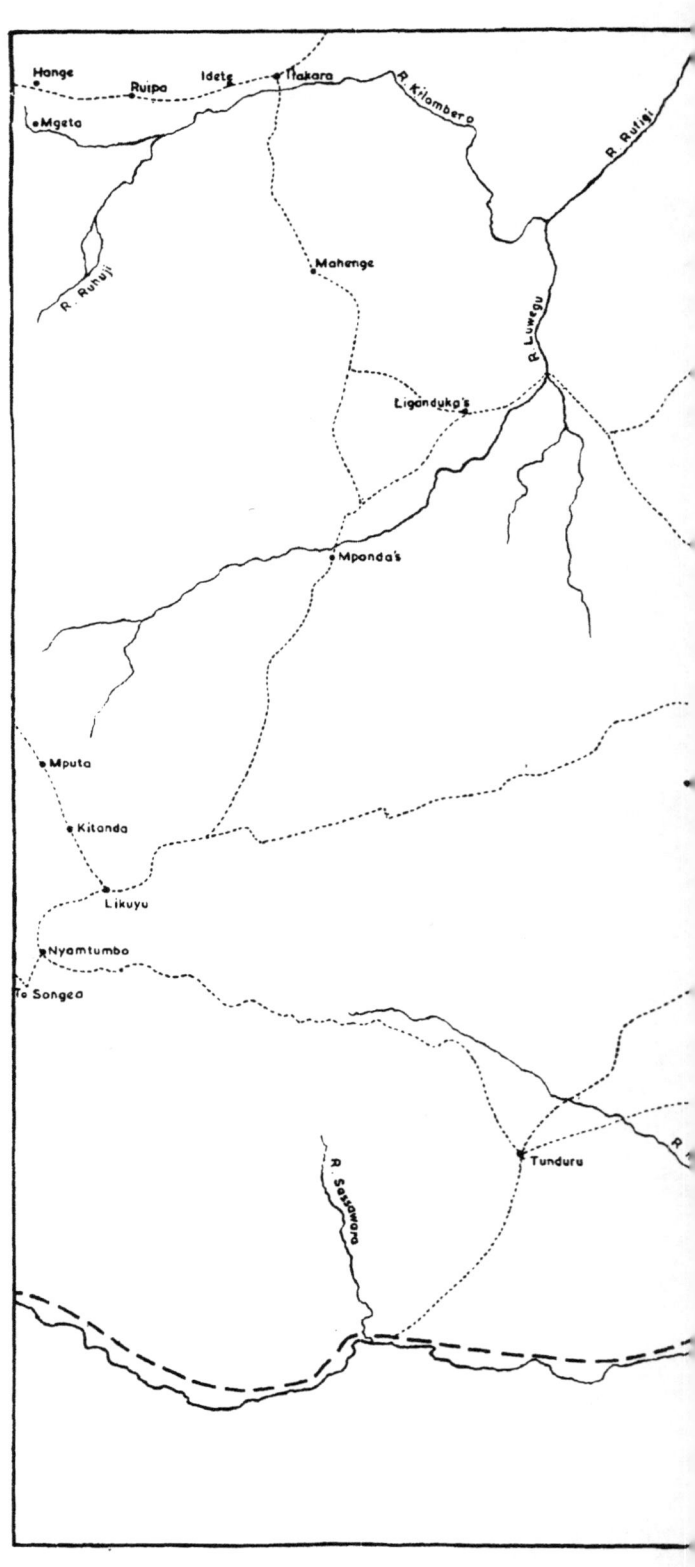

VI. **German East Africa. Southern Sheet**
(a) Campaigns of the Kilwa and Lindi Columns, October, 1916-November, 1917
(b) Area of Operations, Northey's Force, 1916
(c) Movements on Northey's eastern flank, August-September, 1916
(d) The Songea Area
(e) The Lukuledi Valley

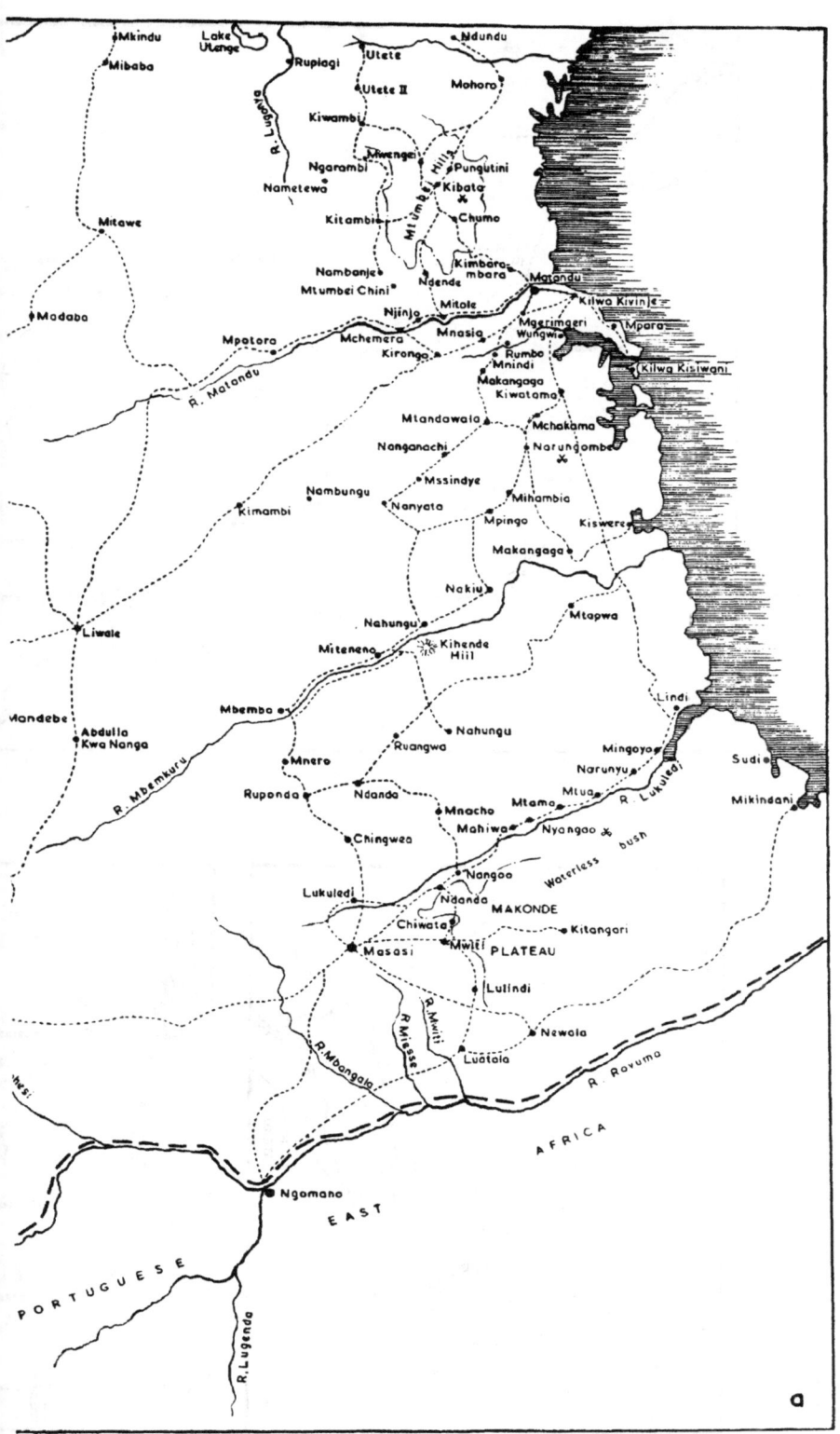

L. RUKWA
Iwungu
Masanga
St Moritz (Galula)
Nev Utengule
Buhora
Ilongo
Brandt
Ruiwa
Itaka
Utengule
Magje
Igale Pass
POROTO MTS
Mbozi
Mwakaleli
Rungwe
Luwiwa
Neu Langenburg
Ulongwe
Fife
Masoko
R. Songwe
Alt Langenberg
Igamba
Mwaya
Ipiana
Nsessi
Fort Hill
L. NYASA
Ngaramu
To Karonga

Iringa
Boma Himbu
Muhanga
Hange
R. Kilombero
Escarpment
Makua
D COY 1 KAR
MAHENGE PLATEAU
Twange
Mkapira
R. Mnyera
Kisingo
Lupembe
HAWTHORN
R. Nyoma
Njombe
Mfirika
R. Ruhuje
C

Weidhaven

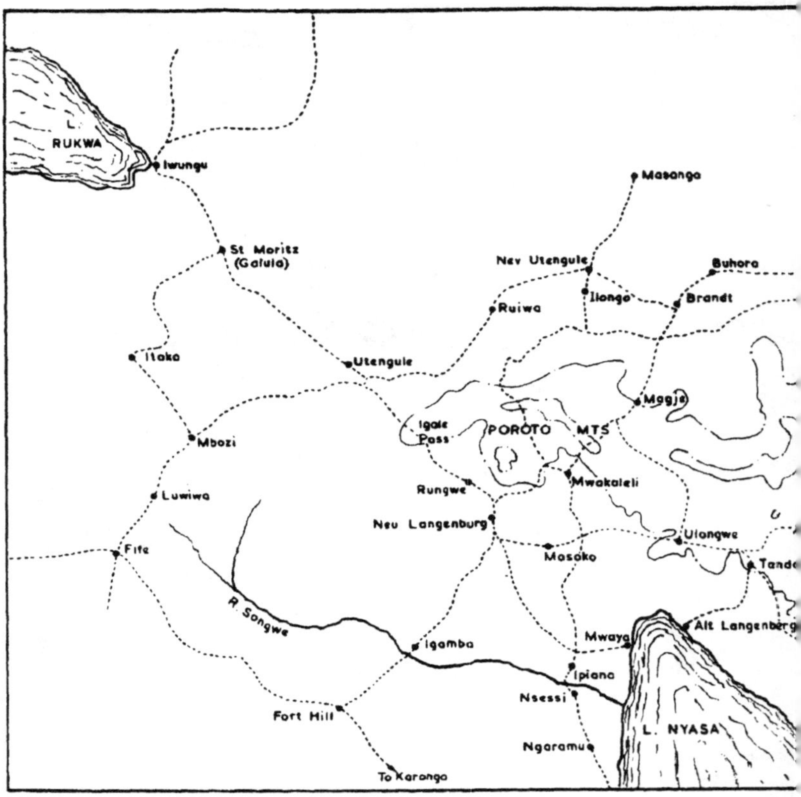

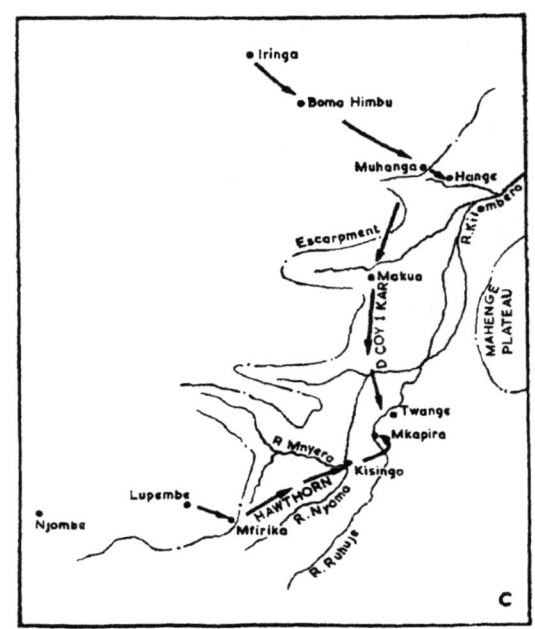

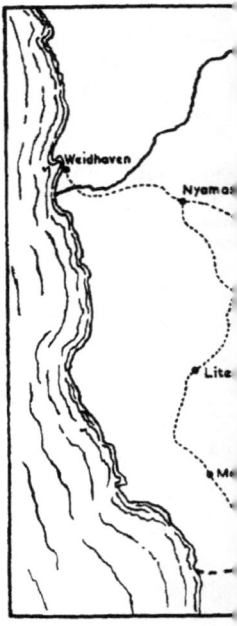

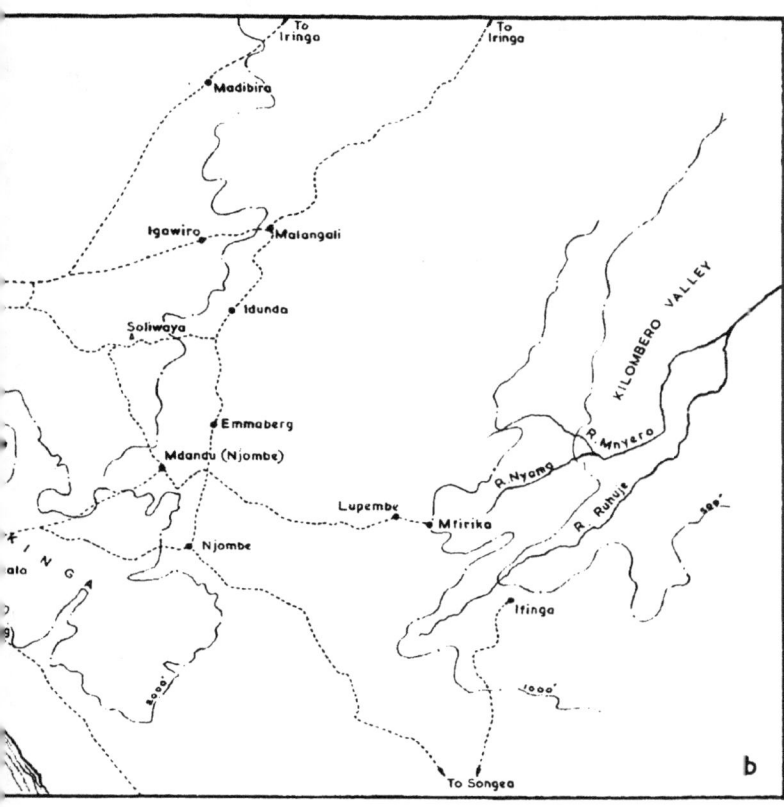

Face page 388

CHAPTER 13

The Pursuit through Portuguese East Africa
NOVEMBER, 1917-NOVEMBER, 1918

(i) *Preliminary Dispositions.* Map VII.

WHEN news reached England that the whole of German East Africa was in British hands, it was assumed that the campaign was over at last. Yet von Lettow's very purpose in crossing the frontier was to obtain the ammunition and supplies needed to prolong his resistance. Van Deventer was under no misapprehension about the difficulties of the task ahead. 'An equally arduous campaign,' he wrote at the conclusion of his despatch describing the enemy's expulsion from German territory, 'though on a very much smaller scale, will, however, probably still be necessary before the German force in Portuguese East Africa is finally brought to book, for the country is vast and communications are difficult.'[1]

Von Lettow began putting his intentions into effect as soon as he reached Portuguese soil. At Ngomano he found the Rovuma about 1,200 yards wide, fordable at chest height. The Portuguese post there was scattered by a sudden attack, and von Lettow re-armed many of his troops with rifles and machine guns, destroying those weapons of his own for which no ammunition remained. With the main body of his force he then ascended the Lugenda to Nanguare, where he settled in the centre of a fertile area, secure once more until the end of the rains. Another party under Wahle went west via the Mkula Hills to Mwembe, and a third under Köhl[2] eastward to the area around Mwalia and Medo.

To invade the country south of the Rovuma a complete reorganization of the East Africa Force was essential, and for this purpose van Deventer took advantage of the respite afforded by the rains. He decided to dispense entirely with Indian infantry units and to fight the final stage of the campaign with African troops alone. The old columns were accordingly broken up and those K.A.R. battalions which had been in the forefront withdrew to rest and re-equip. At the end of November the composite battalion marched back to Masasi, constructed a camp and began cutting a new road through the bush, expecting to remain on the site for several months. Early in December Lieutenant-Colonel Giffard, who had been with the battalion since it took the field in the previous year, went back to Nairobi on duty. 1/2 and 3/2 K.A.R. separated and once more became independent units. 2/2 K.A.R. also moved to Masasi, and the three battalions were then formed into the 1st Brigade, afterwards to be known as KARTUCOL. Similarly a 2nd Brigade was formed from 1/3, 2/3 and 3/3

---

[1] Van Deventer: despatch dated 21.i.18. (Lond. Gaz. Supp. 30611, 5.iv.18.)

[2] It was Köhl, a Bavarian gunner, who had persuaded von Lettow to salvage the guns from the *Königsberg*.

K.A.R. (known later as KARTRECOL). In the latter part of December these battalions were withdrawn to the Mingoyo area to ease the difficulties of supply. A large camp was built around Schaedel's Farm, where reorganization and the training of new drafts continued in preparation for the next advance.

For the time being von Lettow was free to roam throughout a country nearly the size of France. The central districts of Portuguese East Africa were fertile and healthy though difficult of approach for columns operating from fixed points of supply. The Lugenda and Lurio were considerable rivers, not everywhere fordable; tracks were few and maps poor and inaccurate. Van Deventer's plans were made with three objects: to fight the enemy wherever and whenever he could in a war of attrition that would steadily whittle down his remaining Europeans and destroy and capture his arms and ammunition; to prevent him from invading Nyasaland; and to forestall any attempt to break back into German East Africa.

The preventive dispositions were made first. Northey continued to hold the Songea area in strength, and 3/4 K.A.R. went to garrison Tunduru. Meanwhile a column under Hawthorn, consisting of 1/1, 2/1 and 3/1 K.A.R., concentrated south of Lake Nyasa in December and moved towards Namweras. Von Lettow was then at Mtarika with approximately five companies; three more were in the Mwembe area and three near Luambala. By mid-January, 1918, Hawthorn had crossed the Lugenda, which was already in flood, and was approaching Luambala. The post was occupied on the 15th, after slight opposition. At first sight the boma looked large and well defended, but it consisted only of a few huts, walled and floored with brick and surrounded by a mound of turf and a ditch. While Hawthorn's advance continued down-river, a column of the Cape Corps advanced through Mwembe to Mtarika, which was occupied on 3rd February. Subjected to this pressure, and attracted by reports from Köhl of ripening crops in the Medo area, von Lettow abandoned the left bank of the Lugenda and withdrew east. The immediate threat to Nyasaland was thus removed.

The task of preventing the enemy from re-entering his former territory was allotted to KARTRECOL, under the command of Lieutenant-Colonel Fitzgerald. After the end of January the headquarters of the column was stationed at Ndanda with 1/3 and 2/3 K.A.R. 3/3 K.A.R. was at Masasi. By that time the rains had broken with all their usual violence. Operations everywhere were limited to steady pressure on the enemy outposts, seeking constantly to diminish the areas available to foraging patrols. The whole Rovuma district from Ngomano westward, where the foodless belt between Portuguese and German territory was narrowest, was divided into sectors, and plans were made to depopulate the area and destroy the crops. Fortunately this drastic measure was never needed, and for some months KARTRECOL was employed in building roads up the Lugenda valley to Nanguare and west towards Tunduru, so that motor transport could be used in the area if needed.

The main lines of attack, as in the previous year, were to be based upon the sea. The Portuguese, anxious for the safety of Port Amelia when the presence of Köhl's troops became known, requested van Deventer to

Transport of a K.A.R. battalion on the line of march, Portuguese East Africa, 1918

[Photo: Lt.-Col. G. C. Hill

occupy the port. The Gold Coast Regiment landed in December, and was joined later by 4/4 K.A.R. and a section of 22 Mountain Battery. This column, known as ROSECOL, began to develop a line of attack towards Medo. On 22nd February the advanced troops of Hawthorn's column fought an indeterminate action against two companies of the enemy at Mtende, seventy-five miles east of Luambala. Four days later ROSECOL occupied Meza. By the end of February, therefore, these two columns were beginning to press von Lettow's main forces, which were now around Medo, Nanungu, and the River Msalu, seeking to bring him to battle or drive him southward across the Lurio. But the Germans were well supplied[1] and had no intention of being dislodged too easily.

In February Lieutenant-Colonel Giffard returned to the field to take command of KARTUCOL. Mingoyo was unhealthy, and the troops suffered greatly from malaria, but hard training continued. This was particularly for the young African N.C.Os., as the numbers of the British were again dwindling. Orders to move came in the middle of March. Van Deventer had assumed command of all allied forces, and now sent 3/2 K.A.R. to Mozambique to support the Portuguese troops at Nampula. The rest of KARTUCOL was ordered by half-battalions to Port Amelia. By 8th April Giffard had concentrated his column (1/2 K.A.R., 2/2 K.A.R. and the mountain guns) at Manumbiri and was ready to follow ROSECOL inland. The two columns operating from Port Amelia were then designated PAMFORCE, under the command of Brigadier-General W. F. S. Edwards.

(ii) KARTUCOL: *The Advance from Port Amelia to Munevalia, April-June, 1918.* Maps VII, 25.

ROSECOL had advanced as far as Ankuabe, and by the beginning of April was encamped upon a plateau overlooking a wide belt of bush that stretched away towards a line of hazy mountains in the far distance. Upon this ridge, just north of the Portuguese boma at Medo, through which ran the main track inland, Köhl had established his principal camp, manned by about six companies, with defensive positions round the base of Chirimba Hill, a rocky outcrop south of the track. Between the opposing forces lay an area of thick forest and tangled undergrowth, interspersed with elephant grass and tall bamboo, and pierced by occasional sharp crags of rock. Edwards' plan was to advance with KARTUCOL on the left to get astride the Mloco road and attack Medo from the south.

ROSECOL reached the extreme easterly tip of the Medo ridge on the night of 10th April. The march of KARTUCOL had begun on the previous day in pouring rain, immediately after the concentration of the column at Manumbiri. On the late afternoon of the 11th, after a brief halt, KARTUCOL left camp for a night march preparatory to the flank attack at dawn next day. 2/2 K.A.R. had the farther to go and were on the road first, with No. 1 Company as advance guard and No. 3 in support. By 3 a.m. next morning the battalion was in position and lay down to rest in column of route, waiting for daylight.

---

[1] 'Never,' said a captured German diary, 'have we fared so well during the last four years.' (Quoted in Wienholt, *Story of a Lion Hunt*, p. 208.)

Action at Medo, 12th April, 1918.—At dawn on 12th April 2/2 K.A.R. moved forward through the bush on a compass bearing. No. 1 Company (Major G. S. Goldsworthy, Spec. List) was still in advance, with two platoons, each with a Lewis gun, as frontal screen under Lieutenant G. G. de C. Drury (R. S. Fus.) and a third platoon behind with connecting files to the support company. Small parties of scouts moved 50-100 yards ahead. At 10 a.m. the advance guard crossed a wide open swamp and halted beyond. The sound of ROSECOL's mountain guns was already audible, bombarding the hills to the right, and a German field gun could be heard in reply.

A quarter of an hour later the flank patrol of No. 4 Company opened fire on the extreme left of the column. A pause ensued for several minutes, and then heavy fire from hidden machine guns struck the British left. Nos. 3 and 4 Companies deployed, No. 4 joining the left flank of the forward screen almost at a right angle, forming two sides of a square. The screen wheeled left to straighten the angle; No. 2 Company came up on the right again, after some trouble with the porters, many of whom were in action for the first time. The whole column thus came rapidly into action across the swamp in the formation of an inverted U.

The situation was extremely unfavourable, with KARTUCOL caught on difficult ground with a poor field of fire. To prevent the enemy from realizing this, strenuous efforts were made to hold him at a distance from the left flank, where the Germans continued to bring up machine guns and press the attack. Nos. 1 and 4 Companies were soon hotly engaged and ran short of ammunition. Orderlies sent back for more were all shot while crossing open ground to the rear. By the time fresh supplies came forward the men were down to about five rounds each and had bayonets fixed and bombs ready to hold the enemy in a hand-to-hand encounter.

Medo was truly a 'soldiers' battle'. By 1.30 p.m. the enemy had fully developed his counter-attack, made by three companies which had been held ready to the west of Chirimba Hill. From then onward repeated attempts were made to break into the K.A.R. position near the junction of the two battalions. Field cables were cut and the signallers were hard put to maintain communications. Many of the more experienced N.C.Os. were absent, but the new recruits fought well and saved the situation by their steadiness. In places the swamp was knee-deep in water, and some companies had to scoop their rifle-pits out of the mud. In these conditions Lance-Corporal Sowera, D.C.M., of 2/2 K.A.R., decided to climb a tree with his Lewis gun, where he remained nearly all day doing excellent work while his No. 1 handed up the drums from below. The tree was repeatedly hit and on one occasion a burst of machine-gun fire lopped off a branch above his head. Later on Sowera took command of a section that had become shaky after losing its N.C.O. and danced an *ngoma* up and down the firing line to hearten his men. Other African N.C.Os. were seen similarly steadying their recruits, some of them calmly taking pinches of snuff in the intervals of shouting their fire orders.[1]

[1] Sowera was awarded a bar to his D.C.M. Lieutenant Drury, experiencing his first engagement in command of African troops, was greatly impressed by the steadiness of his askaris under fire and recorded in his diary many individual acts of bravery.

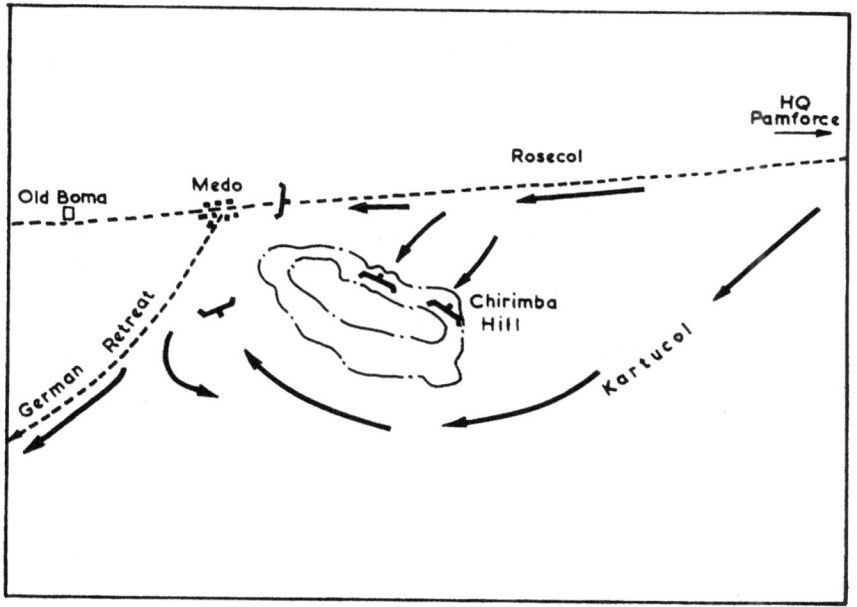

25. Action at Medo, 12th April, 1918

At 4 p.m. the attack slackened. An attempt to renew it an hour later was stopped by No. 2 Company, 2/2 K.A.R., aided by the leading troops of the Gold Coast Regiment, who had fought their way around Chirimba Hill. KARTUCOL and ROSECOL thus joined forces, and when darkness fell the enemy was in full retreat to the south-west.

Medo was a hard-fought action in which both sides maintained for many hours a considerable volume of fire, the Germans exploiting to the full the accurate shooting of their well-trained askaris and changing the position of their machine guns with a skill that struck some recently joined officers, who had no previous experience of bush fighting, as uncanny. When daylight came on the 13th, KARTUCOL set about clearing the battlefield and evacuating the wounded. Every tree and bush within sight was scarred with bullet marks; blood, dirt and flies abounded. The dead were laid in rows and the equipment was stripped from their stiffened bodies. The field hospital was packed with men, white bandages gleaming upon naked black limbs. It was late afternoon before the dead were buried, the wounded carried to the motor-road, the abandoned loads collected, and the column left the battlefield to camp at Medo boma, two miles away on drier ground.

On 15th April ROSECOL resumed the advance towards Mwalia. On the afternoon of the 17th, 4/4 K.A.R., the leading battalion, became heavily engaged with three German companies hidden in tall elephant grass. Though new troops with little operational experience, the askaris maintained the attack, supported by a company of the Gold Coast Regiment, which took over the position on the following day. KARTUCOL had now come forward, and finding a threat developing to his flank, the enemy withdrew. On the 19th KARTUCOL passed through the ROSECOL camp, and with its two battalions alternately in the lead, pressed the enemy rearguard back in a series of minor actions, and on 20th April entered Mwalia, a deserted, tumbledown boma in a valley between two ranges of hills. From there a raiding force consisting of Nos. 2 and 4 Companies, 2/2 K.A.R., under Major F. R. Bradstock (Spec. List) made a circuitous march through unknown bush to raid a food and ammunition store on the River Mkuti, in the rear of the German position. The store was rushed and captured, and besides prisoners and rifles the expedition rejoined the battalion well burdened with pigs and chickens.

The advance beyond Medo had lain through unusually difficult country, where the bamboo thickets and elephant grass grew so high that the tracks, which were often under water, became in places mere swampy tunnels through the bush. The Germans were apparently making for Nanungu, and on 21st April the advance from Mwalia was resumed, with 1/2 K.A.R. leading. On the morning of the 24th, 'A' Company reached the Chiha River and began working on a compass bearing through the bush towards Mbalama Hill. 'C' Company continued down the track towards the village and fought a sharp little action with the enemy rearguard before the rest of the battalion came up. At 3 p.m. 'A' Company got within 500 yards of the Mbalama—Koronje road to the west of the hill, surprised a food convoy and attacked again. But the company had been observed by a large enemy force concealed in the hills and was counter-attacked in such strength that it was obliged to retire.

Next morning patrols discovered the enemy posted in a strong position on the eastern side of Mbalama Hill, with a good field of fire ready cleared to the front. 'B' Company (Captain P. T. Brodie, Spec. List) was ordered to approach from the south-east. Before attacking, Brodie went out to reconnoitre with Sergeant R. Morris, two African ranks and some porters carrying grenades. With great daring Brodie worked forward to the top of the hill, where he suddenly stumbled at point-blank range on an observation post armed with a machine gun. Instead of retiring he stood his ground, flung the grenades and drove the enemy out.[1] 'B' Company then came forward and made good the hill, thus undoubtedly saving the whole column from certain casualties, as the enemy was well posted in the heights around, waiting to attack. Seeing the K.A.R. already in possession of the hill, the Germans speedily withdrew.

For the next few days ROSECOL took the lead. The advance had now reached more open country, where the bamboo thickets were smaller and the plain was dotted with isolated hills. The German rearguard left observation posts to watch the movements of the British columns. By 1st May KARTUCOL was again in the lead, with 1/2 K.A.R. as tactical advance guard, 'A' and 'B' Companies forming the screen. At 9 a.m. that morning the enemy was sighted near the base of Koronje Hill, facing open country with the grass well beaten down. 1/2 K.A.R. came under heavy machine-gun and artillery fire and moved off the track into the

[1] Brodie was later awarded the D.S.O., Morris the D.C.M., and the askaris the M.M. The porters received monetary awards.

bush. The mountain guns were brought into action, and under their cover 'A' Company gained about 200 yards. There the advance halted, as the position was too open to rush with a frontal attack; 'B' Company, deployed on 'A' Company's left, and platoons of 'C' Company were dispatched to locate the enemy's right flank. By early afternoon the fighting had become general. 2/2 K.A.R. began a wide encircling movement to the left, but this move was noted by the enemy, who attacked the Mountain Battery so vigorously that the guns were nearly lost. 2/2 K.A.R. was recalled and the Germans withdrew, though they maintained their fire until dusk and twice renewed it during the night.

At daylight on 2nd May 2/2 K.A.R. moved to the right of the German position, but apart from a few picquets found no sign of the enemy. Next day the battalion progressed for about six miles along the Nanungu road, with flanking platoons out to clear the hills on either side. The spearhead of the advance was now over thirty miles from Mwalia; supplies were becoming difficult, and KARTUCOL had been almost continuously in action for seventeen days. While ROSECOL continued to press the enemy, KARTUCOL was therefore withdrawn for a few days' rest at Koronje, where bandas were built, stores collected, and a large draft of troops arrived by motor convoy. On 12th May 1/2 K.A.R. took over the forward position from the Gold Coast Regiment, the rest of the column following four days later.

The enemy was now at Nanungu, thirty miles west of Koronje, where he was threatened by attack from the west as well as the north. Northey's troops had occupied Mahua on 5th April. A few days later a detachment of 2/1 K.A.R. under Captain G. A. Debenham (Norf. R.) dispersed an enemy company forty miles south-east of Mtarika. By the 11th two companies of 3/1 K.A.R. were in action twenty-five miles south-west of Nanungu. While the western columns were thus steadily closing in, 3/3 K.A.R. of KARTRECOL crossed the Rovuma to occupy Nanguare. On 4th May Lieutenant-Colonel C. W. Barton (Northants. R.), succeeded later by Lieutenant-Colonel A. H. Griffiths (D.C.L.I.), began an advance from Mahua with 3/1 K.A.R. and half 2/1 K.A.R. This column fought two actions against an enemy force west of Nanungu, inflicting very heavy casualties.

With columns closing in from several directions, hopes once more soared of cornering von Lettow and dealing him a blow that might terminate the campaign. ROSECOL made an encircling movement up the left bank of the Msalu to contact Griffiths' column, while KARTUCOL pressed the advance with all speed, travelling as light as practicable with porters reduced to a minimum. All heavy kit was left in camp, with the expectation that it would be recovered within a week at the latest.[1]

KARTUCOL resumed the advance on 17th May. On the following evening, with 2/2 K.A.R. in the lead, camp was made under the lee of a rocky hill some eight miles short of Nanungu. On the 19th the place was found to have been evacuated, except for a large hospital full of sick and wounded. For some time Nanungu had been the German head-

[1] Actually it was December before the officers of KARTUCOL saw their kit again

quarters, and contained a well-designed and comfortable camp, standing on the slope of a hill among a fine grove of trees. From an observation post on top of the hill the surrounding country could be seen for many miles.

Next day KARTUCOL passed through Nanungu, following the enemy south-west. Towards midday on the 21st 'A' and 'C' Companies, 1/2 K.A.R., bumped the rearguard, which was posted along a ridge. The enemy had apparently expected attack from a different direction, and after a smart action withdrew to a second prepared position. At 2.30 p.m. he counter-attacked on the left flank, but was repulsed and resumed his withdrawal, to stand again on some high ground beyond a stream. The action continued until darkness, when the Germans retired out of touch. The rest of 1/2 K.A.R. then crossed the river and was joined by a company of 4/4 K.A.R. from ROSECOL.

KARTUCOL had now reached the Korewa area, some twenty-four miles beyond Nanungu, in a country of tangled rocks and hills. The bush was again very dense, and the road, flanked by precipitous heights, ran ahead for two miles within a narrow gorge containing a dry river-bed. The Germans were not slow to take advantage of this, realizing that small rifle detachments with a few well-posted machine guns could deny the passage of the gorge for a considerable time.

Action at Korewa, 22nd May, 1918.—On the morning of 22nd May KARTUCOL approached the entrance to the gorge, with 2/2 K.A.R. leading. No. 1 Company was advance guard, with a platoon forward as screen and another on either flank. No. 2 Company was in support, and No. 4 in reserve. The first enemy picquet was driven back at 8 a.m., and an hour later No. 1 Company contacted a detachment of about 50 rifles and two machine guns, holding the lip of the narrow pass. The mountain guns came up, a lively fire action developed, and then, as the K.A.R. were preparing to charge, the enemy suddenly withdrew, leaving his wounded behind.

For a time the advance was not pressed. Griffiths' column and ROSECOL were approaching from the west to cut the retreat, and provided the time of the combined attack could be co-ordinated Edwards felt confident of success. Then No. 1 Company found a second enemy detachment, this time of 20 rifles with one machine gun, about 300 yards farther on, in a place where the pass was still narrower. The Stokes mortars drove them out, and a pause ensued while ammunition was brought forward. This enabled the enemy to settle down half a mile beyond in greater strength. Again the mountain guns and Stokes mortars came into action, and the process was repeated. No. 2 Company, 2/2 K.A.R., came forward to join No. 1 Company in the firing line, and 'B' Company, 1/2 K.A.R., was sent to the left flank, reinforced later by the Stokes guns.

At the end of the pass Griffiths with 3/1 K.A.R. had come upon the enemy reserve companies, eating a meal while the rest of the force was defending the pass. Patrols of 'B' Company, 1/2 K.A.R., also worked round the right flank and reached the German rear. The enemy was taken by surprise and fought hard to secure his line of retreat. Meanwhile, hearing the sound of heavy firing, KARTUCOL continued to press the frontal attack. By late afternoon the whole enemy force had broken and scattered, mainly through the gap between 'B' Company, 1/2 K.A.R., and 3/1 K.A.R., which 'B' Company was too weak to close.

Had ROSECOL and the K.A.R.M.I., who were hampered by inaccurate maps and ignorance of the country, arrived in time to close the gap, Edwards might have achieved his object and practically ended the campaign at Korewa. As it was, the Germans suffered their most serious reverse for many months. Though their casualties were not high (11 Germans and 49 askaris killed or taken prisoner) they lost practically all their transport, 100,000 rounds of small-arms ammunition, their last 67 rounds for the captured Portuguese guns, and a great deal of food and baggage, including Governor Schnee's personal kit.

Next day the deserted pass presented a desolate scene of dead askaris, shell-holes and splintered trees. KARTUCOL established contact with GRIFCOL, and the two columns rested while ROSECOL continued the pursuit towards the River Lurio.

Korewa ended the first phase of the campaign in Portuguese East Africa. When it became plain that despite the junction of the K.A.R. columns from Nyasaland and the coast von Lettow had slipped away, van Deventer lost no time in revising his strategy. The Germans were now believed to number about 240 Europeans and 1,300-1,400 askaris, with one field gun and at least 30 machine guns. As they had no fixed food depôts and were seriously short of ammunition, van Deventer decided to establish a line of defended posts from Port Amelia through Medo and Mahua to Fort Johnston, to prevent the enemy from heading to the north, and meanwhile to press the pursuit as vigorously as possible. ROSECOL was broken up; the Gold Coast Regiment was detailed to hold the line of posts, and Giffard's mobile column of 1/2 and 2/2 K.A.R. took up the pursuit, with Griffiths, again under Northey's command, moving in parallel to the west.

KARTUCOL resumed the advance on 24th May, and for the next five weeks pressed forward daily in a monotonous series of seemingly endless marches, interspersed with minor actions against a rearguard that never stood for long. The Germans were now retreating rapidly through the mountainous bush-covered country west of Mozambique. Von Lettow had nothing to gain by attacking until he could obtain fresh stores of ammunition and food from the Portuguese posts along his route. KARTUCOL could only follow in the hope of catching him before he could capture too much.

1/2 K.A.R. and 2/2 K.A.R. led the advance alternately, while the Mounted Infantry operated ahead. All ranks were now very tired and the going was bad, through thick bush and swamp crossed by numerous small rivers. At midnight on 30th May the column found an abandoned hospital full of wounded. The Germans had lost most of their medical stores at Korewa, and were using native bark cloth as bandages. Patrols of 1/2 K.A.R. made a wide reconnaissance to the south but found no sign of the enemy.

Von Lettow crossed the Lurio on 1st June. On the same day 'A' and

'D' Companies, 1/2 K.A.R., reached the north bank of the river and reported the enemy in strength on the far side. The stream was 300-400 yards wide and four feet deep, and divided at this point by two small islands into three channels. After a day spent in reconnaissance, KARTUCOL crossed at another ford upstream on the night of 3rd/4th June. Contact was made with 3/1 K.A.R. from GRIFCOL, operating on the right. While 2/2 K.A.R. camped in the long grass on the south bank, 1/2 K.A.R. continued the advance parallel to the river bank. On the 5th an enemy rearguard opened fire on the right flank of the battalion, but was driven off without difficulty by 'A' Company. On the 6th and 7th 2/2 K.A.R. took over the lead, fighting several small actions along the Malema road. Then 1/2 K.A.R. resumed the advance, through bush country broken by welcome patches of mtama. Progress continued until the 13th, when KARTUCOL camped for two days' foraging, a mile or two north of Malema.

In front lay the barrier of the Inagu Hills, where precipitous groups of lofty rocks were penetrated by several narrow passes. 2/4 K.A.R. had already approached from the west in an unsuccessful attempt to block the enemy's retreat. 'B' Company of that battalion had reached Malema in time to see the German advance guard attacking the Portuguese boma. The company attacked with great courage and suffered severe casualties, but was too weak to affect the issue. Reconnaissance revealed only one enemy patrol in one of the Inagu passes, and on the 15th KARTUCOL passed safely through.

Three days later an unfortunate incident occurred south of the Ligonha River. 1/2 K.A.R. had crossed the stream at 10 a.m. on the 18th and that afternoon, with 'A' Company in the lead, was advancing through dense bush when it unexpectedly bumped a company of 2/4 K.A.R. The troops opened fire immediately, and before the mistake was discovered the company commanders on both sides and several of their men had been wounded.

The Portuguese boma at Vacha was reached on 20th June. KARTUCOL made a short halt for supplies, as many of the askaris had been without food for thirty-six hours and were now exhausted. Foraging parties searched the district for sweet potatoes, mtama and muhogo. When the ration convoy caught up, the European issue was found to consist mainly of coffee, and the officers and B.N.C.Os. were obliged to subsist on native food for the next eighteen days.[1]

From Vacha patrols entered Alto Molocque and found the boma deserted and burnt. KARTUCOL passed through on the 26th and crossed the Melele River. On the 30th the column camped at Munevalia. Since the beginning of May it had made a fighting advance of 304 miles.

(iii) *Operations North of Quelimane, July, 1918.* Maps VII, 26.

By the beginning of June it was apparent that von Lettow's rapid retreat into the fertile country between the Molocque and the Licungo

---

[1] At this period the troops were far worse off than at any other time during the war. Europeans had to subsist on sweet potatoes, manioc, rice, mealie flour, some meat and a little jam.

might constitute a serious threat to Quelimane. Van Deventer arranged for the dispatch of Portuguese troops, and transferred his base from Port Amelia to Mozambique. The whole area of operations had shifted to the south, and it was no longer considered necessary for KARTRECOL to man the Rovuma line.

On 20th April headquarters 1/3 K.A.R. had moved from Ndanda to Masasi. The battalion was now ordered to relieve the companies of 3/3 K.A.R. operating south of the Rovuma. 2/3 K.A.R. remained at Ndanda until 10th June, when the battalion was ordered to Lindi for transit by sea to Quelimane to support the Portuguese. 3/3 K.A.R. marched via Nanguare to Mbalama to join 4/4 K.A.R. as FITZCOL, a new addition to the columns under Brigadier-General Edwards (EDFORCE). FITZCOL left Mbalama on 19th June, crossed the Lurio at Nanripo by a single pontoon bridge, and after a long and exhausting march joined Edwards at Nampula on the 30th.

Two companies of 2/3 K.A.R., under Major E. A. Gore-Browne (Dorset R.), embarked at Lindi in advance of the rest of the battalion and reached Quelimane on 25th June. After consultation with the Portuguese commander, Gore-Browne went inland to reinforce the garrison at Nhamacurra, where a sugar factory stood at the terminus of a short line of railway. There he found three Portuguese infantry companies and one artillery company, numbering about 50 Europeans and 580 African troops, holding a position 3,000 yards in extent, with the left on the River Nhamacurra and the right at the railway station. Gore-Browne decided to complete the arc by covering the railway terminus and bringing his right flank back on to the river. The rear of the position was thus covered by this natural obstacle and the swampy ground bordering its banks. On the left it was fordable in places, but behind the K.A.R. the water ran deep up to the landing-stage.

The defences were divided into three sectors. One Portuguese company manned the first or left sector, which lay between the Nhamacurra and a small tributary stream. This company was responsible for all patrols and picquets west of the river. The second or central sector, also defended by a Portuguese company, lay between the tributary stream and the railway. The third or K.A.R. sector, on the right flank between the railway and the river, was defended by No. 4 Company, 2/3 K.A.R. (150 men and two Lewis guns). The other Portuguese company and No. 3 Company, 2/3 K.A.R., were in reserve. All positions were dug in and made as strong as possible.

Action at Nhamacurra, 1st-3rd July, 1918.—With three companies in advance under Captain Müller, and the main body following under von Lettow, the enemy crossed the Lugella and made some important captures of food and supplies, though without finding the ammunition he so urgently required. Early on the afternoon of 1st July a native reported that the Nhamacurra telegraph line had been cut and that the marks of many booted feet were visible near the spot. Gore-Browne instructed his allies to stand-to and patrol to the front, an order which they appear to have disregarded. In a few minutes the first sector was attacked by a force estimated at one company. The Portuguese quick-firing guns came into action, and apparently also their reserve company on the left flank, but shortly afterwards telephone communication ceased. Gore-Browne moved a platoon to his left rear and sent Lieutenant C. G. W. Anderson to reconnoitre. The central sector was intact but there was no sign of the Portuguese on the left. A few stragglers arrived with the news that their comrades had broken in panic, and that the factory was in German hands. Darkness was now approaching, but Gore-Browne sent a patrol into the sisal plantations across the stream, where enemy forces were located. He therefore decided to defend his own position and at midnight drew back the Portuguese in the central sector to complete the perimeter. By daylight this move had been completed and the force was well entrenched.

Patrols sent out in the early morning killed three enemy askaris and returned with their rifles. The Germans were now approaching the perimeter and about 10 a.m. opened fire on the north face with a machine gun. This attack was silenced, but shortly afterwards was renewed in greater force. For the rest of the day fire in greater or less intensity was maintained upon the position.

On the morning of 3rd July the enemy renewed the attack with several bursts of heavy fire. Gore-Browne sent patrols to locate the flanks, but without success. Rifle and machine-gun fire continued until 3 p.m., when it died down for a time. Then came an artillery bombardment. The first shell struck the station and a number of Portuguese white troops and civilians came rushing out. About 30 Portuguese askaris held in reserve on the north-west of the perimeter then evacuated their trench and fled through the camp, causing a panic among the porters. Before anything could be done the Portuguese troops manning the forward trenches were retiring in disorder, drawing intense fire from the enemy machine guns as they went. Seizing the opportunity thus offered, the Germans dashed forward, occupied the northern face of the perimeter, and brought a cross-fire to bear on the K.A.R. trenches that rapidly made them untenable.

Gore-Browne had no option but to save the remnant of his force as best he could. Ordering a platoon to face north and cover the retirement, he began to withdraw in the only direction possible, i.e. along the river bank in the hope of finding a ford. Many of the troops plunged into the water to swim across. The stream was about ninety yards wide with a strong current, and a number were drowned or shot in crossing, including Gore-Browne himself.

To fight back to the river in the hope of defending the factory and station had from the first placed the K.A.R. in a difficult position. Lack of proper patrolling and reconnaissance had taken the whole force by surprise. Owing to the small resources at his command, Gore-Browne had placed too much reliance upon his allies, and although the three platoons of No. 4 Company who bore the brunt of the action fought well, they were inevitably affected by the flight of the Portuguese. The retirement became a rout, and it was then that most of the casualties occurred. The K.A.R. lost one officer, one B.N.C.O. and 16 African ranks killed, and 28 African ranks wounded. In addition to this known casualty list a further three B.N.C.Os. and 174 African ranks were missing.

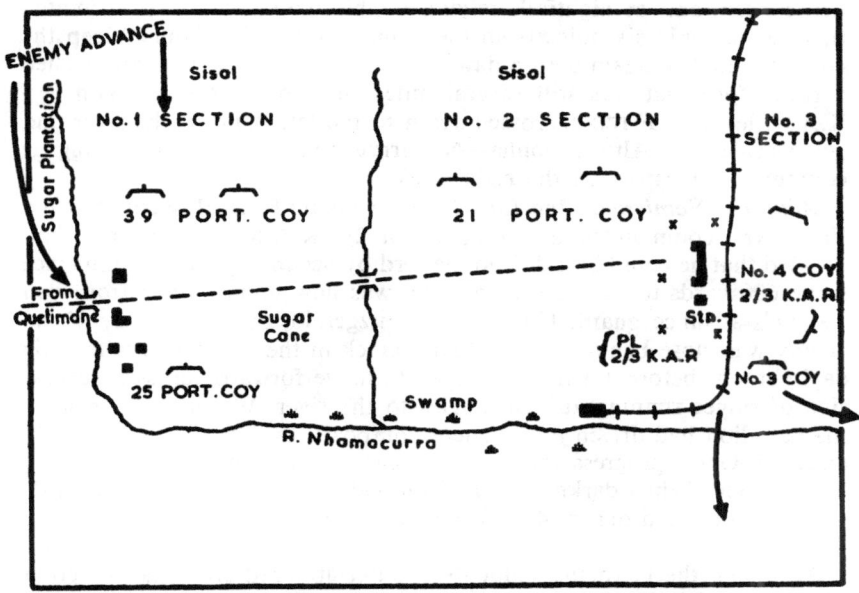

26. Action at Nhamacurra, 1st-3rd July, 1918

At Nhamacurra von Lettow at last obtained what he sought. The factory was full of sugar, clothing and other supplies, but far more important was the capture of arms and ammunition. The two Portuguese guns taken by the Germans on 1st July were used with great effect in the attack, and von Lettow boasted afterwards that he was able to discard nearly all his remaining 1871 pattern rifles. Van Deventer ordered all his columns to converge on Nhamacurra, hoping to pin the enemy against the sea, but von Lettow, too astute to deliver an attack on Quelimane, doubled back to the north-east and made for Ociva, seeking the supplies of ammunition and stores that he believed to exist in that area. For the time being all contact was lost.

July, 1918, was a disastrous month for 2/3 K.A.R. Shortly after the arrival of the rest of the battalion at Quelimane, a company was sent north to garrison the Portuguese boma at Namirrue, to protect the river crossing and cover the parties engaged in road construction. It was not until the middle of the month that it became known for certain that von Lettow was at Ociva and that his advanced companies were making for Tipe to cross the River Molocque on their way north. By that time FITZCOL had reached Alto Ligonha. When news of the direction of von Lettow's movement reached him, Lieutenant-Colonel Fitzgerald made for Namirrue, some thirty miles distant, hoping to bring the enemy to action in the vicinity of the river crossing.

On 20th July FITZCOL reached the Namirrue stream at a ford about twenty-five miles west of the boma. When the march was resumed on the morning of the 21st, heavy firing was heard from the direction of Namirrue. The advance continued all day along narrow tracks through dense bush, and at nightfall, relying on his map, Fitzgerald estimated that he was only six miles from the boma. After a few hours' sleep the column marched again before dawn on the 22nd, and at 11 a.m. reached a rocky ford that was still several miles short of Namirrue. With 3/3 K.A.R. leading, FITZCOL crossed again to the left bank of the river and got astride the Alto Ligonha—Namirrue road, leaving the baggage column under escort on the right bank.

Action at Namirrue, 22nd July, 1918.—Captain F. H. Bustard (North'd Fus.), who commanded the company of 2/3 K.A.R. at Namirrue, had decided that he could best defend the ford by occupying a rocky eminence some 600 yards to the north, where he was now under attack from von Lettow's advance guard. Unknown to Fitzgerald, the main body of the enemy was close behind. It was four o'clock in the afternoon, with little daylight left, before 3/3 K.A.R. began to move forward across a succession of ridges running at right angles to the river. Within half an hour the battalion had driven in the enemy outposts; by 5 p.m. it was heavily engaged. Good progress followed, the enemy apparently evacuating the high ground. When darkness fell Fitzgerald gave orders for 3/3 K.A.R. to form camp and dig in. 4/4 K.A.R. did the same, about 800 yards to the rear.

At 7 p.m. the Germans suddenly counter-attacked from the direction of the river. 3/3 K.A.R. had not yet completed the right face of the perimeter, and within a few minutes the enemy were inside the camp, rushing through it and scattering the battalion. Fitzgerald's first intimation of the affair came when a few stragglers reached 4/4 K.A.R., just in time to give warning of the impending attack. A desperate action followed, but at 9 p.m. the enemy drew off. To prevent the loss of his baggage Fitzgerald then withdrew to the ford. There in the middle of the night the enemy attacked him again, but without success.

It was now plain that FITZCOL had run into the main body of von Lettow's force. 3/3 K.A.R. had ceased to exist as a battalion. Lieutenant-Colonel H. C. Dickinson was a prisoner[1] and most of his officers were missing. 4/4 K.A.R., which had been weakened by detachments and escort duties, numbered fewer than 200 men, barely enough to defend the porters and baggage. Fitzgerald therefore withdrew all his troops to the right bank of the river and retired upstream to his previous camp. Fortunately the enemy made no serious attempt to follow, as FITZCOL had been marching and fighting without sleep and practically without food for nearly two days. But this retreat was disastrous for the company of 2/3 K.A.R. at Namirrue. Massing in ever-increasing strength, the enemy plastered the rocky outpost with a howitzer, and with their water supply cut off and most of the defenders killed or wounded the remnant of the little force was taken.

3/3 K.A.R., reduced at the time to about half a company, was withdrawn from the field and placed on the line of communication until the end of the war. What remained of 2/3 K.A.R. was concentrated at Quelimane. 1/3 K.A.R., who had relieved 3/3 K.A.R. some time before,

---

[1] Dickinson was compelled to march with the German column for the rest of the war. Shortly after regaining his liberty he died of influenza at Dar-es-Salaam.

was now ordered to Lindi. On 16th July headquarters with about half the battalion embarked for Mozambique, and marched thence via Nampula and Murrupula towards Namirrue. Reconnaissance showed that the enemy still occupied the crossing. At the end of the month contact was made with KARTUCOL.

Von Lettow's disappearance after his victory at Nhamacurra and the unexpected reversal of his progress to the south had involved KARTUCOL in a month of strenuous marching. False reports of the enemy's presence were constantly arriving and long-range patrols were often away from the column, searching the bush for several days. At times lack of food brought all the British columns to a halt, while European ranks, like askaris, lived on the mtama and muhogo collected by foraging parties. Mtama meal could be made into porridge or baked as a substitute for bread.

KARTUCOL left Munevalia at midnight on 2nd/3rd July, *en route* for the Licungo, which von Lettow was reported to have crossed. On the late afternoon of the 5th the river was forded breast-deep, and camp made on the right bank in pouring rain. The Germans were still believed to be making for Quelimane, and 2/2 K.A.R. continued down-river, following a column of 1/4 K.A.R. half a day's march ahead. The Licungo was forded on the 6th, and contact made with 3/1 K.A.R. When the column reached the partly-constructed extension of the railway, news was received of the disaster sustained at Nhamacurra. KARTUCOL then returned to Munevalia, which was reached on 14th July after covering 187 miles at an average rate of seventeen miles per marching day. All ranks were extremely tired, but without pause KARTUCOL turned east towards Tipe in an effort to head von Lettow before he could cross the Molocque. On 20th July 2/2 K.A.R. reached Tipe, to find the main body of the enemy already north of the river, with the rearguard holding the ford. After a brief action the Germans retired and KARTUCOL followed, driving the rearguard along the road.

1/2 K.A.R. led the advance on the 22nd, with 'B' and 'C' Companies moving on the flanks of the retreating enemy. Similar tactics continued on the 23rd, with 2/2 K.A.R. in the lead. Heavy firing was heard from the direction of Namirrue, but patrols sent forward on the 24th reported that the action was over and the enemy in camp around the boma and ford. After waiting for 3/2 K.A.R. and a convoy of food, KARTUCOL moved forward again on the 27th to find Namirrue evacuated and the boma burnt. Hearing that von Lettow had turned east, Giffard made a forced march of thirty miles to Calipo, north-east of Namirrue, hoping to prevent the enemy from breaking north. By the end of July KARTUCOL and FITZCOL had concentrated there in a district where food was plentiful. A brief rest followed after a strenuous month in which KARTUCOL had covered some 330 miles, practically without rations and with no blankets or kit.

(iv) *The Break to the North-West, August-September, 1918*. Map VII.

After the fight at Namirrue the main body of the enemy continued north-east to Chalaua, the centre of a very rich district beyond the Ligonha. As the natives there were strongly opposed to the Portuguese and von Lettow was well supplied with trade goods, he met with an enthusiastic welcome, and if left to himself might have remained in the area indefinitely.

Van Deventer was still anxious lest the Germans should break north once more and re-enter their former territory. Partly for this reason and partly to forestall an attack on the new base at Mozambique, road communications were improved along the route Mozambique—Nampula—Malema—Zomba. During the first week of August van Deventer carried out a major regrouping of forces, designed to pen von Lettow to the south of this line while subjecting him to another converging attack. One column moved to Namezeze to intercept any movement from Chalaua towards Nampula; others were concentrated at Murrupula and Calipo; and Hawthorn, who had succeeded Northey in the Nyasaland command, was ordered to concentrate his battalions between Malokotera and Munevalia.

Von Lettow was not left in peace for long. The initiative again fell to KARTUCOL, now joined by 3/2 K.A.R. from Mozambique and again at a strength of three battalions. On 8th August 1/2 and 2/2 K.A.R. left Calipo for Nametil, eighteen miles to the east. On arrival the enemy was reported to be still at Chalaua. KARTUCOL continued the advance on the 9th, 3/2 K.A.R. moving across country from Calipo to join the other two battalions. On the 10th patrols reported an enemy detachment in camp farther along the track, and the column moved south-east for a flank approach through the bush. The camp was found but the enemy had already retired towards Chalaua. Von Lettow had been warned so the need for haste was urgent, but difficult conditions slowed the pace of the advance. On the 11th, 3/2 K.A.R. led the column in pouring rain across patches of black cotton soil the consistency of glue, against the opposition of a strong enemy rearguard. A porter captured that evening said that the enemy was making for Namezeze, north-east of Chalaua. Giffard therefore resumed the advance at midnight, but the night was very dark, touch was hard to maintain, and by daylight only six miles had been covered. Soon afterwards a patrol of the K.A.R.M.I. met the column and reported that the enemy was still at Chalaua, about four miles to the south. KARTUCOL doubled back through the tall elephant grass and swamps of blue mud, and halted preparatory to an attack next day.

At 6.15 a.m. on 13th August KARTUCOL moved off with high hopes of catching the enemy. The camp was reached before noon, but was found to be deserted. After a brief rest KARTUCOL set off again, following the trail through the bush, first east, then east-south-east, then south-east. After five miles or so the column halted, as nothing could be seen but a patrol and it was evident that the main body of the enemy could not be overtaken by direct pursuit. A porter captured by the K.A.R.M.I. said that von Lettow was going either west or north-west. As Mozambique was no longer threatened, Giffard returned to Tipe, which he reached a week later. For the last few days of the march his men were fed on half a pound of meat per day only. The local muhogo had caused some form

[Photo: Lt.-Col. G. C. Hill]
Column of 2/4 K.A.R. moving along a flooded road in Portuguese East Africa, 1918

of food poisoning, and on the final day of the march no food was available at all.

Von Lettow had crossed the Molocque above Tipe and was withdrawing west into the area Ille—Munevalia. FITZCOL, which had moved on Chalaua at the same time as KARTUCOL, chased the enemy for thirteen days, marching at the rate of eighteen to twenty miles per day, and reached Ille on 25th August. There an enforced halt was made to await the ration convoy, as the country traversed by the enemy had been swept practically bare and many of the men were sick from eating muhogo. Meanwhile another column under Lieutenant-Colonel Durham (DURCOL), consisting of the Northern Rhodesia Police and of 1/3 K.A.R., had been formed on 8th August and marched via Namezeze, Nametil, and Calipo to Alto Ligonha. The situation was extremely confused, but the enemy was apparently moving towards Regone. DURCOL and KARTUCOL were ordered to strike north and advance towards the Inagu Hills in parallel with his right flank, in order to head any attempt to reach the Rovuma. KARTUCOL therefore left Tipe on 22nd August and covered the sixty-four miles to Alto Molocque in a little over three days by long, hard marches into the cold air of the hills. Inagu was reached on the 28th.

Lieutenant-Colonel Baxter's column was at Regone, where a large supply dump had been established consisting of thousands of bags made from a local bark cloth, filled with food from the surrounding countryside. These bags were now used to protect the boma on the hill, stacked in barricades four feet high around the perimeter and at right angles across the camp. Outside this breastwork and the trenches and dug-outs that surrounded it sharpened stakes of sisal stalks had been planted.

Action at Numarroe, 24th August, 1918.—On 23rd August Major P. Garrard (Lond. R.) was sent south-east from Regone to Numarroe with 'A' and 'B' Companies, 2/4 K.A.R., two machine guns and four Lewis guns. The boma was still occupied by the Portuguese Resident with a few irregular troops, who professed no knowledge of the approaching enemy. On the 24th Captain R. H. Harris (R. Munster Fus.) left with 100 men of 'A' Company to patrol the track to the River Lugella. Two hours after leaving Numarroe Harris met the enemy advance guard of three companies and was forced to make a fighting retreat. Garrard sent up reinforcements, but the enemy was too strong to be denied and gradually surrounded the boma. Repeated attacks were driven off, but shortly after dark the Germans gained a lodgment in the trenches and the K.A.R. force was split in two. Garrard was taken prisoner, but Harris broke out and withdrew his troops towards Regone.

3/4 K.A.R. had reached Regone while the action was in progress and at midnight on 24th/25th moved out towards Numarroe. At dawn the battalion reached a pass through the hills south-east of Regone. Contact was made with the enemy advance guard, which avoided a direct action and worked through the hills to the British left. 3/4 K.A.R. therefore retired to assist in the defence of Regone.

An anxious day followed on the 26th, with patrols out to discover the enemy's whereabouts and the direction of his movements. During the night of 26th/27th, however, instead of attacking Regone as expected, he drew off towards Lioma, followed by 3/4 K.A.R. and SHORTCOL (1/4 K.A.R. and the Rhodesia Native Regiment under Lieutenant-Colonel Shorthose).

1/1 K.A.R. and the Northern Rhodesia Police were then near Malokotera where 2/1 K.A.R. was also concentrating. 3/1 K.A.R. (less one company at Malokotera) was at Munevalia. Once again von Lettow was surrounded, and it was evident that in the next few days his main body could not avoid a major action. On the evening of the 28th the enemy advance guard was near Mogomo. 1/1 K.A.R. had moved to Lioma and was occupying an entrenched position south of the village. KARTUCOL was divided, with 1/2 K.A.R. still at Inagu and 2/2 and 3/2 K.A.R. at Muanhupa *en route* for Lioma, where the action was expected to take place.

Action at Lioma, 30th-31st August, 1918.—During the next two days strenuous efforts were made by the KARTUCOL battalions to reach Lioma in time. 3/2 K.A.R. arrived first and made contact with 1/1 K.A.R. The enemy attacked the position in force on 30th August, surrounding and annihilating a platoon of 1/1 K.A.R. and attacking the entrenched camp from three directions. 3/2 K.A.R. counter-attacked and the assault was driven off with heavy loss. Marching again at midnight on 30th/31st August, 2/2 K.A.R. reached the scene at 4 a.m., closely followed by 1/2 K.A.R. after a difficult night march. Fires had to be lit to guide the battalion across the steep river-beds in pitch darkness.

2/2 K.A.R. had barely camped to await daylight when a large force of the enemy was reported to be moving across the front of the column from the direction of Lioma. It was impossible to tell what part of the enemy was involved, but with Nos. 1 and 3 Companies in the lead under Major Bradstock, 2/2 K.A.R. went into action. At 11 a.m. 1/2 K.A.R., defending the pass to prevent the enemy from escaping, was ordered up to support 2/2 K.A.R. With 'D' Company as screen the battalion crossed the Malema River and advanced towards Lioma. At 2.30 p.m. touch was gained with the enemy, who was retiring in disorder across the battalion front. While 'D' Company drove the enemy before them, 'A' Company came forward to form the front face and 'C' Company deployed on the left, where the enemy had opened fire and stampeded some of the porters. At 3 p.m. the Germans broke off the action on the left and disappeared into the bush. Meanwhile 'D' Company had driven them out of the hills. The advance continued cautiously as another four enemy companies were reported to be retreating from Lioma. The KARTUCOL battalions joined forces later in the afternoon and formed a perimeter camp.

Von Lettow said afterwards that Lioma had been his narrowest escape. In the two days' engagement he lost 17 Europeans killed and 11 captured, and about 200 askaris, with a quantity of ammunition and stores. Continuing north he entered a tangled area of rugged country and thick bush, making for the River Lurio. For the time being he had made good his escape, after a month's heavy marching in which KARTUCOL had followed on his track for 435 miles.[1]

---

[1] Van Deventer paid Lieutenant-Colonel Giffard and KARTUCOL a special tribute in his despatch of 30th September, 1918, in which he wrote that no column had 'marched farther or fought more'.

At the beginning of September the German force was north of Muanhupa, marching towards Mahua. Its total strength was estimated at 170 Europeans, 900 askaris, 40 machine guns and one field gun. Actually the number of askaris was nearer 1,200, all first-class troops whose morale was high, despite the rough handling they had received at Lioma. Moreover, the Germans possessed some of the best porters in East Africa and were thus able to accomplish extremely rapid marches. North of the Lurio von Lettow entered a country where supplies were short and his columns were often obliged to separate. His usual method was to march with advance guard and rearguard in considerable strength, separated by several days from the main body, with strong foraging parties ranging the countryside far and wide in advance to collect food.[1] In this way supplies were always awaiting the main body, and after the passage of the rearguard the pursuing K.A.R. columns were obliged to traverse a route devastated on either side for a distance well beyond the reach of their patrols.

While SHORTCOL attempted to bar the German passage of the Lurio, the direct pursuit again fell to KARTUCOL. On 1st September 1/2 K.A.R. with an advance guard under Major R. G. H. Wilson, pressed the enemy for eighteen miles along the Muanhupa road. New tactics were adopted, the troops dashing forward and firing from the hip as soon as the rearguard was bumped. This rattled the enemy and correspondingly encouraged the K.A.R., whose morale always rose when in contact with the enemy, despite the hardships of the past few months.

On 2nd September 2/2 K.A.R. took over the advance and continued the same tactics. 3/2 K.A.R. was operating on the left flank in an effort to cut the rearguard off, but the enemy retreat was even more rapid than usual. The countryside was now very dry, with a great deal of the bush burnt off, and part of each night had to be spent in a search for water. On the 3rd, 3/2 K.A.R. led the column. The Lurio, now only a trickle running between dense banks of tropical bush through which a way had to be cut, was crossed on the 4th and 5th September. Contact was made with Shorthose, who said that the enemy was retiring north-east. Leaving the direct pursuit to him, Giffard continued the advance on his left, making for the fords over the Lugenda in the hope of forestalling von Lettow there, or at least of overtaking his main body.

On 6th September the battalions of KARTUCOL were marching in their usual formation with an interval of a mile or more between each battalion. 3/2 K.A.R. led the way through a country of dry river-beds and tangled brakes of bamboo. 1/2 K.A.R. marched in the centre and 2/2 K.A.R. in the rear, with Nos. 1 and 3 Companies in front of the transport column, No. 4 split into platoons escorting the ammunition, and No. 2 as rearguard. Von Lettow's force lay to the east, and was assumed still to be marching in a north-easterly direction.

Affair at Pere Hills, 6th September, 1918.—Shortly before midday the sound of firing was heard from the rear. KARTUCOL had overrun the

[1] Von Lettow possessed a bicycle, on which he paid unexpected visits to his outlying columns and reconnoitred the country in advance.

German main body, the head of which, unexpectedly wheeling to the west, struck 2/2 K.A.R. Seeing the transport, the enemy assumed that he had discovered a convoy, and rushed forward at once, almost cutting off No. 2 Company from the rest of the battalion.

Close at hand there ran the deep channel of a dry river-bed, which the two battalions in front had already crossed. The transport and ammunition columns were hurried into shelter, which averted a panic among the porters. By this time both officers with No. 2 Company had been wounded. C.S.M. Goode took command and with the help of the African N.C.Os. extricated the company by withdrawing in a wide detour through the bush, eventually joining forces with 3/2 K.A.R.

Meanwhile the enemy force, constantly growing in strength, had wheeled to the left and was developing the attack with great speed, driving No. 4 Company before it. The situation was critical, as by this time 1/2 K.A.R. was about two miles and 3/2 K.A.R. nearly four miles ahead. A request for reinforcements went forward, while No. 3 Company formed a firing line in support of No. 4. By 1.30 a.m. No. 1 Company was also in the line and only the battalion signallers and a few orderlies were left in reserve. At least ten enemy machine guns were in action and the battalion was rapidly being outflanked. The enemy was within fifty yards of the transport when R.S.M. Bird collected the signallers and other details, led them into the firing line on the left and held off the attack.

1/2 K.A.R. had halted and closed up at the sound of firing. When news of the engagement came forward, 'A' and 'C' Companies were sent back in support, and at 2 p.m. gained touch with the enemy about 1,000 yards to the rear. Colonel Giffard now reached the scene, ordered back the remainder of 1/2 K.A.R. and brought the battalion into action on both flanks. This held the German attack, and finding opposition growing they realized the true situation and began to withdraw. At 5 p.m. 3/2 K.A.R. came up on the right and began a counter-attack, 'B' Company, 1/2 K.A.R., advancing with them and following the German retreat for some distance. Giffard then broke off the action and camped with 1/2 and 3/2 K.A.R. manning the perimeter and 2/2 K.A.R. in reserve.

Pere Hills was an unexpected action. For 2/2 K.A.R., owing to the heavy losses in European personnel, it was a battle in which the courage, initiative and leadership of the African N.C.Os. were seen at their best. No. 2 Company came away with all their wounded, guns and ammunition. No. 4 Company lost three officers, their C.S.M., C.Q.M.S., and senior sergeant, and fought the later stages of the action under the command of a junior British sergeant whose experience was very limited. Altogether the battalion lost one officer, one B.N.C.O. and six African ranks killed, and six officers, four B.N.C.Os. and 61 African ranks wounded.

For the time being KARTUCOL was unable to continue. On 7th September a company of 3/2 K.A.R. was detailed to maintain touch with the enemy and SHORTCOL continued the pursuit. While fresh ammunition was awaited the porters built hospital bandas and stretchers for the wounded,[1] who were escorted back to the Lurio two days later by 2/2 K.A.R. to meet a motor ambulance convoy. When 2/2 K.A.R. rejoined the column on 13th September the advance was resumed, heading for the upper Rovuma near its junction with the Lugenda. During the march 1/2 K.A.R. left the column to proceed to Port Amelia for transport to Dar-es-Salaam, *en route* to Tabora in reserve. The rest of the column reached the Lugenda on the 28th. Von Lettow crossed the Rovuma on the same day.

A new phase of the campaign had begun. The long chase through Portuguese East Africa was over, and van Deventer began a general movement of his troops to the north. If von Lettow reoccupied the Mahenge Plateau he might prolong his resistance for many months. Another possible route lay through Songea, one of the richest districts in German East Africa, where food was plentiful and cattle on the hoof could accompany marching columns. Possessing the power of swift movement on interior lines, the initiative still lay in von Lettow's hands.

DURCOL had reached Inagu and Malema early in September. When von Lettow crossed the Lurio the column was disbanded and 1/3 K.A.R. was ordered by march route to Lindi, in transit for Dar-es-Salaam and Morogoro. 2/3 K.A.R., who since the action at Nhamacurra had been employed on garrison duty, went by march route via Ngomano to Ndanda. FITZCOL was disbanded at Dar-es-Salaam on 29th September, and most of the units were transferred to a new organization, known as CENFORCE, under Fitzgerald's command. This Force was distributed along the Central Railway from Morogoro to Dodoma, and included the area south of the railway to Mahenge and Iringa. KARTUCOL, after its gallant pursuit of 1,600 miles through the forests and swamps of Portuguese East Africa, in the course of which 29 large rivers had been crossed and 32 engagements had been fought, was also broken up. After crossing the river at Ngomano the battalions were sent first to Masasi and then to Ndanda on garrison duty.

(v) *The Final Phase, October-November, 1918.* Map VI (b).

The final operations of the East Africa Campaign fell upon two of the Uganda battalions, 1/4 and 2/4 K.A.R. As soon as the direction of von Lettow's northward flight was definitely established, van Deventer instructed Hawthorn to take up the pursuit and to transfer troops via Lake Nyasa to Songea.

Early in September Hawthorn ordered 2/4 K.A.R. by march route to Fort Johnston, to embark for Mbamba Bay. The battalion had been marching and fighting continually since the previous March; no issues of clothing had been made, and the men were in a most disreputable state. Embarkation began on 18th September and the battalion landed at Mbamba at the end of the month.

Von Lettow had been reported near Mwembe, and in the hope of disputing his passage of the Rovuma, 'D' Company, 2/4 K.A.R., followed by the Northern Rhodesia Police, went to Songea, where a column was

[1] There were 200 stretcher cases, as all the enemy wounded had to be tended as well as the British.

to be formed under the command of Lieutenant-Colonel G. C. Hill (Wilts. R.). On 25th September Captain R. W. Hodson (Spec. List) with a patrol from Mitimoni discovered that the German columns were crossing the Rovuma. He had a narrow escape from capture, losing all his baggage and only regaining Mitimoni after two days in the bush without food. Two companies were ordered to move north along the enemy's flank, harrying him whenever opportunity offered, but many of their carriers deserted as they had been recently recruited in warmer areas and sent through the hills without blankets and on an unaccustomed diet. Only 'D' Company, half 'C' Company and the Lewis guns could therefore take up the pursuit, leaving the rest of 'C' Company and the machine guns at Mitimoni.

On 4th October patrols of 'C' and 'D' Companies gained contact with the enemy rearguard sixteen miles south of Songea. On the same day the Northern Rhodesia Police fought an action with the main body about fifteen miles to the west. Hill went out in support, but von Lettow, aware that Songea was occupied, drew off to the north. 'C' and 'D' Companies made a night march to Songea and rejoined the battalion.

2/4 K.A.R. and a company of the Northern Rhodesia Police then continued the pursuit. The country was rough and difficult, and the Angoni askaris and porters with the German columns began to desert, entering the K.A.R. camp to surrender or disappearing into the bush. North of Gumbiro the enemy struck the Songea—Njombe road. By this time 2/4 K.A.R. had outrun supplies and the pursuit had to be continued by 'B' Company (Captain G. A. Grant, R. High.) alone. On 17th October Grant surprised the enemy rearguard near Njombe and hustled it out of camp, with the loss of two Europeans and several askaris killed. The Germans had left von Wahle and other wounded and sick in a field hospital to await capture.

Von Lettow continued his march at remarkable speed. His stocks of food were dwindling, so deciding that the best chance of replenishment lay in raiding the British supply dumps he turned west. Some captures were made near Brandt, and following in the wake of his patrols, which were foraging in advance as usual, he made for Fife, where he expected to find a large depôt that might enable him to reach Angola.

Meanwhile van Deventer had been making fresh dispositions to head the German advance. 1/2 K.A.R., now a part of CENFORCE, was ordered from Tabora to Bismarckburg, where a defensive position was taken up early in November.[1] 2/2 and 3/2 K.A.R. were ordered from Ndanda to Lindi for transit via Beira to Broken Hill.[2] 1/4 K.A.R. had been transported to the head of the lake, but two of the three steamers, worn out by continual use, broke down *en route* and it was 18th October before the last company of the battalion reached Alt Langenburg. Next day 1/4 K.A.R. concentrated at Tandala and took over the chase from 2/4 K.A.R., who were sent to Neu Langenburg in reserve and stripped of

---

[1] 3/4 K.A.R. had first been detailed for this, but the battalion was immobilized by Spanish 'flu.

[2] These battalions were overtaken by news of the Armistice while at Schaeffer's Farm.

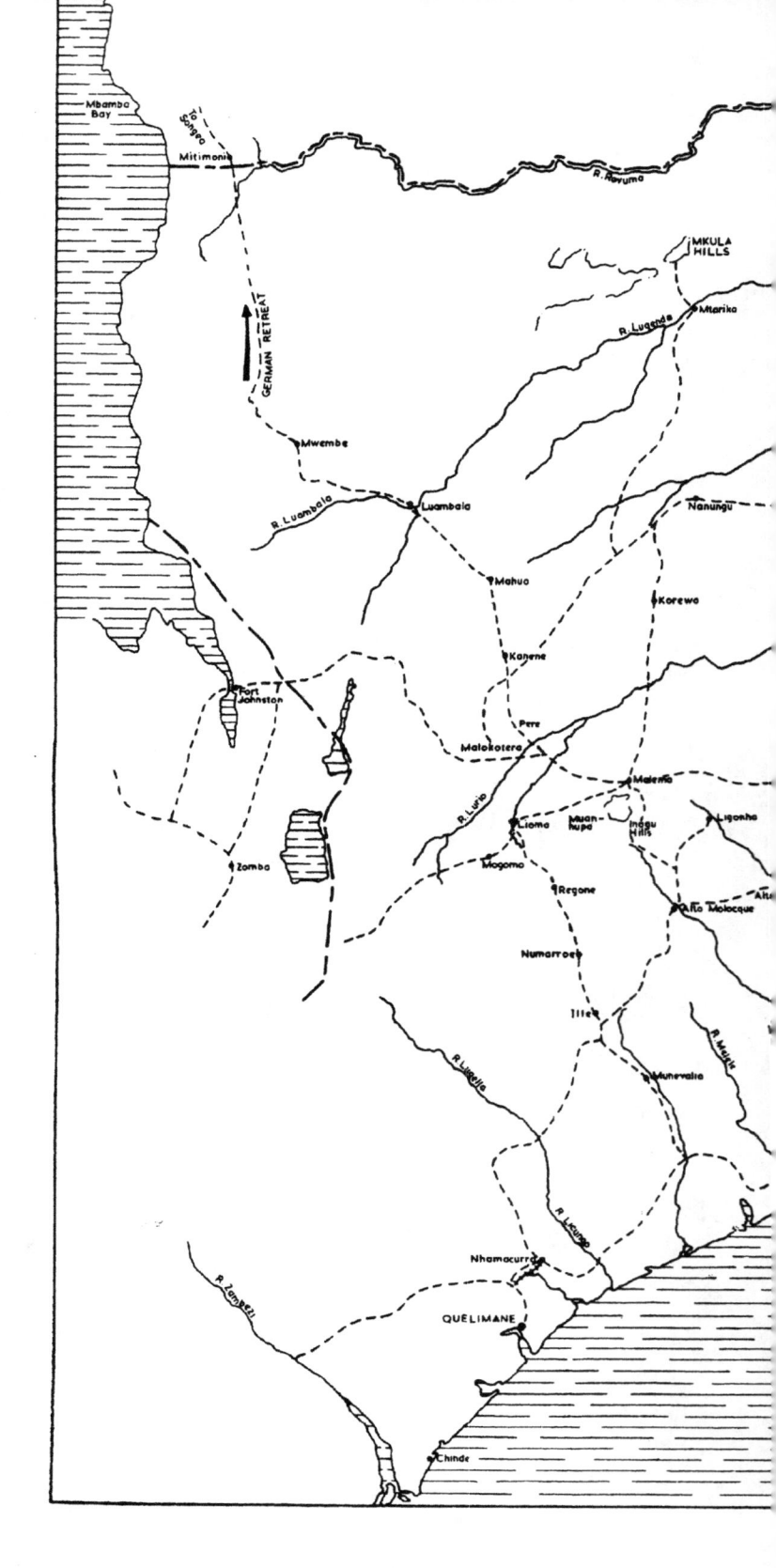

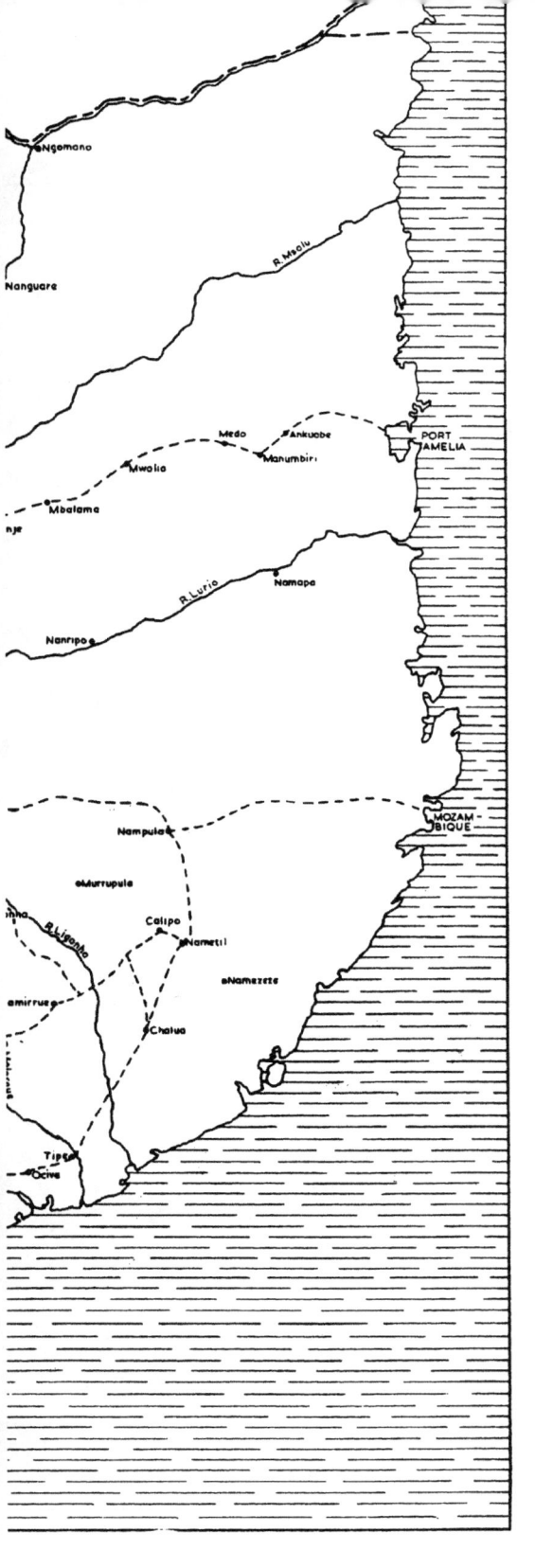

VII. Portuguese East Africa: The Pursuit of von Lettow, 1918

porters to make 1/4 K.A.R. mobile. The Northern Rhodesia Police went by steamer to Mwaya and marched direct on Fife.

1/4 K.A.R. left Tandala on 20th October, following a track for sixty miles over the mountains in the effort to intercept the German column near Brandt. The way lay across a high range scored by deep ravines and bordered by steep escarpments. But von Lettow had a good start along a motorable road, and contact was gained only with his rearguard. Following through New Utengule, on 2nd November 1/4 K.A.R. was still twenty-three miles short of Fife when natives reported that heavy firing had been heard near Fife that morning. Von Lettow had arrived to find two companies of the Northern Rhodesia Police well entrenched, but after bombarding them with his artillery had decided not to risk a general assault.[1] 1/4 K.A.R. followed along the road to Kasama, where von Lettow arrived on the 9th, to find a vehicle repair shop and a quantity of food, but little ammunition.

Pursuer and pursued were now in country unknown to them. Von Lettow was afraid of being trapped among the rivers and marshes, and Major E. B. B. Hawkins, who commanded the pursuing column, had only a small atlas of the world at 200 miles to the inch.[2] On 8th November the column was joined by a local settler, Lionel Smith, who warned Hawkins that he was approaching the deep River Chambezi, where von Lettow would undoubtedly burn the bridge and leave his rearguard to dispute the crossing. Smith suggested an alternative track that crossed the river by a ford twelve miles below the bridge. Hawkins took his advice and crossed the Chambezi unopposed on the evening of the 9th.

During the next two days Hawkins pressed forward, far outstripping his supplies and knowing that he would be unable to continue beyond Kasama without waiting for food. Though realizing that the enemy greatly outnumbered his column of 750 rifles, he hoped to strike a heavy blow before von Lettow once more withdraw out of reach. On 12th November he gained contact with several companies of the enemy at the River Milina. Attacked unexpectedly in the rear, the Germans retired across the valley. After a brisk engagement the K.A.R. got across the river, pressing the attack until long after darkness, when the Germans retreated into the bush. It was the final action of the East Africa Campaign, and as it was fought after the signing of the Armistice in Europe, the last also of the first world war.

That night the German rearguard reached Kasama. Von Lettow had sent his advance guard under Captain Spangenberg south to the Chambezi; on the 13th November he followed with the main body. News of the Armistice had reached von Deventer on the 11th, but an interruption in telephone communication caused some delay. Hawkins had heard nothing when at 11.30 a.m. on 13th November a patrol of askaris posted on the main road reported that two motor-cyclists carrying white flags

---

[1] Von Lettow said that this occasion was his narrowest escape from personal danger. He lay on the ground for half an hour while machine-gun fire almost parted the hair on the back of his head. (War Diary, N.R.P.)

[2] At Kasama, however, the Germans captured some excellent maps of North-East Rhodesia and Angola.

had come from the direction of Abercorn, and in spite of their warning shouts had gone forward towards the enemy at Kasama. At 2.42 p.m. the advance point of the column, then four miles from Kasama, met two German askaris with a large white flag, bearing the telegram that von Lettow had received from the motor-cyclists, announcing the Armistice. British and African ranks heard the news with the greatest enthusiasm, the men shouting their war-cries and dancing around their officers.[1]

That evening Hawkins received a letter from Köhl saying that von Lettow had gone ahead by bicycle to confer with Spangenberg at the Chambezi crossing. There he received the news, and a further message from van Deventer instructing him to march to Abercorn, where his surrender would be formally received. His acceptance of these terms was handed to Hawkins on the morning of the 16th,[2] and a few hours later the German column marched back through the K.A.R. camp.[3]

1/4 K.A.R. set out for Abercorn at dawn on the 17th. The battalion entered the town on the 24th, having marched 1,830 miles in the last six months. The German column entered next day, and at 11 a.m. that morning von Lettow's surrender was received by Brigadier-General W. F. S. Edwards. 1/4 K.A.R. and the Northern Rhodesia Police formed the guard of honour at the ceremony. The German force then comprised 155 Europeans (including Dr. Schnee, the Governor), 1,168 askaris, 1,522 porters and many women and followers. The troops were well disciplined and in excellent condition. German officers were allowed to retain their swords and German other ranks their arms until they reached Dar-es-Salaam.

(vi) *The K.A.R. in the East Africa Campaign.*

Neither before nor since has the K.A.R. been faced with a campaign at once so prolonged, arduous and stubborn as that of the first world war.[4] During the years 1917 and 1918, when in popular estimation the fighting was virtually over, it was in fact increasing in severity, and the last four months of 1917 saw the heaviest fighting of the whole campaign. Terrain and climate remained as formidable as ever, and the absence of definite objectives, other than the scattered forces of a very mobile enemy

---

[1] Account of von Lettow's surrender by Major Hawkins. *The Times*, February, 1919.

[2] This document is now in the possession of 4 K.A.R.

[3] 'Not far north of Kasama we came up with the enemy with whom we had fought our last engagement. They were the 1st battalion of the 4th King's African Rifles. I had to refuse the invitation of Colonel Hawkins (their estimable commander, who was barely thirty years old), communicated to me on the march by Colonel Dickinson, to bring all the German officers to lunch, much though I appreciated such an expression of chivalry. . . . I must record that the officers of this battalion, even in the somewhat difficult circumstances in which they were placed, behaved with great tact, and with that regard which is due to an honourable foe.' (Von Lettow, *My Reminiscences of East Africa*, pp. 319-20.)

[4] It should be noted, however, that the maximum war effort ever achieved by East Africa as a whole was the provision and maintenance of a complete division plus two brigades in Burma during the operations of 1944-45, at a time when the internal security of vast territories on the Continent and in Madagascar had also to be safeguarded. (See Part V.)

> Majestät Berlin
> General Deventer teilt offiziell mit, daß
> nach den von Deutschland unterzeichne-
> ten Waffenstillstandsbedingungen bedin-
> gungslose Übergabe der Schutztruppe zu
> erfolgen hat Ich werde entsprechend
> verfahren
>   Lettow
>   14. 11. 18

> Written in my presence, on the bank of the
> Chambeze river, Northern Rhodesia, on the
> morning of the 14th day of November 1918.
>
>   H. Croad.
>   Provincial Commissioner
>   retired.

Facsimile of von Lettow's surrender

who had no bases, made forward planning very difficult. The troops suffered accordingly. When KARTUCOL recrossed the Rovuma the askaris had marched and fought to a standstill. Stripped for inspection they looked like the victims of famine.

Some statistics of the troops engaged and casualties incurred will place in perspective the contribution made by the K.A.R. to the campaign as a whole. Excluding allied and naval forces, about 114,000 troops were engaged. The greatest number in the field at any time was 55,000 during Smuts' campaign of 1916. At that time the K.A.R. was represented only by the three regular battalions, and in the later stages also by 1/2 K.A.R. and 2/2 K.A.R. The smallest number of troops engaged was about 10,000 during the pursuit of von Lettow in 1918, practically all of whom were K.A.R. At the end of the campaign, when the Regiment stood at its maximum strength, it numbered 1,423 British officers, 2,046 British N.C.Os, and 31,955 African ranks.[1]

[1] Strength returns for 1st November, 1918.

The full casualty list for the campaign (exclusive of sickness and invaliding) totalled nearly 18,000. Casualties in respect of East and Central African forces amounted to 294 officers,[1] 136 B.N.C.Os., and 7,795 Africans, more than 45 per cent. of the total. Carriers also were liable to battle casualties, and in addition about 40,000 of the 494,936 non-combatants enrolled for service during the war fell victims to disease.

Endurance was the keynote of the campaign, and the young askaris accomplished some remarkable feats. The territory in which they fought could hardly have suited their enemy's evasive tactics better. In the thick bush and swamp that formed the scene of so many actions in German and Portuguese East Africa, opposing columns often passed unseen within a few miles of each other. Constant and intensive patrolling was therefore a vital preliminary to tactical success. In this the well-trained African N.C.Os. could be taught to excel, and in the later stages of the campaign, when many officers and B.N.C.Os., though present in greater numbers, were new to bush warfare, considerable dependence had to be placed upon them.

In the early stages of the campaign, full realization of the nature of the operations to come was only appreciated by officers with personal experience of soldiering in local conditions. For a long time the idea persisted that success was only a question of competent leadership and sufficiently large forces, without regard to their suitability for the purpose in hand. The primary difficulty—the battle against Africa—was too little regarded. In consequence, the conquest of the German colony was accomplished at the cost of a disproportionate expenditure of men and materials. Had the expansion of the K.A.R. been accepted as the foundation of future forces and pressed with energy when it was first discussed during the comparative stagnation of 1915, the new battalions that played so large a part in the prolonged campaign of the last two years would not have been handicapped by the lack of experienced European personnel and the rawness of the young recruits in battle. What von Lettow could achieve in the training of askaris—which was something very good indeed—the K.A.R. could always match, given an equal start. The additional advantages of undisturbed recruiting areas and assured (even though inadequate) supplies of war material would have made it possible to meet von Lettow on favourable terms with African troops alone, fighting what was essentially an African war.

The value of the askari as a fighting soldier did eventually receive recognition. In 1917 the C.I.G.S. raised for the second time the possibility of a K.A.R. expeditionary force for service in Egypt, Palestine or Mesopotamia. Early in the following year a definite request was made for two infantry brigades with ancillary troops for the Palestine operations. Plans were made for the dispatch of eight battalions, and for their reinforcement from certain training units to be maintained in East Africa, but the collapse of the Turkish armed forces came before the battalions ear-

[1] Detailed figures of officers killed or died of wounds while serving with infantry battalions of the K.A.R. were: 1st Regt. 39; 2nd Regt. 39; 3rd Regt. 28; M.I. 1; 4th Regt. 24; 5th Regt. 1; 6th Regt. 4; 7th Regt. 2. These casualties, which are a fair reflection of the fighting service of the battalions, occurred mainly during 1917-18.

marked for service abroad could be withdrawn from their own theatre of war. More important still was the recognition accorded to the askari within the colonial territories. Before the war he had played a notable part in the support of British administration and the extension of ordered government; now he was accepted as a soldier in a wider sense. The march-past of the K.A.R. battalions held at Nairobi in the first flush of victory evoked an acclamation of a kind never before experienced in the history of the Regiment.

www.ingramcontent.com/pod-product-compliance
Lightning Source LLC
Chambersburg PA
CBHW050546160426
43199CB00015B/2557